THE ULTIMATE SHORTCUT COOKIE BOOK

745 SCRUMPTIOUS RECIPES
THAT START WITH REFRIGERATED COOKIE DOUGH, CAKE MIX, BROWNIE MIX, OR READY-TO-EAT CEREAL

Camilla V. Saulsbury

CUMBERLAND HOUSE™
AN IMPRINT OF SOURCEBOOKS, INC.®
WWW.SOURCEBOOKS.COM

Published by Cumberland House, an imprint of Sourcebooks, Inc.
P.O. Box 4410, Naperville, Illinois 60567-4410
(630) 961-3900
Fax: (630) 961-2168
www.sourcebooks.com

Library of Congress Cataloging-in-Publication Data

Saulsbury, Camilla V.
   The ultimate shortcut cookie book : 745 scrumptious recipes that start with refrigerated cookie dough, cake mix, brownie mix, or ready-to-eat cereal / by Camilla V. Saulsbury.
      p. cm.
   Includes bibliographical references and index.
   (hardcover : alk. paper) 1. Cookies. I. Title.
   TX772.S2587 2009
   641.8'654—dc22
                                          2009025687

Printed and bound in the United States of America.
LB 10 9 8 7 6 5 4 3 2 1

PRAISE FOR *THE ULTIMATE SHORTCUT COOKIE BOOK*:

"Camilla is no stranger to the kitchen, and in her own easy breezy style, these recipes will inspire the shyest of bakers to try their hand. In fact, my new challenge is keeping the book out of my daughter's grasp, as all of a sudden she fancies herself quite the little baker!"
—Daisy Martinez, Food Network star of *Viva Daisy!* and author of *Daisy Cooks*

"Always a winner, Camilla Saulsbury scores again with *The Ultimate Shortcut Cookie Book*. Her creativity turns convenience-food products into treats so delectable no one would know they weren't baked from scratch. I've followed Camilla's food career ever since she was a finalist in Sutter Home Winery's Build a Better Burger, her first cooking competition, and was thrilled when she returned to win our Grand Prize in 2006. She's been racking up prizes and turning out winning cookbooks ever since!"

—James McNair, cookbook author and head judge of Sutter Home
Winery's Build a Better Burger annual recipe contest

"This book got my sweet tooth going immediately, with titles like Toffee Cream, Caramel Rocky Road, and Coconut Cashew. I'm preheating the oven!"

—Dianne Jacob, author of Will Write for Food

PRAISE FOR CAMILLA'S PREVIOUS COOKIE BOOKS:

"The only hard task regarding this collection will be choosing which recipe to make first."
—*Milwaukee Journal Sentinel*

"Her book appeals to the accomplished baker and the student who has never wielded a wooden spoon."

—*Houston Chronicle*

"As we paged through...we found ourselves first intrigued, then hooked. Many of the recipes are unexpectedly sophisticated."

—*Boston Herald*

"Seems like homemade—although it's much less trouble...adults will probably like...these cookies as much as the kids."

—*St. Louis Post-Dispatch*

TO RON PITKIN

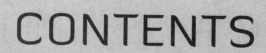

CONTENTS

ACKNOWLEDGMENTS

I cannot sing enough praises for the people I have worked with at Cumberland House Publishing. Special thanks to Ron Pitkin, Julie Pitkin, Lisa Taylor, Paul Mikos, Paige Lakin, Tracy Ford, and Chris Bauerle. Thank you for shaping and guiding my writing career in so many ways.

To my husband, Kevin West, for eating more than his fair share of baking experiments (the good, the bad, and the ugly) and keeping his critiques constructive and kind.

To Nicholas, for making every day beautiful.

To my dear friend Lindsey Vineyard, for promoting the virtues of all of my shortcut cookie books more than any other lone person possibly could—I think you missed your calling as a publicist! There's still plenty of time…Thank you for all of your support and for being such an inspiring friend.

And to my new publishing team at Sourcebooks—I am thrilled to be part of such a dynamic and talented group of people.

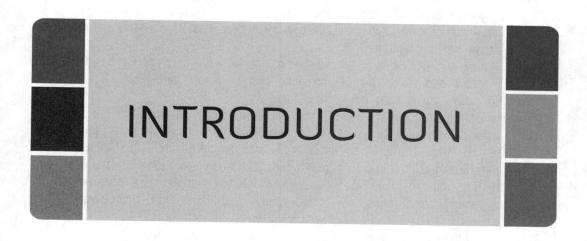

INTRODUCTION

Time. It's in short supply these days, especially when it comes to cookie baking. It's far too easy to turn to cellophane packages of cookies from the supermarket, despite their absence of flavor and soul.

But a sweet solution exists, one that will leave you rich with homemade cookies from here on out: *The Ultimate Shortcut Cookie Book: 745 Scrumptious Recipes That Start with Refrigerated Cookie Dough, Cake Mix, Brownie Mix, or Ready-to-Eat Cereal.*

It's more than OK to make cookie shortcuts. Home bakers have always taken advantage of newly available shortcuts, whether in the form of pre-shelled and chopped nuts, shredded coconut, pureed pumpkin, measured sticks of butter, or the uniform bits of chocolate we know so well as "chips." In short, making quick, easy, and delicious cookies from cake mix, brownie mix, or a roll of refrigerated cookie dough is not about abandoning traditional cookie and dessert recipes but celebrating a host of new options.

I had all levels of home baking ability in mind as I developed the recipes for this book: novice bakers, including kids of all ages, can delight in the assured success of taking a few shortcuts in the kitchen; even the most experienced home baker gets pinched for time. Here you'll find a variety of treats to meet both your needs and your tastes, whether for a bake sale, baby shower, birthday party, care package, afternoon fun, and everything in between, including my favorite cookie occasion: curling up with a good book and a cup of tea.

Each recipe in this collection has been streamlined for easy, everyday baking—if you can wield a wooden spoon, you have all the skills necessary to start turning out any of the scrumptious treats herein. Beginning with a box of cake mix, brownie mix, refrigerated cookie dough—or opting for an equally easy no-bake cookie—is not only easier than pie but also leads to sweet success time and time again. Delicious proof is mere minutes away.

These recipes are filled with color—vibrant oranges, scarlet cranberries, fresh green mint, deep brown chocolate…with texture—crunchy nuts, silken frostings, gooey chocolate, crisp cereals…with spices—sweet cinnamon, exotic cardamom, fiery chili peppers, piquant ginger…and fruits—bright lime, rich dates, homey raisins, and creamy bananas. An abundance of tastes and flavors awaits your experimentation.

I begin with my mini-manifesto on great cookie baking, including smart cookie tips, equipment and ingredient lists, and a wide range of advice on baking, cooling, storing, and shipping. You'll feel like a pro before you ever set foot in the kitchen.

The recipe chapters follow with over 750 very special quick and easy options. You'll find drop cookies, shaped cookies, bars, brownies, biscotti, and so much more. All-American favorites are well represented—Blue Ribbon Chocolate Chip, Chewy Oatmeal Raisin, Jam Thumbprints, and Dark Chocolate Brownies are but a few. International and fresh new cookie ideas are also well represented—for example, Italian Biscotti, French Madeleines, and Viennese Teacakes illustrating the former, and Caramel Apple Cookies, Blackberry Lemon Bars, and Ginger Jeweled Butter Cookies the latter. Of course, soon enough, you will have your own favorites.

At the back of the volume you will find several appendices: a general index of recipes, a glossary of baking terms, and online/mail order sources for ingredients and equipment. And last, an appendix for converting U.S. standard measurements to metric.

One final thought: be sure to let everyone know how quick and easy it was to create your masterpieces. They'll still feel pampered, but they'll be doubly thrilled by your sweet and generous revelation.

ULTIMATE RECIPE SHOWDOWN WINNING COOKIE RECIPE

EXOTIC SPICE COOKIES WITH GINGER, CARDAMOM, AND ROSE WATER

I am 100 percent certain that all of my years of developing, testing, and writing the hundreds of shortcut cookie recipes for my books led directly to my dreaming up what, for me, was the ultimate cookie: a quick and easy spice cookie with exotic flair in the forms of a sprinkle of cardamom, a splash of rosewater, and a few turns of freshly cracked pepper. What sweet satisfaction it was to have my very favorite cookie chosen as the grand prize winner in the Food Network's Ultimate Recipe Showdown in 2008, earning me a perfect score of 100 points, $25,000, and the ultimate cookie bragging rights. And while it's a from-scratch recipe, I had to include it in this collection, because I know you'll find it every bit as easy (and, I hope, delicious!) as the shortcut cookies you'll find in the pages to follow.

2¼ cups all-purpose flour
2¼ teaspoons ground ginger
2 teaspoons baking soda
¾ teaspoon ground cardamom
¾ teaspoon ground cinnamon

½ teaspoon ground coriander
¼ teaspoon freshly ground black pepper
¾ teaspoon salt
¾ cup chopped crystallized ginger
1 cup packed dark brown sugar
½ cup vegetable shortening, room temperature
¼ cup (½ stick) unsalted butter, room temperature
1 large egg
¼ cup honey
1 teaspoon rosewater
¾ cup turbinado (raw) sugar, for rolling

Whisk the flour, ground ginger, baking soda, cardamom, cinnamon, coriander, pepper, and salt in a medium bowl until blended. Mix in the crystallized ginger. Set aside momentarily.

In a large bowl beat the brown sugar, shortening, and butter with an electric mixer until fluffy (do not overbeat—it will add too much air). Add the egg, honey, and rosewater and beat until blended. Stir in the flour mixture with a wooden spoon, mixing until just until blended. Cover and refrigerate 1 hour.

Preheat oven to 350°F. Lightly spray 2 cookie sheets with nonstick cooking spray. Spoon the turbinado sugar in thick layer onto a small plate. Using wet hands, form dough into 1¼-inch balls; roll in sugar to coat completely. Place balls on prepared sheets, spacing 2–3 inches apart.

Bake cookies until cracked on top but still soft to touch, 11–13 minutes. Cool on cookie sheets for 1 minute. Carefully transfer cookies to wire racks; cool completely.

MAKES 24 COOKIES.

COOKIES 101

To ensure that all your cookie baking is blissful, I offer here some tips, guidelines, and a smattering of personal opinions about getting started, selecting, prepping, and measuring ingredients, and choosing equipment. But the best advice I can offer is to share your baking with the people you love and care about, by inviting them into the kitchen to assist, chat, keep you company, or anticipate the sweet goodness soon to come, and then, of course, sharing the freshly baked fruits of your labor.

SMART COOKIE TIPS

- Read the recipe thoroughly. Note the required ingredients, equipment needed, as well as the chilling, baking, and cooling times.
- Gather the necessary ingredients, checking for freshness (see the "Ingredients" section that follows for tips for specific ingredients).
- Gather the necessary equipment, including oven mitts and cooling racks.
- Prep the ingredients as needed, chopping nuts, zesting lemons, softening cream cheese, or melting butter, for example.
- Prepare any baking pans or cookie sheets as specified in the recipe. If no advanced preparation is needed, set the pan or sheet aside so that it is ready to be used when needed.

- Reread the recipe.
- Preheat the oven. Turn the oven to the specified temperature for 10–15 minutes prior to baking to give the oven adequate time to heat up to the correct temperature.
- Use an oven thermometer. Indispensable, inexpensive, and readily available in the baking sections of most supermarkets or at any kitchen supply store, these handy devices allow you to check the accuracy and consistency of your oven temperature. Oven temperatures tend to be too high or too low; armed with the correct information from your thermometer, you can adjust accordingly.
- Precisely measure all of the ingredients. Baking is a science, hence small variations can have a significant effect on the final product. See the "Measuring Ingredients" section for tips on measuring dry, liquid, and moist ingredients.
- Mix ingredients according to recipe specifications.
- Use a kitchen timer. This allows for precision and helps ensure the end product is not overcooked. One or two minutes can make a world of difference in cookie baking, so ensure your results with a reliable timer.
- Check the baked good at the earliest time specified. For example, if a recipe reads "Bake for 30–35 minutes until toothpick inserted near the center comes clean," then check for doneness at 30 minutes. Continue baking if needed and continue checking every minute.

EQUIPMENT

Baking Pans and Sheets
Aluminum cookie sheets (at least two)
8-inch-square pan
9-inch-square pan
Jelly roll pan (10 x 15-inches)
Standard 12-cup muffin pan
Miniature muffin pan
Madeleine pan (3 x 1¼-inch shell molds)
Deep-dish pie pan (9-inch)
Springform pan (9- or 10-inch)

Measuring and Mixing
Dry measuring cups in graduated sizes ¼, 1/3, ½, and 1 cup
Liquid measuring cup (preferably clear glass or plastic)
Measuring spoons in graduated sizes 1/8, ¼, ½, and 1 teaspoon as well as 1 tablespoon
Wooden spoon(s)
Mixing bowls (at least one each of small, medium, and large sizes)
Rubber or silicone spatula (for scraping the sides of a mixing bowl)

Appliances

Electric mixer (handheld or stand mixer)
Food processor
Kitchen timer

Utensils

Rolling pin or mallet (for crushing cookies, graham crackers, and candies)
Wire whisk
Chef's knife
Kitchen spoons (everyday place-setting soup and teaspoons for drop cookies)
Small offset metal spatula (ideal for frosting both cookies and bars)
Metal pastry scraper (the perfect tool for cutting bars into perfect squares and bars)
Cookie scoops (look like small ice cream scoops—use for perfectly measured drop cookies)
Zester
Metal (or plastic if you are using a nonstick-coated pan) spatula or pancake turner for
     removing cookies from sheets
Pastry brush (a clean 1-inch paintbrush from the hardware store works fine)
Rolling pin (only for a few recipes)
Assorted cookie cutters
Metal icing spatula
Melon baller (for making perfect thumbprint cookie impressions)

Miscellaneous

Wire cooling racks
Cutting board(s)
Oven mitts or holders (for holding hot saucepans and skillets)
Aluminum foil
Plastic wrap
Wax paper
Parchment paper

INGREDIENTS

Cake Mixes

All of the recipes in this book calling for cake mix were tested using an 18.25-ounce box of cake mix. These included name-brand mixes such as Betty Crocker, Duncan Hines, and Pillsbury® cake mixes, as well as store-brand mixes such as Kroger and Safeway. Flavors vary slightly by manufacturer, so take note if you prefer one brand over another.

Cake mixes contain flour, sugar, leavening (baking powder and baking soda), fat, salt, flavoring, and coloring in precise, pre-measured proportions. They have a one-year shelf life, so it is a great idea to stock up, particularly when cake mixes are on sale (which is often). For spur of the moment cookie baking, try keeping one or two each of chocolate, yellow, lemon, white, and spice cake mixes in the pantry.

Brownie Mixes

All of the recipes in this book calling for brownie mix were tested using a 19.5 to 19.8-ounce box of brownie mix. These included name-brand mixes such as Betty Crocker Fudge Brownie mix and Pillsbury Brownie Classics Traditional Fudge Brownie Mix, as well as store-brand mixes such as the Kroger label brownie mix. Check the weight, and then double-check that the mix does not include stir-ins such as chocolate syrup, nuts, caramel, or baking chips.

Several brands of brownie mix come in slightly larger sizes, such as Martha White Chewy Fudge Brownie Mix (22.5 ounces), Krusteaz Fudge Brownie Mix (22 ounces), Ghirardelli Brownie Mix (20 ounces), Duncan Hines Family Style Chewy Fudge Brownie Mix (21 ounces), and the Safeway store-brand Fudge Brownie Mix (21.5 ounces). All of these are still suitable for any of the recipes in this book. However, for best success, use only 4 cups of the mix for the equivalent of a 19.5 to 19.8-ounce package.

Refrigerated Cookie Dough

All of the recipes in this book that call for refrigerated cookie dough rely on a 16.5-ounce roll of either sugar or chocolate chip cookie dough. Either name-brand or store-brand varieties may be used for the recipes herein.

For added convenience, rolls of refrigerated cookie dough can be frozen (stock up when they go on sale). Freeze unopened rolls of refrigerated cookie dough in the freezer for two to four months. When you're ready to use them, place the frozen rolls of refrigerated cookie dough in the refrigerator and thaw overnight; microwave thawing is not recommended.

The cookie dough can also be stored once ingredients have been added. Tightly wrap the dough in plastic wrap or in an airtight zip-top bag and place in the refrigerator or freezer. Use dough within one week if placed in refrigerator and within one month if stored in the freezer.

Ready-to-Eat-Cereals

A variety of ready-to-eat cereals are used for a majority of the no-bake cookie options in this collection. The varieties include crisp rice cereal, cornflakes, wheat and barley nuggets (e.g., Grape Nuts), graham cracker cereal, and crisp honey-nut flakes and clusters cereal. Both name-brand and store-brand cereals were used to test recipes in this collection; either variety may be used. Use only fresh, crisp cereal for best results.

Oats

Two types of oats are used throughout this collection: old-fashioned and quick-cooking oats. Old-fashioned oats are rolled and are made from the entire oat kernel. With quick-cooking oats the oat kernel is cut into pieces before being rolled thinly. Use the oats specified in the recipe for best results. Avoid using instant oatmeal, which consists of oats that have been very finely cut and processed. Store oats in a cool, dry place in a tightly covered container for up to six months. Oats may also be frozen in a zip-top plastic freezer bag for up to one year. Oats do not spoil but may become stale with age.

Cookie Crumbs

A variety of store-bought cookies are used in crushed and crumbled form throughout this collection, particularly for the no-bake cookie options. Both name-brand and store-brand cookies were used to test recipes in this collection; either variety may be used. Use only fresh, crisp cookies for best results.

Graham Crackers

Both whole graham crackers and graham cracker crumbs are used throughout this collection, particularly for the no-bake cookie options. Graham crackers are rectangular- shaped, whole-wheat crackers that have been lightly sweetened. Use only fresh, crisp graham crackers for best results. Where graham cracker crumbs are specified in a recipe, readymade graham cracker crumbs may be used. Look for them in the baking section of the grocery store where flour is shelved.

Butter

Butter is used in many of the recipes throughout the book to bolster the flavor of the cookies, brownies, and bars. Either unsalted or lightly salted butter may be used where butter is listed as an ingredient in this book.

Fresh butter should have a delicate cream flavor and pale yellow color. Butter quickly picks up off-flavors during storage and when exposed to oxygen; once the carton is opened, place it in a resealable plastic storage bag or airtight container. Store it away from foods with strong odors, especially items such as onions or garlic.

Avoid using butter to coat baking pans and sheets. Because butter melts at a lower temperature than other "greasing" ingredients, such as vegetable shortening, it may leave ungreased gaps on cookie sheets and pans, causing baked goods to stick. Second, butter can burn, particularly when baking above 350°F. At best, what you're baking will be overly brown; at worst, scorched.

MELTING BUTTER: Melted butter is used in many recipes throughout this book. For best results, cut the specified amount of butter into small pieces, place in a small saucepan, and allow to melt over the lowest heat setting of the burner. Once the butter has melted, remove pan from heat and cool. To speed the cooling pour the melted butter into a small bowl or liquid measuring cup.

SOFTENING BUTTER: Softened butter is also required in several recipes throughout the book. The traditional method for softening butter is to remove the needed amount from the refrigerator and let it stand for 30–45 minutes at room temperature. Cutting the butter into small chunks will reduce the softening time to about 15 minutes. If time is really limited, try grating the cold butter on the large holes of a cheese grater. The small bits of butter will be soft in just a few minutes. Alternatively, place the cold butter between sheets of wax paper and hit it several times with a rolling pin. Avoid softening butter in the microwave. It will typically melt at least part of the butter, even if watched closely.

Chocolate

Two general types of chocolate are used throughout this book. The first type is chocolate chips, available in semisweet, milk, white, and miniature semisweet. Some premium brands offer bittersweet chocolate chips, which may be used interchangeably with semisweet chocolate chips. The second general type of chocolate is baking chocolate, which is typically available in 6- or 8-ounce packages, with the chocolate most often individually wrapped in 1-ounce squares or occasionally in 2-ounce bars. It is available in unsweetened, bittersweet, semisweet, milk, and white chocolate varieties.

CHOCOLATE STORAGE: Store both chocolate chips and baking chocolate in a dry, cool place between 60°F and 78°F. Wrapping chocolate in moisture-proof wrap or in a zip-top plastic bag is a good idea if the temperature is higher or the humidity is above 50 percent. Chocolate can also be stored in the fridge, but let it stand at room temperature before using.

BLOOMING CHOCOLATE: If the chocolate from your pantry has a white, crusty-looking film on it, don't toss it. This is commonly called "bloom" and develops when the chocolate is exposed to varying temperatures, from hot to cold. The change in heat allows the cocoa butter to melt and rise to the surface of the chocolate. Bloom does not affect the quality or flavor of the chocolate. The chocolate will look normal again once it is melted or used in baking.

Cream Cheese

All of the recipes in this book use "brick"-style cream cheese, which is typically packaged in 3-ounce and 8-ounce rectangular packages. For best results avoid using soft-spread, flavored, or whipped cream cheese.

To soften cream cheese, unwrap it and cut it into chunks with a sharp knife. Let it stand at room temperature for 30–45 minutes until softened. For speed softening, place the chunks of cream cheese on a microwavable plate or in a microwavable bowl and microwave on high for 15 seconds. If necessary, microwave 5 or 10 seconds longer.

Eggs

Use large eggs in all of the recipes in this book. Select clean, fresh eggs that have been handled properly and refrigerated. Do not use dirty, cracked, or leaking eggs that may have a bad odor or unnatural color when cracked open. They may have become contaminated with harmful bacteria such as salmonella. Cold eggs are easiest to separate; eggs at room temperature beat to high volume.

Eggs may be checked for freshness by filling a deep bowl with enough cold water to cover an egg. Place the egg in the water. If the egg lies on its side on the bottom of the bowl, it is fresh. If the egg stands up and bobs on the bottom, it isn't quite as fresh, but is still acceptable for baking. If the egg floats on the surface, it should be discarded.

Margarine

Margarine may be substituted for butter, but it is not recommended because it lacks the rich flavor that butter offers. However, if using margarine in place of butter, it is essential that it is a 100 percent vegetable oil, solid stick.

Margarine spreads—in tub or stick form—will alter the liquid and fat combination of the recipe, leading to either unsatisfactory or downright disastrous results. You can determine the fat percentage in one of two ways. In some cases, the percentage is printed on the box. If it reads anything less than 100 percent oil, it is a spread and should be avoided for baking purposes. If the percentage is not printed on the outside of the box, flip it over and check the calories. If it is 100 calories per tablespoon, it is 100 percent vegetable oil; any less, and it is less than 100 percent and should not be used.

Granulated White Sugar

Granulated white sugar is the most common sweetener used throughout this collection. It is refined cane or beet sugar. If a recipe in the book calls for sugar without specifying which one, use granulated white sugar. Once opened, store granulated sugar in an airtight container in a cool, dry place.

Brown Sugar

Brown sugar is granulated sugar that has some molasses added to it. The molasses gives the brown sugar a soft texture. Light brown sugar has less molasses and a more delicate flavor than dark brown sugar. If a recipe in the book calls for brown sugar without specifying which one, use light brown sugar. If you are out of brown sugar, substitute 1 cup granulated white sugar plus 2 tablespoons molasses for each cup of brown sugar. Once opened, store brown sugar in an airtight container or zip-top plastic bag to prevent clumping.

Powdered Sugar

Powdered sugar (also called confectioner's sugar) is granulated sugar that has been ground to a fine powder. Cornstarch is added to prevent the sugar from clumping together. It is used in recipes where regular sugar would be too grainy. If you are out of powdered sugar, place 1 cup granulated white sugar plus 1/8 teaspoon cornstarch in a food processor or blender, then process on high speed until finely powdered. Once opened, store powdered sugar in an airtight container or zip-top plastic bag to prevent clumping.

Corn Syrup

Corn syrup is a thick, sweet syrup made by processing cornstarch with acids or enzymes. Light corn syrup is further treated to remove any color. Light corn syrup is very sweet but does not have much flavor. Dark corn syrup has coloring and flavoring added to make it caramel-like. Unopened containers of corn syrup may be stored at room temperature. After opening, store corn syrup in the refrigerator to protect against mold. Corn syrup will keep indefinitely when stored properly.

Honey

Honey is the nectar of plants that has been gathered and concentrated by honeybees. Unopened containers of honey may be stored at room temperature. After opening, store honey in the refrigerator to protect against mold. Honey will keep indefinitely when stored properly.

Maple Syrup

Maple syrup is a thick, liquid sweetener made by boiling the sap from maple trees. Maple syrup has a strong, pure maple flavor. Unopened containers of maple syrup may be stored at room temperature. After opening, store maple syrup in the refrigerator to protect against mold. Maple syrup will keep indefinitely when stored properly.

Molasses

Molasses is made from the juice of sugar cane or sugar beets that is boiled until a syrupy mixture remains. Light molasses is lighter in flavor and color and results from the first boiling of the syrup. Dark molasses, dark in both flavor and color, is not as sweet as light molasses. It comes from the second boiling of the syrup. Light and dark molasses may be used interchangeably in the recipes in this collection. Blackstrap molasses is thick, very dark, and has a bitter flavor; it is not recommended for the recipes in this collection. Unopened containers of molasses may be stored at room temperature. After opening, store molasses in the refrigerator to protect against mold. Molasses will keep indefinitely when stored properly.

Nonstick Cooking Spray

I prefer to use nonstick cooking spray, such as PAM, for "greasing" pans because of its convenience. However, solid vegetable shortening, such as Crisco, may also be used. Both are flavorless and coat pans and cookie sheets evenly.

When spraying or greasing baking pans for brownies, be sure to coat only the bottom of the pan. If the inside walls of the pan are coated, the brownies will not rise properly. When making bars, the entire inside of the pan may be coated in cooking spray. Cookie sheets should be given only a very light spraying or greasing for best results.

Shelled Nuts

Use plain, unsalted nuts unless specified otherwise in the recipe. To determine whether shelled nuts are fresh, taste them: they should taste and smell fresh, not rancid with an off-flavor. Frozen nuts are prone to freezer burn if stored improperly and may taste old or stale (old, stale, or rancid nuts will ruin the baked product). Shelled nuts should also have a crisp texture, should be relatively uniform in color, and should not be shriveled or discolored in spots.

TOASTING NUTS: Toasting nuts before adding them to a recipe can greatly intensify their flavor and hence their contribution to a recipe. To toast without turning on the oven, place them in an ungreased skillet over medium heat (3–4 minutes), stirring frequently, until golden brown (note that this method works best with chopped, as opposed to whole, nuts). To oven-toast, spread the nuts in a single layer in a baking pan or on a cookie sheet. Bake at 350°F for 10–15 minutes, stirring occasionally, or until golden brown. Cool the nuts before adding them to the recipe.

Spices

All of the recipes in this book use ground, as opposed to whole, spices. Freshness is everything with ground spices. The best way to determine if a ground spice is fresh is to open the container and smell it. If it still has a strong fragrance, it is still acceptable for use. If not, toss it and make a new purchase.

Vanilla Extract

Vanilla extract adds a sweet, fragrant flavor to baked goods and is particularly good for enhancing the flavor of chocolate. It is produced by extracting the flavor of dried vanilla beans with an alcohol and water mixture. It is then aged for several months. The three most common types of beans used to make vanilla extract are Bourbon-Madagascar, Mexican, and Tahitian.

Store vanilla extract in a cool, dark place, with the bottle tightly closed to prevent it from evaporating and losing flavor. It will stay fresh for about two years unopened and for one year after being opened. Imitation vanilla flavoring can be substituted for vanilla extract, but it may have a slight or prominent artificial taste depending on the brand. It is about half the cost of real vanilla extract; however, it's worth the extra expense of splurging on the real thing.

Other Extracts and Flavorings

Other extracts and flavorings, such as maple, rum, lemon and brandy, are used in recipes throughout this book. They can be found in the baking aisle alongside the vanilla extract. Store in a cool, dark place to maintain optimal flavor.

Peanut Butter

Peanut butter is a spreadable blend of ground peanuts, vegetable oil, and salt. Two types of peanut butter are used throughout this collection: creamy and chunky. Avoid using natural or old-fashioned peanut butter in all of the recipes in this book because the consistency is significantly different from the commercial styles of peanut butter.

Marshmallows and Marshmallow Creme

Marshmallows are white, spongy, pillow-shaped confections made from sugar, corn syrup, gelatin, and egg whites. They are available readymade in both large and miniature sizes. Opened packages of marshmallows should be placed in a large, zip-top plastic bag to preserve their freshness. Marshmallow creme (also called marshmallow fluff) is available in jar form and looks like melted marshmallow.

Evaporated Milk

Evaporated milk is a canned milk product that is made by evaporating milk to half of its volume, producing a creamy texture and rich taste. All of the recipes in this book that require evaporated milk were tested using regular (as opposed to low-fat) evaporated milk.

Sweetened Condensed Milk

Sweetened condensed milk is canned evaporated milk that has been reduced further and sweetened with sugar. It is available in fat-free varieties, too; either the regular or fat-free varieties may be used.

Coconut

To toast coconut without turning on the oven, place 1 cup of coconut at a time in a large, nonstick skillet. Cook and stir over medium heat for 3–4 minutes until golden-brown and fragrant. Cool the coconut before adding to the recipe.

READY, SET, BAKE!

Well, almost. Before you begin, I'm going to stand on my soapbox and make a plea for attention to the following four baking issues, each of which is elementary to cookie baking, yet frequently taken for granted, if not overlooked entirely. I'm talking about choosing the correct cookie sheets and baking pans, getting to know your oven, and using an oven thermometer. So if you're looking to make every batch of cookies, brownies, bars, and biscotti edible perfection, read on.

A Few Words about Cookie Sheets

People have strong opinions about their preferred cookie sheet, so consider the following recommendations as guidelines rather than inflexible rules. I find that the more information I have about the baking process, the easier it is to "foolproof" recipes. For example, knowing that different sheets and pans can produce different results, and why, can reduce the possibility of your favorite recipe tasting wonderful one time, okay the next, and positively inedible on the occasion you plan to share it at a potluck party.

When baking cookies, choose light-colored, dull-finished, heavy-gauge cookie sheets. Shiny sheets work best for cookies that should not brown too much on the bottom.

Except for bar cookies, avoid using cookie sheets with high sides. Such pans can deflect heat as well as make it difficult to remove the cookies for cooling. As a general rule, cookie sheets should be two inches narrower and shorter than the oven to allow for even baking.

It is best to avoid dark aluminum cookie sheets. These sheets have a brown or almost black finish and may absorb heat, causing bottoms of cookies to brown more quickly. If using these sheets is the only option, decrease the baking time and lower the temperature slightly (about 25°).

Nonstick cookie sheets are easier to clean and help ensure even baking; however, the dough may not spread as much and you may end up with a thicker cookie. On the other hand, rich cookies can spread if baked on a greased sheet. Follow the manufacturer's instructions if using a cookie sheet with a nonstick coating; the oven temperature may need to be reduced by 25°.

Also follow the manufacturer's instructions if using insulated cookie sheets, which are made from two sheets of metal with a layer of air between for insulation. Cookies will not brown as much on the bottom, so it may hard to tell when the cookies are done. Also, cookies may take slightly longer to bake. If you don't have enough cookie sheets, you can invert a jelly roll pan or use heavy-duty foil.

Selecting the Right Baking Pan

Just as the right cookie sheet is essential for drop and shaped cookies, so too is using the correct size baking pan for brownies and bars. Brownies and bars made in too-large pans, for example, will be over-baked, and those in too-small pans will be under-baked.

If you only have a few pans, and none are the pan size specified, a solution still exists. Use the pan size that you have. If it's larger than what is called for, use a shorter bake time. If it's smaller than what is called for, use a longer bake time and reduce the oven temperature 25°.

For best results, use shiny metal pans for all of the bar recipes in this book. Not only are the bars easier to remove but metal pans allow the crusts of layered bars to become crispy. If possible, avoid using dark pans. If a dark pan is all you have, reduce the oven temperature 25°.

Know Thy Oven

Whether used a little or a lot, it is worth taking a few minutes to familiarize yourself with your oven's myriad functions. Some ovens have specialty features specific to baking, such as precision temperature settings and extra-large interior capacities that allow for multiple items baking at once, so take advantage of these for delicious baked results. Also, give the interior a good cleaning. This is especially important if you have no idea when it last got a thorough wipe-down or if you recently baked or roasted something particularly aromatic. Lingering odors or scents can alter the flavor and smell of your cookies and desserts.

The three most common types of baking ovens for the home kitchen are conventional (gas or electric), convection, and toaster.

CONVENTIONAL OVEN: This is the most common type of oven. All of the recipes in this book were tested using a standard, conventional oven. The heat source is located in the bottom of conventional ovens, allowing for the heat to rise up through the oven in a more or less even manner.

CONVECTION OVEN: By contrast, the heat source in a convection oven is located behind the oven wall. In addition, convection ovens have a fan that continuously circulates air through the oven cavity. When hot air is blowing onto food, as opposed to merely surrounding it (as in a conventional oven), the food tends to cook more quickly and evenly, ideal for baking perfect, evenly browned cookies. The circulating air may alter the amount of time needed for baking, so you may need to do a small experimental batch to get a sense of how to adjust the baking time.

TOASTER OVEN: I do not recommend baking any of the cookies or other desserts in this book in a toaster oven. The exception to this rule is the more recent combination toaster/convection ovens that have appeared on the market in the last few years. These ovens offer more even circulation of heat than traditional toaster ovens. Drop cookies are the best option for baking small batches of cookies in these ovens, but follow the manufacturer's guidelines for adapting recipe baking times.

The Best Baking Investment You May Ever Make: An Oven Thermometer

If I could make a single plea to home bakers it would be this: buy an oven thermometer to check your oven temperature. Unless you have a state-of-the-art oven (and even then, temperature discrepancies can still occur), it is very likely that your oven temperature is inaccurate. It may be off as few as five degrees or as many as fifty degrees, but whatever the discrepancy, it will affect your results.

The good news is that an easy, inexpensive, readily available remedy exists: an oven thermometer. You can find this simple tool in the baking section of most supermarkets or superstores (e.g., Kmart, Target, and Wal-Mart), kitchen stores, and hardware stores (typically if they have a pots and pans section they will carry oven thermometers).

Simply place or attach the oven thermometer in your oven (see package instructions) and preheat. Once your oven indicates that it has reached the temperature setting, check your oven thermometer. If the oven temperature is higher on the thermometer than the setting you selected, you will need to set your oven that many degrees lower. For example, if the thermometer reads 375°F and you had set your oven for 350°F, you know that you will need to set your oven to 325° in the future for it to reach 350°F. Leave the oven thermometer in the oven and check it every time you preheat the oven to monitor temperature accuracy.

While few ovens are precise, most are consistent. That is, if it is 25° hotter than the selected temperature, it tends to stay 25° too hot all of the time. This may shift slightly at extremely high temperatures (exceeding 400°F). However, temperatures lower than 400°F are used for all of the baking recipes in this book.

MEASURING INGREDIENTS

Measuring Dry Ingredients
When measuring a dry ingredient such as sugar, spices, or salt, spoon it into the appropriate-size dry measuring cup or measuring spoon, heaping it up over the top. Next, slide a straight-edged utensil, such as a knife, across the top to level off the extra. Be careful not to shake or tap the cup or spoon to settle the ingredient or you will have more than you need.

Measuring Liquid Ingredients
Use a clear plastic or glass measuring cup or container with lines up the sides to measure liquid ingredients. Set the container on the counter and pour the liquid to the appropriate mark. Lower your head to read the measurement at eye level.

Measuring Syrups, Honey, and Molasses
Measure syrups, honey, and molasses as you would other liquid ingredients, but lightly spray the measuring cup or container with nonstick cooking spray before filling. The syrup, honey, or molasses will slide out of the cup without sticking, allowing for both accurate measuring and easy cleanup.

Measuring Moist Ingredients

Some moist ingredients, such as brown sugar, coconut, and dried fruits, must be firmly packed into the measuring cup to be measured accurately. Use a dry measuring cup for these ingredients. Fill the measuring cup to slightly overflowing, then pack down the ingredient firmly with the back of a spoon. Add more of the ingredient and pack down again until the cup is full and even with the top of the measure.

Measuring Butter

Butter is typically packaged in stick form with markings on the wrapper indicating tablespoon and cup measurements. Use a sharp knife to cut off the amount needed for a recipe.

¼ cup = ½ stick = 4 tablespoons = 2 ounces
½ cup = 1 stick = ¼ pound = 4 ounces
1 cup = 2 sticks = ½ pound = 8 ounces
2 cups = 4 sticks = 1 pound = 16 ounces

Measuring Cream Cheese

Like sticks of butter, bricks of cream cheese are typically packaged with markings on the wrapper indicating tablespoon and cup measurements. Use a sharp knife to cut off the amount needed for a recipe.

Measuring Spices, Salt, Baking Powder, and Baking Soda

Use the standard measuring spoon size specified in the recipe and be sure the spoon is dry when measuring. Fill a standard measuring spoon to the top and level with a spatula or knife. When a recipe calls for a dash of a spice or salt, use about $1/16$ of a teaspoon. A pinch is considered to be the amount of salt that can be held between the tips of the thumb and forefinger, and is also approximately $1/16$ of a teaspoon.

Measuring Nuts

Spoon nuts into a dry measuring cup to the top. Four ounces of whole nuts is the equivalent of 1 cup chopped nuts.

Measuring Extracts and Flavorings

Fill the standard measuring spoon size specified in the recipe to the top, being careful not to let any spill over. It's a good idea to avoid measuring extracts or flavorings over the mixing bowl because the spillover will go into the bowl and you will not know the amount of extract or flavoring you have added.

MAKING, BAKING, AND STORING

Preheating the Oven

For perfectly baked cookies, preheat the oven, which takes about ten to fifteen minutes, depending on your oven.

Center of the Oven

If baking just one sheet or pan of cookies at a time, place it on a rack set in the center of the oven and change from back to front halfway through the baking cycle. Leave at least 2 inches of space on all sides between the edge of the sheet and the oven walls for proper air circulation.

Foil-Line Your Baking Pans

Lining baking pans with aluminum foil is a great way to avoid messy cleanup whenever you bake bar cookies and brownies. Doing so also makes it easy to remove the entire batch of brownies or bars from the pan, making the cutting of perfectly uniform squares and bars a snap. When bars are cool or nearly cool, simply lift them out of the pan, peel back the foil and cut. Foil-lining is also a boon during holiday baking seasons, allowing for the production of multiple batches of bars and brownies in no time, with virtually no clean-up.

Foil-lining is simple. Begin by turning the pan upside down. Tear off a piece of aluminum foil longer than the pan, and shape the foil over the pan. Carefully remove the foil and set aside. Flip the pan over and gently fit the shaped foil into the pan, allowing the foil to hang over the sides (the overhanging ends will work as "handles" when the brownies or bars are removed).

Two Cookie Sheets at a Time: Switch the Racks

It's okay to bake more than one sheet of cookies at a time. Use the upper and lower thirds of the oven, reversing sheets from upper to lower and front to back about halfway through the baking period to ensure even baking. Even the best ovens can build up hot spots in certain areas.

Keep in mind, too, that two sheets of cookies in the oven may require a slightly longer baking time than one sheet. One of the pans may be ready sooner than the other. Reverse the pans in the oven for evenly baked cookies.

Checking for Doneness

Bake cookies the minimum amount of time, even though the center may look slightly under-baked. To check cookies for doneness, press down lightly in the middle to see if it bounces back. Bake sliced cookies until the edges are firm and the bottoms are lightly browned. Generally, cookies are done when the edges begin to brown, or when they are golden. Every pan bakes differently, depending on the material, thickness, weight, and surface reflection.

Remember to open and close the oven door quickly to maintain the proper baking temperature. Most importantly, watch carefully, especially batches of individual cookies that bake for very short amounts of time. While a watched pot may never boil, unwatched cookies will likely burn.

Cooling Cookie Sheets in between Batches

Always cool the cookie sheet before baking another batch. A warm pan causes the dough to melt, which can cause overspreading, deformed cookies, or altered baking times. To cool cookie sheets quickly between baking, rinse under cold water until the sheet is completely cooled. Dry and proceed with the next batch of cookies.

Cooling

Remove baked cookies immediately from the cookie sheet with a wide spatula, unless the recipe states other cooling directions. Place cookies in a single layer on wire racks to cool evenly, so the bottoms don't get soggy. You can transfer some cookies immediately to the wire racks, while others need a couple minutes to cool on the cookie sheet. If the cookie bends or breaks when transferring, wait another minute before trying. Thoroughly cool cookies before storing them to prevent them from becoming soggy.

Quick Cookie Sheet Q&A: Why Do Cookies Stick?

If cookies stick, it is most likely due to one of the following, and easily remedied, problems:

- The cookie sheets were not sufficiently cleaned between uses.
- The cookie sheets were not greased or sprayed with nonstick spray and the recipe called for greasing or spraying.
- The cookies were under-baked.
- The cookies were left on cookie sheets too long before removal.
- The cookie batter was too warm.
- The cookie sheets were warm or hot before baking.

Storing Cookies

Once cookies are baked, keep them delicious by taking care with their storage. Most importantly, store them in an airtight container for optimal freshness. Sturdier cookies, such as drop cookies, can be placed in a zip-top plastic bag, but more delicate filled and formed cookies are better off stacked between layers of wax paper in a plastic container.

Bar cookies can be stacked in a container between layers of wax paper or stored in their baking pan. I prefer to cut them first and then place them back in the pan for easy removal. Cover the top tightly with aluminum foil, wrap, or a lid. For delicate, crisp cookies, store in a sturdy container such as a cookie jar or tin.

Lay extra-fragile cookies flat in a wide container with parchment or wax paper between the layers. If you have iced or decorated cookies, let them dry before storing. (If freezing, freeze on a pan in a single layer, and then carefully stack layers with wax paper between layers).

Freezing Already-Baked Cookies

To enjoy your cookies for several weeks, or even months, freeze them. For best results, freeze the cookies as soon as possible after they are completely cooled. Both individual and bar cookies can be frozen with equal success. With either type, it is best to frost at a future date when the cookies have been thawed. Place the cookies in freezer bags or airtight freezer containers for up to 12 months. Double-wrap cookies to prevent them from getting freezer burn or absorbing odors from the freezer. Label the cookies clearly with the name of the cookie and the date. Cookies can be frosted after thawing at room temperature for 15 minutes.

Shipping Cookies

A care package full of home-baked cookies may be the best gift ever. To ensure perfect delivery, follow my tips below:

- Biscotti, bar, and drop cookies can best withstand mailing; tender, fragile cookies are apt to crumble when shipped.
- Line a heavy cardboard box, cookie tin, or empty coffee can with aluminum foil or plastic wrap. Wrap four to six cookies of the same size together in aluminum foil, plastic wrap, or plastic food bags and seal securely with tape; repeat until the container is full.
- Place the heaviest cookies at the bottom of the container and layer the wrapped cookies with bubble wrap or crumpled paper towels. Use either of these to line the container. Seal the container with tape.

DROP COOKIES

ALMOND APRICOT DROPS

These crisp cookies disappear quickly whenever I make them, and I make them often because they are so simple to prepare and the recipe can easily be doubled for large gatherings, pitch-ins, or cookie trays.

- 2 cups Corn Chex cereal, coarsely crushed
- ½ cup slivered almonds
- ½ cup chopped, dried apricots
- 1¼ cups white chocolate chips
- ¼ teaspoon almond extract

Line cookie sheets with wax paper.

Combine the cereal, almonds, and apricots in a large bowl. Set aside momentarily.

In a microwave-safe medium mixing bowl, melt the white chocolate chips on high for 2 minutes, stirring after 1 minute. Stir in the almond extract and then stir mixture into cereal mixture.

Working quickly, drop by tablespoonfuls onto wax-paper-lined sheets. Let cool until firm. Store in airtight container between sheets of wax paper.

MAKES ABOUT 28 COOKIES.

ALMOND JOYFUL COOKIES

This outstanding milk chocolate–coconut cookie is extremely simple to make and especially wonderful to eat. The finished product strongly resembles a delicious candy bar of a similar name.

- 1 (16.5-ounce) roll refrigerated sugar cookie dough
- ¾ cup shredded coconut
- 1 cup milk chocolate chips
- ¾ cup whole almonds, coarsely chopped

Preheat oven to 350°F. Spray cookie sheets with nonstick cooking spray.

Break up the cookie dough into large bowl; let stand for 10–15 minutes to soften. Add the coconut, milk chocolate chips, and almonds; mix well with your fingers, the paddle attachment of an electric stand mixer, or a wooden spoon.

Drop dough by kitchen teaspoons, 2 inches apart, onto prepared cookie sheets.

Bake for 10–13 minutes or until just set and golden at edges. Transfer cookies to wire racks and cool completely.

MAKES 30 COOKIES.

Baker's Note

Sliced or slivered almonds, coarsely chopped, may be substituted for the chopped whole almonds.

APPLE-CRANBERRY HARVEST COOKIES

Cranberries, apples, and nuts, covered in a quick and spicy dough, make for a festive, fuss-free cookie. If other nuts, such as almonds or pecans, are what you have on hand, use them interchangeably with the walnuts, or leave them out altogether if you prefer.

- 1 (18.25-ounce) package spice cake mix
- 1 teaspoon ground cinnamon
- 1/3 cup vegetable oil
- 2 large eggs
- 1 cup peeled and finely chopped tart apple (e.g., Granny Smith)
- 2/3 cup dried cranberries
- 1 cup chopped walnuts

Preheat oven to 350°F. Position oven rack in middle of oven. Spray cookie sheets with nonstick cooking spray.

Place half of the cake mix in a large mixing bowl along with the cinnamon, oil, and eggs. Blend with an electric mixer set on medium-high speed for 1–2 minutes, until smooth. Stir in the remaining cake mix, apple, and cranberries with a wooden spoon until all dry ingredients are moistened.

Drop dough by teaspoonfuls, 2 inches apart, on prepared cookie sheets. Sprinkle tops with a few chopped walnuts; gently press into the dough.

Bake for 9–12 minutes or until set at edges and just barely set at center when lightly touched. Cool for 1 minute on cookie sheets. Transfer to wire racks with metal spatula and cool completely.

MAKES ABOUT 54 COOKIES.

APPLESAUCE COOKIES

This slightly spicy, nostalgic cookie is simple and good, with lots of familiar flavors and a soft, old-fashioned texture—just what you want to bake on a cool autumn day.

- 1 (18.25-ounce) package spice cake mix
- 1/2 cup vegetable oil
- 1/2 cup applesauce
- 1 large egg
- 1 cup raisins (or dried cranberries)

Preheat oven to 350°F. Position oven rack in middle of oven. Spray cookie sheets with nonstick cooking spray.

Place the cake mix, oil, applesauce, and egg in a large mixing bowl. Blend with an electric mixer set on medium-high speed for 1–2 minutes, until smooth. Stir in the raisins or dried cranberries.

Drop by teaspoonfuls, 2 inches apart, onto prepared cookie sheets.

Bake for 9–12 minutes or until edges are firm and center is just barely set when lightly touched. Cool for 1 minute on cookie sheets. Transfer to wire racks with metal spatula and cool completely.

MAKES ABOUT 48 COOKIES.

APPLE SCOTCHIES

Two harmonious flavors—apple and butterscotch—are united in these vanilla cream-frosted bars. Apple cider is the perfect accompaniment.

- 9 tablespoons butter, softened, divided
- 1 cup butterscotch baking chips, divided
- 1/3 cup firmly packed light brown sugar
- 2 cups graham cracker crumbs
- 1 cup very finely chopped dried apples

- ½ cup finely chopped pecans
- 2 cups powdered sugar, sifted
- 1 (3-ounce) package cream cheese, softened
- 2½ tablespoons milk
- 1 teaspoon vanilla extract

Lightly spray a 9 x 9 x 2-inch pan with nonstick cooking spray; set aside.

Melt 8 tablespoons (1 stick) of the butter with ½ cup of the butterscotch chips in a medium saucepan. Remove from the heat and stir in the brown sugar, graham cracker crumbs, dried apples, and pecans. Press mixture into prepared pan with a large square of wax paper. Chill for 1 hour.

Blend the powdered sugar, cream cheese, milk, and vanilla in a medium bowl with an electric mixer set on medium speed until mixture has an icing-like consistency; spread over the chilled bars. Chill for 30 minutes.

Melt the remaining butter with the remaining ½ cup butterscotch chips, stirring until mixture is smooth. Spread or drizzle over the top of the bars. Chill for 1–2 hours. Cut into 16 squares by dipping a sharp knife in hot water and let it melt through the butterscotch. Store in covered containers between layers of wax paper.

MAKES 16 SQUARES.

APRICOT CHEWS

Apricot fans rejoice—this is an exceptional cookie, chewy and rich with fruit.

- 1 (8-ounce) package cream cheese, softened
- ¼ cup (½ stick) butter, softened

- 1 large egg yolk
- 2 tablespoons milk
- 1 tablespoon grated orange zest
- 1 (18.25-ounce) package vanilla cake mix
- 1 cup chopped dried apricots
- ½ cup sweetened flaked coconut

Preheat oven to 350°F. Position oven rack in middle of oven.

Beat the softened cream cheese and butter in a large bowl with an electric mixer set on low speed until smooth. Beat in egg yolk, milk, and orange zest. Beat in half of the cake mix until well blended. Stir in the remaining cake mix, apricots, and coconut with a wooden spoon.

Drop dough by rounded teaspoonfuls, 2 inches apart, onto ungreased cookie sheets.

Bake for 10–12 minutes or until just set and bottoms of cookies are lightly browned. Remove cookies to wire racks to cool completely.

MAKES ABOUT 54 COOKIES.

BABY RUTHY CLUSTERS

For a backyard barbecue or a fun-in-the-sun picnic, these cookie clusters have all the right ingredients (which can also be found in a favorite candy bar of similar name): milk chocolate, salty peanuts, and a hearty dose of gooey caramel to hold everything together.

- 12 caramels, unwrapped
- ½ cup milk chocolate chips
- 2 tablespoons milk
- 2 cups honey graham cereal, slightly crushed (yields about 1½ cups crushed cereal)

- ¾ cup very coarsely chopped lightly salted, roasted peanuts

Line cookie sheets with wax paper. Lightly spray with nonstick cooking spray. Set aside momentarily.

Combine the caramels, milk chocolate chips, and milk in a heavy medium saucepan. Stir over low heat until caramels are melted. Remove from heat. Stir in the cereal and peanuts.

Working quickly, drop mixture from a teaspoon onto wax-paper-lined sheets. Let stand until firm. Store cookies in refrigerator up to 1 week.

MAKES ABOUT 26 COOKIES.

BANANA-CHIP CHIPPERS

No monkey business here, just a bunch of delicious chocolate-chip cookies with a welcome new crunch of flavor. You can find banana chips in one or more places in the supermarket: the health food section, the dried fruits section, or in the bulk foods section. If you cannot find them there, a health food store is sure to sell them.

- 1 (16.5-ounce) roll refrigerated chocolate-chip cookie dough
- 1 cup crushed banana chips

Preheat oven to 350°F. Spray cookie sheets with nonstick cooking spray.

Break up the cookie dough into large bowl; let stand for 10–15 minutes to soften. Add the banana chips; mix well with your fingers, the paddle attachment of an electric stand mixer, or a wooden spoon.

Drop dough by kitchen teaspoons, 2 inches apart, onto prepared cookie sheets.

Bake for 10–13 minutes or until just set and golden at edges. Transfer cookies to wire racks and cool completely.

MAKES 26 COOKIES.

Baker's Note

To crush the banana chips, place in a small zippered plastic bag. Cover bag with dishtowel and pound with a meat mallet, rolling pin, or soup can.

BANANARAMA SOFTIES

How is it that such simple foods, like these soft, nutmeg-scented banana cookies, have such wide appeal? My guess is that it's because, like many favorite things, the familiar comforts are what we like best.

- 1 medium, ripe banana
- 1 large egg
- 2 tablespoons vegetable oil
- 1 (18.25-ounce) package yellow cake mix
- ½ teaspoon ground nutmeg
- 1 cup chopped walnuts (or pecans), optional

Preheat oven to 350°F. Position oven rack in middle of oven. Spray cookie sheets with nonstick cooking spray.

Mash the banana in a large mixing bowl. Add the egg, oil, half of the cake mix, and the nutmeg. Blend with an electric mixer set on medium-high speed for 1–2 minutes, until smooth. Stir in the remaining cake mix with a wooden spoon until all dry ingredients are moistened.

Drop by teaspoonfuls, 2 inches apart, onto prepared cookie sheets. If desired, sprinkle tops of cookies with chopped nuts; gently press nuts into dough.

Bake for 10–13 minutes or until set at edges and just barely set at center when lightly touched (do not overbake). Cool for 1 minute on cookie sheets. Transfer to wire racks with metal spatula and cool completely.

MAKES ABOUT 48 COOKIES.

BANANAS FOSTER CLUSTERS

You can make these yummy treats without the alcohol by replacing the rum or brandy with 1½ tablespoons water combined with 1½ teaspoons rum-flavored or brandy-flavored baking extract.

- 12 caramels, unwrapped
- ½ cup white, milk, or semisweet chocolate chips
- 2 tablespoons dark rum or brandy
- 2 cups honey graham cereal, slightly crushed (about 1½ cups)
- ¾ cup coarsely crushed banana chips

Line cookie sheets with wax paper.

Combine the caramels, chocolate chips, and rum in a heavy medium saucepan. Stir over low heat until caramels are melted and mixture is smooth. Remove from heat. Stir in the cereal and banana chips until blended.

Working quickly, drop mixture from a kitch-en teaspoon onto wax-paper-lined sheets. Let stand until firm (about 30 minutes). Store in covered container between sheets of wax paper.

MAKES ABOUT 26 CLUSTERS.

BIG BROWNIE COOKIES

So easy, so good, and so very chocolate—who can resist a cookie with those credentials? These cookies are great last-minute makers because an entire batch comes together in well under an hour and the results are so very impressive. If you wish to make smaller cookies, drop by heaping teaspoons (rather than tablespoons) and proceed as directed, baking for 9–13 minutes, until set. This will make about 36 cookies. If you choose to add nuts, sprinkle them on top of each cookie rather than stirring them into the batter. The nuts will get toasted this way, deepening their flavor.

- 1 (19.5- to 19.8-ounce) package brownie mix
- ⅓ cup vegetable oil or melted unsalted butter
- 2 large eggs
- 1½ cups semisweet chocolate chips or chunks
- 1 cup chopped nuts, any variety, sprinkled on top of cookies before baking (optional)

Preheat oven to 350°F. Spray cookie sheets with nonstick cooking spray.

Combine the brownie mix, oil, and eggs in a

large mixing bowl with a wooden spoon until just blended and all dry ingredients are moistened; stir in chocolate chips.

Drop dough by heaping tablespoonfuls, 2 inches apart, onto prepared cookie sheets. Sprinkle with nuts, if desired.

Bake for 11–14 minutes until cracked in appearance and just barely set at center when lightly touched. Cool for 1 minute on cookie sheets. Transfer to wire racks with metal spatula and cool completely.

MAKES ABOUT 30 BIG COOKIES.

BIG FAT OATMEAL-RAISIN COOKIES

Oatmeal cookies are a nostalgic choice anytime. The brown sugar, vanilla extract, and butter heighten the rich, old-fashioned flavor of these easily assembled goodies. And if you're fond of a little innovation, try one or both of the variations, too, for a delicious punch of new flavor.

- 1 (18.25-ounce) package spice cake mix
- 1/3 cup packed dark brown sugar
- 1 cup (2 sticks) butter, softened
- 2 large eggs
- 2 teaspoons vanilla extract
- 1¼ cups raisins
- 2 cups quick-cooking oats

Preheat oven to 350°F. Spray cookie sheets with nonstick cooking spray.

Place half of the cake mix in a large mixing bowl along with the brown sugar, softened butter, eggs, vanilla extract, and raisins. Blend

with an electric mixer set on medium-high speed for 1–2 minutes, until smooth. Stir in the remaining cake mix and oats with a wooden spoon until all dry ingredients are well blended (dough will be very stiff).

Drop dough by level ¼-cupfuls, 2 inches apart, onto prepared cookie sheets; flatten slightly with your palm or a spatula.

Bake for 13–17 minutes or until set at edges and just barely set at center when lightly touched. Cool for 1 minute on cookie sheets. Transfer to wire racks with metal spatula and cool completely.

MAKES 24 BIG COOKIES.

Variations:

CRANBERRY-ORANGE OATMEAL COOKIES: Prepare as directed above but replace raisins with dried cranberries and add 1 tablespoon grated orange zest.

TROPICAL OATMEAL COOKIES: Prepare as directed above but replace raisins with dried tropical fruit bits and add 1 teaspoon ground ginger and 1 tablespoon grated lime zest.

BITTERSWEET CHOCOLATE BLACKOUT COOKIES

The list of what's great about these very chocolate, crisp-chewy cookies is long. In addition to an over-the-top chocolate intensity, they're quite practical: you can make several dozen premium cookies with a few flicks of a spoon and have a delicious chocolate bounty ready and waiting.

- 2 tablespoons instant espresso or coffee powder
- 1/3 cup water
- 1 (18.25-ounce) package devil's food cake mix
- 1/4 cup (1/2 stick) butter, melted
- 1 large egg
- 1 (8-ounce) package bittersweet baking chocolate, coarsely chopped into chunks

Preheat oven to 350°F. Position oven rack in middle of oven. Spray cookie sheets with nonstick cooking spray.

Combine the espresso powder and water in a large mixing bowl, stirring to dissolve. Add half of the cake mix along with the melted butter and egg to the same bowl. Blend with an electric mixer set on medium-high speed for 1–2 minutes, until smooth. Stir in the remaining cake mix and chopped chocolate with a wooden spoon until all dry ingredients are moistened.

Drop dough by teaspoonfuls, 2 inches apart, on prepared cookie sheets.

Bake for 9–12 minutes or until set at edges and just barely set at center when lightly touched. Cool for 1 minute on cookie sheets. Transfer to wire racks with metal spatula and cool completely.

MAKES ABOUT 48 COOKIES.

Variation:

BLACK AND WHITE BLACKOUT COOKIES:
Prepare as directed above but substitute 1 (6-ounce) package chopped white chocolate baking bars for bittersweet chocolate.

BLACK FOREST OATMEAL COOKIES

The combination of chocolate and cherry is always a crowd pleaser, which is why these easily assembled cookies are a guaranteed hit. Be sure to make an extra batch during the holiday season—a plateful will only last so long.

- 1 (18.25-ounce) package devil's food cake mix
- 1/2 cup vegetable oil
- 2 large eggs
- 1/2 teaspoon almond extract
- 1 cup quick-cooking oats
- 1 cup miniature semisweet chocolate chips
- 1 cup tart dried cherries (or dried cranberries)

Preheat oven to 375°F. Position oven rack in middle of oven. Spray cookie sheets with nonstick cooking spray.

Place half of the cake mix along with the oil, eggs, and almond extract in a large mixing bowl. Blend with an electric mixer set on medium-high speed for 1–2 minutes, until smooth. Stir in the remaining cake mix, oats, miniature chocolate chips, and dried cherries with a wooden spoon until all dry ingredients are moistened (dough will be stiff).

Drop dough by heaping teaspoonfuls, 2 inches apart, onto prepared cookie sheets.

Bake for 9–12 minutes or until set at edges and just barely set at center when lightly touched (do not overbake). Cool for 1 minute on cookie sheets. Transfer to wire racks with metal spatula and cool completely.

MAKES ABOUT 48 COOKIES.

BLUE-RIBBON CHOCOLATE-CHIP COOKIES

Hats off to Ruth Wakefield. Back in the 1930s the clever home baker and proprietor of the Toll House Inn "invented" (whether by mistake or design—the jury is still out on this one) what we now know as the chocolate-chip cookie. American cookie baking has never been the same since, and thank goodness. This quick and easy cake mix version of Mrs. Wakefield's classic creation earns its blue-ribbon tag.

- 1 (18.25-ounce) package yellow cake mix
- ½ cup (1 stick) butter, softened
- 3 tablespoons packed dark brown sugar
- 2 large eggs
- 2 teaspoons vanilla extract
- 1½ cups semisweet chocolate chips
- 1 cup chopped pecans (or walnuts), optional

Preheat oven to 350°F. Position oven rack in middle of oven. Spray cookie sheets with nonstick cooking spray.

Place half of the cake mix along with the softened butter, brown sugar, eggs, and vanilla extract in a large mixing bowl. Blend with an electric mixer set on medium-high speed for 1–2 minutes, until smooth. Stir in the remaining cake mix, chocolate chips, and nuts, if desired, with a wooden spoon until all dry ingredients are moistened.

Drop by teaspoonfuls, 2 inches apart, onto prepared cookie sheets.

Bake for 10–13 minutes or until golden at the edges and just barely set at center when lightly touched. Cool for 1 minute on cookie sheets. Transfer to wire racks with metal spatula and cool completely.

MAKES ABOUT 54 COOKIES.

Variations:

GINGER CHOCOLATE CHIPPERS: Prepare as directed above but do not use nuts and add 1½ teaspoons ground ginger and ½ cup chopped crystallized ginger to the dough.

TART CHERRY MILK CHOCOLATE CHIPPERS: Prepare as directed above but replace semisweet chocolate chips with milk chocolate chips and add 2/3 cup dried tart cherries or dried cranberries instead of nuts.

CHOCOLATE MINT CHOCOLATE CHIPPERS: Prepare as directed above but replace the vanilla extract with ¾ teaspoon peppermint extract. Sprinkle cookie tops with crushed red and white striped peppermint candies or candy canes just before baking (about 1 cup total).

MOCHA CHOCOLATE CHIPPERS: Prepare as directed above but dissolve 1 tablespoon instant espresso or coffee powder in the vanilla extract before adding.

TOFFEE CHOCOLATE CHIPPERS: Prepare as directed above but add ¾ cup toffee baking bits to the dough instead of nuts.

BRANDIED FRUITCAKE JUMBLES

There's no middle ground when it comes to fruitcake—one person's beloved portent of the Christmas season is another's bitter pill. But there's no better cookie than this brandy-accented one to convince even the most stalwart of skeptics.

- 1 (18.25-ounce) package yellow cake mix
- ¼ cup brandy or dark rum
- ¼ cup (½ stick) butter, melted
- 1 large egg
- ½ cup quick-cooking oats
- ⅔ cup raisins
- 1 cup candied cherries, chopped
- 1 cup chopped walnuts (or pecans)

Preheat oven to 350°F. Position oven rack in middle of oven. Spray cookie sheets with nonstick cooking spray.

Place half of the cake mix in a large mixing bowl along with the brandy or rum, melted butter, egg, and oats. Blend with an electric mixer set on medium-high speed for 1–2 minutes, until smooth. Stir in the remaining cake mix, raisins, and candied cherries with a wooden spoon until all dry ingredients are moistened.

Drop dough by teaspoonfuls, 2 inches apart, onto prepared cookie sheets. Sprinkle cookie tops with nuts; gently press nuts into dough.

Bake for 10–13 minutes or until just barely set at center when lightly touched. Cool for 1 minute on cookie sheets. Transfer to wire racks with metal spatula and cool completely.

MAKES ABOUT 48 COOKIES.

BROWNED BUTTER-FROSTED CASHEW COOKIES

The short list of ingredients here belies the unique goodness of this simple drop cookie. It is far more than the sum of its parts and is sure to dazzle die-hard dessert-aholics. The nutty-sweet flavor of browned butter—butter you melt until it turns a light caramel hue—is made for cashews.

- 1 (16.5-ounce) roll refrigerated sugar cookie dough
- 1 cup coarsely chopped roasted, lightly salted cashews
- 2 tablespoons dark brown sugar
- 1 recipe Browned Butter Frosting (see page 360)

Preheat oven to 350°F. Spray cookie sheets with nonstick cooking spray.

Break up the cookie dough into large bowl; let stand for 10–15 minutes to soften. Add the cashews and brown sugar; mix well with your fingers, the paddle attachment of an electric stand mixer, or a wooden spoon.

Drop dough by kitchen teaspoons, 2 inches apart, onto prepared cookie sheets.

Bake for 10–13 minutes or until just set and golden at edges. Transfer cookies to wire racks.

While cookies bake, prepare Browned Butter Frosting. Immediately spoon about 1 teaspoon icing over each warm cookie. If icing becomes too thick, reheat over low heat. Cool cookies completely.

MAKES 26 COOKIES.

BROWNIES AND CREAM SANDWICH COOKIES

These humble sandwich cookies have what it takes to bring on the smiles: rich brownie cookies, creamy filling, and a big comfort factor. For a chocolate sandwich cookie, substitute Chocolate Cream Cheese Frosting (see page 361) or Chocolate Fudge Frosting (see page 362) for the cream cheese frosting.

- 1 (19.5- to 19.8-ounce) package brownie mix
- 1/3 cup vegetable oil
- 2 large eggs
- 1 recipe Cream Cheese Frosting (see page 366)

Preheat oven to 350°F. Spray cookie sheets with nonstick cooking spray.

Mix the brownie mix, oil, and eggs in a large mixing bowl with wooden spoon until just blended and all dry ingredients are moistened.

Drop by teaspoonfuls, 2 inches apart, onto prepared cookie sheet.

Bake for 7–8 minutes or until cookies are set at edges and just barely set at center when lightly touched. Cool for 1 minute on cookie sheets. Transfer to wire racks with metal spatula and cool completely.

Prepare Cream Cheese Frosting. Spread frosting on the bottoms of half of the cooled cookies. Top each frosted cookie with another cookie. Gently press together.

MAKES ABOUT 30 SANDWICH COOKIES.

BROWN SUGAR PECAN DATE DROPS

I am a full-fledged brown sugar fiend. As a child I was notorious for eating it straight out of the box. These days I have (a modicum) more self-restraint—except perhaps when it comes to these cookies. Chopped dates, brown sugar, pecans, and vanilla create a perfect coalescence of crisp-chewy, brown sugar-y goodness that is unmatched.

- 1 (16.5-ounce) roll refrigerated sugar cookie dough
- 2 tablespoons packed brown sugar
- 3/4 cup chopped pitted dates
- 1/2 cup chopped lightly toasted pecans (or walnuts), cooled
- 1 teaspoon vanilla extract

Preheat oven to 350°F. Spray cookie sheets with nonstick cooking spray.

Break up the cookie dough into large bowl; let stand for 10–15 minutes to soften. Add the brown sugar, dates, nuts, and vanilla; mix well with your fingers, the paddle attachment of an electric stand mixer, or a wooden spoon.

Drop dough by kitchen teaspoons, 2 inches apart, onto prepared cookie sheets.

Bake for 10–13 minutes or until just set and golden at edges. Transfer cookies to wire racks and cool completely.

MAKES 28 COOKIES.

BUTTERED RUM RAISIN COOKIES

One of my favorite college professors loved to bake. He made the best breads and cookies and, luckily for me and his other students, often brought the results of his late-night baking experiments to class for all of us to enjoy. As an added bonus, he also shared his recipes. This is an adaptation of one of his (and now my) favorites. Delicious plain, they are positively scrumptious frosted with a rum-laced browned-butter icing.

- 1 (16.5-ounce) roll refrigerated sugar cookie dough
- 1 cup raisins
- 1 recipe Butter-Rum Icing (see page 375)

Preheat oven to 350°F. Spray cookie sheets with nonstick cooking spray.

Break up the cookie dough into large bowl; let stand for 10–15 minutes to soften. Add the raisins; mix well with your fingers, the paddle attachment of an electric stand mixer, or a wooden spoon. Drop dough by kitchen teaspoons, 2 inches apart, onto prepared cookie sheets.

Bake for 10–13 minutes or until just set and golden at edges. Immediately remove from cookie sheets; place on wire racks.

Spoon about 1 teaspoon Butter-Rum Icing over each warm cookie. If icing becomes too thick, reheat over low heat.

MAKES 26 COOKIES.

BUTTERSCOTCH PECAN COOKIES

Butter pecan to the max! These cookies have magical properties—they disappear almost as quickly as they are made.

- 1 (18.25-ounce) package butter pecan cake mix
- 1/3 cup butter, melted
- 2 large eggs
- 1½ cups butterscotch baking chips
- 1⅓ cups chopped pecans

Preheat oven to 350°F. Position oven rack in middle of oven. Spray cookie sheets with nonstick cooking spray.

Place half of the cake mix in a large mixing bowl along with the melted butter and eggs. Blend with an electric mixer set on medium-high speed for 1–2 minutes, until smooth. Stir in the remaining cake mix and butterscotch baking chips with a wooden spoon until all dry ingredients are moistened.

Drop dough by teaspoonfuls, 2 inches apart, onto prepared cookie sheets. Sprinkle the chopped pecans onto cookie tops; gently press nuts into dough.

Bake for 9–12 minutes until set at edges and just barely set at center when lightly touched. Cool for 1 minute on cookie sheets. Transfer to wire racks with metal spatula and cool completely.

MAKES ABOUT 54 COOKIES.

CARAMEL APPLE COOKIES

In general, and as a guiding rule, tamper with tradition and that wonderful thing called nostalgia only up to a certain point. Case in point, these cookies, which showcase all the best flavors of classic caramel apples but in convenient cookie form.

- 2 (1.7-ounce) packages chewy chocolate-covered caramel candies (e.g., Rolos), unwrapped and quartered
- 1 (18.25-ounce) package yellow cake mix
- ½ cup vegetable oil
- ¼ cup packed light brown sugar
- 2 large eggs
- 1 teaspoon vanilla extract
- 1 (6-ounce) package dried apples, chopped

Preheat oven to 350°F. Position oven rack in middle of oven.

In a small bowl toss the chopped candies with 2 tablespoons of the cake mix (to prevent sticking).

Place half of the cake mix in a large mixing bowl along with the oil, brown sugar, eggs, and vanilla extract. Blend with an electric mixer set on medium-high speed for 1–2 minutes, until smooth. Stir in the remaining cake mix, caramel candies, and dried apples with a wooden spoon until all dry ingredients are moistened.

Drop by teaspoonfuls, 2 inches apart, onto ungreased cookie sheets.

Bake for 10–13 minutes or until just barely set at center when lightly touched. Cool for 2 minutes on cookie sheets. Transfer to wire racks with metal spatula and cool completely.

MAKES ABOUT 54 COOKIES.

CARAMEL-LOADED CHOCOLATE-CHOCOLATE-CHIP COOKIES

Chocolate-coated caramel candies sweeten the deal in these incredible double chocolate chippers. They are over-the-top good when eaten slightly warm, while the caramel and chocolate are still a bit gooey.

- 1 cup quartered chocolate-covered caramel candies (e.g., Rolos)
- 1 (18.25-ounce) package yellow or chocolate cake mix
- 1/3 cup vegetable oil
- 2 large eggs
- 1 cup semisweet or milk chocolate chips

Preheat oven to 350°F. Position oven rack in middle of oven. Spray cookie sheets with nonstick cooking spray.

Toss the chopped candies with 2 tablespoons of the cake mix (to prevent sticking).

Place half of the cake mix in a large mixing bowl along with the oil and eggs. Blend with an electric mixer set on medium-high speed for 1–2 minutes, until smooth. Stir in the remaining cake mix, flour-coated candies, and chocolate chips with a wooden spoon until all dry ingredients are moistened.

Drop dough by teaspoonfuls, 2 inches apart, onto prepared cookie sheets.

Bake for 9–12 minutes or until set at edges and just barely set at center when lightly touched. Cool for 1 minute on cookie sheets. Transfer to wire racks with metal spatula and cool completely.

MAKES ABOUT 54 COOKIES.

CARAMEL PECAN TURTLE COOKIES (BROWNIE MIX)

If you like the candies called Turtles—milk chocolate, pecan, and caramel clusters—you'll do a cartwheel when you taste these cookies.

- 1 (19.5- to 19.8-ounce) package brownie mix
- 1/3 cup unsweetened cocoa powder, sifted
- 1/4 cup (1/2 stick) unsalted butter, melted
- 2 teaspoons vanilla extract
- 2 large eggs
- 2 cups whole pecan halves
- 24 milk caramels, unwrapped
- 3 tablespoons milk

In a medium mixing bowl mix the brownie mix, sifted cocoa powder, melted butter, vanilla, and eggs with a wooden spoon until all dry ingredients are moistened and dough is well blended. Cover bowl with plastic wrap and refrigerate dough for at least 1 hour.

Preheat oven to 350°F. Spray cookie sheets with nonstick cooking spray.

Shape dough into 1-inch balls. Place balls 2 inches apart on prepared cookie sheets. Press one whole pecan half in center of each cookie.

Bake for 9–11 minutes, until firm to the touch at the edges. Cool for 1 minute on cookie sheets. Transfer to wire racks with metal spatula and cool completely.

Melt the caramels with the milk in a small saucepan set over low heat, stirring until melted and smooth; remove from heat and let cool.

Drizzle caramel across cooled cookies using a spoon or fork.

MAKES ABOUT 54 COOKIES.

CARDAMOM CURRANT TEA COOKIES

A smidgen of cardamom gives these refined cookies a unique flavor reminiscent of Scandinavian breads and pastries. The dried currants and cardamom create a sweet and spicy balance, but you may, if you wish, substitute ground nutmeg for the cardamom. If you have the time and inclination, soak the currants in sweet cooking wine, such as sherry or Marsala (just enough to cover), for about 30 minutes to plump up the fruit. Drain thoroughly, pat dry with paper towels, and proceed as directed.

- 1 (16.5-ounce) roll refrigerated sugar cookie dough
- 1 cup dried currants
- 1 teaspoon ground cardamom (or nutmeg)

Preheat oven to 350°F. Spray cookie sheets with nonstick cooking spray.

Break up the cookie dough into large bowl; let stand for 10–15 minutes to soften. Add the currants and cardamom; mix well with your fingers, the paddle attachment of an electric stand mixer, or a wooden spoon.

Drop dough by kitchen teaspoons, 2 inches apart, onto prepared cookie sheets.

Bake for 10–13 minutes or until just set and golden at edges. Transfer cookies to wire racks and cool completely.

MAKES 26 COOKIES.

CARROT CAKE COOKIE JUMBLES

Restraint is a concept I refuse to associate with cookies. Hence "jumble" cookies—baked goodies chock full of all sorts of yummy ingredients—suit me to a T. These carrot-y cookies are moist and flavorful, just like a slice or square of homemade carrot cake. For the "icing on the cake," add icing to the cookie—specifically, Cream Cheese Frosting.

- 1 (16.5-ounce) roll refrigerated chocolate-chip cookie dough (or sugar cookie dough)
- 1 (8-ounce) package cream cheese, softened
- 1¾ cups peeled, shredded carrots
- 1½ cups shredded coconut
- ¾ cup raisins (or dried cranberries)
- 1 teaspoon ground cinnamon
- 1 recipe Cream Cheese Frosting (see page 366), optional

Preheat oven to 350°F. Spray cookie sheets with nonstick cooking spray.

Break up the cookie dough into large bowl; let stand for 10–15 minutes to soften. Add the cream cheese. Mix well with an electric mixer on medium speed until well combined. Add the carrots, coconut, raisins, and cinnamon; mix well with a wooden spoon.

Drop dough by kitchen teaspoons, 2 inches apart, onto prepared cookie sheets.

Bake for 10–13 minutes or until just set and golden at edges. Quickly transfer cookies to wire racks and cool completely. If desired, frost with Cream Cheese Frosting.

MAKES 42 COOKIES.

CARROT CAKE JUMBLES WITH CREAM CHEESE FROSTING

Looking for a friendly good time? Few things could be more conducive to such than, perhaps, the pure congeniality that comes from baking a batch of these carrot cookies, plump with fruit and spices and finished with a swirl of Cream Cheese Frosting.

- 1 (18.25-ounce) package carrot cake mix
- ⅓ cup vegetable oil
- 2 large eggs
- 1 teaspoon pumpkin pie spice
- 1½ cups grated peeled carrot (about 2 medium)
- 1 cup raisins (or dried cranberries)
- ½ cup canned crushed pineapple, well drained
- 1¼ cups finely chopped walnuts (or pecans), optional
- 1 recipe Cream Cheese Frosting (see page 366)

Preheat oven to 350°F. Position oven rack in middle of oven. Spray cookie sheets with nonstick cooking spray.

Place half of the cake mix in a large mixing bowl along with the oil, eggs, and pumpkin pie spice. Blend with an electric mixer set on medium-high speed for 1–2 minutes, until smooth. Stir in the remaining cake mix, grated carrot, raisins, and drained pineapple with a wooden spoon until all dry ingredients are moistened (dough will be stiff).

Drop dough by teaspoonfuls, 2 inches apart, onto prepared cookie sheets. If desired, sprinkle cookie tops with nuts; gently press nuts into dough.

Bake for 11–14 minutes or until set at edges and just barely set at center when lightly touched. Cool for 1 minute on cookie sheets. Transfer to wire racks with metal spatula and cool completely.

Prepare Cream Cheese Frosting. Spread frosting over cooled cookies.

MAKES ABOUT 54 COOKIES.

CASHEW BRICKLE COOKIES (CAKE MIX)

Toffee fans beware; these cookies are highly addictive. Other roasted nuts may be substituted, but buttery cashews make for a very special confection.

- 1 (18.25-ounce) package vanilla cake mix
- ½ cup (1 stick) butter, melted
- 3 tablespoons dark brown sugar
- 2 large eggs
- ⅔ cup quick-cooking oats
- 1 cup coarsely chopped, lightly salted roasted cashews
- ¾ cup English toffee baking bits

Preheat oven to 350°F. Position oven rack in middle of oven.

Mix the cake mix, melted butter, brown sugar, eggs, oats, cashews, and toffee bits in a large mixing bowl with a wooden spoon until all dry ingredients are moistened.

Drop by teaspoonfuls, 2 inches apart, onto ungreased cookie sheets.

Bake for 10–13 minutes or until cracked in appearance and just barely set at center when

lightly touched. Cool for 1 minute on cookie sheets. Transfer to wire racks with metal spatula and cool completely.

MAKES ABOUT 54 COOKIES.

CASHEW BRICKLE COOKIES (COOKIE DOUGH)

No doubt about it, anything with toffee in it, on it, or around it is just right by me. The butterscotch brickle flavor of these crisp cookies is accentuated by the saltiness of the roasted cashews.

- 1 (16.5-ounce) roll refrigerated sugar cookie dough
- 1 cup chopped lightly salted, roasted cashews
- ½ cup almond toffee baking bits

Preheat oven to 375°F. Spray two cookie sheets with nonstick cooking spray.

Cut cookie dough in half. Roll out half of the dough between two sheets of wax paper to form a 10 x 6-inch rectangle.

Remove top sheet of wax paper. Invert dough onto one of the prepared cookie sheets. Remove remaining sheet of wax paper. Sprinkle dough evenly with half of the nuts and half of the toffee bits. Repeat with remaining dough, nuts, and toffee bits on second cookie sheet.

Bake cookies, one sheet at a time, for 10–12 minutes or until golden. Cool on cookie sheets on a wire rack. Remove cookies to cutting board using two spatulas. Use a sharp

THE ULTIMATE SHORTCUT COOKIE BOOK

knife to cut cooled cookies into irregular shapes.

MAKES ABOUT 42 COOKIES.

CASHEW BUTTER BRICKLE BROWNIE COOKIES

Packed with buttery cashews and toffee baking bits, these newfangled chocolate cookies are a saving grace when I want to make an impressive cookie for a gift or gathering but don't have much time. Be prepared to share the recipe!

- 1 (19.5- to 19.8-ounce) package brownie mix
- ½ cup (1 stick) unsalted butter, melted
- ¼ cup packed light brown sugar
- 2 large eggs
- 2 teaspoons vanilla extract
- 1 cup lightly salted roasted cashews, coarsely chopped
- 1 cup English toffee baking bits

Preheat oven to 350°F. Position racks in lower and upper thirds of oven. Spray cookie sheets with nonstick cooking spray.

Mix the brownie mix, melted butter, brown sugar, eggs, vanilla, cashews, and toffee bits in a large mixing bowl with a wooden spoon until all dry ingredients are moistened.

Drop by teaspoonfuls, 2 inches apart, onto prepared cookie sheets.

Bake for 10–13 minutes, until cracked in appearance and just barely set at center when

lightly touched. Cool for 1 minute on cookie sheets. Transfer to wire racks with metal spatula and cool completely.

MAKES ABOUT 54 COOKIES.

CASHEW BUTTERSCOTCHIES

These four-ingredient treats are certain to liven up your lunch bag and become part of your favorite-cookie repertoire.

- 2 cups butterscotch baking chips
- 1 teaspoon vanilla extract
- 1½ cups quick-cooking oats, uncooked
- 1 cup chopped, lightly salted, roasted cashews

Line cookie sheets with wax paper.

Place the butterscotch chips in a medium microwave-safe bowl. Microwave on high for 30–90 seconds or until mixture is melted and smooth, stirring every 30 seconds. Stir in the vanilla, oats, and cashews; mix until well blended.

Working quickly, drop by heaping teaspoonfuls onto wax-paper-lined sheets. Chill until firm. Store tightly covered in refrigerator.

MAKES ABOUT 32 COOKIES.

CHAI SPICE COOKIES

These quick cookies capture the unique flavor of chai, an aromatic spiced tea drink long favored in the East Indies. Warm and wonderful, they will fill the house with their distinctive fragrance as they bake.

- 1 (18.25-ounce) package spice cake mix
- 1/3 cup butter, melted
- 2 large eggs
- 2 teaspoons pumpkin pie spice
- 1/2 teaspoon ground cardamom
- 1 cup slivered almonds
- 1 recipe Vanilla Icing (see page 376), optional

Preheat oven to 350°F. Position oven rack in middle of oven. Spray cookie sheets with nonstick cooking spray.

Place half of the cake mix along with the melted butter, eggs, pumpkin pie spice, and cardamom in a large mixing bowl. Blend with an electric mixer set on medium-high speed for 1–2 minutes, until smooth. Stir in the remaining cake mix with a wooden spoon until all dry ingredients are moistened.

Drop dough by teaspoonfuls, 2 inches apart, onto prepared cookie sheets. Sprinkle the cookie tops with a few slivered almonds.

Bake for 9–12 minutes or until set at edges and just barely set at center when lightly touched. Cool for 1 minute on cookie sheets. Transfer to wire racks with metal spatula and cool completely.

If desired, prepare Vanilla Icing; drizzle over cooled cookies.

MAKES ABOUT 54 COOKIES.

CHERRY RUM DROPS

Buttery, chewy, and fruity—I find the taste and texture of these cookies especially appealing. Equally appreciated during winter holidays and summer picnics, they are as easy to make as they are to eat.

- 1 (16.5-ounce) roll refrigerated sugar cookie dough
- 1/2 cup finely chopped maraschino cherries, well-drained
- 1/2 cup finely chopped raisins
- 1 recipe Butter-Rum Icing (see page 375)

Preheat oven to 350°F. Spray cookie sheets with nonstick cooking spray.

Break up the cookie dough into large bowl; let stand for 10–15 minutes to soften. Meanwhile, place the chopped cherries between double sheets of paper towels; gently press out excess liquid. Add the cherries and raisins to dough; mix well with your fingers, the paddle attachment of an electric stand mixer, or a wooden spoon.

Drop dough by kitchen teaspoons, 2 inches apart, onto prepared cookie sheets.

Bake for 10–13 minutes or until just set and golden at edges. Transfer cookies to wire racks and cool completely. Frost or drizzle with Butter-Rum Icing.

MAKES 26 COOKIES.

CHOCOLATE-CHIP COCOA COOKIES

If chocolate chip cookies are wonderful, then these chocolate-chocolate-chip cookies are sublime. If you want to take them all the way over the top, consider dipping or drizzling the cooled cookies in the Chocolate Drizzle or Dip on page 361.

- 1 (16.5-ounce) roll refrigerated chocolate-chip cookie dough
- 2 tablespoons unsweetened cocoa powder
- 1½ teaspoons vanilla extract

Preheat oven to 350°F. Spray cookie sheets with nonstick cooking spray.

Break up the cookie dough into large bowl; let stand for 10–15 minutes to soften. Add the cocoa powder and vanilla to the cookie dough; mix well with your fingers, the paddle attachment of an electric stand mixer, or a wooden spoon.

Drop dough by kitchen teaspoons, 2 inches apart, onto prepared cookie sheets.

Bake for 10–13 minutes or until just set in the centers. Transfer cookies to wire racks and cool completely.

MAKES 22 COOKIES.

CHOCOLATE-CHIP CREAM CHEESE SOFTIES

My mother used to make a cookie just like this one every Christmas. This version takes about a quarter of the time and effort but yields the same delicious results.

- 1 (16.5-ounce) roll refrigerated chocolate-chip cookie dough
- 6 ounces (¾ of an 8-ounce package) cream cheese, cut into bits

Preheat oven to 350°F. Spray cookie sheets with nonstick cooking spray.

Break up the cookie dough into large bowl; add the cream cheese bits to bowl and let stand for 10–15 minutes to soften.

Mix the dough and cream well with your fingers, the paddle attachment of an electric stand mixer, or a wooden spoon.

Drop dough by kitchen teaspoons, 2 inches apart, onto prepared cookie sheets.

Bake for 10–13 minutes or until just set and golden at edges. Transfer cookies to wire racks.

MAKES 36 COOKIES.

Baker's Note

For a delicious accent, add 1 tablespoon grated orange or lemon zest to the dough.

CHOCOLATE-CHIP PEANUT BUTTER COOKIES

Your only dilemma with these cookies will be deciding with whom to share them.

- 1 cup creamy peanut butter
- 1 cup powdered sugar
- ½ cup milk
- 2 teaspoons vanilla extract
- 2 cups quick-cooking oats, uncooked
- 2 cups semisweet chocolate chips

Line cookie sheets with wax paper.

Stir together the peanut butter, powdered sugar, milk, and vanilla in a large bowl with a wooden spoon, mixing until well blended. Stir in the oats and chocolate chips.

Drop by teaspoonfuls onto wax-paper-lined sheets. Store tightly covered in an airtight container between layers of wax paper.

MAKES ABOUT 42 COOKIES.

CHOCOLATE-CHIP RAISIN COOKIES

These are exceptional cookies—in taste, time, brevity of ingredients, and absolute ease of preparation. They taste just like a big box of chocolate-covered raisins, all wrapped up in brown sugary dough. While chocolate-raisin is a classic combination, you can substitute other dried fruit—dried cranberries, golden raisins, chopped tropical fruit bits, chopped apricots, or cranberries—for an equally tasty variation.

- 1 (16.5-ounce) roll refrigerated chocolate-chip cookie dough
- 1 cup raisins
- ½ teaspoon ground cinnamon

Preheat oven to 350°F. Spray cookie sheets with nonstick cooking spray.

Break up the cookie dough into large bowl; let stand for 10–15 minutes to soften. Add the raisins and cinnamon; mix well with your fingers, the paddle attachment of an electric stand mixer, or a wooden spoon.

Drop dough by kitchen teaspoons, 2 inches apart, onto prepared cookie sheets.

Bake for 10–13 minutes or until just set and golden at edges. Transfer cookies to wire racks and cool completely.

MAKES 28 COOKIES.

CHOCOLATE-COVERED RAISIN COOKIES

As good as these cookies are, you can also vary the flavor by using other types of chocolate or baking chips (e.g., milk or white chocolate chips, butterscotch chips, cinnamon chips, peanut butter chips) and the dried fruit of your choice.

- 1 cup semisweet chocolate chips
- 5 tablespoons butter
- 16 large marshmallows
- 1 teaspoon vanilla extract
- 2 cups quick-cooking oats, uncooked
- ¾ cup raisins

Line cookie sheets with wax paper.

Melt the chocolate chips with the butter and marshmallows in a large saucepan over low heat, stirring until smooth. Remove from heat; cool for 5 minutes. Stir in the vanilla, oats, and raisins.

Working quickly, drop by rounded teaspoonfuls onto wax-paper-lined sheets. Cover and refrigerate for 2–3 hours. Let stand at room temperature for about 15 minutes before serving. Store tightly covered in refrigerator.

MAKES ABOUT 32 COOKIES.

CHOCOLATE FUDGE-FROSTED RASPBERRY SOFTIES

Here thick raspberry fudge frosting gilds almond-accented, cream cheese chocolate cookies for an irresistible treat. During summer berry season, consider adding a fresh raspberry to the center of each frosted cookie.

- 1 (19.5- to 19.8-ounce) package brownie mix
- ¼ cup (½ stick) unsalted butter, melted
- 4 ounces (½ of an 8-ounce) package) cream cheese, softened
- 1 large egg
- ½ teaspoon almond extract
- 1 recipe Chocolate-Raspberry Frosting (see page 363)

Preheat oven to 350°F.

Mix the brownie mix, melted butter, cream cheese, egg, and almond extract in a medium mixing bowl with a wooden spoon until all dry ingredients are moistened and well blended (dough will be sticky).

Drop dough by teaspoonfuls, 2 inches apart, onto ungreased cookie sheets; smooth edge of each to form round cookie.

Bake for 10–14 minutes or until edges are set. Transfer to wire rack and cool completely.

Prepare Chocolate Raspberry Frosting. Frost cooled cookies.

MAKES 48 BIG COOKIES.

CHOCOLATE HERMITS

Hermits are spicy, spunky, cake-like cookies that date back to the early 1800s. Here their appeal is boosted with a double dose of chocolate.

- 1 (19.5- to 19.8-ounce) package brownie mix
- ¼ cup packed light brown sugar
- 2 teaspoons pumpkin pie spice
- ½ cup (1 stick) unsalted butter, melted
- 2 large eggs
- 1 cup semisweet chocolate chips
- ½ cup raisins or currants
- 1 cup chopped walnuts or pecans

Preheat oven to 350°F. Spray cookie sheets with nonstick cooking spray.

Mix the brownie mix, brown sugar, pumpkin pie spice, melted butter, and eggs in a large mixing bowl with a wooden spoon until just blended and all dry ingredients are moistened; mix in chocolate chips and raisins.

Drop by teaspoonfuls, 2 inches apart, onto prepared cookie sheets. Sprinkle tops with nuts.

Bake for 9–12 minutes, until edges are firm and center is just barely set when lightly touched. Cool for 1 minute on cookie sheets. Transfer to wire racks with metal spatula and cool completely.

MAKES ABOUT 54 COOKIES.

CHOCOLATE OATMEAL COOKIES (ANY WAY YOU LIKE THEM)

This recipe is fun to play around with—add your favorite ingredient from the list below or mix up an eclectic combination of stir-ins to suit your fancy. It's virtually impossible to miss with this very versatile cookie.

- 1 (19.5- to 19.8-ounce) package brownie mix
- ½ cup vegetable oil or melted butter
- 2 large eggs
- 1¼ cups old-fashioned or quick-cooking oats
- 1 or 2 stir-in options (see below)
- ½ cup sugar

Preheat oven to 375°F. Spray cookie sheets with nonstick cooking spray.

Mix the brownie mix, oil, and eggs in a large mixing bowl until blended and all the dry ingredients are moistened. With a wooden spoon, stir in the oats and one or two of the stir-in options, if desired; stir until well blended.

Roll dough into 1½-inch balls; place on the prepared cookie sheets. Place sugar in a shallow dish. Dip bottom of a plastic tumbler in sugar and use to flatten one of the cookies. Repeat with remaining cookies.

Bake for 9–12 minutes until set at edges and just barely set at center when lightly touched (do not overbake). Cool for 1 minute on cookie sheets. Transfer to wire racks with metal spatula and cool completely.

Optional Stir-Ins:

(Stir in one or two of any of the following):

- 1 cup baking chips or chunks (e.g., semisweet chocolate chips or chunks, milk chocolate chips or chunks, white chocolate chips or chunks, butterscotch chips, peanut butter chips, cinnamon chips, or English toffee baking bits)
- 1 cup dried fruit bits (e.g., cranberries, raisins, coconut, or chopped dried apricots)
- 1 cup chopped nuts (e.g., pecans, walnuts, macadamia nuts, or peanuts)

MAKES ABOUT 36 COOKIES WITH NO STIR-INS, ABOUT 42 WITH 1 STIR-IN AND ABOUT 48 WITH 2 STIR-INS.

CHOCOLATE OATMEAL NO-BAKES

Cocoa, butter, and oats make for a dandy of a chocolate cookie. Once these treats set up, they have a rich, fudgy taste and consistency.

- 2 cups packed light brown sugar
- ½ cup (1 stick) butter
- ½ cup canned evaporated milk
- ⅓ cup unsweetened cocoa powder
- 1 teaspoon vanilla extract
- 3 cups quick-cooking oats, uncooked

Line cookie sheets with wax paper.

Combine the brown sugar, butter, evaporated milk, and cocoa powder in a large saucepan. Bring to a boil over medium heat, stirring frequently. Continue boiling for 3 minutes, stirring frequently. Remove from heat and stir in the vanilla and oats.

Working quickly, drop by tablespoonfuls onto waxpaper-lined sheets. Let stand until firm. Store tightly covered.

MAKES ABOUT 32 COOKIES.

HOMEMADE AND DELICIOUS— IN A SNAP!

Baking mouth-watering cookies has never been easier. Genius shortcuts like cake mix, a roll of cookie dough, brownie mix, no-bake ingredients, and ready-to-eat cereal create the perfect foundation for cookies that taste—and look—like they came fresh from the pastry shop.

PAGE 20

Chocolate-Chip Raisin Cookies

TIME-SAVING SHORTCUT: Cookie Dough

ALL-AMERICAN FAVORITES

*n*o cookie recipe collection would be complete without these lovable classics. The perfect treat for anything from a barbeque to a baby shower, these All-American Favorites are sure to please every time.

Blue-Ribbon Chocolate-Chip Cookies

TIME-SAVING SHORTCUT: Cake Mix

Gingerbread People

TIME-SAVING SHORTCUT:
Cake Mix

Granola Chocolate Chunkers

TIME-SAVING SHORTCUT:
Cake Mix

Big Fat Oatmeal-Raisin Cookies

TIME-SAVING SHORTCUT:
Cake Mix

Chocolate Hermits

TIME-SAVING SHORTCUT:
Brownie Mix

PAGE 161, 83

Stained Glass Cookie Cutouts and Basic Rolled Sugar Cookies

TIME-SAVING SHORTCUT:
Cookie Dough (both)

PAGE 57

Peanut Butter Cookies

TIME-SAVING SHORTCUT:
Cake Mix

Sean's Very Chocolate Cookies

PAGE 66

TIME-SAVING SHORTCUT: Brownie Mix

Toasted Almond Cookies

PAGE 70

TIME-SAVING SHORTCUT: Cake Mix

Chocolate-Kissed Cookies

PAGE 98

TIME-SAVING SHORTCUT: Cookie Dough

Jumbo Jumble Chocolate Oatmeal Cookies

PAGE 41

TIME-SAVING SHORTCUT: Cake Mix

YOU-BETTER-BELIEVE-IT! BROWNIES

*O*zing with chocolatey goodness, no one will suspect these yummy homemade treats started with a mix out of the box. For extra indulgence, serve warm with a scoop of ice cream.

Classic Brownies PAGE 328

TIME-SAVING SHORTCUT: Brownie Mix

PAGE 86 *Brownie Biscotti*

TIME-SAVING SHORTCUT: Brownie Mix

PAGE 323 *Caramelicious Turtle Brownies*

TIME-SAVING SHORTCUT: Brownie Mix

Big Brownie Cookies

TIME-SAVING SHORTCUT: Brownie Mix

Milk Chocolate Malt Brownies

PAGE 338

TIME-SAVING SHORTCUT: Brownie Mix

PAGE 354 *Truffle-Topped Brownies*
TIME-SAVING SHORTCUT: Brownie Mix

PAGE 340 *Mocha Buttercream Brownies*
TIME-SAVING SHORTCUT: Brownie Mix

Sour Cream Brownies with Chocolate Velvet Frosting

PAGE 350

TIME-SAVING SHORTCUT:
Brownie Mix

PAGE 327

Chocolate-Glazed Mint-Frosted Brownies

TIME-SAVING SHORTCUT:
Brownie Mix

CHOCOLATE RAISIN COOKIES

Forget the fuss—whip up a batch of these simple and oh-so-homey chocolate raisin cookies and get cozy. They're easy enough to justify a party for one and fancy enough to serve on a platter to share with guests.

- 1 (19.5- to 19.8-ounce) package brownie mix
- 1/3 cup vegetable oil
- 2 large eggs
- 1/2 teaspoon ground cinnamon
- 1 cup raisins
- 1 cup miniature semisweet chocolate chips

Preheat oven to 350°F. Spray cookie sheets with nonstick cooking spray.

Mix the brownie mix, vegetable oil, eggs, and cinnamon in a medium mixing bowl with a wooden spoon until just blended and all dry ingredients are moistened; stir in raisins and chocolate chips.

Drop dough by teaspoonfuls, 2 inches apart, onto prepared cookie sheets.

Bake for 9–11 minutes, until set at edges and just barely set at center when lightly touched. Cool for 1 minute on cookie sheets. Transfer to wire racks with metal spatula and cool completely.

MAKES ABOUT 54 COOKIES.

CHOCOLATE SNICKERDOODLES

Sugar and spice and everything nice are what old-fashioned snickerdoodles are made of. Here the soft, cake-like cookies get a chocolate twist before being rolled in their traditional coating of cinnamon sugar.

- 1 (19.5- to 19.8-ounce) package brownie mix
- 1/4 cup (1/2 stick) unsalted butter, melted
- 3 large eggs, lightly beaten
- 1 cup chopped walnuts, preferably lightly toasted
- 1/2 cup dried currants
- 2/3 cup sugar
- 1 tablespoon ground cinnamon
- 1/2 teaspoon ground nutmeg

Preheat oven to 350°F. Position racks in lower and upper thirds of oven. Spray cookie sheets with nonstick cooking spray.

Mix the brownie mix, melted butter, and eggs in a large mixing bowl with a wooden spoon until just blended and all dry ingredients are moistened; stir in the chopped walnuts and currants. Chill dough for at least 1 hour.

Combine the sugar, cinnamon, and nutmeg in a shallow dish or bowl. Form dough into 1-inch balls; roll in cinnamon sugar. Place 2 inches apart on prepared cookie sheets.

Bake for 9–12 minutes, until set at edges and just barely set at center when lightly touched. Cool for 1 minute on cookie sheets. Transfer to wire racks with metal spatula and cool completely.

MAKES ABOUT 48 COOKIES.

CINNAMON-CHIP CHEWS

When a magic wand—or, perhaps, a magic cinnamon stick—is waved over classic chocolate-chip cookies, this is the sweet and spicy result. Cinnamon chips can be found in the baking aisle of the supermarket alongside chocolate chips. They look and melt like chocolate chips (although tan in color) and are a cinnamon lover's delight.

■ 1 (18.25-ounce) package spice cake mix
■ ½ cup water
■ ¼ cup (½ stick) butter, melted
■ 1 large egg
■ 1 teaspoon ground cinnamon
■ 1½ cups cinnamon baking chips

Preheat oven to 350°F. Position oven rack in middle of oven. Spray cookie sheets with nonstick cooking spray.

Place half of the cake mix along with the water, melted butter, egg, and cinnamon in a large mixing bowl. Blend with an electric mixer set on medium-high speed for 1–2 minutes, until smooth. Stir in the remaining cake mix and cinnamon chips with a wooden spoon until all dry ingredients are moistened.

Drop dough by teaspoonfuls, 2 inches apart, onto prepared cookie sheets.

Bake for 9–12 minutes or until set at edges and just barely set at center when lightly touched. Cool for 1 minute on cookie sheets. Transfer to wire racks with metal spatula and cool completely.

MAKES ABOUT 48 COOKIES.

CINNAMON-CHIP CHOCOLATE COOKIES

Remember the first time you baked a batch of cookies? Chances are they were some sort of permutation of either chocolate or cinnamon. These double cinnamon chocolate cookies are bound to bring back warm fuzzy memories, both as they bake and as you eat them.

■ 1 (19.5- to 19.8-ounce) package brownie mix
■ ⅓ cup vegetable oil
■ 2 large eggs
■ ¾ teaspoon ground cinnamon
■ 1½ cups cinnamon baking chips

Preheat oven to 350°F. Spray cookie sheets with nonstick cooking spray.

Mix the brownie mix, oil, eggs, cinnamon, and cinnamon chips in a medium mixing bowl with a wooden spoon until blended and all dry ingredients are moistened.

Drop dough by teaspoonfuls, 2 inches apart, onto prepared cookie sheets.

Bake for 9–12 minutes, until set at edges and just barely set at center when lightly touched. Cool for 1 minute on cookie sheets. Transfer to wire racks with metal spatula and cool completely.

MAKES ABOUT 48 COOKIES.

CINNAMON-ORANGE CHOCOLATE CHIPPERS

Perhaps it's time to modify the old adage "As American as apple pie." By my measure, it's chocolate-chip cookies that most fittingly define dessert "Americana" these days. Here a lively dose of cinnamon and orange zest lends everyone's favorite cookie a subtly spicy, citrus edge.

- 1 (16.5-ounce) roll refrigerated chocolate-chip cookie dough
- 1 teaspoon ground cinnamon
- 2 tablespoons grated orange zest

Preheat oven to 350°F. Spray cookie sheets with nonstick cooking spray.

Break up the cookie dough into large bowl; let stand for 10–15 minutes to soften. Add the cinnamon and orange zest; mix well with your fingers, the paddle attachment of an electric stand mixer, or a wooden spoon.

Drop dough by kitchen teaspoons, 2 inches apart, onto prepared cookie sheets.

Bake for 10–13 minutes or until just set and golden at edges. Transfer cookies to wire racks and cool completely.

MAKES 22 COOKIES.

CINNAMON PECAN COOKIES

Nothing beats the undeniable comfort and unmistakable flavor of cinnamon. It's hard to believe that this rich and homey cookie comes together with such ease. Pecans add a nutty sweetness, but almonds or walnuts can substitute if that's what you have on hand.

- 1 (16.5-ounce) roll refrigerated sugar cookie dough
- 1½ teaspoons cinnamon
- ½ teaspoon ground nutmeg
- 1 teaspoon vanilla extract
- 1 cup chopped pecans

Preheat oven to 350°F. Spray cookie sheets with nonstick cooking spray.

Break up the cookie dough into large bowl; let stand for 10–15 minutes to soften. Add the cinnamon, nutmeg, vanilla, and pecans; mix well with your fingers, the paddle attachment of an electric stand mixer, or a wooden spoon.

Drop dough by teaspoons, 2 inches apart, onto prepared cookie sheets.

Bake for 10–13 minutes or until just set and golden at edges. Remove from oven and cool on cookie sheets for 2 minutes; transfer to wire racks and cool completely.

MAKES 26 COOKIES.

COCONUT, CASHEW, AND WHITE CHOCOLATE CHEWIES

Newfangled has never been better than with this delectable cookie. Crunchy cashews, chewy coconut, butter, and white chocolate? Hooray for innovation!

- ¼ cup butter, softened
- 1 (8-ounce) package cream cheese, softened
- 1 (14-ounce) can sweetened condensed milk
- 1 large egg
- 2 teaspoons vanilla extract
- 1 cup all-purpose flour
- 1 (18.25-ounce) package yellow cake mix
- 1½ cups chopped, lightly salted roasted cashews
- 1⅓ cups shredded coconut
- 1½ cups white chocolate chips

Preheat oven to 375°F. Position oven rack in middle of oven. Spray cookie sheets with nonstick cooking spray.

Beat the butter and cream cheese in a large mixing bowl with electric mixer set on high until smooth. Add the sweetened condensed milk, egg, and vanilla extract; beat until blended. Add the flour and cake mix; stir with wooden spoon until blended and all dry ingredients are moistened. Stir in the cashews, coconut, and white chocolate chips.

Drop dough by teaspoonfuls, 1 inch apart, onto prepared cookie sheets.

Bake for 9–12 minutes or until set at edges and just barely set at center when lightly touched. Cool for 1 minute on cookie sheets. Transfer to wire racks with metal spatula and cool completely.

MAKES ABOUT 60 COOKIES.

COCONUT CASHEW COOKIES

Cashews are as tropical as coconut, originating in South America but also widely cultivated in many tropical countries. The two flavors pair deliciously in these easy drops that require no cooking at all.

- 1 cup cashew butter or creamy peanut butter
- 1 cup powdered sugar
- ½ cup milk
- 1 teaspoon vanilla extract
- 2 cups uncooked oats (quick or old-fashioned)
- 1 cup coarsely chopped, lightly salted roasted cashews
- 1 cup sweetened flake coconut

Line cookie sheets with wax paper.

Combine the cashew butter, powdered sugar, milk, and vanilla in a large bowl with a wooden spoon until well blended. Stir in the oats, cashews, and coconut until mixture is well blended.

Drop by kitchen teaspoonfuls onto prepared wax-paper-lined sheets. Store tightly covered in a cool, dry place.

MAKES ABOUT 42 COOKIES.

COCONUT MACAROONIES

I don't know whether "nature" or "nurture" best explains why my mother and I share the same dessert preferences. Whatever the reason, our mutual confection affections sure make our time together all the sweeter. We both love macaroons, whether they are crispy or chewy. This simple version is both—crispy at the edges, chewy toward the center. Find coconut extract where you find vanilla extract in the baking section of the supermarket. It really adds "oomph" to the flavor of these cookies.

- 1 (16.5-ounce) roll refrigerated sugar cookie dough
- 1 (3-ounce) package cream cheese, softened
- 1½ teaspoons coconut extract (or vanilla extract)
- 1 (7-ounce) package shredded coconut

Preheat oven to 350°F. Spray cookie sheets with nonstick cooking spray.

Break up the cookie dough into large bowl; let stand for 10–15 minutes to soften. Add the cream cheese and extract. Mix well with an electric mixer on medium speed until well combined. Add the coconut; mix well with a wooden spoon.

Drop dough by kitchen teaspoons, 2 inches apart, onto prepared cookie sheets.

Bake for 10–13 minutes or until just set and golden at edges. Quickly transfer cookies to wire racks and cool completely.

MAKES 32 COOKIES.

COFFEE AND CREAM WHITE CHOCOLATE CHUNKERS

Coffee-enriched and loaded with white chocolate chips, these luxurious cookies are reminiscent of a perfectly rendered cup of cappuccino. For a bit of crunch, try adding a handful of chopped almonds or hazelnuts.

- 1 (16.5-ounce) roll refrigerated sugar cookie dough
- 1 (3-ounce) package cream cheese, cut into bits
- 1 teaspoon vanilla extract
- 2½ teaspoons instant espresso (or coffee) powder
- 1 (6-ounce) white chocolate baking bar, coarsely chopped (or 1 cup white chocolate chips)

Preheat oven to 350°F. Spray cookie sheets with nonstick cooking spray.

Break up the cookie dough into large bowl; add the cream cheese to bowl and let stand for 10–15 minutes to soften.

Combine the vanilla and espresso powder in a small cup. Add the vanilla mixture and white chocolate to the cookie dough and cream cheese bowl; mix well with your fingers, the paddle attachment of an electric stand mixer, or a wooden spoon.

Drop dough by teaspoons, 2 inches apart, onto prepared cookie sheets.

Bake for 10–13 minutes or until just set and golden at edges. Transfer cookies to wire racks.

MAKES 26 COOKIES.

COFFEE TOFFEE COOKIES

This is a rich, comforting cookie, reminiscent of favorite flavored espresso drinks from the local coffee shop. Tuck one of these in your lunch bag or briefcase for a late-afternoon pick-me-up.

- 2 cups packed dark brown sugar
- ¾ cup (1½ sticks) butter
- 1 (5-ounce) can (⅔ cup) evaporated milk
- 1 (4-serving-size) package instant butterscotch pudding mix
- 2¼ teaspoons instant coffee or espresso powder
- 2½ cups quick-cooking oats, uncooked

Line cookie sheets with wax paper.

Combine the brown sugar, butter, and evaporated milk in a large heavy saucepan. Cook and stir until mixture comes to a full rolling boil. Remove the pan from heat. Stir in the pudding mix, coffee powder, and oats, mixing well.

Working quickly, drop the mixture by tablespoonfuls onto wax-paper-lined sheets. Allow to cool and become firm, about 30 minutes.

MAKES ABOUT 22 COOKIES.

CRANBERRY CORNMEAL COOKIES

If ever there was a Thanksgiving cookie, this is it. Cornmeal adds both crunch and color, a fine counterpoint to tart, red, chewy bits of cranberry.

- 1 (18.25-ounce) package yellow cake mix
- ⅔ cup plain yellow cornmeal
- ⅓ cup vegetable oil
- 2 large eggs
- 1 tablespoon grated lemon or orange zest
- 1¼ cups sweetened dried cranberries, chopped

Preheat oven to 350°F. Position oven rack in middle of oven. Spray cookie sheets with nonstick cooking spray.

Place half of the cake mix in a large mixing bowl along with the cornmeal, oil, eggs, and zest. Blend with an electric mixer set on medium-high speed for 1–2 minutes, until smooth. Stir in the remaining cake mix and dried cranberries with a wooden spoon until all dry ingredients are moistened.

Drop dough by teaspoonfuls, 2 inches apart, onto prepared cookie sheets.

Bake for 9–12 minutes or until set at edges and just barely set at center when lightly touched. Cool for 1 minute on cookie sheets. Transfer to wire racks with metal spatula and cool completely.

MAKES ABOUT 48 COOKIES.

CREAM CHEESE CHOCOLATE SOFTIES

You're only four ingredients away from a batch of heavenly, soft chocolate cookies. Cream cheese adds a distinctive tanginess to these cookies, a fine foil to the chocolate. You can up the chocolate ante by adding a cup of semisweet, milk, or white chocolate chips.

- 1 (19.5- to 19.8-ounce) package brownie mix
- ¼ cup (½ stick) unsalted butter, melted
- 4 ounces (half of an 8-ounce package) cream cheese, softened
- 1 large egg

Preheat oven to 350°F.

Beat the brownie mix, melted butter, cream cheese, and egg in a medium mixing bowl with a wooden spoon until all dry ingredients are moistened and well blended (dough will be sticky).

Drop dough by teaspoonfuls, 2 inches apart, onto ungreased cookie sheets; smooth edge of each to form round cookie.

Bake for 9–12 minutes or until set at edges and just barely set at center when lightly touched (do not overbake; cookies will become more firm as they cool). Transfer to wire rack and cool completely.

MAKES 48 COOKIES.

DARK CHOCOLATE HAZELNUT COOKIES

The confectionary combination of hazelnuts and chocolate is very popular throughout Europe, particularly Italy, where it is known as gianduia. Deep and rich in chocolate flavor, these cookies are sure to top your list of chocolate favorites.

- ½ cup (1 stick) butter
- 2 (1-ounce) squares unsweetened baking chocolate, chopped

- 1¾ cups sugar
- ⅓ cup milk
- ½ cup chocolate hazelnut spread (e.g., Nutella)
- 1 teaspoon vanilla extract
- 3 cups quick-cooking oats, uncooked

Line cookie sheets with wax paper.

Melt the butter and unsweetened chocolate in a large heavy saucepan over medium heat, stirring constantly until melted and smooth. Add the sugar and milk; continue stirring until mixture comes to a full rolling boil. Let mixture boil for exactly 3 minutes without stirring. Immediately remove the pan from heat.

Stir in the hazelnut spread and vanilla, stirring until the hazelnut spread has melted. Quickly stir in the oats, mixing well.

Working quickly, drop the mixture by tablespoonfuls onto wax-paper-lined sheets. Allow to cool for about 30 minutes until cookies are firm. Store tightly covered between sheets of wax paper.

MAKES ABOUT 22 COOKIES.

DOUBLE-CHIP CHIPPERS

Sweet tooth that I am, I always feel that most chocolate-chip cookie recipes have too much cookie and not enough chips. This recipe remedies the problem. I guarantee a hearty dose of gooey goodness in every bite.

- 1 (16.5-ounce) roll refrigerated chocolate-chip cookie dough
- ⅔ cup milk chocolate, white

chocolate, peanut butter, cinnamon, or butterscotch chips

Preheat oven to 350°F. Spray cookie sheets with nonstick cooking spray.

Break up the cookie dough into large bowl; let stand for 10–15 minutes to soften. Add the baking chips; mix well with your fingers, the paddle attachment of an electric stand mixer, or a wooden spoon.

Drop dough by kitchen teaspoons, 2 inches apart, onto prepared cookie sheets.

Bake for 10–13 minutes or until just set and golden at edges. Transfer cookies to wire racks and cool completely.

MAKES 26 COOKIES.

DOUBLE FUDGE CHEWIES WITH COCONUT AND PECANS

These cookies are dense and fudgy thanks to the addition of cream cheese and sweetened condensed milk. The coconut and pecans add just the right amount of toothsome chewiness. For an even more chocolate-chocolate cookie, substitute 1 cup sifted, unsweetened cocoa powder for the flour.

- ¼ cup (½ stick) unsalted butter, softened
- 1 (8-ounce) package cream cheese, softened
- 1 (14-ounce) can sweetened condensed milk
- 1 large egg
- 1 cup all-purpose flour

- 1 (19.5- to 19.8-ounce) package brownie mix
- 1 cup coarsely chopped pecans
- 1⅓ cups shredded sweetened coconut
- 2 cups semisweet chocolate chips

Preheat oven to 375°F. Spray cookie sheets with nonstick cooking spray.

Beat the butter and cream cheese in a large mixing bowl with electric mixer set on high until smooth. Add the condensed milk and egg; beat until blended. Add the flour and brownie mix; stir with wooden spoon until blended and all dry ingredients are moistened. Stir in the pecans, coconut, and chocolate chips.

Drop dough by teaspoonfuls, 1 inch apart, onto prepared cookie sheets.

Bake for 9–12 minutes or until set at edges and just barely set at center when lightly touched. Cool for 1 minute on cookie sheets. Transfer to wire racks with metal spatula and cool completely.

MAKES ABOUT 60 COOKIES.

DOUBLE LEMON GINGER GEMS

Ginger and lemon lovers, take note—this is destined to become your favorite cookie, bar none. It is also the perfect summer cookie—simple to make and simply delicious.

- 1 (16.5-ounce) roll refrigerated sugar cookie dough
- 6 ounces (¾ of an 8-ounce package) cream cheese, cut into bits
- ½ cup finely chopped crystallized/ candied ginger

- 2 teaspoons ground ginger
- 2 teaspoons grated lemon zest
- 1 recipe Lemon Icing (see page 368)

Preheat oven to 350°F. Spray cookie sheets with nonstick cooking spray.

Break up the cookie dough into large bowl; add the cream cheese bits to bowl and let stand for 10–15 minutes to soften. Add the chopped crystallized ginger, ground ginger, and lemon zest; mix well with your fingers, the paddle attachment of an electric stand mixer, or a wooden spoon.

Drop dough by kitchen teaspoons, 2 inches apart, onto prepared cookie sheets.

Bake for 10–13 minutes or until just set and golden at edges. Transfer cookies to wire racks and cool completely. Drizzle with Lemon Icing.

MAKES 42 COOKIES.

Baker's Note

Lime zest or orange zest may be substituted in place of the lemon zest. Prepare the icing using lime or orange juice in place of the lemon juice.

DRIED APPLE CIDER COOKIES

While fresh apples lead to soft, sometimes cake-like cookies, dried apples create a slightly chewy, toothsome treat. The apple flavor is intensified here with apple cider. All in all, it's a cookie that epitomizes autumn.

- 1 (18.25-ounce) package yellow cake mix

- ¼ cup apple cider (or apple juice)
- ¼ cup vegetable oil
- ½ teaspoon ground cinnamon
- 1 large egg
- 1⅓ cups chopped dried apples
- 1¼ cups chopped walnuts, optional

Preheat oven to 350°F. Position oven rack in middle of oven. Spray cookie sheets with nonstick cooking spray.

Place half of the cake mix along with the apple cider, oil, cinnamon, and egg in a large mixing bowl. Blend with an electric mixer set on medium-high speed for 1–2 minutes, until smooth. Stir in the remaining cake mix and dried apples with a wooden spoon until all dry ingredients are moistened.

Drop dough by teaspoonfuls, 2 inches apart, onto prepared cookie sheets. If desired, sprinkle cookie tops with chopped nuts; gently press nuts into dough.

Bake for 10–13 minutes or until set at edges and just barely set at center when lightly touched. Cool for 1 minute on cookie sheets. Transfer to wire racks with metal spatula and cool completely.

MAKES ABOUT 48 COOKIES.

EGGNOG COOKIES

Here that homogenous blend of eggs, cream, spices, spirits, and plenty of holiday cheer finds form in a delectable, streamlined cookie. For a dazzling finish, drizzle with or dip in melted white or dark chocolate (see page 361).

- 1 (18.25-ounce) package yellow cake mix
- ⅓ cup butter, melted

- 2 large eggs
- 2 teaspoons brandy or rum-flavored extract
- 2 teaspoons ground nutmeg, divided
- ½ teaspoon ground cinnamon
- ⅓ cup sugar

Preheat oven to 350°F. Position oven rack in middle of oven. Spray cookie sheets with nonstick cooking spray.

Place half of the cake mix along with the melted butter, eggs, extract, 1 teaspoon nutmeg, and cinnamon in a large mixing bowl. Blend with an electric mixer set on medium-high speed for 1–2 minutes, until smooth. Stir in the remaining cake mix with a wooden spoon until all dry ingredients are moistened.

In a small dish combine the sugar and remaining teaspoon nutmeg. Drop dough by teaspoonfuls, 2 inches apart, onto prepared cookie sheets; sprinkle cookie tops with the nutmeg sugar.

Bake for 9–12 minutes or until set at edges and just barely set at center when lightly touched. Cool for 1 minute on cookie sheets. Transfer to wire racks with metal spatula and cool completely.

MAKES ABOUT 54 COOKIES.

EXOTIC SPICE COOKIES WITH CARDAMOM, WHITE CHOCOLATE, AND GINGER

At once sophisticated and homey, this spicy little cookie will surprise and delight. A hot cup of tea is the perfect accompaniment.

- 1 (16.5-ounce) roll refrigerated sugar cookie dough, softened
- ¼ cup packed dark brown sugar
- ¾ teaspoon ground cinnamon
- ½ teaspoon ground cardamom
- ½ teaspoon ground ginger
- ¼ teaspoon ground coriander
- 1 cup (6 ounces) white chocolate chips
- ¾ cup chopped macadamia nuts
- ⅓ cup finely chopped crystallized ginger
- glaze
- ½ cup powdered sugar
- ⅛ teaspoon ground cardamom
- 1 tablespoon milk

Break up the cookie dough into a large bowl. Sprinkle the brown sugar, cinnamon, ½ teaspoon cardamom, ground ginger, coriander, white chocolate, macadamia nuts, and crystallized ginger over dough. Mix well with fingers until blended. Chill 20 minutes.

Preheat oven to 350°F.

Drop dough by ¼-cupfuls 3 inches apart on an ungreased cookie sheets.

Bake for 13–17 minutes or until edges are golden brown. Cool for 2 minutes on cookie sheets. Transfer cookies to cooling racks and cool completely.

Combine the powdered sugar, ⅛ teaspoon cardamom, and enough of the milk to blend for drizzling consistency in a small bowl. Drizzle glaze over cooled cookies. Let stand until glaze is set.

MAKES 12 LARGE COOKIES.

FRESH APPLE COOKIES

Apples just seem made for brown sugar and butter. With a combination this good, you won't need much else, save for time to enjoy.

- ½ cup (1 stick) butter
- 2 cups packed brown sugar
- 2 tablespoons flour
- 1 cup peeled, grated tart apple (e.g., Granny Smith)
- ½ teaspoon ground cinnamon
- 3 cups quick-cooking oats, uncooked
- ⅔ cup chopped walnuts or pecans
- 1 teaspoon vanilla extract

Line cookie sheets with wax paper.

Melt the butter in a medium saucepan over medium heat. Add the brown sugar, flour, grated apple, and cinnamon. Bring mixture to a boil; boil for 1 minute. Remove from heat and immediately add the oats, nuts, and vanilla, mixing until well blended.

Working quickly, drop by heaping teaspoonfuls onto wax-paper-lined sheets. Loosely cover with plastic wrap and refrigerate for at least 1 hour until firm. Store tightly covered in refrigerator.

MAKES ABOUT 36 COOKIES.

Variation:
FRESH PEAR AND NUTMEG COOKIES:
Prepare as directed above but substitute 1 cup grated fresh pear for the apple and ¼ teaspoon ground nutmeg for the cinnamon.

FRESH PEAR COOKIES WITH BROWNED BUTTER ICING

Here a great cookie, loaded with fresh pears and a sprinkle of nutmeg, gets even better with the addition of a quick slick of Browned Butter Icing. Be sure to use real butter—margarine does not get brown and nutty the way real butter will. It's not necessary to peel the pears before chopping and adding to the dough.

- 1 (18.25-ounce) package vanilla cake mix
- ½ cup (1 stick) butter, softened
- ¼ cup packed light brown sugar
- 2 large eggs
- ¾ teaspoon ground nutmeg
- 1½ cups coarsely chopped fresh pears (about 2 medium pears)
- 1 cup finely chopped pecans
- 1 recipe Browned Butter Icing (see page 360)

Preheat oven to 350°F. Position oven rack in middle of oven. Spray cookie sheets with nonstick cooking spray.

Place half of the cake mix in a large mixing bowl along with the softened butter, brown sugar, eggs, and nutmeg. Blend with an electric mixer set on medium-high speed for 1–2 minutes, until smooth. Stir in the remaining cake mix and pears with a wooden spoon until all dry ingredients are moistened.

Drop by teaspoonfuls, 2 inches apart, onto prepared cookie sheets. Sprinkle cookie tops with pecans.

Bake for 10–13 minutes or until cracked in appearance and just barely set at center when lightly touched. Cool for 1 minute on cookie sheets. Transfer to wire racks with metal spatula and cool completely.

Prepare Browned Butter Icing; drizzle over cooled cookies.

MAKES ABOUT 48 COOKIES.

Variations:

FRESH CRANBERRY COOKIES: Prepare as directed above but replace the fresh pears with an equal amount of coarsely chopped fresh cranberries and replace the nutmeg with an equal amount of ground ginger.

FRESH APPLE COOKIES: Prepare as directed above but replace the fresh pears with an equal amount of coarsely chopped peeled tart apples and replace the nutmeg with an equal amount of ground cinnamon.

FROSTED DOUBLE-APRICOT DROP COOKIES

If you are not already an apricot lover, you will be converted—instantly—after tasting these fruit-packed gems.

- 1 (16.5-ounce) roll refrigerated sugar cookie dough
- 1 (3-ounce) package cream cheese, cut into bits
- 1 cup chopped dried apricots
- 1 recipe Apricot Frosting (see page 360)

Preheat oven to 350°F. Spray cookie sheets with nonstick cooking spray.

Break up the cookie dough into large bowl; add the cream cheese to bowl and let stand for 10–15 minutes to soften. Add the dried apricots to bowl with cream cheese and cookie dough; mix well with your fingers, the paddle attachment of an electric stand mixer, or a wooden spoon.

Drop dough by kitchen teaspoons, 2 inches apart, onto prepared cookie sheets.

Bake for 10–13 minutes or until just set and golden at edges. Transfer cookies to wire racks and cool completely. Frost with Apricot Frosting.

MAKES 26 COOKIES.

FROSTED ORANGE BLOSSOMS

Enhanced with orange zest and a swipe of orange frosting, these delicate citrus cookies are bursting with flavor. The addition of ground coriander lends a distinctive flavor reminiscent of Northern European baked goods. Serve them during the winter holidays as a festive addition to any cookie platter. They are right at home, year-round, as part of an everyday tea ritual, too.

- 1 (16.5-ounce) roll refrigerated sugar cookie dough
- 1 tablespoon grated orange zest
- ¾ teaspoon ground coriander (or nutmeg)
- 1 recipe Orange Icing (see page 368)

Preheat oven to 350°F. Spray cookie sheets with nonstick cooking spray.

Break up the cookie dough into large bowl; let stand for 10–15 minutes to soften. Add the orange zest and coriander; mix well with your fingers, the paddle attachment of an electric stand mixer, or a wooden spoon.

Drop dough by kitchen teaspoons, 2 inches apart, onto prepared cookie sheets.

Bake for 10–13 minutes or until just set and golden at edges. Transfer cookies to wire racks and cool completely. Spread cooled cookies with Orange Icing.

MAKES 22 COOKIES.

Baker's Note

For a fanciful presentation, garnish each frosted cookie with a few strips of candied orange zest. For a simpler enhancement, sprinkle with colored decorating sugars.

GERMAN CHOCOLATE COOKIES

These milk chocolate, toffee, and coconut cookies have all of the great flavor of German chocolate cake in drop cookie form and just a few minutes of preparation. Serve them up and wait for the "oohs" and "ahhs."

- 1 cup milk chocolate chips
- 5 tablespoons butter
- 16 large marshmallows
- 1 teaspoon vanilla
- 2 cups quick-cooking oats, uncooked
- 1 cup sweetened flake coconut
- ½ cup toffee baking bits
- ½ cup chopped pecans

Line cookie sheets with wax paper.

Melt the chocolate chips with the butter

and marshmallows in a large saucepan over low heat, stirring until smooth. Remove from heat; cool slightly. Stir in vanilla, oats, coconut, toffee bits, and pecans.

Working quickly, drop by rounded teaspoonfuls onto wax-paper-lined sheets. Cover and refrigerate for 2–3 hours. Let stand at room temperature for about 15 minutes before serving. Store tightly covered in refrigerator.

MAKES ABOUT 32 COOKIES.

GIANT CHOCOLATE-CHIP CRANBERRY OATMEAL COOKIES

I suppose plain oatmeal cookies are fine, but I am of the mindset that "more is more" when it comes to cookies. Loaded with chocolate chips and dried cranberries, these fit the bill, beautifully. They make great travelers, too, whether across town or across the country.

- 1 (16.5-ounce) roll refrigerated chocolate-chip cookie dough
- 1 teaspoon ground cinnamon
- ⅔ cup old-fashioned or quick oats
- ⅔ cup chopped dried cranberries (or tart cherries)

Preheat oven to 350°F. Spray cookie sheets with nonstick cooking spray.

Break up the cookie dough into large bowl; let stand for 10–15 minutes to soften. Add the cinnamon, oats, and cranberries; mix well with wooden spoon or fingers just until combined (dough will be stiff).

Drop dough by rounded ¼ cupfuls, 2 inches

apart, onto prepared cookie sheet. Flatten to ½-inch thickness.

Bake for 13–18 minutes or until cookies are slightly puffed and edges are golden brown. Cool for 1 minute. Transfer to wire racks and cool completely.

MAKES 9 GIANT COOKIES.

GINGERBREAD CHEWS

These chewy drops have the lovely flavor of old-fashioned gingerbread. Scented with ginger, cinnamon, and cloves, they're are all about cozy.

- ½ cup packed dark brown sugar
- ½ cup dark corn syrup
- ¾ cup creamy peanut butter
- 1 teaspoon vanilla extract
- 1¼ teaspoons ground ginger
- ¾ teaspoon ground cinnamon
- ⅛ teaspoon ground cloves
- 4 cups crisp rice cereal

Line cookie sheets with wax paper.

Combine the brown sugar and corn syrup in a medium-size saucepan. Bring the mixture to a boil, cooking and stirring constantly, until sugar is completely dissolved. Remove from heat. Stir in the peanut butter, vanilla, ginger, cinnamon, and cloves until blended and smooth. Add the cereal to the peanut butter mixture, stirring until well coated.

Working quickly, drop the mixture by heaping teaspoonfuls onto the wax paper.

Let stand in cool place to harden. Store tightly covered between layers of wax paper.

MAKES ABOUT 22 COOKIES.

GINGERBREAD SOFTIES

As the weather grows colder and the holidays head in, there's no better time to bake a batch of the kind of cookies that fill every room in the house with the familiar scents of good things to come. These cookies, redolent with sweet vanilla, spicy ginger, and cinnamon, fit the bill.

- 1 (18.25-ounce) package spice cake mix
- 1 (8-ounce) package cream cheese, softened
- ¼ cup (½ stick) butter, melted
- 1 large egg
- ¼ cup packed dark brown sugar
- 2 teaspoons ground ginger
- ¾ teaspoon ground cinnamon
- 2 teaspoons vanilla extract
- 1 recipe Orange or Lemon Icing (page 368), optional

Preheat oven to 350°F. Position oven rack in middle of oven. Spray cookie sheets with nonstick cooking spray.

Place half of the cake mix in a large mixing bowl along with the softened cream cheese, melted butter, egg, brown sugar, ginger, cinnamon, and vanilla extract. Blend with an electric mixer set on medium-high speed for 1–2 minutes, until smooth.

Stir in the remaining cake mix with a wooden spoon until all dry ingredients are moistened.

Drop by teaspoonfuls, 2 inches apart, onto prepared cookie sheets.

Bake for 10–13 minutes or until just barely set at center when lightly touched. Cool for 1 minute on cookie sheets. Transfer to wire racks with metal spatula and cool completely.

If desired, prepare Orange or Lemon Icing. Drizzle icing over cooled cookies.

MAKES ABOUT 54 COOKIES.

GINGER-JEWELED BUTTER COOKIES

These cookies warrant singular attention. When you taste them—rich with butter, bejeweled with bits of peppery, candied ginger—you will understand why. Don't forget the pot of strong Indian black tea.

- 1 (18.25-ounce) package yellow cake mix
- 1/3 cup butter, softened
- 1 large egg
- 1 teaspoon ground ginger
- 2/3 cup chopped crystallized ginger

Preheat oven to 350°F. Position oven rack in middle of oven.

Place half of the cake mix in a large mixing bowl along with the softened butter, egg, and ginger. Blend with an electric mixer set on medium-high speed for 1–2 minutes, until smooth. Stir in the remaining cake mix and crystallized ginger with a wooden spoon until all dry ingredients are moistened.

Drop by teaspoonfuls, 2 inches apart, onto ungreased cookie sheets.

Bake for 9–12 minutes or until edges are firm and center is just barely set at center when lightly touched. Cool for 1 minute on cookie sheets. Transfer to wire racks with metal spatula and cool completely.

MAKES ABOUT 48 COOKIES.

GINGER-MACADAMIA TROPI-CLUSTERS

Anyone with a sweet tooth and a penchant for the peppery flavor of ginger will be delighted with these tropical-inspired cookies.

- 5 cups cornflakes cereal
- 1 cup sweetened flake coconut
- 1/2 cup chopped, lightly salted macadamia nuts
- 1/2 cup (1 stick) butter
- 4 1/2 cups miniature marshmallows
- 2 teaspoons ground ginger
- 1 1/2 teaspoons rum-flavored extract

Line cookie sheets with wax paper.

Mix the cornflakes, coconut, and macadamia nuts in a large bowl. In large saucepan set over low heat melt the butter. Add the marshmallows; stir until marshmallows are melted and mixture is smooth. Remove from heat and stir in the ginger and rum extract. Pour over the cornflakes mixture; toss until well coated.

Working quickly, drop by tablespoonfuls onto prepared wax-paper-lined sheets. Cool completely. Store in covered container between sheets of wax paper.

MAKES ABOUT 36 COOKIES.

GRANOLA CHOCOLATE CHUNKERS

Excellent travelers, these sturdy cookies are a good choice for care packages, lunch boxes, and also backpacks when heading out on a hike or picnic.

- 1 (18.25-ounce) package yellow cake mix
- ¼ cup packed brown sugar
- ½ cup vegetable oil
- 2 large eggs
- 2 teaspoons vanilla extract
- 1½ cups granola
- ¾ cup dried fruit of choice (e.g., raisins, dried cranberries, chopped dried apricots)
- 1 cup semisweet chocolate chunks

Preheat oven to 350°F. Position oven rack in middle of oven. Spray cookie sheets with nonstick cooking spray.

Place half of the cake in a large mixing bowl mix along with the brown sugar, oil, eggs, and vanilla extract. Blend with an electric mixer set on medium-high speed for 1–2 minutes, until smooth. Stir in the remaining cake mix, granola, dried fruit, and chocolate chunks with a wooden spoon until all dry ingredients are moistened.

Drop dough by teaspoonfuls, 2 inches apart, onto prepared cookie sheets.

Bake for 9–12 minutes or until set at edges and just barely set at center when lightly touched. Cool for 1 minute on cookie sheets. Transfer to wire racks with metal spatula and cool completely.

MAKES ABOUT 66 COOKIES.

HAYSTACKS

The crunch of crisp chow mein noodles and the smooth, rich taste of chocolate makes these long-standing favorites worth making time and time again.

- 1 (3-ounce) can chow mein noodles or 2 cups pretzel sticks, broken into ½-inch pieces
- 1 cup dry-roasted peanuts
- 2 cups semisweet chocolate chips
- 1 (14-ounce) can sweetened condensed milk

Line cookie sheets with wax paper.

In a large bowl combine the noodles and peanuts; set aside.

Melt the chocolate chips with the condensed milk in a heavy medium saucepan set over low heat, stirring until melted and smooth. Remove from heat.

Stir warm chocolate mixture into noodle-peanut mixture. Working quickly, drop by tablespoonfuls onto prepared baking sheet; chill 2 hours or until firm. Store in covered container between sheets of wax paper.

MAKES ABOUT 32 COOKIES.

Variations:

MILK CHOCOLATE CASHEW HAYSTACKS:
Prepare as directed above but use milk chocolate chips in place of the semisweet chocolate chips and coarsely chopped roasted cashews in place of the peanuts.

WHITE CHOCOLATE ALMOND HAYSTACKS:
Prepare as directed above but use white chocolate chips in place of the semisweet chocolate chips. Add ½ teaspoon almond extract to the melted chocolate mixture

and use coarsely chopped roasted almonds in place of the peanuts.

HOLIDAY HAYSTACKS: Prepare as directed above but use white chocolate chips in place of the semisweet chocolate chips and a combination of ½ cup dried cranberries plus ½ cup coarsely chopped roasted almonds in place of the peanuts.

BUTTERSCOTCH HAYSTACKS: Prepare as directed above but use butterscotch baking chips in place of the semisweet chocolate chips.

HONEY-PEANUT BUTTER PUFFS

Sweet and wholesome, these are Mom and kid favorites. They are a delicious and healthful alternative to candy and a frugal substitute for purchased energy bars.

- ½ cup firmly packed brown sugar
- ¼ cup honey
- 1 tablespoon butter
- ½ cup creamy peanut butter
- 2 cups sweetened puffed wheat cereal

Line cookie sheets with wax paper.

Combine the brown sugar and honey in a medium-size saucepan. Cook over medium heat, stirring frequently, until sugar is dissolved and mixture begins to bubble, about 4 minutes. Remove from heat.

Blend in the butter and peanut butter, stirring until melted and smooth. Add the cereal, stirring only until cereal is well coated. Working quickly, drop mixture by teaspoonfuls onto wax-paper-lined sheets. Let stand in cool place to harden. Store in airtight container between sheets of wax paper.

MAKES ABOUT 22 COOKIES.

ICED MAPLE-PECAN COOKIES

Looking for a new Christmas cookie? Give these double-maple treats a try—they're sure to become a fast family favorite, especially if you pair them with mugs of hot cocoa.

- 1 (18.25-ounce) package butter pecan cake mix
- ⅓ cup butter, softened
- 2 large eggs
- 2 teaspoons maple extract
- 1 cup chopped pecans
- 1 recipe Maple Icing (see page 369)

Preheat oven to 350°F. Position oven rack in middle of oven. Spray cookie sheets with nonstick cooking spray.

Place half of the cake mix in a large mixing bowl along with the softened butter, eggs, and maple extract. Blend with an electric mixer set on medium-high speed for 1–2 minutes, until smooth. Stir in the remaining cake mix and pecans with a wooden spoon until all dry ingredients are moistened.

Drop dough by teaspoonfuls, 2 inches apart, onto prepared cookie sheets.

Bake for 9–12 minutes or until set at edges and just barely set at center when lightly touched. Cool for 1 minute on cookie sheets. Transfer to wire racks with metal spatula and cool completely.

Prepare Maple Icing. Drizzle icing over cookies.

MAKES ABOUT 54 COOKIES.

"I LOVE LIME" WHITE CHOCOLATE COOKIES

If ever a match was made in culinary heaven, it is lime and white chocolate. These particular cookies, as their eponym suggests, are loaded with lime—both the juice in the icing and the zest in the cookies—and balanced by the smooth sweetness of the white chocolate chips that stud each treat.

- 1 (18.25-ounce) package vanilla cake mix
- ½ cup (1 stick) butter, softened
- 2 large eggs
- 1 tablespoon grated lime zest
- 1¼ cups white chocolate chips
- 1 recipe Lime Icing (see page 368)

Preheat oven to 350°F. Position oven rack in upper third of oven. Spray cookie sheets with nonstick cooking spray.

Place half of the cake mix in a large mixing bowl with the softened butter, eggs, and lime zest. Blend with an electric mixer set on medium-high speed for 1–2 minutes, until smooth. Stir in the remaining cake mix and white chocolate chips with a wooden spoon until all dry ingredients are moistened.

Drop dough by teaspoonfuls, 2 inches apart, onto prepared cookie sheets.

Bake for 10–13 minutes or until set at edges and just barely set at center when lightly touched. Cool for 1 minute on cookie sheets. Transfer to wire racks with metal spatula and cool completely.

Prepare Lime Icing. Drizzle icing over cooled cookies.

MAKES ABOUT 48 COOKIES.

Variation:

"I LOVE LEMON" WHITE CHOCOLATE COOKIES: Prepare as directed above but substitute lemon zest for the lime zest and Lemon Icing (see page 368) for the Lime Icing.

IRISH CREAM–FROSTED MILK CHOCOLATE COOKIES

Because I love frosting, it's not surprising that this yummy, liqueur-frosted chocolate cookie tops my list. Depending on your preference and what you have available, change out the liqueur in both the cookie and the frosting (although the Irish cream version is wickedly good). The best way to eat them is with complete abandon, with no thoughts of calories and not a twinge of guilt.

- 1 (19.5- to 19.8-ounce) package brownie mix
- ¼ cup (½ stick) unsalted butter, melted
- ¼ cup Irish cream liqueur
- 1 large egg

- 1½ cups milk chocolate chips
- 1 recipe Irish Cream Frosting (see page 368)

Preheat oven to 350°F. Spray cookie sheets with nonstick cooking spray.

Mix the brownie mix, melted butter, liqueur, and egg in a large mixing bowl with a wooden spoon until just blended and all dry ingredients are moistened; stir in the chocolate chips.

Drop dough by teaspoonfuls, 2 inches apart, onto prepared cookie sheets.

Bake for 10–13 minutes, until cracked in appearance and just barely set at center when lightly touched. Cool for 1 minute on cookie sheets. Transfer to wire racks with metal spatula and cool completely.

Prepare Irish Cream Frosting; frost cooled cookies.

MAKES ABOUT 54 COOKIES

JUMBO JUMBLE CHOCOLATE OATMEAL COOKIES

When the kitchen is warm from baking and the cookie jar is full with these everything-but-the-kitchen-sink chocolate cookies, who cares if it's cold outside?

- 1 (18.25-ounce) package chocolate or devil's food cake mix
- 1 cup vegetable oil
- 3 large eggs
- 2 cups quick-cooking oats
- 1 cup semisweet or milk chocolate chips
- 1 cup miniature candy-coated chocolate baking pieces (e.g., baking M&Ms)
- ½ cup raisins (or dried cranberries)

Place the cake mix, oil, and eggs in a large mixing bowl. Blend with an electric mixer set on medium-high speed for 1–2 minutes, until smooth. Stir in the oats, chocolate chips, baking pieces, and raisins with a wooden spoon until well blended. Let stand 30 minutes (oats will absorb some of the liquid).

Preheat oven to 350°F. Position oven rack in middle of oven. Spray cookie sheets with nonstick cooking spray.

Drop dough by level ¼-cupfuls, 2 inches apart, onto prepared cookie sheets; flatten slightly with your palm or a spatula.

Bake for 13–17 minutes or until set at edges and just barely set at center when lightly touched. Cool for 1 minute on cookie sheets. Transfer to wire racks with metal spatula and cool completely.

MAKES 24 BIG COOKIES.

JUMBO TRIPLE-CHOCOLATE OATMEAL COOKIES

Here's a real treat for the lunch box or bag (for both kids and adults). A chocolate cookie dough and two kinds of chocolate chips turn plain oatmeal cookies into something new and exciting.

- 1 (19.5- to 19.8-ounce) package brownie mix
- 2 cups quick-cooking oats, uncooked

- ½ cup (1 stick) unsalted butter, melted
- 3 large eggs
- 1 cup white chocolate chips
- 1 cup semisweet chocolate chips

Preheat oven to 350°F. Spray cookie sheets with nonstick cooking spray.

Combine brownie mix, oats, melted butter, eggs, white chocolate chips, and semisweet chocolate chips in a large mixing bowl. Stir with a wooden spoon until well blended (dough will be very stiff).

Drop dough by level ¼-cupfuls, 2 inches apart, onto prepared cookie sheets; flatten slightly with your palm or a spatula.

Bake for 13–17 minutes, until set at edges and just barely set at center when lightly touched. Cool for 1 minute on cookie sheets. Transfer to wire racks with metal spatula and cool completely.

MAKES 24 BIG COOKIES.

KAHLUA COOKIES

Impressive to serve yet simple to prepare, these caffeinated cookies are definitely for adults. The type of chocolate chip chosen really makes a difference in the result. Semisweet chips make for a European-tasting cookie (consider adding ½ teaspoon ground cinnamon), milk chocolate chips an American-style mocha flavor, and white chocolate chips create a coffee and cream cookie.

- ⅓ cup Kahlua or other coffee liqueur
- 2 teaspoons instant coffee or espresso powder
- 1 (18.25-ounce) package vanilla cake mix
- ¼ cup (½ stick) butter, melted

- 1 large egg
- 1¼ cups semisweet, milk, or white chocolate chips

Preheat oven to 350°F. Position oven rack in middle of oven. Spray cookie sheets with nonstick cooking spray.

Mix the Kahlua and coffee powder in a large mixing bowl until blended. Add half of the cake mix to the same bowl, along with the melted butter and egg. Blend with an electric mixer set on medium-high speed for 1–2 minutes, until smooth. Stir in the remaining cake mix and chocolate chips with a wooden spoon until all dry ingredients are moistened.

Drop dough by teaspoonfuls, 2 inches apart, onto prepared cookie sheets.

Bake for 10–13 minutes until set at edges and just barely set at center when lightly touched. Cool for 1 minute on cookie sheets. Transfer to wire racks with metal spatula and cool completely.

MAKES ABOUT 48 COOKIES.

KAHLUA WHITE CHOCOLATE CHUNK CHEWIES

These incredible cookies, rich with white chocolate chunks and Kahlua, got a high approval rating first from my husband, then from everyone at work. While testing recipes, I made sure to send lots of "samples" to friends and co-workers, and they gave this particular recipe an approval rating of 100 percent.

- ¼ cup Kahlua or other coffee liqueur
- 1 tablespoon instant coffee or espresso powder
- 1 (19.5- to 19.8-ounce) package brownie mix
- ¼ cup (½ stick) unsalted butter, melted
- 1 large egg
- 1 (6-ounce) box white chocolate baking bars, chopped into chunks
- 1 recipe Kahlua Coffee Icing (see page 369)

Preheat oven to 350°F. Spray cookie sheets with nonstick cooking spray.

Mix the Kahlua and coffee powder in a large mixing bowl. Mix in the brownie mix, melted butter, and egg with a wooden spoon, until just blended and all dry ingredients are moistened; mix in the white chocolate chunks.

Drop dough by teaspoonfuls, 2 inches apart, onto prepared cookie sheets.

Bake for 10–13 minutes, until set at edges and just barely set at center when lightly touched. Cool for 1 minute on cookie sheets. Transfer to wire racks with metal spatula and cool completely.

Prepare Kahlua Coffee Icing. Drizzle icing over cooled cookies.

MAKES ABOUT 48 COOKIES.

KEY LIME COOKIES

These cookies have a marvelous flavor with a bright citrus edge that's just tart enough to nicely offset the richness of the sugar cookie dough. You can substitute lemon or orange for the lime.

- 1 (16.5-ounce) roll refrigerated sugar cookie dough
- 1 tablespoon grated lime zest
- 1 recipe Lime Icing (see page 368)

Preheat oven to 350°F. Spray cookie sheets with nonstick cooking spray.

Break up the cookie dough into large bowl; let stand for 10–15 minutes to soften. Add the lime zest; mix well with your fingers, the paddle attachment of an electric stand mixer, or a wooden spoon.

Drop dough by kitchen teaspoons, 2 inches apart, onto prepared cookie sheets.

Bake for 10–13 minutes or until just set and golden at edges. Transfer cookies to wire racks and cool completely. Drizzle with Lime Icing.

MAKES 22 COOKIES.

KONA COCONUT AND COFFEE COOKIES

Basic sugar cookie dough becomes something altogether extraordinary when blended with espresso, coconut, and nuts. Baked to a perfect golden brown, these cookies have the power to transport you to a Hawaiian paradise in just a few nibbles.

- 1 (16.5-ounce) roll refrigerated sugar cookie dough
- 1 tablespoon instant coffee (or espresso) powder
- 2 teaspoons rum (or vanilla) extract
- 1 (8-ounce) package cream cheese, softened
- 1 (7-ounce) package shredded coconut

- 1 cup sliced, lightly toasted almonds, cooled (optional)

Preheat oven to 350°F. Spray cookie sheets with nonstick cooking spray.

Break up the cookie dough into large bowl; let stand for 10–15 minutes to soften.

Dissolve the coffee powder in the extract in a small cup. Add the coffee mixture, cream cheese, coconut, and nuts, if desired, to cookie dough; mix well with your fingers, the paddle attachment of an electric stand mixer, or a wooden spoon.

Drop dough by kitchen teaspoons, 2 inches apart, onto prepared cookie sheets.

Bake for 10–13 minutes or until just set and golden at edges. Remove from oven and cool on cookie sheets for 2 minutes; transfer to wire racks and cool completely.

MAKES 36 COOKIES.

LADY BALTIMORE COOKIES

This recipe is inspired by a traditional Southern white cake of the same name. According to one story, the cake was first baked by Alicia Rhett Mayberry of Charleston, South Carolina, for novelist Owen Wister. Wister was supposedly so smitten by the cake, he described it in his next book and even named the novel *Lady Baltimore*, published in 1906. The icing, loaded with fruits, nuts, and a splash of spirits, is the secret to this cookie's unique appeal.

- 1 (16.5-ounce) roll refrigerated sugar cookie dough
- 1 (3-ounce) package cream cheese, cut into bits
- 1 cup chopped pecans, preferably lightly toasted
- 1 teaspoon almond extract
- 1 recipe Lady Baltimore Frosting (see page 369)

Preheat oven to 350°F. Spray cookie sheets with nonstick cooking spray.

Break up the cookie dough into large bowl. Add the cream cheese to the bowl; let stand for 10–15 minutes to soften. Add the pecans and almond extract to bowl with dough and cream cheese; mix well with your fingers, the paddle attachment of an electric stand mixer, or a wooden spoon.

Drop dough by kitchen teaspoons, 2 inches apart, onto prepared cookie sheets.

Bake for 10–13 minutes or until just set and golden at edges. Transfer cookies to wire racks and cool completely. Generously frost each cookie with a heaping tablespoon of the icing.

MAKES 32 COOKIES.

Baker's Note

You can substitute the nuts of your choice—almonds, walnuts, hazelnuts—in place of pecans.

LEMON-GINGER CREAM CHEESE SOFTIES

The pleasant bite of ginger coupled with the zing of lemon gives these cookies grown-up appeal.

- 1 (18.25-ounce) package lemon cake mix
- 2 teaspoons ground ginger
- ¼ cup (½ stick) butter, melted
- 4 ounces (half of an 8-ounce) package) cream cheese, softened
- 1 large egg
- 1 recipe Lemon Icing (see page 368), optional

Preheat oven to 350°F. Position oven rack in middle of oven.

Place half of the cake mix in a large mixing bowl along with the ginger, melted butter, softened cream cheese, and egg. Blend with an electric mixer set on medium-high speed for 1–2 minutes, until smooth. Stir in the remaining cake mix with a wooden spoon until all dry ingredients are moistened (dough will be sticky).

Drop dough by teaspoonfuls, 2 inches apart, onto ungreased cookie sheets; smooth edge of each to form round cookie.

Bake for 9–12 minutes or until edges are set and just barely set at center when lightly touched (do not overbake; cookies will become more firm as they cool). Transfer to wire rack and cool completely. If desired, prepare lemon icing; drizzle over cooled cookies.

MAKES 48 COOKIES.

LEMON-GINGER WHITE CHOCOLATE SOFTIES

One of my lemon-loving friends informs me that these soft and tender cookies are now near the top of her list of all-time favorite cookies. Combining the cookie dough with the cream cheese could not be easier—just be sure to soften the cream cheese to room temperature for easy mixing. A wooden spoon will work, but for best results, use an electric mixer. If you have a stand mixer, opt for the paddle attachment.

- 1 (16.5-ounce) roll refrigerated sugar cookie dough
- 6 ounces (¾ of an 8-ounce package) cream cheese, softened
- 2 tablespoons grated lemon zest
- 2 teaspoons ground ginger
- 1 cup white chocolate chips
- 1 recipe Lemon Icing (see page 368)

Preheat oven to 350°F. Spray cookie sheets with nonstick cooking spray.

Break up the cookie dough into large bowl; let stand for 10–15 minutes to soften. Add the cream cheese, lemon zest, and ginger. Mix well with an electric mixer on medium speed until well combined. Add the white chocolate chips; mix well with a wooden spoon.

Drop dough by kitchen teaspoons, 2 inches apart, onto prepared cookie sheets.

Bake for 10–13 minutes, until just set and golden at edges. Quickly transfer cookies to wire racks and cool completely. If desired, drizzle with Lemon Icing.

MAKES 36 COOKIES.

LEMON-HONEY CLUSTERS

Ready for a new taste treat? Try these lemony, crispy clusters, scented with coriander, citrus zest, and honey.

- 5¼ cups honey-nut cornflakes cereal
- ½ cup sliced almonds
- ½ cup (1 stick) butter
- 3¾ cups miniature marshmallows
- ⅓ cup honey
- 1 tablespoon grated lemon zest
- ½ teaspoon ground coriander (optional)

Line cookie sheets with wax paper.

Mix the cornflakes and almonds in a large bowl.

Melt the butter in a large saucepan on low heat. Add the marshmallows and honey; cook and stir until marshmallows are completely melted and mixture is smooth.

Remove from heat and stir in the lemon zest and ground coriander, if desired, until blended. Pour marshmallow mixture over corn flake mixture, tossing to coat well.

Working quickly, drop by rounded table-spoonfuls onto prepared wax-paper-lined sheets. Cool completely. Store, tightly covered, in a cool, dry place.

MAKES ABOUT 36 CLUSTERS.

LEMON POPPYSEED COOKIES

Here's proof positive that joy can be shared in small, sweet ways. Impressive to serve, these lemon-y treats are equally easy to prepare.

- 1 (18.25-ounce) package lemon cake mix
- ⅓ cup vegetable oil
- 2 large eggs
- 1½ tablespoons grated lemon zest
- 3 tablespoons poppyseeds
- 1 recipe Lemon Icing (see page 368), optional

Preheat oven to 350°F. Position oven rack in middle of oven. Spray cookie sheets with nonstick cooking spray.

Place half of the cake mix in a large mixing bowl along with the oil, eggs, lemon zest, and poppyseeds. Blend with an electric mixer set on medium-high speed for 1–2 minutes, until smooth. Stir in the remaining cake mix with a wooden spoon until all dry ingredients are moistened.

Drop dough by teaspoonfuls, 2 inches apart, onto prepared cookie sheets.

Bake for 9–12 minutes or until set at edges and just barely set at center when lightly touched. Cool for 1 minute on cookie sheets. Transfer to wire racks with metal spatula and cool completely.

If desired, prepare Lemon Icing; drizzle icing over cooled cookies.

MAKES ABOUT 48 COOKIES.

LEMON-THYME SUGAR COOKIES

Part of the fun of making cookies is sharing them and showing off a little. You may be mistaken for a pastry chef when you present these elegant cookies, yet they could not be easier to make. They are just the thing for an afternoon pick-me-up alongside a cup of coffee or tea.

- 1 (16.5-ounce) roll refrigerated sugar cookie dough
- 1 cup finely chopped lightly toasted walnuts (or almonds), cooled
- 2 teaspoons chopped thyme leaves or 1 teaspoon dried thyme
- 1 tablespoon grated lemon zest
- 1 recipe Lemon Icing (see page 368)

Preheat oven to 350°F. Spray cookie sheets with nonstick cooking spray.

Break up the cookie dough into large bowl; let stand for 10–15 minutes to soften. Add the nuts, thyme, and lemon zest; mix well with your fingers, the paddle attachment of an electric stand mixer, or a wooden spoon.

Drop dough by kitchen teaspoons, 2 inches apart, onto prepared cookie sheets.

Bake for 10–13 minutes or until just set and golden at edges. Transfer cookies to wire racks and cool completely. Drizzle cooled cookies with Lemon Icing.

MAKES 26 COOKIES.

MACADAMIA AND TOASTED COCONUT CHOCOLATE COOKIES

This island-inspired cookie is just the thing for warm summer days, beach parties, outdoor barbecues, and lazy twilit picnics. Don't forget the lemonade and iced tea.

- 1 2/3 cups sweetened shredded coconut
- 1 (19.5- to 19.8-ounce) package brownie mix
- 1/3 cup canned unsweetened coconut milk
- 1/4 cup (1/2 stick) unsalted butter, melted
- 1 large egg
- 1 cup coarsely chopped roasted, lightly salted macadamia nuts

Preheat oven to 350°F.

Spread coconut evenly over an ungreased cookie sheet. Place sheet on lower rack and toast coconut for 7–8 minutes until golden brown and fragrant. Transfer to a large mixing bowl and cool completely.

Spray cookie sheets with nonstick cooking spray. Add the brownie mix, coconut milk, melted butter, egg, and macadamia nuts to the bowl with the coconut. Mix with a wooden spoon until blended and all dry ingredients are moistened.

Drop by teaspoonfuls, 2 inches apart, onto prepared cookie sheets.

Bake for 10–13 minutes until set at edges and just barely set at center when lightly touched. Cool for 1 minute on cookie sheets. Transfer to wire racks with metal spatula and cool completely.

MAKES ABOUT 54 COOKIES.

MANDARIN ORANGE COOKIES

Looking for a very special cookie? Sweet-tart mandarin oranges and a bit of orange zest dress up a basic cake mix dough, transforming it from ordinary to extraordinary with minimal effort and expense.

- 1 (18.25-ounce) package yellow cake mix
- 1/3 cup vegetable oil
- 1 large egg
- 1 tablespoon grated orange zest
- 1 (10-ounce) can mandarin oranges, well drained, coarsely chopped
- 1 recipe Orange Icing (see page 368)

Preheat oven to 350°F. Position oven rack in middle of oven. Spray cookie sheets with nonstick cooking spray.

Place half of the cake mix in a large mixing bowl along with the oil, egg, and orange zest. Blend with an electric mixer set on medium-high speed for 1–2 minutes, until smooth. Stir in the remaining cake mix with a wooden spoon until all dry ingredients are moistened. Gently fold in the chopped mandarin oranges.

Drop dough by teaspoonfuls, 2 inches apart, onto prepared cookie sheets.

Bake for 9–12 minutes until set at edges and just barely set at center when lightly touched. Cool for 1 minute on cookie sheets. Transfer to wire racks with metal spatula and cool completely.

Prepare Orange Icing; drizzle icing over cooled cookies.

MAKES ABOUT 48 COOKIES.

MAPLE CRANBERRY COOKIES

The aromatic flavor of maple makes for a particularly fine fall cookie, especially when punctuated with tart-sweet bits of dried cranberries.

- 2 cups white chocolate chips
- 1/4 cup creamy peanut butter
- 2 teaspoons maple-flavored extract
- 3 cups crisp rice cereal
- 1 cup dried cranberries

Line cookie sheets with wax paper.

Place the white chocolate chips and peanut butter in a large, uncovered, microwavable bowl. Microwave on medium-high (70 percent power) for 1 minute; stir. If necessary, microwave at additional 10- to 15-second intervals, stirring just until chips are melted. Stir in the maple extract. Stir in the cereal and cranberries until combined.

Working quickly, drop by rounded tablespoonfuls onto prepared wax-paper-lined sheets; let stand until set. Store tightly covered in a cool, dry place.

MAKES 32 COOKIES.

MAPLE PRALINE COOKIES

The taste of fall, all wrapped up in a heavenly cookie, is deceptively easy to prepare. To increase the autumnal experience, add 1/2 cup chopped dried cranberries to the mix along with the oats.

- 1¼ cups maple syrup
- ¼ cup light corn syrup
- ¼ cup (½ stick) butter
- 1 cup chopped pecans
- 1 teaspoon vanilla extract
- 3 cups quick-cooking oats, uncooked

Line cookie sheets with wax paper.

Combine the maple syrup and corn syrup in a large saucepan. Bring to a boil over medium heat, stirring frequently. Continue boiling for 3 minutes, stirring frequently.

Remove from heat. Stir in butter until melted. Stir in the pecans, vanilla, and oats. Working quickly, drop by tablespoonfuls onto wax-paper-lined sheets. Let stand until firm. Store tightly covered.

MAKES ABOUT 32 COOKIES.

MINT CHOCOLATE CHIPPERS

A batch of chocolate-chip cookies still warm from the oven is reason enough for celebration. But if you add a dose of peppermint to the cookies and accompany them with several mugfuls of hot chocolate, you have a full-fledged party.

- 1 (16.5-ounce) roll refrigerated chocolate-chip cookie dough
- 1 teaspoon peppermint extract

Preheat oven to 350°F. Spray cookie sheets with nonstick cooking spray.

Break up the cookie dough into large bowl; let stand for 10–15 minutes to soften. Add the peppermint extract; mix well with your fingers, the paddle attachment of an electric stand mixer, or a wooden spoon.

Drop dough by kitchen teaspoons, 2 inches apart, onto prepared cookie sheets.

Bake for 10–13 minutes or until just set and golden at edges. Transfer cookies to wire racks and cool completely.

MAKES 22 COOKIES.

MINT JULEP COOKIES

The arrival of spring brings both the Kentucky Derby and the mint julep, a very elegant, very potent potion made of bourbon and fresh mint. Here the libation takes cookie form in a quick, but equally elegant cookie. Be warned—they're potent!

- 1 (18.25-ounce) package vanilla cake mix
- ⅓ cup bourbon (or whiskey)
- ¼ cup (½ stick) butter, melted
- ¾ teaspoon peppermint extract
- 1 large egg
- 1 (6-ounce) white chocolate baking bar, chopped

Preheat oven to 350°F. Spray cookie sheets with nonstick cooking spray.

Place half of the cake mix in a large mixing bowl along with the bourbon, melted butter, peppermint extract, and egg. Blend with an electric mixer set on medium-high speed for 1–2 minutes, until smooth. Stir in the remaining cake mix and chopped white chocolate with a wooden spoon until all dry ingredients are moistened.

Drop dough by teaspoonfuls, 2 inches apart, onto prepared cookie sheets.

Bake for 10–13 minutes or until set at edges and just barely set at center when lightly touched. Cool for 1 minute on cookie sheets. Transfer to wire racks with metal spatula and cool completely.

MAKES ABOUT 48 COOKIES.

Variation:

BITTERSWEET CHOCOLATE MINT JULEP COOKIES: Prepare as directed above but substitute chocolate cake mix for the vanilla cake mix and 6 ounces bittersweet baking chocolate for the white chocolate.

Mix the brownie mix, oil, eggs, espresso powder, almond extract, and chocolate chips in a medium mixing bowl with a wooden spoon until well blended.

Drop dough by teaspoonfuls, 2 inches apart, onto prepared cookie sheets. Sprinkle tops with a few sliced almonds; gently press almonds into dough.

Bake for 9–12 minutes, until set at edges and just barely set at center when lightly touched. Cool for 1 minute on cookie sheets. Transfer to wire racks with metal spatula and cool completely.

Prepare the Kahlua Coffee Icing; drizzle over cooled cookies.

MAKES ABOUT 48 COOKIES.

MOCHA ALMOND FUDGE COOKIES

Yes, these fudgy cookies are very rich, but they're worth every bite. They're perfect for afternoon (or, if you cannot wait, morning) coffee breaks.

- 1 (19.5- to 19.8-ounce) package brownie mix
- 1/3 cup vegetable oil
- 2 large eggs
- 1 tablespoon espresso or coffee powder
- 1 teaspoon almond extract
- 1 cup semisweet chocolate chips
- 1 cup sliced almonds
- 1 recipe Kahlua Coffee Icing (see page 369)

Preheat oven to 350°F. Spray cookie sheets with nonstick cooking spray.

MOCHA BUTTERCREAM–FILLED DOUBLE CHOCOLATE SANDWICH COOKIES

I tend to like things gussied up, sometimes to excess. Here's a case where it works to perfection. Two essentials for the success of these cream-filled coffee confections are (1) make sure the filling is semi-set (if fully set, it will be too hard to spread) and (2) make sure the cookies are completely cooled before assembly to avoid melting the buttery filling.

- 2 cups semisweet chocolate chips, divided
- 1/2 cup heavy whipping cream
- 1½ tablespoons instant espresso or coffee powder, divided
- 6 tablespoons (¾ stick) unsalted

butter, room temperature
- ¾ cup powdered sugar
- 1 teaspoon vanilla extract
- 1 (19.5- to 19.8-ounce) package brownie mix
- ⅓ cup vegetable oil
- 3 tablespoons water
- 2 large eggs
- 1 cup coarsely chopped pecans

Stir ½ cup of the chocolate chips, cream, and 1 tablespoon espresso powder in a medium, heavy-bottomed saucepan set over medium-low heat until chocolate melts and coffee dissolves. Remove from heat and cool to room temperature, about 20 minutes.

Beat the butter, powdered sugar, and vanilla in a medium mixing bowl with an electric mixer until blended. Beat in chocolate mixture. Refrigerate until slightly firm but not hard, about 10 minutes.

Preheat oven to 350°F. Spray cookie sheets with nonstick cooking spray. In a large mixing bowl mix the brownie mix, oil, water, eggs, and remaining espresso powder with a wooden spoon until just blended and all dry ingredients are moistened. Stir in pecans and remaining chocolate chips.

Drop by teaspoonfuls, 2 inches apart, onto prepared cookie sheets. Bake for 7–8 minutes or until set at edges and just barely set at center when lightly touched. Cool for 1 minute on cookie sheets. Transfer cookies to wire racks with metal spatula and cool completely.

Spread filling on half the cookies. Top each frosted cookie with another cookie. Gently press together.

MAKES ABOUT 30 SANDWICH COOKIES.

MOCHA CHOCOLATE-CHIP COOKIES

If food marriages are made in heaven, then surely chocolate-coffee is one of the select matches. Given how the two flavors bring out the best in each other, you will be hard-pressed finding someone to turn down an offer of one or more of these cookies. More likely, you will need to conceal a stash for yourself before they evaporate into thin air.

- 1 (16.5-ounce) roll refrigerated chocolate-chip cookie dough
- 1½ teaspoons vanilla extract
- 2½ teaspoons instant espresso (or coffee) powder
- 2 tablespoons unsweetened cocoa powder
- ½ teaspoon ground cinnamon

Preheat oven to 350°F. Spray cookie sheets with nonstick cooking spray.

Break up the cookie dough into large bowl; let stand for 10–15 minutes to soften.

In a small cup combine the vanilla and espresso powder. Add the vanilla mixture, cocoa powder, and cinnamon to the cookie dough; mix well with your fingers, the paddle attachment of an electric stand mixer, or a wooden spoon.

Drop dough by kitchen teaspoons, 2 inches apart, onto prepared cookie sheets.

Bake for 10–13 minutes or until just set and golden at edges. Transfer cookies to wire racks and cool completely.

MAKES 26 COOKIES.

MOCHA PUFFS

Chocolate and coffee team up for a simple, and simply delicious, little cookie.

- 4 (1-ounce) squares semisweet baking chocolate, chopped
- 2 tablespoons chocolate hazelnut spread (e.g., Nutella)
- 1 teaspoon instant espresso or coffee powder
- 2½ cups sweetened puffed wheat cereal

Line cookie sheets with wax paper.

Microwave the chocolate, hazelnut spread, and espresso powder on high in a large microwavable bowl for 1½–2 minutes or until chocolate is almost melted, stopping and stirring every 30 seconds. Stir until chocolate is completely melted. Stir in cereal.

Working quickly, drop by teaspoonfuls onto prepared wax-paper-lined sheets.

Refrigerate until firm. Store in tightly covered container in refrigerator.

MAKES ABOUT 28 COOKIES.

NEAPOLITAN COOKIES

These tricolor cookies are as delightful and delicious as the brick ice cream by the same name.

- 1 (18.25-ounce) package cherry chip cake mix
- ¼ cup vegetable oil
- 2 tablespoons water
- 2 large eggs
- ½ teaspoon almond extract
- ¾ cup finely chopped maraschino cherries (patted dry between paper towels)
- 1 cup miniature semisweet chocolate chips

Preheat oven to 350°F. Position oven rack in middle of oven. Spray cookie sheets with nonstick cooking spray.

Place half of the cake mix in a large mixing bowl along with the oil, water, eggs, and almond extract. Blend with an electric mixer set on medium-high speed for 1–2 minutes, until smooth. Stir in the remaining cake mix, cherries, and chocolate chips with a wooden spoon until all dry ingredients are moistened.

Drop by teaspoonfuls, 2 inches apart, onto prepared cookie sheets.

Bake for 10–12 minutes or until golden brown at edges. Cool for 1 minute on cookie sheets. Transfer to wire racks with metal spatula and cool completely.

MAKES ABOUT 54 COOKIES.

OATMEAL RAISIN COOKIES

On a cold winter evening, cozy up with one of these cookies in one hand and a steaming mug of cocoa in the other.

- 1 cup butterscotch baking chips
- 5 tablespoons butter
- 16 large marshmallows
- ½ teaspoon ground cinnamon

- 2 cups quick-cooking oats, uncooked
- 1 cup raisins
- ½ cup sweetened flake coconut

Line cookie sheets with wax paper.

Melt the butterscotch chips with the butter, marshmallows, and cinnamon in a large saucepan set over low heat, stirring until smooth. Remove from heat; cool for 5 minutes. Stir in the oats, raisins, and coconut.

Working quickly, drop by rounded teaspoonfuls onto wax-paper-lined sheets. Loosely cover with plastic wrap and refrigerate for 2–3 hours. Let stand at room temperature about for 15 minutes before serving. Store tightly covered in refrigerator.

MAKES ABOUT 32 COOKIES.

OLD-FASHIONED HERMITS

Hermits—spicy drop cookies filled with fruits and nuts—have been filling American cookie jars since colonial times. Here they are better than ever—and simplified with the help of cake mix.

- 1 (18.25-ounce) package spice cake mix
- 1 teaspoon pumpkin pie spice
- ⅓ cup butter, softened
- 1 (3-ounce) package cream cheese, softened
- 2 large eggs
- 1 tablespoon grated orange zest
- 1 cup snipped dates, raisins, or currants
- 1 cup chopped walnuts (or pecans)

Preheat oven to 350°F. Position oven rack in middle of oven. Spray cookie sheets with nonstick cooking spray.

Place half of the cake mix in a large mixing bowl along with the pumpkin pie spice, softened butter, softened cream cheese, eggs, and orange zest. Blend with an electric mixer set on medium-high speed for 1–2 minutes, until smooth. Stir in the remaining cake mix and dried fruit with a wooden spoon until all dry ingredients are moistened.

Drop by teaspoonfuls, 2 inches apart, onto prepared cookie sheets. Sprinkle tops with nuts.

Bake for 9–12 minutes or until firm at edges and center is just barely set when lightly touched. Cool for 1 minute on cookie sheets. Transfer to wire racks with metal spatula and cool completely.

MAKES ABOUT 54 COOKIES.

ORANGE CHOCOLATE-CHIP CREAM CHEESE DROPS

Here's a cookie with a delicate, tender texture and a subtle tang. Both qualities are owed to the addition of cream cheese to the dough—it's a fine foil for the dark, miniature chocolate chips scattered throughout. Lemon zest may be interchanged for the orange zest with equal success.

- 1 (18.25-ounce) package vanilla cake mix
- ¼ cup (½ stick) butter, melted
- 1 (8-ounce) package cream cheese, softened
- 1 large egg

- 1 tablespoon grated orange zest
- 1 cup miniature semisweet chocolate chips

Preheat oven to 350°F. Position oven rack in middle of oven.

Place half of the cake mix in a large mixing bowl along with the melted butter, softened cream cheese, egg, and orange zest. Blend with an electric mixer set on medium-high speed for 1–2 minutes, until smooth. Stir in the remaining cake mix and miniature chocolate chips with a wooden spoon until all dry ingredients are moistened.

Drop dough by teaspoonfuls, 2 inches apart, onto ungreased cookie sheets.

Bake for 9–12 minutes or until set at edges and just barely set at center when lightly touched (do not overbake; cookies will become more firm as they cool). Transfer to wire rack and cool completely.

MAKES ABOUT 48 COOKIES.

ORANGE CREAM CLUSTERS

Ramen noodles may sound like an unusual ingredient for cookies, but you'll be convinced after your first nibble. They add a delicate crispiness that deliciously complements the citrus-cream flavor of these teatime treats.

- 3 (3-ounce) packages ramen noodles (any flavor)
- ½ cup sliced almonds
- ¼ cup (½ stick) butter
- 1 tablespoon grated orange zest
- 1 cup white chocolate chips

Line cookie sheets with wax paper.

Place the uncooked noodles in a large bowl. Discard noodle seasoning packets or save for another use. Break up the noodles into small pieces (½ inch or smaller) with fingers or a wooden spoon. Add the almonds to the bowl.

Melt the butter in a large skillet set over medium heat. Add the noodle mixture. Cook over medium heat, stirring constantly, for about 5 minutes or until noodles and almonds just begin to brown. Transfer mixture from skillet back to large bowl; add the orange zest, stirring to combine. Cool slightly.

Melt the white chocolate chips on medium-high (70 percent power) for 1 minute in a medium, uncovered, microwave-safe bowl; stir. Microwave at additional 10- to 15-second intervals, stirring just until chocolate is melted. Pour melted chocolate over noodle mixture in bowl. Toss until noodle mixture is completely coated.

Working quickly, drop by rounded teaspoonfuls into mounds onto prepared wax-paper-lined sheets (mixture will appear loose, but will set as it cools). Let stand for 45–60 minutes or until set. Store in covered container between sheets of wax paper.

MAKES 22 COOKIES.

Variations:

LIME CREAM COOKIES: Prepare as directed above but substitute lime zest for the orange zest.

BUTTER PECAN COOKIE CLUSTERS: Prepare as directed above but omit the orange zest. Use chopped pecans in place of the almonds and add 1 teaspoon vanilla extract to the melted white chocolate before adding the ramen noodle mixture.

ORANGE DREAMSICLE COOKIES

Remember those orange and vanilla cream pops from summer vacations past? Vanilla ice cream inside, orange sherbet outside, they always topped my list of ice pop favorites. Recapture that summertime flavor with these orange and vanilla cookies. But don't limit them to the summer months—they are delicious year-round.

- 1 (18.25-ounce) package yellow cake mix
- ½ cup (1 stick) butter, melted
- 1 large egg
- 1 tablespoon grated orange zest
- 1½ cups white chocolate chips
- 1 recipe Orange Icing (see page 368)

Preheat oven to 350°F. Position oven rack in middle of oven.

Place half of the cake in a large mixing bowl mix along with the melted butter, egg, and orange zest. Blend with an electric mixer set on medium-high speed for 1–2 minutes, until smooth. Stir in the remaining cake mix and white chocolate chips with a wooden spoon until all dry ingredients are moistened.

Drop dough by teaspoonfuls, 2 inches apart, onto ungreased cookie sheets.

Bake for 10–13 minutes or until just barely set at center when lightly touched. Cool for 1 minute on cookie sheets. Transfer to wire racks with metal spatula and cool completely.

Prepare Orange Icing. Drizzle icing over cooled cookies.

MAKES ABOUT 48 COOKIES.

PEACHES AND CREAM COOKIES

You'll taste the best of summer in these peachy-keen cookies. Although irresistible frosted, they are excellent straight-up, too.

- 1 (18.25-ounce) package vanilla cake mix
- ½ cup vegetable oil
- ½ cup peach preserves
- 1 tablespoon grated lemon zest
- 1 large egg
- 1 recipe Cream Cheese Frosting (see page 366)

Preheat oven to 350°F. Position oven rack in upper third of oven. Spray cookie sheets with nonstick cooking spray.

Place half of the cake mix in a large mixing bowl along with the oil, preserves, lemon zest, and egg. Blend with an electric mixer set on medium-high speed for 1–2 minutes, until smooth. Stir in the remaining cake mix with a wooden spoon until all dry ingredients are moistened.

Drop dough by teaspoonfuls, 2 inches apart, onto prepared cookie sheets.

Bake for 11–13 minutes or until set at edges and just golden brown. Cool for 1 minute on cookie sheets. Transfer to wire racks with metal spatula and cool completely.

Prepare Cream Cheese Frosting; frost cookies.

MAKES ABOUT 48 COOKIES.

FROSTED APRICOT COOKIES: Prepare as directed above but use apricot preserves in place of the peach preserves and add ¼ teaspoon ground nutmeg to the dough along with the other ingredients.

MARMALADE SPICE COOKIES: Prepare as directed above but eliminate the lemon zest, use a spice cake mix in place of the vanilla cake mix, use orange marmalade in place of the peach preserves, and add ¾ teaspoon ground cinnamon to the dough along with the other ingredients.

PEANUT BRITTLE COOKIES

My husband claims that his maternal grandmother makes the very best versions of several Southern classics, including, but not limited to, pecan pie, candied sweet potatoes, and peanut brittle. The latter inspired me to develop this finger-licking, lickity-split cookie. If you want to add a subtle hint of chocolate to this already delicious cookie, replace the toffee baking bits with finely chopped chocolate-covered toffee candy bars.

- 1 (16.5-ounce) roll refrigerated sugar cookie dough
- ½ cup toffee baking bits
- ¾ cup very coarsely chopped salted, dry roasted peanuts

Preheat oven to 350°F. Spray cookie sheets with nonstick cooking spray.

Break up the cookie dough into large bowl; let stand for 10–15 minutes to soften. Add the toffee bits and peanuts; mix well with your fingers, the paddle attachment of an electric stand mixer, or a wooden spoon.

Drop dough by kitchen teaspoons, 2 inches apart, onto prepared cookie sheets.

Bake for 10–13 minutes or until just set and golden at edges. Transfer cookies to wire racks.

MAKES 28 COOKIES.

PEANUT BUTTER-CHIP CHOCOLATE COOKIES

My favorite way to make these peanut-buttery chocolate cookies is with peanut butter chips, but I also think they are pretty incredible made with semisweet or milk chocolate chips. If you can't decide, go half and half: ¾ cup chocolate chips and ¾ cup peanut butter chips. You can't go wrong!

- 1 (19.5- to 19.8-ounce) package brownie mix
- 1 cup creamy peanut butter (not old-fashioned or natural style)
- ½ cup (1 stick) unsalted butter, melted
- ¼ cup packed dark brown sugar
- 2 large eggs
- 2 teaspoons vanilla extract
- 1½ cups peanut butter–flavored baking chips

Preheat oven to 350°F. Spray cookie sheets with nonstick cooking spray.

Mix the brownie mix, peanut butter, melted butter, brown sugar, eggs, and vanilla in a medium mixing bowl with a wooden spoon until well blended. Stir in peanut butter baking chips.

Drop dough by teaspoonfuls, 2 inches apart, onto prepared cookie sheets.

Bake for 10–13 minutes, until set at edges and just barely set at center when lightly touched. Cool for 1 minute on cookie sheets. Transfer to wire racks with metal spatula and cool completely.

MAKES ABOUT 60 COOKIES.

PEANUT BUTTER CHOCOLATE CHUNKERS

A scrumptious pairing of dark chocolate and peanut butter, these chunky cookies call for tall glasses of cold milk and lots of good cheer.

- 1 (18.25-ounce) package chocolate cake mix
- ½ cup chunky-style peanut butter (not old-fashioned or natural style)
- ½ cup (1 stick) butter, softened
- 3 large eggs
- 1 cup semisweet chocolate chips or chunks

Preheat oven to 350°F. Position oven rack in middle of oven. Spray cookie sheets with nonstick cooking spray.

Place half of the cake mix in a large mixing bowl along with the peanut butter, softened butter, and eggs. Blend with an electric mixer set on medium-high speed for 1–2 minutes,

until smooth. Stir in the remaining cake mix and chocolate chips with a wooden spoon until all dry ingredients are moistened.

Drop dough by teaspoonfuls, 2 inches apart, onto prepared cookie sheets.

Bake for 10–13 minutes or until set at edges and just barely set at center when lightly touched. Cool for 1 minute on cookie sheets. Transfer to wire racks with metal spatula and cool completely.

MAKES ABOUT 48 COOKIES.

PEANUT BUTTER COOKIES (CAKE MIX)

There's a time for discovering new flavors and a time for savoring old favorites. When you're in the mood for the latter, whip up a batch of these peanut butter cookies.

- 1 cup creamy peanut butter (not old-fashioned or natural style)
- 2 large eggs
- ⅓ cup milk
- 1 (18.25-ounce) package yellow cake mix
- ⅓ cup granulated sugar

Preheat oven to 375°F. Position oven rack in middle of oven. Spray cookie sheets with nonstick cooking spray.

Mix the peanut butter, eggs, milk, and half of the cake mix in a large mixing bowl with a wooden spoon until well blended. Mix in remaining cake mix with a spoon until blended and all dry ingredients are moistened.

Place sugar in a shallow dish. Drop dough by tablespoonfuls onto prepared cookie sheets.

Gently press a crisscross pattern on top of cookies with fork dipped in the sugar.

Bake for 10–12 minutes or until set at edges and just barely set at center when lightly touched. Cool for 3–4 minutes on cookie sheets to firm the cookies. Transfer to wire racks with metal spatula and cool completely.

MAKES ABOUT 48 COOKIES.

PEANUT BUTTER COOKIES (NO-BAKE)

Peanut butter was one of the original health foods, invented in 1890 by a St. Louis doctor for an ailing patient and promoted in 1904 at the St. Louis Universal Exposition. It's been a favorite American food ever since. Celebrate its goodness with this delicious, no-bake take on peanut butter cookies.

- ½ cup (1 stick) butter
- 2 cups packed dark brown sugar
- ½ cup canned evaporated milk
- ½ cup creamy peanut butter
- 1 teaspoon vanilla extract
- 3 cups quick-cooking oats, uncooked
- 1 cup roasted peanuts (optional)

Line cookie sheets with wax paper.

Combine the butter, brown sugar, and evaporated milk in a large heavy saucepan. Bring mixture to a boil over medium heat, stirring occasionally, until mixture comes to a full boil.

Let mixture boil, without stirring, for exactly 3 minutes. remove from heat immediately. Stir in peanut butter and vanilla, stirring until peanut butter has melted. Quickly stir in the oats

and, if desired, peanuts; mix well.

Working quickly, drop mixture by kitchen tablespoonfuls onto wax-paper-lined sheets. Allow to cool and become firm, for about 30 minutes. Store in covered container between sheets of wax paper in a cool, dry place.

MAKES ABOUT 32 COOKIES.

PEANUT BUTTER SCOTCHIES

In my book, few things are as comforting, reassuring, and just plain delicious as the flavor of butterscotch. Add a hefty dollop of creamy peanut butter and you've got an irresistible homespun treat. Delicious anytime, these cookies are especially excellent dunked in a cold glass of milk in the middle of the afternoon or as a late-night snack.

- 1 (16.5-ounce) roll refrigerated sugar cookie dough
- ½ cup creamy-style peanut butter
- 3 tablespoons packed dark brown sugar
- 1½ teaspoons vanilla extract
- 1¼ cups butterscotch morsels

Preheat oven to 350°F. Spray cookie sheets with nonstick cooking spray.

Break up the cookie dough into large bowl; let stand for 10–15 minutes to soften. Add the peanut butter, brown sugar, vanilla, and butterscotch morsels; mix well with your fingers, the paddle attachment of an electric stand mixer, or a wooden spoon.

Drop dough by kitchen teaspoons, 2 inches apart, onto prepared cookie sheets.

Bake for 10–13 minutes or until just set and

golden at edges. Transfer cookies to wire racks and cool completely.

MAKES 30 COOKIES.

PEANUT BUTTERY CHOCOLATE CHIP-LOADED COWBOY COOKIES

If you crave a simple, sturdy cookie, free of pretension and full of homey goodness, here you are. The cookie may sound new-fangled, but the taste is entirely old-fashioned. Loaded with so many good things, you almost need an excuse not to make these cookies.

- 1 (16.5-ounce) roll refrigerated chocolate-chip cookie dough
- ½ cup shredded coconut
- ⅔ cup creamy-style peanut butter
- ½ cup quick or old-fashioned oats
- ½ cup chopped roasted peanuts

Preheat oven to 350°F. Spray cookie sheets with nonstick cooking spray.

Break up the cookie dough into large bowl; let stand for 10–15 minutes to soften. Add the coconut, peanut butter, oats, and peanuts to the cookie dough; mix well with your fingers, the paddle attachment of an electric stand mixer, or a wooden spoon.

Drop dough by kitchen teaspoons, 2 inches apart, onto prepared cookie sheets.

Bake for 10–13 minutes or until just set and golden at edges. Transfer to wire racks and cool completely.

MAKES 36 COOKIES.

PECAN AND WHITE CHOCOLATE CHUNK BROWNIE COOKIES

White chocolate, pecans, brown sugar, and dark chocolate dough—cookies don't get much better than this. Ready from start to finish in well under an hour, they're terrific with a cappuccino or glass of ice-cold milk.

- 1 (19.5- to 19.8-ounce) package brownie mix
- ½ cup (1 stick) unsalted butter, melted
- ¼ cup packed dark brown sugar
- 2 large eggs
- 1 (6-ounce) package white chocolate baking squares, coarsely chopped into chunks
- 1 cup coarsely chopped pecans

Preheat oven to 350°F. Spray cookie sheets with nonstick cooking spray.

Mix the brownie mix, melted butter, brown sugar, eggs, and white chocolate chunks in a medium mixing bowl with a wooden spoon until well blended.

Drop dough by teaspoonfuls, 2 inches apart, onto prepared cookie sheets. Sprinkle tops with a few pecans.

Bake for 9–12 minutes, until set at edges and just barely set at center when lightly touched. Cool for 1 minute on cookie sheets. Transfer to wire racks with metal spatula and cool completely.

MAKES ABOUT 54 COOKIES.

PEPPERMINT WHITE CHOCOLATE CRINKLES

A batch of these minty chocolate cookies makes a wonderful winter holiday gift, but chances are you'll want to keep them for yourself. Perhaps you'll succumb to the spirit of the season and share them with friends nonetheless. Or make two batches!

- 1 (19.5- to 19.8-ounce) package brownie mix
- 1/3 cup vegetable oil
- 2 large eggs
- 1 teaspoon peppermint extract
- 1½ cups white chocolate chips
- 12 red and white striped round peppermint hard candies, crushed

Preheat oven to 350°F. Spray cookie sheets with nonstick cooking spray.

Mix the brownie mix, oil, eggs, and peppermint extract in a medium mixing bowl with a wooden spoon until just blended and all dry ingredients are moistened; stir in white chocolate chips.

Drop dough by teaspoonfuls, 2 inches apart, onto prepared cookie sheets. Sprinkle tops with crushed candies.

Bake for 9–12 minutes, until set at edges and just barely set at center when lightly touched. Cool for 1 minute on cookie sheets. Transfer to wire racks with metal spatula and cool completely.

MAKES ABOUT 54 COOKIES.

PEPPERY GINGER CHOCOLATE COOKIES

These simple cookies celebrate one of my favorite flavors: ginger. Fragrant and speckled with bits of candied ginger and miniature chocolate chips, these cookies are the ticket for anyone who likes a bit of spice with their chocolate.

- 1 (19.5- to 19.8-ounce) package brownie mix
- 2 teaspoons ground ginger
- ½ teaspoon ground black pepper
- ½ cup (1 stick) unsalted butter, melted
- ¼ cup packed dark brown sugar
- 2 large eggs
- 2/3 cup very finely chopped crystallized ginger
- 1 cup semisweet chocolate chips

Preheat oven to 350°F. Spray cookie sheets with nonstick cooking spray.

Mix the brownie mix, ground ginger, black pepper, melted butter, brown sugar, and eggs in a large mixing bowl with a wooden spoon until just blended and all dry ingredients are moistened; mix in crystallized ginger and chocolate chips.

Drop by teaspoonfuls, 2 inches apart, onto prepared cookie sheets.

Bake for 9–12 minutes, until cracked in appearance and just barely set at center when lightly touched. Cool for 1 minute on cookie sheets. Transfer to wire racks with metal spatula and cool completely.

MAKES ABOUT 48 COOKIES.

PIÑA COLADA COOKIES

All of the flavors of the cool, creamy tropical drink come together in this easy, breezy cookie.

- 1 (8-ounce) package cream cheese, softened
- ¼ cup (½ stick) butter, softened
- 1 large egg yolk
- ½ cup pineapple juice
- 2 teaspoons rum-flavored extract
- 1 (18.25-ounce) package yellow cake mix
- 1 cup sweetened flaked coconut

Place the softened cream cheese and softened butter in a large mixing bowl. Blend with an electric mixer set on medium-high speed for 1–2 minutes, until smooth. Add the egg yolk, pineapple juice, rum extract, and half of the cake mix; blend with an electric mixer set on medium-high speed for 1–2 minutes, until smooth. Stir in the remaining cake mix and coconut with a wooden spoon until all dry ingredients are moistened. Chill the dough, covered, for 30 minutes.

Preheat oven to 375°F. Position oven rack in middle of oven. Spray cookie sheets with non-stick cooking spray.

Drop dough by teaspoonfuls, 2 inches apart, onto prepared cookie sheets.

Bake for 9–11 minutes or until set at edges and just barely set at center when lightly touched. Cool for 1 minute on cookie sheets. Transfer to wire racks with metal spatula and cool completely.

MAKES ABOUT 48 COOKIES.

PIÑA COLADA PINEAPPLE DROPS

Pineapple and coconut create a fresh burst of flavor for this harmonious little cookie. For some added crunch, stir in ⅓ cup chopped macadamia nuts or blanched almonds. For a beautiful summer dessert platter, serve them up surrounded by a sliced assortment of the season's finest fruit.

- 1 (16.5-ounce) roll refrigerated sugar cookie dough
- ⅔ cup chopped dried pineapple
- ½ cup shredded coconut
- 1 teaspoon rum flavor (or vanilla extract)

Preheat oven to 350°F. Spray cookie sheets with nonstick cooking spray.

Break up the cookie dough into large bowl; let stand for 10–15 minutes to soften. Add the dried pineapple, coconut, and extract; mix well with your fingers, the paddle attachment of an electric stand mixer, or a wooden spoon.

Drop dough by kitchen teaspoons, 2 inches apart, onto prepared cookie sheets.

Bake for 10–13 minutes or until just set and golden at edges. Transfer cookies to wire racks and cool completely.

MAKES 26 COOKIES.

PINE NUT COOKIES

Pine nuts, also known as pignola, pignoli, Indian nuts, and piñon, come from the pinecones of several varieties of pine trees.

Sweet and delicate in flavor, the ivory-colored, torpedo-shaped nuts are used in a wide array of savory and sweet dishes in many cuisines. They are particularly delicious in baked goods, like these subtly spiced, Italian-inspired cookies. Anise is a traditional flavoring in Italian baked goods, but ½ teaspoon ground nutmeg, mace, or coriander may be substituted.

- 1 (18.25-ounce) package vanilla cake mix
- ½ cup (1 stick) butter, softened
- 2 large eggs
- 1 teaspoon vanilla extract
- 1 teaspoon anise seed, coarsely crushed in a mortar and pestle
- 1 cup pine nuts

Preheat oven to 350°F. Position oven rack in upper third of oven. Spray cookie sheets with nonstick cooking spray.

Place half of the cake mix in a large mixing bowl along with the softened butter, eggs, vanilla extract, and anise seed. Blend with an electric mixer set on medium-high speed for 1–2 minutes, until smooth. Stir in the remaining cake mix with a wooden spoon until all dry ingredients are moistened.

Drop dough by teaspoonfuls, 2 inches apart, onto prepared cookie sheets. Sprinkle cookie tops with a few pine nuts; gently press nuts into dough.

Bake for 9–12 minutes or until set at edges and just barely set at center when lightly touched. Cool for 1 minute on cookie sheets. Transfer to wire racks with metal spatula and cool completely.

MAKES ABOUT 54 COOKIES.

PINEAPPLE SOFTIES

This friendly cookie is an ideal choice for giving to new friends and neighbors because it is lush with pineapple, the historic symbol of welcome.

- 1 (18.25-ounce) package spice cake mix
- 1 (8-ounce) can crushed pineapple, drained, juice reserved
- ¼ cup vegetable oil
- 1 large egg
- 1 cup sweetened flaked coconut, optional

Preheat oven to 350°F. Position oven rack in middle of oven. Spray cookie sheets with nonstick cooking spray.

Place half of the cake mix in a large mixing bowl along with the pineapple, 2 tablespoons of the reserved juice, oil, and egg. Blend with an electric mixer set on medium-high speed for 1–2 minutes, until smooth. Stir in the remaining cake mix with a wooden spoon until all dry ingredients are moistened.

Drop dough by teaspoonfuls, 2 inches apart, onto prepared cookie sheets. If desired, sprinkle cookie tops with coconut; gently press into dough.

Bake for 10–13 minutes or until set at edges and just barely set at center when lightly touched. Cool for 1 minute on cookie sheets. Transfer to wire racks with metal spatula and cool completely.

MAKES ABOUT 48 COOKIES.

PRALINE COOKIES

This is one great cookie. The dough will spread out relatively thin as it bakes because the butter recipe cake mix has a higher fat content than other cake mixes. It is very important to let the cookies rest on the sheets before transferring them to cooling racks (they will be too soft when they first come out of the oven). The result is a thin, crispy cookie that really does taste like a praline. For a perfectly round cookie, try using a cookie scoop—it looks like a mini ice cream scooper. I bet once you taste these you'll agree that a praline in cookie form tastes just as sweet.

- 1 (18.25-ounce) package butter recipe cake mix
- ½ cup (1 stick) butter, softened
- ¼ cup packed dark brown sugar
- 2 large eggs
- 1 teaspoon vanilla extract
- 1¼ cups toffee baking bits
- 2 cups chopped pecans

Preheat oven to 350°F. Position oven rack in middle of oven. Spray cookie sheets with nonstick cooking spray.

Place half of the cake mix in a large mixing bowl along with the softened butter, brown sugar, eggs, and vanilla extract. Blend with an electric mixer set on medium-high speed for 1–2 minutes, until smooth. Stir in the remaining cake mix and toffee bits with a wooden spoon until all dry ingredients are moistened.

Drop by teaspoonfuls, 2 inches apart, onto prepared cookie sheets. Generously sprinkle cookie tops with chopped pecans; gently press into cookies.

Bake for 10–12 minutes or until golden brown at edges. Cool for 2 minutes on cookie sheets. Transfer to wire racks with metal spatula and cool completely.

MAKES ABOUT 54 COOKIES.

PUMPKIN SPICE SOFTIES

Rediscover a family favorite—in minutes—with this quickly assembled cookie. They keep well—that is, if you can keep them from being gobbled up.

- 1 (18.25-ounce) package spice cake mix
- ⅔ cup canned pumpkin purée
- 1 large egg
- 2 tablespoons vegetable oil
- 1 teaspoon pumpkin pie spice
- 1 cup raisins (or dried cranberries), optional
- 1 cup finely chopped pecans or walnuts, optional
- 1 recipe Vanilla Icing (see page 376), optional

Preheat oven to 350°F. Position oven rack in middle of oven. Spray cookie sheets with nonstick cooking spray.

Place half of the cake mix in a large mixing bowl along with the pumpkin, egg, oil, and pumpkin pie spice. Blend with an electric mixer set on medium-high speed for 1–2 minutes, until smooth. Stir in the remaining cake mix and optional raisins with a wooden spoon until all dry ingredients are moistened.

Drop by teaspoonfuls, 2 inches apart, onto prepared cookie sheets. If desired, sprinkle tops of cookies with chopped nuts; gently press nuts into dough.

Bake for 10–13 minutes or until set at edges and just barely set at center when lightly touched (do not overbake). Cool for 1 minute on cookie sheets. Transfer to wire racks with metal spatula and cool completely. If desired, drizzle with Vanilla Icing.

MAKES ABOUT 48 COOKIES.

RANGER COOKIES

Chock-full of everything, ranger cookies are old-time favorites, and with good reason: they taste like home, keep well, and are great travelers for lunch boxes and picnics. Make a batch and there's just one thing left to do—sit, eat, and enjoy.

- 1 (18.25-ounce) package **yellow cake mix**
- ¾ cup **vegetable oil**
- ⅓ cup **chunky peanut butter** (not old-fashioned or natural style)
- 3 large **eggs**
- 1½ cups **quick-cooking oats**
- ⅔ cup **semisweet chocolate chips, raisins, or dried cranberries**
- ½ cup **sweetened flaked coconut**

Preheat oven to 350°F. Position oven rack in middle of oven.

Place the cake mix, oil, peanut butter, and eggs in a large mixing bowl. Blend with an electric mixer set on medium-high speed for 1–2 minutes, until smooth. Stir in the oats, chocolate chips (or dried fruit), and coconut with a wooden spoon until all dry ingredients are moistened (dough will be very stiff).

Drop dough by level ¼-cupfuls, 2 inches apart, onto ungreased cookie sheets; flatten slightly with your palm or a spatula.

Bake for 13–17 minutes or until set at edges and just barely set at center when lightly touched. Cool for 1 minute on cookie sheets. Transfer to wire racks with metal spatula and cool completely.

MAKES 30 BIG COOKIES.

RICOTTA COOKIES

Somewhat similar to cottage cheese, ricotta is a slightly grainy, very soft, and smooth Italian cheese used in a variety of sweet and savory dishes like cheesecake and lasagna. Here it creates a rich, cake-like cookie with a crisp shell and soft, snowy interior. For a citrus variation, substitute 2 teaspoons of freshly grated lemon, lime, or orange zest for the vanilla.

- 1 (18.25-ounce) package **vanilla cake mix**
- ¼ cup (½ stick) **butter,** melted
- ¾ cup **ricotta cheese**
- 1 large **egg**
- 2 teaspoons **vanilla extract**
- 1 recipe **Vanilla Icing** (see page 376)

Preheat oven to 350°F. Position oven rack in middle of oven.

Place half of the cake mix in a large mixing bowl along with the melted butter, ricotta cheese, egg, and vanilla extract. Blend with an electric mixer set on medium-high speed for 1–2 minutes, until smooth. Stir in the remaining cake mix with a wooden spoon until all dry ingredients are moistened (dough will be somewhat stiff).

Drop dough by teaspoonfuls, 2 inches apart, onto ungreased cookie sheets.

Bake for 9–12 minutes or until golden at edges and just barely set at center when lightly touched (do not overbake; cookies will become more firm as they cool). Transfer to wire rack and cool completely.

Prepare Vanilla Icing. Drizzle cooled cookies with icing.

MAKES 48 COOKIES.

ROCKY ROAD DROPS

If you like marshmallows, chocolate chips, and peanuts, you'll love this cookie version of rocky road.

- 2 cups sugar
- ½ cup (1 stick) butter
- ½ cup milk
- ⅓ cup unsweetened cocoa powder
- 3 cups quick-cooking oats, uncooked
- ⅓ cup chopped roasted, salted peanuts
- ⅓ cup semisweet chocolate chips
- 2 cups miniature marshmallows

Line cookie sheets with wax paper.

Combine sugar, butter, milk, and cocoa in a large saucepan. Bring to a boil over medium heat, stirring frequently. Continue boiling for 3 minutes. Remove from heat.

Stir in the oats, peanuts, chocolate chips, and marshmallows; mix well.

Working quickly, drop by tablespoonfuls onto wax-paper-lined sheets. Let stand until set. Store tightly covered at room temperature.

MAKES ABOUT 42 COOKIES.

RUM RAISIN COOKIES

Enhanced with the flavors of rum and nutmeg, these easy raisin cookies are fit for both company and comfort on a cold, chilly night.

- 1 (18.25-ounce) package yellow cake mix
- ½ teaspoon ground nutmeg
- ⅓ cup vegetable oil
- 2 large eggs
- 1½ teaspoons rum extract
- 1½ cups raisins
- 1 recipe Rum Icing (see page 374)

Preheat oven to 350°F. Position oven rack in middle of oven. Spray cookie sheets with nonstick cooking spray.

Place half of the cake mix in a large mixing bowl along with the nutmeg, oil, eggs, and rum extract. Blend with an electric mixer set on medium-high speed for 1–2 minutes, until smooth. Stir in the remaining cake mix and raisins with a wooden spoon until all dry ingredients are moistened.

Drop dough by teaspoonfuls, 2 inches apart, on prepared cookie sheets.

Bake for 9–12 minutes or until set at edges and just barely set at center when lightly touched. Cool for 1 minute on cookie sheets. Transfer to wire racks with metal spatula and cool completely.

Prepare Rum Icing. Drizzle icing over cooled cookies.

MAKES ABOUT 54 COOKIES.

Variation:

BRANDIED APRICOT COOKIES: Prepare as directed above but substitute snipped dried apricots for the raisins, brandy extract for the rum extract, and Brandy Icing (see page 360).

SALTY-SWEET CHOCOLATE CRISPY CHEWS

If you have a penchant for the combination of salty and sweet, this is your cookie.

- 2 cups semisweet, milk, or white chocolate chips or butterscotch baking chips
- ½ cup chunky peanut butter
- 1 teaspoon vanilla extract
- 1½ cups miniature marshmallows
- 1 cup lightly salted mixed nuts, coarsely chopped
- 1 cup crisp rice cereal

Line cookie sheets with wax paper.

Melt the chips on high for 2 minutes in a microwave-safe medium mixing bowl, stirring every 30 seconds. Stir in the peanut butter and vanilla until blended. Stir in the marshmallows, nuts, and cereal.

Working quickly, drop by small spoonfuls onto prepared wax-paper-lined sheets. Store in a covered container in a cool place.

MAKES ABOUT 22 COOKIES.

SEAN'S VERY CHOCOLATE COOKIES

When it comes to birthdays, my brother Sean is easy to satisfy. All he really wants is his favorite birthday cake, known by my family as "Very Chocolate Cake." It's a simple yet intensely chocolate pound cake that starts with a chocolate cake mix. These cookies follow the same basic formula as the cake but start with brownie mix. One bite and you'll understand why the name is so very fitting.

- 1 (19.5- to 19.8-ounce) package brownie mix
- 1 (5½-ounce) package instant chocolate pudding mix
- ¼ cup dark rum
- ½ cup (1 stick) butter, melted
- 2 large eggs
- 1½ cups semisweet chocolate chunks or chips

Preheat oven to 350°F. Position racks in lower and upper thirds of oven. Spray cookie sheets with nonstick cooking spray.

Mix the brownie mix, pudding mix, rum, melted butter, and eggs in a large mixing bowl with a wooden spoon until just blended and all dry ingredients are moistened; mix in chocolate chunks.

Drop by teaspoonfuls, 2 inches apart, onto prepared cookie sheets.

Bake for 10–13 minutes, until cracked in appearance and just barely set at center when lightly touched. Cool for 1 minute on cookie sheets. Transfer to wire racks with metal spatula and cool completely.

MAKES ABOUT 54 COOKIES.

S'MORES CLUSTERS

Kids of all ages will appreciate the decadent campfire combination of chocolate, marshmallows, and graham crackers in these easily assembled cookie clusters.

- 2 cups semisweet chocolate chips
- 3 cups miniature marshmallows
- 12 whole honey graham crackers, coarsely crushed

Line cookie sheets with wax paper.

Place chocolate chips in large microwave-safe bowl. Microwave on high for 2 minutes, stopping every 30 seconds to stir chocolate, until chocolate is melted.

Stir the marshmallows and graham pieces into the melted chocolate until evenly coated.

Working quickly, drop tablespoonfuls of the s'more mixture onto wax-paper-lined cookie sheets. Refrigerate for 30 minutes or until chocolate is set. Store in covered container in refrigerator.

MAKES ABOUT 32 CLUSTERS.

SOFT BANANA BROWNIE COOKIES

Chocolate and banana are clearly made for each other in these soft, cake-like cookies. They're great to pack into lunchbags. Moreover, it's quite likely you have all the ingredients you need in your kitchen right now.

- 1 medium-sized, ripe banana
- 1 large egg
- 1 tablespoon vegetable oil
- 1 (19.5- to 19.8-ounce) package brownie mix
- 1 cup milk or white chocolate chips
- 1 cup chopped walnuts (optional)

Preheat oven to 350°F. Spray cookie sheets with nonstick cooking spray.

Mash the banana in a medium mixing bowl. Add the egg, oil, and brownie mix. Mix with a wooden spoon until just blended and all the dry ingredients are moistened. Stir in chocolate chips.

Drop by teaspoonfuls, 2 inches apart, onto prepared cookie sheets. Sprinkle with chopped walnuts, if desired.

Bake for 10–13 minutes, until set at edges and just barely set at center when lightly touched (do not overbake). Cool for 1 minute on cookie sheets. Transfer to wire racks with metal spatula and cool completely.

MAKES ABOUT 48 COOKIES.

SPECIAL K CHEWIES

These classic caramel–peanut butter chews are an all-time favorite at my graduate school alma mater, Indiana University, where they have been prepared and served on campus for more than a generation. The mixture hardens quickly, so be sure to prep the cookie sheets before you start cooking.

- ½ cup sugar
- ½ cup corn syrup
- ¾ cup creamy peanut butter
- 1 teaspoon vanilla extract
- 4 cups Kellogg's Special K cereal

Line cookie sheets with wax paper.

Combine the sugar and corn syrup in a medium-size saucepan. Bring mixture to a boil, cooking and stirring constantly, until sugar is completely dissolved.

Remove from heat. Stir in the peanut butter and vanilla until smooth.

Add the cereal to the peanut butter mixture,

stirring until well coated. Working quickly, drop the mixture by heaping teaspoonfuls onto the wax paper. Let stand in cool place to harden. Store tightly covered between layers of wax paper.

MAKES ABOUT 22 COOKIES.

SPICY DOUBLE-GINGER CHOCOLATE CHIPPERS

This version is spicy and robust thanks to a double dose of ginger and a dash of pepper.

- 1 (16.5-ounce) roll refrigerated chocolate-chip cookie dough
- ½ cup finely chopped crystallized/ candied ginger
- 1 teaspoon ground ginger
- ¼ teaspoon cracked black pepper (optional)

Preheat oven to 350°F. Spray cookie sheets with nonstick cooking spray.

Break up the cookie dough into large bowl; let stand for 10–15 minutes to soften. Add the crystallized ginger, ground ginger, and pepper, if desired; mix well with your fingers, the paddle attachment of an electric stand mixer, or a wooden spoon.

Drop dough by kitchen teaspoons, 2 inches apart, onto prepared cookie sheets.

Bake for 10–13 minutes or until just set and golden at edges. Transfer cookies to wire racks and cool completely.

MAKES 26 COOKIES.

TEXAS-SIZED RED VELVET SOFTIES WITH CREAM CHEESE FROSTING

Texas-sized indeed—these great big, bright red cookies are more like little cakes than cookies. As big as they are, most people will still want more than one.

- 1 cup jarred applesauce
- ⅓ cup butter, softened
- 1 (18.25-ounce) package red velvet cake mix
- 2 large eggs
- ½ cup milk
- 1 recipe Cream Cheese Frosting (see page 366)

Preheat oven to 375°F. Position oven rack in middle of oven. Line a cookie sheet with parchment paper or foil (if using foil, grease it).

Beat applesauce and softened butter in a large mixing bowl with an electric mixer on medium speed until smooth. Add the cake mix, eggs, and milk; beat on low speed until combined and then on medium speed for 1 minute. Drop mounds of batter by heaping tablespoonfuls, 3 inches apart, onto prepared cookie sheet; keep remaining batter chilled.

Bake for 15 minutes or until set and lightly browned around edges. Carefully remove from parchment or foil; cool on wire rack. Repeat with remaining batter, lining cooled cookie sheets each time with new parchment or foil. Place cookies in a covered storage container with wax paper between layers, if desired.

Prepare Cream Cheese Icing. Frost the cookies.

MAKES ABOUT 30 BIG COOKIES.

TEXAS-SIZE TOFFEE SCOTCHIE COOKIES

These abundantly stuffed beauties are a butterscotch lover's dream come true. Be sure to bake just a few at a time on each sheet—they bake up big, hence the eponymous "Texas-size."

- 1 (16.5-ounce) roll refrigerated sugar cookie dough
- ¼ cup firmly packed brown sugar
- 1 teaspoon vanilla extract
- ⅓ cup old-fashioned or quick oats
- ¾ cup butterscotch chips
- 2 (1.4-ounce) milk chocolate covered toffee candy bars, chopped

Preheat oven to 350°F. Spray cookie sheets with nonstick cooking spray.

Break up the cookie dough into large bowl; let stand for 10–15 minutes to soften. Add the brown sugar, vanilla, oats, butterscotch chips, and chopped candy bars; mix well with your fingers, the paddle attachment of an electric stand mixer, or a wooden spoon.

Drop dough by rounded ¼ cupfuls, 2 inches apart, onto prepared cookie sheets.

Bake for 15–18 minutes or until cookies are slightly puffed and edges are golden brown. Cool for on cookie sheets 1 minute. Transfer to wire racks and cool completely.

MAKES 9 BIG COOKIES.

Baker's Note

To make regular-size cookies, prepare cookies as directed above but drop cookies by tablespoons onto prepared cookie sheets. Bake for 10–13 minutes or until just set and golden at edges. Transfer cookies to wire racks. Makes about 28 cookies.

THANKSGIVING CRANBERRY WHITE CHOCOLATE JUMBLES

Don't be fooled by the name—these cookies are appealing at any time of the year. The mildly spiced dough is a fine foil for plump, sweet cranberries. They are arguably the perfect bag-lunch cookie and are destined to be the first to disappear from the holiday cookie tray.

- 1 (16.5-ounce) roll refrigerated sugar cookie dough
- ¾ cup white chocolate chips
- ½ cup dried cranberries
- ½ cup sliced almonds, coarsely chopped
- 2 teaspoons grated orange zest
- 1 teaspoon pumpkin pie spice (or ground cinnamon)

Preheat oven to 350°F. Spray cookie sheets with nonstick cooking spray.

Break up the cookie dough into large bowl; let stand for 10–15 minutes to soften. Add the white chocolate chips, cranberries, almonds, orange zest, and spice; mix well with your fingers, the paddle attachment of an electric stand mixer, or a wooden spoon.

Drop dough by kitchen teaspoons, 2 inches apart, onto prepared cookie sheets.

Bake for 10–13 minutes or until just set and golden at edges. Transfer cookies to wire racks and cool completely.

MAKES 28 COOKIES.

TOASTED ALMOND COOKIES

Five ingredients—that's all it takes to produce these elegant almond cookies. They are a fine choice for teatime.

- 1 (18.25-ounce) package vanilla cake mix
- 1/3 cup vegetable oil
- 2 large eggs
- 1 teaspoon almond extract
- 1 1/3 cups sliced almonds

Preheat oven to 350°F. Position oven rack in middle of oven. Spray cookie sheets with nonstick cooking spray.

Place half of the cake mix along with the oil, eggs, and almond extract in a large mixing bowl. Blend with an electric mixer set on medium-high speed for 1–2 minutes, until smooth. Stir in the remaining cake mix with a wooden spoon until all dry ingredients are moistened.

Drop dough by teaspoonfuls, 2 inches apart, onto prepared cookie sheets. Sprinkle cookie tops with sliced almonds; gently press almonds into dough.

Bake for 9–12 minutes or until set at edges and just barely set at center when lightly

touched. Cool for 1 minute on cookie sheets. Transfer to wire racks with metal spatula and cool completely.

MAKES ABOUT 48 COOKIES.

TOASTED COCONUT CHOCOLATE CHIPPERS

A tropical twist on good old-fashioned chocolate-chip cookies is only minutes away with a hot oven, a cookie sheet, and a few basic pantry items. Toasting the coconut is well worth the minimal effort: it brings out the rich, full flavor of the coconut, transforming these chippers into five-star treats.

- 1 cup shredded coconut
- 1 (16.5-ounce) roll refrigerated chocolate-chip cookie dough
- 1 teaspoon coconut (or rum) extract (optional)

Preheat oven to 350°F. Spread coconut evenly onto ungreased cookie sheet.

Toast coconut for 9–12 minutes or until golden brown; remove from oven and cool completely on sheet.

Spray cookie sheets with nonstick cooking spray. Break up the cookie dough into large bowl; let stand for 10–15 minutes to soften. Add the cooled toasted coconut and coconut or rum extract, if desired; mix well with your fingers, the paddle attachment of an electric stand mixer, or a wooden spoon.

Drop dough by kitchen teaspoons, 2 inches apart, onto prepared cookie sheets.

Bake for 10–13 minutes or until just set and

golden at edges. Transfer cookies to wire racks and cool completely.

MAKES 26 COOKIES.

TO-DIE-FOR CHOCOLATE HAZELNUT SANDWICH COOKIES

I personally refer to these as "true believer" cookies because they have turned many foodie friends and acquaintances into brownie mix converts in just a few nibbles. They nearly flip when I tell them the recipe is made with only four ingredients. Sophisticated and intensely chocolate, they are as pretty as they are easy to make. The flavor of chocolate and hazelnut may not be familiar to many Americans, but it is a common, and much loved, European combination. But you only need to love chocolate to go nuts over these cookies. You can find chocolate hazelnut spread in most supermarkets these days, right next to the peanut butter or in the international foods section.

- 1 (19.5- to 19.8-ounce) package brownie mix
- 1²/₃ cup chocolate-hazelnut spread (e.g., Nutella), divided
- ¹/₃ cup unsalted butter, melted
- 2 large eggs

Preheat oven to 350°F. Spray cookie sheets with nonstick cooking spray.

Mix the brownie mix, 1 cup chocolate-hazelnut spread, melted butter, and eggs in a large mixing bowl with a wooden spoon until well blended (mixture will be very thick).

Roll dough into ¾-inch balls and place 2 inches apart on prepared cookie sheets. Flatten slightly with the your palm, a spatula, or the tines of a fork.

Bake for 8–11 minutes until set at edges and just barely set at center when lightly touched and cookies have a cracked appearance (cookies will be flat and round). Cool for 1 minute on cookie sheets. Transfer to wire racks with metal spatula and cool completely.

Spread bottom side of one cookie with a teaspoon of remaining chocolate-hazelnut spread; sandwich with a second cookie. Repeat with remaining cookies.

MAKES ABOUT 36 SANDWICH COOKIES.

TOFFEE APPLE CHOCOLATE COOKIES

I've made this same cookie with a sugar cookie dough for years, but I have to admit that it is even better made with chocolate dough. The dried apples together with the toffee bits give these cookies a crunchy-chewy consistency, making them great partners for tall glasses of milk on cool autumn afternoons. To send these cookies over the top, dip or drizzle them with melted white chocolate, place on wax paper–lined cookie sheets, and refrigerate until chocolate is set. Outstanding!

- 1 (19.5- to 19.8-ounce) package brownie mix
- ½ cup (1 stick) unsalted butter, melted
- ¼ cup packed light brown sugar
- 2 large eggs

- 2 teaspoons vanilla extract
- 1 (6-ounce) package dried apples, chopped
- 1¼ cups English toffee baking bits

Preheat oven to 350°F. Position racks in lower and upper thirds of oven. Spray cookie sheets with nonstick cooking spray.

Mix the brownie mix, melted butter, brown sugar, eggs, vanilla, dried apples, and toffee bits in a large mixing bowl with a wooden spoon until all dry ingredients are moistened.

Drop by teaspoonfuls, 2 inches apart, onto prepared cookie sheets.

Bake for 10–13 minutes, until just barely set at center when lightly touched. Cool for 2 minutes on cookie sheets. Transfer to wire racks with metal spatula and cool completely.

MAKES ABOUT 54 COOKIES.

TOFFEE APPLE COOKIES

My better half, Kevin, is such a cookie lover that he prefers a fresh-baked batch to birthday cake. I'm happy to oblige him with these easy drop cookies inspired by one of my favorite confections.

- 1 (16.5-ounce) roll refrigerated sugar cookie dough
- 1 (6-ounce) package dried apples, chopped
- ½ cup English toffee baking bits
- 1 recipe Chocolate Drizzle or Dip (see page 361), optional

Preheat oven to 350°F. Spray cookie sheets with nonstick cooking spray.

Break up the cookie dough into large bowl; let stand for 10–15 minutes to soften. Add the dried apples and toffee bits; mix well with your fingers, the paddle attachment of an electric stand mixer, or a wooden spoon.

Drop dough by kitchen teaspoons, 2 inches apart, onto prepared cookie sheets.

Bake for 10–13 minutes or until just set and golden at edges. Transfer cookies to wire racks and cool completely.

If desired, dunk one end of each cookie into Chocolate Dip; place dipped cookies on wax-paper-lined cookie sheet. Place cookies in refrigerator until chocolate is set.

MAKES 30 COOKIES.

Baker's Note

These cookies are outstanding dipped or drizzled in any variety of chocolate— semisweet, white, or milk chocolate. It's your call!

TRAIL MIX COOKIES

A great portable cookie, these oat-, fruit-, and seed-filled treats will keep your energy going for a hike up the mountain or a stroll across town. Packages of assorted dried fruit bits can be found alongside raisins in your supermarket. If you cannot find them, raisins, dried cranberries, or chopped dried apricots may be substituted.

- 1 (19.5- to 19.8-ounce) package brownie mix
- ½ cup vegetable oil
- 2 large eggs
- ⅔ cup quick-cooking oats
- ½ cup miniature chocolate chips

- ½ cup mixed dried fruit bits
- ½ cup roasted, lightly salted sunflower seeds

Preheat oven to 350°F. Position racks in lower and upper thirds of oven. Spray cookie sheets with nonstick cooking spray.

Mix the brownie mix, oil, eggs, oats, chocolate chips, fruit bits, and sunflower seeds in a large mixing bowl with a wooden spoon until all dry ingredients are moistened.

Drop by teaspoonfuls, 2 inches apart, onto prepared cookie sheets.

Bake for 10–12 minutes until cracked in appearance and just barely set at center when lightly touched. Cool for 1 minute on cookie sheets. Transfer to wire racks with metal spatula and cool completely.

MAKES ABOUT 54 COOKIES.

TRIPLE CHOCOLATE CHIPPERS

Chocolate times three equals cookie perfection in these fast and fudgy cookies.

- 1½ cups sugar
- ½ cup (1 stick) butter
- 1 (5-ounce) can (2/3 cup) evaporated milk
- 1 1/3 cups miniature semisweet chocolate chips, divided use
- 1 (4-serving-size) package instant chocolate pudding mix
- 1 teaspoon vanilla extract
- 2½ cups quick-cooking oats, uncooked

Line cookie sheets with wax paper.

Combine the sugar, butter, and evaporated milk in a large heavy saucepan. Cook and stir until mixture comes to a full rolling boil. Remove the pan from heat and stir in 1/3 cup of the chocolate chips until melted and smooth.

Stir in the pudding mix, vanilla, and oats, mixing well. Stir in the remaining 1 cup chocolate chips.

Working quickly, drop the mixture by tablespoonfuls onto wax-paper-lined sheets. Allow to cool for about 30 minutes until firm.

MAKES ABOUT 22 COOKIES.

ULTIMATE ALMOND COOKIES

Rich, classic sugar cookie dough, enriched with both almonds and almond extract, makes for simple, and simply wonderful, cookies for almond lovers.

- 1 (16.5-ounce) roll refrigerated sugar cookie dough
- 1 (3-ounce) package cream cheese, cut into bits
- ¾ teaspoon almond extract
- 1 cup whole almonds, lightly toasted, cooled and coarsely chopped
- 1 recipe Almond Icing (see page 360), optional

Preheat oven to 350°F. Spray cookie sheets with nonstick cooking spray.

Break up the cookie dough into large bowl; add the cream cheese to bowl and let stand for 10–15 minutes to soften. Add the almond extract and almonds to the cookie dough and cream cheese bowl; mix well with your fingers, the paddle attachment of an electric stand mixer, or a wooden spoon.

Drop dough by kitchen teaspoons, 2 inches apart, onto prepared cookie sheets.

Bake for 10–13 minutes or until just set and golden at edges. Transfer cookies to wire racks. If desired, drizzle with Almond Icing.

MAKES 28 COOKIES.

WALNUT-DATE COOKIES

Dates are one of the first confections, going back more than 5,000 years in culinary history. Although native to the Middle East, they are also plentiful in my home state of California. For anyone who loves brown sugar (me!), dates are a favorite cookie ingredient. Here they add a toothsome chewiness, a delicious foil to the nutty crunch of walnuts.

- 1 (18.25-ounce) package vanilla cake mix
- ¾ cup (1½ sticks) butter, melted
- ⅓ cup all-purpose flour
- 2 large eggs
- 1 teaspoon ground cinnamon
- 1 cup quick-cooking oats
- 1 cup chopped dates
- 1 cup chopped walnuts

Preheat oven to 375°F. Position oven rack in middle of oven. Spray cookie sheets with nonstick cooking spray.

Place half of the cake mix in a large mixing bowl along with the melted butter, flour, eggs, and cinnamon. Blend with an electric mixer set on medium-high speed for 1–2 minutes, until smooth. Stir in the remaining cake mix, oats,

and dates with a wooden spoon until all dry ingredients are moistened.

Drop dough by teaspoonfuls, 2 inches apart, onto prepared cookie sheets. Sprinkle cookie tops with a few chopped walnuts.

Bake for 9–11 minutes or until set at edges and just barely set at center when lightly touched. Cool for 1 minute on cookie sheets. Transfer to wire racks with metal spatula and cool completely.

MAKES ABOUT 66 COOKIES.

WHITE CHOCOLATE CHERRY COOKIES

This is one of my signature cookie concoctions. The cookies taste like a temptation you might find at a high-end specialty store or bakery but are quick and easy to make—perfect when you need to make or bring an impressive dessert in short order.

- 1 (19.5- to 19.8-ounce) package brownie mix
- ⅓ cup vegetable oil
- 2 large eggs
- ½ teaspoon almond extract
- 1 cup tart dried cherries or dried cranberries
- 1 cup white chocolate chips

Preheat oven to 350°F. Spray cookie sheets with nonstick cooking spray.

Mix the brownie mix, oil, eggs, almond extract, cherries, and white chocolate chips in a medium bowl with a wooden spoon until well blended.

Drop dough by teaspoonfuls, 2 inches apart, onto prepared cookie sheets.

Bake for 9–12 minutes, until set at edges and

just barely set at center when lightly touched. Cool for 1 minute on cookie sheets. Transfer to wire racks with metal spatula and cool completely.

MAKES ABOUT 54 COOKIES.

WHITE CHOCOLATE, COCONUT, AND LIME COOKIES

Both coconut and lime lovers will delight in these drops, rich in the flavors of the tropics.

- 1 cup white chocolate chips
- 5 tablespoons butter
- 16 large marshmallows
- 1 tablespoon fresh lime juice
- 2 teaspoons grated lime zest
- 1 teaspoon ground ginger
- 2 cups quick-cooking oats, uncooked
- 1 cup sweetened flake coconut

Line cookie sheets with wax paper.

Melt the white chocolate chips in a large saucepan with the butter, marshmallows, and lime juice over low heat, stirring until smooth. Remove from heat; cool for 5 minutes. Stir in the lime zest, ginger, oats, and coconut.

Working quickly, drop by rounded tea-spoonfuls onto wax-paper-lined sheets. cover loosely with plastic wrap and refrigerate for 2–3 hours. Let stand at room temperature for about 15 minutes before serving. Store tightly covered in refrigerator.

MAKES ABOUT 32 COOKIES.

WHITE CHOCOLATE PEPPERMINT SNOWDROPS

When I moved from California to the Midwest to attend graduate school, I found myself longing for a winter-wonderful cookie to spur me on through gray, slushy December and January weather. These easy treats quickly became my hot cocoa companions.

- 1 (16.5-ounce) roll refrigerated sugar cookie dough
- 1 cup white chocolate chips
- 1 recipe Peppermint Icing (see page 374)
- 1 cup crushed peppermint candies (or candy canes)

Preheat oven to 350°F. Spray cookie sheets with nonstick cooking spray.

Break up the cookie dough into large bowl; let stand for 10–15 minutes to soften. Add the white chocolate chips; mix well with your fingers, the paddle attachment of an electric stand mixer, or a wooden spoon.

Drop dough by measuring tablespoonfuls onto prepared cookie sheets.

Bake for 10–13 minutes or until just set and golden at edges. Cool for 2 minutes; transfer to wire racks and cool completely. Drizzle cookies with Peppermint Icing and sprinkle with crushed peppermint candies.

MAKES 26 COOKIES.

Prepare Chocolate Whiskey Frosting. Generously frost cooled cookies.

MAKES ABOUT 48 COOKIES.

WICKED WHISKEY CHOCOLATE COOKIES

It's pretty easy to take your favorite feel-good chocolate cookies from standard to sensational when you add more chocolate and a generous splash of whiskey.

- 1 (19.5- to 19.8-ounce) package brownie mix
- ¼ cup whiskey
- ¼ cup (½ stick) unsalted butter, melted
- 1 large egg
- 1½ cups semisweet chocolate chunks or chips
- 1 recipe Chocolate Whiskey Frosting (see page 364)

Preheat oven to 350°F. Position racks in lower and upper thirds of oven.

Spray cookie sheets with nonstick cooking spray. Mix the brownie mix, whiskey, melted butter, and egg in a large bowl with a wooden spoon until just blended and all dry ingredients are moistened; mix in chocolate chunks.

Drop dough by teaspoonfuls, 2 inches apart, onto prepared cookie sheets.

Bake for 9–12 minutes, until cracked in appearance and just barely set at center when lightly touched. Cool for 1 minute on cookie sheets. Transfer to wire racks with metal spatula and cool completely.

FORMED, FILLED, AND FANCY COOKIES

ALMOND COFFEE COOKIE BALLS

For an extra-special presentation, consider drizzling some melted white or dark chocolate over each cookie ball. Refrigerate for 30 minutes until set and then serve.

- 2 cups finely crushed plain sugar cookies (about 8 ounces)
- 1 cup sliced almonds, finely chopped
- ¼ cup light corn syrup
- 2 tablespoons coffee-flavored liqueur
- ½ teaspoon almond extract
- 2 tablespoons butter, melted
- 1⅔ cups sifted powdered sugar, divided

Combine the crushed cookies, chopped almonds, corn syrup, coffee liqueur, almond extract, butter, and 1 cup of the powdered sugar in a large mixing bowl with a wooden spoon until well blended. Shape mixture into 1-inch balls.

Place remaining ⅔ cup powdered sugar in shallow dish or bowl. Roll balls in powdered sugar; loosely cover with plastic wrap. Let stand for 2 hours. roll again in additional powdered sugar if desired. Chill for up to 1 week or freeze for up to 3 months.

MAKES ABOUT 36 COOKIE BALLS.

ALMOND CRESCENTS

My mother made nut crescents every Christmas when I was a girl. This simplified variation captures all of the flavor, and the nostalgia.

- 1 (16.5-ounce) roll refrigerated sugar cookie dough, softened
- ½ cup all-purpose flour
- ⅔ cup sliced almonds
- ¼ teaspoon almond extract
- 1 cup powdered sugar

Break up the cookie dough into a large bowl. Sprinkle the flour, almonds, and almond extract over dough. Mix well with fingers until blended.

Roll dough into 1-inch balls, then shape each ball into a 1½-inch crescent. Place 2 inches apart on ungreased cookie sheets. Preheat oven to 350°F. Chill crescents on cookie sheets for 15 minutes.

Bake cookies for 11–13 minutes or until light golden brown. Cool on cookie sheets for 2 minutes.

Place the powdered sugar in a small, shallow dish. Roll warm cookies in powdered sugar. Cool on cooling rack. Roll in powdered sugar again.

MAKES 42 COOKIES.

ALMOND MACAROON-TOPPED COOKIES

I am particularly fond of macaroons of all varieties. This version is no exception.

- 1 (16.5-ounce) roll refrigerated sugar cookie dough
- ⅓ cup sugar
- 1 tablespoon all-purpose flour
- ¼ teaspoon almond extract
- 1 large egg white
- 1½ cups sweetened flake coconut
- 30 whole blanched almonds

Place cookie dough in freezer for 30 minutes.

Preheat oven to 350°F. Whisk the sugar, flour, almond extract, and egg white in a medium bowl until well blended and slightly frothy. Stir in the coconut.

Cut the chilled cookie dough into 30 slices. Place cookie slices 2 inches apart on ungreased cookie sheets. Spoon 1 rounded teaspoon coconut mixture onto each slice, spreading slightly over dough with back of spoon. Press 1 almond into center of each cookie.

Bake for 12–15 minutes or until edges are light golden brown. Cool for 1 minute on cookie sheets. Transfer cookies to cooling racks and cool completely.

MAKES 30 COOKIES.

ALMOND-ORANGE CHOCOLATE BISCOTTI

Combining two classic biscotti flavors in a dark chocolate dough, these biscotti are great for tea and coffee breaks, not to mention gift-giving.

- 1 (19.5- to 19.8-ounce) package brownie mix
- 1 cup all-purpose flour
- ½ cup (1 stick) unsalted butter, melted and cooled
- 2 large eggs
- 1 tablespoon grated orange zest
- 1 teaspoon almond extract
- 1 cup coarsely chopped whole almonds

Preheat oven to 350°F. Position rack in center of oven. Line a cookie sheet with parchment paper.

Combine the brownie mix, flour, melted butter, eggs, orange zest, almond extract, and almonds in a large mixing bowl. Blend with an electric mixer set on low for 1–2 minutes until well blended, scraping down sides of bowl (mixture will be stiff).

Transfer dough to prepared cookie sheet. With floured hands, shape dough into two 14 x 3-inch rectangles, ¾-inch thick, spacing them 4–5 inches apart on sheet. Mound the dough so it is slightly higher in the center than at the edges. Place cookie sheet in oven.

Bake for 30–35 minutes, until firm to touch; remove from oven and cool on sheet for 10 minutes (leave oven on).

Transfer logs to cutting board using a spatula. Use a sharp knife to slice each rectangle on the diagonal into ¾-inch slices. Return to sheet, on their sides.

Return baking sheet to oven. Bake biscotti for 10 minutes. Turn oven off and let biscotti remain in oven until crisp, about for 30–40 minutes longer.

Remove from oven and transfer biscotti to a rack. Cool completely. Store in an airtight container or plastic zip-top bag for up to 3 weeks.

MAKES ABOUT 32 BISCOTTI.

APPLE COBBLER COOKIES

Reminiscent of apple crisp or streusel-topped apple pie, these apple-packed treats are made for autumn eating. They are equally delicious warm or cold, so you can bake a batch to enjoy with a cup of cocoa on the weekend and savor the rest during the week.

- 1 (16.5-ounce) roll refrigerated sugar cookie dough
- 1 cup peeled, finely chopped tart green apple such as Granny Smith (about 1 large apple)
- ½ cup chopped pecans
- 1¾ teaspoons cinnamon, divided
- ¼ cup packed brown sugar
- ⅓ cup quick-cooking oats
- 2 tablespoons (⅛ stick) butter, melted

Break up the cookie dough into large bowl; let stand for 10–15 minutes to soften. Add the apple, pecans, and 1 teaspoon cinnamon; mix well with your fingers, the paddle attachment of an electric mixer, or a wooden spoon. Chill dough for 1 hour in refrigerator or for 20–25 minutes in freezer.

Preheat oven to 350°F. Spray cookie sheets with nonstick cooking spray.

Combine the brown sugar, oats, remaining 1 teaspoon cinnamon, and butter in a small bowl. Roll dough into 1-inch balls. Roll each ball in crumb mixture until well coated. Place cookies on prepared cookie sheets.

Bake for 10–13 minutes or until cookie is firm to the touch and crumb mixture begins to brown. Transfer to wire racks and cool completely.

MAKES 30 COOKIES.

APRICOT-ALMOND BISCOTTI

Despite a reputation as a temperamental treat, biscotti is simply a few basic ingredients blended into a dough and baked twice to create an impressive cookie perfect for dunking or nibbling along with a favorite hot drink. These particular biscotti, accented with bits of dried apricot and almond in each bite, are made all the easier thanks to cake mix. And they aren't as time-consuming as you might think. Surprisingly, you can make and bake an entire batch in under an hour.

- 1 (18.25-ounce) package vanilla cake mix
- 1 cup all-purpose flour
- 1 teaspoon almond extract
- ½ cup (1 stick) butter, melted and cooled
- 2 large eggs
- 1 cup chopped dried apricots
- 1 cup coarsely chopped almonds

Preheat oven to 350°F. Position rack in center of oven. Spray cookie sheet with nonstick cooking spray.

Combine the cake mix, flour, almond extract, melted butter, eggs, apricots, and almonds in a large mixing bowl. Blend with an electric mixer set on low speed for 2–3 minutes until well-blended, scraping down sides of bowl (dough will be very stiff).

Transfer dough to prepared cookie sheet. Shape dough, with floured hands, into two 14 x 3-inch rectangles, ¾-inch thick, spacing them 4–5 inches apart on sheet. Mound the dough so it is slightly higher in the middle than at the edges.

Bake for 30–35 minutes, until firm to touch; remove from oven (leave oven on) and cool on sheet for 10 minutes.

Transfer logs to a cutting board, and use a sharp knife to slice each rectangle into ¾-inch slices on the diagonal. Carefully return slices, cut sides up, to cookie sheets. Return cookie sheet to oven. Bake biscotti for 10 minutes. Turn oven off and let biscotti remain in oven until crisp, 30–40 minutes longer.

Remove from oven and transfer biscotti to a rack. Cool completely.

MAKES ABOUT 32 BISCOTTI.

Variation:

RAISIN AND CINNAMON BISCOTTI:

Prepare as directed above but substitute raisins for the apricots, chopped pecans for the almonds, vanilla extract for the almond extract, and add 2 teaspoons ground cinnamon to the dough.

Bake for 10–12 minutes or until light golden at edges. Remove cookies from oven and immediately make a depression in each cookie with thumb or cork; fill each with ½ teaspoon of apricot preserves. Transfer to wire racks and cool completely.

Prepare Milk Chocolate Drizzle; drizzle over cookies. Place in refrigerator until chocolate is set.

MAKES 24 COOKIES.

APRICOT MILK CHOCOLATE THUMBPRINTS

Typically unassuming little cookies, thumbprints go glamorous in this delectable combination of apricot and milk chocolate, accented with a smidgeon of nutmeg. They make a great finish for a sit-down dinner party. The problem here is keeping enough around until the guests arrive. This justifies making a double batch.

- 1 (16.5-ounce) roll refrigerated sugar cookie dough, well chilled
- ⅓ cup sugar
- 1 teaspoon nutmeg
- ½ cup apricot preserves
- 1 recipe Milk Chocolate Drizzle (see page 370)

Preheat oven to 350°F. Spray cookie sheets with nonstick cooking spray.

Cut the cookie dough into 12 equal slices. Cut each slice in half. Roll each piece into a ball.

Combine the sugar and nutmeg in a shallow dish; roll balls in sugar mixture. Place balls 2 inches apart on the prepared cookie sheets.

APRICOT PETITES

Lush, fragrant apricots show off their versatility in these quick-to-assemble cookies.

- 2 cups crushed vanilla wafers (40–45 wafers)
- ½ cup finely chopped dried apricots
- ½ cup finely chopped pecans or walnuts
- ¼ teaspoon ground nutmeg
- 1⅔ cups powdered sugar, divided
- ¼ cup apricot nectar or orange juice
- 3 tablespoons light corn syrup
- 2 tablespoons (¼ stick) butter, melted

Combine vanilla wafers, dried apricots, pecans, nutmeg, and 1 cup of the powdered sugar in a medium bowl; mix well. Add the apricot nectar, corn syrup, and melted butter; mix well with a wooden spoon.

Place the remaining ⅔ cup powdered sugar in a pie plate or other shallow dish. Shape mixture into 1-inch balls. Roll in powdered sugar. Cover tightly. Let stand for 24 hours to blend flavors. Store in airtight container in refrigerator.

MAKES ABOUT 32 COOKIES.

BAHAMAS BISCOTTI

The flavors of the Caribbean—toasted coconut, ginger, and lime—enrich this simple biscotti dough for a unique crispy-crunchy cookie.

- 1 (18.25-ounce) package white cake mix
- 2 teaspoons ground ginger
- 1 tablespoon oil
- 2 large eggs
- 1 cup sweetened flaked coconut, lightly toasted
- ½ cup slivered almonds, lightly toasted
- 1 tablespoon grated lime zest
- 1 recipe Lime Icing (see page 368) or White Chocolate Dip (see page 361), optional

Preheat oven to 350°F. Position rack in center of oven. Set aside an ungreased cookie sheet.

Stir together the cake mix, ginger, oil, and eggs in a large bowl with a wooden spoon until blended and all dry ingredients are incorporated. Stir in the coconut, almonds, and lime zest by hand (dough will be stiff).

On the ungreased cookie sheet shape dough into a 15 x 4-inch rectangle.

Bake for 22–25 minutes, until golden and just set at the center when touched. Transfer log to a cutting board, and cut log crosswise into ½-inch-thick slices. Return the slices to the cookie sheet, and turn them onto their sides.

Bake 10 minutes longer. Remove from oven and let cool on cookie sheets for 5 minutes. Transfer biscotti to a wire rack with a metal spatula and cool completely. If desired, prepare Lime Icing or White Chocolate Dip; drizzle over cooled biscotti. Place on wax- paper-lined cookie sheet and refrigerate for at least 1 hour to set icing or chocolate. Store in an airtight container or plastic zip-top bag for 1–2 weeks.

MAKES ABOUT 30 BISCOTTI.

BAKLAVA BITES

This recipe is based on one of my favorite desserts: baklava. For anyone who shares my affection for the flavorsome combination of nuts, spices, and honey, but fears working with phyllo dough, this is your sweet solution.

- ¼ cup (½ stick) butter
- ½ cup sifted powdered sugar
- 3 tablespoons honey
- ¾ cup finely chopped almonds (or walnuts or pistachios)
- ¼ teaspoon cinnamon
- 1 teaspoon finely chopped lemon zest
- 1 (16.5-ounce) roll refrigerated sugar cookie dough, well chilled

Melt the butter in a medium, heavy saucepan over medium heat and then stir in the powdered sugar and honey. Cook and stir until mixture boils; remove from heat. Stir in the nuts, cinnamon, and lemon zest. Cool 30 minutes. Shape mixture by teaspoons into ½-inch balls.

Preheat oven to 350°F. Spray cookie sheets with nonstick cooking spray.

Cut the cookie dough into 12 equal slices. Cut each slice in half. Roll each piece into a ball. Place balls 2 inches apart on cookie sheets.

Bake for 6 minutes; remove from oven and press 1 nut ball into center of each cookie. Bake for 6–7 minutes more until golden at edges. Transfer to wire racks and cool completely.

MAKES 24 COOKIES.

BASIC ROLLED SUGAR COOKIES

These cookies are so easy to make you'll have plenty of time to decorate them to suit your fancy. Whether it's a tasty cream cheese frosting or an assortment of candy trims, you will have a great time letting loose your creative and culinary whims.

- 1 (16.5-ounce) roll refrigerated sugar cookie dough, well chilled
- Flour for dusting rolling pin and rolling surface
- Assorted cookie cutters
- Frosting or decorations of your choice (see the "Icings, Frostings, Fillings, and Extras" chapter)

Preheat oven to 350°F. Spray cookie sheets with nonstick cooking spray.

Cut the dough in half crosswise. Refrigerate one half of the dough. Roll out the other half of dough on a lightly floured surface to 1/8-inch thickness.

Cut out cookies. Place 1/2 inch apart on cookie sheets. Repeat with remaining dough, rerolling as needed.

Bake for 4–6 minutes for small cutter shapes and for 7–12 minutes for medium to large cutter shapes. Transfer cookies to wire racks and cool completely.

MAKES ABOUT 32 SMALL TO MEDIUM-SIZE COOKIE CUTOUTS.

Baker's Note

For thicker cookie cutouts, follow directions above but roll dough to 1/4-inch thickness. Bake for 5–8 minutes for small cutter shapes and 9–14 minutes for medium to large cutter shapes.

BEE HAPPY HONEY SANDWICH COOKIES

Mild honey lends sweetness, while lemon zest adds subtle notes of citrus.

- 3 tablespoons sugar
- 3/4 teaspoon ground nutmeg
- 1 (16.5-ounce) roll refrigerated sugar cookie dough
- 1 (8-ounce) package cream cheese, softened
- 3 tablespoons honey
- 1 teaspoon finely grated lemon zest

Preheat oven to 375°F.

Combine the sugar and nutmeg in a small bowl. Shape cookie dough into 3/4-inch balls. Roll the balls in the nutmeg sugar to coat. Place balls 1 inch apart on an ungreased cookie sheet.

Bake for 7–9 minutes or just until just set at centers. Transfer cookies to a wire rack and cool completely.

Combine the cream cheese, honey, and lemon zest in a medium bowl. Beat with a wooden spoon until smooth.

Spread filling generously on the bottoms of half of the cookies. Top with remaining cookies, flat sides down, gently pressing together.

MAKES ABOUT 22 SANDWICH COOKIES.

BIG BROWNIE BUTTERCREAM "PIES"

It took me a long time to get these dreamy treats exactly as I wanted them—loaded with chocolate chips and rich with buttercream. If time is an issue, you can always substitute ready-to-spread frosting for the homemade filling, but if you have the time, the buttercream is well worth the effort.

- 1 (19.5- to 19.8-ounce) package brownie mix
- ⅓ cup vegetable oil
- 2 large eggs
- 2 cups miniature semisweet chocolate chips, divided

Filling:
- 1 cup (2 sticks) salted butter, softened
- 1 tablespoon vanilla extract
- 4 cups sifted powdered sugar

Preheat oven to 350°F. Spray cookie sheets with nonstick cooking spray.

Combine brownie mix, oil, eggs, and 1 cup of the chocolate chips in a large mixing bowl until well blended. Shape dough into 24 balls (about 1½ inches). Place 2 inches apart on prepared cookie sheets. Flatten slightly with your palm or a spatula.

Bake for 12–14 minutes, until set at edges and just barely set at center when lightly touched. Cool for 1 minute on cookie sheets. Transfer to wire racks with metal spatula and cool completely.

Prepare the filling while the cookies cool. Beat the butter with electric mixer in a large mixing bowl for 2 minutes, scraping sides with a rubber spatula. Add the vanilla and powdered sugar and beat for 2–3 minutes longer; scrape down sides of the bowl and beat for an additional 2 minutes, until light and fluffy. Stop the mixer, add the remaining chocolate chips, and mix for 30 seconds to combine.

Place half of the cookies, top side down, onto wax paper. Spoon 3 tablespoons of filling onto center of each cookie. Place remaining cookies top side up onto the filling to make a sandwich. Gently but firmly press down on the top cookie to spread the filling to the edges. Serve immediately or wrap in plastic wrap and store in tightly sealed plastic container.

MAKES 12 BIG PIES.

BIG BUNNY COOKIE

Be sure to include this at your next Easter gathering. Bake the big cookie ahead of time and have the kids decorate, if you like. To make decorating this fun and yummy cookie extra easy, place the different decorations and candies in each cup of a muffin tin.

- 1 (16.5-ounce) roll refrigerator sugar cookie dough, well chilled
- 1 cup canned strawberry or other pink cake frosting
- ¾ cup shredded coconut
- Assorted small candies

Preheat oven to 350°F. Line a cookie sheet with aluminum foil; spray foil with nonstick cooking spray.

Cut the cookie roll crosswise into thirds. pat 1 portion into a 5-inch circle on the bottom half of the lined sheet, to form the bunny's head.

Position the remaining 2 portions of dough atop head, and pat into two 7-inch-long bunny ears, connecting the ears to the bunny head.

Bake for 13–16 minutes or until edges are golden and center is just barely set. Carefully transfer bunny cookie to a flat surface or wire rack by lifting foil from cookie sheet. Cool completely before decorating.

Spread frosting over bunny to within 1 inch

of edges; sprinkle with coconut. Use candies to decorate bunny's face as desired.

MAKES 12 TO 14 SERVINGS.

BLACK AND WHITE COOKIES

Whatever the occasion, an offering of elegant cookies at the end seems to make any meal—from a simple barbecue to a salad supper to a classic afternoon tea with friends—more special. This ebony and ivory offering fits the bill in high style.

- 1 (19.5- to 19.8-ounce) package brownie mix
- ⅓ cup unsweetened cocoa powder, sifted
- ¼ cup (½ stick) unsalted butter, melted
- 2 teaspoons vanilla extract
- 2 large eggs
- 1½ cups white chocolate chips
- 3 tablespoons vegetable shortening, divided
- 1½ cups semisweet chocolate chips

Mix the brownie mix, sifted cocoa powder, melted butter, vanilla, and eggs in a medium mixing bowl with a wooden spoon until all dry ingredients are moistened and dough is well blended. Cover bowl with plastic wrap. Refrigerate dough for at least 1 hour.

Preheat oven to 350°F. Spray cookie sheets with nonstick cooking spray.

Shape dough into 1-inch balls and position 2 inches apart on prepared cookie sheets. Flatten each ball to ¼-inch thickness with the your palm or a spatula.

Bake for 8–10 minutes, until firm to the touch at the edges. Cool for 1 minute on cookie sheets. Transfer to wire racks with metal spatula and cool completely.

Line cooled cookie sheets with wax paper. In a small, heavy-bottomed saucepan set over low heat melt the white chocolate chips with 1½ tablespoons shortening, stirring until smooth. Dip one half of each cooled cookie in white chocolate; place on wax paper. Refrigerate for 30 minutes.

In a small heavy-bottomed saucepan set over low heat, melt the semisweet chocolate chips with remaining 1½ tablespoons shortening, stirring until smooth. Dip other half of each cooled cookie in semisweet chocolate; place on wax paper. Refrigerate for 30 minutes to 1 hour to set the chocolate.

MAKES ABOUT 54 COOKIES.

BLACKBERRY SAGE THUMBPRINTS

Blackberries and sage? Absolutely. This cookie was inspired by one of my favorite teas of the same name. The combination of the earthy flavor of sage and the bright flavor of blackberry is a winning match.

- ⅓ cup sugar
- 2 teaspoons rubbed dry sage
- 1 (16.5-ounce) roll refrigerated sugar cookie dough, well chilled
- ½ cup blackberry preserves or jam

Preheat oven to 350°F. Spray cookie sheets with nonstick cooking spray.

Combine the sugar and sage in a small dish; set aside.

Cut cookie dough into 12 equal slices. Cut each slice in half. Roll each piece into a ball; roll balls in sugar mixture. Place balls 2 inches apart on cookie sheets.

Bake for 10–12 minutes or until golden at edges. Remove cookies from oven and immediately make a depression in each cookie with thumb or cork; fill each with a teaspoon of jam. Transfer to wire racks and cool completely.

MAKES 24 COOKIES.

BRANDIED FRUITCAKE COOKIES

Here's an easily assembled cookie with all of the rich flavor, but none of the fuss, of homemade fruitcake.

- 1 (9-ounce) package condensed mincemeat, finely crumbled (e.g., None Such brand)
- 2 cups vanilla wafer crumbs
- 1 cup sweetened flake coconut
- 5 tablespoons brandy, bourbon, or rum
- 3 tablespoons light corn syrup
- 1 2/3 cups powdered sugar, divided use

Line two cookie sheets with wax paper.

Combine the mincemeat, crumbs, coconut, brandy, corn syrup, and 1 cup powdered sugar in a large bowl until well blended. Cover and chill 4 hours or as long as overnight.

Place remaining 2/3 cup powdered sugar in a shallow dish or pie plate. Roll heaping teaspoonfuls of cookie mixture into 1-inch balls. Roll in powdered sugar to coat evenly. Place

on prepared sheets. Chill at least 1 day in airtight container to blend flavors.

MAKES ABOUT 42 COOKIES.

BROWNIE BISCOTTI

Prepare for the best chocolate biscotti you have ever tasted. These biscotti are exactly the way I prefer all biscotti: dense, crunchy, and very dunk-able. For complete chocolate euphoria, dip, spread, or drizzle each biscotto with melted semisweet, milk, or white chocolate. These make great gifts because they keep well and look festive wrapped in tinted cellophane bags tied with a silk ribbon or raffia, or packed into petite holiday bags.

- 1 (19.5- to 19.8-ounce) package brownie mix
- 1 cup all-purpose flour
- ½ cup (1 stick) unsalted butter, melted and cooled
- 2 large eggs
- 1 cup very coarsely chopped nuts (e.g., walnuts, pecans, macadamia nuts), optional
- 1 recipe Chocolate Dip (see page 361), optional

Preheat oven to 350°F. Position rack in center of oven. Line a cookie sheet with parchment paper.

Combine the brownie mix, flour, melted butter, eggs, and nuts, if desired, in a large mixing bowl. Blend with an electric mixer set on low for 1–2 minutes until well blended, scraping down sides of bowl (mixture will be stiff).

Transfer dough to prepared cookie sheet. Shape dough, with floured hands, into two 14 x 3-inch rectangles, ¾-inch thick, spacing them

4–5 inches apart on sheet. Mound the dough so it is slightly higher in the center than at the edges. Place cookie sheet in oven.

Bake for 30–35 minutes, until firm to touch; remove from oven and cool on sheet for 10 minutes, leaving oven on.

With spatula, transfer logs to cutting board. Use a sharp knife to slice each rectangle on the diagonal into ¾-inch slices. Return slices to sheet, cut sides down. Return sheet to oven. Bake biscotti for 10 minutes.

Turn oven off and let biscotti remain in oven until crisp, 30–40 minutes longer. Remove from oven and transfer biscotti to a rack. Cool completely.

If desired, prepare Chocolate Dip and with a butter knife or small offset spatula spread over one side of each biscotto. Place on wax paper–lined cookie sheet and refrigerate for at least 1 hour to set chocolate.

Store in an airtight container or plastic zip-top bag for up to 3 weeks.

MAKES ABOUT 32 BISCOTTI.

BROWNIE MACAROONS

I love a good macaroon, especially one with a slightly crisp exterior and a chewy interior. Rich and delicious, this version does it. The added bonus of chocolate takes these macaroons in a delectable new direction.

- 1 (19.5- to 19.8-ounce) package brownie mix
- 1 (7-ounce) package (2²/₃ cups) sweetened shredded coconut
- 3 tablespoons vegetable oil
- 2 tablespoons water
- 2 large eggs

- 1 teaspoon almond extract

Preheat oven to 350°F. Spray cookie sheets with nonstick cooking spray.

Combine brownie mix and coconut in a large mixing bowl; stir well. Mix in the oil, water, eggs, and almond extract with a wooden spoon until all dry ingredients are moistened (dough will be stiff).

Shape dough into 1-inch balls. Place 2 inches apart on prepared cookie sheets; flatten slightly with your palm or a spatula.

Bake for 10–12 minutes or until edges are set (centers will be slightly soft). Transfer cookies to wire rack with metal spatula and cool completely.

MAKES ABOUT 60 COOKIES.

BUTTER PECAN THUMBPRINTS

Some cookies transcend their short list of ingredients—you can't imagine how delicious they are until you taste the final product. These are such cookies.

- 1 (16-ounce) container prepared caramel-flavored frosting
- ¼ cup (½ stick) butter, softened
- 2½ cups graham cracker crumbs
- 1 teaspoon butter pecan extract
- 1 cup very finely ground pecans
- 42 white chocolate-striped "Hugs" kisses, unwrapped

Line a cookie sheet with wax paper.

Beat the frosting and butter in a large bowl with an electric mixer set on medium speed until well blended and smooth. Mix in graham cracker crumbs and butter pecan extract with a wooden spoon until combined.

Place ground pecans in a pie pan or shallow dish. Shape graham cracker mixture into 1-inch balls. Roll each ball in pecans to coat. Place balls on prepared sheets. Press one chocolate candy into the center of each cookie.

Refrigerate for 30 minutes or until cold. Store leftovers tightly covered in refrigerator for up to 1 week.

MAKES 42 COOKIES.

Variation:
DOUBLE CHOCOLATE KISS COOKIES:
Prepare as directed above but use chocolate frosting in place of caramel frosting, vanilla extract in place of butter pecan extract, and milk chocolate kisses in place of "Hugs."

BUTTERSCOTCH CRISPY COOKIES

Part crispy rice treat, part cookie, 100 percent yummy—these indispensable treats are ideal mates for tall, cold glasses of milk.

- 1 (18.25-ounce) package yellow cake mix
- ¼ cup packed dark brown sugar
- 1 cup (2 sticks) butter, softened
- 2 large eggs
- 2 tablespoons milk
- 1½ cups butterscotch baking chips
- 3 cups crisp rice cereal, divided

Preheat oven to 350°F. Position oven rack in middle of oven. Spray cookie sheets with nonstick cooking spray.

Place the cake mix, brown sugar, softened butter, eggs, and milk in a large bowl. Blend with an electric mixer set on low speed for 2 minutes, until well blended. Fold in butterscotch chips and 1½ cups cereal. Refrigerate 1 hour.

Crush remaining cereal into coarse crumbs; place in shallow dish.

Shape dough into 1-inch balls. Roll in crushed cereal. Place on prepared cookie sheets about 1 inch apart.

Bake for 11–13 minutes or until set at edges and just barely set at center when lightly touched. Cool for 1 minute on cookie sheets. Transfer to wire racks with metal spatula and cool completely.

MAKES ABOUT 54 COOKIES.

Variation:
CHOCOLATE CRISPY COOKIES: Prepare
as directed above but use chocolate cake mix in place of yellow cake mix and semisweet chocolate chips in place of butterscotch baking chips.

BUTTERSCOTCHIES

The sum of this crunchy little cookie belies its short list of ingredients. Good luck eating just one. Or two. Or three.

- 1 (16.5-ounce) roll refrigerated sugar cookie dough, softened
- 1¼ cups cornflakes, crushed (about ¾ cup, crushed)

- ⅔ cup butterscotch baking chips
- ⅓ cup sweetened flake coconut
- ½ cup powdered sugar

Preheat oven to 350°F. Spray cookie sheets with nonstick cooking spray.

Break up the cookie dough into a large bowl. Sprinkle with the cornflakes, butterscotch chips, and coconut. Mix well with fingers until blended.

Place powdered sugar in a shallow dish. Shape dough into 1-inch balls and roll in powdered sugar. Place balls 2 inches apart on cookie sheets.

Bake for 11-14 minutes or until edges are golden brown. Cool for 1 minute on cookie sheets. Transfer from cookie sheets to cooling racks.

MAKES 48 COOKIES.

BUTTERY CUTOUT COOKIES

You can't please all of the people all of the time—unless, that is, you're a warm butter cookie, fresh from the oven.

- 1 (18.25-ounce) package vanilla cake mix
- ¾ cup (1½ sticks) butter, softened
- 1 large egg
- 1 teaspoon vanilla extract
- 1 recipe Cookie Decorating Icing (see page 365)

Place the cake mix, butter, egg, and vanilla extract in a large bowl. Blend with an electric mixer set on low speed for 2 minutes, until mixture comes together as a dough (dough will be very thick). Scrape the dough off the beaters and wrap the bowl in plastic wrap. Chill, covered, at least 4 hours or overnight.

Preheat oven to 350°F. Position racks to upper and lower positions of oven. Sprinkle a work surface with a thin layer of flour. Set out rolling pin, cookie cutters, metal spatula, two cookie sheets, and cooling racks.

Remove the dough from the refrigerator and divide into fourths. Place ¼ of the dough on floured surface (cover and return remaining dough to refrigerator). Flour the rolling pin and roll dough to ¼-inch thickness. Flour cookie cutters and cut out shapes. Transfer dough to ungreased cookie sheets with spatula. Reroll any scraps, then repeat with remaining dough, rolling one-fourth at a time.

Place one sheet on each oven rack. Bake for 4 minutes. Rotate the sheets (place the sheet from the bottom rack on the top rack and the sheet from the top rack on the bottom rack; this ensures even baking). Bake 2–3 minutes longer for small shapes, or 5–7 minutes for large shapes, until center is puffed and sinks back.

Remove from oven and let cookies rest on cookie sheets for 1 minute. Transfer with metal spatula to racks and cool completely. Prepare cookie decorating icing, or other icing of choice. Decorate cookies with icing.

MAKES ABOUT 60 2½-INCH COOKIES.

Variation:
BUTTERY CHOCOLATE CUTOUTS: Prepare as directed above but use chocolate cake mix in place of the vanilla cake mix.

CAFÉ BRÛLOT BISCOTTI

Café Brûlot is a traditional New Orleans coffee drink, often served flaming, flavored with spices, orange peel, lemon peel, and brandy. Here it is in crunchy biscotti form.

- 2½ teaspoons instant espresso or coffee powder
- 2 teaspoons vanilla extract
- 1 (18.25-ounce) package vanilla cake mix
- 1 cup all-purpose flour
- 1 tablespoon grated lemon zest
- 1 tablespoon grated orange zest
- ½ cup (1 stick) butter, melted and cooled
- 2 large eggs
- ½ teaspoon ground cinnamon
- ¼ teaspoon ground cloves
- 1 recipe Brandy Icing (see page 360)

Preheat oven to 350°F. Position rack in center of oven. Spray cookie sheet with nonstick cooking spray.

Dissolve the espresso powder in the vanilla extract in a large bowl. Add the cake mix, flour, lemon zest, orange zest, melted butter, eggs, cinnamon, and cloves. Blend with an electric mixer set on low speed for 2–3 minutes until well blended, scraping down sides of bowl (dough will be very stiff).

Transfer dough to prepared cookie sheet. With floured hands, shape dough into two 14 x 3-inch rectangles, ¾-inch thick, spacing them 4–5 inches apart on sheet. Mound the dough so it is slightly higher in the middle than at the edges.

Bake for 30–35 minutes, until firm to touch; remove from oven (leave oven on) and cool on sheet for 10 minutes.

Transfer rectangles to a cutting board, and use a sharp kitchen knife to slice each rectangle into ¾-inch slices on the diagonal. Carefully turn these slices onto their sides and move them back to the cookie sheet. Return cookie sheet to oven. Bake biscotti 10 minutes. Turn oven off and let biscotti remain in oven until crisp, 30–40 minutes longer. Remove from oven and transfer biscotti to a rack.

Cool completely.

Prepare Brandy Icing and with a butter knife or small offset spatula spread over one side of each biscotto. Place on wax paper–lined cookie sheet and refrigerate at least 30 minutes to set the icing. Store in an airtight container or plastic zip-top bag for 2–3 weeks.

MAKES ABOUT 32 BISCOTTI.

CANDY BAR COOKIE POPS

Be sure to wait until the cookies are completely cooled before picking them up by the stick (or the stick will pull right out of the cookie!).

- 22 flat wooden sticks with round ends (popsicle sticks)
- 22 miniature candy bars (any variety), unwrapped
- 1 (16.5-ounce) roll refrigerated sugar cookie dough
- ½ cup semisweet chocolate chips, optional

Preheat oven to 350°F.

Cut cookie dough into 22 equal slices. Place wooden stick on dough with end at center; top with candy bar. Wrap dough around stick and candy, covering and sealing completely.

Place the cookies 2 inches apart on ungreased cookie sheets, overlapping wooden sticks if needed.

Bake for 10–12 minutes or until edges are light golden brown. Cool for 5 minutes on cookie sheets. Remove from cookie sheets to cooling racks. Cool completely.

If desired, melt the chocolate chips according to package directions and drizzle over cooled cookies to decorate.

MAKES 22 COOKIES.

CARAMEL DELIGHTFULS

Perfect lunch-box or after-school treats, these caramel-coconut cookies will be surefire hits with one and all.

- 30 square shortbread cookies (e.g., Lorna Doones)
- 6 tablespoons (¾ stick) butter
- ½ cup packed dark brown sugar
- ½ cup light corn syrup
- ½ cup sweetened condensed milk
- ½ teaspoon vanilla extract
- 4 cups sweetened flake coconut, skillet toasted (see page xx) and cooled
- 1 cup semisweet chocolate chips

Place each shortbread cookie on cookie sheets lined with wax paper.

Combine the butter, brown sugar, and corn syrup in medium saucepan set over medium-low heat. Bring mixture to a full boil, stirring constantly with a wooden spoon. Boil for 3 minutes, stirring constantly.

Add sweetened condensed milk slowly, stirring constantly. Continue cooking over low heat for 5 minutes, stirring constantly. Remove the pan from the heat; stir in the vanilla. Beat with an electric mixer set on medium-high speed for 3–4 minutes until creamy.

Immediately stir in toasted coconut and mix well. Spoon mixture by teaspoonfuls over shortbread cookies. Cool completely.

Melt chocolate chips in small microwavable bowl in microwave for 1–2 minutes; drizzle thinly in stripes over cookies and let chocolate harden at room temperature. Store in airtight container.

MAKES ABOUT 28 COOKIES.

CARAMEL-MALLOW GOODIES

Part cookie, part candy, entirely delicious.

- ½ cup (1 stick) butter
- 1 (14-ounce) bag caramels, unwrapped
- 1 (14-ounce) can sweetened condensed milk
- 1 (16-ounce) bag regular marshmallows
- 5–7 cups crisp rice cereal

Line cookie sheets with wax paper.

Melt the butter and caramels in a medium saucepan set over low heat, stirring constantly. Remove from heat. Whisk in the condensed milk until smooth.

Spread the cereal in ¼-inch layer in a jelly

roll pan. Using a fork, dip one marshmallow at a time in caramel mixture (coating thoroughly). Roll dipped marshmallows in cereal until well coated.

Place coated marshmallows on prepared cookie sheets. Refrigerate coated marshmallows for 30 minutes before serving. Store in the refrigerator in an airtight container for up to 4 days.

MAKES ABOUT 32 COOKIES.

CARAMEL PECAN TURTLE COOKIES (CAKE MIX)

Turtles are caramel and pecan candy clusters that are then covered in a thick swath of milk chocolate. To caramel lovers, like myself, they are heaven. Here's a quick and easy cookie version of the irresistible treat. Warning: do not leave yourself alone with a fresh batch.

- 1 (18.25-ounce) package chocolate cake mix
- ¼ cup (½ stick) butter, softened
- 2 large eggs
- 2 cups whole pecan halves
- 24 milk caramels, unwrapped
- 3 tablespoons milk

Place half of the cake mix in a large bowl along with the softened butter and eggs. Blend with electric mixer on low speed for 1 minute; stop mixer and scrape down bowl. Blend on low speed 1 minute longer. Stir in remaining cake mix. Cover bowl with plastic wrap and refrigerate dough for at least 1 hour.

Preheat oven to 350°F. Position oven rack in

middle of oven. Spray cookie sheets with non-stick cooking spray.

Shape dough into 1-inch balls. Place 2 inches apart on prepared cookie sheets. Press one whole pecan half in center of each cookie.

Bake for 9–11 minutes or until firm to the touch at the edges. Cool for 1 minute on cookie sheets. Transfer to wire racks with metal spatula and cool completely.

Melt the caramels with the milk in a small saucepan set over low heat, stirring until smooth; remove from heat. Drizzle caramel across cooled cookies using spoon or fork.

MAKES ABOUT 54 COOKIES.

CARAMEL TOFFEE TASSIES

Perfect for pitch-ins, these caramel-toffee-loaded treats both travel and keep well.

- ¼ cup (½ stick) butter
- 1 (10-ounce) package miniature marshmallows
- 1 teaspoon vanilla extract
- 7 cups crisp rice cereal
- 4 chocolate-covered English toffee candy bars
- 1 cup caramel apple dip

Lightly spray the cups of two 12-count muffin tins with nonstick cooking spray; set aside.

Melt the butter in a medium saucepan set over low heat. Add the marshmallows and continue to cook and stir until the marshmallows are completely melted and the mixture is well blended. Remove from heat and stir in the vanilla. Mix in the cereal and toffee bars, stirring to coat well.

Press cereal mixture firmly into prepared muffin tins, using a wooden spoon, to form tassies. Make an indentation in each tassie by pressing gently with the back of a rounded tablespoon. Cool for at least 30 minutes; remove from pans. Fill each indentation with caramel apple dip.

Refrigerate for 30 minutes. Store in the refrigerator.

MAKES 24 TASSIES.

CHARLOTTE'S DATE-FILLED COOKIE TARTS

To this day my mother reminisces about the brown sugar tarts she ate as a child on afternoon tea trips to downtown Winnipeg. This streamlined rendition is just for her. You don't have to love dates—just the unmistakable flavor combination of brown sugar and butter—to love these cookie tarts.

- ½ cup chopped dates
- ¼ cup packed brown sugar
- 2 tablespoons butter
- 2 tablespoons water
- 1 (16.5-ounce) roll refrigerated sugar cookie dough, well chilled

Combine the dates, brown sugar, butter, and water in a medium saucepan. Bring to a boil over medium-high heat; reduce heat to low and simmer for 10 minutes, stirring frequently. Transfer to a small bowl and cool completely.

Preheat oven to 350°F. Spray cookie sheets with nonstick cooking spray.

Cut dough in half; refrigerate remaining dough. Cut dough half into 22 thin slices with a sharp knife,. Place slices 2 inches apart on cookie sheets. Place 1 generous teaspoon of cooled date mixture in center of each cookie slice. Set aside.

Cut remaining dough into 22 thin slices. Place cookie slices on jam-topped cookie slices; press edges with tines of fork to decorate and seal.

Bake for 10–12 minutes or until edges are light golden brown. Cool for 1 minute on cookie sheets. Transfer to wire racks and cool completely.

MAKES 22 COOKIES.

CHARLOTTE'S GINGER-JEWELED CHOCOLATE BISCOTTI

My mother is as crazy about ginger as I am, so this boldly spiced biscotti recipe is just for her. Two kinds of ginger give these cookies a lively hit of heat.

- 1 (19.5- to 19.8-ounce) package brownie mix
- 1 cup all-purpose flour
- 2½ teaspoons ground ginger
- ½ cup (1 stick) unsalted butter, melted and cooled
- 2 large eggs
- 2/3 cup finely chopped crystallized ginger

Preheat oven to 350°F. Position rack in center of oven. Line a cookie sheet with parchment paper.

Combine the brownie mix, flour, ground ginger, melted butter, eggs, and crystallized ginger in a large bowl. Blend with an electric mixer set on low for 1–2 minutes until well blended, scraping down sides of bowl (mixture will be stiff).

Transfer dough to prepared cookie sheet. Shape dough, with floured hands, into two 14 x 3-inch rectangles, ¾-inch thick, spacing them 4–5 inches apart on sheet. Mound the dough so it is slightly higher in the center than at the edges. Place cookie sheet in oven.

Bake for 30–35 minutes until firm to touch; remove from oven and cool on sheet for 10 minutes (leave oven on).

With spatula, transfer logs to cutting board. Use a sharp knife to slice each rectangle into ¾-inch slices on the diagonal. Return to sheet, cut sides down. Return baking sheet to oven. Bake biscotti for 10 minutes. Turn oven off and let biscotti remain in oven until crisp, 30–40 minutes longer.

Remove from oven and transfer biscotti to a rack. Cool completely. Store in an airtight container or plastic zip-top bag for up to 3 weeks.

MAKES ABOUT 32 BISCOTTI.

CHERRY CHOCOLATE THUMBPRINTS

Cherries are great with chocolate and thumbprints are just plain great. Hence, this is nothing short of a great cookie, by any measure.

- ⅓ cup sugar
- 1½ teaspoons cinnamon
- 1 (16.5-ounce) roll refrigerated sugar cookie dough, well chilled
- ⅓ cup miniature semisweet chocolate chips
- ⅓ cup cherry preserves

Preheat oven to 350°F. Spray cookie sheets with nonstick cooking spray.

Combine sugar and cinnamon in a small dish. Cut cookie dough into 12 equal slices. Cut each slice in half. Roll each piece into a ball; roll balls in sugar mixture. Place balls 2 inches apart on cookie sheets.

Bake for 10–12 minutes or until golden at edges. Remove cookies from oven and immediately make a depression in each cookie with thumb or cork; fill each with ½ teaspoon of miniature chocolate chips; return to oven for 30 seconds.

Remove cookies from oven and place a teaspoon of preserves on top of the chocolate filling. Transfer to wire racks and cool completely.

MAKES 24 COOKIES.

CHOCOLATE CANDY TREASURE COOKIES

What happens when you cover a candy bar nugget in sugar cookie dough and bake it until silken in the center? Magic. Even though it is a test of will to wait for these treasures, be sure to let them cool completely before serving.

- 1 (16.5-ounce) roll refrigerated sugar cookie dough, well chilled
- 12 miniature peanut butter cups (or any chocolate-covered nugget-size candies), unwrapped
- ½ cup semisweet chocolate chips
- 1 teaspoon vegetable shortening

Preheat oven to 350°F. Spray cookie sheets with nonstick cooking spray.

Cut cookie dough into 12 equal pieces. Wrap 1 piece of dough around each candy, completely covering candy; roll in hands to form ball.

Place 6 dough balls on cookie sheet. Refrigerate remaining 6 dough balls until ready to bake.

Bake for 12–15 minutes or until golden brown. Cool for 2 minutes on cookie sheets. Transfer to wire racks and cool completely. Repeat with remaining 6 dough balls.

Combine chocolate chips and shortening in small saucepan over low heat,; cook over low heat until melted and smooth, stirring constantly. Drizzle over cooled cookies in crisscross pattern. Let stand until glaze is set before storing.

MAKES 12 BIG COOKIES.

CHOCOLATE-CHIP CHERRY CHEESECAKE TARTLETS

Beyond being a delicious recipe, this is also a template for any miniature cheesecake. Vary the type of fruit topping, for example, or leave it off altogether and flavor the filling with anything from coffee powder, citrus zest, or liqueur.

- 1 (16.5-ounce) roll refrigerated chocolate-chip cookie dough
- 1 (8-ounce) package cream cheese, softened
- ½ cup sweetened condensed milk
- 1 large egg
- 1 teaspoon vanilla extract
- 1 (21-ounce) can cherry pie filling

Preheat oven to 325°. Line 12 muffin cups with paper liners.

Slice cookie dough into 12 equal pieces. Place one piece in each muffin cup. Bake for 10–12 minutes or until cookie has spread to edge of cup (dough will appear slightly puffed). Remove from the oven and press an indentation into the center of each cup with the back of a spoon.

Meanwhile, combine the cream cheese, condensed milk, egg, and vanilla in a medium bowl; beat with an electric mixer on high until smooth. Spoon cream cheese mixture over each cookie in cup.

Bake an additional 13–17 minutes or until cream cheese filling is just set. Cool completely in pan on wire rack. Top with pie filling. Refrigerate for 1 hour until chilled.

MAKES 12 CHEESECAKE TARTLETS.

CHOCOLATE-CHIP COOKIE S'MORES

Who needs a campfire? You can have an amped-up s'more anytime of the year, fresh from your own oven with a chocolate-chip cookie surprise.

- 44 graham cracker squares, divided
- 1 (16.5-ounce) roll refrigerated chocolate chip cookie dough
- 11 large marshmallows, cut in half crosswise

Preheat oven to 350°F.

Line a cookie sheet with foil. Arrange 22 graham cracker squares on prepared cookie sheet.

Bake cookie dough on another cookie sheet according to package instructions to make 22 cookies. Cool for 2 minutes on cookie sheet. Remove cookies from cookie sheet and place one warm cookie on each of the graham cracker squares on the foil. Top each cookie with one marshmallow half.

Bake cookie-marshmallow topped graham crackers for 1–2 minutes or until marshmallows are soft. Immediately top each marshmallow with remaining graham cracker squares, pressing down slightly. Cool.

MAKES 22 COOKIES.

CHOCOLATE-CHIP COOKIE TRUFFLES

For perfect truffles, bake the cookies a little longer than the package states so they are crispier than usual. Watch them closely so they don't burn!

- ▪ 1 (16.5-ounce) roll refrigerated chocolate chip cookie dough
- ▪ ½ (8-ounce) package cream cheese, softened
- ▪ 1 cup bittersweet or semisweet chocolate chips
- ▪ 1 tablespoon vegetable shortening
- ▪ 2–3 tablespoons unsweetened cocoa powder

Preheat oven to 350°.

Prepare cookies according to package instructions. Bake cookies for 3–4 minutes longer than directed until crisp and golden brown but not burnt. Transfer cookies to cooling racks. Cool completely.

Line a cookie sheet with wax paper or foil.

Crumble the cookies into the bowl of a large food processor. Process until cookies resemble coarse meal. Add the cream cheese and process until mixture begins to hold together (mixture will be dark in color).

Measure off dough, using a 2-tablespoon cookie scoop, and roll into 1-inch balls. Place on prepared cookie sheet. Loosely cover with plastic wrap and chill for at least 1 hour.

Microwave the chocolate chips and shortening in a small, uncovered, microwave-safe bowl on high for 1 minute. Stir until chips are completely melted and mixture is smooth. If necessary, microwave at additional 10- to 15-second intervals, stirring just until chips are melted.

Dip the cookie balls completely into melted chocolate with fork. Use side of bowl or shake gently to remove excess chocolate. Return to cookie sheet. Sift cocoa powder over the truffles. Refrigerate for 30 minutes or until set. Store in tightly covered container in refrigerator.

MAKES 32 TRUFFLES.

CHOCOLATE-DIPPED PECAN PRALINE BISCOTTI

- ▪ 1 (16.5-ounce) roll refrigerated sugar cookie dough
- ▪ ½ cup all-purpose flour
- ▪ 1 cup chopped pecans, lightly toasted, cooled
- ▪ 1 cup English toffee baking bits
- ▪ 1 teaspoon vanilla extract
- ▪ 1 recipe Chocolate Drizzle or Dip (see page 361), optional

Preheat oven to 350°F. Lightly spray a cookie sheet with nonstick cooking spray.

Break up the cookie dough into large bowl; let stand for 10–15 minutes to soften. Add flour, pecans, toffee bits, and vanilla extract to the cookie dough; mix well with your fingers, the paddle attachment of an electric stand mixer, or a wooden spoon.

Divide dough into two equal halves. On the cookie sheet, shape each dough half into a 12 x 2-inch, ¾-inch-high rectangle, spacing the dough halves about 3 inches apart.

Bake for 26–28 minutes until the logs are deep golden brown and spring back in the center when touched. Remove sheet from oven; keep oven on.

Using two pancake turners, lift logs, one at a time, from the cookie sheet to a cutting board. Using a sharp knife, cut one of the logs into ¾-inch-wide slices. Note: for longer biscotti, cut at a deep diagonal; for shorter biscotti, cut log crosswise. Repeat with second log. Place slices on the same cookie sheet (do not worry about the spacing).

Bake slices for 5 minutes; remove from oven and turn over all of the slices. Return cookie sheet to oven and bake 5 minutes longer. Remove sheet from oven and immediately transfer biscotti to a wire rack; cool completely. If desired, dip one end of each biscotti in 1 recipe of the Chocolate Dip; place on wax-paper-lined cookie sheet and refrigerate until chocolate is firm.

MAKES 28 BISCOTTI.

CHOCOLATE-FILLED AZTEC COOKIES

Offer a plate of these cookies along with an assortment of fresh fruit as a fitting finale to a Mexican-style meal. Leftovers are great additions to weekday lunchbags, too.

- 1 (16.5-ounce) roll refrigerated sugar cookie dough, well chilled
- ¼ cup yellow cornmeal
- ¾ teaspoon ground cinnamon
- ⅛ teaspoon ground cayenne pepper
- 1 teaspoon grated orange zest
- 18 dark chocolate candy miniatures, unwrapped

Preheat oven to 375°. Spray cookie sheets with nonstick cooking spray.

Crumble the cookie dough into large bowl. Let stand for 10–15 minutes to soften. Add the cornmeal, cinnamon, cayenne, and orange zest; mix well with fingers or wooden spoon.

Shape rounded tablespoon of dough around each candy, covering completely. Place 2 inches apart on cookie sheets.

Bake for 8–11 minutes or until edges are light golden brown. Cool for 1 minute on cookie sheets. Transfer to wire racks and cool completely.

MAKES 18 COOKIES.

CHOCOLATE-FRECKLED SNOWBALL COOKIES

It's a good idea to have a napkin handy when eating these crackle-top chocolate cookies—the powdered-sugar coating can get all over the place. But they are so very worth the mess!

- 1 (16.5-ounce) roll refrigerated sugar cookie dough, softened
- ⅓ cup all-purpose flour
- ¾ cup slivered almonds, lightly toasted and chopped fine

- ½ cup miniature semisweet chocolate chips
- ½ teaspoon almond extract
- 1 cup powdered sugar

Break up the cookie dough into a large bowl. Sprinkle the flour, almonds, chocolate chips, and almond extract over dough. Mix well with fingers until blended. Chill 20 minutes.

Preheat oven to 350°F. Shape dough into 1-inch balls. Place 1 inch apart on ungreased cookie sheets.

Bake for 11–14 minutes or until just set but not brown. Remove from cookie sheets. Cool slightly on cooling rack.

Place powdered sugar in a small, shallow dish. Roll warm cookies in powdered sugar. Cool on cooling rack. Roll in powdered sugar again.

MAKES 42 COOKIES.

CHOCOLATE-KISSED COOKIES

Who doesn't want to be "kissed" by chocolate? These pretty little cookies are familiar to holiday cookie jars everywhere. Here they are made extra easy with a short list of three ingredients. If the kids are handy, recruit them to help with the rolling of the cookie dough and the placing of the chocolate kisses. Be warned, though: you may need to keep close guard over the chocolates, or else buy an extra bag.

- ⅓ cup sugar
- 1 (16.5-ounce) roll refrigerated sugar cookie dough, well chilled
- 24 milk chocolate "kiss" candies, unwrapped

Preheat oven to 350°F. Spray cookie sheets with nonstick cooking spray.

Place sugar in a shallow dish.

Cut the cookie dough into 12 equal slices. Cut each slice in half. Roll each piece into a ball; roll balls in sugar. Place balls 2 inches apart on cookie sheets.

Bake for 10–13 minutes or until golden at edges.

Remove cookie sheet from oven and immediately top each cookie with 1 milk chocolate candy, pressing down firmly so cookie cracks around edges. Transfer cookies to wire racks and cool completely.

MAKES 24 COOKIES.

CHOCOLATE-KISSED PEANUT BUTTER THUMBPRINTS

Every baker needs a few recipes they can rely on as all-around pleasers, whether it's for a bake sale, potluck, picnic, or after-school treats for the kids. This cute cookie is one such recipe. Traditional milk chocolate "kisses" are always wonderful, but the white chocolate-milk chocolate striped "hugs" candies look especially pretty perched atop the dark chocolate dough.

- 1 (19.5- to 19.8-ounce) package brownie mix
- 1 (14-ounce) can sweetened condensed milk
- 1 cup creamy-style peanut butter
- 1 large egg
- 2 teaspoons vanilla extract

■ 72 chocolate "kiss" or "hugs" candies (from a 13-ounce bag), unwrapped

Preheat oven to 350°F. Combine the brownie mix, condensed milk, peanut butter, egg, and vanilla in a large mixing bowl with an electric mixer set on low speed for 1–2 minutes, until all dry ingredients are moistened and dough is well blended (dough will be very thick).

Shape dough into 1-inch balls and position 2 inches apart on ungreased cookie sheets.

Bake for 8–10 minutes, until firm to the touch at the edges and slightly puffed in appearance. Remove sheets from the oven and immediately push a kiss candy, flat side down, into the center of each cookie. Cool for 1 minute on cookie sheets. Transfer cookies to wire racks with metal spatula and cool completely.

MAKES ABOUT 72 COOKIES.

CHOCOLATE MADELEINES

Always a favorite in my book, these deeply ridged, delicate madeleines taste like tender little chocolate cakes and look like little shells. They are sure to garner attention on any cookie platter. A madeleine pan is a metal mold with scallop-shaped indentations (like a muffin tray), sold at cookware stores.

■ Vegetable shortening and all-purpose flour to coat pans.
■ 1 (19.5- to 19.8-ounce) package brownie mix
■ ½ cup (1 stick) unsalted butter, melted
■ ¼ cup water

■ 4 large eggs, separated
■ 2–3 tablespoons powdered sugar or unsweetened cocoa powder

Preheat oven to 350°F. Grease molds of large madeleine pan (3 x 1¼-inch shell molds) with vegetable shortening. Sprinkle with flour to coat pan, shaking off excess.

Combine brownie mix, melted butter, water, and egg yolks in a large mixing bowl until well blended; set aside.

Beat egg whites in a medium mixing bowl with electric mixer set on high until soft peaks form. Stir ¼ of the beaten egg whites into the brownie batter to lighten it; fold remaining whites into batter.

Spoon 1 heaping tablespoon batter into center of each indentation in pan (do not overfill; batter will spread as it bakes).

Bake for 8–10 minutes until puffed and set at center. Cool in pan for 5 minutes; gently remove madeleines to wire rack. Repeat process, greasing and flouring pan before each batch. Sift powdered sugar or cocoa powder over cooled cookies.

MAKES ABOUT 28 MADELEINES.

CHOCOLATE PEPPERMINT COOKIE HEARTS

It may seem calculated, but the fact is that planning for love in a modern world is essential. Your calculations are destined to add up if you make someone who matters a plate of these whimsical heart cookies.

■ 1 (16.5-ounce) roll refrigerated sugar cookie dough

- 2 tablespoons unsweetened cocoa
- 1 recipe Dark Chocolate Frosting (see page 367)
- 1/8 teaspoon peppermint extract
- 1/2 cup coarsely crushed peppermint candies or candy canes

Break up the cookie dough into large bowl; let stand for 10–15 minutes to soften. Add the cocoa; mix with wooden spoon or fingers until well blended. Chill for 1 hour in refrigerator or 20–25 minutes in freezer.

Preheat oven to 350°F. Spray cookie sheets with nonstick cooking spray.

On lightly floured surface, roll out half of the dough at a time to 1/4-inch thickness. With 2½-inch heart-shaped cookie cutter, cut out cookies.

Place ½ inch apart on prepared cookie sheets. Repeat with remaining dough, rerolling as needed. Bake for 10–12 minutes or until golden at edges and just set. Remove cookies from cookie sheets; place on wire racks. Cool completely.

Prepare Dark Chocolate Frosting, stirring in the peppermint extract. Spread about 2 teaspoons of icing onto each cookie. Sprinkle each with crushed candies.

MAKES 28 COOKIES.

CHOCOLATE-RAISIN COOKIE TARTLETS

Serve these rich chocolate tartlets warm or cold. They are perfect with coffee at the end of dinner, or out in the sunshine on a springtime picnic.

- 1/2 cup chopped raisins
- 1/2 cup water
- 1/4 cup firmly packed brown sugar

- 1/2 teaspoon grated orange peel
- 1/4 cup semisweet chocolate chips
- 1 (16.5-ounce) roll refrigerated sugar cookie dough, well chilled

Combine the raisins, water, brown sugar, and orange peel in small saucepan and bring to a boil. Cook over low heat for 11–13 minutes or until liquid is almost completely absorbed, stirring frequently. Remove from heat and immediately stir in chocolate chips. Cool completely.

Preheat oven to 350°F. Spray cookie sheets with nonstick cooking spray.

Cut the dough in half crosswise; refrigerate one half. With sharp knife, cut dough half into 20 thin slices. Place slices 2 inches apart on cookie sheets. Place 1 generous teaspoon chocolate-raisin mixture in center of each cookie slice. Set aside.

Cut remaining dough into 20 thin slices. Place cookie slices on filling-topped cookie slices; press edges with tines of fork to decorate and seal.

Bake for 10–12 minutes or until edges are light golden brown. Cool for 1 minute on cookie sheets. Transfer to wire racks and cool completely.

MAKES 20 COOKIES.

Baker's Note

Other chopped dried fruit, such as dried cranberries or dried apricots, may be substituted for the chopped raisins.

CHOCOLATE RANCHO ROUNDUP COOKIES

Corral the kids or some friends for a night of old-fashioned movies and a roundup of these rancho cookies, some hot buttered popcorn, and big mugs of hot cocoa.

- 1 (19.5- to 19.8-ounce) package brownie mix
- ¾ cup old-fashioned or quick-cooking oats
- ⅔ cup vegetable oil
- 1 cup creamy peanut butter
- 2 large eggs
- 1 cup roasted lightly salted or honey roasted peanuts
- 1 cup semisweet chocolate chips

Preheat oven to 350°F. Spray cookie sheets with nonstick cooking spray.

Combine the brownie mix, oats, oil, peanut butter, and eggs in a large mixing bowl until well blended; mix in peanuts and chocolate chips. Chill for 1 hour.

Shape dough into 2-inch balls; place 2 inches apart on prepared cookie sheets. Flatten slightly with your palm or a spatula.

Bake for 11–14 minutes, until set at edges and just barely set at center when lightly touched. Cool for 1 minute on cookie sheets. Transfer to wire racks with metal spatula and cool completely.

MAKES ABOUT 30 LARGE COOKIES.

CHOCOLATE RICE CRISPY COOKIES

This homespun cookie is a sweet combination of crispy and chewy highlighted with a double dose of chocolate.

- 1 (19.5- to 19.8-ounce) package brownie mix
- 1 cup (2 sticks) butter, softened
- 2 large eggs

- 2 tablespoons water
- 1 cup miniature semisweet chocolate chips
- 3 cups crisp rice cereal, divided

Preheat oven to 350°F. Spray cookie sheets with nonstick cooking spray.

Beat the brownie mix, butter, eggs, and water in a large mixing bowl with an electric mixer set on low for 2 minutes until well blended. Fold in the chocolate chips and 1½ cups cereal. Refrigerate for at least 1 hour or up to overnight. Crush the remaining cereal into coarse crumbs; place in shallow dish.

Shape the dough into 1-inch balls. Roll in crushed cereal. Place balls about 1 inch apart on prepared cookie sheets.

Bake for 11–13 minutes, until set at edges and just barely set at center when lightly touched. Cool for 1 minute on cookie sheets. Transfer to wire racks with metal spatula and cool completely.

MAKES ABOUT 54 COOKIES.

CHOCOLATE-VANILLA PINWHEEL COOKIES

These pretty cookies may take a few more steps than other options in this book, but the results are well worth it. Get ready for the compliments!

- ½ cup vegetable shortening
- ⅓ cup plus 1 tablespoon butter, softened, divided
- 2 large egg yolks
- 1 teaspoon vanilla extract
- 1 (18.25-ounce) package vanilla cake mix

2½ tablespoons unsweetened cocoa powder

Place the shortening, ⅓ cup softened butter, egg yolks, and vanilla extract in a large bowl. Blend with an electric mixer set on medium-high speed for 1–2 minutes, until smooth. Add the cake mix to bowl; blend on low speed for 1–2 minutes, until all dry ingredients are incorporated.

Divide the dough in half. To one half of the dough, add remaining tablespoon butter and cocoa powder; knead until chocolate-colored and thoroughly blended.

Place yellow dough between 2 pieces of wax paper and roll into an 18 x 12-inch rectangle, ⅛-inch thick. Repeat with chocolate dough. Remove top piece of wax paper from each piece of dough. Place one rectangle on top of the other and roll up like a jelly roll, beginning with long side. Tightly wrap in plastic wrap and refrigerate at least 2 hours.

Preheat oven to 350°F. Position oven rack in middle of oven. Spray cookie sheets with non-stick cooking spray.

With a sharp knife slice dough into ⅛-inch-thick slices; place 1 inch apart on prepared cookie sheets. Bake for 9–11 minutes. Cool 2 minutes on cookie sheets. Transfer to wire racks with metal spatula and cool completely.

MAKES ABOUT 42 COOKIES.

CHOCOLATE WHISKEY BALLS

If you think this is just another cookie, think again—you may be surprised by the magic wrought by combining chocolate and whiskey.

- 1 cup pecans
- 1 cup chocolate wafer cookie crumbs
- 1½ tablespoons light corn syrup
- ¼ cup whiskey
- 1½ cups powdered sugar, divided use

Grind the pecans and the chocolate wafers coarsely in a large food processor. Transfer mixture to a large bowl. Mix in the corn syrup, whiskey, and 1 cup of the powdered sugar with wooden spoon or hands until well blended.

Place remaining powdered sugar in shallow dish or bowl. Roll balls in powdered sugar; cover. Let stand for 2 hours. If desired, roll again in additional powdered sugar. Refrigerate for up to 1 week or freeze for up to 3 months.

MAKES ABOUT 22 COOKIE BALLS.

Variation:
CHOCOLATE GRAND MARNIER BALLS:
Prepare as directed above but use Grand Marnier or other orange liqueur in place of the whiskey and add 2 teaspoons grated orange zest to the mixture along with the cookie crumbs.

CHRISTMAS CRANBERRY-PISTACHIO BISCOTTI

Dotted with ruby-red cranberries and bright green pistachios, these bejeweled biscotti are a must-make when the temperature goes down and the holiday decorations go up.

- 1 (19.5- to 19.8-ounce) package brownie mix

- 1 cup all-purpose flour
- ½ cup (1 stick) unsalted butter, melted and cooled
- 2 large eggs
- ¾ cup coarsely chopped dried cranberries
- 1 cup shelled pistachios
- 2 teaspoons grated orange zest
- 1 recipe White Chocolate Dip (see page 361), optional

Preheat oven to 350°F. Position rack in center of oven. Line a cookie sheet with parchment paper.

Combine the brownie mix, flour, melted butter, eggs, cranberries, pistachios, and orange zest in a large mixing bowl. Blend with an electric mixer set on low for 1–2 minutes until well blended, scraping down sides of bowl (mixture will be stiff).

Transfer dough to prepared cookie sheet. With floured hands, shape dough into two 14 x 3-inch rectangles, ¾-inch thick, spacing them 4–5 inches apart on sheet. Mound the dough so it is slightly higher in the center than at the edges. Place cookie sheet in oven.

Bake for 30–35 minutes, until firm to touch; remove from oven and cool for 10 minutes (leave oven on).

With spatula, transfer logs to cutting board. Use a sharp knife to slice each rectangle into (approximately) ¾-inch slices on the diagonal. Return slices to sheet, cut sides down. Return baking sheet to oven. Bake biscotti for 10 minutes. Turn oven off and let biscotti remain in oven until crisp, 30–40 minutes longer. Remove from oven and transfer biscotti to a rack. Cool completely.

If desired, prepare White Chocolate Dip, and with a butter knife or small offset spatula spread over one side of each biscotti. Place on wax-paper-lined cookie sheet and refrigerate for at least 1 hour to set chocolate. Store in an airtight container or plastic zip-top bag for up to 3 weeks.

MAKES ABOUT 32 BISCOTTI.

CHUNKY CHOCOLATE WALNUT BISCOTTI

A cup of espresso. An inspiring view. And one of these very chocolate biscotti. These cookies can make a coffee break a quick escape.

- 1 (18.25-ounce) package chocolate cake mix
- 1 cup all-purpose flour
- ½ cup (1 stick) butter, melted and cooled
- 2 large eggs
- 1⅓ cups semisweet chocolate chunks
- 1 cup coarsely chopped walnuts

Preheat oven to 350°F. Position rack in center of oven. Spray cookie sheet with nonstick cooking spray.

Place cake mix, flour, melted butter, eggs, chocolate chunks, and walnuts in a large mixing bowl. Blend with an electric mixer set on low speed for 2–3 minutes until well-blended, scraping down sides of bowl (dough will be very stiff).

Transfer dough to prepared cookie sheet. With floured hands, shape dough into two 14 x 3-inch rectangles, ¾-inch thick, spacing them 4–5 inches apart on sheet. Mound the dough so it is slightly higher in the middle than at the edges.

Bake for 30–35 minutes until firm to touch; remove from oven and cool on sheet for 10 minutes, leaving oven on.

Cutting on the cookie sheet, use a sharp knife to slice each rectangle into ¾-inch slices on the diagonal. Carefully turn these slices onto their sides. Return cookie sheet to oven. Bake biscotti for 10 minutes. Turn oven off and let biscotti remain in oven until crisp, 30–40 minutes longer. Remove from oven and transfer biscotti to a rack.

Cool completely.

MAKES ABOUT 32 BISCOTTI.

CINNAMON SLICES

When these cookie are baking in the oven, it's easy to understand why the ancient Romans used cinnamon as a perfume—the scent is decidedly aphrodisiacal.

- 1 (18.25-ounce) package spice cake mix
- ½ cup shortening
- ⅓ cup butter, softened
- 1 large egg
- 2 teaspoons ground cinnamon
- 1½ cups raw sugar, optional

Place the cake mix, shortening, softened butter, egg, and cinnamon in a large bowl. Blend with an electric mixer set on low speed for 1 minute (dough will be very thick). Scrape the dough off the beaters.

Divide dough in half; shape each half into 12 x 2-inch roll.

If desired, place raw sugar on a shallow plate; roll each log in the sugar, pressing gently to adhere. Wrap each roll in plastic food wrap; refrigerate until firm (at least 3 hours).

Preheat oven to 350°F. Position rack in center of oven. Cut rolls into ¼-inch slices with a sharp knife. Place 2 inches apart on ungreased cookie sheets.

Bake for 7–8 minutes or until edges are lightly browned. Let stand on cookie sheets 1 minute. Transfer to wire rack and cool completely.

MAKES ABOUT 60 COOKIES.

Variation:

CARAMEL-SPICE SANDWICH COOKIES:
Prepare cookies as directed above. Prepare 1 recipe of Quick Caramel Frosting (see page 374); sandwich a tablespoon of frosting between two cookies. Repeat with remaining cookies and frosting.

CINNAMON STICK CHOCOLATE BISCOTTI

After a brisk winter day, these cinnamon-laced biscotti, paired with steaming mugs of marshmallow-topped cocoa, are just the ticket to warm up a crowd.

- 1 (19.5- to 19.8-ounce) package brownie mix
- 1 cup all-purpose flour
- 1½ teaspoons ground cinnamon
- ½ cup (1 stick) unsalted butter, melted and cooled
- 2 large eggs
- 1 recipe Chocolate Dip made with cinnamon chips (see page 361)

Preheat oven to 350°F. Position rack in center of oven. Line a cookie sheet with parchment paper.

Place the brownie mix, flour, cinnamon, melted butter, and eggs in a large mixing bowl. Blend with an electric mixer set on low for 1–2 minutes until well blended, scraping down sides of bowl (mixture will be stiff).

Transfer dough to prepared cookie sheet. With floured hands, shape dough into two 14 x 3-inch rectangles, ¾-inch thick, spacing them

4–5 inches apart on sheet. Mound the dough so it is slightly higher in the center than at the edges. Place cookie sheet in oven.

Bake for 30–35 minutes, until firm to touch; remove from oven and cool on sheet for 10 minutes (leave oven on).

With spatula, transfer logs to cutting board. Use a sharp knife to slice each rectangle into (approximately) ¾-inch slices on the diagonal. Return slices to sheet, cut sides down. Return baking sheet to oven. Bake biscotti for 10 minutes. Turn oven off and let biscotti remain in oven until crisp, 30–40 minutes longer. Remove from oven and transfer biscotti to a rack. Cool completely.

If desired, prepare Cinnamon Chocolate Dip and with a butter knife or small offset spatula spread over one side of each biscotti. Place on wax-paper-lined cookie sheet and refrigerate for at least 1 hour to set melted chips. Store in an airtight container or plastic zip-top bag for up to 3 weeks.

MAKES ABOUT 32 BISCOTTI.

CLASSIC MADELEINES

French writer Marcel Proust praised the tender, buttery sponge cakes known as madeleines in his work *Remembrance of Things Past*. You, too, will sing their praises once this recipe is tried. A few standard pantry items transform a box of yellow cake mix into these classic cookies, worthy of a Parisian patisserie.

■ Vegetable shortening and all-purpose flour to grease pans.
■ 1 (18.25-ounce) package yellow cake mix
■ ½ cup (1 stick) butter, melted
■ ¼ cup milk
■ 4 large eggs, separated
■ 2–3 tablespoons powdered sugar

Preheat oven to 350°F. Position oven rack in middle of oven. Grease molds of large madeleine pan (3 x 1¼-inch shell molds) with vegetable shortening. Sprinkle with flour to coat pan, shaking off excess.

In a large bowl place the cake mix, melted butter, milk, and egg yolks. Blend for 1–2 minutes with an electric mixer set on medium speed until well blended and smooth. Set aside momentarily. Clean beaters.

Beat the egg whites in another large mixing bowl with an electric mixer set on high speed until soft peaks form. Stir ¼ of the beaten egg whites into the cake batter to lighten it; fold remaining whites into batter.

Spoon 1 heaping tablespoon batter into each indentation in pan (do not overfill; batter will spread as it bakes). Bake until puffed and set at center, 8–10 minutes. Cool in pan 5 minutes; gently remove madeleines to wire rack. Repeat process, greasing and flouring pan before each batch. Sift powdered sugar over cooled cookies.

MAKES ABOUT 30 MADELEINES.

Variation:

ALMOND MADELEINES: Prepare as directed above but use vanilla cake mix in place of the yellow cake mix and add ¾ teaspoon almond extract to the batter.

COCONUT MACAROONS

I'm a bit of a snob about macaroons—I like the kind that strike a good balance between chewy and crisp with just a slight nuance of almond flavor. This recipe fits the bill. Better still, you can bang out a batch in well under an hour.

- 1 (18.25-ounce) package white cake mix
- 1 cup water
- ⅓ cup vegetable oil
- 3 large egg whites
- ¾ teaspoon almond extract
- 2 (14-ounce) packages sweetened flaked coconut

Preheat oven to 350°F. Position oven rack in middle of oven. Grease cookie sheets with vegetable shortening.

Place the cake mix, water, oil, egg whites, and almond extract in a large bowl. Blend with an electric mixer set on medium speed for 1–2 minutes; stop mixer and scrape down sides of bowl with rubber spatula. Blend for 1 minute longer on medium-high speed until smooth and all dry ingredients are moistened. Stir in coconut with a wooden spoon until blended.

Drop dough by rounded tablespoonfuls onto prepared sheets.

Bake for 12–14 minutes or until golden brown. Transfer cookies to wire rack with metal spatula and cool completely.

MAKES ABOUT 72 COOKIES.

Variation:

CHOCOLATE-CHIP MACAROONS: Prepare as directed above but add 2 cups miniature semisweet chocolate chips to the batter along with the coconut.

COFFEE TOFFEE CHOCOLATE BISCOTTI

You'll want to keep a stash of these handy for yourself or for very, very good friends.

- 1 (19.5- to 19.8-ounce) package brownie mix
- 1 cup all-purpose flour
- 1 tablespoon instant coffee or espresso powder
- ½ cup (1 stick) unsalted butter, melted and cooled
- 2 large eggs
- 1 cup English toffee baking bits
- 1 recipe Chocolate Dip (see page 361), optional

Preheat oven to 350°F. Position rack in center of oven. Line a cookie sheet with parchment paper.

Combine the brownie mix, flour, coffee powder, melted butter, eggs, and toffee bits in a large mixing bowl. Blend with an electric mixer set on low until well blended, for 1–2 minutes, scraping down sides of bowl (mixture will be stiff).

Transfer dough to prepared cookie sheet. With floured hands, shape dough into 2 rectangles, 14 x 3-inch, ¾-inch thick, spacing them 4–5 inches apart on sheet. Mound the dough so it is slightly higher in the center than at the edges. Place cookie sheet in oven.

Bake for 30–35 minutes, until firm to touch; remove from oven and cool on sheet for 10 minutes (leave oven on).

With spatula, transfer logs to cutting board. Use a sharp knife to slice each rectangle into (approximately) ¾-inch slices on the diagonal. Return slices to sheet, cut sides down. Return sheet to oven. Bake biscotti for 10 minutes. Turn oven off and let biscotti remain in oven until crisp, 30–40 minutes longer. Remove from oven and transfer biscotti to a rack. Cool completely.

If desired, prepare Chocolate Dip and with a butter knife or small offset spatula spread over one side of each biscotti. Place on wax-paper-lined cookie sheet and refrigerate for at least 1 hour to set chocolate. Store in an airtight container or plastic ziplock bag for up to 3 weeks.

MAKES ABOUT 32 BISCOTTI.

COOKIE DOMINOES

Who says you can't play with your food? These whimsical cookies are both charming and child's play.

- 1 (16.5-ounce) roll refrigerated sugar cookie dough, well chilled
- ½ cup semisweet chocolate chips

Preheat oven to 350°F. Spray cookie sheets with nonstick cooking spray.

Cut the dough in half lengthwise; refrigerate one half. Roll out dough on a lightly floured surface to ¼-inch thickness to form a 10 x 6-inch rectangle. Cut into 10 equal-size rectangles.

Place rectangles 2 inches apart on cookie sheet. With a sharp knife, score each rectangle in half, crosswise. Gently press morsels, point side down, into dough to form domino numbers. Repeat with remaining dough.

Bake for 8–11 minutes or until edges are golden. Cool on cookie sheets for 1 minute. Transfer to wire racks and cool completely.

MAKES 20 COOKIES.

Baker's Note

To score each cookie in half, cut approximately one-third to halfway through the dough, being careful not to cut all the way through.

COOKIE POPS FOR COOKIE BOUQUETS

A bouquet of flowers is always lovely, but a "bouquet" of delicious, decorated cookies is all the sweeter. Consider delivering your gift in a vase, bundled with pretty ribbon, or placed in a box surrounded by pastel tissue paper. This is also a great activity for children's birthday parties. Bake the cookies ahead of time then have the children decorate their individual "bouquets" with an assortment of colored frostings, sprinkles, and candies for a memorable and delectable takeaway gift.

- 1 (16.5-ounce) roll refrigerated sugar cookie dough (or chocolate-chip cookie dough), well chilled
- 8 long, flat wooden craft sticks (popsicle sticks)
- Assorted decorations: icing, frosting, small candies, melted chocolate (see the "Icings, Frostings, Fillings, and Extras" chapter)

Preheat oven to 375°F. Spray cookie sheets with nonstick cooking spray.

Slice the cookie dough into 8 equal pieces; roll each slice into a ball. Place 4 balls at a time onto prepared cookie sheet, spacing far apart.

Insert wooden sticks into each ball to resemble a lollipop; flatten dough to ½-inch thickness with your palm or a spatula.

Bake for 13–15 minutes or until edges are golden and centers are just set. Cool on cookie sheet for 1 minute. Remove to wire racks and cool completely. Decorate as desired.

MAKES 8 COOKIES, ENOUGH FOR
1 COOKIE BOUQUET.

Baker's Note

Wooden craft sticks can be found at craft stores. To make a bouquet, bundle cookies together and tie colorful ribbons around sticks. For easier handling, place sticks in a vase or in a box.

CORIANDER LEMON COOKIES

Coriander leaves (cilantro) are well known and much used in contemporary kitchens, but the delicious seeds, though readily available, are far less familiar. The ground seeds have a mild fragrance, which some describe as a combination of lemon, sage, and cardamom. The spice is an exquisite enhancement in delicate baked goods such as these elegant slice-and-bake lemon cookies. The dough may also be rolled out and cut out with decorative cookie cutters.

- 1 (18.25-ounce) package lemon cake mix
- ½ cup vegetable shortening
- ⅓ cup butter, softened
- 1 large egg
- 1 tablespoon grated lemon zest
- ½ teaspoon ground coriander or ¼ teaspoon ground nutmeg
- 3–4 tablespoons powdered sugar or 1 recipe Lemon Icing (see page 368), optional

Place the cake mix, shortening, softened butter, egg, lemon zest, and ground coriander in a large bowl. Blend with an electric mixer set on low speed for 1 minute until blended (dough will be very thick). Scrape the dough off the beaters. Divide dough in half; shape each half into a 12 x 2-inch roll. Wrap each roll in plastic food wrap; refrigerate until firm (at least 4 hours).

Preheat oven to 350°F. Position rack in center of oven. Cut rolls into ¼-inch slices with a sharp knife. Place 2 inches apart on ungreased cookie sheets.

Bake for 7–8 minutes or until edges are lightly browned. Let stand on cookie sheets 1 minute. Transfer to wire rack and cool completely. Sprinkle with powdered sugar or ice with Lemon Icing, if desired.

MAKES ABOUT 60 COOKIES.

CRANBERRY-ALMOND SLICES

These marshmallow and cranberry-flecked treats look like miniature mosaics.

- 1 cup butterscotch baking chips
- 2 tablespoons (¼ stick) butter
- 1 (14-ounce) can sweetened condensed milk
- ¾ teaspoon almond extract
- 3 cups graham cracker crumbs

- 2 cups miniature marshmallows
- ¾ cup coarsely chopped honey-roasted almonds
- ¾ cup chopped dried cranberries

Set aside two 20-inch pieces of wax paper.

Melt the butterscotch chips and butter with the condensed milk in a heavy saucepan set over low heat, stirring until blended and smooth. Stir in the almond extract.

Combine the graham cracker crumbs, marshmallows, almonds, and cranberries in a large bowl; stir in the butterscotch mixture. Divide mixture in half. Place each portion on a piece of the prepared wax paper; let stand 10 minutes.

Using the wax paper as an aid, shape each portion into a 12-inch log. Wrap each log tightly; chill for 2 hours or until firm. Remove paper and cut each log into 15 slices. Store covered in refrigerator.

MAKES ABOUT 30 COOKIES.

CRANBERRY CEREAL WREATHS

Delight everyone on your gift list with these irresistible treats. They're the perfect way to show how much you care.

- 4½ cups cornflakes
- 1 cup miniature marshmallows
- ⅓ cup chopped almonds
- ⅔ cup dried cranberries
- 3 cups vanilla baking chips or white chocolate chips
- ¾ teaspoon almond extract
- Small tubes (purchased) of green and/or red decorating icing (optional)

Line cookie sheets with wax paper.

Combine the cornflakes, marshmallows, almonds, and dried cranberries in a large mixing bowl.

Melt the vanilla chips in a heavy medium saucepan over very low heat, stirring until completely melted and smooth; stir in almond extract. Pour this mixture over cereal mixture; stir gently until well coated.

Drop mixture by ¼-cupfuls onto the prepared cookie sheets. Flatten mixture slightly to form circles about 2 inches wide. Using the handle of a wooden spoon, make a ¾-inch hole in the center of each cookie to form a wreath shape, spreading the cookies to about 3 inches in diameter.

When cool, decorate with frosting, if desired. Place wreaths in an airtight container with wax paper between layers. Seal and store at room temperature up to 3 days.

MAKES ABOUT 15 COOKIE WREATHS.

CRANBERRY EGGNOG BISCOTTI

- 1 (16.5-ounce) roll refrigerated sugar cookie dough
- ⅓ cup all-purpose flour
- ¾ cups dried cranberries, coarsely chopped
- 2 tablespoons grated orange zest
- ¾ teaspoon ground cinnamon
- ½ teaspoon ground nutmeg
- 1 teaspoon vanilla extract

Preheat oven to 350°F. Lightly spray a cookie sheet with nonstick cooking spray.

Break up the cookie dough into large bowl; let stand for 10–15 minutes to soften. Add flour, cranberries, orange zest, cinnamon, nutmeg, and vanilla extract to the cookie dough; mix well with your fingers, the paddle attachment of an electric stand mixer, or a wooden spoon.

Divide dough into two equal halves. On the cookie sheet, shape each dough half into a 12 x 2-inch rectangle, ¾-inch high, spacing the dough halves about 3 inches apart.

Bake for 26–28 minutes or until the logs are deep golden brown and spring back in the center when touched. Remove sheet from oven; keep oven on.

Using two pancake turners, lift logs, one at a time, from the cookie sheet to a cutting board. Using a sharp knife, cut one of the logs into ¾-inch-wide slices. Note: for longer biscotti, cut at a deep diagonal; for shorter biscotti, cut log crosswise. Repeat with second log. Place slices on the same cookie sheet (do not worry about the spacing).

Bake slices for 5 minutes; remove from oven and turn over all of the slices. Return cookie sheet to oven and bake for 5 minutes longer. Remove sheet from oven and immediately transfer biscotti to a wire rack; cool completely.

MAKES 28 BISCOTTI.

- ¼ cup orange marmalade
- ¼ teaspoon ground allspice
- 1 (16.5-ounce) roll refrigerated sugar cookie dough, well chilled

Combine the cornstarch, cranberry sauce, and marmalade in a small saucepan. Bring to a boil over medium heat, stirring constantly. Transfer to a small bowl and stir in the allspice. Cool completely.

Using a lightly floured rolling pin on a lightly floured surface, roll dough into a 16 x 8-inch rectangle. Spoon and spread cooled filling evenly over dough to within ½ inch of edges.

Starting with 16-inch side, roll up dough jellyroll fashion; cut in half to form two 8-inch rolls. Wrap each in plastic wrap or foil; freeze for 2 hours until firm.

Preheat oven to 350°F. Spray cookie sheets with nonstick cooking spray.

Using a sharp knife, cut each dough log in half crosswise; cut each piece into 8 even slices. Place slices 2 inches apart on prepared sheets.

Bake for 10–13 minutes or until light golden brown. Immediately transfer cookies to wire cooling racks and cool completely.

MAKES 32 COOKIES.

CRANBERRY-ORANGE PINWHEELS

Here's a cookie I love to add to holiday cookie gift plates. It's a grab-bag of many of my favorite fall flavors: cranberry, orange, and allspice.

- 1 tablespoon cornstarch
- ½ cup whole-berry cranberry sauce

CREAM CHEESE CANDY CANE COOKIES

These whimsical cookies are equally cute and delicious. For an added flavor twist, add a drop or two of peppermint extract to the dough along with the cream cheese and butter.

- ¼ cup (½ stick) butter, softened
- 1 (3-ounce) package cream cheese, softened

- 1 large egg
- 1 (18.25-ounce) package white cake mix
- ¼ teaspoon red gel or paste icing color

Preheat oven to 350°F.

Beat the butter, cream cheese, and egg in large bowl with an electric mixer on medium until blended. Add the cake mix. Stir in with a wooden spoon until well blended.

Divide dough in half. Add the food color to one half of the dough; blend well for even red color.

Measure a scant 1 teaspoon white dough and scant 1 teaspoon red dough for each cookie. Roll out each into 4-inch rope. Place ropes side by side. Lightly roll together into twist. Place cookie twists 2 inches apart on ungreased cookie sheet, then shape each into a hook to resemble candy cane.

Bake for 7–9 minutes or just until edges are golden brown. Immediately remove from cookie sheets to cool.

MAKES 36 COOKIES.

CRÈME DE MENTHE COOKIES

This classic cookie combines three of my favorite sweets: cookie, mint, and chocolate. The crisp, clean texture makes these the perfect accompaniment to a glass of cold milk or a mug of hot cocoa.

- 1 (16.5-ounce) roll refrigerated sugar cookie dough, softened
- 2 cups chopped unwrapped thin rectangular crème de menthe

candies, divided
- 2¼ cups powdered sugar
- ¼ cup (½ stick) butter, softened
- 1–2 drops green food color, if desired
- 2–3 tablespoons milk

Preheat oven to 350°F.

Break up the dough into a medium bowl. Sprinkle with ¾ cup of the chopped candies. Mix well with fingers until blended.

Shape teaspoons of dough into balls. Place balls 1 inch apart on ungreased cookie sheets.

Bake cookies 10–12 minutes or until just set and edges are light golden brown. Cool for 1 minute on cookie sheets. Transfer to cooling racks and cool completely.

In a small bowl, mix the powdered sugar, butter, and food color until smooth, adding enough of the milk, 1 teaspoon at a time, until desired spreading consistency.

Spread 1 teaspoon frosting on each cooled cookie. Sprinkle with some of the remaining chopped candies.

MAKES 22 COOKIES.

DATE DAINTIES

Dates are so sweet and flavorful, why relegate them to granola and holiday breads alone? The rich flavor here is far greater than the sum of this cookie's parts.

- 1 cup sweetened flake coconut
- 1 cup packed light brown sugar
- 1 cup finely chopped, pitted dates
- 2 large eggs, lightly beaten
- 1 teaspoon vanilla extract
- 3 cups crisp rice cereal

Line cookie sheets with wax paper.

Place the coconut into a shallow dish or pie plate; set aside.

In a cold, 12-inch frying pan, combine the brown sugar, dates, and eggs. Cook for about 10 minutes over medium heat, stirring constantly, or until mixture starts to thicken and sugar is dissolved. Remove from heat. Stir the vanilla and cereal into the hot date mixture, mixing until well blended.

Working quickly, dip a teaspoon in ice water, then drop rounded teaspoonfuls of mixture onto prepared sheets. Roll each cookie in coconut. Chill for at least 1 hour before serving. Store in airtight container i n refrigerator.

MAKES ABOUT 32 COOKIES.

DECADENT CHOCOLATE-DIPPED TOFFEE CHIPPERS

You can stop with the addition of the toffee bits to the cookie dough and you will still have a delectable cookie. But if you give the cookies a dunk in melted chocolate and sprinkle with extra toffee you will have cookies that live up to their name.

- 1 (16.5-ounce) roll refrigerated chocolate-chip cookie dough
- 1½ cups toffee baking bits, divided
- 1 recipe Chocolate Drizzle or Dip (see page 361)

Break up the cookie dough into large bowl; let stand for 10–15 minutes to soften. Add ½ cup

of the toffee bits; mix well with wooden spoon or fingers. Chill for 1 hour in refrigerator or 20–25 minutes in freezer.

Preheat oven to 350°F. Spray cookie sheets with nonstick cooking spray.

Shape dough into 26 walnut-size balls. Space 2 inches apart on prepared cookie sheets; flatten slightly using your palm or a spatula.

Bake for 11–13 minutes or until light golden brown at edges. Cool for 2 minutes on cookie sheets. Transfer cookies to wire racks and cool completely. Cover cookie sheet with wax paper or foil; spray with nonstick cooking spray.

Prepare chocolate dip. Dip one half of each cookie in chocolate; generously sprinkle with remaining 1 cup toffee bits. Place cookies on prepared sheet. Place sheet in refrigerator for 30 minutes to set chocolate. Store in refrigerator.

MAKES 26 COOKIES.

DELUXE SALTED NUT CHOCOLATE BISCOTTI

Chocolate, nuts, and a bit of salt—this is a cookie experience for those who welcome a double dose of chocolate with a spike of grown-up flair.

- Nonstick baking spray with flour
- 1 (16.5-ounce) roll refrigerated chocolate chip cookie dough, softened
- 2 teaspoons vanilla extract
- 1½ cups chopped deluxe salted mixed nuts (e.g., blend of almonds, Brazil nuts, hazelnuts, pecans)
- 1 cup (6 ounces) semisweet chocolate chips

Spray a large cookie sheet with nonstick baking spray with flour.

Break up the cookie dough into a large bowl. Sprinkle vanilla and nuts over dough. Mix well with fingers until blended.

Divide dough into 4 equal portions; shape each into an 8 x 1-inch log. Place logs 3 inches apart on prepared cookie sheet. Flatten each log to about 1½ inches wide. Chill on cookie sheet for 15 minutes.

Preheat oven to 350°F.

Bake cookie logs for 15–20 minutes or until golden brown. Cool on sheet for 15 minutes. Reduce oven temperature to 200°.

Transfer cookie logs to cutting board. With serrated knife, carefully cut each log into 10 (¾-inch thick) slices. Place slices on same cookie sheet, cut side down.

Return cookies to oven and bake for 1 hour. Transfer cookies from cookie sheet to cooling rack. Cool completely.

Meanwhile, microwave the chocolate chips in a small microwavable bowl on high for 1 minute. Stir. Microwave 1 minute longer, stirring every 15 seconds, until chocolate is melted and smooth.

Line cookie sheet with wax paper. Dip ¼ of each cookie into melted chocolate, then place on prepared cookie sheet. Refrigerate until chocolate is set, about 10 minutes.

MAKES 40 BISCOTTI.

DEVIL'S FOOD WHOOPIES WITH COCOA FLUFF FILLING

These showstoppers reward a little bit of work with a whole heap of praise. Kids can help with the final assembly of the whoopies—they'll love saying the name as much as eating their efforts.

- 1 cup jarred, unsweetened applesauce
- ⅓ cup butter, plus ½ cup (1 stick), softened, divided
- 1 (18.25-ounce) package devil's food cake mix
- 2 large eggs
- ½ cup milk
- 1 cup miniature semisweet chocolate chips, optional
- 1 (8-ounce) package cream cheese, softened
- 1⅔ cups powdered sugar, sifted
- ⅓ cup unsweetened cocoa powder, sifted
- ½ (7-ounce) jar marshmallow creme
- 1 teaspoon vanilla extract

Preheat oven to 375°F. Position oven rack in middle of oven. Line a cookie sheet with parchment paper or foil (grease foil, if using).

Beat applesauce and ⅓ cup softened butter in a large mixing bowl with an electric mixer on medium speed until smooth. Add the cake mix, eggs, and milk; beat on low speed until combined, and then on medium speed for 1 minute. Stir in the miniature chocolate chips, if desired. Drop mounds of batter by heaping tablespoonfuls, 3 inches apart, onto cookie sheet; keep remaining batter chilled. Bake for 15 minutes or until set and lightly browned around edges.

Carefully remove from parchment or foil; cool on wire rack. Repeat with remaining batter, lining cooled cookie sheets each time with new parchment or foil. If desired, place cookies in a covered storage container with wax paper between layers to prevent sticking. Store cookies at room temperature for 24 hours.

In a medium bowl beat remaining ½ cup

(1 stick) softened butter and softened cream cheese with an electric mixer set on high until smooth. Add the sifted powdered sugar, cocoa powder, marshmallow creme, and vanilla; beat until blended and smooth.

Spread about 2½ tablespoons of filling on flat side of one cookie; top with a second cookie. Repeat. Serve immediately or cover and chill up to 2 hours.

MAKES 15 WHOOPIES.

DOWN ISLAND COCONUT LIME COOKIES

Bursting with the tropical flavors of ginger, rum, lime, and coconut, these are definitely cookies for summer days when the livin'—and the cookie-makin'—should be easy.

- 1 (7-ounce) bag sweetened flake coconut
- 1 (12-ounce) package vanilla wafers, finely crushed
- 2 cups sifted powdered sugar
- 2 teaspoons rum flavored extract
- 1½ teaspoons ground ginger
- 1 (6-ounce) can frozen limeade concentrate, thawed and undiluted

Place the coconut in a shallow dish or pie plate; set aside momentarily.

Combine the vanilla wafer crumbs, powdered sugar, rum extract, ginger, and enough of the limeade concentrate to make the mixture stick together in a medium bowl; mix well.

Form the mixture into ½-inch balls. Roll balls in the coconut to coat, pressing gently to ad-

here. Store in covered containers between layers of wax paper. Chill 1 day before serving.

MAKES ABOUT 60 COOKIES.

DULCE DE LECHE CRISPS

A favorite confection in Latin American countries, dulce de leche is made by slowly reducing fresh milk and sugar until the mixture thickens into a luscious caramel. Here the beloved treat finds new life as a charming cookie that bakes up much like a crisp brandy snap with a lacy, brown-sugary center.

- 1 cup packed dark brown sugar
- 1 cup canned evaporated milk
- ½ cup (1 stick) plus ⅓ cup butter, softened, divided
- 3 large egg yolks, lightly beaten with a fork
- 1 teaspoon vanilla extract
- 1⅓ cups toffee baking bits
- 2 cups chopped pecans, walnuts, or almonds
- 1 (18.25-ounce) package white cake mix

Combine the brown sugar, evaporated milk, ½ cup softened butter, and egg yolks in a heavy-bottomed medium saucepan. Cook over medium heat for 10–13 minutes or until thickened and bubbly, whisking frequently. Stir in vanilla extract. Remove from heat; cool completely. Stir the toffee bits and nuts into cooled mixture. Reserve 1¼ cups toffee mixture. Set aside.

Preheat oven to 350°F. Position oven rack in middle of oven. combine the cake mix, remaining ⅓ cup softened butter, and remaining toffee mixture in a large mixing bowl. Stir by hand until all dry ingredients are thoroughly moistened.

Shape dough into 1-inch balls. Place 2 inches apart on ungreased cookie sheets. With thumb or back of a teaspoon measure, make an indentation in center of each ball and fill with mounded ½ teaspoonful of the reserved brown sugar mixture.

Bake for 10–13 minutes or until just barely set. Cool for 2 minutes on cookie sheets. Transfer cookies with spatula to wire racks and cool completely.

MAKES ABOUT 54 COOKIES.

DUTCH SPICE COOKIES

Rich with spices, these cookies are wonderful any time of year. However, you're likely to enjoy them most when the temperature dips and the air turns crisp. The combination of dark brown sugar and spices transforms the basic sugar cookie dough, resulting in a cookie evocative of European bakeries.

- 1 (16.5-ounce) roll refrigerated sugar cookie dough
- 3 tablespoons packed dark brown sugar
- 1½ teaspoons ground cinnamon
- ½ teaspoon ground nutmeg
- ½ teaspoon ground ginger
- ¼ teaspoon ground cloves
- ¼ cup sugar

Break up the cookie dough into large bowl; let stand for 10–15 minutes to soften. Add the brown sugar, cinnamon, nutmeg, ginger, and cloves; mix well with your fingers, the paddle attachment of an electric mixer, or a wooden spoon. Chill dough for 1 hour in refrigerator or 20–25 minutes in freezer.

Preheat oven to 350°F. Spray cookie sheets with nonstick cooking spray.

Place the sugar in small flat dish. Form the dough into 1-inch balls and roll in the sugar.

Place balls about 2 inches apart on prepared cookie sheets. Flatten with your palm or a spatula.

Bake for 8–10 minutes or until light brown on bottom. Transfer cookies to wire racks and cool completely.

MAKES ABOUT 30 COOKIES.

EASY ROLL AND GO SLICED COOKIES

Edged in chopped nuts, toffee bits, candies, or coloring sugar, these easy roll-slice-and-bake cookies are a fast fix for dressing up sugar cookies.

- 1 (16.5-ounce) roll refrigerated sugar cookie dough (or chocolate-chip cookie dough), well chilled
- 1 cup any of the following: finely chopped nuts (any variety), toffee bits, colored sugar, or small decorator candies

Preheat oven to 350°F. Spray cookie sheets with nonstick cooking spray. Place the chopped nuts or candies on a large plate; gently shake plate to distribute evenly.

Carefully remove wrapper from the sugar cookie dough, keeping log of dough intact. Immediately roll dough in chopped nuts or candy, gently pressing dough to adhere to the bits. Transfer dough to a cutting board and slice into 22 even slices. Space slices 2 inches apart on prepared cookie sheets.

Bake cookies for 10–12 minutes or until

golden at edges; cool on cookie sheets for 1 minute. Transfer cookies to wire racks and cool completely.

MAKES 22 COOKIES.

EGGNOG THUMBPRINTS

These delicately spiced cookies are bound to stir up memories of favorite holidays spent with family and friends. Be sure to store them in the refrigerator once they are filled.

- ½ cup soft spread-style honey nut cream cheese
- ¾ teaspoon rum extract
- ¾ teaspoon nutmeg, divided
- 1 teaspoon cinnamon
- ⅓ cup granulated sugar
- 1 (16.5-ounce) roll refrigerated sugar cookie dough, well chilled

Preheat oven to 350°F. Spray cookie sheets with nonstick cooking spray.

Mix the cream cheese, rum extract, and ¼ teaspoon nutmeg in a small bowl; mix well and set aside. Combine cinnamon, remaining nutmeg, and sugar in a small dish.

Cut cookie dough into 12 equal slices. Cut each slice in half. Roll each piece into a ball; roll balls in sugar mixture. Place balls 2 inches apart on cookie sheets.

Bake for 10–12 minutes or until golden at edges. Remove cookies from oven and immediately make a depression in each cookie with thumb or cork; fill each with a spoonful of cream cheese mixture. Transfer to wire racks and cool completely. Store in refrigerator.

MAKES 24 COOKIES.

FAST AND FUDGY MINI TARTS

These scrumptious bites of fudge are as impressive as they are easy to prepare. For a holiday-inspired peppermint variation, substitute ½ teaspoon mint extract for the vanilla extract. Garnish each chocolate mint tart with crushed red and white peppermint candies.

- 1 (16.5-ounce) roll refrigerated sugar cookie dough, well chilled
- 1 cup semisweet chocolate chips
- ½ cup canned sweetened condensed milk
- ½ teaspoon vanilla extract

Preheat oven to 350°F. Spray 24 mini muffin pan cups (1¾-inch size) with nonstick cooking spray.

Slice the cookie dough in half; refrigerate half. Cut remaining half into 6 equal pieces; cut each piece into 4 equal pieces (a total of 24 pieces). Press each dough piece into bottoms and up the sides of prepared muffin cups.

Bake dough cups for 8–10 minutes or until golden (dough will not be completely set). Remove from oven and press an indentation into center of each cup with the back of a ½-teaspoon measuring spoon.

Bake 2 minutes longer until golden. Place pans on wire racks and cool for 15–20 minutes. Carefully remove tart cups from the pans.

Remove second half of dough from refrigerator and repeat, making a total of 48 cups. Cool all cups completely while making filling.

Combine the chocolate chips and condensed milk in a small saucepan over medium-high heat. Cook and stir until chocolate melts and mixture is smooth; stir in vanilla.

Fill each tart cup with a teaspoon of filling. Let stand until filling sets.

MAKES 48 MINI TARTS.

FLORIDA CITRUS MADELEINES

I love these madeleines for their lightness and intense citrus flavor. The most difficult thing about making them is remembering to take it easy when folding the egg whites into the batter—the gentler the folding, the airier the madeleines. For a fancier final flourish, consider dipping each madeleine in melted white chocolate instead of dusting with powdered sugar.

- Vegetable shortening and all-purpose flour to grease pans.
- 1 (18.25-ounce) package lemon cake mix
- ½ cup (1 stick) butter, melted
- ¼ cup orange juice
- 1 tablespoon grated orange zest
- 4 large eggs, separated
- 2–3 tablespoons powdered sugar

Preheat oven to 350°F. Position oven rack in middle of oven. Grease molds of large madeleine pan (3 x 1¼-inch shell molds) with vegetable shortening. Sprinkle with flour to coat pan, shaking off excess.

Place the cake mix, melted butter, orange juice, orange zest, and egg yolks in a large bowl. Blend with an electric mixer set on medium speed for 1–2 minutes, until well blended and smooth. Set aside momentarily. Clean beaters.

Beat egg whites in a large mixing bowl with electric mixer set on high speed until soft peaks form. Stir ¼ of the beaten egg whites into the cake batter to lighten it; fold remaining whites into batter.

Spoon 1 heaping tablespoon batter into each indentation in pan (do not overfill; batter will spread as it bakes).

Bake until puffed and set at center, 8–10 minutes. Cool in pan for 5 minutes; gently remove madeleines to wire rack. Repeat process, greasing and flouring pan before each batch. Sift powdered sugar over cooled cookies.

MAKES ABOUT 30 MADELEINES.

Variations:

ORANGE MADELEINES: Prepare as directed above but use orange cake mix in place of the lemon cake mix and, if desired, add ½ teaspoon ground coriander or cardamom to the batter.

LEMON MADELEINES: Prepare as directed above but replace the orange juice with 2 tablespoons water and 2 tablespoons fresh lemon juice and use grated lemon zest in place of the orange zest. If desired, drizzle madeleines with Lemon Icing (see page 368).

LEMON-LIME MADELEINES: Prepare as directed above but replace the orange juice with 2 tablespoons water and 2 tablespoons fresh lime juice and use grated lime zest in place of the orange zest. If desired, drizzle madeleines with Lime Icing (see page 368).

pieces. Wrap each in plastic wrap or foil. Store in refrigerator to keep filling firm.

MAKES 16 COOKIE SANDWICHES.

FLUFFERNUTTER CHOCOLATE-CHIP COOKIE SANDWICHES

Peanut butter and marshmallow? Oh yes. Fluffernutter aficionados know that something so right can never be wrong. Here the traditional peanut butter and marshmallow fluff sandwich gets a newfangled twist with chocolate-chip cookies in place of white bread.

■ 1 (16.5-ounce) roll refrigerated chocolate-chip cookie dough, well chilled
■ ½ cup creamy-style peanut butter
■ 1 cup marshmallow creme

Preheat oven to 350°F. Line two 8-inch pans with foil; spray with nonstick cooking spray.

Cut cookie dough into ¼-inch-thick slices. Divide slices between the two pans. With floured fingers, press dough evenly to form crust.

Bake for 13–17 minutes or until golden brown and set at the center. Remove from oven and cool completely. Use foil to lift cookies from pans; remove foil.

Place cookies, bottom side up, on work surface. Spread one cookie with peanut butter; spread second cookie with marshmallow creme. Place cookie, marshmallow creme side down, on top of peanut butter-spread cookie. Cut into 16

FROSTED MAPLE-NUT MINIS

"You must try these!" a friend wrote on the card enclosed in a box of frosted maple cookies. She procured the cookies at a newly opened bakery in her hometown, and, knowing my fondness for cookies, brown sugar, and maple, she felt compelled to send some along for sampling. What a friend! This is my version of the mouthwatering cookie.

■ 1 (16.5-ounce) roll refrigerated sugar cookie dough
■ ⅔ cup creamy-style peanut butter
■ 2 teaspoons maple extract
■ 3 tablespoons packed brown sugar
■ ¼ teaspoon ground cinnamon
■ 1 recipe Maple Icing (see page 369)

Preheat oven to 350°F. Spray cookie sheets with nonstick cooking spray.

Break up the cookie dough into large bowl; let stand for 10–15 minutes to soften. Add the peanut butter, maple extract, brown sugar, and cinnamon; mix well with your fingers or a wooden spoon.

Shape dough into 1-inch balls; place 2 inches apart on prepared cookie sheets.

Bake for 10–12 minutes or until golden brown. Cool for 2 minutes on cookie sheets; remove from cookie sheets and cool completely. When cool, frost or drizzle with Maple Icing.

MAKES 32 COOKIES.

FRUIT AND NUT STRUDEL COOKIES

Utterly eye-pleasing, these well-dressed cookie twirls are a breeze to assemble. They are as fitting on a holiday dessert buffet as a summer picnic table. Be sure that the dough is very well chilled to make the rolling easy.

- 1 (16.5-ounce) roll refrigerated sugar cookie dough
- ⅔ cup apricot preserves
- ¾ cup flaked sweetened coconut
- ¾ cup chopped walnuts
- ½ cup raisins

Using a lightly floured rolling pin on a lightly floured surface, roll dough into a 14 x 8-inch rectangle. Spread dough with preserves; sprinkle with coconut, walnuts, and raisins to within ½ inch of edges.

Starting with 14-inch side, roll up dough jellyroll fashion; cut in half to form two 7-inch rolls. Wrap each in plastic wrap or foil; freeze for 2 hours until firm.

Preheat oven to 350°F. Spray cookie sheets with nonstick cooking spray.

Using a sharp knife, cut each dough log in half crosswise; cut each piece into 7 even slices. Place slices 2 inches apart on prepared sheets.

Bake for 10–13 minutes or until light golden brown. Immediately transfer cookies to wire cooling racks and cool completely.

MAKES 28 COOKIES.

GERMAN CHOCOLATE THUMBPRINT COOKIES (BROWNIE MIX)

These cookies top my list for holiday cookie plates, and although they take a bit more time to make (with the cooling and cooking times), the overall effort is well worth it. I've found, in particular, that people who claim they do not like coconut are easily converted with these thumbprints, each of which tastes like a miniature German chocolate cake.

- 1 cup packed light brown sugar
- 1 cup canned evaporated milk
- ½ cup (1 stick) plus ⅓ cup butter, softened, divided
- 3 large egg yolks, lightly beaten with a fork
- 1 teaspoon vanilla extract
- 1½ cups sweetened shredded coconut
- 1½ cups chopped pecans
- 1 (19.5- to 19.8-ounce) package brownie mix

Combine brown sugar, evaporated milk, ½ cup butter, and beaten egg yolks in a medium, heavy-bottomed saucepan. Cook over medium heat for 10–13 minutes or until thickened and bubbly, whisking frequently. Stir in vanilla, coconut, and pecans. Remove from heat and cool to room temperature. Reserve 1¼ cups topping mixture. Set aside.

Preheat oven to 350°F. Position a rack in the lower third of the oven. Combine the brownie mix, remaining ⅓ cup softened butter, and re-maining topping mixture in a medium mixing bowl. Stir with a wooden spoon until all dry ingredients are thoroughly moistened.

Shape dough into 1-inch balls. Place 2 inches apart on ungreased cookie sheets. With thumb or back of a ¼ teaspoon measure, make an indentation in center of each ball and fill with mounded ½ teaspoonful of reserved topping.

Bake for 10–13 minutes or until just barely set. Cool on cookie sheets for 2 minutes. Transfer cookies with spatula to wire racks and cool completely.

MAKES ABOUT 54 THUMBPRINTS.

GERMAN CHOCOLATE THUMBPRINT COOKIES (CAKE MIX)

These decadent mouthfuls are worth every calorie.

- 1 cup packed light brown sugar
- 1 cup canned evaporated milk
- ½ cup (1 stick) plus ⅓ cup butter, softened, divided
- 3 large egg yolks, lightly beaten with a fork
- 1 teaspoon vanilla extract
- 1½ cups sweetened flaked coconut
- 1½ cups chopped pecans
- 1 (18.25-ounce) package German chocolate cake mix

Combine the brown sugar, evaporated milk, ½ cup softened butter, and egg yolks in a heavy-bottomed medium saucepan. Cook over medium heat for 10–13 minutes or until

thickened and bubbly, whisking frequently. Stir in vanilla extract, coconut, and pecans. Remove from heat; cool completely. Reserve 1¼ cups topping mixture; set aside.

Preheat oven to 350°F. Position oven rack in middle of oven. combine cake mix, remaining ⅓ cup softened butter, and remaining coconut-pecan mixture in a large mixing bowl. Stir by hand until all dry ingredients are thoroughly moistened.

Shape dough into 1-inch balls. Place 2 inches apart on ungreased cookie sheets. With thumb or back of a teaspoon measure, make an indentation in center of each ball and fill with mounded ½ teaspoonful of reserved coconut-pecan mixture.

Bake for 10–13 minutes or until just barely set. Cool for 2 minutes on cookie sheets. Transfer cookies with spatula to wire racks and cool completely.

MAKES ABOUT 54 THUMBPRINTS.

GINGER AND LIME CHEESECAKE TARTLETS

I enjoyed the most delicious cheesecake ever at one of the most unlikely spots: a food court at a mall in Indianapolis. Turns out the proprietor's mother supplied the sandwich stand's scrumptious desserts. These mini ginger-lime gems are my best approximation of the remarkable slice of heaven I enjoyed that day.

- 1 (16.5-ounce) roll refrigerated sugar cookie dough, well chilled
- 1 (8-ounce) package cream cheese, softened
- ½ cup sweetened condensed milk
- 1 large egg

- 2 teaspoons fresh lime juice
- 1 teaspoon grated lime zest
- 1 teaspoon ground ginger

Preheat oven to 350°F. Line 12 muffin cups with paper liners.

Slice cookie dough into 12 equal pieces. Place one piece in each muffin cup. Bake for 10–12 minutes or until cookie has spread to edge of cup (dough will appear slightly puffed). Remove from the oven and press an indentation into the center of each cup with the back of a spoon.

Meanwhile, combine the cream cheese, condensed milk, egg, lime juice, lime zest, and ginger in a medium bowl; beat with an electric mixer on high until smooth. Spoon cream cheese mixture over each cookie in cup.

Bake for an additional 13–17 minutes or until cream cheese filling is just set. Cool completely in pan on wire rack. Refrigerate for 1 hour until chilled.

MAKES 12 CHEESECAKE TARTLETS.

GINGERBREAD PEOPLE

An afternoon spent making, baking, and decorating these nostalgic cutout cookies is perfect for preheating memories, folding in both friends and family, and baking up good times.

- 1 (18.25-ounce) package spice cake mix
- ¾ cup all-purpose flour
- 2½ teaspoons ground ginger
- 1 teaspoon ground cinnamon
- 2 large eggs
- ⅓ cup vegetable oil
- ⅓ cup molasses
- 1 recipe Vanilla Icing (see page 376)
- Red Hots cinnamon candies or raisins, optional

Place the cake mix, flour, ginger, and cinnamon in a large bowl; stir to combine. Add the eggs, oil, and molasses. Mix with a wooden spoon until well blended and all dry ingredients are moistened. Chill, covered, for at least 4 hours or up to overnight.

Preheat oven to 375°F and spray cookie sheets with nonstick cooking spray. Position racks to upper and lower positions of oven.

Sprinkle a work surface with a thin layer of flour. Set out rolling pin, 4-inch gingerbread person cookie cutters, metal spatula, and cooling racks.

Remove the dough from the refrigerator and divide into fourths. Place ¼ of the dough on floured surface (cover and return remaining dough to refrigerator). Flour the rolling pin and roll dough to ¼-inch thickness. Flour cookie cutters and cut out shapes. Transfer dough to prepared cookie sheets with spatula. Re-roll any scraps, then repeat with remaining dough, rolling one fourth at a time.

Place one sheet on each oven rack. Bake for 4 minutes. Rotate the sheets (place the sheet from the bottom rack on the top rack and the sheet from the top rack on the bottom rack. This ensures even baking). Bake for 4–7 minutes for large shapes or until center is puffed and sinks back.

Remove from oven and let cookies rest on cookie sheets for 1 minute. Transfer with metal spatula to racks and cool completely. Prepare Vanilla Icing, or other icing of choice. Decorate cookies with icing and candies or raisins, if desired.

MAKES ABOUT 24 4-INCH COOKIES.

GINGER LIME BISCOTTI

- 1 (16.5-ounce) roll refrigerated sugar cookie dough
- ⅓ cup all-purpose flour
- ¾ cup finely chopped candied ginger
- 1 teaspoon ground ginger
- 2 tablespoons grated lime zest
- 1 teaspoon vanilla extract
- 1 recipe Lime Icing (see page 368), optional

Preheat oven to 350°F. Lightly spray a cookie sheet with nonstick cooking spray.

Break up the cookie dough into large bowl; let stand for 10–15 minutes to soften. Add the flour, candied ginger, ground ginger, lime zest, and vanilla extract to the cookie dough; mix well with your fingers, the paddle attachment of an electric stand mixer, or a wooden spoon.

Divide dough into two equal halves. On the cookie sheet, shape each dough half into a 12 x 2-inch rectangle, ¾-inch high, spacing the dough halves about 3 inches apart.

Bake for 26–28 minutes or until the logs are deep golden brown and spring back in the center when touched. Remove sheet from oven; keep oven on.

Using two pancake turners, lift logs, one at a time, from the cookie sheet to a cutting board. Using a sharp knife, cut one of the logs into ¾-inch-wide slices. Note: for longer biscotti, cut at a deep diagonal; for shorter biscotti, cut log crosswise. Repeat with second log. Place slices on the same cookie sheet; do not worry about the spacing.

Bake slices 5 minutes; remove from oven and turn over all of the slices. Return cookie sheet to oven and bake 5 minutes longer. Remove sheet from oven and immediately transfer biscotti to a wire rack; cool completely. If desired, drizzle each biscotti with Lime Icing.

MAKES 28 BISCOTTI.

GINGER LOVER'S BISCOTTI

One of my favorite family rituals is afternoon tea. We stop what we're doing, plug in the kettle, and load up a tray with an assortment of nibbles. This biscotti is a favorite with my ginger-loving parents and siblings. Don't be put off by the addition of black pepper to the dough—it enhances the peppery bite of the ginger.

- 1 (18.25-ounce) package vanilla cake mix
- 1 cup all-purpose flour
- 2½ teaspoons ground ginger
- ¼ teaspoon finely ground black pepper
- ½ cup (1 stick) butter, melted and cooled
- 2 teaspoons vanilla extract
- 2 large eggs
- ⅔ cup finely chopped crystallized ginger

Preheat oven to 350°F. Position rack in center of oven. Spray cookie sheet with nonstick cooking spray.

Place the cake mix, flour, ground ginger, ground pepper, melted butter, vanilla extract, eggs, and crystallized ginger in a large mixing bowl. Blend with an electric mixer set on low speed for 2–3 minutes until well-blended, scraping down sides of bowl.

Transfer dough to prepared cookie sheet. With floured hands, shape dough into two 14 x 3-inch rectangles, each ¾-inch thick, spacing them 4–5 inches apart on sheet. Mound the dough so it is slightly higher in the middle than at the edges.

Bake for 30–35 minutes, until firm to touch; remove from oven (leave oven on) and cool on sheet for 10 minutes.

Transfer rectangles to a cutting board, and use a sharp knife to slice each rectangle into ¾-inch slices on the diagonal. Carefully return these slices to the cookie sheet, and turn them onto their sides. Return cookie sheet to oven. Bake biscotti 10 minutes. Turn oven off and let biscotti remain in oven until crisp, 30–40 minutes longer.

Remove from oven and transfer biscotti to a rack. Cool completely. Store in an airtight container or plastic zip-top bag for 2–3 weeks.

MAKES ABOUT 32 BISCOTTI.

GINGERSNAP CRINKLES

Turbinado sugar (sometimes called "raw" sugar) adds a sophisticated sparkle and crunch to these spicy favorites. If you cannot find it, regular sugar works just fine as a substitute. Be sure to make these in fall and serve with mugfuls of hot apple cider.

- 1 (18.25-ounce) package spice cake mix
- 2 large eggs
- 1¾ cups frozen whipped topping, thawed
- 1½ teaspoons ground ginger
- ½ teaspoon ground cinnamon
- ⅛ teaspoon ground black pepper
- ¾ cup turbinado sugar

Place the cake mix, eggs, thawed whipped topping, ginger, cinnamon, and black pepper in a large bowl. Blend for 1–2 minutes with an electric mixer set on medium speed until well blended and all dry ingredients are moistened (dough will be stiff). Refrigerate dough, covered, for 30 minutes.

Preheat oven to 350°F. Position oven rack in middle of oven. Set aside ungreased cookie sheets. Place the turbinado sugar into a small, shallow dish.

Shape dough into 1-inch balls. Roll cookies in sugar to coat. Place 2 inches apart on ungreased cookie sheet.

Bake for 10–12 minutes or until cookies are puffed in appearance and firm at edges (centers will still be slightly soft). Let cookies rest on cookie sheets for 2 minutes (cookies will fall, giving them a cracked appearance). Transfer cookies to wire rack with metal spatula and cool completely.

MAKES ABOUT 60 COOKIES.

GLOREO COOKIES

Think of a favorite sandwich cookie that rhymes with "gloreo" and you'll know what these yummy treats are all about. The cookies are softer than their store-bought cousins, making for a homey, old-fashioned cookie.

- 1 (18.25-ounce) package devil's food cake mix
- 2 large eggs
- 6 tablespoons cold water, divided
- 2 tablespoons vegetable oil
- ¼ cup unsweetened cocoa powder
- 1 packet unflavored gelatin
- 1 cup vegetable shortening
- 2 teaspoons vanilla extract
- 1 (16-ounce) package powdered sugar

Preheat oven to 350°F. Position oven rack in upper third of the oven. Spray cookie sheets with nonstick cooking spray.

Place the cake mix, eggs, 2 tablespoons

water, and oil in a large bowl. Blend with an electric mixer set on low speed for 1–2 minutes until mixture is blended.

Place the cocoa powder in a small dish. Shape dough into marble-size balls; place 2 inches apart on greased cookie sheets. Dip bottom of a plastic drinking glass into cocoa powder; press to slightly flatten each ball.

Bake for 7–8 minutes, until just set. Remove at once from cookie sheet to paper towels; immediately flatten each cookie with a smooth spatula. Cool completely.

Meanwhile, soften gelatin in remaining 4 tablespoons of cold water in a small heatproof cup. Place cup in a pan of hot water until gelatin is melted and transparent. Cool completely.

Beat the shortening in a medium bowl with an electric mixer set on high speed until fluffy; add vanilla extract and powdered sugar a little at a time. Beat in gelatin mixture. Refrigerate for 30 minutes.

Shape the filling into 1-inch balls. Place between the two bottom sides of the cooled cookies and press gently until the filling has spread to edges of cookie.

MAKES 48 COOKIES.

GORGEOUS WHITE CHOCOLATE–DIPPED COCONUT BROWNIE BISCOTTI

If you decide to give these decked-out beauties as gifts, package them prettily, perhaps in decorative tins or in clear cellophane bags festooned with ribbons. For a bonus, include the recipe on the gift card.

- 1 (7-ounce) bag (about 2²/₃ cups) shredded coconut, divided
- 1 (19.5- to 19.8-ounce) package brownie mix
- 1 cup all-purpose flour
- ½ cup (1 stick) unsalted butter, melted and cooled
- 2 large eggs
- 1 recipe White Chocolate Dip (see page 361)

Preheat oven to 350°F. Position rack in center of oven. Line a cookie sheet with parchment paper.

Finely chop 1 cup of the coconut by hand or in food processor. Combine the chopped coconut, brownie mix, flour, melted butter, and eggs in a large bowl. Blend with an electric mixer set on low for 1–2 minutes until well blended, scraping down sides of bowl (mixture will be stiff).

Transfer dough to prepared cookie sheet. With floured hands, shape dough into two 14 x 3-inch rectangles, ¾-inch thick, spacing them 4–5 inches apart on sheet. Mound the dough so it is slightly higher in the center than at the edges. Place cookie sheet in oven.

Bake for 30–35 minutes, until firm to touch; remove from oven and cool on sheet for 10 minutes (leave oven on).

With spatula, transfer logs to cutting board. Use a sharp knife to slice each rectangle into (approximately) ¾-inch slices on the diagonal. Return slices to sheet, cut sides down. Return sheet to oven. Bake biscotti for 10 minutes. Turn oven off and let biscotti remain in oven until crisp, 30–40 minutes longer. Remove from oven and transfer biscotti to a rack; cool completely.

Spread cookie sheet with wax paper. Prepare White Chocolate Dip. With a butter knife or small offset spatula, spread one side of each biscotti with melted chocolate. Immediately sprinkle with some of the remaining coconut, shaking off excess. Place on wax paper. Refrigerate for at least 1 hour to set chocolate.

Store in an airtight container or plastic zip-top bag for up to 3 weeks.

MAKES ABOUT 32 BISCOTTI.

GRANOLA MACAROONS

This is one of those cookies that delights children and adults with equal ease.

- 1 (16.5-ounce) roll refrigerated sugar cookie dough, softened
- 1 (7-ounce) package almond paste
- ¾ cup almond granola, coarsely crushed
- 2½ cups sweetened flake coconut
- 1 teaspoon almond extract
- ½ cup turbinado (raw) sugar

Preheat oven to 350°F. Spray cookie sheets with nonstick cooking spray.

Break up the cookie dough and almond paste into a large bowl. Mix well with fingers until blended. Mix in the crushed granola, coconut, and almond extract.

Place turbinado sugar in a shallow dish. Shape dough into 1¼-inch balls and roll in the sugar. Place 2 inches apart on prepared cookie sheets.

Bake for 12–14 minutes or until edges are light golden brown. Cool for 1 minute on cookie sheets. Use a spatula to transfer from cookie sheets to cooling racks. Cool completely.

MAKES 42 COOKIES.

GRAN'S CHOCOLATE-COVERED CHERRY COOKIES

No holiday could pass without my gran receiving multiple boxes of her favorite candy, chocolate-covered cherries, from her children, grandchildren, friends, and admirers. Given her equal affection for cookies, I know she would have loved this twist on her favorite bonbon. The union of rich chocolate fudge, cherries, and sugar cookie bottoms is irresistible.

- 1 (16.5-ounce) roll refrigerated sugar cookie dough, well chilled
- 28 maraschino cherries (about one (10-ounce) jar, with juice)
- 1 cup semisweet chocolate chips
- ½ cup canned sweetened condensed milk

Preheat oven to 350°F. Spray cookie sheets with nonstick cooking spray.

Cut cookie dough into 14 equal slices. Cut each slice in half. Roll each piece into a ball. Place balls 2 inches apart on prepared cookie sheets. Press down center of each ball with thumb or cork. Drain maraschino cherries, reserving juice. Place a cherry in the center of each cookie.

Combine the chocolate pieces and sweetened condensed milk in a small saucepan; cook and stir over low heat until chocolate is melted. Stir in 1 tablespoon of the reserved cherry juice. Spoon about 1 teaspoon of the frosting over each cherry, spreading to cover cherry. (Frosting may be thinned with additional cherry juice, if necessary.)

Bake for 9–12 minutes. Transfer cookies to wire racks and cool completely. Cover and store at room temperature for up to 2 days.

MAKES 28 COOKIES.

HAZELNUT ORANGE COOKIES

Madame Kanyuk, my sister's childhood piano teacher, was as talented in the kitchen as at the keyboard. When it came time for her annual piano recitals, her house was filled with the sweet harmony of both music and baked treats from her native Hungary. I will never forget her hazelnut-orange cookies, a crisp-chewy confection with a generous measure of orange zest and a hint of ground coriander. If you do not have coriander, substitute ground nutmeg or mace.

- 1 (16.5-ounce) roll refrigerated sugar cookie dough
- 1 cup chopped hazelnuts (or almonds)
- 2 teaspoons grated orange zest
- ½ teaspoon ground coriander (or nutmeg)
- ⅓ cup granulated sugar
- 1 recipe Orange Icing (see page 368), optional

Break up the cookie dough into large bowl; let stand for 10–15 minutes to soften. Add hazelnuts, orange zest, and coriander. Mix well with your fingers, the paddle attachment of an electric mixer, or a wooden spoon. Chill dough for 1 hour in refrigerator or 20–25 minutes in freezer.

Preheat oven to 350°F. Spray cookie sheets with nonstick cooking spray.

Place sugar in shallow dish. Roll dough into 1-inch balls; roll in sugar. Arrange balls 2 inches apart on prepared cookie sheets; flatten to ¼-inch thickness by pressing with the bottom of a plastic drinking glass, dipping the glass into granulated sugar for each round.

Bake for 10–12 minutes or until edges begin to brown. Transfer cookies to wire racks and cool completely.

If desired, drizzle with Orange Icing.

MAKES ABOUT 28 COOKIES.

ITALIAN MELTAWAYS

These are elegant, refined cookies with a slightly fruity essence thanks to the extra virgin olive oil.

- ½ cup extra virgin olive oil
- 1¼ cups quick-cooking oats
- 1 (18.25-ounce) package white cake mix
- 2 large eggs
- 1 teaspoon vanilla
- ½ cup finely chopped, lightly toasted walnuts
- 1 cup powdered sugar, sifted

Preheat oven to 350°F.

Combine the olive oil and oats in a medium bowl. Let stand 5 minutes. Stir in the cake mix, eggs, and vanilla until well blended. Fold in the nuts.

Form dough into 1-inch balls and place about 2 inches apart on ungreased cookie sheets.

Bake for 8–10 minutes or until just set. Cool on cookie sheets for 1 minute. Remove cookies to cooling rack. Roll in powdered sugar while still slightly warm.

MAKES 32 COOKIES.

JAM THUMBPRINTS

It just doesn't get much easier than this. Yet the results are heartwarming, delectable, and endlessly variable.

- 1 (16.5-ounce) roll refrigerated sugar cookie dough, softened
- 1/3 cup all-purpose flour
- 1 teaspoon vanilla extract
- 1/4 cup raspberry, strawberry or apricot jam or preserves

Preheat oven to 350°.

Break up the cookie dough into a large bowl. Sprinkle the flour and vanilla over dough. Mix well with fingers until blended. Roll dough into 1-inch balls.

Place balls 2 inches apart on ungreased cookie sheets. Press thumb into tops to make deep depression. Fill each depression with about 1/4 teaspoon jam.

Bake for 11–13 minutes or until light golden brown. Cool on cookie sheets for 2 minutes. Transfer to cooling racks and cool completely.

MAKES 28 COOKIES.

JUMBO CHOCOLATE-CHIP PEANUT BUTTER SANDWICH COOKIES

If you're making these sandwich cookies ahead of time, store the filling and cookies separately until you're ready to eat. Once assembled, the cookies should be eaten immediately (never a problem!), or you can store them in a single layer, tightly covered in refrigerator for 3–4 hours (they become softer the longer they sit).

- 1 (8-ounce) package cream cheese, softened
- 1/2 cup creamy peanut butter
- 1 cup powdered sugar
- 2 teaspoons vanilla extract
- 1 (16.5-ounce) roll refrigerated chocolate chip cookie dough
- 1 1/4 cups honey roasted peanuts, coarsely chopped

Beat the cream cheese, peanut butter, powdered sugar, and vanilla in a large bowl with an electric mixer on medium speed until smooth. Cover and refrigerate for at least 1 hour while baking and cooling cookies.

Preheat oven to 350°F. Cut cookie dough into 16 equal slices. Place slices 2 inches apart on ungreased cookie sheets.

Bake for 11–15 minutes until golden at edges and set at centers. Transfer to cooling racks and cool completely.

Spread 1/3 cup cream cheese mixture on bottom of a cooled cookie. Top with another cookie, bottom side down. Press cookies together slightly so filling comes just past edges of cookies. Roll edge of cream cheese mixture in chopped peanuts. Repeat with remaining cookies, filling, and peanuts.

MAKES 8 BIG SANDWICH COOKIES.

JUNGLE CRUNCH CHOCOLATE-CHIP COOKIES

The lumpy-bumpy appearance of these cookies comes courtesy of a heaping handful of chopped banana chips, cashews, toffee baking bits, and chocolate chips. They are guaranteed pleasers.

- 1 (16.5-ounce) roll refrigerated chocolate-chip cookie dough
- ½ cup coarsely chopped banana chips
- ½ cup coarsely chopped lightly salted roasted cashews (or peanuts)
- 1 cup toffee baking bits

Break up the cookie dough into large bowl; let stand for 10–15 minutes to soften. Add the banana chips and cashews; mix well with your fingers or a wooden spoon. Chill dough for 1 hour in refrigerator or 20–25 minutes in freezer.

Preheat oven to 350°F. Spray cookie sheets with nonstick cooking spray.

Place the toffee bits in a small bowl. Roll dough into 1-inch balls. Roll each ball in toffee bits, pressing gently so that toffee adheres to dough. Place cookies on prepared cookie sheets.

Bake for 10–12 minutes or until just golden at edges. Cool for 2 minutes on cookie sheets. Transfer to wire racks and cool completely.

MAKES 30 COOKIES.

LEMON COCONUT THUMBPRINTS

The combination of citrus and toasted coconut coalesce to create this scrumptious summer cookie, perfect for pairing with long, cold glasses of iced tea or lemonade.

- 1 (16.5-ounce) roll refrigerated sugar cookie dough, well chilled
- ¾ cup shredded coconut
- ½ cup lemon curd (or canned lemon pie filling)
- ½ cup white chocolate chips
- 1 teaspoon vegetable shortening

Preheat oven to 350°F. Spray cookie sheets with nonstick cooking spray.

Cut cookie dough into 12 equal slices. Cut each slice in half. Roll each piece into a ball.

Place coconut into shallow dish; roll balls in coconut, pressing gently so that coconut adheres. Place balls 2 inches apart on cookie sheets.

Bake for 10–12 minutes or until coconut turns light golden. Remove cookies from oven and immediately make a depression in each cookie with thumb or cork; fill each with spoonful of lemon curd or pie filling. Transfer to wire racks and cool completely.

Meanwhile, melt the white chocolate chips with shortening in a small saucepan set over low heat, stirring until melted and smooth. Drizzle over cookies.

MAKES 24 COOKIES.

LEMON CURD TASSIES

A double dose of lemon—both zest in the cookie and a lemon curd filling—means these are must-makes on hot, sultry summer days. For a triple lemon experience, serve with tall glasses of ice-cold lemonade.

- ¼ cup (½ stick) butter
- 1 (10-ounce) package miniature marshmallows
- 1¼ cups jarred lemon curd
- 1 teaspoon vanilla extract
- 1 tablespoon grated lemon zest
- 7 cups crisp rice cereal

Lightly spray the cups of two 12-count muffin tins; set aside.

Melt the butter in a medium saucepan set over low heat. Add the marshmallows; mix to coat. Continue to cook and stir until the marshmallows are completely melted and the mixture is well blended. Remove from heat and stir in the vanilla and lemon zest. Mix in the cereal, stirring to coat well.

Press cereal mixture firmly into prepared muffin tins with a wooden spoon; gently press an indentation into each tassie using the back of a rounded tablespoon. Cool for at least 30 minutes; remove from pans. Fill each indentation with lemon curd.

Refrigerate for 30 minutes. Store in the refrigerator.

MAKES 24 TASSIES.

LEMON-LIME SUGAR COOKIES

Bright with a double dose of citrus, these very easy, very citrus-y cookies are hands-down winners. Be sure to use real butter for optimal results.

- ¾ cup (1½ sticks) butter, softened
- 1 large egg
- 2 tablespoons grated lime zest
- 1 (18.25-ounce) package lemon cake mix with pudding in the mix
- 1 cup yellow cornmeal
- ½ cup coarse sugar or granulated sugar for rolling

Preheat oven to 375°F. Position oven rack in middle of oven. Set aside ungreased cookie sheets.

Beat the softened butter, egg, and lime zest in a large bowl on high speed for about 1 minute until blended. Add the cake mix gradually until blended and all dry ingredients are incorporated. Stir in the cornmeal by hand (dough will be stiff).

Place the sugar in a shallow dish. Shape dough into 1-inch balls; roll in sugar to coat. Position 2 inches apart on ungreased cookie sheets.

Bake for 9–10 minutes or until just set and bottoms are lightly browned. Remove from oven and let cool on cookie sheets for 1 minute. Transfer cookies to a wire rack with a metal spatula and cool completely.

MAKES 42 COOKIES.

LEMON-ROSEMARY OR LEMON-THYME SUGAR COOKIES: Prepare as directed above but replace the lime zest with 2 tablespoons lemon zest and add 1 tablespoon chopped fresh rosemary or thyme leaves to the dough.

DOUBLE-LIME SUGAR COOKIES: Prepare as directed above but use vanilla cake mix. Prepare Lime Icing (see page 368) and drizzle over cooled cookies.

ORANGE SUGAR COOKIES: Prepare as directed above but use orange flavor or yellow cake mix and 2 tablespoons grated orange zest in place of the lime zest.

VANILLA SUGAR COOKIES: Prepare as directed above but use vanilla cake mix and 2 teaspoons vanilla extract in place of the lime zest.

LEMON PISTACHIO BISCOTTI

- 1 (16.5-ounce) roll refrigerated sugar cookie dough
- 1/3 cup all-purpose flour
- 1¼ cups shelled, roasted pistachios
- 2 tablespoons grated lemon zest
- 1 teaspoon vanilla extract
- 1 recipe Lemon Icing (see page 368), optional

Preheat oven to 350°F. Lightly spray a cookie sheet with nonstick cooking spray.

Break up the cookie dough into large bowl; let stand for 10–15 minutes to soften. Add flour, pistachios, lemon zest, and vanilla extract to the cookie dough; mix well with your fingers, the paddle attachment of an electric stand mixer, or a wooden spoon.

Divide dough into two equal halves. On the cookie sheet, shape each dough half into a 12 x 2-inch rectangle, ¾-inch high, spacing the dough halves about 3 inches apart.

Bake for 26–28 minutes or until the logs are deep golden brown and spring back in the center when touched. Remove sheet from oven; keep oven on.

Using two pancake turners, lift logs, one at a time, from the cookie sheet to a cutting board. Using a sharp knife, cut one of the logs into ¾-inch-wide slices. Note: for longer biscotti, cut at a deep diagonal; for shorter biscotti, cut log crosswise. Repeat with second log. Place slices on the same cookie sheet (do not worry about the spacing).

Bake slices for 5 minutes; remove from oven and turn over all of the slices. Return cookie sheet to oven and bake for 5 minutes longer. Remove sheet from oven and immediately transfer biscotti to a wire rack; cool completely. If desired, drizzle one side of each biscotti with Lemon Icing.

MAKES 28 BISCOTTI.

LEMON POPPYSEED PETITES

Poppyseeds are more than decoration in these petite morsels—they have a subtle, slightly earthy, slightly spicy flavor, not to mention a delicate crunch. Their flavor finds perfect complement here with the rich sugar cookie dough and familiar tang of lemon zest.

- 1 (16.5-ounce) roll refrigerated sugar cookie dough
- 1½ tablespoons poppyseeds
- 2 teaspoons grated lemon zest
- 1 cup sifted powdered sugar

Break up the cookie dough into a large bowl; let stand for 10–15 minutes to soften. Add the poppyseeds and lemon zest; mix well with your fingers or a wooden spoon. Chill dough for 1 hour in refrigerator or 20–25 minutes in freezer.

Preheat oven to 350°F. Spray cookie sheets with nonstick cooking spray. Shape dough into 1-inch balls; place 2 inches apart on prepared cookie sheets.

Bake for 10–12 minutes or until golden brown. Cool for 2 minutes on cookie sheets; remove from cookie sheets.

Place powdered sugar in a plastic bag. transfer several cookies at a time to the bag while still warm. Gently shake until coated. Transfer cookies to a wire rack to cool. When completely cooled, gently shake cookies again in powdered sugar.

MAKES 28 COOKIES.

LEMON TASSIES

These dainty treats are fabulous for a wedding or baby shower. If summer berries are in season, top with a raspberry or blackberry and a fresh mint sprig.

- 1 (16.5-ounce) package refrigerated sugar cookie dough, well chilled
- 1 cup jarred lemon curd (or canned lemon pie filling)

Preheat oven to 350°F. Place paper liners in 28 miniature muffin cups.

Cut cookie dough in quarters lengthwise. Cut each quarter into 7 pieces. Place 1 piece into each prepared muffin cup and press down center to form a small well.

Bake for 7–11 minutes or until edges are deep golden (dough will appear slightly puffed). Remove to wire racks and cool completely.

Remove tart shells in their paper cups from tin. Fill each tart shell with spoonful of lemon curd. Chill at least 30 minutes or until ready to serve.

MAKES 28 TASSIES.

Baker's Note

For a pretty presentation, consider drizzling with White Chocolate Drizzle on page 361.

LEMONY HIDDEN KISS COOKIES

When I'm feeling self-indulgent on trips home to California, I stop in at a small bakery just blocks from my parents' home. There I pick up a double mocha (with extra whipped cream) and one of their specialties, a lemon cookie drizzled with milk chocolate. This is my own sweet version. The milk chocolate is both snuggled inside the dough and drizzled on top.

- 1 (16.5-ounce) roll refrigerated sugar cookie dough, well chilled
- 1 teaspoon lemon extract
- 20 milk chocolate candy kisses, unwrapped

■ ½ cup milk (or semisweet) chocolate chips

■ 1 tablespoon vegetable shortening

Preheat oven to 375°F. Spray cookie sheets with nonstick cooking spray.

Crumble cookie dough into large bowl. Sprinkle with lemon extract; mix well with fingers or wooden spoon.

Shape about 1 tablespoon dough around each candy kiss, covering completely. Roll in hands to form a ball; place on cookie sheets.

Bake for 8–11 minutes or until cookies are set and bottoms are light golden brown. Cool for 1 minute on cookie sheets. Transfer to wire racks and cool completely.

Combine chocolate chips and shortening in a small saucepan; cook, stirring, over low heat until melted and smooth. Drizzle over cooled cookies. Let stand until set. Store in tightly covered container.

MAKES 20 COOKIES.

Baker's Note

You can use any other flavor of extract—orange, maple, mint, rum, brandy—in place of the lemon, or leave it out altogether.

LOLLIPOP COOKIES

Looking for a great birthday party activity for a group of little girls? Make several batches of these cookies, set out the icing, candies, and sprinkles, and you'll have a great party all wrapped up. For an even fancier, festive option, buy extra-long wooden sticks (found in craft stores), place the finished cookies in small vases, and tie with ribbon.

■ 1 (18.25-ounce) package vanilla cake mix

■ ⅓ cup vegetable oil

■ 2 large eggs

■ 24 wooden sticks with rounded ends

■ 1 recipe Cookie Decorating Icing (see page 365)

Assorted decorating candies and nonpareils

Preheat oven to 375°F. Position oven rack in middle of oven. Set aside an ungreased cookie sheet.

Place the cake mix, oil, and eggs in a large bowl. Blend with an electric mixer set on low speed for 1–2 minutes, until mixture is blended and all dry ingredients are moistened.

Drop dough by heaping, rounded tablespoonfuls, 3 inches apart, onto cookie sheet. Insert wooden stick in edge of dough until tip is in center.

Bake for 8–11 minutes or until puffed and almost no indentation remains when touched. Cool for 1 minute on cookie sheet. Transfer to wire rack and cool completely.

Frost and decorate as desired.

MAKES 24 COOKIE POPS.

MADELEINES

Part cake, part cookie, madeleines get their shell shape from madeleine pans, which come in both large and small sizes. Look for pans with a nonstick finish for easy removal. If you want to gild the lily, dip the cooled madeleines in melted chocolate.

■ 1 (16.5-ounce) roll refrigerated sugar cookie dough

■ 1 (8-ounce) package cream cheese, cut into small bits

- 1 large egg
- 2 tablespoons grated lemon zest
- 1 teaspoon vanilla extract
- 1 cup sifted powdered sugar

Preheat oven to 350°F. Position oven rack to highest position in oven. Spray madeleine pan with nonstick cooking spray.

Break up the cookie dough into large bowl; add cream cheese and let stand for 10–15 minutes to soften. Add the eggs, lemon zest, and vanilla. Mix with an electric mixer until well blended and smooth.

Spoon the batter into prepared madeleine molds, filling about two-thirds full.

Bake on highest oven rack for 6–7 minutes for small madeleine molds, 8–9 minutes for large madeleine molds, or until the edges are golden and centers are puffed. Turn the madeleines out onto wire racks and cool completely. Sift powdered sugar over the cooled madeleines.

MAKES 24 LARGE OR 38 SMALL MADELEINES.

Baker's Note

If you decide to dip the madeleines in melted chocolate (see page 361), dip the plain side (as opposed to the shell side) for a pretty finish.

MAPLE CINNAMON SPIRALS

It's worth splurging on real maple syrup for this recipe—nothing else tastes quite like it. Once you experience the winning combination of maple and cinnamon in these pretty cookies, you will want to add them to your list of favorites.

- 1 (16.5-ounce) roll refrigerated sugar cookie dough, well chilled
- ¼ cup granulated sugar
- 2 tablespoons ground cinnamon
- ¼ cup pure maple syrup

Using a lightly floured rolling pin on a lightly floured surface, roll dough into a 16 x 8-inch rectangle. combine the sugar and cinnamon in a small dish; sprinkle evenly over rolled dough.

Starting with the 16-inch side, roll up dough jellyroll fashion; cut in half to form two 8-inch rolls. Tightly wrap each roll in plastic wrap or foil; freeze for 2 hours until firm.

Preheat oven to 350°F. Spray cookie sheets with nonstick cooking spray.

Using a sharp knife, cut each dough log in half crosswise; cut each piece into 8 even slices. Place slices 2 inches apart on prepared sheets; brush with maple syrup.

Bake for 10–13 minutes or until light golden brown and just set at centers. Immediately transfer cookies to wire cooling racks and cool completely.

MAKES 32 COOKIES.

MAPLE SUGAR COOKIES

Maple has been a favorite American flavoring since Native Americans first taught the early colonists how to tap trees for their sap.

- 1 (18.25-ounce) package yellow cake mix
- ¼ cup packed light brown sugar

- ¼ teaspoon baking soda
- 2 tablespoons butter, melted
- 1 large egg yolk
- ¼ cup pure maple syrup
- 2 teaspoons maple-flavored extract
- ⅔ cup turbinado (or "raw") sugar

Place half of the cake mix in a large bowl along with the brown sugar, baking soda, melted butter, egg yolk, maple syrup, and maple extract. Blend for 1–2 minutes with an electric mixer set on medium speed until well combined and all dry ingredients are moistened (dough will be stiff). Stir in remaining cake mix. Chill dough for 1 hour.

Preheat oven to 375°F. Position oven rack in middle of oven. Spray cookie sheets with non-stick cooking spray.

Place the turbinado sugar in shallow dish. Form dough into 1-inch balls. Roll each ball in sugar to coat. Place balls 2 inches apart on prepared cookie sheets. Flatten slightly.

Bake for 9–10 minutes or until surface cracks and cookies are firm. Transfer to wire racks and cool completely.

MAKES ABOUT 36 COOKIES.

MAPLE WALNUT CRISPS

- 1 (18.25-ounce) package yellow cake mix
- ⅓ cup vegetable shortening
- ⅓ cup maple syrup
- 1 large egg
- 1 cup chopped walnuts
- 1½ tablespoons sugar
- 3 tablespoons finely chopped walnuts

- 1 large egg white, beaten

Preheat oven to 375°F. Spray cookie sheets with nonstick cooking spray.

Combine the cake mix and shortening in a medium bowl with an electric mixer at medium speed until a coarse meal forms. Add the syrup, egg, and the 1 cup of chopped walnuts, mixing on low, until a smooth dough forms.

Shape dough into 1-inch balls. Place balls 2 inches apart on prepared cookie sheets. Spray bottom of cup with nonstick cooking spray, then use to flatten dough to 2 inches in diameter.

Combine the sugar and 3 tablespoons finely chopped walnuts in a small bowl. Brush tops of cookies with egg white, then sprinkle with walnut mixture.

Bake for 7–9 minutes or until edges are light golden brown. Cool for 1 minute. Remove to cooling rack.

MAKES 42 COOKIES.

MARBLED CHOCOLATE AND VANILLA COOKIES

With a gorgeous presentation and the rich, classic flavor combination of chocolate and vanilla, these cookies are showstoppers.

- 1 (18.25-ounce) package white cake mix
- ⅔ cup vegetable oil, divided
- 8 tablespoons (1 stick) butter, melted, divided
- 2 large eggs
- 3 teaspoons vanilla extract, divided
- 1 (18.25-ounce) package devil's food cake mix

■ 1½ cups toasted pecans (or walnuts), divided

Preheat oven to 400°. Position oven rack in middle of oven. Set aside an ungreased cookie sheet.

Place half of the white cake mix in a large bowl along with ⅓ cup oil, 4 tablespoons melted butter, 1 egg, and 1 teaspoon vanilla. Beat with an electric mixer set on medium speed for 1–2 minutes, until blended. Stir in the remaining cake mix and ¾ cup of the nuts.

Place half of the devil's food cake mix in a second large bowl, along with the remaining ⅓ cup oil, remaining 4 tablespoons melted butter, remaining egg, and remaining 2 teaspoons vanilla extract. Blend with an electric mixer set on medium speed for 1–2 minutes, until blended. Stir in the remaining cake mix and ¾ cup nuts.

Scoop 1 teaspoon of vanilla dough into ball. Scoop 1 teaspoon of chocolate dough into ball. Gently press dough balls together, then roll gently to form one ball. Place balls 2 inches apart on the ungreased cookie sheet.

Bake for 10 minutes or just until cookies begin to brown (be careful not to overbake). Cool cookies on cookie sheets for 2 minutes. Transfer cookies to cooling racks and cool completely. Repeat with remaining chocolate and vanilla dough.

MAKES 72 COOKIES.

Variations:
MOCHA CHIP MARBLE COOKIES:
Prepare as directed above but dissolve 1 tablespoon instant espresso or coffee powder in the 1 teaspoon vanilla before adding to the white cake mix and substitute 1½ cups miniature semisweet chocolate chips for the chopped nuts.

LEMON MACADAMIA MARBLE COOKIES:
Prepare as directed above but use lemon cake mix in place of devil's food cake mix, substitute 3 teaspoons grated lemon zest for the vanilla extract, and use roasted, lightly salted chopped macadamia nuts instead of walnuts or pecans.

MEXICAN WEDDING CAKES

Baked to golden perfection, then dunked in powdered sugar, these melt-in-your-mouth treats won't last more than a few minutes when offered to a crowd. No one will believe they began with a roll of cookie dough.

■ 1 (16.5-ounce) roll refrigerated sugar cookie dough
■ ½ cup all-purpose flour
■ ¾ cup finely chopped pecans or walnuts
■ ½ teaspoon vanilla extract
■ 1 cup powdered sugar

Break up the cookie dough into a large bowl. Sprinkle the flour, nuts, and vanilla over dough. Mix well with fingers until blended. Chill for 20 minutes.

Preheat oven to 350°. Shape dough into 1-inch balls. Place 1 inch apart on ungreased cookie sheets.

Bake for 11–14 minutes or until just set but not brown. Remove from cookie sheets. Cool slightly on cooling rack.

Roll warm cookies in powdered sugar; cool on cooling rack. Roll in powdered sugar again.

MAKES 50 COOKIES.

MILK CHOCOLATE CHERRY BISCOTTI

■ 1 (16.5-ounce) roll refrigerated sugar cookie dough
■ 1/3 cup all-purpose flour
■ 2/3 cup coarsely chopped dried cherries (or dried cranberries)
■ 2/3 cup milk chocolate chips
■ 1 teaspoon pure almond extract

Preheat oven to 350°F. Lightly spray a cookie sheet with nonstick cooking spray.

Break up the cookie dough into large bowl; let stand for 10–15 minutes to soften. Add the flour, dried fruit, milk chocolate chips, and almond extract to the cookie dough; mix well with your fingers, the paddle attachment of an electric stand mixer, or a wooden spoon.

Divide dough into two equal halves. On the cookie sheet, shape each dough half into a 12 x 2-inch, rectangle, 3/4-inch high, spacing the dough halves about 3 inches apart.

Bake for 26–28 minutes or until the logs are deep golden brown and spring back in the center when touched. Remove sheet from oven; keep oven on.

Using two pancake turners, lift logs, one at a time, from the cookie sheet to a cutting board. Using a sharp knife, cut one of the logs into 3/4-inch-wide slices. Note: for longer biscotti, cut at a deep diagonal; for shorter biscotti, cut log crosswise. Repeat with second log. Place slices on the same cookie sheet (do not worry about the spacing).

Bake for slices 5 minutes; remove from oven and turn over all of the slices. Return cookie sheet to oven and bake for 5 minutes longer. Remove sheet from oven and immediately transfer biscotti to a wire rack; cool completely.

MAKES 28 BISCOTTI.

MINT CHOCOLATE-CHIP MADELEINES

Peppermint gives these tender, chocolate-dotted madeleines a cool accent of refreshing flavor. Be sure to use miniature chocolate chips in the recipe—regular-size chips will sink in the batter.

■ Vegetable shortening and all-purpose flour to grease pans.
■ 1 (18.25-ounce) package vanilla cake mix
■ 1/2 cup (1 stick) butter, melted
■ 1/4 cup milk
■ 4 large eggs, separated
■ 1 teaspoon peppermint extract
■ 1 cup miniature semisweet chocolate chips
■ 2–3 tablespoons powdered sugar

Preheat oven to 350°F. Position oven rack in middle of oven. Grease molds of large madeleine pan (3 x 1 1/4-inch shell molds) with vegetable shortening. Sprinkle with flour to coat pan, shaking off excess.

Place the cake mix, melted butter, milk, egg yolks, and peppermint extract in a large bowl. Blend for 1–2 minutes with an electric mixer set on medium speed until well blended and smooth; stir in miniature chocolate chips. Set aside momentarily. Clean beaters.

Beat the egg whites in a large mixing bowl with electric mixer set on high speed until soft peaks form. Stir 1/4 of the beaten egg whites into the cake batter to lighten it; fold remaining whites into batter.

Spoon 1 heaping tablespoonful of batter into each indentation in pan (do not overfill; batter will spread as it bakes).

Bake until puffed and set at center, 8–10 minutes. Cool in pan for 5 minutes; gently remove madeleines to wire rack. Repeat process, greasing and flouring pan before each batch. Sift powdered sugar over cooled cookies.

MAKES ABOUT 36 MADELEINES.

Variations:

DOUBLE CHOCOLATE MINT MADELEINES: Prepare as directed above but use chocolate cake mix in place of the vanilla cake mix.

MOCHA CHIP MADELEINES: Prepare as directed above but use chocolate cake mix in place of the vanilla cake mix. Eliminate the peppermint extract and in its place use 2½ teaspoons instant espresso or coffee powder that has been dissolved in 1½ teaspoons vanilla extract.

MOCHA-HAZELNUT SANDWICH COOKIES

An elegant, contemporary cookie with European flair thanks to the chocolate-hazelnut spread. Look for the spread in one of two places in the supermarket: in the international foods section or the aisle where peanut butter can be found.

- 2 teaspoons instant coffee or espresso powder
- 2 teaspoons vanilla extract
- 1 (18.25-ounce) package German chocolate cake mix
- ⅓ cup vegetable oil
- 2 large eggs
- ¾ cup chocolate-hazelnut spread (e.g., Nutella)

Preheat oven to 350°F. Position oven rack in middle of oven. Spray cookie sheets with nonstick cooking spray.

Dissolve the espresso powder in the vanilla extract in a large bowl. Add half of the cake mix along with the oil and eggs. Blend with an electric mixer set on medium-high speed for 1–2 minutes, until smooth. Stir in remaining cake mix.

Drop dough by teaspoonfuls on prepared cookie sheets.

Bake for 8–10 minutes or until set at edges and just barely set at center when lightly touched and cookies have a cracked appearance (cookies will be flat and round). Cool for 1 minute on cookie sheets. Transfer to wire racks with metal spatula and cool completely.

Spread bottom half of one cookie with a teaspoon of chocolate-hazelnut spread; sandwich with a second cookie. Repeat with remaining cookies.

MAKES ABOUT 36 SANDWICH COOKIES.

MOCHA MELTAWAYS

No one will ever guess that these sophisticated, melt-in-your-mouth morsels begin with a roll of sugar cookie dough.

- 1 (16.5-ounce) roll refrigerated sugar cookie dough, softened
- ¼ cup unsweetened baking cocoa (not Dutch process)
- 1 tablespoon instant espresso powder

- 1 cup very finely chopped walnuts or pecans
- 42 milk chocolate candy pieces, unwrapped
- 1 cup powdered sugar, sifted

Break up the cookie dough into a large bowl. Sprinkle cocoa powder, espresso powder, and pecans over dough. Mix well with fingers until blended. Chill 20 minutes.

Preheat oven to 375°F. Shape dough into forty-two 1-inch balls. Wrap each around 1 piece of milk chocolate candy. Place cookies 2 inches apart on ungreased cookie sheets.

Bake for 8–10 minutes or until set. Immediately transfer from cookie sheets to wire racks. Cool for 5 minutes.

Place the powdered sugar in a shallow dish. Roll the warm cookies in the sugar to coat. Cool completely, about 15 minutes. Re-roll cookies in powdered sugar.

MAKES 42 COOKIES.

MOCHA WHITE CHOCOLATE CHUNK BISCOTTI

- 1 (16.5-ounce) roll refrigerated sugar cookie dough
- 2½ teaspoons instant espresso (or coffee) powder
- 1 teaspoon vanilla extract
- 1/3 cup all-purpose flour
- 1½ tablespoons unsweetened cocoa powder
- 1 (6-ounce) white chocolate baking bar, chopped into chunks

Preheat oven to 350°F. Lightly spray a cookie sheet with nonstick cooking spray.

Break up the cookie dough into large bowl; let stand for 10–15 minutes to soften. Combine espresso powder and vanilla in a small cup. Add vanilla mixture, flour, cocoa powder, and white chocolate chunks to the cookie dough; mix well with your fingers, the paddle attachment of an electric stand mixer, or a wooden spoon.

Divide dough into two equal halves. On the cookie sheet, shape each dough half into a 12 x 2-inch rectangle, ¾-inch high, spacing the dough halves about 3 inches apart.

Bake for 26–28 minutes until the logs are deep golden brown and spring back in the center when touched. Remove sheet from oven; keep oven on.

Using two pancake turners, lift logs, one at a time, from the cookie sheet to a cutting board. Using a sharp knife, cut one of the logs into ¾-inch-wide slices. Note: for longer biscotti, cut at a deep diagonal; for shorter biscotti, cut log crosswise. Repeat with second log. Place slices on the same cookie sheet; do not worry about the spacing.

Bake slices for 5 minutes; remove from oven and turn over all of the slices. Return cookie sheet to oven and bake for 5 minutes longer. Remove sheet from oven and immediately transfer biscotti to a wire rack; cool completely.

MAKES 28 BISCOTTI.

Baker's Note

For half-batches of biscotti, follow all of the directions above but halve the ingredients. Make one biscotti log instead of two and proceed as directed above. Or make a full batch and wrap and freeze the second half of dough for a future batch of biscotti or cookies.

MOLASSES SPICE COOKIES

Here is a homespun cookie that tastes like gingerbread—perfect for feeling cozy on cold days and nights.

- 1 (18.25-ounce) package spice cake mix
- ¾ teaspoon ground cinnamon
- ¾ teaspoon ground ginger
- ⅛ teaspoon ground cloves
- ¼ teaspoon baking soda
- 2 tablespoons vegetable oil
- 1 large egg yolk
- ¼ cup dark molasses
- 2 teaspoons vanilla extract
- ⅔ cup granulated sugar

Place half of the cake mix along with the cinnamon, ginger, cloves, baking soda, oil, egg yolk, molasses, and vanilla extract in a large bowl. Blend with an electric mixer set on medium-high speed for 1–2 minutes, until smooth. Stir in remaining cake mix. Chill dough for 1 hour.

Preheat oven to 375°F. Position oven rack in middle of oven. Spray cookie sheets with non-stick cooking spray.

Place sugar in shallow dish. Roll dough into 1-inch balls; roll in sugar to coat. Place balls 2 inches apart on prepared cookie sheets. Flatten slightly with your palm or a spatula.

Bake for 9–10 minutes or until surface cracks and cookies are firm. Transfer to wire racks and cool completely.

MAKES ABOUT 36 COOKIES.

NUTTY CHOCOLATE CARAMEL BULL'S-EYES

Not sure which cookie to make for the kids? This is it. They will clamor for this yummy cookie, especially if you get them involved in unwrapping and pressing the chocolate-covered caramel "bull's-eyes" into the center of each treat. And for the record, grown-up "kids" love these cookies, too. Do be sure, however, to cool the cookies completely before serving (the hot caramel may burn tender mouths).

- 1 (19.5- to 19.8-ounce) package brownie mix
- ⅓ cup unsweetened cocoa powder, sifted
- ¼ cup (½ stick) unsalted butter, melted
- 2 teaspoons vanilla extract
- 2 large eggs
- 1 cup finely chopped nuts (e.g., pecans, peanuts, walnuts, almonds, or macadamia nuts)
- 54 chocolate-covered caramel candies (e.g., Rolos), unwrapped

Combine the brownie mix, sifted cocoa powder, melted butter, vanilla, and eggs in a medium mixing bowl with a wooden spoon until all dry ingredients are moistened and dough is well blended. Cover bowl with plastic wrap and refrigerate dough for at least 1 hour.

Preheat oven to 350°F. Spray cookie sheets with nonstick cooking spray.

Place chopped nuts into a shallow dish. Shape dough into 1-inch balls; roll each ball in nuts to coat evenly. Place balls 2 inches apart on prepared cookie sheets.

Bake for 9–11 minutes, until firm to the touch at the edges. Remove from oven and immediately press one candy into center of each cookie. Return to oven for 1 minute to melt candy slightly; remove from oven. Cool for 1 minute on cookie sheets. Transfer to wire racks with metal spatula and cool completely.

MAKES ABOUT 54 COOKIES.

NUTTY COFFEE-TOFFEE BISCOTTI

These nut-studded biscotti, enriched further with both coffee and toffee, stand strong on their own but are also quite fine alongside your favorite coffee or espresso drink.

- 1 (18.25-ounce) package vanilla cake mix
- 1 cup all-purpose flour
- 1 tablespoon instant coffee or espresso powder
- ½ cup (1 stick) butter, melted and cooled
- 2 large eggs
- ½ teaspoon almond extract
- 1 cup English toffee baking bits
- 1½ cups very coarsely chopped almonds

Preheat oven to 350°F. Position rack in center of oven. Spray cookie sheet with nonstick cooking spray.

Place the cake mix, flour, coffee powder, melted butter, eggs, almond extract, toffee bits, and almonds in a large mixing bowl. Blend with an electric mixer set on low speed for 2–3 minutes until well-blended, scraping down sides of bowl (dough will be very stiff).

Transfer dough to prepared cookie sheet. With floured hands, shape dough into two 14 x 3-inch rectangles, each ¾-inch thick, spacing them 4–5 inches apart on sheet. Mound the dough so it is slightly higher in the middle than at the edges.

Bake for 30–35 minutes or until firm to touch; remove from oven (leave oven on) and cool on sheet for 10 minutes.

Cutting on the cookie sheet, use a sharp knife to slice each rectangle into ¾-inch slices on the diagonal. Carefully turn these slices onto their sides. Return cookie sheet to oven. Bake biscotti for 10 minutes. Turn oven off and let biscotti remain in oven until crisp, 30–40 minutes longer. Remove from oven and transfer biscotti to a rack.

Cool completely.

MAKES ABOUT 32 BISCOTTI.

NUTTY JAM GEMS

A generous coating of nuts adds just the right amount of crunch to transform these bite-sized morsels into jam-filled treasures.

- 1 (16.5-ounce) roll refrigerated sugar cookie dough, well chilled
- 1 cup finely chopped almonds, pecans, walnuts, or peanuts
- ½ cup jam or preserves, any flavor

Preheat oven to 350°F. Spray cookie sheets with nonstick cooking spray.

Cut cookie dough into 12 equal slices. Cut each slice in half. Roll each piece into a ball. Place chopped nuts into a shallow dish; roll balls in the nuts, pressing gently so that the nuts adhere. Place balls 2 inches apart on prepared cookie sheets.

Bake for 10–12 minutes or until golden at

edges. Remove cookies from oven and immediately make a depression in each cookie with thumb or cork; fill each with a spoonful of preserves. Transfer to wire racks and cool completely.

MAKES 24 COOKIES.

OLD-FASHIONED BLACKBERRY THUMBPRINTS

Wheat germ lends an extra-toasty, old-fashioned flavor to these tea-wonderful cookies. Be sure to use toasted wheat germ as opposed to raw wheat germ—the latter will impart an unpleasant flavor to the dough. Blackberry is a delicious flavor contrast to the rich dough, but you can substitute the jam, preserves, or jelly of your choice.

- 1 (18.25-ounce) package yellow cake mix
- 1 cup toasted wheat germ (e.g., Kretschmer's)
- ¼ cup (½ stick) butter, softened
- 1 (3-ounce) package cream cheese, softened
- 2 large egg yolks
- 1 teaspoon vanilla extract
- ⅔ cup blackberry jam, stirred to loosen

Preheat oven to 350°F. Position oven rack to upper third of the oven. Set aside two ungreased cookie sheets.

Place the cake mix, wheat germ, softened butter, and cream cheese in a large bowl. Blend with an electric mixer set on low speed for 1–2 minutes, until mixture is blended and resembles fresh bread crumbs. Add the egg yolks and vanilla extract; beat on low speed for 1–2 minutes longer, until dough comes together into a ball.

Shape dough into 1-inch balls. Position 2 inches apart on cookie sheets. Push an indentation into the center of each cookie with your thumb, the back of a rounded ¼-teaspoon measuring spoon, or cork. Fill each indentation with ¼ teaspoon jam.

Bake for 8–10 minutes until firm to the touch at the edges and slightly puffed in appearance. Cool for 1 minute on cookie sheets. Transfer to wire racks with metal spatula and cool completely.

MAKES ABOUT 42 COOKIES.

Variation:

NUTTY THUMBPRINTS: Prepare as directed above but roll dough balls in 1 cup finely chopped nuts (e.g., walnuts, pecans, almonds, or peanuts). Use any variety of jam, preserves, or jelly.

ONE BIG PARTY COOKIE

You need only be a kid at heart to enjoy a party devoted to decorating—and eating—these giant cookies. Place some of the icings in ketchup-style squirt bottles (available at craft and kitchen stores) to allow for abstract impressionism or precision lettering and drawing. For a great potluck party, bake multiple giant cookies (one per guest), prepare the icings ahead of time and have guests bring their favorite candies for decorating.

- 1 (16.5-ounce) roll refrigerated sugar cookie dough (or chocolate-chip cookie dough), well chilled
- Assorted decorations: icing, frosting, small candies, melted chocolate (see the "Icings, Frostings, Fillings, and Extras" chapter)

Preheat oven to 350°F. Line a cookie sheet or a 12- or 14-inch pizza pan with aluminum foil; spray foil with nonstick cooking spray.

Slice dough into ¼-inch-thick slices. With floured fingers, press slices evenly into the prepared pan or cookie sheet, pressing edges together to form one large circle.

Bake for 15–18 minutes or until edges are golden and center is just barely set. Remove from oven and place pan on top of wire rack. Cool completely on pan.

Decorate with frosting and candies as desired.

MAKES 12 TO 14 SERVINGS.

ORANGE AND CARDAMOM COOKIE BALLS

Looking for a different kind of cookie? Try whipping up a batch of these elegant little cookies perfumed with cardamom and citrus.

- 2 cups finely crushed plain sugar cookies
- 1 cup sliced almonds, finely chopped
- ¼ cup light corn syrup
- 2 tablespoons thawed orange juice concentrate (undiluted)

- 2 teaspoons grated orange zest
- ½ teaspoon ground cardamom
- 2 tablespoons butter, melted
- 1⅔ cup sifted powdered sugar, divided use

Combine the crushed cookies, chopped almonds, corn syrup, orange juice concentrate, orange zest, cardamom, melted butter, and 1 cup of the powdered sugar in a large mixing bowl with a wooden spoon until well blended. Shape mixture into 1-inch balls.

Place remaining ⅔ cup powdered sugar in shallow dish or bowl. Roll balls in powdered sugar; loosely cover with plastic wrap. Let stand for 2 hours. If desired, roll again in additional powdered sugar. Keep refrigerated for up to 1 week or freeze up to 3 months.

MAKES ABOUT 36 COOKIE BALLS.

ORANGE AND HONEY CUTOUTS

Any honey will work here, but a light-flavored honey such as orange blossom or clover honey is especially delicious in these delicately flavored cutout cookies.

- 1 (18.25-ounce) package orange or yellow cake mix
- ¾ cup all-purpose flour
- 2 large eggs
- ⅓ cup butter, melted
- ⅓ cup honey
- 1 tablespoon grated orange zest
- 1 recipe Orange Icing (see page 368)
- 2–3 tablespoons orange-colored decorating sugar, optional

Place the cake mix, flour, eggs, melted butter, honey, and orange zest in a large bowl. Mix with a wooden spoon until well blended and all dry ingredients are moistened. Chill, covered, for at least 4 hours or overnight.

Preheat oven to 375°F and spray cookie sheets with nonstick cooking spray. Position racks to upper and lower positions of oven.

Sprinkle a work surface with a thin layer of flour. Set out rolling pin, 2-inch cookie cutters, metal spatula, and cooling racks.

Remove the dough from the refrigerator and divide into fourths. Place one-fourth of the dough on floured surface (cover and return remaining dough to refrigerator). Flour the rolling pin and roll dough to ¼-inch thickness. Flour cookie cutters and cut out shapes. Transfer dough to prepared cookie sheets with spatula. Re-roll any scraps, then repeat with remaining dough, rolling one fourth at a time.

Place one sheet on each oven rack. Bake for 4 minutes. Rotate the sheets (place the sheet from the bottom rack on the top rack and the sheet from the top rack on the bottom rack. This ensures even baking). Bake 2–3 minutes longer.

Remove from oven and let cookies rest on cookie sheets for 1 minute. Transfer with metal spatula to racks and cool completely. Prepare Orange Icing; decorate cookies with icing and sprinkle with colored sugar, if desired.

MAKES ABOUT 24 4-INCH COOKIES.

ORANGE POPPYSEED BISCOTTI

Poppyseeds—perhaps due to their polka-dotting potential—have a natural charm that always appeals. Here they grace a simple, orange-scented biscotti that comes together with ease. Like all biscotti, they are good candidates for a picnic since they travel well, and deliciously.

- 1 (18.25-ounce) package yellow cake mix
- 1 cup all-purpose flour
- ¼ cup poppyseeds
- 1½ tablespoons grated orange zest
- ½ cup (1 stick) butter, melted and cooled
- 2 large eggs
- 1 recipe Orange Icing (see page 368), optional

Preheat oven to 350°F. Position rack in center of oven. Spray cookie sheet with nonstick cooking spray.

Place cake mix, flour, poppyseeds, orange zest, melted butter, and eggs in a large mixing bowl. Blend with an electric mixer set on low speed for 2–3 minutes until well-blended, scraping down sides of bowl (dough will be very stiff).

Transfer dough to prepared cookie sheet. With floured hands, shape dough into two 14 x 3-inch rectangles, ¾-inch thick, spacing them 4–5 inches apart on sheet. Mound the dough so it is slightly higher in the middle than at the edges.

Bake for 30–35 minutes, until firm to touch; remove from oven (leave oven on) and cool on sheet for 10 minutes.

Cutting on the cookie sheet, use a sharp knife to slice each rectangle into (approximately) ¾-inch slices on the diagonal. Carefully turn these slices onto their sides.

Return cookie sheet to oven. Bake biscotti for 10 minutes. Turn oven off and let biscotti remain in oven until crisp, 30–40 minutes longer. Remove from oven and transfer biscotti to a rack. Cool completely.

If desired, prepare Orange Icing and with a

butter knife or small offset spatula spread over one side of each biscotti. Place on wax paper–lined cookie sheet and refrigerate for at least 30 minutes to set the icing. Store in an airtight container or plastic zip-top bag for 2–3 weeks.

MAKES ABOUT 32 BISCOTTI.

Variation:

LEMON POPPYSEED BISCOTTI: Prepare as directed above but substitute lemon zest for the orange zest and Lemon Icing (see page 368) for the Orange Icing.

PASTEL MINT MELTAWAYS

For a classy little tea party, an occasion is required—pretty linens, some fresh flowers, and, of course, an assortment of delicious and delicate cakes and cookies. These pastel mint dainties hit the mark.

- 1 (18.25-ounce) package white cake mix
- 1 (8-ounce) package cream cheese, softened
- ¼ cup (½ stick) butter, softened
- 1 large egg
- 1 teaspoon peppermint extract
- 1½ cups coarsely chopped pastel mints

Preheat oven to 375°F. Position oven rack in middle of oven. Spray cookie sheets with nonstick cooking spray.

Place the half of the cake mix, along with the softened cream cheese, butter, egg, and peppermint extract in a large bowl. Blend with an electric mixer set on medium speed for 1–2 minutes, until well blended and smooth. Stir in remaining cake mix and pastel mints until blended.

Shape dough into 1-inch balls. Place balls 2 inches apart on prepared cookie sheets.

Bake for 10–12 minutes or until set at edges and just barely set at center when lightly touched. Cool for 3–4 minutes on cookie sheets (cookies will firm as they cool). Transfer to wire racks with metal spatula and cool completely.

MAKES ABOUT 48 COOKIES.

PEANUT BUTTER CHOCOLATE KISS THUMBPRINTS

This favorite recipe makes enough to feed a small army of cookie monsters. Although delicious when eaten right away, these cookies taste even better if you have the time to make them a day ahead.

- 1 (18.25-ounce) package yellow cake mix
- 1 (14-ounce) can sweetened condensed milk
- 1 cup chunky-style peanut butter
- 1 large egg
- 2 teaspoons vanilla extract
- 1 (13-ounce) package chocolate "kiss" candies, unwrapped

Preheat oven to 350°F. Position oven rack in middle of oven. Set aside two ungreased cookie sheets.

Combine the cake mix, condensed milk, peanut butter, egg, and vanilla extract in a large mixing bowl with an electric mixer set on low speed for 1–2 minutes, until all dry ingredients are moistened and dough is well blended (dough will be very thick).

Shape dough into 1-inch balls and position 2 inches apart on cookie sheets.

Bake for 8–10 minutes, until firm to the touch at the edges and slightly puffed in appearance. Remove sheets from the oven and immediately push a kiss candy, flat side down, into the center of each cookie. Cool for 1 minute on cookie sheets. Transfer to wire racks with metal spatula and cool completely.

MAKES ABOUT 72 COOKIES.

Variation:

PEANUT BUTTER CARAMEL THUMBPRINTS:

Prepare as directed above but use chocolate-covered caramel candies (e.g., Rolos) in place of the kiss candies.

PEANUT BUTTER-FROSTED DOUBLE CHOCOLATE COOKIES

This is a cookie I know I can count on time and again, year in and year out. With the all-American combination of chocolate and peanut butter, the appeal is decidedly old-fashioned and downhome. It's just what you want from a cookie.

- 1 (19.5- to 19.8-ounce) package brownie mix

- ⅓ cup unsweetened cocoa powder, sifted
- ⅓ cup vegetable oil or melted butter
- 1 large egg
- 2 cups creamy peanut butter, divided
- 2 cups miniature semisweet chocolate chips, divided
- ¼ cup powdered sugar

Preheat oven to 350°F. Spray cookie sheets with nonstick cooking spray.

Combine the brownie mix, sifted cocoa powder, oil, egg, and 1 cup of the peanut butter in a large mixing bowl with a wooden spoon until well blended (mixture will be very stiff). Mix in 1 cup of the chocolate chips. Cover bowl with plastic wrap and chill for 1 hour.

Shape dough into 1-inch balls; place 2 inches apart on prepared cookie sheets. Flatten slightly with your palm or a spatula.

Bake for 9–11 minutes, until set at edges and just barely set at center when lightly touched. Cool for 1 minute on cookie sheets. Transfer to wire racks with metal spatula and cool completely.

Make the icing, while cookies cool, by combining the remaining peanut butter and the powdered sugar in a small mixing bowl. Mix by hand or with electric mixer until smooth. Spread cooled cookies with icing and sprinkle with remaining mini chocolate chips.

MAKES ABOUT 60 COOKIES.

PEANUT BUTTER HONEY BEES

Involve the entire family with this recipe. Even the youngest members of the family can help shape the bee bodies or stick in a few chow mein antennae.

- ◼ 1¾ cups creamy-style peanut butter
- ◼ ½ cup (1 stick) butter, softened
- ◼ ¼ cup honey
- ◼ 1¾ cups powdered sugar
- ◼ 3 cups graham cracker crumbs
- ◼ ½ cup semisweet real chocolate chips
- ◼ 1 teaspoon vegetable shortening
- ◼ ⅓ cup sliced almonds
- ◼ ½ cup chow mein noodles

Line two cookie sheets with wax paper.

Combine the peanut butter and butter in a large bowl. Beat with an electric mixer set on medium speed for 1–2 minutes scraping bowl often, until creamy. Add the honey and powdered sugar; reduce speed to low. Beat for 1–2 minutes until well mixed. Stir in the graham cracker crumbs with a wooden spoon.

Shape rounded tablespoonfuls of mixture into 1½-inch ovals. Place onto prepared cookie sheets.

Combine the chocolate chips and shortening in a small microwave-safe bowl. Microwave on high for 30 seconds; stir. Continue microwaving at 10-second intervals, stirring until mixture is melted and smooth. Cool for 2 minutes.

Place chocolate in small plastic zip-top bag. Cut very small tip from one corner of bag. For each honey bee, pipe 3 chocolate stripes crosswise on each oval; insert 2 almond slices in each side for wings. Insert 2 chow mein noodles in head for antenna; insert 1 short chow mein noodle for tail. Dot with chocolate for eyes, if desired.

Refrigerate until firm, about 30 minutes. Store in refrigerator in a tightly covered container.

MAKES ABOUT 50 "BEES."

Baker's Note

If dough is too soft, stir in additional powdered sugar, 1 tablespoon at a time, until desired consistency is reached.

PECAN SANDIES

- ◼ ¾ cup (1½ sticks) butter, softened
- ◼ 1 large egg
- ◼ 2 teaspoons vanilla extract
- ◼ 1 (18.25-ounce) package yellow cake mix with pudding in the mix
- ◼ 1¼ cups very finely chopped pecans
- ◼ ½ cup coarse sugar or granulated sugar for rolling

Preheat oven to 375°F. Position oven rack in middle of oven. Set aside ungreased cookie sheets.

Beat the butter, egg, and vanilla extract in a large bowl on high speed for about 1 minute, until blended. Add the cake mix gradually until blended and all dry ingredients are incorporated. Stir in the pecans by hand (dough will be stiff).

Place the sugar in a shallow dish. Shape the dough into 1-inch balls; roll in sugar to coat. Position balls 2 inches apart on ungreased cookie sheets.

Bake for 9–10 minutes or until just set and bottoms are lightly browned. Remove from oven and let cool on cookie sheets 1 minute. Transfer cookies to a wire rack with a metal spatula and cool completely.

MAKES 42 COOKIES.

ALMOND SANDIES: Prepare as directed above but substitute finely chopped almonds for the pecans and replace the vanilla extract with ¾ teaspoon almond extract.

PEANUT BRITTLE SANDIES: Prepare as directed above but substitute finely chopped peanuts for the pecans. Just before baking, roll dough balls in toffee baking bits (you will need 1 (10-ounce) package).

PEPPERY PECAN-CHOCOLATE CRACKLES

Take a walk on the spicy side with a kick of cayenne and a dash of cinnamon in these easy chocolate cookies. If you like, add a slick of Chocolate Ganache (see page 362) to cool things down.

- 1 (18.25-ounce) package devil's food cake mix
- ¼ cup unsweetened cocoa powder
- ⅛ teaspoon cayenne pepper
- 2 large eggs, lightly beaten
- 2 tablespoons butter, softened
- 2 tablespoons milk
- 1 cup finely chopped pecans

Preheat oven to 375°F. Position oven rack in middle of oven. Set aside ungreased cookie sheet.

Place half of the cake mix in a large bowl along with the cocoa powder, cayenne pepper, eggs, and softened butter. Beat with an electric mixer set on low speed for 1–2 minutes, until mixture is blended. Stir in remaining cake mix until all dry ingredients are blended (dough will be stiff).

Place milk in a shallow dish. Place pecans in another shallow dish. Roll dough into 1-inch balls. Dip balls in milk, then roll in nuts to coat. Place 2 inches apart on ungreased cookie sheet.

Bake for 8–9 minutes or until tops appear cracked. Cool for 1 minute on sheet. Transfer to a wire rack and let cool completely.

MAKES 30 COOKIES.

"PICK YOUR FILLING" COOKIE SANDWICHES

Satisfy your kid cravings with these yummy cookies, personalized with your favorite filling. Try filling them with any one of the thick frosting recipes—such as Irish Cream or Dark Chocolate Frosting—in the "Icings, Frostings, Fillings, and Extras" chapter. Or use any one of the "no-prep" fillings, such as peanut butter or canned cake frosting.

- 1 (16.5-ounce) roll refrigerated chocolate-chip cookie dough (or sugar cookie dough), well chilled
- 1 recipe frosting or filling of your choice, see the "Icings, Frostings, Fillings, and Extras" chapter

Preheat oven to 350°F. Spray cookie sheets with nonstick cooking spray.

With a sharp knife cut cookie dough crosswise into 4 equal pieces; cut each piece into 8 equal slices. Arrange slices 2 inches apart on cookie sheets.

Bake for 8–11 minutes or until golden at

edges and just set at the center. Transfer to wire racks and cool completely.

Generously spread bottom side of one cookie with frosting or filling of choice; place second cookie, bottom side down, on top. Gently press together. Repeat with remaining cookies and marshmallow mixture.

MAKES 16 COOKIE SANDWICHES.

Baker's Note

If using cream cheese as a filling, be sure to store cookies in refrigerator.

"PICK YOUR FILLING" THUMBPRINTS

With just two ingredients and minimal preparation steps, this is one of the handiest cookies to make. Children can help in the production by making the "thumbprint" in each warm cookie and filling the impressions with any number of delicious options.

- ▨ 1 (16.5-ounce) roll refrigerated chocolate-chip cookie dough, well chilled
- ▨ ½ cup filling of choice (see options below)

Preheat oven to 350°F. Spray cookie sheets with nonstick cooking spray.

Cut cookie dough into 12 equal slices. Cut each slice in half. Roll each piece into a ball. Place balls 2 inches apart on cookie sheets.

Bake for 10–12 minutes or until golden at edges. Remove cookies from oven and immediately make a depression in each cookie with thumb or cork; fill each with a teaspoonful of filling. Transfer to wire racks and cool completely.

Filling Options:
Any flavor preserves, jam, jelly, marmalade, or apple butter
Lemon curd
Smooth-style peanut butter
Chocolate-hazelnut spread
Sweetened soft-spread-style cream cheese, any flavor
Canned cake frosting, any flavor

MAKES 24 COOKIES.

Baker's Note

If using cream cheese as a filling, be sure to store cookies in refrigerator.

PINWHEELS

You'll feel like a pastry chef when you pull these out of the oven—yet you'll have plenty of time to kick up your feet, too. Look for larger crystal sugars in a wide range of colors in cooking stores and the baking sections of superstores.

- ▨ 1 (16.5-ounce) roll refrigerated sugar cookie dough
- ▨ ½ cup all-purpose flour
- ▨ 6 tablespoons colored sugar

Cut cookie dough in half. Sprinkle ¼ cup of the flour onto work surface. Roll out half of dough to 12 x 7-inch rectangle. Repeat with remaining half of dough and ¼ cup flour. Sprinkle each rectangle evenly with 3 tablespoons colored sugar.

Starting with shortest side, roll up each rectangle jelly-roll fashion. Tightly wrap rolls in plastic wrap and refrigerate for at least 1 hour for easier handling.

Preheat oven to 350°F. Cut each roll into 16 slices. Place slices 1 inch apart on ungreased cookie sheets

Bake for 7–9 minutes or until edges are light golden brown. Cool for 1 minute on cookie sheets. Transfer from cookie sheets to cooling racks.

MAKES 32 COOKIES.

Variation:

NUTTY PINWHEELS: Prepare as directed above, substituting a mixture of 1/3 cup very finely chopped nuts with 2 tablespoons sugar for the colored sugar.

PISTACHIO-LEMON BISCOTTI

Cultivated in Mediterranean climates, pale green pistachios have a delicate flavor that pairs perfectly with lemon. Either raw or roasted unsalted pistachios can be used here with equally successful results.

- 1 (18.25-ounce) package vanilla cake mix
- 1 cup all-purpose flour
- 1 tablespoon grated lemon zest
- ½ cup (1 stick) butter, melted and cooled
- 2 large eggs
- 1⅓ cups shelled natural pistachios
- 1 recipe Lemon Icing (see page 368)

Preheat oven to 350°F. Position rack in center of oven. Spray cookie sheet with nonstick cooking spray.

Place the cake mix, flour, lemon zest, melted butter, eggs, and pistachios in a large mixing bowl. Blend with an electric mixer set on low speed for 2–3 minutes until well combined, scraping down sides of bowl (dough will be very stiff).

Transfer dough to prepared cookie sheet. With floured hands, shape dough into two 14 x 3-inch rectangles, ¾-inch thick, spacing them 4–5 inches apart on sheet. Mound the dough so it is slightly higher in the middle than at the edges.

Bake for 30–35 minutes, until firm to touch; remove from oven (leave oven on) and cool on cookie sheet for 10 minutes.

Cutting on the cookie sheet, use a sharp knife to slice each rectangle into ¾-inch slices on the diagonal. Carefully turn these slices onto their sides.

Return cookie sheet to oven. Bake biscotti 10 minutes. Turn oven off and let biscotti remain in oven until crisp, 30–40 minutes longer. Remove from oven and transfer biscotti to a rack. Cool completely.

Prepare Lemon Icing and with a butter knife or small offset spatula spread over one side of each biscotti. Place on wax-paper-lined cookie sheet and refrigerate for at least 30 minutes to set the icing. Store in an airtight container or zip-top bag for 2–3 weeks.

MAKES ABOUT 32 BISCOTTI.

PUMPKIN WHOOPIES WITH CINNAMON FLUFF FILLING

These fluff-filled, hand-held "pies" are festive fun for kids and adults alike. The flavors of pumpkin and cinnamon fit the bill for all sorts of fall festivities from Halloween to hay rides.

- 1 cup canned pumpkin purée
- 1/3 cup butter, plus 1/2 cup (1 stick), softened, divided
- 1 (18.25-ounce) package spice cake mix
- 2 large eggs
- 1/2 cup milk
- 1 (8-ounce) package cream cheese, softened
- 2 cups sifted powdered sugar
- 1/2 (7-ounce) jar marshmallow creme
- 1 teaspoon vanilla extract
- 1 teaspoon ground cinnamon

Preheat oven to 375°F. Position oven rack in middle of oven. Line a cookie sheet with parchment paper or foil (grease foil, if using).

Beat pumpkin and 1/3 cup softened butter in a large mixing bowl with an electric mixer on medium speed until smooth. Add cake mix, eggs, and milk; beat on low speed until combined, and then on medium speed for 1 minute. By the heaping tablespoonfuls, drop mounds of batter, 3 inches apart, onto cookie sheet; keep remaining batter chilled.

Bake 15 minutes or until set and lightly browned around edges. Carefully remove from parchment or foil; cool on wire rack. Repeat with remaining batter, lining cooled cookie sheets each time with new parchment or foil. If desired, place cookies in a covered storage container with wax paper between layers to prevent sticking. Store cookies at room temperature for 24 hours.

Beat the remaining 1/2 cup (1 stick) butter and cream cheese in a medium bowl with an electric mixer set on high until smooth. Add the sifted powdered sugar, marshmallow creme, vanilla extract, and cinnamon; beat until blended and smooth.

Spread about 2 1/2 tablespoons filling on flat side of one cookie; top with a second cookie.

Repeat. Serve immediately or cover and chill up to 2 hours.

MAKES 15 WHOOPIES.

QUARESIMALE (LOADED ALMOND BISCOTTI)

- 1 (16.5-ounce) roll refrigerated sugar cookie dough
- 1/3 cup all-purpose flour
- 1 1/4 cups whole almonds, lightly toasted, cooled, very coarsely chopped
- 3/4 teaspoons pure almond extract
- 3/4 teaspoon ground cinnamon

Preheat oven to 350°F. Lightly spray a cookie sheet with nonstick cooking spray.

Break up the cookie dough into large bowl; let stand for 10–15 minutes to soften. Add the flour, almonds, almond extract, and cinnamon to the cookie dough; mix well with your fingers, the paddle attachment of an electric stand mixer, or a wooden spoon.

Divide dough into two equal halves. On the cookie sheet, shape each dough half into a 12 x 2-inch, 3/4-inch-high rectangle, spacing the dough halves about 3 inches apart.

Bake for 26–28 minutes until the logs are deep golden brown and spring back in the center when touched. Remove sheet from oven; keep oven on.

Using two pancake turners, lift logs, one at a time, from the cookie sheet to a cutting board. Using a very sharp knife, cut one of the logs into 3/4-inch-wide slices. Note: for longer biscotti, cut at a deep diagonal; for shorter biscotti, cut log crosswise. Repeat with second log. Place slices on the same cookie sheet; do not worry about the spacing.

Bake slices for 5 minutes; remove from oven and turn over all of the slices. Return cookie sheet to oven and bake 5 minutes longer. Remove sheet from oven and immediately transfer biscotti to a wire rack; cool completely.

MAKES 28 BISCOTTI.

QUICK CARAMEL-PECAN TURTLE COOKIES

My abiding affection for turtle candies—caramel-pecan clusters covered in milk chocolate—can be traced to my childhood spending habits. On more than one occasion I blew my entire allowance on a bag full of turtles alone. The combination of flavors inspired me to create these cookies, which are child's play to make and to eat.

- 1 (16.5-ounce) roll refrigerated chocolate-chip cookie dough, well chilled
- 30 chewy chocolate-coated caramel candies, unwrapped
- 30 pecan halves, preferably lightly toasted, cooled

Preheat oven to 350°F. Spray cookie sheets with nonstick cooking spray.

Cut the cookie dough into 15 equal slices. Cut each slice in half. Roll each piece into a ball. Place balls 2 inches apart on ungreased cookie sheets. Flatten slightly with your palm or a spatula.

Bake for 7–10 minutes or until golden at edges. Remove from oven and immediately press one candy into the top of each cookie. Cool for 2 minutes on cookie sheets. Remove from cookie sheets; place on wire racks and cool 2–3 minutes.

With knife, spread softened candy on each cookie to cover; top with a pecan half. Cool completely.

MAKES 30 COOKIES.

RASPBERRY PINWHEELS

This almond-laced, raspberry preserves-filled cookie takes the crispy rice cookie to delectable new heights.

- ¼ cup (½ stick) butter
- 4 cups miniature marshmallows
- ½ teaspoon almond extract
- 6 cups crisp rice cereal
- 1 cup seedless raspberry preserves, room temperature

Spray a 15 x 10 x 1-inch pan with nonstick cooking spray; set aside momentarily.

Melt the butter over low heat in large saucepan. Add the marshmallows and stir until completely melted. Cook over low heat 3 minutes longer, stirring constantly. Remove from heat and stir in almond extract. Add cereal and stir until well combined.

Press mixture evenly into prepared pan using a piece of wax paper. Cool completely.

Stir preserves to loosen. Spread preserves over cereal mixture almost to edges. Cut in half crosswise. Roll up each half jelly-roll fashion, starting with cut edge. Wrap tightly in wax paper, sealing ends. Chill for 1–2 hours or until firm. Cut into ½-inch slices. Best if served the same day.

MAKES ABOUT 36 SLICES.

Baker's Note

For a decorative flair, cut 1-inch star shape out of center of each top cookie slice. Proceed as above. To bake the tiny star cutouts, place on a cookie sheet and bake for 4–6 minutes.

RASPBERRY TART COOKIES

This recipe reminds me of a far more complicated cookie my mother made every Christmas of my childhood. Besides their winning flavor, I remember her making a double batch since we ate about half of the cookies straight from the oven. At once both no-nonsense and elegant, they can be made with any jam or preserve of your choosing. To dress them up further, dust them with sifted powdered sugar just before serving.

- 1 (16.5-ounce) roll refrigerated sugar cookie dough, well chilled
- ½ cup seedless raspberry jam or preserves

Preheat oven to 350°F. Spray cookie sheets with nonstick cooking spray.

Cut dough in half; refrigerate remaining dough. With sharp knife, cut dough half into 22 thin slices. Place slices 2 inches apart on cookie sheets. Place 1 teaspoon jam in center of each cookie slice. Set aside momentarily.

Cut remaining dough into 22 thin slices. Place cookie slices on jam-topped cookie slices; press edges with tines of fork to decorate and seal.

Bake for 10–12 minutes or until edges are light golden brown. Cool for 1 minute on cookie sheets. Transfer to wire racks and cool completely.

MAKES 22 COOKIES.

REINDEER PRETZEL TREATS

At holiday time, everyone needs a few cookie recipes that are extra good and extra easy. That way, a gift-worthy cookie plate for a friend, neighbor, teacher, or colleague can be assembled in short order. These adorable reindeer cookies fit the bill—they're as cute as they are delicious.

- 32 large pretzel twists
- ½ cup (1 stick) butter
- 1 (10-ounce) bag miniature marshmallows
- 3 tablespoons unsweetened cocoa powder
- 5 cups chocolate or plain crisp rice cereal
- 32 red cinnamon candies
- 64 mini chocolate chips or candies

Line two cookie sheets with wax paper.

Carefully break off the very top of the two curved loops on each pretzel so that each pretzel resembles a pair of antlers; set aside.

Melt the butter and marshmallows with the cocoa powder in a large saucepan or Dutch oven set over low heat, stirring constantly, until marshmallows are melted and mixture is well blended. Add cereal; gently stir until well blended. Add cereal; gently stir until well coated.

Drop cereal mixture by buttered tablespoonfuls onto prepared sheets (32 mounds total). Using buttered hands, shape each mound into an oval shape (to resemble a reindeer head). Quickly push 2 pretzel pieces into top of each oval to resemble the antlers. Press in cinnamon candy for its red nose and 2 chocolate chips for its eyes. Cool completely. Store between sheets of wax paper in airtight container.

MAKES 32 COOKIES.

ROCKY ROAD SLICES

Part cookie, part candy, these rocky road slices make a yummy special occasion treat for kids of all ages.

- 1 cup semisweet chocolate chips
- 2 tablespoons (¼ stick) butter
- 1 (14-ounce) can sweetened condensed milk
- 3 cups graham cracker crumbs
- 3 cups miniature marshmallows
- 1½ cups finely chopped peanuts

Set aside two 20-inch pieces of wax paper.

Melt the chocolate chips and butter with the condensed milk in a heavy saucepan set over low heat, stirring until smooth.

Combine the graham cracker crumbs and marshmallows in a large bowl; stir in the chocolate mixture.

Divide mixture in half. Place each portion on a piece of the prepared wax paper; let stand 10 minutes.

Using the wax paper as an aid, shape each portion into a 12-inch log. Place the peanuts on a flat surface covered with wax paper. Roll

each log in nuts. Wrap each log tightly; chill for 2 hours or until firm.

Remove paper; cut each log into 15 slices. Store covered in refrigerator.

MAKES 30 SLICES.

RUM RAISIN COOKIE BALLS

Oh-so-delicious, these grown-up cookies are guaranteed favorites thanks to a hearty dose of dark rum.

- ½ cup quick-cooking oats
- ⅓ cup dark rum
- 2 cups powdered sugar
- ⅔ cup sweetened flake coconut
- ⅔ cup ground pecans
- ⅔ cup golden raisins
- 3 tablespoons unsweetened cocoa
- ¼ teaspoon ground nutmeg
- 6 tablespoons (3/4 stick) butter, melted
- ⅓ cup sugar

Combine the oats and rum in a large bowl. Cover; let stand 1 hour.

Add the powdered sugar, coconut, pecans, raisins, cocoa, nutmeg, and butter to the rum-oats mixture; mix well with a wooden spoon or hands. Cover with plastic wrap and refrigerate until firm, for at least 2 hours.

Place the sugar in a shallow dish. Form heaping teaspoonfuls of cookie mixture into 1-inch balls. Roll in sugar to coat evenly. Store at least 2 days in airtight container at room temperature to blend flavors.

MAKES ABOUT 42 COOKIE BALLS.

RUSSIAN SOUR CREAM TARTS

Rich and elegant, this is a cookie for company. Be sure the almonds are absolutely fresh for the best flavor—a good sniff test for staleness will work. To heighten their flavor, toast the nuts in a 350°F oven for 8–10 minutes until fragrant. Cool the nuts completely before chopping and adding to the recipe.

- 1 (16.5-ounce) roll refrigerated sugar cookie dough, well chilled
- 1¼ cups blanched almonds, finely chopped
- 2 tablespoons powdered sugar
- 3 tablespoons sour cream
- 2 tablespoons apricot preserves
- 2 large eggs, separated
- ¼ cup granulated sugar

Preheat oven to 350°F. Spray cookie sheets with nonstick cookie spray.

Cut cookie dough crosswise into 4 equal pieces with a sharp knife; cut each piece into 6 equal slices. Arrange slices 2 inches apart on cookie sheets.

Combine the almonds, powdered sugar, sour cream, preserves, and egg yolks in a small bowl; mix well. Spoon and spread 1 teaspoon filling onto each cookie slice.

Beat egg whites in a small bowl until soft peaks form. Gradually add sugar, beating until stiff peaks form. Top each cookie with 1 teaspoon meringue; swirl top.

Bake for 10–12 minutes or until meringue is lightly golden brown. Transfer to wire racks and cool completely.

MAKES 24 COOKIES.

SALTED CARAMEL CASHEWIES

Salt and caramel? Oh yes—it's a match made in heaven. And it is easily accomplished in perfect combination with these three-ingredient cookies that will wow one and all.

- 1 (16.5-ounce) roll refrigerated sugar cookie dough
- 1 cup salted cashews, chopped
- 42 chocolate-covered caramel candies (e.g., Rolos), unwrapped

Preheat oven to 350°F.

Break up dough into a large bowl. Sprinkle with the cashews. Mix well with fingers until blended.

Shape dough into 1-inch balls. Wrap each ball of dough around a piece of candy. Place balls on ungreased cookie sheets, about 2 inches apart.

Bake for 9–11 minutes or until cookies are set and edges are light golden brown. Cool for 1 minute; remove from cookie sheets to racks. Cool for 15 minutes.

MAKES 42 COOKIES.

SANTA'S WHISKERS COOKIES

These festive cookies are especially handy at holiday time—several batches can be made at once, refrigerated, then sliced and baked as needed.

- 1 (18.25-ounce) package white cake mix
- ½ cup shortening
- ⅓ cup butter, softened
- 1 large egg
- 1 cup red or green candied cherries (or combination of both), halved
- 1 tablespoon all-purpose flour
- ½ cup finely chopped pecans
- 2 cups sweetened flaked coconut

Place the cake mix, shortening, butter, and egg in a large bowl. Blend with an electric mixer set on low speed for 1 minute (dough will be very thick). Scrape the dough off the beaters.

Combine cherries and tablespoon flour in a small bowl; toss to coat. Add cherry mixture and pecans into dough by hand until combined.

Divide dough in half. Shape each dough piece into a 12 x 2-inch roll. Roll each in 1 cup coconut, pressing gently to adhere. Wrap each roll in plastic food wrap; refrigerate until firm (at least 4 hours).

Preheat oven to 350°F. Position rack in center of oven. Cut rolls into ¼-inch slices with a sharp knife. Place 2 inches apart on ungreased cookie sheets.

Bake for 7–8 minutes or until edges are lightly browned. Let stand on cookie sheets for 1 minute. Transfer to wire rack and cool completely.

MAKES ABOUT 60 COOKIES.

My family invariably ended the weekend excursion sipping tea and nibbling cookies at the park's Japanese tea gardens. This ginger-spiked sesame cookie strongly resembles a delicate tea cookie that always appeared in the tea garden's assorted offerings.

- 1 (16.5-ounce) roll refrigerated sugar cookie dough
- 1½ teaspoons ground ginger
- ¾ teaspoon almond extract
- ½ cup sesame seeds

Break up the cookie dough into large bowl; let stand for 10–15 minutes to soften. Add the ginger and almond extract; mix well with your fingers, the paddle attachment of an electric stand mixer, or a wooden spoon. Chill dough for 1 hour in refrigerator or 25 minutes in freezer.

Preheat oven to 350°F. Spray cookie sheets with nonstick cooking spray.

Spread the sesame seeds in a small, flat dish. Shape dough into 1-inch balls and roll in sesame seeds to coat. Place balls onto prepared sheets. Gently flatten (slightly) with your palm or a spatula.

Bake for 9–12 minutes or until golden brown at edges. Cool for 2 minutes; transfer to wire racks and cool completely.

MAKES 30 COOKIES.

SESAME GINGER COOKIES

One of my most cherished childhood memories is spending Sunday afternoons in San Francisco's Golden Gate Park.

SESAME HONEY CRINKLES

Culinary historians contend that sesame is one of the first recorded seasonings, dating back to 3000 B.C. In addition to a traditional role in Middle Eastern and Indian cuisines, sesame also has a rich culinary role in the cuisine of the American South (where it is also known as "benne"). One bite of these cookies reveals that sesame is quintessentially suited to honey, making this recipe an all-American winner.

- 1 (18.25-ounce) package yellow cake mix
- 1 cup all-purpose flour
- ½ cup (1 stick) butter, melted
- ¼ cup honey
- 2 large eggs
- ¾ cup sesame seeds

Preheat oven to 375°F. Position oven rack in middle of oven. Spray cookie sheets with nonstick cooking spray.

Place half of the cake mix in a large bowl along with the flour, melted butter, honey, and eggs. Blend with electric mixer set on low speed for 1 minute; stop mixer and scrape bowl. Beat on low speed 1–2 minutes longer, until well blended. Stir in remaining cake mix. Chill dough for 1 hour.

Place sesame seeds in shallow dish. Roll dough into 1-inch balls. Roll each ball in sesame seeds to coat. Place balls 2 inches apart on prepared cookie sheets. Flatten slightly.

Bake for 9–10 minutes or until cookies are golden at the edges and just barely set at center. Transfer to wire racks and cool completely.

MAKES ABOUT 48 COOKIES.

Variation:

HONEY AND LEMON CRINKLES: Prepare as directed above but use lemon cake mix in place of yellow cake mix and roll cookies in granulated sugar rather than sesame seeds.

SLICE-AND-BAKE TOASTED COCONUT COOKIES

No need to pre-toast the coconut here—because the cookies are sliced thin, the coconut toasts in the dough as it bakes. Delicious plain, these cookies are also heavenly drizzled with Citrus Icing (see page 368).

- 1 (18.25-ounce) package white cake mix
- ½ cup vegetable shortening
- ⅓ cup butter, softened
- 1 large egg
- 1½ teaspoons rum-flavored extract, optional
- 1½ cups sweetened flaked coconut

Place the cake mix, shortening, butter, egg, and rum extract, if desired, in a large bowl. Blend with an electric mixer set on low speed for 1 minute or until blended (dough will be very thick). Scrape the dough off the beaters. Stir in the coconut by hand.

Divide dough in half; shape each half into a 12 x 2-inch roll. Wrap each roll in plastic food wrap; refrigerate until firm (at least 4 hours).

Preheat oven to 350°F. Position rack in center of oven. Cut rolls into ¼-inch slices with a sharp knife. Place 2 inches apart on ungreased cookie sheets.

Bake for 7–8 minutes or until edges are lightly browned. Let stand on cookie sheets for 1 minute. Transfer to wire rack and cool completely.

MAKES ABOUT 60 COOKIES.

SLIM MINT CHOCOLATE WAFERS

Smooth and cool, these chocolate-mint wafers—a variation on a favorite Girl Scout cookie—are always winners, even with people who claim they do not like mint.

- 1 (12-ounce) bag (2 cups) semisweet chocolate chips
- 1 tablespoon vegetable shortening
- 1 teaspoon peppermint extract
- 32 round buttery crackers (e.g., Ritz)

Line two cookie sheets with wax paper.

Melt the chocolate chips and shortening in a large heavy saucepan over low heat, stirring until melted and smooth; stir in peppermint extract until blended.

Working quickly, drop crackers, one at a time, into melted chocolate, coating completely. Remove with 2 forks and place on prepared cookie sheets. (if chocolate mixture becomes too thick, re-warm for 1–2 minutes over low heat, stirring until melted).

Refrigerate for 20 minutes or until set. Store leftovers, tightly covered, in refrigerator for up to 1 week.

MAKES 32 COOKIES.

S'MORE SANDWICHES

The original campfire treat undergoes a tasty transformation in this easy chocolate-chip sandwich cookie.

- 1 (16.5-ounce) roll refrigerated chocolate-chip cookie dough, well chilled
- 1 cup sifted powdered sugar
- 1 (7-ounce) jar (about 1⅓ cups) marshmallow creme

Preheat oven to 350°F. Spray cookie sheets with nonstick cooking spray.

With a sharp knife cut cookie dough crosswise into 4 equal pieces; cut each piece into 8 equal slices. Arrange slices 2 inches apart on cookie sheets.

Bake for 8–11 minutes or until golden at edges and just set at the center. Transfer to wire racks and cool completely.

Meanwhile, combine the powdered sugar and marshmallow creme in a medium bowl; mix with a wooden spoon until well blended. Place 1 heaping tablespoon marshmallow mixture on bottom side of one cookie; place second cookie, bottom side down, on top. Gently press together. Repeat with remaining cookies and marshmallow mixture.

MAKES 16 COOKIE SANDWICHES.

SNICKERDOODLES (CAKE MIX)

Snickerdoodles, favorite American cookies dating back to nineteenth-century New England, are likely beloved for their whimsical name as much as their old-fashioned good taste. Whatever the case, these cinnamon-spiked, crisp-soft cookies have never been easier to prepare than with a package of cake mix.

- 1 (18.25-ounce) package white cake mix
- ¼ cup vegetable oil
- 2 large eggs, lightly beaten
- ½ teaspoon ground nutmeg
- ¼ cup sugar
- 2 teaspoons ground cinnamon

Preheat oven to 350°F. Position oven rack in middle of oven. Spray cookie sheets with nonstick cooking spray.

Place the cake mix, oil, eggs, and nutmeg in a large bowl. Mix with a wooden spoon until just blended and all dry ingredients are moistened (dough will be stiff).

Combine the sugar and cinnamon in a shallow dish or bowl. Form dough into 1-inch balls; roll in cinnamon sugar. Place 2 inches apart on prepared cookie sheets.

Bake for 10–12 minutes, until set at edges and just barely set at center when lightly touched. Cool for 1 minute on cookie sheets. Transfer to wire racks with metal spatula and cool completely.

MAKES ABOUT 48 COOKIES.

SNICKERDOODLES (COOKIE DOUGH)

Like a good book, a broken-in pair of slippers, or an old easy chair, snickerdoodles are a sure bet for finding instant calm. So when you want to strike a comforting note—for yourself or someone special—this is your cookie.

- ⅓ cup sugar
- 2 teaspoons ground cinnamon
- 1 teaspoon ground nutmeg
- 1 (16.5-ounce) roll refrigerated sugar cookie dough, well chilled

Preheat oven to 350°F. Spray cookie sheets with nonstick cooking spray.

Combine sugar, cinnamon, and nutmeg in small bowl.

Cut cookie dough in half. Cut each half into 11 slices. Roll each slice into a ball; roll balls in sugar mixture. Place balls 2 inches apart on cookie sheets.

Bake for 10–13 minutes or until edges are golden and centers are just set. Cool on cookie sheets for 2 minutes. Transfer cookies to wire racks and cool completely.

MAKES 22 COOKIES.

SNICKERY CRISPY COOKIE BALLS

Tempt the candy lovers you know with these crispy, candy bar treats. The cookies can also be made in bar form. Simply press the mixture into a 13 x 9 x 2-inch baking pan that has been lightly sprayed with cooking spray, bake, and then cut into bars when cool.

- ½ cup (1 stick) butter
- 1 (10-ounce) bag miniature marshmallows
- 2 (2.15-ounce) chocolate-covered caramel and nougat candy bars, chopped (e.g., Snickers)

- 6 cups crisp rice cereal
- Decorator sugars, decorator candies, sprinkles, or miniature semisweet chocolate chips (optional)

Melt butter over medium-low heat in 4-quart saucepan. Stir in marshmallows until melted.

Remove from heat; stir in candy bars and cereal until blended.

Shape mixture into 1-inch balls with buttered hands. If desired, roll the balls in decorator sugars, decorator candies, sprinkles, or miniature chocolate chips. Place on wax paper. Store in airtight containers between sheets of wax paper.

MAKES ABOUT 42 SMALL COOKIE BALLS.

SNICKERY HIDDEN TREASURE COOKIES

These cookies are so easy and so delicious—and you can "hide" just about any variety of chocolate candy bar inside the dough. Do be sure to cool the cookies before eating to avoid burning tender tongues on the hot filling.

- 1 (18.25-ounce) package yellow cake mix
- 2 large eggs
- 1/3 cup vegetable oil
- 1 bag mini-size chocolate-covered caramel nougat candy bar pieces (e.g., Snickers), unwrapped

Preheat oven to 400°F. Position oven rack in middle of oven. Set aside an ungreased cookie sheet.

Place half of the cake mix in a large bowl along with the eggs and oil. Beat with an electric mixer set on medium-high speed for 1–2 minutes, until blended. Stir in the remaining cake mix until all dry ingredients are moistened.

Cut candy bars in half to create square-shaped pieces. Shape dough into 1½ inch balls.

Place a candy bar half into the center of a ball of dough, shaping the dough around the candy to cover completely. Place dough balls 2 inches apart on ungreased cookie sheet.

Bake for 9–11 minutes or until dough is just set. Transfer to a wire rack and cool completely.

MAKES ABOUT 36 COOKIES.

Variation:

PEANUT BUTTER CUP COOKIES: Prepare as directed above but use chocolate cake mix in place of yellow cake mix and miniature peanut butter cups in place of chocolate caramel nougat candies.

SNOW-CAPPED CHOCOLATE CRINKLES

My friend Abby wanted to know who first hypothesized that combining frozen whipped topping and cake mix could lead to a great cookie. Good question. And while I don't have the answer, I do know that these easy cookies are loved by one and all and are a last-minute saving grace when a batch of cookies is needed in a pinch. They get their "snow-capped" appearance when the powdered sugar tops crack as they bake.

- 1 (18.25-ounce) package chocolate cake mix

- 2 large eggs
- 1¾ cups frozen whipped topping, thawed
- 1 cup powdered sugar, sifted

Place the cake mix, eggs, and thawed whipped topping in a large bowl. Blend for 1–2 minutes with an electric mixer set on medium speed until well blended and all dry ingredients are moistened (dough will be stiff). Refrigerate dough, covered, for 30 minutes.

Preheat oven to 350°F. Position oven rack in middle of oven. Set aside ungreased cookie sheets. Place sifted powdered sugar in a small, shallow dish.

Shape dough into 1-inch balls. Roll cookies in powdered sugar to coat. Place 2 inches apart on ungreased cookie sheet.

Bake for 10–12 minutes or until cookies are puffed in appearance and firm at edges (centers will still be slightly soft). Let cookies rest on cookie sheets for 2 minutes (cookies will fall, giving them a cracked appearance). Transfer cookies to wire rack with metal spatula and cool completely.

MAKES ABOUT 60 COOKIES.

SPICED PECAN BOURBON BALLS

Looking for a special-occasion cookie? This is it. Coffee, cocoa, pecans, bourbon? Few things could make these any better, except perhaps the addition of a lazy summer afternoon.

- 2½ cups finely ground vanilla wafers
- 2 tablespoons unsweetened cocoa powder
- 1 cup finely chopped pecans

- 1 tablespoon instant espresso or coffee powder
- ¼ teaspoon ground cinnamon
- 3 tablespoons light corn syrup
- 1⅔ cups powdered sugar, divided use
- ⅓ cup bourbon

Combine the vanilla wafer crumbs, cocoa powder, chopped pecans, espresso powder, cinnamon, corn syrup, and 1 cup powdered sugar in a large bowl. Stir in enough of the bourbon for mixture to hold together easily. Shape mixture into 1-inch balls.

Place remaining ⅔ cup powdered sugar in shallow dish or bowl. Roll balls in powdered sugar; cover. Let stand for 2 hours.

If desired, roll again in additional powdered sugar. Refrigerate for up to 1 week or freeze up to 3 months in an airtight container between layers of wax paper.

MAKES ABOUT 32 COOKIE BALLS.

STACKED, PACKED PEANUT BUTTER-FUDGE CHOCOLATE CHIPPERS

This just may be the quintessential indulgence for chocolate and peanut butter lovers.

- 2 (16.5-ounce) rolls refrigerated chocolate-chip cookie dough, well chilled
- 1 cup canned chocolate cake frosting
- ¾ cup creamy peanut butter

Preheat oven to 350°F. Spray cookie sheets with nonstick cooking spray.

Cut each cookie dough roll crosswise into 4 equal pieces, using a sharp knife; cut each piece into 7 equal slices. Arrange slices 2 inches apart on cookie sheets.

Bake for 8–11 minutes or until golden at edges and just set at the center. Transfer to wire racks and cool completely.

Combine frosting and peanut butter in small bowl; blend well. Spread about 1 heaping tablespoon peanut butter-fudge mixture on bottom side of each cookie; top each with a second cookie, bottom side down. Press gently. Store in refrigerator.

MAKES 28 SANDWICH COOKIES.

STAINED GLASS COOKIE CUTOUTS

Looking for a cookie that is a first-prize winner in looks as well as taste? These stained glass cookies look as though made by an expert, but even the youngest of children can help make them. I give directions below for punching a hole in the cookies, so that they may be hung in the window or on a tree as ornaments. This step is not necessary if the only plan is to eat the cookies. Use one color per "pane" or sprinkle two or three different colors of crushed candy in each "pane" for a kaleidoscope effect. Just make sure to crush the candies fine to ensure even melting.

- 12 pieces (about 2 ounces) clear hard fruit candies, unwrapped
- 1 (16.5-ounce) roll refrigerated sugar cookie dough, well chilled
- ¼ cup all-purpose flour
- Assorted decorations: icing, frosting, small candies, melted chocolate (see the "Icings, Frostings, Fillings, and Extras" chapter)
- 6 to 8 yards of ribbon, optional

Preheat oven to 350°F. Line cookie sheets with parchment paper or foil. (If using foil, smooth out all wrinkles.)

Place 3 to 4 candies of the same color in small plastic bag; seal bag and gently pound to crush candy, using a hammer or the flat side of a meat mallet,. Repeat with remaining candies, using several different colors.

Cut chilled dough in half; wrap and refrigerate one-half until needed. Remove wrapper from remaining half roll; coat sides of dough with 2 tablespoons of the flour. Roll out dough to ⅛-inch thickness, using additional flour as needed to prevent sticking. Cut out dough with floured 2-inch cookie cutter. With smaller cookie cutter or sharp knife, cut out center of cookie, leaving about ½-inch frame.

Place small center cutouts on separate cookie sheet sprayed with nonstick cooking spray. Bake for 4–6 minutes or until light golden brown.

Brush excess flour from cutout cookies. With spatula, place cutout shapes 2 inches apart on paper-lined cookie sheets. With drinking straw, make hole in top of each cookie. Place ½ teaspoon crushed candy in center ("pane") of each cutout cookie, making sure candy touches edges of cookie. (Do not mound candy in centers of cookies.)

Bake for 5–9 minutes or until edges of cookies are light golden brown and candy is melted and fills center of cookie. Cool for 5 minutes on cookie sheets or until candy is hardened. Reshape holes for ribbon, if necessary. Remove cookies from cookie sheets. Cool completely. Repeat with remaining half of dough and candy.

Frost and decorate cookies. Cut ribbon into 9- to 12-inch lengths. Insert piece of ribbon through hole of each cookie; tie in knot or bow.

MAKES 32 COOKIES.

Store leftovers tightly covered in refrigerator for up to 1 week.

MAKES ABOUT 45 COOKIES.

STRAWBERRY CHEESECAKE THUMBPRINTS

The tanginess of cream cheese partners deliciously with strawberry jam in these rich and pretty cookies.

- 1 (16-ounce) container prepared cream cheese frosting
- 4 ounces (½ of an 8-ounce package) cream cheese, softened
- 2½ cups crisp sugar cookie or crisp macaroon crumbs
- ½ teaspoon almond extract
- 1 cup very finely ground almonds
- ½ cup strawberry jam, room temperature

Line a cookie sheet with wax paper.

Beat the frosting and cream cheese in a large bowl with an electric mixer set to medium speed until well blended and smooth. Mix in cookie crumbs and almond extract with a wooden spoon until combined.

Place the ground almonds in a pie pan or shallow dish. Shape cookie mixture into 1-inch balls. Roll each ball in almonds to coat. Place balls on cookie sheet. Make an indentation with thumb or back of a ¼-teaspoon measure into the center of each cookie. Fill each indentation with ¼ teaspoon jam.

Refrigerate for 30 minutes or until cold.

STRAWBERRY-CREAM CHEESE THUMBPRINTS

These sweet cookies are pretty-as-a-picture perfect, as welcome in a lunchbox as they are at a bridal shower. You can use the basic dough as a blueprint for your own thumbprint designs, varying the cake mix flavor and filling choice in endless permutations.

- 1 (18.25-ounce) package white cake mix
- 1 cup all-purpose flour
- ¼ cup (½ stick) butter, softened
- 1 (3-ounce) package cream cheese, softened
- 2 large egg yolks
- 1 teaspoon almond extract
- ⅔ cup strawberry jam, stirred to loosen

Preheat oven to 350°F. Position oven rack to upper third of the oven. Set aside two ungreased cookie sheets.

Place the cake mix, flour, softened butter, and cream cheese in a large bowl. Blend for 1–2 minutes with an electric mixer set on low speed until mixture is blended and resembles fresh bread crumbs. Add the egg yolks and almond extract; beat on low speed for 1–2 minutes longer until dough comes together into a ball.

Shape dough into 1-inch balls and position 2 inches apart on cookie sheets. Push an indentation into the center of each cookie with your thumb, the back of a rounded ¼-teaspoon measuring spoon, or a cork. Fill each indentation with ¼ teaspoon jam.

Bake for 8–10 minutes or until firm to the touch at the edges and slightly puffed in appearance. Cool for 1 minute on cookie sheets. Transfer to wire racks with metal spatula and cool completely.

MAKES ABOUT 42 COOKIES.

Variations:

CHOCOLATE COVERED STRAWBERRY THUMBPRINTS: Prepare as directed above but add ¾ cup miniature semisweet chocolate chips to the dough along with the egg yolks.

PINEAPPLE COCONUT THUMBPRINTS: Prepare as directed above but use 1 teaspoon rum-flavored extract in place of the almond extract and add 2 teaspoons ground ginger to the dough. Roll dough balls in 1 cup flaked sweetened coconut, pressing to coat. Use pineapple preserves in place of the strawberry jam.

LEMON HEAVEN THUMBPRINTS: Prepare as directed above but use lemon cake mix in place of white cake mix, 2 teaspoons grated lemon zest in place of almond extract, and jarred lemon curd in place of jam.

CHOCOLATE RASPBERRY THUMBPRINTS: Prepare as directed above but use chocolate cake mix in place of white cake mix and seedless raspberry preserves in place of jam.

TART CHERRY-DATE SKILLET COOKIES

Need lots of treats in a hurry for a party or potluck? Here's the solution. You don't need to like dates to love these cookies. The dates create a brown sugar-butter complement to the tart dried cherries, making for a cookie to be enjoyed by all.

- 1 cup (2 sticks) butter
- 1 cup firmly packed light or dark brown sugar
- 1 (8-ounce) package chopped dates
- 1 large egg, lightly beaten
- 3 cups crisp rice cereal
- 1 cup chopped tart dried cherries or dried cranberries
- 1 tablespoon vanilla extract
- 3½ cups sweetened flake coconut

Melt the butter in a large skillet; stir in the brown sugar and dates. Remove from heat. Stir in the egg; return to heat. Cook over medium heat for 4–6 minutes, stirring constantly, until mixture comes to a full boil. Boil, stirring constantly, for 1 minute.

Remove from heat; stir in the cereal, dried cherries, vanilla, and 1 cup of the coconut until blended. Let stand for 10 minutes.

Place the remaining coconut in a shallow dish or pie plate. Shape rounded teaspoonfuls into 1-inch balls and roll in remaining coconut.

MAKES ABOUT 60 COOKIES.

TUSCAN CORNMEAL COOKIES

Cornmeal may seem an unusual cookie ingredient to most Americans, but it is a common dessert ingredient in Northern Italy. This sugar-coated cookie, with its rustic cornmeal crunch and citrus-rosemary infused flavor, is destined to turn questioners into converts.

Both hearty and heartwarming, these cookies are not-too-sweet companions to coffee or a terrific finish to any simple pasta dinner.

- 1 (16.5-ounce) roll refrigerated sugar cookie dough
- 2 tablespoons light brown sugar
- ¼ cup yellow or white cornmeal
- 2 tablespoons minced fresh rosemary (or 1 teaspoon dried, crumbled rosemary)
- 1 tablespoon grated lemon zest
- 1 teaspoon vanilla extract
- 1 recipe Lemon Icing (see page 368), optional

Break up the cookie dough into large bowl; let stand for 10–15 minutes to soften. Add the brown sugar, cornmeal, rosemary, lemon zest, and vanilla extract; mix well with your fingers or a wooden spoon. Chill dough for 1 hour in refrigerator or 20–25 minutes in freezer.

Preheat oven to 350°F. Spray cookie sheets with nonstick cooking spray.

Shape dough into 1-inch balls; place 2 inches apart on prepared cookie sheets. Flatten cookies with a fork dipped in sugar.

Bake for 10–12 minutes or until golden brown. Cool for 2 minutes on cookie sheet. Transfer to wire racks and cool completely. If desired, drizzle with Lemon Icing.

MAKES 28 COOKIES.

VALENTINE'S DAY CHOCOLATE-MINT HEARTS

You're sure to win a few hearts with these pretty and very delicious crispy cookies.

- 1 cup semisweet chocolate chips
- ¼ cup light corn syrup
- 2 tablespoons butter
- ½ teaspoon peppermint extract
- 3 cups crisp rice cereal
- Small tubes, purchased, of pink and/ or red decorating icing (optional)

Line cookie sheets with wax paper.

Melt the chocolate chips with the corn syrup and butter in a heavy medium saucepan set over low heat, stirring with a wooden spoon until melted and smooth. Remove from heat and stir in peppermint extract. Gently stir in rice cereal with a wooden spoon until the cereal is evenly coated with chocolate.

Immediately turn the chocolate-coated cereal out onto the wax-paper-lined cookie sheet. Pat mixture into a 12 x 6-inch rectangle. Chill for about 20 minutes or until slightly firm.

Cut cereal mixture into heart shapes with a 3-inch heart-shaped cookie cutter. Decorate with frosting, if desired. Chill until firm; wrap each heart in plastic wrap. Store cookies in refrigerator up to 1 week.

MAKES 8 OR 9 COOKIES.

VANILLA BLISS COOKIES

All you need to make and enjoy these cookies is a big sweet tooth and a fondness for vanilla.

- 1 (18.25-ounce) package vanilla cake mix
- 1 (3.4-ounce) package instant vanilla pudding mix
- ½ cup vegetable oil
- 1 egg
- ½ cup sour cream (not reduced fat)
- 2 teaspoons vanilla extract
- ⅔ cup quick-cooking oats
- 1½ cups vanilla baking chips or white chocolate chips

Preheat oven to 350°F. Position oven rack in middle of oven. Spray cookie sheets with nonstick cooking spray.

Place half of the cake mix in a large bowl along with the instant pudding mix, oil, egg, sour cream, and vanilla extract. Blend with an electric mixer set on low speed for 1–2 minutes until mixture is blended and smooth. Stir in oats and chips.

Shape dough into 1½ inch balls; place 2 inches apart on the prepared cookie sheets.

Bake for 11–13 minutes until golden at edges and just barely set at center. Cool cookies on cookie sheet for 5 minutes (cookies will continue to firm). Transfer to a wire rack; cool completely.

MAKES ABOUT 48 COOKIES.

Variations:

BUTTERSCOTCH BLISS COOKIES: Prepare as directed above but use yellow cake mix, instant butterscotch pudding, and butterscotch baking chips.

TRIPLE-CHOCOLATE BLISS COOKIES: Prepare as directed above but use chocolate cake mix, instant chocolate pudding, and semisweet chocolate chips.

PEANUT BUTTER BLISS COOKIES: Prepare as directed above but use yellow cake mix, instant butterscotch pudding, and peanut butter–flavored baking chips. Additionally, use ½ cup creamy peanut butter in place of the sour cream.

WALNUT RAISIN BISCOTTI

- 1 (16.5-ounce) roll refrigerated sugar cookie dough
- ⅓ cup all-purpose flour
- ¾ cup chopped walnuts, lightly toasted, cooled
- ¾ cup coarsely chopped raisins
- 1 teaspoon vanilla extract

Preheat oven to 350°F. Lightly spray a cookie sheet with nonstick cooking spray.

Break up the cookie dough into large bowl; let stand for 10–15 minutes to soften. Add the flour, walnuts, raisins, and vanilla extract to the cookie dough; mix well with your fingers, the paddle attachment of an electric stand mixer, or a wooden spoon.

Divide dough into two equal halves. On the cookie sheet, shape each dough half into a 12 x 2-inch, ¾-inch-high rectangle, spacing the dough halves about 3 inches apart.

Bake for 26–28 minutes or until the logs are deep golden brown and spring back in the center when touched. Remove sheet from oven; keep oven on.

Using two pancake turners, lift logs, one at a time, from the cookie sheet to a cutting board. Using a sharp knife, cut one of the logs into ¾-inch-wide slices. Note: for longer biscotti, cut at a deep diagonal; for shorter biscotti, cut log crosswise. Repeat with second log. Place slices on the same cookie sheet (do not worry about the spacing).

Bake slices for 5 minutes; remove from oven and turn over all of the slices. Return cookie sheet to oven and bake 5 minutes longer. Remove sheet from oven and immediately transfer biscotti to a wire rack; cool completely.

MAKES 28 BISCOTTI.

Baker's Note

For half batches of biscotti, follow all of the directions above but halve the ingredients. Make one biscotti log instead of two and proceed as directed above. Or make a full batch and wrap and freeze the second half of dough for a future batch of biscotti or cookies.

WHITE CHOCOLATE– CRANBERRY BISCOTTI

This biscotto is as beautiful as it is delicious and makes an especially appealing gift. You can transform this recipe into a dark chocolate treat by substituting chocolate cake mix for the vanilla cake mix and semisweet chocolate-chips for the white chocolate chips.

- 1 (18.25-ounce) package vanilla cake mix
- 1 cup all-purpose flour
- ½ cup (1 stick) butter, melted and cooled
- 2 large eggs
- 1 teaspoon almond extract
- 1 cup dried cranberries
- 1 cup white chocolate chips

Preheat oven to 350°F. Position rack in center of oven. Spray cookie sheet with nonstick cooking spray.

Place the cake mix, flour, melted butter, eggs, almond extract, cranberries, and white chocolate chips in a large mixing bowl. Blend with an electric mixer set on low speed for 2–3 minutes until well-blended, scraping down sides of bowl (dough will be very stiff).

Transfer dough to prepared cookie sheet. With floured hands, shape dough into two 14 x 3-inch rectangles, ¾-inch thick, spacing them 4–5 inches apart on sheet. Mound the dough so it is slightly higher in the middle than at the edges.

Bake for 30–35 minutes until firm to touch; remove from oven (leave oven on) and cool on sheet for 10 minutes.

Cutting on the cookie sheet, use a sharp knife to slice each rectangle into ¾-inch slices on the diagonal. Carefully turn these slices onto their sides.

Return cookie sheet to oven. Bake biscotti 10 minutes. Turn oven off and let biscotti remain in oven until crisp, 30–40 minutes longer. Remove from oven and transfer biscotti to a rack. Cool completely. Store in an airtight container or plastic zip-top bag for 2–3 weeks.

MAKES ABOUT 32 BISCOTTI.

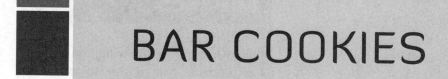

BAR COOKIES

ALMOND BRICKLE BROWNIE BARS

These bars showcase two favorite flavors—chocolate and toffee—in all their delicious glory. The peanut butter in the filling adds a creamy nuttiness, but the almond extract makes the filling distinctively almond, a delicious complement to the toffee.

- 1 (19.5- to 19.8-ounce) package brownie mix
- 2⅓ cups quick-cooking oats
- 1 cup (2 sticks) unsalted butter, melted
- 1 (14-ounce) can sweetened condensed milk
- ¾ cup creamy peanut butter
- 1 teaspoon almond extract
- ⅔ cup English toffee baking bits
- ½ cup slivered almonds

Preheat oven to 350°F (325° for dark-coated metal pan). Position a rack in the lower third of the oven. Spray the bottom only of a 13 x 9-inch baking pan with nonstick cooking spray (or foil-line pan; see page xxiv).

Mix the brownie mix, oats, and melted butter in a medium mixing bowl with a wooden spoon until just blended and all dry ingredients are moistened. Press ⅔ of mixture evenly into prepared pan.

Beat condensed milk, peanut butter, and almond extract in a large mixing bowl with electric mixer set on medium until smooth. Spread evenly over base layer.

Combine reserved crumb mixture with toffee bits and almonds in a medium mixing bowl. Sprinkle mixture evenly over filling; press down firmly.

Bake for 30–34 minutes or until topping is firm. Transfer to a wire rack and cool completely. Cut into bars.

MAKES 24 LARGE OR 36 SMALL BARS.

ALMOND BUTTERSCOTCH SQUARES

Regardless of your feelings about nuts in desserts, you're sure to love these sweet treats.

- 2 cups butterscotch baking chips
- 2 tablespoons vegetable shortening
- ½ teaspoon almond extract
- 1 cup miniature marshmallows
- 1 cup coarsely chopped honey-roasted almonds
- 2 cups crisp rice cereal

Lightly spray an 8 x 8 x 2-inch square baking pan with nonstick cooking spray; set aside.

Stir the butterscotch chips and shortening in a medium saucepan over low heat until chips are melted and mixture is smooth. Remove from heat; stir in the almond extract, marshmallows, almonds, and cereal. Mix well.

Spread mixture into the prepared pan with a wooden spoon. Chill until set. Cut into 24 small squares. Store in covered containers between layers of wax paper.

MAKES 24 SQUARES.

ALMOND JOYFUL BARS

As the name implies, these simple-to-make—and simply delicious—cookies bear a strong resemblance to the delectable candy with a similar name.

- ¼ cup (½ stick) butter
- 30 large marshmallows
- 1 teaspoon almond extract
- 1 cup very coarsely chopped, roasted, lightly salted almonds
- 2 cups sweetened flake coconut, divided use
- 3½ cups cornflakes cereal
- 1⅓ cups milk chocolate chips
- 1 tablespoon vegetable shortening

Lightly spray a 13 x 9 x 2-inch baking pan with nonstick cooking spray; set aside.

Combine the butter and marshmallows in a large saucepan. Cook over medium heat, stirring occasionally, until melted and smooth. Stir in the almond extract, almonds, 1 cup of the coconut, and cornflakes. Using a large square of wax paper, press into the prepared pan and let sit for 30 minutes.

Melt the milk chocolate chips with the vegetable shortening in a small saucepan set over low heat, stirring until melted and smooth. Spread chocolate mixture over cooled bars and sprinkle with remaining coconut. Refrigerate for 30 minutes to set the chocolate. Cut into 36 bars. Store in covered containers between layers of wax paper.

MAKES 36 BARS.

ALMOND SQUARES WITH DRIED CHERRIES

I don't like to turn on the oven in the sweltering heat, but sometimes I want to bypass baking in the fall, too, especially when I'm pressed for time. These almond-accented bars, balanced with the tart-sweet taste of dried cherries, are a perfect solution.

- 3 cups bite-sized pieces shredded wheat cereal, coarsely crushed
- ¾ cup dried tart cherries or dried cranberries
- ½ cup chopped, lightly salted roasted almonds
- ½ cup light corn syrup or honey
- ½ cup firmly packed brown sugar
- ½ cup almond butter
- 1 teaspoon almond extract

Lightly spray an 8 x 8 x 2-inch square baking pan with nonstick cooking spray; set aside.

Place cereal, cherries, and almonds in a large bowl; set aside.

Bring the corn syrup, brown sugar, and almond butter to a boil in a medium saucepan over medium heat, stirring occasionally. Remove from heat and stir in almond extract. Pour almond butter mixture over cereal mixture, stirring until blended.

Using a large square of wax paper, press firmly into prepared pan. Cool completely. Cut into 24 small squares. Store in covered containers between layers of wax paper.

MAKES 24 SQUARES.

ALMOND TOFFEE BARS

Who would guess that such a short list of ingredients could lead to such sweet success? It's easy to keep all of the ingredients on hand, too, for spur-of-the-moment splurges. Earmark this one as a sure bet for group gatherings both for its brief preparation requirements and universal appeal.

- 1 (16.5-ounce) roll refrigerated sugar cookie dough, well chilled
- 1 cup semisweet (or milk) chocolate chips
- 1 cup toffee baking bits
- 1 cup sliced (or chopped) almonds
- 1 (14-ounce) can sweetened condensed milk

Preheat oven to 350°F. Spray a 13 x 9-inch pan with nonstick cooking spray or line with foil.

Cut cookie dough into ¼-inch-thick slices. Arrange slices in bottom of the prepared pan. With floured fingers, press dough evenly to form crust. Sprinkle the chocolate chips, toffee bits, and almonds evenly over prepared crust. Drizzle evenly with sweetened condensed milk.

Bake 25–28 minutes or until edges are bubbly and center is just lightly browned. Remove from oven and immediately run a narrow metal spatula or table knife around edges of pan to loosen. Cool completely in pan on a wire rack; cut into bars.

MAKES 36 BARS.

AMBROSIA BARS

Consider cutting this cookie version of the "food of the gods" into diamonds or triangles to create little works of art on your cookie tray.

- 1¼ cups crisp macaroon cookie crumbs
- ¼ cup (½ stick) butter, melted
- ⅔ cup canned unsweetened coconut milk
- 2 teaspoons unflavored gelatin
- 1 (8-ounce) package cream cheese, softened
- 1 (6-ounce) container frozen orange juice concentrate, thawed
- 1 cup sweetened flake coconut
- ½ cup coarsely chopped maraschino cherries

Line an 8 x 8 x 2-inch baking pan with foil (see page xxiv); lightly spray with nonstick cooking spray. Set aside.

Combine the cookie crumbs and melted butter in a medium bowl with a fork or fingers until well blended. Transfer crumb mixture to prepared pan. Press firmly into bottom of pan with a large square of wax paper. Freeze until ready to use.

Place ⅓ cup of the coconut milk in a small saucepan; sprinkle gelatin over (do not stir). Let stand 10 minutes to soften. Add the remaining ⅓ cup coconut milk to saucepan and turn the heat under saucepan to medium. Whisk and stir until coconut milk is very hot (but not boiling) and gelatin is completely dissolved. Remove from heat and cool for 15 minutes.

Beat the cream cheese and thawed orange juice concentrate in a large bowl with an electric mixer on medium speed until creamy.

Add gelatin mixture gradually, beating on low speed and occasionally scraping sides of bowl with spatula, until well blended.

Pour and spread filling evenly over prepared crust. Sprinkle coconut and cherries over bars, pressing gently into filling. Refrigerate for 3 hours or until firm. Use foil lining to remove uncut bars from pan to cutting board. Cut into 16 bars. Store, loosely covered with foil or plastic wrap, in refrigerator.

MAKES 16 BARS.

APPLE-CRANBERRY SNACK BARS

These sound like ideal autumn bars, and indeed they are. But don't wait until the leaves turn to give them a try—they are year-round winners.

- 1 (18.25-ounce) package spice cake mix
- ¾ cup mayonnaise
- 2 large eggs
- 1 cup chopped peeled tart apples (e.g., Granny Smith)
- 1 cup dried cranberries (or raisins)
- ½ cup (1 stick) butter, softened
- 3½ cups powdered sugar
- 2 tablespoons lemon juice

Preheat oven to 350°F (or 325° for dark-coated metal pan). Position oven rack in middle of oven. Spray the bottom only of a 15 x 10 x 1-inch jelly roll pan with nonstick cooking spray (or foil-line pan; see page xxiv).

Place the cake mix, mayonnaise, and eggs in a large bowl. Blend for 2 minutes with an elec-

tric mixer set on medium speed until smooth. Stir in the apples and dried cranberries. Pour and spread batter into prepared baking pan.

Bake for 18–20 minutes or until toothpick inserted in center comes out clean. Transfer to wire rack and cool completely.

Beat the softened butter, powdered sugar, and lemon juice in a medium bowl with the electric mixer set on low speed for 2 minutes. Beat on high speed until light and fluffy. Spread over cooled bars. Cut into bars. Store leftover bars in refrigerator.

MAKES 36 LARGE OR 48 SMALL BARS.

APRICOT AMBROSIA BARS

I have fond memories of my maternal grandmother making her special version of ambrosia, a mesmerizing concoction of vanilla custard, apricots, whipped cream, almonds, and toasted coconut. Just as the name implies, it was heaven. This easy bar lives up to its namesake and is nothing short of a showstopper. It's bound to bring cheers at any gathering.

- 1 (16.5-ounce) roll refrigerated sugar cookie dough, well chilled
- 2 (8-ounce) packages cream cheese, softened
- ⅔ cup granulated sugar
- 2 large eggs
- ¾ teaspoon almond extract
- ¾ cup apricot preserves
- 1 cup shredded coconut
- ½ cup sliced almonds

Preheat oven to 350°F. Spray a 13 x 9-inch pan with nonstick cooking spray or line with foil.

Cut cookie dough into ¼-inch-thick slices. Arrange slices in bottom of the prepared pan. With floured fingers, press dough evenly to form crust.

Bake for 10–13 minutes or until dough is golden brown (dough will appear slightly puffed). Remove from oven.

Meanwhile, beat the cream cheese, granulated sugar, eggs, and almond extract in another bowl with an electric mixer set on high until smooth, stopping mixer occasionally to scrape the sides of the bowl with a rubber spatula.

Spread over partially baked crust. Dollop preserves over cream cheese layer (does not need to completely cover cream cheese layer). Sprinkle coconut and almonds over preserves. Return to oven and bake for 22–25 minutes, until coconut is golden.

Cool completely; cut into bars. Serve room temperature or chilled. Store in refrigerator.

MAKES 36 BARS.

APRICOT COCONUT BARS

Whenever I return home to the San Francisco Bay Area to visit family, I try to stop by Yanni's produce store on College Avenue in Oakland to pick up a bag of apricot candies from their large bin selection of natural foods. They are so good because they are so very apricot: finely chopped dried apricots pressed together and rolled in shredded coconut. These bars capture the same ambrosial combination of apricot and coconut with the added, unbeatable base layer of chocolate.

- 1 (19.5- to 19.8-ounce) package brownie mix
- ½ cup (1 stick) unsalted butter, melted
- 1 (14-ounce) can sweetened condensed milk
- 2 large eggs
- 1½ cups sweetened shredded coconut
- 1½ cups finely chopped dried apricots

Preheat oven to 350°F (325° for dark-coated metal pan). Position a rack in the lower third of the oven. Spray the bottom only of a 13 x 9-inch baking pan with nonstick cooking spray (or foil-line pan; see page xxiv).

Combine the brownie mix and melted butter in a medium mixing bowl with a wooden spoon until just blended and all dry ingredients are moistened. Press mixture into prepared pan. Bake for 15 minutes. Remove from oven (leave oven on).

Meanwhile, whisk condensed milk and eggs in a medium mixing bowl until blended. Stir in coconut and apricots. Spread mixture evenly over hot crust.

Return to oven and bake 22–25 minutes longer or until golden around edges. Transfer to a wire rack and cool completely. Cut into bars.

MAKES 24 LARGE OR 36 SMALL BARS.

APRICOT MOUSSE BARS

Delicate and lovely, these light and creamy bars are one-of-a-kind. If you like, substitute canned peaches or fresh mangoes for the apricots.

- 2 cups crushed creme-filled lemon sandwich cookies (about 24 cookies)

- 1/3 cup butter, melted
- 1 cup canned, drained apricot halves
- 1/2 cup orange juice, divided
- 2 1/4 teaspoons unflavored gelatin
- 1/3 cup sugar
- 2/3 cup heavy whipping cream

Line an 8 x 8 x 2-inch baking pan with foil (see page xxiv); lightly spray with nonstick cooking spray. Set aside.

Combine the cookie crumbs and melted butter in a medium bowl with a fork or fingers until well blended. Transfer crumb mixture to prepared pan. Press firmly into bottom of pan with a large square of wax paper. Freeze until ready to use.

In a blender or food processor puree the apricots with 1/4 cup of the orange juice; set aside. Place the remaining 1/4 cup orange juice in a small saucepan. Sprinkle gelatin over (do not stir). Let stand 5 minutes to soften.

Add sugar and apricot puree to saucepan. Stir over low heat for 4–6 minutes until both the sugar and gelatin are dissolved. Remove from heat. Let cool for 20–25 minutes until it reaches room temperature.

Beat the whipping cream in a medium bowl with an electric mixer set on high speed until soft peaks form. Gently stir in cooled apricot mixture until just blended. Pour mixture over chilled crust. Refrigerate for 3 hours until firm. Use foil lining to remove uncut bars from pan to cutting board. Cut into 24 small squares. Store, loosely covered with plastic wrap, in the refrigerator.

MAKES 24 BARS.

BACKPACKER BARS

Just one of these bars is enough to help you hit the trail running—with a big smile, to boot. Carob chips are my preference for these energy-boosting bars. You can find them at your local health food store and at some supermarkets in the baking, health food, or bulk foods section. Of course, chocolate chips are always a very fine substitute.

- 1 (19.5- to 19.8-ounce) package brownie mix
- 1/2 cup vegetable oil or 1/2 cup (1 stick) unsalted butter, melted
- 1/3 cup milk
- 3 large eggs
- 1 1/3 cups quick-cooking or old-fashioned oats, divided
- 1 1/2 cups carob chips or semisweet chocolate chips, divided
- 1 1/2 cups lightly salted mixed nuts, coarsely chopped, divided
- 1 cup dried cranberries

Preheat oven to 350°F (325° for dark-coated metal pan). Position a rack in the lower third of the oven. Spray the bottom only of a 13 x 9-inch baking pan with nonstick cooking spray (or line pan with foil; see page xxiv).

Combine the brownie mix, oil, milk, and eggs in a large mixing bowl with a wooden spoon until just blended and all dry ingredients are moistened. Stir in 1 cup of the oats, 1 cup of the chips, 1 cup of the nuts, and the dried cranberries. Spread batter into prepared pan. Sprinkle with remaining 1/3 cup oats, remaining 1/2 cup chips, and remaining 1/2 cup nuts; gently press into batter.

Bake for 28–30 minutes or until a toothpick inserted 2 inches from side of pan comes out clean or almost clean (do not overbake).

Transfer to a wire rack and cool completely. Cut into squares.

MAKES 24 LARGE OR 36 SMALL BARS.

BAKLAVA BARS

The flavor of baklava—a butter-rich, many-layered Greek pastry, rich with spices, nuts, and lemon—is simplified here in an easy-to-prepare bar recipe.

- 1 (18.25-ounce) package yellow cake mix
- ¾ cup (1½ sticks) butter, melted, divided
- 4 large eggs
- 1 cup packed light brown sugar
- 1 cup honey
- 2 teaspoons grated lemon zest
- 2 teaspoons vanilla extract
- ½ teaspoon ground cinnamon
- 1½ cups chopped walnuts

Preheat oven to 350°F (or 325° for dark-coated metal pan). Position oven rack in middle of oven. Spray a 13 x 9-inch metal baking pan with nonstick cooking spray (or foil-line pan; see page xxiv).

Place the cake mix and ½ cup melted butter in a large bowl. Blend with an electric mixer set on medium speed until blended and crumbly. Press mixture into the prepared pan. Bake for 15 minutes.

Beat the eggs in a large mixing bowl with a fork while crust bakes. Whisk in the brown sugar, honey, remaining melted butter, lemon zest, vanilla extract, and cinnamon; stir in the walnuts. Spread mixture evenly over warm base layer.

Bake for an additional 40–45 minutes or until filling is set. Transfer to a wire rack and cool completely. Cut into bars.

MAKES 24 LARGE OR 36 SMALL BARS.

BAKLAVA CRISPY BARS

Baklava is a butter-rich, layered Greek pastry, filled with spices, lemon, honey and nuts. While this crispy, no-bake bar is a significant departure from the original in terms of form, it captures the much beloved combination of flavors.

- 2 tablespoons butter
- ⅓ cup honey
- 4 cups miniature marshmallows
- 1½ teaspoons ground cinnamon
- 1 tablespoon grated lemon zest
- 6 cups oats and honey crispy cereal
- 1 cup chopped walnuts

Lightly spray a 13 x 9 x 2-inch baking pan with nonstick cooking spray; set aside.

Melt the butter with the honey in a large saucepan or Dutch oven set over low heat, stirring until blended. Add the marshmallows, cinnamon, and lemon zest; cook and stir until melted and blended. Add the cereal and walnuts; mix well.

With a large square of wax paper, press cereal mixture firmly into prepared pan. Cool completely. Cut into bars. Store in covered containers between layers of wax paper.

MAKES 24 BIG BARS.

BANANA BARS

These delicious confections are just as delightful eaten during a midmorning coffee break as they are devoured as a midnight snack. If you are not a coconut fan, leave it out and substitute an extra ½ cup of cereal in its place.

- ¼ cup (½ stick) butter
- 1 (10-ounce) bag marshmallows
- 6 cups crisp rice cereal
- 1 cup coarsely crushed dried banana chips
- 1 cup coarsely chopped, lightly salted roasted cashews, peanuts, or macadamia nuts
- ½ cup sweetened flake coconut

Lightly spray a 13 x 9 x 2-inch baking pan with nonstick cooking spray; set aside.

Melt the butter in a large saucepan or Dutch oven set over medium heat. Add the marshmallows and stir until marshmallows are melted. Remove from heat.

Stir in the cereal, banana chips, nuts, and coconut until evenly coated. With a large square of wax paper, press evenly into prepared pan. Cool for 30 minutes. Cut into bars. Store in covered containers between layers of wax paper.

MAKES 36 BARS.

Baker's Note

To crush banana chips easily, place in a large, resealable plastic bag. Place on a flat surface and use a rolling pin or mallet to crush the chips.

BANANA BLISS GOOEY CHESS SQUARES

Who would have guessed that such commonly available, reasonably priced ingredients—a cake mix, a few bananas, and a package of cream cheese—could lead to such a supreme treat, with such little effort to boot? Kids of all ages will line up for seconds (and thirds!).

- 1 cup (2 sticks) butter, divided
- 1 (18.25-ounce) package yellow or chocolate cake mix
- 4 large eggs
- 1 (8-ounce) package cream cheese, softened
- 1½ cups mashed banana (about 2 large bananas)
- 2 teaspoons vanilla extract
- 1 (16-ounce) box powdered sugar
- ½ teaspoon ground nutmeg

Preheat oven to 350°F (or 325° for dark-coated metal pan). Position oven rack in middle of oven. Spray the bottom only of a 13 x 9-inch metal baking pan with nonstick cooking spray (or foil-line pan; see page xxiv).

Melt ½ cup (1 stick) of the butter in a small saucepan set over low heat. beat the cake mix, melted butter, and 1 egg in a large bowl with an electric mixer set on medium speed until well blended (mixture will come together as a thick dough). Pat evenly into the prepared pan. Set aside momentarily.

Melt the remaining stick of butter in a small saucepan set over low heat. Beat the cream cheese and mashed banana in a large bowl with an electric mixer set on medium speed until smooth, scraping down sides of bowl occasionally. Add the melted butter, remaining eggs, and vanilla extract; blend until smooth. Add the powdered sugar and nutmeg; blend until smooth.

Spread the banana mixture over prepared crust. Bake for 42–45 minutes (do not overbake; bars should be slightly gooey). Transfer to a wire rack and cool completely. Cut into bars or squares. Cover and store in refrigerator.

MAKES 24 LARGE OR 36 SMALL BARS.

BANANA CRUNCH BARS

These make a great ending to a warm-weather gathering. And because bananas are available year-round, you can enjoy them no matter what the season. Be sure to select bananas that are ripe, but still firm, for best results.

- ½ cup plus 2 tablespoons (1¼ sticks) butter, softened, divided use
- ¼ cup packed brown sugar
- 2 cups chocolate wafer or chocolate graham cracker crumbs
- 3 tablespoons light corn syrup
- 2 medium firm bananas, peeled and diced (about 1½ cups)
- 1 teaspoon rum-flavored extract
- 1 cup milk or semisweet chocolate chips
- 1 teaspoon vegetable shortening

Set aside an ungreased 8 x 8 x 2-inch baking pan.

In a small saucepan set over low heat melt ½ cup (1 stick) of the butter. combine the melted butter, brown sugar, and chocolate wafer crumbs in a medium mixing bowl, using fingers or a wooden spoon, until well blended. With a large square of wax paper, press mixture into the bottom of prepared pan. Chill for about 20 minutes or until firm.

Combine the corn syrup and remaining butter in a small saucepan. Stir over medium heat until melted and bubbly. Remove from heat; stir in bananas and rum extract. Spoon banana mixture in an even layer over prepared crust.

Melt the chocolate chips and shortening over low heat in a small saucepan, stirring until melted and smooth; drizzle over the banana layer. Cover and chill until set. Cut into 16 bars. Store, loosely covered with plastic wrap, in the refrigerator.

MAKES 16 BARS.

BANANAS FOSTER BARS

A sprinkle of rum extract imparts a note of extravagance to the bananas in these bars; rich, buttery caramel adds a layer of luxury.

- 1 (8-ounce) package cream cheese, softened
- ½ cup mashed, ripe banana (about 1 medium banana)
- 1½ tablespoons all-purpose flour
- 6 tablespoons thick caramel ice cream topping, divided
- 1 large egg yolk
- 1½ teaspoons rum (or brandy) extract
- 1 (16.5-ounce) roll refrigerated sugar cookie dough, well chilled
- ½ cup chopped pecans

Preheat oven to 350°F. Spray an 8 x 8-inch baking

pan with nonstick spray or line with foil.

Beat the cream cheese, mashed banana, flour, 2 tablespoons caramel topping, egg yolk, and rum extract in a medium bowl with electric beaters until smooth; set aside.

Cut cookie dough in half. Press half of the dough in bottom of the prepared pan. Spread cream cheese mixture over dough. Crumble and sprinkle remaining half of cookie dough and pecans over cream cheese mixture; gently press into cream cheese layer.

Bake for 33–36 minutes or until the crust is golden brown and firm to the touch. Cool completely. Drizzle with remaining caramel topping. Cut into bars. Serve room temperature or chilled. Store in refrigerator.

MAKES 16 BARS.

Baker's Note

For a chocolate twist, use chocolate-chip cookie dough in place of sugar cookie dough.

BANANA MONKEY BARS

What are you waiting for? Any time is a good time to get together with friends and family—and bring along a great recipe you can share and you'll soon be known for. Like these quick and delicious banana bars that are made with ingredients likely in your pantry already.

- 1 (18.25-ounce) package yellow cake mix
- 1/3 cup vegetable oil
- 1 large egg
- 1 cup chopped nuts (e.g., peanuts, walnuts, or pecans)
- 1 (14-ounce) can sweetened condensed milk
- 1 cup mashed banana (about 2 medium bananas)
- 1 cup butterscotch baking chips (or milk chocolate chips)
- 1 1/3 cups sweetened flaked coconut

Preheat oven to 350°F (or 325° for dark-coated metal pan). Position oven rack in middle of oven. Spray the bottom only of a 13 x 9-inch metal baking pan with nonstick cooking spray (or foil-line pan; see page xxiv).

Beat cake mix, oil, and egg in a large bowl with electric mixer set on medium speed until well blended and crumbly. Stir in the nuts. Set aside 1 cup of the crumb mixture. Firmly press remaining crumb mixture on bottom of prepared pan.

Combine the condensed milk and mashed banana in a small bowl; pour evenly over crust. Top with butterscotch chips and coconut; press down firmly. Sprinkle with reserved crumb mixture.

Bake for 25–28 minutes or until lightly browned. Transfer to wire rack and cool completely. Cut into bars.

MAKES 24 LARGE OR 36 SMALL BARS.

BERRY-BERRY CHOCOLATE STREUSEL BARS

When the next pitch-in party comes along, make a batch of these bars and prepare for accolades. I guarantee you won't be bringing any home.

- 1 (19.5- to 19.8-ounce) package brownie mix
- 2¼ cups quick-cooking oats
- 2 teaspoons ground cinnamon
- 1 cup (2 sticks) unsalted butter, melted
- 1 (12-ounce) package frozen blueberries, thawed
- ¾ cup seedless raspberry jam
- 2 tablespoons all-purpose flour
- 1 tablespoon grated lemon peel

Preheat oven to 350°F (325°F for dark-coated metal pan). Position a rack in the lower third of the oven. Spray the bottom only of a 13 x 9-inch baking pan with nonstick cooking spray (or foil-line pan; see page xxiv).

Mix the brownie mix, oats, cinnamon, and melted butter in a large mixing bowl with a wooden spoon until just blended and all dry ingredients are moistened. Press half of mixture evenly into prepared pan.

Stir together the blueberries, jam, flour, and lemon peel in a medium mixing bowl. Spoon and spread berry mixture over prepared crust; top with reserved crumb mixture and press down gently.

Bake for 30–34 minutes or until topping is set and firm to the touch. Transfer to wire rack and cool completely.

MAKES 24 LARGE OR 36 SMALL BARS.

BLACK AND TAN ESPRESSO BARS

The symphony of chocolate and espresso in these sublime bars is sure to get a standing ovation. For a coffee-lover's gift, pair these grown-up bars with a bag of coffee beans or a gift certificate to the local coffeehouse.

- 2 cups crushed creme-filled chocolate cookies (e.g., Oreos)
- ⅓ cup butter, melted
- ⅓ cup milk
- 2 teaspoons unflavored gelatin
- 2 tablespoons instant espresso or coffee powder
- 1 (14-ounce) can sweetened condensed milk, chilled in refrigerator overnight
- ¾ cup sour cream

Line an 8 x 8 x 2-inch baking pan with foil (see page xxiv); lightly spray with nonstick cooking spray. Set aside.

Combine the cookie crumbs and melted butter in a medium bowl with a fork or fingers until well blended. Transfer crumb mixture to prepared pan. Press firmly into bottom of pan with a large square of wax paper. Freeze until ready to use.

Place the milk in a small saucepan; sprinkle gelatin over (do not stir). Let stand 10 minutes to soften. Add the espresso powder to saucepan and turn the heat under saucepan to medium. Whisk and stir until liquid is very hot (but not boiling) and the gelatin is completely dissolved. Remove from heat and cool for 15–20 minutes until lukewarm.

Whisk the chilled sweetened condensed milk and sour cream in a medium bowl until blended. Gradually add gelatin mixture, whisking until well blended. Pour and spread evenly over prepared crust. Refrigerate for 3 hours or until firm. Use foil lining to remove uncut bars from pan to cutting board. Cut into 24 bars. Store, loosely covered with foil or plastic wrap, in refrigerator.

MAKES 24 BARS.

BLACKBERRY MASCARPONE BARS

Extra-rich and creamy mascarpone, a soft Italian cheese similar to cream cheese, teams up with the bright flavor of fresh blackberries in these stylish cookies. If mascarpone is unavailable, substitute one (8-ounce) package of cream cheese.

- 1¼ cups crisp sugar cookie crumbs
- ¼ cup (½ stick) butter, melted
- ½ cup milk
- 2¼ teaspoons unflavored gelatin
- 1 (8-ounce) container mascarpone cheese, room temperature
- ½ cup sour cream
- ¾ cup powdered sugar
- 1 teaspoon vanilla extract
- ¼ teaspoon ground cardamom
- 1 cup fresh blackberries

Line an 8 x 8 x 2-inch baking pan with foil (see page xxiv); lightly spray with nonstick cooking spray. Set aside.

Combine the cookie crumbs and melted butter in a medium bowl with a fork or fingers until well blended. Transfer crumb mixture to prepared pan. Press firmly into bottom of pan with a large square of wax paper. Freeze until ready to use.

Place the milk in a small saucepan; sprinkle gelatin over (do not stir). Let stand 10 minutes to soften. Turn the heat under saucepan to medium. Whisk and stir until milk is very hot (but not boiling) and gelatin is completely dissolved. Remove from heat and set aside momentarily.

Beat the mascarpone cheese, sour cream, powdered sugar, vanilla, and cardamom in a large bowl with electric mixer on medium speed until creamy. Gradually add gelatin-milk mixture, beating on low speed and occasionally scraping sides of bowl with rubber spatula, until well blended.

Pour and evenly spread mascarpone mixture over prepared crust. Press the blackberries into the top of the bars. Refrigerate for 3 hours or until firm. Use foil lining to remove uncut bars from pan to cutting board. Cut into 16 bars. Store, loosely covered with foil or plastic wrap, in refrigerator.

MAKES 16 BARS.

BLACK-BOTTOMED BUTTERSCOTCH BARS

These showy cookies feature a rich, dark chocolate bottom, a smooth butterscotch top and a crunchy crown of peanuts. They'll surely attract a following of enthusiasts whenever you make them.

- 6 tablespoons (¾ stick) butter, melted
- 1 cup creamy peanut butter
- 1½ cups sifted powdered sugar
- 1 (9-ounce) package chocolate wafers, crushed into crumbs

- 1 (11-ounce) package (about 2 cups) butterscotch baking chips
- ¼ cup heavy whipping cream
- ¾ cup chopped roasted, lightly salted peanuts or cashews

Set aside an ungreased 13 x 9 x 2-inch baking pan.

Mix the melted butter, peanut butter, and powdered sugar in a large mixing bowl with a wooden spoon until blended. Stir in the chocolate wafer crumbs until combined. Press evenly into baking pan, pressing down and smoothing surface with a square of wax paper. Refrigerate while preparing topping.

Melt the butterscotch chips with the whipping cream in a heavy medium saucepan set over low heat, stirring until melted and smooth. Spoon and spread butterscotch mixture over crumb mixture; sprinkle with the nuts. Refrigerate until set, about 2 hours. Cut into 48 bars. Store in covered containers between layers of wax paper.

MAKES 48 BARS.

BLACK FOREST BITES

These cookies are based on the flavors of a far more complicated chocolate and cherry torte called Schwarzwalder Kirschtorte. It hails from the Black Forest region of Germany—hence the shortened name, Black Forest Torte. The classic flavor combination still holds tremendous appeal when simplified into these no-bake petites.

- 2 cups semisweet chocolate chips
- 2 tablespoons vegetable shortening
- 1 cup miniature marshmallows

- ½ teaspoon almond extract
- ⅔ cup dried cherries or cranberries
- 2 cups crisp rice cereal

Lightly spray an 8 x 8 x 2-inch square baking pan with nonstick cooking spray; set aside.

Place the chocolate chips and shortening in a medium saucepan over low heat. Stir until chips are melted and mixture is smooth. Remove from heat and stir in the marshmallows, almond extract, cherries, and cereal. Mix well.

Using a large square of wax paper, press and spread mixture into the prepared pan. Chill until set. Cut into 24 small squares. Store in covered containers between layers of wax paper.

MAKES 24 "BITES."

BLACKBERRY CHEESECAKE BARS

The popularity of cheesecake doesn't seem to end. Thank goodness. This version gives the tried-and-true classic a contrasting cookie base and a delicious swirl of blackberry jam. Cut them small and serve in the most casual of circumstances or cut them big and plate them with a handful of fresh berries for a sophisticated dinner finale.

- 1 (16.5-ounce) roll refrigerated sugar cookie dough, well chilled
- 2 (8-ounce) packages cream cheese, softened
- ⅔ cup granulated sugar
- 2 large eggs
- 1 teaspoon vanilla extract
- ¾ cup blackberry (or other fruit) preserves, room temperature

Preheat oven to 350°F. Spray a 13 x 9-inch pan with nonstick cooking spray or line with foil.

Cut cookie dough into ¼-inch-thick slices. Arrange slices in bottom of the prepared pan. With floured fingers, press dough evenly to form crust.

Bake for 10–13 minutes or until dough is golden brown (dough will appear slightly puffed). Remove from oven.

Meanwhile, beat the cream cheese and sugar in a medium bowl with electric beaters on high until smooth. Add eggs and vanilla; beat until just combined. Spread cream cheese mixture evenly over hot cookie base; dollop with teaspoons of blackberry jam. Swirl cream cheese filling and jam slightly with the tip of a knife.

Bake in middle of oven until slightly puffed, 22–25 minutes. Cool completely in pan and cut into bars; chill.

MAKES 24 BIG BARS.

Baker's Note

The preserves will be easier to swirl if they are room temperature instead of chilled.

BLACK-BOTTOM BANANA CHEESECAKE BARS

Looking for a stylish dessert to wrap up a casual summer gathering? You can both cool things down and fire things up when you pull these pretty (and very chocolate) cheesecake bars out of the icebox.

- 1 (18.25-ounce) package devil's food cake mix
- 3 (8-ounce) packages cream cheese, softened
- 3 large eggs
- ½ cup (1 stick) butter, melted
- 1 cup miniature semisweet chocolate chips
- 1 cup mashed ripe banana (about 2 large bananas)
- 1 cup powdered sugar, plus 1–2 tablespoons for garnish
- 1½ teaspoons vanilla extract

Preheat oven to 350°F (or 325°F for dark-coated metal pan). Position oven rack in middle of oven. Spray the bottom only of a 13 x 9-inch metal baking pan with nonstick cooking spray (or foil-line pan; see page xxiv).

Place the cake mix, 4 ounces (half of one 8-ounce package) of the softened cream cheese, 1 of the eggs, and the melted butter in a large bowl. Blend for 2 minutes with an electric mixer set on low speed until well blended. Stir in chocolate chips. Press mixture into bottom of prepared pan. Bake crust for 15 minutes.

While crust bakes, place the remaining cream cheese, mashed banana, 1 cup powdered sugar, and vanilla extract in a medium bowl. Blend for 2 minutes with electric mixer set on medium speed until smooth. Add remaining eggs, one at a time, beating only until incorporated. Spread cream cheese mixture evenly over chocolate crust.

Bake for 25–28 minutes or until just set. Transfer to wire rack and cool completely. Refrigerate for at least 2 hours before serving. Cut into bars and sprinkle with remaining 1–2 tablespoons powdered sugar.

MAKES 24 LARGE OR 36 SMALL BARS.

BLUEBERRY BARS

Showcase plump, fresh blueberries in these gorgeous bars during the summer months, or make them year-round with frozen berries. Either way, you're sure to receive rave reviews.

- 1¼ cups crisp sugar cookie crumbs
- ¼ cup (½ stick) butter, melted
- 3 tablespoons fresh lemon juice
- 2¼ teaspoons unflavored gelatin
- 1½ cups fresh blueberries or frozen (thawed) blueberries
- ½ cup sugar
- 1 (8-ounce) package cream cheese, softened

Line an 8 x 8 x 2-inch baking pan with foil (see page xxiv); lightly spray with nonstick cooking spray. Set aside.

Combine the cookie crumbs and melted butter in a medium bowl with a fork or fingers until well blended. Transfer crumb mixture to prepared pan. Press firmly into bottom of pan with a large square of wax paper. Freeze until ready to use.

Place the lemon juice in a small cup; sprinkle gelatin over (do not stir). Let stand 5 minutes to soften.

Puree the blueberries and sugar in a blender or food processor until smooth. Transfer mixture to a small saucepan. Heat over medium-high heat until hot but not boiling. Add gelatin mixture to saucepan. Whisk until gelatin is completely dissolved. Remove from heat and cool 20 minutes.

Beat the cream cheese in a large bowl with electric mixer on medium speed until creamy. Gradually add blueberry mixture, beating until well blended. Pour and evenly spread over prepared crust. Refrigerate 3 hours or until firm.

Use foil lining to remove uncut bars from pan to cutting board. Cut into 16 bars. Store, loosely covered with foil or plastic wrap, in refrigerator.

MAKES 16 BARS.

BLUEBERRY SOUR CREAM KUCHEN BARS

As the name implies, these easily assembled bars are inspired by German kuchen (pronounced KOO-khehn), which is a cheese- or fruit-filled bread that can be eaten for breakfast or dessert. The blueberries can be substituted for with your favorite fruit of choice, from apricots to apples to fresh or frozen peaches.

- 1 (18.25-ounce) package yellow cake mix
- ½ cup (1 stick) butter, softened
- 1 (3-ounce) package cream cheese, softened
- 2 large eggs
- 2 cups sour cream (not reduced fat)
- ¼ cup sugar
- ½ teaspoon cinnamon
- 2 cups fresh or frozen (thawed) blueberries

Preheat oven to 350°F. Position oven rack in middle of oven. Set aside an ungreased 13 x 9-inch baking pan.

Place the cake mix, softened butter, cream cheese, and 1 of the eggs in a large bowl. Blend with electric mixer for 1–2 minutes on low speed until a dough forms. Gather dough together and press into ungreased pan. Bake crust for 10–12 minutes or until light golden.

Whisk the sour cream with the sugar, cinnamon, and remaining egg in a medium bowl until smooth; mix in the blueberries. Spread mixture over partially baked crust.

Bake for 13–15 minutes, until sour cream layer is just set. Transfer to a wire rack and cool completely. Cut into bars. Store, covered, in refrigerator.

MAKES 36 SMALL OR 24 LARGE BARS.

BROWN SUGAR AND TOFFEE CHEESECAKE BARS

This cookie is dedicated to all of my fellow brown sugar lovers. Restraint is futile here, so be sure to invite a gaggle of good friends over to share the joy.

- 1 (19.5- to 19.8-ounce) package brownie mix
- ½ cup (1 stick) unsalted butter, melted
- 4 large eggs
- 3 (8-ounce) packages cream cheese, softened
- ¾ cup packed dark brown sugar
- 2 teaspoons vanilla extract
- 1 (10-ounce) package English toffee baking bits, divided

Preheat oven to 350°F (325°F for dark-coated metal pan). Position a rack in the lower third of the oven. Spray the bottom only of a 13 x 9-inch baking pan with nonstick cooking spray (or foil-line pan; see page xxiv).

Combine the brownie mix, melted butter, and 1 egg in a medium mixing bowl with a wooden spoon until just blended and all dry ingredients are moistened. Press mixture into prepared pan. Bake for 18 minutes. Remove from oven (leave oven on).

While crust bakes, beat the cream cheese and brown sugar with an electric mixer set on high until smooth. Add the remaining eggs and vanilla; beat until just blended. Stir in 1 cup of the toffee bits; pour mixture over hot crust and sprinkle with remaining toffee bits.

Return to oven and bake 25–28 minutes, until center is just barely set. Transfer to a wire rack and cool completely. Refrigerate for at least 3 hours until chilled.

MAKES 24 LARGE OR 36 SMALL BARS.

BROWN SUGAR- MILK CHOCOLATE MERINGUE BARS

Growing up, I loved lemon meringue pie, but only the lemon filling and crust—I thought the puffy meringue was some sort of penance for an otherwise heavenly dessert. Some years later, I had my first crisp meringue at a neighborhood bakery. Crisp and crunchy—it was nothing like the seepy version I was used to, and I was instantly hooked. These bars have the same crispy meringue, made even better with brown sugar, wrapped around a milk chocolate and almond filling.

- 1 (18.25-ounce) package German chocolate cake mix
- ½ cup (1 stick) butter, melted
- 2 large egg yolks
- 1 (12-ounce) package (2 cups) milk chocolate chips
- 1 cup sliced almonds, divided
- 4 large egg whites, room temperature
- 1 cup packed dark brown sugar

Preheat oven to 375°F (or 350°F for dark-coated metal pan). Position oven rack in middle of oven. Spray the bottom only of a 13 x 9-inch metal baking pan with nonstick cooking spray (or foil-line pan; see page xxiv).

Place the cake mix, melted butter, and egg yolks in a large bowl. Blend for 1–2 minutes with an electric mixer set on low speed until well blended. Press mixture evenly into prepared pan.

Bake crust for 20 minutes. Remove pan from oven (leave oven on). Sprinkle with chocolate chips and ½ cup of the almonds. Transfer to wire rack while preparing meringue.

In a large mixing bowl beat the egg whites with an electric mixer set on high until frothy. Gradually add brown sugar; beat until stiff peaks form. Carefully spread meringue over chips and nuts. Sprinkle with remaining ½ cup almonds.

Bake for an additional 13–15 minutes or until meringue is golden brown. Transfer to a wire rack and cool completely. Cut into bars.

MAKES 24 LARGE OR 36 SMALL BARS.

Variation:

DARK CHOCOLATE–RASPBERRY MERINGUE BARS: Prepare as directed above but use semisweet chocolate chips in place of the milk chocolate chips and eliminate the almonds. After sprinkling crust with chocolate chips, dollop ½ cup seedless raspberry preserves, by teaspoons, over the chips. Use plain white granulated sugar in place of the brown sugar in the meringue.

BURST OF LIME BARS

Imagine your favorite silken lemon bar; add a twist of lime and a kick of ginger and you know what this bar tastes like. It's an incomparable cookie for any occasion with an incredible flavor unlike any other.

- 1 (16.5-ounce) roll refrigerated sugar cookie dough, well chilled
- 4 large eggs
- 1½ cups granulated sugar
- ¾ cup fresh lime juice
- ⅓ cup all-purpose flour
- 1 teaspoon ground ginger
- 3 tablespoons sifted powdered sugar

Preheat oven to 350°F. Spray a 13 x 9-inch pan with nonstick cooking spray or line with foil.

Cut cookie dough into ¼-inch-thick slices. Arrange slices in bottom of the prepared pan. With floured fingers, press dough evenly to form crust.

Bake for 10–13 minutes or until light golden brown (dough will appear slightly puffed). Remove from oven.

Meanwhile, whisk together eggs and granulated sugar in a medium bowl until blended; whisk in lime juice, flour, and ginger. Pour mixture over warm, partially baked crust.

Reduce oven temperature to 300° and bake bars in middle of oven until just set, about 30 minutes. Cool completely in pan; cut into bars. Sift powdered sugar over bars before serving.

MAKES 36 BARS.

BUTTER RUM BARS WITH COCONUT AND MACADAMIA NUTS

End your next summer BBQ on a sweet note with these easy, island-inspired bars.

- 1 (18.25-ounce) package yellow cake mix
- ½ cup (1 stick) butter, melted
- 1 (14-ounce) can sweetened condensed milk
- 2 large eggs
- 2 tablespoons dark rum (or 2 teaspoons rum-flavored extract)
- 1½ cups sweetened shredded coconut
- 1 cup chopped macadamia nuts
- 1 cup milk or white chocolate chips
- 1 tablespoon vegetable shortening

Preheat oven to 350°F (or 325°F for dark-coated metal pan). Position oven rack in middle of oven. Spray the bottom only of a 13 x 9-inch metal baking pan with nonstick cooking spray (or foil-line pan; see page xxiv).

Place cake mix and melted butter in a large bowl. Blend for 1–2 minutes with an electric mixer set on low speed until well blended and crumbly. Press mixture into bottom of prepared pan. Bake for 15 minutes.

While crust bakes, whisk the condensed milk, eggs, and rum in a medium bowl until blended; stir in coconut and macadamia nuts. Pour mixture over partially baked crust.

Bake for 18–20 minutes longer or until golden at edges and just set at the center. Transfer to a wire rack.

In small saucepan set over low heat melt the chocolate chips with the shortening until melted and smooth. Drizzle over bars; cool completely.

MAKES 24 LARGE OR 36 SMALL BARS.

BUTTERSCOTCH BLONDIES

The brownie has legions of loyal fans, but the blondie has a multitude of equally steadfast enthusiasts. The reasons are clear: a rich and chewy butterscotch bar, studded with more butterscotch or a contrast of chocolate chips, and highly transportable to boot.

- 1 (18.25-ounce) package yellow cake mix
- ¼ cup packed dark brown sugar
- 2 large eggs
- ½ cup (1 stick) butter, melted
- 1 teaspoon vanilla extract
- 1 cup semisweet chocolate chips or butterscotch baking chips
- 1 cup chopped pecans, optional

Preheat oven to 350°F. Position oven rack in center of oven. Set aside a 13 x 9-inch baking pan.

Blend the cake mix, brown sugar, eggs, melted butter, and vanilla extract in a large mixing bowl with electric mixer on low speed for 1–2 minutes until all dry ingredients are moistened. Mix in the chocolate chips or butterscotch chips (dough will be stiff).

Spoon the dough into the ungreased pan; spread dough evenly with rubber spatula or fingers (dough will puff and spread as it bakes). If desired, sprinkle with chopped pecans; gently press into dough.

Bake for 22–25 minutes or until the bars are golden brown but still soft. Transfer pan to a wire rack and cool completely. Cut into bars or squares.

MAKES 24 LARGE OR 36 SMALL
BARS OR SQUARES.

Variations:

APPLE BLONDIES WITH CARAMEL FROSTING: Prepare as directed above but substitute 1 cup peeled, chopped tart apple (about 1 large apple) for the chocolate chips (pecans are still optional). Frost cooled blondies with Caramel Frosting (see page 374).

WHITE CHOCOLATE BLONDIES: Prepare as directed above but eliminate the brown sugar, substitute vanilla cake mix for the yellow cake mix, use white chocolate chips in place of semisweet chocolate chips, and use ½ teaspoon almond extract in place of the vanilla extract. If nuts are desired, substitute an equal amount of sliced or slivered almonds for the pecans.

BUTTERSCOTCH PUDDING BARS

Rich and creamy, these bars dazzle with their deep butterscotch flavor. It's a great way to enjoy the comforts of pudding in hand-held form.

- 11 tablespoons butter, divided
- 2 cups crushed creme-filled vanilla sandwich cookies (about 24 cookies)
- ¼ cup cornstarch
- 2½ cups half and half, divided use
- ⅔ cup packed dark brown sugar
- 1 teaspoon vanilla extract

Line an 8 x 8 x 2-inch baking pan with foil (see page xxiv); lightly spray with nonstick cooking spray. Set aside.

Melt 6 tablespoons of the butter in a large nonstick skillet set over medium-high heat. Combine the melted butter and cookie crumbs in a medium bowl with a fork or fingers until well blended. Transfer crumb mixture to prepared pan. Press firmly into bottom of pan with a large square of wax paper. Freeze until ready to use.

In a small bowl whisk the cornstarch and ½ cup of the half and half until the cornstarch is dissolved; set aside.

Combine the brown sugar and remaining butter in a medium saucepan. Cook over low heat, whisking constantly, until the butter is melted. Whisk in the remaining half and half until smooth and blended. Add cornstarch mixture. Stir over medium-high heat until mixture is thick and bubbly. Remove from heat and whisk in vanilla. Cool for 20 minutes, whisking occasionally to prevent skin from forming on top.

Pour and spread mixture evenly over prepared crust. Place a piece of plastic wrap directly on filling. Refrigerate for 4–6 hours or until firm. Use foil lining to remove uncut bars from pan to cutting board. Cut into 16 bars. Store, loosely covered with foil or plastic wrap, in refrigerator.

MAKES 16 BARS.

BUTTERY GOOEY CHESS SQUARES

When your kitchen is filled with the enticing aroma of vanilla and butter, you'll know that weekend baking will never be the same. These delectable treats are made with a buttery cake mix dough on the bottom and a generous layer of more butter, cream cheese, and vanilla on top—irresistible!

- 1 cup (2 sticks) butter, divided
- 1 (18.25-ounce) package yellow cake mix
- 4 large eggs
- 1 (8-ounce) package cream cheese, softened
- 2 teaspoons vanilla extract
- 1 (16-ounce) box powdered sugar

Preheat oven to 350°F (or 325°F for dark-coated metal pan). Position oven rack in middle of oven. Spray the bottom only of a 13 x 9-inch metal baking pan with nonstick cooking spray (or foil-line pan; see page xxiv).

Melt ½ cup (1 stick) of the butter in a small saucepan set over low heat. Beat the cake mix, melted butter, and 1 egg in a large bowl with an electric mixer set on medium speed until well blended (mixture will come together as a thick dough). Pat the dough evenly into the prepared pan. Set aside momentarily.

Melt the remaining butter in a small saucepan set over low heat. Beat the softened cream cheese and vanilla extract in a large bowl with an electric mixer set on medium speed until smooth, scraping down sides of bowl occasionally. Add the melted butter and remaining 3 eggs; blend until smooth. Add the powdered sugar; blend until smooth.

Spread cream cheese mixture over prepared crust. Bake for 42–45 minutes (do not overbake; bars should be slightly gooey). Transfer to a wire rack and cool completely. Cut into bars or squares. Cover and store in refrigerator.

MAKES 24 LARGE OR 36 SMALL BARS.

CALIFORNIA DRIED FRUIT AND NUT BARS

Dried fruit makes a great, wholesome cookie in short order. Any combination of chopped dried fruit will work here. To avoid the chopping step, look for pre-chopped dried fruit mixes in the supermarket where raisins are shelved. They are typically packaged in traditional blends (e.g., dried raisins, cranberries, apricots, and plums) or in unusual blends such as tropical fruit medleys.

- ½ cup (1 stick) butter
- ½ cup firmly packed light brown sugar
- 2 large egg yolks, slightly beaten
- 1 cup mixed dried fruits, chopped
- 1 cup lightly salted, coarsely chopped roasted nuts
- 2 cups crisp rice cereal

Lightly spray a 9 x 9 x 2-inch baking pan with nonstick cooking spray; set aside.

Melt the butter in a large nonstick skillet. Remove from heat and add the brown sugar and egg yolks. Return to low heat and cook and stir until mixture simmers and thickens slightly. Remove from heat and stir in the dried fruits, nuts, and cereal. Cool for 5 minutes.

With a large square of wax paper, firmly press mixture into prepared pan. Cool completely.

Cut into 16 bars. Store in covered containers between layers of wax paper.

MAKES 16 BARS.

CANDY BAR BARS

These over-the-top bars are intense, rich, and chocolate to the max.

- 1 (19.5- to 19.8-ounce) package brownie mix
- ⅓ cup vegetable oil
- ¼ cup water
- 2 large eggs
- 30 caramels, unwrapped
- 1 (14-ounce) can sweetened condensed milk
- ½ cup (1 stick) butter
- 2 cups coarsely chopped chocolate candy bars (e.g., Snickers, Butterfinger, or Heath)
- 1½ cups pecan halves, coarsely chopped

Preheat oven to 350°F. Foil-line a 13 x 9-inch baking pan.

Combine the brownie mix, oil, water, and eggs in a medium bowl with a wooden spoon until just blended and all dry ingredients are moistened. Spread 1½ cups of the batter into prepared pan. Bake for 10–15 minutes or until center is set.

Combine the caramels, sweetened condensed milk, and butter in a medium saucepan. Cook over medium-low heat until caramels are almost melted. Whisk until smooth.

Gently spread caramel mixture over partially baked brownie. Sprinkle caramel with candy bars. Spread remaining unbaked brownie batter evenly over candy bars. Sprinkle with pecan halves.

Bake 20–25 minutes longer until top is just set. Transfer to a wire tack and cool completely. Cover and refrigerate. Lift chilled brownies from pan onto cutting board. Cut into 48 small bars.

MAKES 48 SMALL BROWNIES.

CAPPUCCINO BARS

If you love coffee or espresso drinks, you'll savor the flavor of these rich, layered bars.

- 9 tablespoons butter, softened, divided use
- 6 (1-ounce) squares semisweet chocolate, divided use
- ⅓ cup firmly packed light brown sugar
- 2 cups chocolate wafer or chocolate graham cracker crumbs
- 1 cup finely chopped walnuts
- 1 teaspoon vanilla extract
- 2 teaspoons instant espresso or coffee powder
- 2 cups powdered sugar, sifted
- 1 (3-ounce) package cream cheese, softened
- 2½ tablespoons milk

Lightly spray an 9 x 9 x 2-inch pan with nonstick cooking spray; set aside.

Melt 8 tablespoons (1 stick) of the butter with 3 squares of the chocolate in a medium saucepan. Remove from the heat; stir in the brown sugar, chocolate wafer crumbs, and walnuts. Press mixture into prepared pan with a large square of wax paper. Chill for 1 hour.

Combine the vanilla and espresso powder

in a small cup, stirring until dissolved. Blend the espresso mixture, powdered sugar, cream cheese, and milk in a medium bowl with an electric mixer set on medium until mixture has an icing-like consistency; spread over bars. Chill for 30 minutes.

Melt the remaining butter with the remaining chocolate, stirring until mixture is smooth. Spread over the top of the bars. Chill for 1–2 hours. Cut into 16 squares by dipping a sharp knife in hot water and let it melt through the chocolate.

Store in covered containers between layers of wax paper.

MAKES 16 SQUARES.

bowl for 2 minutes or until caramels are melted, stirring every minute. Immediately pour over cereal mixture; mix lightly until well coated.

With a large square of wax paper, press into the prepared pan. Refrigerate for 30 minutes or until firm. Cut into 24 bars. Store in covered containers between layers of wax paper.

MAKES 24 BARS.

Variation:

CARAMEL NUT BARS: Replace the dried apples and ½ cup almonds with 1½ cups lightly salted roasted nuts, any variety, coarsely chopped. Use 3 tablespoons milk in place of the juice concentrate.

CARAMEL APPLE BARS

So easy and so good, these really do taste like caramel apples thanks to the apple juice concentrate and dried apples.

- 8 cups sweetened puffed wheat cereal
- 1½ cups chopped dried apples
- ½ cup chopped roasted almonds or peanuts
- 1 (14-ounce) package caramels, unwrapped
- ½ (6-ounce) container frozen apple juice concentrate, thawed

Lightly spray a 13 x 9 x 2-inch baking pan with nonstick cooking spray; set aside.

In a large bowl mix the cereal, dried apples, and nuts.

Microwave the caramels and apple juice concentrate on high in a medium microwavable

CARAMEL APPLE CHOCOLATE CRUMBLE BARS

We all know what a ho-hum cookie is; we've had many too many of them in our times. These cookie bars are the exact opposite. Like a chocolate-dipped caramel apple, they are pure panache.

- 1 (19.5- to 19.8-ounce) package brownie mix
- 2¼ cups quick-cooking oats
- 1 cup (2 sticks) unsalted butter, melted
- 1 cup semisweet or milk chocolate chips
- 4½ cups coarsely chopped peeled tart apples (about 4 large apples)
- 3 tablespoons all-purpose flour

- 1 (14-ounce) bag caramels, unwrapped
- 2 tablespoons cream or milk

Preheat oven to 350°F (325°F for dark-coated metal pan). Position a rack in the lower third of the oven. Spray the bottom only of a 13 x 9-inch baking pan with nonstick cooking spray (or foil-line pan; see page xxiv).

Combine the brownie mix, oats, and melted butter in a large mixing bowl with a wooden spoon until just blended and all dry ingredients are moistened. Press half of mixture evenly into prepared pan. Add chocolate chips to remaining crumbs.

Toss together the chopped apples and flour in another large mixing bowl. Spread over prepared crust; set aside.

Melt caramels with cream in a medium saucepan set over low heat, stirring occasionally, until melted. Pour caramel mixture evenly over apples. Top with reserved crumb mixture and press down gently.

Bake for 30–34 minutes or until topping is set and firm to the touch. Transfer to wire rack and cool completely.

MAKES 24 LARGE OR 36 SMALL BARS.

CARAMEL APPLE STREUSEL BARS

Surprise your favorite apple aficionado with these caramel apple bars to convey the extent of your good wishes.

- 1 (18.25-ounce) package yellow cake mix
- 1 cup (2 sticks) butter, melted

- 2¼ cups quick-cooking oats
- 4 cups coarsely chopped, peeled tart apples (about 4 large apples)
- 1 (16-ounce) container caramel apple dip

Preheat oven to 350°F (or 325°F for dark-coated metal pan). Position oven rack in middle of oven. Spray the bottom only of a 13 x 9-inch metal baking pan with nonstick cooking spray (or foil-line pan; see page xxiv).

Reserve 3 tablespoons cake mix. Place the remaining cake mix and melted butter in a large bowl. Blend for 1–2 minutes with an electric mixer set on low speed until smooth. Stir in oats until blended. Press half of mixture evenly into prepared pan.

Toss together the chopped apples and remaining 3 tablespoons cake mix in another large mixing bowl; spread over prepared crust; set aside momentarily. Pour caramel dip evenly over apples. Top with reserved crumb mixture and press down gently.

Bake for 30–34 minutes or until topping is set and firm to the touch. Transfer to wire rack and cool completely.

MAKES 24 LARGE OR 36 SMALL BARS.

Variation:

PEACHY KEEN STREUSEL BARS: Prepare as directed above but substitute chopped fresh (or frozen, thawed) peaches for the apples and 1 (12-ounce) jar of peach preserves for the caramel apple dip.

CARAMEL CHOCOLATE-CHIP BARS

Who doesn't love the combination of caramel and chocolate? By adding brown sugar to caramel cake mix, these simple-to-prepare bars are richly flavored treat

- 1 (18.25-ounce) package caramel cake mix
- 2 large eggs
- ¼ cup water
- ¼ cup firmly packed brown sugar
- ¼ cup butter
- 1 cup semisweet chocolate chips

Preheat oven to 375°F. Spray a 13 x 9-inch baking pan with nonstick cooking spray.

Combine the cake mix, eggs, water, brown sugar, and butter in a large bowl with a wooden spoon until thoroughly blended (dough will be very thick). Stir in chocolate chips. Spread dough into prepared pan.

Bake for 24–27 minutes or until toothpick inserted in center comes out clean. Cool completely in pan. Cut into bars.

MAKES 36 BARS.

CARAMEL CHOCOLATE PECAN BARS

I have long loved the flavors of caramel, chocolate, and pecans, especially in combination. These easy bars satisfy my sweet cravings, without fuss, when my sweet tooth strikes.

- 1 (16.5-ounce) roll refrigerated sugar cookie dough, well chilled
- 1⅓ cups caramel apple dip (or caramel ice cream topping)
- 3 tablespoons all-purpose flour
- 2 cups chopped pecans
- 1⅓ cups semisweet chocolate chips

Preheat oven to 350°F. Spray a 13 x 9-inch pan with nonstick cooking spray or line with foil.

Cut cookie dough into ¼-inch-thick slices. Arrange slices in bottom of the prepared pan. With floured fingers, press dough evenly to form crust. Bake for 10–14 minutes or until light golden brown (dough will appear slightly puffed).

While crust bakes, combine caramel topping and flour in a small bowl; blend until smooth. Remove pan from oven. Immediately sprinkle partially baked crust with pecans and chocolate chips. Drizzle with caramel mixture.

Return to oven; bake for an additional 13–17 minutes or until topping is bubbly. Remove from oven and cool completely. Cut into bars.

MAKES 36 BARS.

"CARAMEL DELIGHTFUL" BARS

These bars were inspired by a scrumptious Girl Scout cookie of similar name, made even better with the addition of a chocolate cookie crust. Perhaps "delirium" would be more apropos than "delightful."

- 1 (19.5- to 19.8-ounce) package brownie mix
- ½ cup (1 stick) unsalted butter, melted
- 1 (7-ounce) package (about 2⅔ cups) sweetened shredded coconut

- 1 (14-ounce) can sweetened condensed milk
- 2 teaspoons vanilla extract
- 1 cup semisweet chocolate chunks or chips
- 1 cup chopped pecans
- 30 caramels, unwrapped
- 2 tablespoons milk

Preheat oven to 350°F (325°F for dark-coated metal pan). Position a rack in the lower third of the oven. Spray a 13 x 9-inch baking pan with nonstick cooking spray (or foil-line pan; see page xxiv).

Combine the brownie mix and melted butter in a medium mixing bowl with a wooden spoon until just blended and all dry ingredients are moistened. Press mixture into prepared pan. Bake for 15 minutes. Remove from oven (leave oven on).

Meanwhile, mix the coconut, condensed milk, and vanilla in a medium mixing bowl until blended; spread over hot crust and sprinkle with the chocolate chunks and pecans.

Bake for an additional 18–20 minutes or until coconut is lightly browned. Transfer to wire rack.

Melt caramels and milk in a medium saucepan set over low heat, stirring until melted and smooth. Drizzle over bars. Transfer to a wire rack and cool completely. Cut into bars.

MAKES 24 LARGE OR 36 SMALL BARS.

CARAMEL FUDGE BARS

With a dream-team combination of caramel and chocolate fudge, these bars could win any popularity contest.

- 54 flaky, buttery rectangular crackers (e.g., Waverly or Club crackers)
- 1 (14-ounce) can sweetened condensed milk
- 1 cup firmly packed dark brown sugar
- ½ cup (1 stick) butter
- 6 tablespoons milk, divided use
- 1 cup graham cracker crumbs
- 1 cup semisweet chocolate chips
- 1 cup creamy peanut butter

Lightly spray a 13 x 9 x 2-inch pan with nonstick cooking spray; set aside. Place half of the crackers in bottom of the prepared pan.

Combine the sweetened condensed milk, brown sugar, butter, and 4 tablespoons (¼ cup) of the milk in a medium saucepan. Cook over low heat until butter is melted, stirring frequently. Increase heat to medium-high; bring to a boil. Boil for 5 minutes, stirring constantly. Remove from heat and stir in the graham cracker crumbs.

Pour and spread half of caramel mixture over crackers in pan. Arrange remaining crackers over caramel. Top with remaining caramel mixture.

Heat the chocolate chips and remaining milk in a small saucepan over low heat, stirring until chocolate is melted and smooth. Stir in the peanut butter until well blended. Spread chocolate mixture over bars. Refrigerate for 30 minutes or until set. Cut into 36 bars. Store in covered containers between layers of wax paper.

MAKES 36 BARS.

CARAMEL MALLOW BROWNIE BARS

Bauer's Candies, Inc., located in Lawrenceburg, Kentucky, makes a special candy that ranks at the very top of my all-time favorites. Known as a "modjeska," it is a caramel-covered marshmallow that tastes like a piece of heaven. These bars were inspired by modjeskas, with an additional tweak of chocolate. You won't be disappointed!

- 1 (19.5- to 19.8-ounce) package brownie mix
- ½ cup (1 stick) unsalted butter, melted
- 1 large egg
- 1 (17-ounce) jar premium caramel ice cream topping
- 3 cups miniature marshmallows

Preheat oven to 350°F (325°F for dark-coated metal pan). Position a rack in the lower third of the oven. Spray the bottom only of a 13 x 9-inch baking pan with nonstick cooking spray (or foil-line pan; see page xxiv).

Combine the brownie mix, melted butter, and egg in a medium mixing bowl with a wooden spoon until just blended and all dry ingredients are moistened. Reserve 2/3 cup of mixture; press remaining mixture into prepared pan.

Bake for 21–24 minutes or until center is set (do not overbake). Pour caramel topping over hot crust. Sprinkle with marshmallows. Spoon remaining brownie mixture randomly over bars.

Bake for an additional 6–8 minutes or until marshmallows are puffed and lightly browned (do not overbake). Transfer to a wire rack and cool completely. Cut into bars.

MAKES 24 LARGE OR 36 SMALL BARS.

CARAMEL MALLOW BUTTERSCOTCH BARS

We all know about the great matches that chocolate and peanut butter, lemon and ginger, and cinnamon and vanilla make. Well, here's another made-for-each-other combination: caramel and marshmallow. Prepare to hoot and holler when you take a bite.

- 1 (18.25-ounce) package yellow cake mix
- ¼ cup (1 stick) butter, melted
- ¼ cup water
- ¼ cup packed light brown sugar
- 2 large eggs
- 3 cups miniature marshmallows
- 1 cup butterscotch baking chips
- ¾ cup caramel ice cream topping

Preheat oven to 350°F (or 325°F for dark-coated metal pan). Position oven rack in middle of oven. Spray the bottom only of a 13 x 9-inch metal baking pan with nonstick cooking spray (or foil-line pan; see page xxiv).

Place the cake mix, melted butter, water, brown sugar, and eggs in a large bowl. Blend with an electric mixer for 1–2 minutes on medium speed, until well blended and crumbly. Press mixture evenly in prepared pan.

Bake for 15–18 minutes or until golden. Remove from oven and sprinkle with marshmallows and butterscotch baking chips.

Bake 5–8 minutes longer or until marshmallows are puffed and golden. Transfer to wire rack and cool completely. Drizzle with caramel topping. Cut into bars.

MAKES 24 LARGE OR 36 SMALL BARS.

CARAMEL MOCHA CRUNCH BARS

Caramel and coffee pair perfectly with chocolate. All three taste wonderful when stirred together in these rich bars. If you prefer to skip the nuts, leave them out and add an extra cup of cereal to the mix. And if you prefer milk or semisweet chocolate to white, go ahead and make the switch.

- 1 (14-ounce) bag caramels, unwrapped
- 2 tablespoons butter
- 2 tablespoons water
- 2 teaspoons instant espresso or coffee powder
- 6 cups cocoa-flavored crisp rice cereal
- 1 cup coarsely chopped roasted, lightly salted cashews or almonds
- 1 cup white chocolate chips, divided

Lightly spray a 13 x 9 x 2-inch baking pan with nonstick cooking spray; set aside.

Microwave the caramels, butter, water, and espresso powder in a large microwave-safe mixing bowl on high for 3 minutes or until melted and smooth, stirring after each minute.

Add the cereal and nuts. Stir until well coated. Add ½ cup white chocolate chips, stirring until combined.

Using a large piece of wax paper, press mixture evenly into prepared pan. Let stand for about 2 minutes. Sprinkle the remaining white chocolate chips over the mixture. Using wax paper, press the chips evenly into the bars. Cut into large bars when cool. Store in covered containers between layers of wax paper.

MAKES 24 BARS.

CARAMEL ROCKY ROAD BARS

Sometimes mistakes are wonderful. Case in point, these bars, which were originally supposed to have chocolate fudge topping. But when I asked a friend to pick up the ingredients to test these one day, she came back with caramel. I decided "what the heck" and gave it a try. What a treat! They are favorites wherever they go. Any caramel topping will do, but for a truly amazing bar, buy a premium brand.

- 1½ cups lightly salted peanuts, divided
- 1 (18.25-ounce) package devils food cake mix
- 1 cup (2 sticks) butter, melted
- 2¼ cups quick-cooking oats
- 1 (17.5-ounce) jar caramel ice cream topping
- 4 cups miniature marshmallows
- 1½ cups semisweet chocolate chips

Preheat oven to 350°F (or 325°F for dark-coated metal pan). Position oven rack in middle of oven. Spray the bottom only of a 13 x 9-inch metal baking pan with nonstick cooking spray (or foil-line pan; see page xxiv).

Coarsely chop ½ cup of the peanuts. Place the chopped peanuts, cake mix, and melted butter in a large bowl. Blend for 1–2 minutes with an electric mixer set on medium speed until well blended. Stir in oats until blended. Press half of mixture evenly into prepared pan.

Pour caramel topping evenly over crust. Sprinkle with marshmallows, remaining 1 cup peanuts, and chocolate chips. Top with reserved oat mixture; press down gently.

Bake for 30–34 minutes or until topping is

set and firm to the touch. Transfer to wire rack and cool completely.

MAKES 24 LARGE OR 36 SMALL BARS.

CARDAMOM, ALMOND, AND ORANGE BARS

Fragrant and flavorful are the catchwords for these elegant bars. Cardamom is often used in Scandinavian baking and is particularly delicious here in combination with chocolate and citrus. If you cannot find it, ground coriander or nutmeg may be substituted. Perfect for spring dining and celebrating, these delicious mouthfuls are sure to awaken your taste buds.

- 1 (19.5- to 19.8-ounce) package brownie mix
- ½ cup (1 stick) unsalted butter, melted
- 3 large eggs
- 3½ tablespoons all-purpose flour
- 2 teaspoons vanilla extract
- ¾ teaspoon ground cardamom
- ¼ teaspoon salt
- 1½ cups sliced almonds
- 1½ cups powdered sugar
- 2 tablespoons freshly squeezed orange juice
- 2 teaspoons grated orange zest

Preheat oven to 350°F (325°F for dark-coated metal pan). Position a rack in the lower third of the oven. Spray the bottom only of a 13 x 9-inch baking pan with nonstick cooking spray (or foil-line pan; see page xxiv).

Combine the brownie mix and melted butter in a medium mixing bowl with a wooden spoon un-til just blended and all dry ingredients are moistened. Press mixture into prepared pan. Bake for 15 minutes. Remove from oven (leave oven on).

Meanwhile, mix the eggs, flour, vanilla, cardamom, and salt in a medium mixing bowl with an electric mixer set on medium about 2 minutes or until smooth; stir in the almonds. Spread the mixture over hot crust.

Bake for 18–21 minutes or until top is golden brown and set around edges. Transfer to wire rack to cool. Whisk the powdered sugar, orange juice, and zest in a small mixing bowl until smooth; spread evenly over bars.

MAKES 24 LARGE OR 36 SMALL BARS.

CARMELITAS (CAKE MIX)

Pick up a good book, brew a pot of coffee, and head to your favorite easy chair with one of these carmelita bars in hand. Don't forget the napkin as these treats are definitely on the (deliciously) gooey side.

- 1 (18.25-ounce) package yellow cake mix
- 1 cup (2 sticks) butter, melted
- 2 cups quick-cooking oats
- 2 cups miniature semisweet chocolate chips, divided
- 1 (16-ounce) container caramel apple dip

Preheat oven to 350°F (or 325°F for dark-coated metal pan). Position oven rack in middle of oven. Spray the bottom only of a 13 x 9-inch metal baking pan with nonstick cooking spray (or foil-line pan; see page xxiv).

Place the cake mix and melted butter in a large bowl. Blend 1–2 minutes with an electric mixer set on low speed until well blended. Stir in oats until blended. Press half of mixture evenly into prepared pan. Add 1 cup miniature chocolate chips to remaining mixture; set aside momentarily.

In a medium bowl stir together the caramel dip and remaining 1 cup chocolate chips. Pour caramel mixture over prepared crust and sprinkle with reserved crumb mixture.

Bake 28–30 minutes or until topping is firm to the touch. Transfer to a wire rack and cool completely. Cut into bars.

MAKES 24 LARGE OR 36 SMALL BARS.

CARMELITAS (COOKIE DOUGH)

For a few selfish moments I came close to dubbing these scrumptious bake-house bars "Camilla-litas." Of all the cookies in this book, I could easily eat these every day without ever tiring of them. I prefer them with milk chocolate chips, but I have also made them with butterscotch, white chocolate, and cinnamon chips, all to rave reviews.

- 2 (16.5-ounce) rolls refrigerated sugar cookie dough
- 1¾ cups quick-cooking oats, divided use
- ⅔ cup packed dark brown sugar, divided
- 2 teaspoons vanilla extract, divided
- 1 (14-ounce) bag caramels, unwrapped
- ½ cup (1 stick) butter
- 1 (14-ounce) can sweetened condensed milk
- 1 cup semisweet chocolate chips

Preheat oven to 350°F.

Break up 1 roll of the cookie dough into a large bowl. Sprinkle with ¾ cup of the oats, ⅓ cup of the brown sugar and 1 teaspoon of the vanilla. Mix well with fingers until blended. Press evenly into bottom of ungreased 13 x 9-inch pan to form crust.

Bake crust for 13–18 minutes or until light golden brown.

Meanwhile, break up remaining roll of the cookie dough in same bowl. Sprinkle with remaining ¾ cup of the oats, ⅓ cup of the brown sugar and 1 teaspoon of the vanilla. Mix well with fingers until blended.

Heat the caramels, butter, and condensed milk in a large heavy saucepan, over medium-low heat, stirring frequently, until caramels are melted and mixture is smooth.

Spread caramel mixture evenly over baked crust and sprinkle with chocolate chips. Crumble remaining cookie dough mixture evenly over caramel.

Bake 20–25 minutes longer or until light golden brown. Cool for 1 hour. Refrigerate for 1 hour or until firm. Cut into bars.

MAKES 36 BARS.

CARROT CAKE BARS

I'd like to convince myself that eating one of these moist, cream cheese–topped bars is not an exercise in indulgence but rather good health. After all, carrots have been revered for their nutritional benefits for more than 2,000 years. You might just have to eat two to be on the safe side.

- 1 (18.25-ounce) package carrot cake or spice cake mix
- ⅔ cup vegetable oil

- 3 large eggs
- 1 cup shredded, peeled carrots
- 1 cup raisins (or dried cranberries)
- 1 cup chopped pecans, optional
- 1 recipe Cream Cheese Frosting (see page 366)

Preheat oven to 350°F (or 325°F for dark-coated metal pan). Position oven rack in middle of oven. Spray the bottom only of a 13 x 9-inch metal baking pan with nonstick cooking spray (or foil-line pan; see page xxiv).

Mix the cake mix, oil, and eggs in a large bowl with an electric mixer on low speed for 30 seconds. Scrape down the sides of the bowl. Increase the mixer speed to medium and beat for 1–2 minutes more, or until batter is smooth and very thick. Stir in the carrots, raisins, and pecans with a wooden spoon.

Spread the batter into the prepared pan, pressing out to cover the bottom (dough will spread as it bakes).

Bake for 22–25 minutes or until just set at center (do not overbake). Transfer to a wire rack and cool completely. Prepare Cream Cheese Frosting; spread over cooled bars. Cut into bars or squares.

MAKES 24 LARGE OR 36 SMALL BARS.

- 2 cups miniature marshmallows
- 1 cup lightly salted roasted cashews, chopped
- 1 cup butterscotch baking chips
- 1 cup canned evaporated milk
- ½ cup light corn syrup
- 1 tablespoon butter
- 1 tablespoon vanilla extract

Lightly spray a 9 x 9 x 2-inch baking pan with nonstick cooking spray; set aside.

Mix the crumbs, marshmallows, and cashews in a large bowl; set aside.

Combine the butterscotch chips, evaporated milk, and corn syrup in a medium saucepan. Stir over low heat until butterscotch chips are melted. Increase heat to medium; bring to a full boil. Boil for 10 minutes, stirring constantly. Remove from heat and stir in butter and vanilla until blended.

Immediately stir butterscotch mixture into the crumb mixture, mixing until well blended. Spread evenly in prepared pan, pressing down and smoothing surface with a square of wax paper. Refrigerate until set, about 3 hours. Cut into bars. Store in covered containers between layers of wax paper.

MAKES 24 BARS.

CASHEW BLONDIES

Butterscotch lovers will love this no-bake rendition of classic blondies. Although scrumptious with cashews, you can substitute the roasted nut of your choice, from almonds to macadamias to peanuts.

- 2½ cups finely crushed graham cracker crumbs

CASHEW CRUNCH BROWNIE BARS

Looking for a showstopper bar cookie? You've turned to the right page, and it couldn't be easier than with this tiered treat. With but a few steps, you can take brownie mix to the ooh-aah level by covering it in layers of marshmallows, nuts, and chow mein noodles. The contrast of crispy and chewy is guaranteed to make this a "Wow!"-inducing dessert.

- 1 (19.5- to 19.8-ounce) package brownie mix
- ½ cup (1 stick) unsalted butter, melted
- 1 large egg
- 3 cups miniature marshmallows
- 1 (14-ounce) can sweetened condensed milk
- ½ cup creamy peanut butter
- 2 teaspoons vanilla extract
- 1 (3-ounce) can chow mein noodles
- 1 cup coarsely chopped roasted, lightly salted cashews or peanuts

Preheat oven to 350°F (325°F for dark-coated metal pan). Position a rack in the lower third of the oven. Spray the bottom only of a 13 x 9-inch baking pan with nonstick cooking spray (or foil-line pan; see page xxiv).

Combine the brownie mix, melted butter, and egg in a medium mixing bowl with a wooden spoon until just blended and all dry ingredients are moistened. Press mixture into prepared pan. Bake for 22–24 minutes, until just set at center (do not overbake).

Transfer to a wire rack and immediately sprinkle with marshmallows. Return to oven and bake 2 minutes longer or until marshmallows begin to puff. Remove from oven; transfer to a wire rack to cool.

Meanwhile, combine condensed milk and peanut butter in heavy saucepan over medium heat,; stir until slightly thickened, 5–6 minutes. Remove from heat; stir in vanilla, noodles, and nuts. Spread evenly over marshmallows. Transfer to wire rack and cool completely. Chill for 1 hour in refrigerator. Cut into bars. Store loosely covered at room temperature.

MAKES 24 LARGE OR 36 SMALL BARS.

CHEESECAKE BARS

A silky layer of vanilla cream cheese atop a buttery cookie crust makes for one fine bar cookie.

- 1¼ cups crisp sugar cookie crumbs
- ¼ cup (½ stick) butter, melted
- ½ cup milk
- 2 teaspoons unflavored gelatin
- 1 (8-ounce) package cream cheese, softened
- 1 cup sour cream
- ¾ cup powdered sugar
- 1½ teaspoons vanilla extract

Line an 8 x 8 x 2-inch baking pan with foil (see page xxiv); lightly spray with nonstick cooking spray. Set aside.

Combine the sugar cookie crumbs and melted butter in a medium bowl with a fork or fingers until well blended. Transfer crumb mixture to prepared pan. Press firmly into bottom of pan with a large square of wax paper. Freeze until ready to use.

Place the milk in a small saucepan; sprinkle gelatin over (do not stir). Let stand for 10 minutes to soften. Turn the heat under saucepan to medium. Whisk and stir until milk is very hot (but not boiling) and gelatin is completely dissolved. Remove from heat and set aside momentarily.

Beat the cream cheese, sour cream, powdered sugar, and vanilla in a large bowl with electric mixer on medium speed until creamy. Gradually add gelatin-milk mixture, beating on low speed and occasionally scraping sides of bowl with rubber spatula, until well blended.

Pour and spread cream cheese mixture evenly over prepared crust. Refrigerate for 3 hours or until firm. Use foil lining to remove uncut bars from pan to cutting board. Cut into bars. Store, loosely covered with foil or plastic wrap, in refrigerator.

MAKES 16 BARS.

CHEESECAKE-FILLED CHOCOLATE STREUSEL BARS

Take heart as you take up spoon and bowl to make these soon-to-be-classic bar cookies. A chocolate crumble cookie bottom and topping with a smooth layer of cheesecake sandwiched in between? Pure comfort.

- 1 (19.5- to 19.8-ounce) package brownie mix
- 2¼ cups quick-cooking oats
- 1 cup (2 sticks) unsalted butter, melted
- 2 (8-ounce) packages cream cheese, softened
- ½ cup sugar
- 2 large eggs
- 1½ teaspoons vanilla extract

Preheat oven to 350°F (325°F for dark-coated metal pan). Position a rack in the lower third of the oven. Spray the bottom only of a 13 x 9-inch baking pan with nonstick cooking spray (or foil-line pan; see page xxiv).

Combine the brownie mix, oats, and melted butter in a large mixing bowl with a wooden spoon until just blended and all dry ingredients are moistened. Press half of mixture evenly into prepared pan.

Beat the cream cheese and sugar in a medium mixing bowl with electric mixer set on high until smooth. Add eggs and vanilla; beat until just blended. Spoon and spread cheesecake mixture over base layer; top with reserved crumb mixture and press down gently.

Bake for 30–34 minutes or until topping is firm to the touch. Transfer to a wire rack and cool completely. Cut into bars.

MAKES 24 LARGE OR 36 SMALL BARS.

CHERRY PIE BARS

Come cherry season, it's hard to escape the allure of the sweet little fruits. But if the notion of baking a pie seems like too much work, consider these simple bars, which offer the pleasure of pie with a lot less effort.

- 1 (18.25-ounce) package vanilla cake mix
- 8 tablespoons (1 stick) butter, melted, divided
- 1¼ cups quick-cooking oats, divided
- 1 large egg
- 1 (21-ounce) can cherry pie filling
- ¼ cup packed light brown sugar
- ½ cup chopped pecans

Preheat oven to 350°F (or 325°F for dark-coated metal pan). Position oven rack in middle of oven. Spray the bottom only of a 13 x 9-inch metal baking pan with nonstick cooking spray (or foil-line pan; see page xxiv).

Combine the cake mix, 6 tablespoons melted butter, and 1 cup of the oats in a large bowl with a wooden spoon until well blended (mixture will be crumbly); reserve 1 cup of crumb mixture. Stir the egg into the remaining mixture until well blended; press into bottom of prepared pan.

Pour the cherry pie filling over crust. Combine

the reserved cake mixture, remaining oats, remaining melted butter, brown sugar, and pecans in small bowl until blended; sprinkle evenly over cherry filling.

Bake for 30–35 minutes or until filling is bubbly and topping is golden. Transfer to wire rack and cool completely. Cut into bars.

MAKES 24 LARGE OR 36 SMALL BARS.

Variation:

CHOCOLATE CHERRY PIE BARS: Prepare as directed above but use chocolate cake mix in place of vanilla cake mix and use 1 cup miniature semisweet chocolate chips in place of the pecans.

CHEWY APRICOT GRANOLA BARS

At my house, these granola bars are standard fare, perfect for snacks, lunch bags, breakfast on the run, and late-night munching. They can be varied in multiple ways by changing out the type of dried fruit (e.g., cranberries, cherries, tropical fruit mixes, and raisins), using baking chips in place of the dried fruit (e.g., chocolate chips, carob chips, or toffee baking bits), and using different types of nuts and seeds in place of the sunflower seeds (roasted pumpkin seeds—also known as pepitas—are a delicious option).

- 1 (10-ounce) bag miniature marshmallows
- ¼ cup (½ stick) butter

- 3¾ cups granola with almonds
- 1½ cups crisp rice cereal
- 1 cup chopped dried apricots
- ½ cup roasted, lightly salted sunflower seeds

Line a 13 x 9 x 2-inch pan with foil (see page xxiv). Lightly spray foil with nonstick cooking spray; set aside.

Combine the marshmallows and butter in a large saucepan. Stir mixture until the marshmallows are melted. Remove from heat.

Stir in granola, cereal, apricots, and sunflower seeds until well blended. With a large square of wax paper, press mixture into the prepared pan. Cool completely.

Use the foil overhang to lift bars out of pan. Peel off foil. Cut into bars. Store in covered containers between layers of wax paper.

MAKES 24 BIG BARS.

CHEWY CINNAMON ROLL BARS

The taste of a rich, chewy caramel cinnamon roll is captured in these delicious bars, which can be assembled in minutes.

- 1 (14-ounce) can sweetened condensed milk
- 1¾ cups white chocolate chips
- 1 (10-ounce) package miniature marshmallows
- 2 teaspoons ground cinnamon
- 1 (15-ounce) package (13 cups) toasted oat O-shaped cereal
- 1 cup toffee baking bits

Line a 15 x 10 x 1-inch jelly roll pan with foil (see page xxiv). Lightly coat foil with nonstick cooking spray.

Cook the condensed milk, white chocolate chips, and marshmallows in a large saucepan or Dutch oven set over medium heat, stirring constantly, until melted and smooth. Stir in cinnamon, cereal, and toffee bits.

Turn mixture into the prepared pan. Using a square of wax paper or moist fingers, press into pan. Cool for 1–2 hours or until firm. Cut into bars. Store in covered containers between layers of wax paper.

MAKES 24 BIG BARS.

CHEWY DATE SQUARES

An old-fashioned flavor gives these squares broad appeal. The amount of water is not set in stone given that some dates are drier than others—so add more water, by the teaspoonful, as needed.

- 3 tablespoons butter
- 1 cup chopped pitted dates
- 1 tablespoon water
- 4 tablespoons packed brown sugar, divided use
- 3 tablespoons coarsely chopped pecans or walnuts
- ½ cup light corn syrup
- 1 teaspoon vanilla extract
- 6 cups multigrain or bran flakes cereal, crushed to 4 cups

Lightly spray a 9 x 9 x 2-inch square baking pan with nonstick cooking spray; set aside.

Combine the butter, dates, water, and 3 tablespoons of the brown sugar in a medium saucepan. Cook over medium heat, stirring constantly until mixture is the consistency of soft paste. Remove from heat. Stir in the nuts; set aside.

Heat the corn syrup and the remaining brown sugar in a large saucepan over medium heat, stirring constantly until mixture comes to a rolling boil. Boil for 1 minute. Remove from heat; stir in vanilla. Add the cereal and mix until well blended.

Using a square of wax paper, press half the mixture evenly and firmly into prepared pan. Spread evenly with date mixture. Press remaining cereal mixture evenly over date layer, pressing lightly. Cool completely. Cut into bars. Store in covered containers between layers of wax paper.

MAKES 16 BARS.

CHEWY HEALTHNUT RAISIN BARS

You'll never buy overpriced cereal bars from the supermarket again once you taste these chewy bars, which are equally loaded with great taste and good health.

- 2 cups 100 percent bran cereal (e.g., All-Bran cereal, not bran flakes)
- ¾ cup raisins or dried cranberries
- ½ cup chopped roasted nuts or roasted, shelled sunflower seeds
- 1 tablespoon butter
- ½ cup honey
- ¼ cup creamy peanut butter
- 1 teaspoon vanilla extract
- ½ teaspoon ground cinnamon

Lightly spray a 9 x 9 x 2-inch square baking pan with nonstick cooking spray; set aside.

In a large bowl stir together the cereal, raisins, and nuts. Set aside.

Combine the butter, honey, and peanut butter in a medium saucepan, over medium heat, stirring until mixture is melted and blended. Remove from heat. Stir in vanilla, cinnamon, and cereal mixture until well blended.

Using wax paper, press mixture evenly into prepared pan. Cool completely. Cut into bars. Store in covered containers between layers of wax paper.

MAKES 16 BARS.

CHEWY MEXICAN CHOCOLATE BARS

If you are bewitched by a bit of spice in your sweets, than these south-of-the-border cookies are must-makes.

- 1 cup creamy peanut butter
- 1 cup light corn syrup
- 1 cup packed light brown sugar
- 1 teaspoon ground cinnamon
- 1/8 teaspoon ground cloves
- 1/8 teaspoon cayenne pepper
- 1¼ cups semisweet chocolate chips, divided use
- 6 cups cornflakes cereal
- 1 cup coarsely chopped roasted peanuts

Lightly spray a 13 x 9 x 2-inch baking pan with nonstick cooking spray; set aside.

Combine the peanut butter, corn syrup, brown sugar, cinnamon, cloves, cayenne, and

¼ cup of the chocolate chips in a large saucepan over medium heat. Cook, stirring occasionally until smooth.

Remove from heat and quickly mix in the cornflakes, peanuts, and remaining chocolate chips until mixture is combined.

With a large square of wax paper, press the mixture into the prepared pan with a wooden spoon. Cool completely. Cut into bars. Store in covered containers between layers of wax paper.

MAKES 36 BARS.

CHOCOLATE CARAMEL PEANUT BARS

You'll savor every bite of these caramel and chocolate-rich bars.

- 1½ cups roasted peanuts, divided use
- 1 sleeve saltine crackers (about 38 crackers), coarsely broken
- 1 cup semisweet miniature chocolate chips
- 1 cup miniature marshmallows
- ½ cup (1 stick) butter
- 1 (14-ounce) package caramels (about 50), unwrapped

Lightly spray a 13 x 9 x 2-inch pan with nonstick cooking spray; set aside.

Chop ½ cup of the peanuts; set aside. Mix remaining 1 cup peanuts, the cracker pieces, miniature chocolate chips, and marshmallows in large bowl; set aside.

Place the butter and caramels in a medium saucepan; cook on low heat until caramels are completely melted and mixture is well blended, stirring frequently. Pour over cracker mixture, tossing to coat well.

Gently press cracker mixture firmly into prepared pan with a square of wax paper. Sprinkle with reserved chopped peanuts; press gently into bars with square of wax paper. Refrigerate 30 minutes or until completely cooled. Cut into bars. Store in covered containers between layers of wax paper.

MAKES 36 BARS.

CHOCOLATE CARAMEL PEANUT BUTTER BARS

If ever there was a pull-out-all-the-stops bar cookie, this is it. Caramel, chocolate, cream cheese, peanut butter—on a scale of 1 to 10, these are an 11.

- 1 (18.25-ounce) package white cake mix
- 1 cup quick-cooking oats
- ½ cup creamy-style peanut butter
- 1 large egg
- 2 tablespoons milk
- 1 (8-ounce) package cream cheese, softened
- 1 (12-ounce) jar caramel ice cream topping
- 2 cups milk or semisweet chocolate chips
- 1 cup cocktail peanuts

Preheat oven to 350°F (or 325°F for dark-coated metal pan). Position oven rack in middle of oven. Spray the bottom only of a 13 x 9-inch metal baking pan with nonstick cooking spray (or foil-line pan; see page xxiv).

Mix the cake mix and oats in a large bowl. Using your fingers or a pastry blender, cut in the peanut butter until mixture resembles fine crumbs. Beat the egg with the milk in a small cup; add to the oat mixture, stirring until well blended. Reserve 1 cup of the oat mixture; press remaining mixture into bottom of prepared pan.

Beat the cream cheese in a medium bowl with an electric mixer set on medium speed until smooth. Add caramel topping; beat until smooth. Spread cream cheese mixture on top of prepared crust. Sprinkle evenly with chocolate chips and peanuts to cover. Sprinkle evenly with reserved oat mixture.

Bake for 28–30 minutes until topping is golden. Transfer to wire rack and cool completely. Cut into bars.

MAKES 24 LARGE OR 36 SMALL BARS.

CHOCOLATE CARMELITAS

When life becomes particularly frantic and stressful, bake a batch of these bars. They have the flavor and richness of your favorite candy bar all wrapped up into a streusel-layered cookie. Once you're done, pour yourself a glass of cold milk, grab the latest issue of your favorite magazine, turn off the telephone ringer, sit in a comfy chair and prop up your feet—and enjoy!

- 1 (19.5- to 19.8-ounce) package brownie mix

- 2¼ cups quick-cooking oats
- 1 cup (2 sticks) unsalted butter, melted
- 1 cup miniature semisweet chocolate chips
- 1 (14-ounce) bag caramels, unwrapped
- 1 (14-ounce) can sweetened condensed milk

Preheat oven to 350°F (325°F for dark-coated metal pan). Position a rack in the lower third of the oven. Spray the bottom only of a 13 x 9-inch baking pan with nonstick cooking spray (or foil-line pan; see page xxiv).

Combine the brownie mix, oats, and melted butter in a medium mixing bowl with a wooden spoon until just blended and all dry ingredients are moistened. Press half of mixture evenly into prepared pan. Stir miniature chocolate chips into remaining mixture; set aside.

Combine the caramels and the sweetened condensed milk in a medium saucepan set over low heat, stirring until melted and smooth. Pour caramel mixture over prepared crust and sprinkle with reserved crumb mixture.

Bake for 28–30 minutes or until topping is firm to the touch. Transfer to a wire rack and cool completely. Cut into bars.

MAKES 24 LARGE OR 36 SMALL BARS.

CHOCOLATE CHEESECAKE BARS

Sure to make chocoholic hearts beat faster, these enticing confections combine a velvet cheesecake and chocolate filling with even more chocolate in the base. Irresistible.

- 1 (18.25-ounce) package chocolate cake mix
- 3 large eggs
- ⅓ cup butter, melted
- 2 (8-ounce) packages cream cheese
- 1 cup sour cream
- 1½ cups semisweet chocolate chips

Preheat oven to 350°F (or 325°F for dark-coated metal pan). Position oven rack in middle of oven. Spray the bottom only of a 13 x 9-inch metal baking pan with nonstick cooking spray (or foil-line pan; see page xxiv).

Reserve 1 cup of cake mix; set aside. Place the remaining cake mix, 1 of the eggs, and melted butter in a medium bowl. Blend with an electric mixer set on medium speed until all dry ingredients are moistened. Press mixture into prepared pan. Bake for 10 minutes.

Meanwhile, beat the reserved cake mix, remaining eggs, cream cheese, and sour cream in a medium bowl with an electric mixer set on medium speed until smooth; fold in chocolate chips. Spread cream cheese mixture over crust.

Bake for 30–35 minutes or until just barely set. Transfer to wire rack and cool completely. Refrigerate at least 2 hours before serving. Cut into bars.

MAKES 24 LARGE OR 36 SMALL BARS.

Variations:

CHOCOLATE-RASPBERRY CHEESECAKE BARS: Prepare as directed above but dollop ⅔ cup seedless raspberry preserves in teaspoons over surface of cheesecake batter before baking; swirl batter and preserves with tip of a kitchen knife.

WHITE CHOCOLATE-LEMON CHEESECAKE BARS: Prepare as directed above but substitute lemon cake mix for the chocolate cake mix. Reduce sour cream to ¾ cup and add ¼ cup fresh lemon juice to cream cheese batter. Substitute white chocolate chips for the semisweet chocolate chips.

WHITE CHOCOLATE-LATTE CHEESECAKE BARS:
Prepare as directed above but substitute vanilla cake mix for the chocolate cake mix. Add 2½ teaspoons instant espresso or coffee powder dissolved in 2 teaspoons vanilla extract into the cream cheese batter and substitute white chocolate chips for the semisweet chocolate chips.

IRISH CREAM–MILK CHOCOLATE CHEESECAKE BARS:
Prepare as directed above but substitute vanilla cake mix for the chocolate cake mix, ½ cup Irish cream liqueur for ½ cup of the sour cream, and milk chocolate chips for the semisweet chocolate chips.

- ⅓ cup sugar
- 1 large egg
- 1 teaspoon vanilla extract
- 1 cup semisweet chocolate chips
- 1 (16.5-ounce) roll refrigerated chocolate-chip cookie dough

Preheat oven to 350°F. Spray an 8-inch pan with nonstick cooking spray or line with foil.

Combine the cream cheese, sugar, egg, and vanilla in a medium bowl; beat with electric beaters on high, stopping to scrape down sides of the bowl with a rubber spatula once or twice, until smooth. Stir in chocolate chips; set aside.

Cut cookie dough in half. With floured fingers, press half of dough in bottom of prepared pan. Spread cream cheese mixture over dough. Crumble and sprinkle remaining half of the cookie dough over cream cheese mixture (need not completely cover cream cheese layer).

Bake for 32–36 minutes or until golden brown and firm to the touch; cool completely. Cut into bars. Serve room temperature or chilled. Store in refrigerator.

MAKES 16 BARS.

CHOCOLATE-CHIP CHEESECAKE CHUBBIES

I am a fool for cheesecake. Lucky for me with these delectable bars I can get all of the richness and flavor of my favorite dessert with minimal fuss and a fraction of the time it takes to make a regular cheesecake. Be sure to cool the pan of bars completely before cutting into squares.

- 1 (8-ounce) package cream cheese, softened

CHOCOLATE-CHIP OATMEAL BARS

Apple pie is often heralded as the favorite American dessert, but a strong case can be made for the chocolate-chip cookie. This no-bake, bar version is a bit of a departure, but it is still scrumptious and rich with the familiar flavors of chocolate, brown sugar, and vanilla.

- 2½ cups crisp rice cereal

- 2 cups quick-cooking oats, uncooked
- ½ cup firmly packed dark brown sugar
- ½ cup light corn syrup
- ½ cup creamy peanut butter
- 1 teaspoon vanilla extract
- 1 cup semisweet or milk chocolate chips

Lightly spray an 8 x 8 x 2-inch baking pan with nonstick cooking spray; set aside.

Combine the rice cereal and oats in a large bowl; set aside.

Bring the brown sugar and corn syrup to a boil in a small saucepan set over medium-high heat, stirring constantly. Remove from heat. Stir in peanut butter and vanilla until blended.

Pour peanut butter mixture over cereal mixture, stirring until coated. Let mixture stand for 2 minutes. Stir in the chocolate chips. With a large square of wax paper, press mixture into prepared pan. Cool completely. Cut into bars. Store in covered containers between layers of wax paper.

MAKES 12 BARS.

CHOCOLATE-CHIP PB AND J BARS

I cannot be left alone with these cookies—they are just that good! And because it's easy to keep all of the ingredients on hand, they are (dangerously!) easy to throw together at a moment's notice.

- 1 (16.5-ounce) roll refrigerated chocolate chip cookie dough
- 3 tablespoons creamy or chunky-style peanut butter
- ¼ cup strawberry jam or grape jelly

- 1 tablespoon all-purpose flour

Preheat oven to 325°F. Spray the bottom of an 8-inch-square baking pan with nonstick cooking spray.

Cut dough crosswise into thirds. Break up ⅔ of the dough into prepared pan. Allow to soften for 5–10 minutes. Pat dough gently to cover bottom using fingertips. Spread with peanut butter, then spread with the jam or jelly.

Crumble remaining dough into small bowl. Sprinkle the flour over dough. Mix well with fingers until blended. Sprinkle dough mixture evenly over the bars.

Bake for 24–28 minutes until golden brown. Cool completely in pan on wire rack. Cut into bars.

MAKES 16 BARS.

CHOCOLATE-CHIP PECAN PIE BARS

This inventive take on pecan pie gets a double dose of chocolate. It's a no-fail pleaser you can always count on for a wide variety of occasions, from casual pitch-ins to formal buffets.

- 1 (19.5- to 19.8-ounce) package brownie mix
- ½ cup (1 stick) plus 3 tablespoons unsalted butter, melted, divided
- 3 large eggs
- 1 cup dark brown sugar
- 1 cup dark corn syrup
- 2 cups coarsely chopped pecans
- 1 cup miniature semisweet chocolate chips

Preheat oven to 350°F (325°F for dark-coated

metal pan). Position a rack in the lower third of the oven. Spray the bottom only of a 13 x 9-inch baking pan with nonstick cooking spray (or foil-line pan; see page xxiv).

Combine the brownie mix and ½ cup (1 stick) melted butter in a medium mixing bowl with a wooden spoon until just blended and all dry ingredients are moistened. Press mixture into prepared pan. Bake for 15 minutes. Remove from oven (leave oven on).

Whisk the eggs, brown sugar, corn syrup, and remaining 3 tablespoons melted butter in a medium mixing bowl until well blended while crust bakes. Stir in the pecans and miniature chocolate chips; pour over hot crust.

Bake for 35–40 minutes longer, until just set and topping is golden brown. Transfer to a wire rack and cool completely. Cut into bars.

MAKES 24 LARGE OR 36 SMALL BARS.

CHOCOLATE-CHIP TOFFEE BARS

Toffee bar recipes are relatively easy to come by. Exceptional toffee bars, on the other hand, are an entirely different matter. For example, this recipe. Decadent with nuts, toffee, and chocolate but still easy to assemble—one bite and I think you'll decide this is the only toffee bar recipe you'll need from now on.

- 1 (18.25-ounce) package yellow cake mix
- ½ cup (1 stick) butter, softened
- 1 large egg
- 1 cup coarsely chopped nuts (e.g., walnuts, pecans, or peanuts)

- 2 cups semisweet chocolate chips, divided
- 1 (14-ounce) can sweetened condensed milk
- 1 (10-ounce) package toffee baking bits, divided

Preheat oven to 350°F (or 325°F for dark-coated metal pan). Position oven rack in middle of oven. Spray the bottom only of a 13 x 9-inch metal baking pan with nonstick cooking spray (or foil-line pan; see page xxiv).

Combine cake mix, softened butter, and egg in a large bowl with an electric mixer set on medium speed until blended and crumbly; stir in nuts and 1½ cups chocolate chips. Set aside 1½ cups of the crumb mixture. Firmly press remaining crumb mixture into bottom of prepared pan. Bake for 15 minutes.

Pour condensed milk evenly over partially baked crust; top with 1½ cups of the toffee bits. Sprinkle the reserved crumb mixture and remaining chocolate chips evenly over top.

Bake for 25–28 minutes or until golden brown. Immediately sprinkle with toffee bits. Transfer to wire rack and cool completely. Cut into bars.

MAKES 24 LARGE OR 36 SMALL BARS.

Variations:

DOUBLE CHOCOLATE TOFFEE BARS: Prepare as directed above but use chocolate cake mix in place of the yellow cake mix.

BEST BUTTERSCOTCH BARS: Prepare as directed above but use pecans for the nuts and use butterscotch baking chips in place of the chocolate chips.

CHOCOLATE, CHOCOLATE, CHOCOLATE-CHIP CHEESECAKE BARS

These bars describe themselves: a crunchy chocolate cookie-like base layer, a luscious chocolate cheesecake layer, and chocolate chips scattered throughout. Yes, they are heavenly, so help yourself—go ahead, you deserve it!

- 1 (19.5- to 19.8-ounce) package brownie mix
- ½ cup (1 stick) unsalted butter, melted
- 3 large eggs
- ½ cup heavy whipping cream
- 2½ cups semisweet chocolate chips
- 2 (8-ounce) packages cream cheese, room temperature
- ⅓ cup sugar
- 1 tablespoon cornstarch
- 2 teaspoons vanilla extract

Preheat oven to 350°F (325°F for dark-coated metal pan). Position a rack in the lower third of the oven. Spray the bottom only of a 13 x 9-inch baking pan with nonstick cooking spray (or foil-line pan; see page xxiv).

Combine the brownie mix, melted butter, and 1 egg in a medium mixing bowl with a wooden spoon until just blended and all dry ingredients are moistened. Press mixture into prepared pan. Bake for 18 minutes or until center is partially set (do not overbake). Remove from oven (leave oven on).

While crust bakes, heat the cream in a medium saucepan set over medium heat until hot but not boiling. Reduce heat to low. Add 1½ cups of the chocolate chips; whisk until chocolate melts and mixture is smooth. Remove from heat and cool for 10 minutes.

Meanwhile, beat cream cheese and sugar in a large mixing bowl with electric mixer set on high until well blended. Beat in cornstarch and vanilla. Add remaining 2 eggs, 1 at a time, beating just until blended after each addition. Whisk 1 cup of the cream cheese mixture into chocolate mixture. Return chocolate mixture to remaining cheese mixture; whisk until smooth. Pour batter over hot crust and sprinkle with remaining chocolate chips.

Bake for 20–25 minutes, until just barely set at center (do not overbake). Transfer to a wire rack and cool completely. Chill for at least 3 hours in refrigerator. Cut into bars. Store in refrigerator.

MAKES 24 LARGE OR 36 SMALL BARS.

CHOCOLATE CINNAMON SANDWICH COOKIES

Eat these sinfully good, intensely chocolate cookies within a few days for the best flavor.

- 4 cups semisweet chocolate chips, divided use
- 1 cup creamy peanut butter
- 2 teaspoons ground cinnamon
- 8 cups crisp rice cereal
- ¼ cup (½ stick) butter
- 1 cup sifted powdered sugar
- 2 tablespoons milk

Foil-line two 13 x 9 x 2-inch baking pans (see page xxiv); lightly spray with nonstick cooking spray. Set aside.

Melt 2 cups of the chocolate chips with the peanut butter in a large saucepan set over low heat, stirring frequently until smooth. Remove from heat and stir in the cinnamon and crisp rice cereal. With a large square of wax paper, press half of the cereal mixture into each of the two prepared pans.

Melt the butter and remaining 2 cups chocolate chips over low heat in a medium saucepan, stirring until melted and smooth. Mix in the powdered sugar and milk, stirring until smooth.

Using the foil overhang, remove the cereal mixture from one of the pans; peel off foil. Spread the chocolate mixture evenly over the cereal layer in the other pan. Top with the remaining cereal layer and press down lightly. Cover loosely with plastic wrap and chill for about 1 hour before cutting into bars. Store in covered containers between layers of wax paper.

MAKES 24 BIG BARS.

CHOCOLATE-COVERED APRICOT BARS

Apricots never had it as good as they do here in this double chocolate cookie bar.

- 1 (16.5-ounce) roll refrigerated chocolate chip cookie dough
- ½ cup chopped dried apricots
- 1 tablespoon all-purpose flour
- ¼ cup apricot preserves
- ½ cup semisweet chocolate chips

Preheat oven to 350°F. Spray an 8-inch-square pan with nonstick cooking spray.

Break up ⅔ of the cookie dough into the prepared pan. With floured fingers, press dough evenly in bottom of pan to form crust.

Break up remaining ⅓ of dough into a small bowl. Add the dried apricots and flour and mix well with fingers until blended.

Spread preserves over dough in pan. Sprinkle with the apricot-cookie dough mixture, pressing mixture lightly into preserves. Sprinkle with chocolate chips.

Bake for 25–28 minutes or until deep golden brown. Cool completely on wire rack. Cut into bars.

MAKES 16 BARS.

CHOCOLATE-COVERED PRETZEL BARS

Everyone who loves the combination of salty and sweet will think these bars are brilliant.

- 1 (18.25-ounce) package German chocolate cake mix
- ½ cup (1 stick) butter, melted
- 1 large egg
- ⅔ cup crushed pretzels
- 1 cup semisweet chocolate chips
- 1 cup butterscotch baking chips
- 1 cup flaked coconut
- 1 cup coarsely chopped lightly salted mixed nuts

- 1 (14-ounce) can sweetened condensed milk

Preheat oven to 350°F (or 325°F for dark-coated metal pan). Position oven rack in middle of oven. Spray the bottom only of a 13 x 9-inch metal baking pan with nonstick cooking spray (or foil-line pan; see page xxiv).

Place the cake mix, melted butter, and egg in a large bowl. Blend with an electric mixer for 1–2 minutes on medium speed until all dry ingredients are moistened and mixture is well blended. Stir in pretzels. Press pretzel mixture into bottom of prepared pan. Bake crust for 15 minutes.

Layer the chocolate chips, butterscotch chips, coconut, and nuts over crust; drizzle with condensed milk.

Bake for 25–28 minutes or until edges are golden brown. Transfer to wire rack and cool completely before cutting into bars.

MAKES 24 LARGE OR 36 SMALL BARS.

CHOCOLATE DATE BARS

Traditional date bars just got better than ever thanks to a chocolate-cinnamon streusel in place of the traditional crumb component. For some additional chocolate revving, stir 1 cup miniature semisweet chocolate chips into the chocolate streusel topping before popping them in the oven.

- 2½ cups water
- ½ cup fresh lemon juice
- 3 cups chopped pitted dates
- 2 teaspoons vanilla extract
- 1 (19.5- to 19.8-ounce) package brownie mix

- 2¼ cups quick-cooking oats
- 2½ teaspoons ground cinnamon
- 1 cup (2 sticks) unsalted butter, melted

Combine water and lemon juice in a medium saucepan. Bring to a boil over medium heat. Add dates; simmer until very soft and thick, stirring occasionally, about 10 minutes. Cool to room temperature. Stir in vanilla.

Preheat oven to 350°F (325°F for dark-coated metal pan). Position a rack in the lower third of the oven. Spray the bottom only of a 13 x 9-inch baking pan with nonstick cooking spray (or foil-line pan; see page xxiv).

Combine the brownie mix, oats, cinnamon, and melted butter in a medium mixing bowl with a wooden spoon until just blended and all the dry ingredients are moistened. Press half of mixture evenly into prepared pan.

Spoon and spread date mixture over prepared crust; top with reserved crumb mixture and press down gently.

Bake for 30–34 minutes or until topping is firm to the touch. Transfer to wire rack and cool completely.

MAKES 24 LARGE OR 36 SMALL BARS.

CHOCOLATE DECADENCE BARS

Got a chocolate lover in your family or circle of friends? If so, ordinary cookies just won't cut it, but these intensely chocolate, triple-layer treats will thrill them through and through.

- 1 (8-ounce) package semisweet baking chocolate, divided
- 10 tablespoons butter, divided use

- 1½ cups graham cracker crumbs
- ⅓ cup water
- 1 (4-serving-size) package chocolate instant pudding and pie filling
- 2 cups powdered sugar
- ½ cup heavy whipping cream

Line a 9 x 9 x 2-inch baking pan with foil (see page xxiv); lightly spray with nonstick cooking spray. Set aside.

Coarsely chop the chocolate. Place half of the chopped chocolate and 5 tablespoons of the butter in a large microwavable bowl. Microwave on high for 2 minutes or until butter is melted (chocolate will not look completely melted). Stir mixture until chocolate is completely melted. Add the graham cracker crumbs; mix well. Transfer crumb mixture to prepared pan. Press firmly into bottom of pan with a large square of wax paper. Refrigerate until ready to use.

Microwave the water and remaining 5 tablespoons butter in a large microwavable bowl on high for 1 minute or until butter is melted. Whisk in dry pudding mix; continue to whisk mixture for 2 minutes or until completely dissolved. Gradually mix in powdered sugar, stirring until well blended after each addition. Spread over crust. Refrigerate for 15 minutes or until firm.

Microwave the remaining chopped chocolate and heavy cream in a medium microwavable bowl on high for 2 minutes. Stir until chocolate is completely melted and mixture is blended and smooth. Spread and smooth evenly over pudding layer. Refrigerate for 2 hours or until set. Use foil lining to remove uncut bars from pan to cutting board. Cut into bars. Store, loosely covered with foil or plastic wrap, in refrigerator.

MAKES 24 BARS.

CHOCOLATE HAZELNUT FUDGE BARS

Chocolate and hazelnut pair perfectly, as these streamlined treats deliciously demonstrate.

- 18 double chocolate fudge sandwich cookies, divided
- 6 squares semisweet baking chocolate squares, divided
- 5 tablespoons butter, divided use
- 1 (4-serving-size) package instant chocolate pudding and pie filling
- 1½ cups powdered sugar
- ⅓ cup boiling water
- ½ cup chocolate-hazelnut spread (e.g., Nutella)

Lightly spray an 8 x 8 x 2-inch pan with nonstick cooking spray; set aside.

Finely crush 12 of the cookies; set aside. Coarsely crush remaining 6 cookies; set aside.

Melt 3 of the chocolate squares and 4 tablespoons (½ stick) butter in a medium saucepan over low heat, stirring until completely melted. Stir until chocolate is completely melted and mixture is well blended. Stir in the finely crushed cookies. With a large square of wax paper, firmly press into prepared pan.

Combine the dry pudding mix and powdered sugar in a medium bowl. Add the boiling water gradually, stirring until well blended. Whisk in the chocolate-hazelnut spread until well blended. Spread evenly to cover bottom of crust.

Melt the remaining chocolate squares and 1 tablespoon butter in a small saucepan; stir until chocolate is completely melted. Spread carefully over the pudding mixture; sprinkle the coarsely crushed cookies over bars. Refrigerate at least 1 hour or until set. Cut into bars. Store in covered containers between layers of wax paper.

MAKES 16 BARS.

CHOCOLATE LINZER BARS

These bars are loosely based on Linzer Torte, an Austrian pastry concoction made with almonds and raspberry jam. For a more pronounced almond accent, mix the preserves with 1 teaspoon almond extract before spreading over bars.

- 1 (19.5- to 19.8-ounce) package brownie mix
- 1½ teaspoons ground cinnamon
- 1½ cups quick-cooking oats
- 1 cup finely chopped almonds
- 1 cup (2 sticks) unsalted butter, melted
- 1 (12-ounce) jar seedless raspberry preserves
- 1 cup miniature semisweet chocolate chips

Preheat oven to 350°F (325°F for dark-coated metal pan). Position a rack in the lower third of the oven. Spray the bottom only of a 13 x 9-inch baking pan with nonstick cooking spray (or foil-line pan; see page xxiv).

Combine the brownie mix, cinnamon, oats, almonds, and melted butter in a medium mixing bowl with a wooden spoon until just blended and all dry ingredients are moistened. Press half of mixture evenly into prepared pan.

Spread base layer with preserves. Add chocolate chips to remaining crumb mixture. Sprinkle crumb mixture over preserves, and press down firmly.

Bake for 28–30 minutes or until topping is firm to the touch. Transfer to a wire rack and cool completely. Cut into bars.

MAKES 24 LARGE OR 36 SMALL BARS.

CHOCOLATE-MARSHMALLOW BARS

Rich and chewy with marshmallows and two kinds of chips, these cookie bars are worth every gooey bite.

- ½ cup (1 stick) butter
- 2 cups semisweet chocolate chips
- 1 cup butterscotch baking chips
- 1 cup creamy peanut butter
- 4 cups crisp rice cereal
- 3 cups miniature marshmallows
- ¾ cup chopped walnuts or pecans, skillet toasted and cooled (see page xviii), optional

Spray a 13 x 9 x 2-inch baking pan with nonstick cooking spray; set aside.

Melt the butter, chocolate chips, and butterscotch chips in a large saucepan or Dutch oven set over low heat, stirring constantly until melted and smooth. Mix in the peanut butter until blended. Remove the saucepan from the heat. Add the cereal, marshmallows, and nuts, if desired, and toss until well coated.

With a large square of wax paper, press mixture onto bottom of prepared pan. Refrigerate for 30 minutes or until firm. Cut into bars. Store in covered containers between layers of wax paper.

MAKES 36 BARS.

CHOCOLATE PEANUT BUTTER CRISP RICE BARS

Always a favorite with kids, these rich bars belie their short list of ingredients.

- 2 cups semisweet chocolate chips
- 2/3 cup creamy peanut butter
- 6 cups crisp rice cereal
- 3 cups miniature marshmallows

Lightly spray a 13 x 9 x 2-inch baking pan with nonstick cooking spray; set aside.

In a large saucepan melt the chocolate chips and peanut butter over low heat, stirring constantly until smooth. Remove from heat. Stir in cereal and marshmallows.

Using a large square of wax paper, press mixture evenly into prepared pan. Chill in refrigerator for about 45 minutes to set. Cut into bars. Store in covered containers between layers of wax paper.

MAKES 18 BIG BARS.

CHOCOLATE RAISIN PECAN BARS

No reason is needed for stirring up a batch of these rich bar cookies—the arrival of the weekend or the end of the workday is grounds enough. Raisins are my favorite for this recipe, but feel free to substitute an equal amount of dried cranberries or chopped dried apricots.

- 1 (19.5- to 19.8-ounce) package brownie mix
- ½ cup (1 stick) unsalted butter, melted
- 1 (14-ounce) can sweetened condensed milk
- ¾ teaspoon ground cinnamon
- 1½ cups raisins
- 2 cups semisweet chocolate chips
- 1 cup coarsely chopped pecans

Preheat oven to 350°F (325°F for dark-coated metal pan). Position a rack in the lower third of the oven. Spray the bottom only of a 13 x 9-inch baking pan with nonstick cooking spray (or foil-line pan; see page xxiv).

Combine the brownie mix and butter in a medium mixing bowl with a wooden spoon until just blended and all dry ingredients are moistened. Press mixture into prepared pan.

Bake for 15 minutes. Remove from oven (leave oven on).

Combine the condensed milk, cinnamon, and raisins in a medium mixing bowl and stir until blended. Spoon and spread mixture over hot crust. Sprinkle with chocolate chips and pecans; gently press into condensed milk layer.

Bake 16–18 minutes longer or until lightly browned at edges. Transfer to a wire rack and cool completely. Cut into bars. Store loosely covered at room temperature.

MAKES 24 LARGE OR 36 SMALL BARS.

CHOCOLATE RASPBERRY LINZER BARS

These intensely chocolate bars are a long way from their Austrian forebears, marrying traditional sense with modern sensibility.

- 1 (18.25-ounce) package chocolate cake mix
- 1 cup finely chopped almonds
- 1/3 cup vegetable oil
- 1 large egg
- 1 teaspoon almond extract
- 1 (12-ounce) jar seedless raspberry preserves
- 1 cup miniature chocolate chips

Preheat oven to 350°F (or 325°F for dark-coated metal pan). Position oven rack in middle of oven. Spray the bottom only of a 13 x 9-inch metal baking pan with nonstick cooking spray (or foil-line pan; see page xxiv).

Combine the cake mix, almonds, oil, egg, and almond extract in a large bowl. Blend with an electric mixer set on medium speed until blended and crumbly. Set aside 1½ cups of the crumb mixture. Firmly press remaining crumb mixture into bottom of prepared pan.

Spread raspberry preserves evenly over crust. Sprinkle with reserved crumb mixture and miniature chocolate chips; gently press into filling layer.

Bake for 25–28 minutes or until topping is

firm to the touch. Transfer to wire rack and cool completely. Cut into bars.

MAKES 24 LARGE OR 36 SMALL BARS.

Variations:

CLASSIC LINZER BARS: Prepare as directed above but use vanilla cake mix in place of chocolate cake mix and eliminate the chocolate chips.

SACHER TORTE BARS: Prepare as directed above but use apricot preserves in place of the raspberry preserves.

CHOCOLATE RASPBERRY TRUFFLE BARS

A combination of rich and richer, these confections are a scrumptious mix of two favorite flavors: chocolate and raspberry. For an extra-special treat, poke 24 fresh raspberries into the chocolate mixture before chilling, then cut into squares with a raspberry in the center of each square.

- ½ cup plus 1 tablespoon butter, divided
- ¼ cup packed light brown sugar
- 2 cups chocolate wafer or chocolate graham cracker crumbs
- 1/3 cup canned sweetened condensed milk
- 3 tablespoons seedless raspberry jam
- 1⅓ cups semisweet chocolate chips
- 1–2 tablespoons powdered sugar

Foil-line an 8 x 8 x 2-inch baking pan (see page xxiv); set aside.

Melt ½ cup (1 stick) of the butter. combine the melted butter, brown sugar, and chocolate wafer crumbs in a medium mixing bowl with a wooden spoon until well blended. With a large square of wax paper, press mixture into bottom of prepared pan; chill about 20 minutes or until firm.

Combine the condensed milk, jam, and remaining tablespoon butter in a medium saucepan. Stir over low heat until mixture is melted and smooth, 2–3 minutes. Stir in chocolate chips; continue stirring until melted and smooth. Pour mixture over prepared crust. Cover and chill for 2 hours until set. Cut into bars and sprinkle with powdered sugar. Store in covered containers between layers of wax paper.

MAKES 24 SMALL BARS.

CHOCOLATE REVEL CRUMBLE BARS

They shouldn't be this easy. They shouldn't be this delicious. But oh, how they are.

- 1 (18.25-ounce) package butter pecan cake mix
- ¼ cup packed dark brown sugar
- 1 cup (2 sticks) butter, melted
- 2 large eggs
- 2½ cups quick-cooking oats
- 2 cups semisweet chocolate chips
- 1 (14-ounce) can sweetened condensed milk
- 2 teaspoons vanilla extract
- ½ cup chopped pecans (or walnuts)

Preheat oven to 350°F (or 325°F for dark-coated metal pan). Position oven rack in middle of oven. Spray the bottom only of a 15 x 10 x 1-inch jelly roll pan with nonstick cooking spray (or foil-line pan; see page xxiv).

Combine the cake mix, brown sugar, melted butter, and eggs in a large bowl. Blend for 1–2 minutes with an electric mixer set on low speed until smooth. Stir in the oats by hand until combined. Press ⅔ of the oat mixture into bottom of prepared pan.

Melt the chocolate chips with the condensed milk in a medium saucepan set over low heat, stirring until smooth. Remove from heat and stir in vanilla extract. Spread chocolate filling evenly over the oat crust. Add the nuts to remaining oat mixture; distribute evenly over the filling.

Bake for 24–27 minutes or until topping is light brown (filling will still look slightly wet). Transfer to wire rack and cool. Cut into bars while still slightly warm.

MAKES 36 LARGE OR 48 SMALL BARS.

CHOCOLATE TRAIL BLAZER BARS

Packaged energy bars? Never again, once you taste these delicious bars. They will power you through the most hectic of days.

- 3 (1-ounce) squares unsweetened chocolate, coarsely chopped
- ¼ cup creamy or crunchy-style peanut butter
- 1 (14-ounce) can sweetened condensed milk
- 1 teaspoon vanilla extract

- 4½ cups granola cereal
- 1⅓ cups sweetened flake coconut

Lightly spray a 13 x 9 x 2-inch baking pan with nonstick cooking spray; set aside.

Melt the chocolate and peanut butter with the condensed milk in a large saucepan or Dutch oven over low heat, stirring until smooth.

Remove saucepan from heat. Stir in the vanilla, granola, and coconut until well blended. With a large square of wax paper, press into prepared pan. Chill for 1–2 hours or until set. Cut into bars. Store in covered containers between layers of wax paper.

MAKES 24 BARS.

CHOCOLATE TRUFFLE CRUMB BARS

An opulent treat for chocolate lovers, this recipe involves a rich chocolate truffle filling sandwiched between two layers of chocolate streusel to create a uniquely delicious chocolate treat.

- 1 (18.25-ounce) package chocolate cake mix
- ⅓ cup butter, melted
- 1 large egg
- 2 cups semisweet chocolate chips, divided
- 1 (14-ounce) can sweetened condensed milk
- 2 teaspoons vanilla extract
- 1 cup chopped walnuts

Preheat oven to 350°F (or 325°F for dark-coated metal pan). Position oven rack in middle of oven. Spray the bottom only of a 13 x 9-inch

metal baking pan with nonstick cooking spray (or foil-line pan; see page xxiv).

Combine the cake mix, melted butter, and egg in a large bowl. Blend for 1–2 minutes with an electric mixer set on medium speed until crumbly. Set aside 1 cup of the crumb mixture. Firmly press remaining crumb mixture into bottom of prepared baking pan. Bake for 15 minutes.

Combine 1 cup of the chocolate chips and condensed milk in a medium saucepan. Warm over low heat, stirring until smooth. Remove from heat and stir in the vanilla; spread over hot crust. Stir the walnuts and remaining chocolate chips into reserved crumb mixture; sprinkle over chocolate filling.

Bake for 25–28 minutes or until topping is firm to the touch. Transfer to wire rack and cool completely. Cut into bars.

MAKES 24 LARGE OR 36 SMALL BARS.

CHUBBY ROCKY ROAD BARS

Whenever I make these bars they disappear instantly. Consequently, I make them often for sharing at potlucks, picnics, and other pitch-ins.

- 1 (16.5-ounce) roll refrigerated chocolate-chip cookie dough
- 1 cup semisweet chocolate morsels, divided
- 1½ cups miniature marshmallows
- ½ cup chopped walnuts (or pecans)

Preheat oven to 350°F. Spray an 8-inch-square baking pan with nonstick cooking spray or line with foil.

Break up dough into the prepared pan; with floured fingers, press dough into pan to form an even layer.

Bake for 27–30 minutes or until toothpick inserted in center comes out clean. Remove from oven and immediately sprinkle with half of the chocolate chips; keep oven on. Let stand 5 minutes until chips are shiny; spread chocolate chips with a knife to cover cookie layer.

Top with marshmallows, remaining morsels, and walnuts. Press down lightly. Bake an additional 5 minutes or until marshmallows begin to puff.

Remove from oven and cool on wire rack 15–20 minutes. Cut warm bars into pieces with wet knife.

MAKES 16 SQUARES.

CINNAMON BARS WITH CREAM CHEESE FROSTING

The down-home flavor of these cream cheese-frosted, cinnamon-y bars will surely bring back memories of cookies past.

- 2 large eggs, lightly beaten
- 1 cup firmly packed dark brown sugar
- ¾ cup (1½ sticks) butter
- 2 teaspoons ground cinnamon
- 2½ cups gingersnap crumbs
- 2 cups miniature marshmallows
- ½ cup finely chopped pecans, preferably skillet-toasted and cooled
- 1 (8-ounce) package cream cheese, softened
- 1 teaspoon vanilla extract
- 2 cups powdered sugar
- 3–4 tablespoons milk

Lightly spray a 9 x 9 x 2-inch pan with nonstick cooking spray; set aside.

Combine the beaten eggs, brown sugar, butter, and cinnamon in a large saucepan. Bring to a boil and let cook on low for 2 minutes, stirring constantly. Remove from heat. Add the gingersnap crumbs, marshmallows, and pecans, mixing until blended.

Transfer mixture to prepared pan, pressing down and smoothing surface with a square of wax paper. Cool completely. Refrigerate while preparing topping.

Beat the cream cheese in a medium bowl, using an electric mixer, until smooth. Add the vanilla and powdered sugar and beat until smooth. Beat in enough of the milk to make frosting of spreading consistency.

Spread frosting over bars. Refrigerate overnight. Cut into small bars. Store in covered containers between layers of wax paper.

MAKES 24 BARS.

CINNAMON-CHIP CRANBERRY WALNUT BARS

Here's a bar cookie that is as versatile as it is delicious. You can vary it in several ways: change the cranberries to another dried fruit (such as dried cherries, raisins, or snipped apricots), vary the choice of chips, or pick your favorite chopped nuts. Any way is a good way here.

- 1 (19.5- to 19.8-ounce) package brownie mix
- ½ cup (1 stick) unsalted butter, melted
- 1 (14-ounce) can sweetened condensed milk
- 1½ cups cinnamon flavored baking chips
- 1⅓ cups sweetened dried cranberries
- 1 cup chopped walnuts

Preheat oven to 350°F (325°F for dark-coated metal pan). Position a rack in the lower third of the oven. Spray the bottom only of a 13 x 9-inch baking pan with nonstick cooking spray (or foil-line pan; see page xxiv).

Combine the brownie mix and melted butter in a medium mixing bowl with a wooden spoon until just blended and all dry ingredients are moistened. Press mixture into prepared pan.

Bake for 15 minutes. Remove from oven (leave oven on).

Spoon and spread condensed milk over partially baked crust. Sprinkle the cinnamon chips, dried cranberries, and nuts over condensed milk layer; press down firmly.

Bake 16–18 minutes longer or until lightly browned at edges. Transfer to a wire rack and cool. Cut into bars while still slightly warm. Store loosely covered at room temperature.

MAKES 24 LARGE OR 36 SMALL BARS.

CINNAMON-RAISIN WALNUT BARS

Cinnamon and spice are extra nice when accompanied by crunchy pecans and plump raisins in a quick cookie bar. For a tart contrast of flavors, substitute dried cranberries or tart dried cherries for the raisins.

- 1 (18.25-ounce) package spice cake mix
- ½ cup (1 stick) butter, melted
- 1 large egg yolk
- 1 (14-ounce) can sweetened condensed milk
- 1¼ teaspoons ground cinnamon
- 1 ½ cups raisins
- 1 cup cinnamon baking chips
- 1 cup coarsely chopped walnuts (or pecans)

Preheat oven to 350°F (or 325°F for dark-coated metal pan). Position oven rack in middle of oven. Spray the bottom only of a 13 x 9-inch metal baking pan with nonstick cooking spray (or foil-line pan; see page xxiv).

In a large bowl place the cake mix, melted butter, and egg yolk. Blend for 1–2 minutes with an electric mixer set on low speed. Press the mixture into prepared pan. Bake crust for 15 minutes.

Meanwhile, combine condensed milk, cinnamon, and raisins in a medium mixing bowl until blended. Spoon and spread mixture over hot crust. Sprinkle with cinnamon chips and nuts; gently press into condensed milk layer.

Bake 16–18 minutes longer or until lightly browned at edges. Transfer to a wire rack and cool completely. Cut into bars. Store loosely covered at room temperature.

MAKES 24 LARGE OR 36 SMALL BARS.

COCONUT CASHEW APRICOT BARS

A short list of yummy ingredients is all it takes for these wickedly delicious bars. The flavor far surpasses the time it will take you to make them.

- 1 (16.5-ounce) roll refrigerated sugar cookie dough, well chilled
- 1 (14-ounce) can sweetened condensed milk
- 1 cup chopped dried apricots
- ¾ cup butterscotch chips
- 1⅓ cups shredded coconut
- 1 cup chopped lightly salted cashews

Preheat oven to 350°F. Spray a 13 x 9-inch baking pan with nonstick cooking spray or line with foil.

Cut cookie dough into ⅛-inch-thick slices. Arrange slices in bottom of the prepared pan. With floured fingers, press dough evenly to form crust. Drizzle condensed milk over dough, spreading evenly. Sprinkle with apricots, butterscotch chips, coconut, and cashews. Press down firmly with back of spoon or spatula.

Bake for 20–23 minutes or until golden brown. Cool completely in pan.

MAKES 64 BARS.

COCONUT CREAM BARS

Top off your next summer soiree with these creamy coconut bars.

- 1⅓ cups white chocolate chips, divided
- 10 tablespoons butter, divided use
- 1½ cups crisp macaroon cookie crumbs
- 1⅓ cups sweetened flake coconut, divided use
- ⅓ cup milk
- 1 (4-serving-size) package vanilla flavor instant pudding and pie filling
- 2 teaspoons coconut-flavored extract
- 2 cups powdered sugar
- ½ cup heavy whipping cream

Line a 9 x 9 x 2-inch baking pan with foil (see page xxiv); lightly spray with nonstick cooking spray. Set aside.

Place ⅔ cup of the white chocolate chips and 5 tablespoons of the butter in a large microwavable bowl. Microwave on high for 2 minutes or until butter is melted (chocolate chips will not look completely melted). Stir mixture until white chocolate chips are completely melted. Add the cookie crumbs and ⅓ cup coconut; mix well. Transfer crumb mixture to prepared pan. Press firmly into bottom of pan with a large square of wax paper. Refrigerate until ready to use.

Microwave the milk and remaining 5 tablespoons butter in a large microwavable bowl on high for 1 minute or until butter is melted. Whisk in dry pudding mix and coconut extract; continue to whisk mixture for 2 minutes or until completely dissolved. Gradually mix in powdered sugar, stirring until well blended after each addition. Spread over crust.

Refrigerate for 15 minutes or until firm.

Microwave the remaining white chocolate chips and heavy cream in a medium microwavable bowl on high for 2 minutes. Stir until chocolate chips are completely melted and mixture is blended and smooth.

Spread and smooth evenly over pudding layer. Sprinkle with the remaining coconut, pressing gently into bars. Refrigerate for 2 hours or until set. Use foil lining to remove uncut bars from pan to cutting board. Cut into bars. Store, loosely covered with foil or plastic wrap, in refrigerator.

MAKES 24 BARS.

COCONUT LIME BARS

The mesmerizing melding of lime and coconut is captured in these silky treats. The dynamic flavor duo is made even dreamier with a coconut cookie crust.

- 1¼ cups crisp macaroon cookie crumbs
- ¼ cup (½ stick) butter, melted
- 1 (6-ounce) container frozen limeade concentrate, thawed
- 2 teaspoons unflavored gelatin
- 1 cup unsweetened coconut milk, chilled
- 1 (8-ounce) package cream cheese, softened

Line an 8 x 8 x 2-inch baking pan with foil (see page xxiv); lightly spray with nonstick cooking spray. Set aside.

Combine the cookie crumbs and melted butter in a medium bowl with a fork or fingers until well blended. Transfer crumb mixture to prepared pan. Press firmly into bottom of pan with a large square of wax paper. Freeze until ready to use.

Place the limeade concentrate in a small saucepan; sprinkle gelatin over (do not stir). Let stand 5 minutes to soften. Turn heat under saucepan to medium and whisk until mixture

is hot but not boiling and gelatin is completely dissolved; let cool for 20 minutes.

In a large bowl beat the coconut milk and cream cheese with electric mixer on medium speed until smooth. Gradually add lime mixture, beating until well blended.

Pour and spread mixture evenly over prepared crust. Refrigerate for 3 hours or until firm. Use foil lining to remove uncut bars from pan to cutting board. Cut into bars. Store, loosely covered with plastic wrap, in the refrigerator.

MAKES 16 BARS.

COCONUT LIME CRISPIES

Who would have thought that crispy rice treats could be transformed into a tropical taste sensation with just a few simple stir-ins? Whip up a batch—the proof of these crispies is in the tasting.

- ¼ cup (½ stick) butter
- 4 cups miniature marshmallows
- 1 tablespoon grated lime zest
- 1 teaspoon ground ginger
- 5 cups crisp rice cereal
- 1½ cups sweetened flake coconut
- ½ cup coarsely chopped roasted, lightly salted macadamia nuts (optional)

Lightly spray a 9 x 9 x 2-inch square baking pan with nonstick cooking spray; set aside.

Melt the butter in a large saucepan set over low heat. Add the marshmallows; stir until completely melted. Remove from heat and stir in the lime zest and ginger. Add the cereal, coconut, and nuts, if desired. Stir until well coated.

Using wax paper, press mixture evenly into prepared pan. Cool in refrigerator for about 30 minutes. Cut into bars. Store in covered containers between layers of wax paper.

MAKES 12 BIG BARS.

COCONUT-PECAN CHOCOLATE FUDGE BARS

Your most vivid chocolate fantasy, these bars walk a fine line between cookie and candy.

- 1 (18.25-ounce) package chocolate cake mix
- ¾ cup butter, melted
- 1 large egg
- 2½ cups quick-cooking oats
- 1 (15-ounce) tub coconut pecan frosting
- 2 cups semisweet chocolate chips
- 1 cup chopped pecans

Preheat oven to 350°F for metal or glass pan. Position oven rack in middle of oven. Spray the bottom only of a 15 x 10 x 1-inch jelly roll pan with nonstick cooking spray (or foil-line pan; see page xxxiv).

Reserve 3 tablespoons of the cake mix. Combine the remaining cake mix, melted butter, and egg in a large bowl. Blend for 1–2 minutes with an electric mixer set on low speed until smooth. Stir in oats until blended. Press ⅔ of cake mix mixture (about 2½ cups) into bottom of prepared pan.

Place frosting in medium microwave-safe bowl; microwave on high for 1 minute. Add reserved 3 tablespoons cake mix; stir until well blended. Drizzle half of frosting mixture over cake mix mixture in pan, spreading evenly. Sprinkle with chocolate chips and pecans. Drizzle with remaining frosting mixture. Crumble remaining cake mix mixture over frosting mixture.

Bake for 25–30 minutes or until top is golden brown and edges are bubbly. Transfer to wire rack and cool completely.

MAKES 36 LARGE OR 48 SMALL BARS.

COCONUT, RUM, AND WHITE CHOCOLATE MACADAMIA BARS

Consider this an island escape bar. For a fruitier bar, consider using dried tropical fruit bits—found in the dried fruit section of the supermarket—in place of all or part of the shredded coconut.

- 1 (19.5- to 19.8-ounce) package brownie mix
- ½ cup (1 stick) unsalted butter, melted
- 1 (14-ounce) can sweetened condensed milk
- 2 large eggs
- 2 tablespoons dark rum or 2 teaspoons rum-flavored extract
- 1½ cups sweetened shredded coconut
- 1 cup chopped macadamia nuts
- 1 cup white chocolate chips
- 1 tablespoon vegetable shortening

Preheat oven to 350°F (325°F for dark-coated metal pan). Position a rack in the lower third of the oven. Spray the bottom only of a 13 x

9-inch baking pan with nonstick cooking spray (or foil-line pan; see page xxiv).

In a medium mixing bowl mix the brownie mix and melted butter with a wooden spoon until just blended and all dry ingredients are moistened. Press mixture into prepared pan.

Bake for 15 minutes. Remove from oven (leave oven on).

Combine the condensed milk, eggs, rum, coconut, and nuts in a medium bowl. Pour over partially baked crust.

Bake for 18–20 minutes longer or until golden at edges and just set at the center. Transfer to a wire rack.

Melt the chocolate chips with the shortening in small saucepan set over low heat until melted and smooth. Drizzle over bars; cool completely.

MAKES 24 LARGE OR 36 SMALL BARS.

COFFEE TOFFEE CHOCOLATE BARS

Prepare to go nuts for these rocky-topped bars. Make a batch whenever you need to celebrate—coffee breaks included.

- 1 (16.5-ounce) roll refrigerated sugar cookie dough, well chilled
- 1 (14-ounce) can sweetened condensed milk
- 2 tablespoons butter
- 1 tablespoon coffee liqueur
- 2 teaspoons instant espresso (or coffee) powder
- 1 cup chopped pecans (or walnuts)
- 1 cup chopped chocolate-covered espresso beans

- 1 cup coarsely chopped chocolate-covered English toffee candy bars

Preheat oven to 350°F. Spray a 13 x 9-inch pan with nonstick cooking spray or line with foil.

Cut cookie dough into ¼-inch-thick slices. Arrange slices in bottom of the prepared pan. With floured fingers, press dough evenly to form crust.

Bake for 10–13 minutes or until dough is golden brown (dough will appear slightly puffed). Remove from oven.

Meanwhile, combine the condensed milk and butter in a medium, heavy saucepan. Bring to a boil over medium heat; cook and stir for 5 minutes. Remove from heat and stir in liqueur and espresso powder. Pour mixture over partially baked crust; sprinkle with nuts.

Bake in middle of oven until slightly puffed, about 12 minutes. Remove from oven and immediately sprinkle with the chopped espresso beans and toffee bars; gently press mixture into uncut bars. Cool completely; chill. Let stand 5 minutes before cutting into bars.

MAKES 48 BARS.

COFFEE TOFFEE CREAM BARS

These charming black and tan bars are infused with the bold flavor of coffee and the double crunch of toffee and toasted almonds—who can (or would want to) resist? A pleasure to eat out of hand, they can also be cut into larger squares and plated for dessert.

- 1 (19.5- to 19.8-ounce) package brownie mix

- ½ cup (1 stick) butter, melted
- 2 tablespoons water
- 2 large eggs
- 4 teaspoons instant espresso or coffee powder, divided
- 6 (1.4-ounce) chocolate covered toffee bars, chopped
- 1 cup slivered lightly toasted almonds, divided
- 2 teaspoons vanilla extract
- 4 ounces (half of an 8-ounce) package) cream cheese, softened
- ⅓ cup packed dark brown sugar
- 1½ cups heavy whipping cream

Preheat oven to 350°F (325°F for dark-coated metal pan). Position a rack in the lower third of the oven. Spray the bottom only of a 13 x 9-inch baking pan with nonstick cooking spray (or foil-line pan; see page xxiv).

Combine the brownie mix, melted butter, water, eggs, and 2 teaspoons espresso powder in a medium mixing bowl with a wooden spoon until just blended and all dry ingredients are moistened; stir in ⅓ of the chopped toffee bars and ½ cup of the toasted almonds. Spread batter into prepared pan. Bake for 24–27 minutes or until just set (do not overbake). Transfer to wire rack and cool completely.

Dissolve the remaining espresso powder in the vanilla in a medium bowl. Add the cream cheese and brown sugar; beat with electric mixer set on medium until smooth. Increase speed to high; beat in the heavy whipping cream until soft peaks form.

Spread the cream mixture over cooled brownie base. Sprinkle remaining chopped toffee bars and toasted almonds over top. Refrigerate for at least 1 hour before serving. Cut into bars. Store, loosely covered, in refrigerator.

MAKES 24 LARGE OR 36 SMALL BARS.

COLOSSAL CRANBERRY PECAN CHUNKERS

Years ago I was stranded in Chicago's O'Hare Airport for most of the day on a Christmas trip home from college. Exhausted and ravenous, I stumbled into a sandwich shop for sustenance and discovered one of the most delectable bar cookies I have ever encountered. Thick, rich, and loaded with dried cranberries, pecans, and white chocolate, I almost wished for an added delay. Here is my shortcut version of that mouthwatering cookie. The vanilla extract is optional, but works wonderfully to bring out the cookie's colossal combination of flavors.

- 1 (16.5-ounce) roll refrigerated sugar cookie dough
- 1 cup coarsely chopped pecans
- ¾ cup dried cranberries
- 1 teaspoon vanilla extract (optional)
- 1¼ cups white chocolate chips, divided
- 1 tablespoon vegetable shortening

Preheat oven to 350°F. Spray an 8-inch square baking pan with nonstick cooking spray or line with foil.

Break up the cookie dough into large bowl; let stand for 10–15 minutes to soften. Add the pecans, cranberries, vanilla, if desired, and ¾ cup white chocolate chips; mix well (mixture will be stiff). With floured hands, press dough into the prepared pan.

Bake for 27–30 minutes or until a toothpick inserted near center comes out clean. Cool completely in pan on wire rack.

Melt reserved ½ cup white chocolate chips

and shortening in a small saucepan set over low heat, stirring constantly until smooth; drizzle over cooled base. Cut into squares.

MAKES 16 CHUNKY SQUARES.

Baker's Note

For an extra-rich variation, frost the bars with White Chocolate Cream Cheese Frosting (see page 377) in place of the white chocolate drizzle.

COOKIES AND CREAM BARS

Semisweet chocolate and vanilla pudding mix transform chocolate sandwich cookies into sublime treats.

- 28 creme-filled chocolate sandwich cookies
- ¼ cup (½ stick) butter
- ⅓ cup milk
- 1 (4-serving-size) package vanilla instant pudding and pie filling
- 1 cup powdered sugar
- 1 teaspoon vanilla extract
- 2 (1-ounce) squares semisweet baking chocolate, coarsely chopped

Lightly spray a 9 x 9 x 2-inch pan with nonstick cooking spray; set aside.

Finely crush 20 of the cookies; set aside. Coarsely crush the remaining 8 cookies; set aside.

Microwave the butter on high in a large microwavable bowl for 30 seconds or until butter is melted. Add the 20 finely crushed cookies; mix well. With a large square of wax paper, press crumb mixture firmly onto bottom of prepared pan.

Microwave the milk in a small microwavable bowl on high for 1 minute or until very hot. Whisk in dry pudding mix, powdered sugar, and vanilla until well blended. Pour over crust; spread to completely cover crust. Sprinkle with reserved coarsely crushed cookies.

Place the chopped chocolate squares in small microwavable bowl. Microwave on high for 45 seconds; stir until chocolate is completely melted. Drizzle melted chocolate over pudding mixture. Refrigerate for 1 hour or until set. Cut into bars. Store in covered containers between layers of wax paper.

MAKES 20 BARS.

COOKIES AND CREAM GOOEY CHESS SQUARES

Life moves quickly these days, but here's a delicious reason to slow down: rich and gooey and oh-so-comforting bar cookies, filled with more chopped creme-filled cookies. They'll bring everyone to the kitchen.

- 1 cup (2 sticks) butter, divided
- 1 (18.25-ounce) package chocolate cake mix
- 4 large eggs
- 1 (8-ounce) package cream cheese, softened
- 1 teaspoon vanilla extract
- 1 (16-ounce) box powdered sugar
- 12 creme-filled chocolate sandwich cookies, coarsely crumbled

Preheat oven to 350°F (or 325°F for dark-coated metal pan). Position oven rack in middle of oven. Spray the bottom only of a 13 x 9-inch metal baking pan with nonstick cooking spray (or foil-line pan; see page xxiv).

Melt ½ cup (1 stick) of the butter in a small saucepan set over low heat. Beat the cake mix, melted butter, and 1 egg in a large bowl with an electric mixer set on medium speed until well blended (mixture will come together as a thick dough). Pat the dough evenly into the prepared pan. Set aside momentarily.

Melt the remaining stick of butter in a small saucepan set over low heat. In a large bowl beat the softened cream cheese and vanilla extract with an electric mixer set on medium speed until smooth, scraping down sides of bowl occasionally. Add the melted butter and remaining eggs; blend until smooth. Add the powdered sugar; blend until smooth. Stir in the crumbled cookies.

Spread cream cheese mixture over prepared crust. Bake for 42–45 minutes (do not overbake; bars should be slightly gooey). Transfer to a wire rack and cool completely. Cut into bars or squares. Cover and store in refrigerator.

MAKES 24 LARGE OR 36 SMALL BARS.

CRANBERRY CARAMEL BARS

Spectacular but easy, thanks to boxed cake mix and canned cranberry sauce.

- 1 (14-ounce) package caramels, unwrapped
- ⅔ cup half and half (light cream), divided
- 1 (18.25-ounce) package white cake mix

- ¼ cup (½ stick) butter, melted
- 1 teaspoon vanilla extract
- 1 (16-ounce) can whole cranberry sauce, stirred to loosen
- ½ cup chopped pecans

Preheat oven to 350°F (or 325°F for dark-coated metal pan). Position oven rack in middle of oven. Spray the bottom only of a 13 x 9-inch metal baking pan with nonstick cooking spray (or foil-line pan; see page xxiv).

Melt caramels with ⅓ cup of the cream in a heavy medium saucepan set over low heat, stirring until melted and smooth. Remove from heat and set aside momentarily.

Meanwhile, beat cake mix, remaining cream, melted butter, and vanilla extract in a large bowl with an electric mixer set on medium speed for 1–2 minutes, until blended. Pat half of the mixture into the bottom of prepared pan.

Bake crust for 10 minutes; remove from oven. Immediately spread with warm caramel mixture. Spoon cranberry sauce over caramel layer. Dot remaining cake mixture over cranberry layer; sprinkle with the chopped pecans.

Bake bars for 25–27 minutes or until topping is firm and deep golden. Transfer to wire rack and cool completely. Cut into bars.

MAKES 24 LARGE OR 36 SMALL BARS.

CRANBERRY-CAROB BACKPACKER BARS

Stow one or two of these high-energy bars in your backpack, and you'll be able to climb mountains big and small.

- 1 cup dried cranberries
- 1½ cups carob chips or semisweet chocolate chips
- ¾ cup roasted, lightly salted shelled sunflower seeds
- 1 cup quick-cooking oats, uncooked
- 7 cups crisp rice cereal
- 1 cup honey
- 1 cup sugar
- 1½ cups crunchy-style peanut butter
- 1 cup powdered milk
- 1 teaspoon vanilla extract
- ½ teaspoon almond extract

Lightly spray a 15 x 10 x 1-inch jelly roll pan with nonstick cooking spray; set aside.

Combine the dried cranberries, carob chips, and sunflower seeds in a food processor. Pulse to chop until coarsely chopped (3–4 pulses). Transfer to a large bowl and mix in the oats and crisp rice cereal.

Mix the honey, sugar, and peanut butter in a medium saucepan. Cook and stir over low heat until blended and bubbly. Remove from heat and stir in the powdered milk, vanilla, and almond extract.

Pour the peanut butter mixture over the cereal mixture; mix with a wooden spoon until evenly coated. With a large square of wax paper, press the mixture into the prepared pan. Cool for 15 minutes. Cut into bars. Cool completely before removing from the pan. Store in covered containers between layers of wax paper.

MAKES 24 BIG BARS.

CRANBERRY CRUMBLE BARS

One bite of these humble, crumble-topped bars can turn my day around. Add a good book and a comfy chair and I'm all set. Sometimes "crumble" bars turn into just that: crumble. But you won't have any problems with this recipe. Sugar cookie dough, mixed with a very short list of stir-ins, makes a sturdy base and topping for the thick layer of tart, whole-berry cranberry sauce. Few recipes are less complicated or more versatile, making these treats suitable for serving year-round.

- 1 (16.5-ounce) roll refrigerated sugar cookie dough, room temperature
- 1 cup regular or quick-cooking oats
- 3 tablespoons firmly packed dark brown sugar
- 1½ cups canned whole cranberry sauce (from a 16-ounce can)
- ½ cup chopped pecans (or walnuts)

Preheat oven to 350°F. Spray an 8-inch square baking pan with nonstick cooking spray or line with foil.

Crumble cookie dough into large bowl; add the oats and brown sugar. Mix with your fingers or a wooden spoon until combined. Reserve 1 cup of the mixture for topping.

Press the remaining oat mixture into the bottom of the prepared pan. Bake for 17–20 minutes or until light golden brown.

Carefully spread the cranberry sauce evenly over the partially baked crust. Stir the nuts into the reserved topping; sprinkle over cranberry sauce. Lightly pat topping into cranberry layer.

Bake for 18–21 minutes more or until top is lightly browned. Cool in pan on a wire rack. Cut into bars.

MAKES 16 BARS.

CRANBERRY ORANGE BARS

Super-saturated with flavor, these easy bars are both cozy in winter and cool in summer.

- 2 tablespoons (1/8 stick) butter
- 3 cups miniature marshmallows
- 2½ cups coarsely crushed crisp sugar cookies
- ¾ cup dried cranberries
- 1 tablespoon grated orange zest
- ½ cup coarsely chopped honey-roasted almonds

Lightly spray an 8 x 8 x 2-inch pan with nonstick cooking spray; set aside.

Melt the butter in a large saucepan set over low heat,. Add the marshmallows; stir until marshmallows are melted and mixture is smooth.

Remove from heat. Stir in the cookie crumbs, cranberries, orange zest, and almonds; spread into prepared pan with a large square of wax paper.

Refrigerate for 1 hour or until firm. Cut into bars. Store in covered containers between layers of wax paper.

MAKES 16 BARS.

CRISPY CARAMEL CASHEW BARS

Can a bar cookie be spectacular? If milk chocolate, caramel, and cashews top your list of favorite flavors, then the answer is a resounding "yes."

- 1 (16.5-ounce) roll refrigerated chocolate-chip cookie dough, well chilled
- 2 cups milk chocolate chips, divided
- 1 (16-ounce) container (about 1½ cups) caramel apple dip, divided
- 3 cups crisp rice cereal
- 1¼ cups chopped lightly salted roasted cashews

Preheat oven to 350°F. Spray a 13 x 9-inch pan with nonstick cooking spray or line with foil.

Slice cookie dough into ¼-inch-thick slices. Arrange slices in bottom of the prepared pan. With floured fingers, press dough evenly to form crust.

Bake for 10–14 minutes or until light golden brown (dough will appear slightly puffed). Remove from oven; cool for 15 minutes.

Combine 1 cup of the chocolate chips and 1 cup of the caramel dip in a large saucepan. Cook over medium heat until melted and smooth, stirring constantly. Remove from heat. Stir in cereal and cashews; immediately spread over cooled crust.

In small saucepan, combine remaining chips and ½ cup caramel dip. Cook over medium heat until melted and smooth, stirring constantly. Spread over cereal mixture. Refrigerate for 30 minutes or until set. Cut into bars.

MAKES 36 BARS.

CRISPY RICE TREATS

It's a good idea to have a few no-nonsense recipes in any cookie collection, and crispy rice treats hit the mark. Everyone loves them, almost anyone can make them, and they can be enhanced in multiple ways with myriad flavors. A short list of variations follows the master recipe here, but you can let your imagine run wild with combinations of your own design.

- 3 tablespoons butter
- 4 cups miniature marshmallows or 1 (7-ounce) jar marshmallow creme
- 6 cups crisp rice cereal

Lightly spray a 13 x 9 x 2-inch baking pan with nonstick cooking spray; set aside.

Melt the butter in a large saucepan set over low heat. Add marshmallows or marshmallow creme and stir with a wooden spoon until completely melted. Remove from heat. Add the cereal, stirring until all of the cereal is well coated.

Using a large square of wax paper, press mixture evenly into prepared pan. Cool completely. Cut into 2-inch squares. Store in covered containers between layers of wax paper.

MAKES 24 SQUARES.

Variations:

PEANUT BUTTER CRISPY TREATS:
Prepare as directed above but stir ½ cup creamy peanut butter into the marshmallow-butter mixture before adding the cereal.

COCOA CRISPY TREATS:
Prepare as directed above but use cocoa-flavored crisp rice cereal in place of regular crisp rice cereal.

"PICK YOUR STIR-IN" CRISPY RICE TREATS:
Prepare as directed above but stir in 1 cup of any of the following when adding the cereal: miniature semisweet chocolate chips, chopped dried fruit, dried cranberries, raisins, chopped nuts, toffee baking bits, or sweetened flake coconut.

CHOCOLATE MINT CHIP TREATS:
Prepare as directed above but stir 1 teaspoon peppermint extract into the marshmallow-butter mixture. Add 1 cup miniature semisweet chocolate chips along with the cereal.

CITRUS TREATS:
Prepare as directed above but stir in 1 tablespoon freshly grated lemon, lime, or orange zest to the marshmallow-butter mixture before adding the cereal.

ALMOND LOVER'S TREATS:
Prepare as directed above but stir in ¾ teaspoon almond extract to the marshmallow-butter mixture. Add 1 cup coarsely chopped honey-roasted almonds along with the cereal.

DARK CHOCOLATE BARS WITH WHITE CHOCOLATE RASPBERRY FILLING

Scrumptious. These decadent, double chocolate, raspberry-rich bars answer the question of what to make when you want to impress a crowd.

- 1 (18.25-ounce) package chocolate cake mix
- ¼ cup (½ stick) butter, melted
- 1 large egg
- 2 cups white chocolate chips, divided
- 1 (14-ounce) can sweetened condensed milk
- ¼ teaspoon almond extract
- ½ cup chopped walnuts (or pecans)
- ½ cup seedless raspberry jam

Preheat oven to 350°F (or 325°F for dark-coated metal pan). Position oven rack in middle of oven. Spray the bottom only of a 13 x 9-inch metal baking pan with nonstick cooking spray (or foil-line pan; see page xxiv).

Combine the cake mix, melted butter, and egg in a large bowl. Blend with an electric mixer set on medium speed until crumbly. Set aside 1 cup of the crumb mixture. Firmly press remaining crumb mixture into bottom of prepared pan. Bake for 15 minutes.

Combine 1 cup white chocolate chips and condensed milk in a medium saucepan. Warm over low heat, stirring until smooth. Remove from heat and stir in almond extract; spread over hot crust.

Stir nuts into reserved crumb mixture; sprinkle over chocolate filling. Drop teaspoonfuls of raspberry jam over crumb mixture. Sprinkle with remaining white chocolate chips.

Bake for 25–28 minutes or until topping is firm to the touch. Transfer to wire rack and cool completely. Cut into bars.

MAKES 24 LARGE OR 36 SMALL BARS.

DATE BARS DELUXE

As a child I painstakingly picked out every date from the granola, trail mix, and gorp my mother offered up as snacks. I'm unsure of my reason, but I think it was because I did not like the look of them. So it came as a surprise to everyone when I went crazy for the date bars delivered on a neighbor's cookie plate one Christmas. Most likely my instant love affair stemmed from my failure to recognize that dates were involved. Date bars remain one of my favorite curl-up-with-a-cup-of-tea cookie options. Although simplified with cake mix, this version tastes nothing short of deluxe.

- 2½ cups water
- ½ cup fresh lemon juice
- 3 cups chopped pitted dates
- 2 teaspoons vanilla extract
- 1 (18.25-ounce) package yellow cake mix
- 1 teaspoon ground cinnamon
- 1 cup (2 sticks) butter, melted
- 2 ¼ cups quick-cooking oats

Combine water and lemon juice in a medium saucepan. Bring to a boil over medium heat. Add dates; simmer until very soft and thick, stirring occasionally, about 10 minutes. Cool to room temperature. Stir in vanilla extract.

Preheat oven to 350°F (or 325°F for dark-coated metal pan). Position oven rack in middle of oven. Spray the bottom only of a 13 x 9-inch baking pan with nonstick cooking spray (or foil-line pan; see page xxiv).

Combine the cake mix, cinnamon, and melted butter in a large bowl. Blend for 1–2 minutes with an electric mixer set on medium speed until smooth. Stir in the oats until blended. Press half of mixture evenly into prepared pan. Spoon and spread date mixture over prepared crust; top with reserved crumb mixture and press down gently.

Bake for 30–34 minutes or until topping is firm to the touch. Transfer to wire rack and cool completely.

MAKES 24 LARGE OR 36 SMALL BARS.

DEEP DARK CHOCOLATE SOUR CREAM BARS

Surrender to the sublime. Smooth and deeply chocolate, chocoholics will be hard-pressed to find a more opulent option.

- 1 (18.25-ounce) package chocolate fudge cake mix
- 4 large eggs
- ¾ cup (1½ sticks) butter, melted, divided
- 1 cup sour cream (not reduced fat)
- ⅓ cup light brown sugar, packed
- 2 cups semisweet chocolate chips
- 1–2 tablespoons unsweetened cocoa powder

Preheat oven to 350°F (or 325°F for dark-coated

metal pan). Position oven rack in middle of oven. Spray the bottom only of a 13 x 9-inch metal baking pan with nonstick cooking spray (or foil-line pan; see page xxiv).

Reserve 1 cup of the cake mix; set aside. Place remaining cake mix, 1 of the eggs, and ¼ cup melted butter in a large bowl. Blend for 1–2 minutes with an electric mixer set on low speed until well blended. Press mixture into prepared pan.

Mix remaining eggs, sour cream, brown sugar, and remaining melted butter in medium bowl with electric mixer set on low speed until well blended. Add reserved cake mix, beating for 2 minutes on medium speed until mixture is smooth; stir in chocolate chips. Pour over prepared crust.

Bake for 35–38 minutes, until just set and light golden on top. Transfer to wire rack and cool completely. Cut into bars and sift with cocoa powder.

MAKES 24 LARGE OR 36 SMALL BARS.

DEEP DARK CHOCOLATE TRUFFLE BARS

These loaded confections are a luxurious coalescence of a crunchy cookie crust and a liqueur-spiked layer of chocolate fudge. All that and they can be made up to a day ahead of time, too.

- 1 (16.5-ounce) roll refrigerated sugar cookie dough, well chilled
- 1½ cups semisweet chocolate chips
- 1 (14-ounce) can sweetened condensed milk

- 1½ tablespoons orange (or coffee) liqueur
- ½ cup white chocolate chips
- 1 tablespoon shortening

Preheat oven to 350°F. Spray a 13 x 9-inch pan with nonstick cooking spray or line with foil. Cut cookie dough into ¼-inch-thick slices. Arrange slices in bottom of the prepared pan. With floured fingers, press dough evenly to form crust.

Bake for 15–18 minutes or until deep golden brown (dough will appear puffed). Cool completely.

Combine semisweet chocolate chips and sweetened condensed milk in medium saucepan over low heat; stir until smooth and chips are melted. Remove from heat and stir in liqueur; spread over cooled crust.

Combine white chocolate chips and shortening in small saucepan over low heat. Stir until melted and smooth. Drizzle over chocolate-liqueur layer. Refrigerate for 1–2 hours or until set. Cut into bars or squares. Store in refrigerator.

MAKES 36 PIECES.

DELUXE CHOCOLATE CARAMEL CANDY BARS

These luscious treats are a cross between a cookie and a candy bar. In other words, to die for. For a birthday treat, serve them warm, topped with a scoop of ice cream, sliced bananas, and fudge sauce for a brownie banana split. Don't forget the whipped cream, cherries, and nuts!

- 1 (18.25-ounce) package butter pecan cake mix
- ½ cup (1 stick) butter, melted
- 1 (14-ounce) can sweetened condensed milk
- 2 teaspoons vanilla extract
- 1½ cups coarsely chopped pecans
- 1½ cups sweetened flaked coconut
- 20 caramels, unwrapped
- 2 tablespoons milk
- 1 cup semisweet chocolate chips

Preheat oven to 350°F (or 325°F for dark-coated metal pan). Position oven rack in middle of oven. Spray an 13 x 9-inch metal baking pan with nonstick cooking spray (or foil-line pan; see page xxiv).

Place the cake mix and melted butter in a large bowl. Blend for 1–2 minutes with an electric mixer set on low speed until well blended and crumbly. Press mixture into bottom of prepared pan. Bake for 10 minutes.

While crust bakes, whisk together the condensed milk and vanilla extract in a large mixing bowl. Sprinkle pecans and coconut over baked crust; pour condensed milk mixture over pecans and coconut.

Bake for an additional 25–28 minutes or until filling is set and golden brown. Transfer to a wire rack and cool 10 minutes.

Meanwhile, melt the caramels with the milk in a small saucepan set over low heat, stirring until smooth; drizzle over partially cooled bars and sprinkle with chocolate chips. Cool completely. Cut into bars.

MAKES 24 LARGE OR 36 SMALL BARS.

DOUBLE BERRY STREUSEL BARS

Looking for the perfect picnic bar cookie? Look no further. Loaded with the flavor of blueberries, raspberries, and the zing of fresh lemon peel, they taste like summer.

- 1 (18.25-ounce) package yellow cake mix
- 1 cup (2 sticks) butter, melted
- 2¼ cups quick-cooking oats
- 1 (12-ounce) package frozen (thawed) blueberries
- ¾ cup seedless raspberry jam
- 1 tablespoon grated lemon zest

Preheat oven to 350°F (or 325°F for dark-coated metal pan). Position oven rack in middle of oven. Spray the bottom only of a 13 x 9-inch metal baking pan with nonstick cooking spray (or foil-line pan; see page xxiv).

Set aside 3 tablespoons of the cake mix. Place the remaining cake mix and melted butter in a large bowl. Blend for 1–2 minutes with an electric mixer set on low speed until smooth. Stir in oats until blended. Press half of mixture evenly into prepared pan.

Stir together the blueberries, jam, reserved 3 tablespoons cake mix, and lemon zest in a large mixing bowl. Spoon and spread berry mixture over prepared crust; top with reserved crumb mixture and press down gently.

Bake for 30–34 minutes or until topping is set and firm to the touch. Transfer to wire rack and cool completely.

MAKES 24 LARGE OR 36 SMALL BARS.

DOUBLE BLUEBERRY SQUARES

This is a "pull out all the stops" pleasure for blueberry lovers. For obvious reasons, leftovers are unlikely.

- 1 (16.5-ounce) roll refrigerated sugar cookie dough, well chilled
- ⅔ cup quick-cooking rolled oats
- 3 tablespoons packed brown sugar
- 1 cup frozen blueberries, thawed
- ½ cup blueberry preserves
- 1 teaspoon grated lemon zest

Preheat oven to 350°F. Spray an 8-inch baking pan with nonstick cooking spray or line with foil.

Crumble cookie dough into a medium mixing bowl; add the oats and brown sugar. Mix with your fingers or a wooden spoon until blended. Reserve 1 cup of the mixture. Press remaining dough mixture into the bottom of the prepared pan.

Bake for 17–20 minutes or until golden brown. Remove from oven.

Combine frozen blueberries, preserves, and lemon peel in a medium mixing bowl. Carefully spread over partially baked crust. Sprinkle with reserved dough mixture, pressing lightly into blueberry mixture.

Bake for 19–23 minutes more or until top is golden and firm to the touch. Cool completely in pan on a wire rack. Cut into squares.

MAKES 16 SQUARES.

DOUBLE PEANUT BUTTER CHOCOLATE-CHIP BARS

Pinched for time? Whip up a batch of these bars, which taste every bit as delicious and decadent as they sound.

- 1 (16.5-ounce) roll refrigerated sugar cookie dough, well chilled
- 2 cups milk or semisweet chocolate chips
- 1 (14-ounce) can sweetened condensed milk
- 1½ cups lightly salted roasted peanuts
- 1 (10-ounce) package peanut butter–flavored baking chips
- 1 recipe Peanut Butter Icing (see page 373)

Preheat oven to 350°F. Spray a 15 x 10 x 1-inch baking pan with nonstick cooking spray or line with foil.

Cut cookie dough into ⅛-inch-thick slices. Arrange slices in bottom of the prepared pan. With floured fingers, press dough evenly to form crust. Sprinkle dough evenly with the chocolate chips; drizzle condensed milk evenly over chips. Sprinkle the peanuts and peanut butter baking chips evenly over condensed milk layer. Gently press down with back of spoon or spatula.

Bake for 24–27 minutes or until edges are set and firm to the touch. Cool completely in pan. Drizzle with Peanut Butter Icing. Let icing set before cutting into bars.

MAKES 64 BARS.

DRIED APPLE-ALMOND BUTTER BARS

To transform ordinary oat cereal into a tasty, homespun treat, hold the baking and try making these apple-almond bars instead.

- ½ cup packed light brown sugar
- ½ cup light corn syrup
- ½ cup almond butter (crunchy peanut butter may be substituted)
- ½ teaspoon cinnamon
- 4 cups honey-nut O-shape oat cereal
- 1 cup chopped dried apples

Lightly spray an 8 x 8 x 2-inch baking pan with nonstick cooking spray; set aside.

Combine the brown sugar and corn syrup in a large saucepan or Dutch oven. Cook over medium heat, stirring constantly, until mixture boils. Remove from heat and stir in the almond butter and cinnamon. Add the cereal and dried apples, stirring until evenly coated.

Press hot cereal mixture evenly into prepared pan with a wooden spoon. Cool completely. Cut into bars. Store in covered containers between layers of wax paper.

MAKES 16 BARS.

DULCE DE LECHE CREAM BARS

Inspired by Latin and South America's beloved dessert, these creamy, caramel-filled bars are inarguably awesome.

- 1 (19.5- to 19.8-ounce) package brownie mix
- ½ cup (1 stick) unsalted butter, melted
- 4 large eggs
- 2 (8-ounce) packages cream cheese, softened
- ½ cup firmly packed brown sugar
- 3 tablespoons flour
- 1 tablespoon vanilla extract
- 1 cup sour cream
- 1 (17-ounce) jar premium caramel ice cream topping

Preheat oven to 350°F (325°F for dark-coated metal pan). Position a rack in the lower third of the oven. Spray a 13 x 9-inch baking pan with nonstick cooking spray (or foil-line pan; see page xxiv).

Combine the brownie mix, melted butter, and 1 egg in a medium mixing bowl with a wooden spoon until just blended and all dry ingredients are moistened. Spread mixture into prepared pan. Bake for 18 minutes. Remove from oven (leave oven on).

Meanwhile, in a large bowl beat the cream cheese, brown sugar, flour, and vanilla with electric mixer set on high until well blended. Add the sour cream; mix until blended. Add remaining eggs, one at a time, mixing on low after each addition until just blended. Add half of the caramel topping; mix on low until blended. Pour over hot crust.

Bake for 32–35 minutes or until center is just barely set. Transfer to a wire rack and cool completely. Refrigerate for at least 4 hours or overnight. Drizzle remaining caramel topping over bars; refrigerate until set. Cut into bars.

MAKES 24 LARGE OR 36 SMALL BARS.

DULCE DE LECHE TRUFFLE BARS

Offer these sophisticated bars with strong cups of coffee or espresso drinks for a grown-up, coffeehouse-style splurge.

- 1 cup (2 sticks) butter, melted, divided use
- 2½ cups finely crushed crisp shortbread cookie crumbs
- 1 cup firmly packed dark brown sugar
- 1 (5-ounce) can evaporated milk (about ⅔ cup)
- 1 (10-ounce) package miniature marshmallows
- 2 cups butterscotch baking chips
- 2 teaspoons vanilla extract
- 1 cup toffee baking bits, divided use

Foil-line a 13 x 9 x 2-inch baking pan (see page xxiv); set aside.

In a large skillet melt ¾ cup (1½ sticks) of the butter over medium heat. In a large bowl mix the melted butter with the cookie crumbs. Transfer mixture to prepared pan, pressing down and smoothing surface with a square of wax paper. Refrigerate while preparing topping.

Place the brown sugar, evaporated milk, marshmallows, and remaining ¼ cup butter in a large saucepan. Cook over medium-high heat, stirring constantly, until mixture comes to a boil. Boil for 5 minutes, stirring constantly. Reduce heat to medium-low and add the butterscotch chips. Stir until chips are completely melted. Remove from heat; stir in the vanilla extract and ½ cup of the toffee bits.

Pour mixture over prepared crust; spread evenly to cover. Sprinkle with the remaining toffee bits. Refrigerate for 2 hours or until firm. Cut into small bars. Store in covered containers between layers of wax paper.

MAKES 36 BARS.

EGGNOG BARS

Rich with rum and spiced with nutmeg, these bars will be a surefire hit with holiday revelers.

- 2 cups crushed creme-filled vanilla sandwich cookies (about 24 cookies)
- 1/3 cup butter, melted
- 1 teaspoon ground cinnamon
- 1/4 cup dark rum
- 2 teaspoons unflavored gelatin
- 1 cup chilled eggnog, divided use
- 1 (8-ounce) package cream cheese, softened
- 2/3 cup powdered sugar
- 1/4 teaspoon ground nutmeg

Line an 8 x 8 x 2-inch baking pan with foil (see page xxiv); lightly spray with nonstick cooking spray. Set aside.

Combine the cookie crumbs, melted butter, and cinnamon in a medium bowl with a fork or fingers until well blended. Transfer crumb mixture to prepared pan. Press firmly into bottom of pan with a large square of wax paper. Freeze until ready to use.

Place the rum in a small saucepan; sprinkle gelatin over (do not stir). Let stand 5 minutes to soften. Add 1/4 cup eggnog to saucepan and turn heat to medium. Whisk until hot but not boiling and gelatin is completely dissolved. Remove from heat and whisk in remaining eggnog. Let cool for 5 minutes.

In a large bowl beat the cream cheese, powdered sugar, and nutmeg with electric mixer on medium speed until creamy and smooth. Gradually add gelatin mixture, beating until well blended. Pour and evenly spread over prepared crust. Refrigerate for 3 hours or until firm. Use foil lining to remove uncut bars from pan to cutting board. Cut into bars. Store, loosely covered with foil or plastic wrap, in refrigerator.

MAKES 16 BARS.

ELEGANT ORANGE BARS WITH ALMOND COOKIE CRUST

I took a batch of these to a graduate school potluck party and the guests inhaled them. Once the crumbs had settled, more than a dozen people asked for the recipe, which I was as happy to share then as I am now. Similar to a traditional lemon bar, the filling is made extra easy with orange juice concentrate. If almonds do not suit your fancy, leave them out or use the nut of your choice—they are delicious any way you choose to serve them.

- 1 (16.5-ounce) roll refrigerated sugar cookie dough, well chilled
- 2/3 cup chopped almonds
- 3 tablespoons all-purpose flour
- 1 (6-ounce) container frozen orange juice concentrate, thawed
- 2 teaspoons grated orange zest
- 2 large eggs
- 3–4 tablespoons sifted powdered sugar, optional

Preheat oven to 350°F. Spray a 13 x 9-inch pan with nonstick cooking spray or line with foil.

Cut dough into ¼-inch-thick slices. Arrange slices in bottom of the prepared pan. With floured fingers, press dough evenly to form crust. Sprinkle with almonds; press firmly into dough.

Bake for 10–13 minutes or until dough is golden brown (dough will appear slightly puffed). Remove from oven.

Meanwhile, whisk together the orange juice concentrate, orange zest, and eggs in a medium bowl; blend until smooth with wire whisk. Carefully pour orange mixture over partially baked crust.

Bake for 18–23 minutes or until edges are golden brown and filling is set. Remove from oven and cool completely. Cut into bars and sprinkle with powdered sugar if desired.

MAKES 36 BARS.

ESPRESSO CHOCOLATE-CHIP CHEESECAKE BARS

Rich and gutsy, and especially delicious when shared with a fellow coffee lover, these bars will deliver you into the lap of luxury in just a few nibbles.

- 1 (16.5-ounce) roll refrigerated chocolate-chip cookie dough, well chilled
- 2 (8-ounce) packages cream cheese, softened
- ½ cup sugar
- 2 large eggs

- 4 teaspoons instant espresso (or coffee) powder
- 2 teaspoons vanilla extract
- ⅔ cup semisweet miniature chocolate chips

Preheat oven to 350°F. Spray a 13 x 9-inch pan with nonstick cooking spray or line with foil.

Cut cookie dough into ¼-inch-thick slices. Arrange slices in bottom of the prepared pan. With floured fingers, press dough evenly to form crust.

Bake for 10–13 minutes or until light golden brown (dough will appear slightly puffed). Remove from oven.

In a medium mixing bowl place the cream cheese, sugar, and eggs; beat on medium speed with an electric mixer until smooth. In a small bowl stir together the instant espresso and vanilla until powder is dissolved. Beat the espresso mixture into cream cheese mixture until combined. Spread cream cheese mixture evenly over warm crust; evenly sprinkle with miniature chocolate chips.

Bake for 19–23 minutes or until just set. Cool in pan on a wire rack; cut into bars and chill. Store in refrigerator.

MAKES 36 BARS.

EXTRA-EASY CHOCOLATE-FROSTED ROCKY ROAD BARS

Yes, comfort can arrive in bar cookie form—here it is.

- 1 (19.5- to 19.8-ounce) package brownie mix

- ½ cup (1 stick) unsalted butter, melted
- 1 large egg
- 1 (16-ounce) tub ready-to-spread chocolate frosting
- 2 cups miniature marshmallows
- 1 cup chopped peanuts

Preheat oven to 350°F (325°F for dark-coated metal pan). Position a rack in the lower third of the oven. Spray the bottom only of a 13 x 9-inch baking pan with nonstick cooking spray (or foil-line pan; see page xxiv).

Combine the brownie mix, melted butter, and egg in a medium mixing bowl with a wooden spoon until all dry ingredients are moistened. Press mixture into prepared pan.

Bake for 22–25 minutes or until center is set (do not overbake). Transfer to a wire rack and cool completely.

Stir frosting in a medium mixing bowl until smooth; stir in marshmallows. Spoon and spread frosting mixture over brownie base. Sprinkle with peanuts. Refrigerate for 1 hour. Cut into bars.

MAKES 24 LARGE OR 36 SMALL BARS.

FIVE-LAYER CHOCOLATE MARSHMALLOW BROWNIE BARS

Versions of this bar—typically with a graham cracker crust—abound. This version surpasses the rest. The bars are big and gooey, and everybody who has one is going to demand seconds.

- 1 (19.5- to 19.8-ounce) package brownie mix
- ½ cup (1 stick) unsalted butter, melted
- 1 large egg
- 3 cups miniature marshmallows
- 1 cup semisweet chocolate chunks or chips
- 1 cup sweetened shredded coconut
- 1 cup chopped pecans or walnuts

Preheat oven to 350°F (325°F for dark-coated metal pan). Position a rack in the lower third of the oven. Spray the bottom only of a 13 x 9-inch baking pan with nonstick cooking spray (or foil-line pan; see page xxiv).

Combine the brownie mix, melted butter, and egg in a medium mixing bowl with a wooden spoon until just blended and all dry ingredients are moistened. Spread mixture into prepared pan.

Bake for 22–25 minutes or until center is just set (do not overbake; leave oven on).

Layer the marshmallows, chocolate chunks, coconut, and nuts over crust; press down gently. Bake for an additional 3–5 minutes or until marshmallows begin to puff. Transfer to a wire rack and cool completely.

Cut into bars.

MAKES 24 LARGE OR 36 SMALL BARS.

FLUFFERNUTTER SANDWICH BARS

The fluffernutter sandwich—peanut butter and marshmallow fluff, sandwiched between two slices of white bread—was invented back in 1961 by Durkee-Mower, Inc., the company that developed the first version of marshmallow fluff. Here it is reinvented in cookie form, with even more peanut butter and more marshmallow.

- ¼ cup (½ stick) butter
- 1 (10-ounce) package miniature marshmallows
- 1 (16-ounce) box honey and nut flakes and clusters cereal
- ½ cup creamy peanut butter
- ⅔ cup jarred marshmallow fluff or creme

Line a 15 x 10 x 1-inch pan with foil; lightly spray foil with nonstick cooking spray. Set aside.

Melt the butter in a large saucepan on low heat. Add the miniature marshmallows; cook until melted, stirring constantly. Remove from heat. Stir in the cereal, mixing until blended. With a large square of wax paper, press firmly into prepared pan. Cool completely.

Remove formed cereal mixture from pan by turning pan upside down on cutting board. Remove pan and peel off foil. Cut rectangle in half lengthwise. Spread one half with peanut butter; spread other half with marshmallow creme. Stack halves, peanut butter and marshmallow creme sides together, to form sandwich. Cut into bars. Store in covered containers between layers of wax paper.

MAKES 24 BARS.

FRESH BLACKBERRY-LEMON CRUMB BARS

Think summer, then think refreshing and sweet. Lemons come to mind? Let this easy lemon bar cookie, bursting with blackberries, celebrate the picnics, parties, and barbecues to come. Raspberries or blueberries may be used in place of the blackberries for delicious variations.

- 1 (18.25-ounce) package yellow cake mix
- ½ cup (1 stick) butter, softened
- 1 large egg
- 1 tablespoon grated lemon zest
- 1 (14-ounce) can sweetened condensed milk
- ½ cup fresh-squeezed lemon juice
- 2 cups fresh or frozen (thawed) blackberries

Preheat oven to 350°F (or 325°F for dark-coated metal pan). Position oven rack in middle of oven. Spray the bottom only of a 13 x 9-inch metal baking pan with nonstick cooking spray (or foil-line pan; see page xxiv).

Place the cake mix, softened butter, and egg in a large bowl. Blend with an electric mixer set on low speed until all dry ingredients are moistened and mixture is well blended and crumbly. Press half of mixture evenly into bottom of prepared pan. Bake for 15 minutes.

Meanwhile, whisk together the lemon zest and condensed milk with the lemon juice in a medium bowl. Stir until well-blended.

Arrange blackberries evenly over surface of partially baked crust. Pour lemon mixture over blackberries as evenly as possible; sprinkle with reserved crumb mixture.

Bake for 20–24 minutes or until topping is golden brown. Transfer to wire rack and cool completely. Cut into bars. Store in the refrigerator.

MAKES 24 LARGE OR 36 SMALL BARS.

FRESH CRANBERRY-CARAMEL STREUSEL BARS

You know that cookie on the Christmas cookie plate that everyone fights over? This is it. You may not have considered the combination of cranberry and caramel before now, but you'll never forget it after tasting these rich treats. They are definitely holiday fare, but if you stow a few bags of fresh cranberries in the freezer, you can make and enjoy them year-round.

- 1 (18.25-ounce) package yellow cake mix
- 1 cup (2 sticks) butter, melted
- 2⅓ cups quick-cooking oats
- 1 (12-ounce) jar caramel ice cream topping
- 1 (10-ounce) package chopped dates
- 1⅓ cups chopped fresh cranberries
- ¾ cup chopped pecans

Preheat oven to 350°F (or 325°F for dark-coated metal pan). Position oven rack in middle of oven. Spray the bottom only of a 13 x 9-inch metal baking pan with nonstick cooking spray (or foil-line pan; see page xxiv).

Set aside ⅓ cup cake mix. Place the remaining cake mix and melted butter in a large bowl. Blend for 1–2 minutes with an electric mixer set on medium speed until well blended and smooth. Stir in oats until blended. Press half of mixture evenly into prepared pan.

Whisk the caramel topping and reserved ⅓ cup cake mix in a medium bowl until blended; mix in the dates and cranberries. Spoon and spread the caramel mixture over prepared crust; top with reserved crumb mixture and pecans and press down gently.

Bake for 30–34 minutes or until topping is firm to the touch. Transfer to wire rack and cool completely.

MAKES 24 LARGE OR 36 SMALL BARS.

FROSTED CHOCOLATE CANDY BAR CHEWS

When the season of potlucks, parties, and pitch-ins rolls around, we all need a few terrific, foolproof recipes to prepare and take in short order. These candy bar-like cookies fit the bill, deliciously.

- 1 cup light corn syrup
- 1 cup packed light brown sugar
- 1 cup peanut butter
- 8 cups crisp rice cereal
- 1 cup milk chocolate chips
- 1 cup butterscotch chips

Lightly spray a 13 x 9 x 2-inch baking pan with nonstick cooking spray; set aside.

Place the corn syrup and brown sugar in a medium-size saucepan. Stir to combine. Cook over medium heat, stirring frequently, until mixture begins to bubble. Remove from heat. Stir in peanut butter.

Add the cereal and stir until evenly coated. With a large square of wax paper, press mixture evenly and firmly in bottom of prepared pan. Cool.

Melt the chocolate and butterscotch chips together in small saucepan over very low heat, stirring constantly. Spread evenly over cereal mixture. Cool completely. Cut into bars. Store in covered containers between layers of wax paper.

MAKES 36 BARS.

FUNKY, CHUNKY CHOCOLATE BANANA CHIP BARS

Banana chips definitely add the "funky" to these chunky bars. Look for them in the health food or dried fruit sections of the supermarket. To break them up for this recipe, place in a large zip-top plastic bag and hit several times with a can or rolling pin.

- 1 (19.5- to 19.8-ounce) package brownie mix
- ½ cup (1 stick) unsalted butter, melted
- 1 large egg
- 2 cups broken banana chips
- 2 cups miniature marshmallows
- 1 cup milk or semisweet chocolate chips
- 1 cup chopped walnuts or pecans

Preheat oven to 350°F (325°F for dark-coated metal pan). Position a rack in the lower third of the oven. Spray the bottom only of a 13 x 9-inch baking pan with nonstick cooking spray (or foil-line pan; see page xxiv).

Combine the brownie mix, melted butter, and egg in a medium mixing bowl with a wooden spoon until just blended and all dry ingredients are moistened. Press mixture into prepared pan. Bake for 20 minutes.

Remove pan from oven and layer with the banana chips, marshmallows, chocolate chips, and nuts; press down gently. Bake for 7–8 minutes more, until marshmallows are puffed and golden. Transfer to a wire rack and cool completely. Cut into bars. Store loosely covered at room temperature.

MAKES 24 LARGE OR 36 SMALL BARS.

GERMAN CHOCOLATE BARS

Delight chocolate aficionados with this gooey cookie bar that showcases chocolate in all its decadent glory.

- 1 (18.25-ounce) package German chocolate cake mix
- ⅓ cup butter, softened
- 2 large eggs
- 1 14-ounce) can sweetened condensed milk
- 1 teaspoon vanilla extract
- 1⅓ cups flaked sweetened coconut, divided
- 1 cup chopped pecans
- 1½ cups milk chocolate chips, divided

Preheat oven to 350°F (or 325°F for dark-coated metal pan). Position oven rack in middle of oven. Spray the bottom only of a 13 x 9-inch metal baking pan with nonstick cooking spray (or foil-line pan; see page xxiv).

Place the cake mix, softened butter, and 1 of the eggs in a large bowl. Blend for 1–2 minutes with an electric mixer set on low speed until well blended. Press mixture in bottom of prepared pan.

Whisk the condensed milk, remaining egg, and vanilla extract in a medium bowl until well blended. Stir in 1 cup of coconut, pecans, and ¾ cup milk chocolate chips. Spread mixture evenly over crust. Sprinkle with the remaining coconut and chocolate chips; lightly press into condensed milk layer.

Bake for 30–32 minutes or until center is almost set. Center will firm when cool. Transfer to wire rack and cool completely. Cut into bars.

MAKES 24 LARGE OR 36 SMALL BARS.

GERMAN CHOCOLATE CAKE BARS

All of the flavors of German Chocolate Cake—milk chocolate, coconut, and pecans—are loaded into this tasty recipe. It's an ooey-gooey confection for anyone in need of a hearty dose of decadence.

- 1 (16.5-ounce) roll refrigerated chocolate-chip cookie dough, well chilled
- 2 large eggs
- 2 teaspoons vanilla extract
- 1 (15-ounce) can coconut pecan frosting
- 1 (14-ounce) can sweetened condensed milk
- 1 cup coarsely chopped pecans
- 1 (11.5-ounce) package milk chocolate chips
- 2 tablespoons vegetable shortening

Preheat oven to 350°F. Spray a 15 x 10 x 1-inch baking pan with nonstick cooking spray or line with foil.

Cut cookie dough into 1/8-inch slices. Arrange slices in bottom of the prepared pan. Using floured fingers, press dough evenly in pan to form crust.

Bake for 8–11 minutes or until light golden brown and slightly puffed. Remove pan from oven and cool for 5 minutes.

Meanwhile, beat the eggs with in a large bowl electric beaters until foamy. Add the vanilla extract, frosting, and condensed milk; beat for 1 minute at medium speed or until well blended. Spoon and spread filling evenly over partially baked crust. Sprinkle with pecans.

Bake for an additional 20–24 minutes or until top is deep golden brown and center is set. Cool for 5 minutes.

Combine the chocolate chips and shortening in a small saucepan. Stir over medium heat until smooth and chips are melted. Carefully pour over filling; gently spread to cover. Refrigerate for 1½ hours or until chocolate is set. Cut into small bars. Store in refrigerator.

MAKES 64 BARS.

GIANDUIA BARS

The rich chocolate-hazelnut flavor of these European-inspired cookies qualifies them as classic. Plus, they're practically foolproof, a fact appreciated by cooks of all experience levels.

- 2 cups crushed creme-filled chocolate sandwich cookies (about 24 cookies)
- 1/3 cup butter, melted
- 1/2 cup heavy whipping cream
- 2 teaspoons unflavored gelatin
- 2/3 cup semisweet chocolate chips
- 1 (13-ounce) jar chocolate-hazelnut spread (e.g., Nutella)

Line an 8 x 8 x 2-inch pan with foil (see page xxiv). Lightly coat foil with nonstick cooking spray.

Combine the cookie crumbs and melted butter in a medium bowl with a fork or fingers until well blended. Transfer crumb mixture to prepared pan. Press firmly into bottom of pan with a large square of wax paper. Freeze until ready to use.

Pour the cream into a small saucepan. Sprinkle gelatin over cream (do not stir). Let stand for 5 minutes to soften. Cook and stir over low heat for 4–6 minutes until cream is hot (but not boiling) and gelatin is dissolved. Remove from heat and add chocolate chips; stir until melted and smooth. Add chocolate-hazelnut spread to mixture; whisk until smooth. Set aside and let cool for 15–20 minutes until room temperature.

Pour and spread filling evenly over chilled crust. Refrigerate for at least 3 hours until firm. Use foil lining to remove uncut bars from pan to cutting board. Cut into bars. Store, loosely covered with foil or plastic wrap, in refrigerator.

MAKES 16 BARS.

GINGER BARS WITH LEMON FROSTING

When it's high time for teatime, head for this recipe. The bite of ginger and brightness of lemon have a natural affinity that is always satisfying.

- ½ cup (1 stick) plus 3 tablespoons butter, divided
- ½ cup packed dark brown sugar
- ½ cup unsweetened canned evaporated milk
- 2¼ teaspoons ground ginger
- 2 teaspoons vanilla extract
- 2 cups uncooked quick oats
- ½ cup toasted wheat germ
- 1 cup sweetened flake coconut
- ⅓ cup white chocolate chips
- 1 (3-ounce) package cream cheese, softened
- 1 teaspoon grated lemon zest
- 1½ teaspoons lemon juice
- 2¼ cups powdered sugar

Lightly spray a 9 x 9 x 2-inch square baking pan with nonstick cooking spray; set aside.

Melt ½ cup (1 stick) of the butter in a medium-size saucepan. Add the brown sugar

and evaporated milk. Cook and stir until over medium heat until sugar is dissolved. Remove from the heat and add the ginger, vanilla, oats, wheat germ, and coconut; mix well. Spread the mixture into a prepared pan with a wooden spoon; set aside.

In a small saucepan set over low heat melt the remaining butter with the white chocolate chips. Transfer mixture to a medium bowl and add the cream cheese, lemon zest, and lemon juice. Beat with an electric mixer set on medium-high speed until blended. Gradually beat in powdered sugar until mixture reaches spreading consistency.

Spread the cream cheese mixture over the bars. Refrigerate until firm. Cut into 16 bars. Store in covered containers between layers of wax paper.

MAKES 16 BARS.

GOLDEN BARS

The refreshing flavor of lemon, together with the subtle mingling of walnuts, coconut, and golden raisins, makes for a guaranteed favorite.

- 1 (16.5-ounce) roll refrigerated sugar cookie dough, well chilled
- 4 large eggs
- 1 cup packed light brown sugar
- 2 teaspoons finely shredded lemon peel
- ¼ cup lemon juice
- ½ teaspoon salt
- 1½ cups chopped walnuts (or pecans)
- 2 cups shredded coconut
- 1 cup golden raisins

Preheat oven to 350°F. Spray a 13 x 9-inch pan with nonstick cooking spray or line with foil.

Cut cookie dough into ¼-inch-thick slices. Arrange slices in bottom of the prepared pan. With floured fingers, press dough evenly to form crust.

Bake for 10–13 minutes or until dough is golden brown (dough will appear slightly puffed). Remove from oven.

Meanwhile, beat the eggs, brown sugar, lemon peel, lemon juice, and salt in a medium bowl with an electric mixer on medium speed for 2 minutes. Stir in the nuts, coconut, and raisins.

Pour this filling over partially baked crust. Bake for 18–21 minutes or until lightly browned around edges and center is set. Cool in pan on a wire rack. Cut into bars.

MAKES 36 BARS.

GRASSHOPPER BARS

Not a mint fan? Customize these gourmet, grown-up bars with the liqueur of your choice. The bars will be impressive and delicious no matter which flavor you choose.

- 1¼ cups chocolate wafer cookie crumbs
- ¼ cup (½ stick) butter, melted
- ⅓ cup crème de menthe liqueur
- 2 teaspoons unflavored gelatin
- ⅔ cup heavy whipping cream
- 1 (8-ounce) package cream cheese, softened
- ¾ cup powdered sugar
- ½ cup miniature semisweet chocolate chips

Line an 8 x 8 x 2-inch baking pan with foil (see page xxiv); lightly spray with nonstick cooking spray. Set aside.

Combine the cookie crumbs and melted butter in a medium bowl with a fork or fingers until well blended. Transfer crumb mixture to prepared pan. Press firmly into bottom of pan with a large square of wax paper. Freeze until ready to use.

Place the liqueur in a small cup; sprinkle gelatin over (do not stir). Let stand for 5 minutes to soften.

Heat the cream in a small saucepan set over medium heat, until hot but not boiling. Add the gelatin mixture. Whisk and stir until gelatin is completely dissolved. Remove from heat and set aside momentarily.

Beat the cream cheese and powdered sugar in a large bowl with electric mixer on medium speed until creamy. Gradually add gelatin-cream mixture, beating on low speed and occasionally scraping sides of bowl with rubber spatula, until well blended. Pour and spread cream cheese mixture evenly over prepared crust; sprinkle with chocolate chips.

Refrigerate for 3 hours or until firm. Use foil lining to remove uncut bars from pan to cutting board. Cut into bars. Store, loosely covered with foil or plastic wrap, in refrigerator.

MAKES 16 BARS.

HIGH-ENERGY DRIED FRUIT BARS

One thing's for certain—you'll expend very little energy making these power-packed treats, which stir together in no time. For a chocolate twist, substitute an equal amount of chocolate-hazelnut spread for the peanut butter.

- 4 cups wheat and barley nugget cereal (e.g., Grape Nuts)
- 1 cup dried fruit, such as raisins, cranberries, cherries, or dried fruit bits
- 1 cup honey
- 1 cup packed light brown sugar
- ¾ cup creamy peanut butter

Lightly spray a 13 x 9 x 2-inch baking pan with nonstick cooking spray; set aside.

Place the cereal and fruit in a large bowl; set aside.

Mix the honey, brown sugar, and peanut butter in a medium saucepan. Bring to a boil over medium-low heat, stirring occasionally. Pour peanut butter mixture over cereal and fruit mixture, stirring until blended.

With a large square of wax paper, press mixture firmly into prepared pan. Cool completely. Cut into bars. Wrap bars individually with plastic wrap. Store in tightly covered container.

MAKES 30 BARS.

HOLIDAY HONEY-GUMDROP BARS

These showy cookies feature the flavors and the colors of Christmas with very little effort.

- 1 (13-ounce) package (about 8 cups) honey graham cereal squares
- 2 cups red and green small spice drops

- 2 cups white chocolate chips or vanilla baking chips
- ⅓ cup butter
- ¼ cup honey
- 1 (10-ounce) package miniature marshmallows
- 1 teaspoon ground ginger
- 1 teaspoon vanilla extract

Lightly spray a 13 x 9 x 2-inch square baking pan with nonstick cooking spray; set aside. Lightly spray a large bowl with nonstick cooking spray. Combine the cereal and spice drops in the bowl; set aside.

Melt the white chocolate chips with the butter and honey in a large saucepan over low heat, stirring until melted and smooth. Add the marshmallows and cook, stirring constantly, until melted and smooth. Remove from heat and stir in the ground ginger and vanilla.

Pour the marshmallow mixture over the cereal mixture in bowl, folding gently to mix. Turn into sprayed pan. With large square of wax paper, press and spread mixture evenly in pan. Cool for 30 minutes. Cut into bars. Store in covered containers between layers of wax paper.

MAKES 36 BARS.

HONEY SESAME CRUNCH BARS

Make lunch extra special by ending it with one of these sweet bars. The honey and sesame add a unique, slightly exotic flavor to the cookie base.

- 1 cup packed dark brown sugar
- ⅔ cup honey
- ½ cup all-purpose flour
- 6 tablespoons (¾ stick) butter
- 2 tablespoons toasted sesame oil
- ⅓ cup milk
- 4 cups toasted honey graham cereal squares
- 3 cups crisp rice cereal
- ¼ cup sesame seeds
- 1 cup coarsely chopped roasted, salted peanuts or cashews
- 2 cups white or milk chocolate chips

Lightly spray a 13 x 9 x 2-inch baking pan with nonstick cooking spray; set aside.

Combine the brown sugar, honey, flour, butter, sesame oil, and milk in a large saucepan or Dutch oven. Cook over medium heat, stirring occasionally, until mixture comes to a full boil. Boil, stirring constantly, for 5 minutes. Remove saucepan from heat. Add the cereals, sesame seeds, and peanuts, tossing until well coated.

Spread mixture into prepared pan with a wooden spoon. Immediately sprinkle the warm bars with chocolate chips. Cover pan with a cookie sheet and let stand 4 minutes. Spread chocolate chips over bars. Cover and refrigerate for 30 minutes or until firm. Cut into bars. Store in covered containers between layers of wax paper.

MAKES 36 BARS.

HONEY-SOUR CREAM BARS

Summer days fly swiftly by, but you can make the most of them by savoring these cool, honey-laced sour cream bars. Add a few tall glasses of iced tea, a handful of good friends, and you're all set.

- 1¼ cups crisp sugar cookie crumbs
- ¼ cup (½ stick) butter, melted
- ⅓ cup milk
- 2 teaspoons unflavored gelatin
- ⅓ cup honey
- 1 (16-ounce) container sour cream
- 1 teaspoon vanilla extract
- ¼ teaspoon ground coriander or nutmeg

Line an 8 x 8 x 2-inch baking pan with foil (see page xxiv); lightly spray with nonstick cooking spray. Set aside.

Combine the cookie crumbs and melted butter in a medium bowl with a fork or fingers until well blended. Transfer crumb mixture to prepared pan. Press firmly into bottom of pan with a large square of wax paper. Freeze until ready to use.

Place the milk in a small saucepan; sprinkle gelatin over (do not stir). Let stand for 10 minutes to soften. Turn the heat under saucepan to medium. Whisk and stir until milk is very hot (but not boiling) and gelatin is completely dissolved. Remove from heat and cool for 15 minutes.

Whisk the honey, sour cream, vanilla, and coriander in a medium bowl until smooth. Gradually whisk in the cooled gelatin-milk mixture until well blended. Pour and spread sour cream mixture evenly over prepared crust. Refrigerate for 3 hours or until firm.

Use foil lining to remove uncut bars from pan to cutting board. Cut into bars. Store, loosely covered with foil or plastic wrap, in refrigerator.

MAKES 16 BARS.

IRISH CREAM MOUSSE BARS

These petite and pretty treats are special enough to stand in for dessert under any circumstances.

- 2 cups crushed creme-filled chocolate sandwich cookies (about 24 cookies)
- ⅓ cup butter, melted
- ½ cup milk, divided use
- 2¼ teaspoons unflavored gelatin
- ⅓ cup sugar
- 3 tablespoons Irish Cream liqueur
- ½ cup heavy whipping cream

Line an 8 x 8 x 2-inch baking pan with foil (see page xxiv); lightly spray with nonstick cooking spray. Set aside.

Combine the cookie crumbs and melted butter in a medium bowl with a fork or fingers until well blended. Transfer crumb mixture to prepared pan. Press firmly into bottom of pan with a large square of wax paper. Freeze until ready to use.

Place ¼ cup of the milk in a small saucepan. Sprinkle gelatin over milk (do not stir). Let stand for 5 minutes to soften. Add sugar and remaining ¼ cup milk to saucepan. Stir over low heat for 4–6 minutes, until both the sugar and gelatin are dissolved.

Remove from heat and stir in liqueur. Let cool for 20–25 minutes until room temperature.

Beat the whipping cream in a medium bowl with an electric mixer set on high speed until soft peaks form. Gently stir in cooled Irish Cream mixture until just blended. Pour mixture over chilled crust.

Refrigerate for at least 1 hour until firm. Use foil lining to remove uncut bars from pan to cutting board. Cut into small squares. Store, loosely covered with plastic wrap, in the refrigerator.

MAKES 24 COOKIES.

Variations:

KAHLUA MOCHA MOUSSE BARS:
Prepare as directed above but substitute Kahlua liqueur for the Irish cream and add 1½ teaspoons instant coffee or espresso powder to the milk mixture along with the sugar.

GRAND MARNIER ORANGE MOUSSE BARS:
Prepare as directed above but substitute Grand Marnier or other orange liqueur for the Irish cream and use vanilla creme-filled sandwich cookies in place of the chocolate sandwich cookies.

IRISH CREAM SWIRLED BARS

Not only are these liqueur-rich bars incredible and incredibly rich, the recipe can be used as a template for countless variations, depending on the cake mix, frosting, and spirits used.

- 1 (18.25-ounce) package vanilla cake mix
- 3 large eggs
- ⅔ cup plus ¼ cup Irish Cream liqueur, divided
- ⅓ cup vegetable oil
- 1 (16-ounce) container cream cheese frosting
- 1½ cups white chocolate chips

Preheat oven to 350°F. Position oven rack in middle of oven. Spray the bottom only of a 15 x 10 x 1-inch jelly roll pan with nonstick cooking spray (or foil-line pan; see page xxiv).

Place the cake mix, eggs, 2/3 cup liqueur, and oil in a large bowl. Blend for 1–2 minutes with an electric mixer set on low speed until well blended and smooth. Reserve ½ cup batter; spread remaining batter into bottom of prepared pan.

In same large bowl used for cake batter (no need to clean it) place the frosting, remaining liqueur, and reserved cake batter. Blend for 1–2 minutes with an electric mixer (no need to clean beaters) set on low speed until well blended and smooth; stir in white chocolate chips. Drop large spoonfuls of this mixture over the cake batter. Swirl with tip of knife to make a marble effect.

Bake for 24–27 minutes, or until the bars are just set and golden. Transfer pan to a wire rack and cool completely. Cut into bars or squares.

MAKES 48 BARS OR SQUARES.

Variation:
CHOCOLATE WHISKEY SWIRL BARS:
Prepare as directed above but use chocolate cake mix in place of vanilla cake mix, chocolate cream cheese frosting in place of cream cheese frosting, whiskey in place of Irish Cream liqueur, and semisweet chocolate chips in place of white chocolate chips.

ITALIAN CHEESECAKE BARS

With their smooth Italian accent, these rich bars are just the thing for special luncheons or afternoon chats over coffee. For a sophisticated supper conclusion, treat your guests to small cups of steaming espresso and bite-sized squares of these rich and creamy cookies.

- 1 (16.5-ounce) roll refrigerated sugar cookie dough, well chilled
- 1 (15-ounce) container ricotta cheese
- 1 large egg
- 1/3 cup granulated sugar
- 2 tablespoons all-purpose flour
- 2 teaspoons grated orange zest
- 1 teaspoon almond extract
- ½ cup golden raisins (or dried cranberries), chopped
- ½ cup sliced almonds (or chopped hazelnuts)

Preheat oven to 350°F. Spray a 13 x 9-inch pan with nonstick cooking spray or line with foil.

Cut cookie dough into ¼-inch-thick slices. Arrange slices in bottom of the prepared pan. With floured fingers, press dough evenly to form crust.

Bake for 10–13 minutes or until dough is golden brown (dough will appear slightly puffed). Remove from oven.

Whisk the ricotta cheese, egg, sugar, flour, orange peel, and almond extract in a medium bowl until smooth; stir in raisins. Carefully spread cheese mixture over warm crust; sprinkle with almonds.

Bake for 22–25 minutes or until edges are puffed and golden. Cool in pan on a wire rack for 1 hour; cover and chill for 2 hours. Cut into bars; store in refrigerator.

MAKES 36 BARS.

ITALIAN CHEESECAKE BARS (NO-BAKE)

A splash of Marsala wine, a sprinkle of lemon zest, and a buttery shortbread crust add up to one decadent bar.

- 1¼ cups crisp sugar cookie crumbs
- ¼ cup (½ stick) butter, melted
- ¼ cup Marsala or sweet sherry wine
- 2 teaspoons unflavored gelatin
- ¼ cup orange juice
- 1 (3-ounce) package cream cheese, softened
- 1 (8-ounce) container ricotta cheese
- ¾ cup powdered sugar
- 1 teaspoon vanilla extract
- 2/3 cup golden raisins
- ½ cup sliced almonds, skillet-toasted (see page xviii), optional

Line an 8 x 8 x 2-inch baking pan with foil (see page xxiv); lightly spray with nonstick cooking spray. Set aside.

Combine the cookie crumbs and melted butter in a medium bowl with a fork or fingers until well blended. Transfer crumb mixture to prepared pan. Press firmly into bottom of pan with a large square of wax paper. Freeze until ready to use.

Place the Marsala in a small saucepan; sprinkle gelatin over (do not stir). Let stand 10 minutes to soften. Add the orange juice to saucepan and turn the heat under saucepan to medium. Whisk and stir until liquid is very hot (but not boiling) and gelatin is completely dissolved. Remove from heat and cool for 15 minutes.

Beat the cream cheese, ricotta cheese, powdered sugar, and vanilla in a large bowl with electric mixer on medium speed until creamy. Gradually add cooled gelatin mixture, beating on low speed and occasionally scraping sides of bowl with rubber spatula, until well blended. Stir in golden raisins.

Pour and spread cheese mixture evenly over prepared crust. Sprinkle top of bars with toasted almonds, if desired. Refrigerate for 3 hours or until firm. Use foil lining to remove uncut bars from pan to cutting board. Cut into bars. Store, loosely covered with foil or plastic wrap, in refrigerator.

MAKES 16 BARS.

ITALIAN PANFORTE PETITES

These dainty cookies capture the flavor of panforte, a dense Italian confection similar to American fruitcake. Cut the baked bars into bite-sized pieces.

- 1 (16.5-ounce) roll refrigerated sugar cookie dough
- 1 cup canned unsalted mixed nuts, coarsely chopped
- ½ cup butterscotch baking chips
- ½ cup mixed dried fruit bits (or chopped dried fruit of choice)
- ½ cup shredded coconut

Preheat oven to 350°F. Spray a 9-inch square baking pan with nonstick cooking spray or line with foil.

Break up the cookie dough into large bowl; let stand for 10–15 minutes to soften. Add the nuts, butterscotch chips, and dried fruit to dough; mix well with your fingers, the paddle attachment of an electric stand mixer, or a wooden spoon. With floured hands press dough into the prepared pan. Sprinkle the coconut over top of dough; gently press into dough.

Bake for 27–30 minutes or until a toothpick inserted near center comes out clean. Cool completely in pan on wire rack. Cut into small squares.

MAKES 32 SQUARES.

KARMA KRUNCH BARS

Here's an innovative twist on the no-bake cookie. Bright with the flavor of citrus, sweet with honey and tropical fruit, and peppery with ginger, they're sure to be favorites at your next picnic pitch-in.

- 2 tablespoons butter
- 1/3 cup honey
- 4 cups miniature marshmallows
- 2 teaspoons ground ginger
- 6 cups oats and honey crispy cereal
- 1 cup dried tropical fruit bits or other dried fruit of choice
- 3/4 cup roasted, lightly salted sunflower seeds
- 1 tablespoon grated lemon or lime zest

Lightly spray a 13 x 9 x 2-inch baking pan with nonstick cooking spray; set aside.

Melt the butter with the honey in a large saucepan or Dutch oven over low heat, stirring until blended. Add the marshmallows and ginger. Cook and stir until marshmallows are melted and mixture is blended.

Add the cereal, dried fruit, sunflower seeds,

and zest to marshmallow mixture; mix well. With a large square of wax paper, press cereal mixture firmly into prepared pan. Cool completely. Cut into bars. Store in covered containers between layers of wax paper.

MAKES 24 BARS.

KEY LIME BARS

Whether the weather is already warm or just heating up, these chilled, tart, creamy bars have immense appeal. And even though they are excellent served cold on a sultry day, they are not exclusively hot-weather fare. It would be a shame to limit such pleasures to only one season of the year!

- 1 (18.25-ounce) package vanilla cake mix
- 1 stick (1/2 cup) butter, melted
- 1 large egg yolk
- 4 large eggs
- 1 (14-ounce) can sweetened condensed milk
- 2/3 cup lime juice
- 1 tablespoon grated lime zest

Preheat oven to 350°F (or 325°F for dark-coated metal pan). Position oven rack in middle of oven. Spray an 13 x 9-inch metal baking pan with nonstick cooking spray (or foil-line pan; see page xxiv).

Reserve 1 tablespoon cake mix. Place the remaining cake mix, melted butter, and egg yolk in a large bowl. Blend for 1–2 minutes with an electric mixer set on low speed until well mixed and crumbly. Press mixture into bottom of prepared pan. Bake for 15 minutes.

While crust bakes, whisk the eggs, condensed milk, lime juice, and reserved tablespoon of cake mix in a large mixing bowl until smooth; stir in lime zest. Carefully spread lime mixture over warm base layer.

Bake for an additional 20–24 minutes or until topping is set and golden brown. Transfer to a wire rack and cool completely. Refrigerate until cold before serving, for at least 2 hours. Cut into bars.

MAKES 24 LARGE OR 36 SMALL BARS.

Variations:

CREAMY LEMON BARS: Prepare as directed above but use lemon juice in place of the lime juice and lemon zest in place of the lime zest.

ORANGE BURST BARS: Prepare as directed above but use ½ cup orange juice plus 2½ tablespoons lemon juice in place of the lime juice and orange zest in place of the lime zest.

KEY LIME BARS (NO-BAKE)

Add some sophisticated, citrus flair to your next cookout with this cool bar cookie, which showcases a tart-sweet lime filling and a buttery vanilla crust.

- 2 cups crushed creme-filled vanilla sandwich cookies (about 24 cookies)
- ⅓ cup butter, melted
- 2 teaspoons unflavored gelatin
- ½ cup Key lime or regular lime juice
- 1 (14-ounce) can sweetened condensed milk

- 1 teaspoon grated lime zest
- ½ cup chilled heavy whipping cream
- Fresh lime slices (optional—for garnish)

Line a 9 x 9 x 2-inch baking pan with foil (see page xxiv); lightly spray with nonstick cooking spray. Set aside.

Combine the cookie crumbs and melted butter in a medium bowl with a fork or fingers until well blended. Transfer crumb mixture to prepared pan. Press firmly into bottom of pan with a large square of wax paper. Freeze until ready to use.

Sprinkle gelatin over the lime juice in a medium bowl; let stand for 5 minutes. Cook over low heat, stirring until gelatin dissolves. Pour the juice into a large bowl; whisk in sweetened condensed milk and grated lime zest.

Place bowl in a larger bowl filled with ice; whisk mixture for 10 minutes or until partially set. Beat the whipping cream in a medium bowl with an electric mixer set on high speed until soft peaks form. Fold whipped cream into lime mixture. Pour evenly over prepared crust; cover and chill for 8 hours.

Use foil lining to remove uncut bars from pan to cutting board. Cut into bars. Garnish with lime slices, if desired. Store, loosely covered with plastic wrap, in the refrigerator.

MAKES 24 BARS.

LAYERED CHOCOLATE-MALLOW YUMMIES

Crisp graham crackers compose the foundation of these very yummy bars, which are part s'more, part crispy rice treat, part peanut butter cup candy.

- 7 graham crackers (whole rectangles)
- 2½ cups miniature marshmallows
- 2 cups semisweet chocolate morsels
- ⅔ cup light corn syrup
- 3 tablespoons butter
- ½ cup crunchy peanut butter
- 3 cups crisp rice cereal

Lightly spray a 13 x 9 x 2-inch baking pan with nonstick cooking spray.

Place six whole graham crackers in single layer in bottom of prepared pan. Cut remaining cracker to fit in bottom. Sprinkle marshmallows evenly over crackers; set aside.

Melt the chocolate chips, corn syrup, and butter in a medium saucepan set over low heat, stirring constantly until smooth. Remove from heat and stir in peanut butter. Add cereal, mixing until combined.

Immediately spread cereal mixture evenly over marshmallows, using a large square of wax paper to help spread. Cover and refrigerate for about 1 hour or until firm. Cut into bars. Store in covered containers between layers of wax paper.

MAKES 36 BARS.

LEMON-BLUEBERRY GOOEY CHESS SQUARES

A box of yellow cake mix is suddenly elegant thanks to a little imagination and a handful of summer berries. You can substitute fresh or frozen (thawed) blackberries or raspberries in this recipe for an equally delicious, decadent result. An equal amount of diced fresh apricots or peaches is also excellent here at the height of the harvest.

- 1 cup (2 sticks) butter, divided
- 1 (18.25-ounce) package yellow cake mix
- 4 large eggs
- 1 (8-ounce) package cream cheese, softened
- 6 tablespoons fresh lemon juice
- 2 tablespoons grated lemon zest
- 1 (16-ounce) box powdered sugar
- 2 cups fresh blueberries or 2 cups frozen (thawed) blueberries, drained and patted dry

Preheat oven to 350°F (or 325°F for dark-coated metal pan). Position oven rack in middle of oven. Spray the bottom only of a 13 x 9-inch metal baking pan with nonstick cooking spray (or foil-line pan; see page xxiv).

Melt ½ cup (1 stick) of the butter in a small saucepan set over low heat. Beat the cake mix, melted butter, and 1 egg in a large bowl with an electric mixer set on medium speed until well blended (mixture will come together as a thick dough). Pat the dough evenly into the prepared pan. Set aside momentarily.

Melt the remaining stick of butter in a small saucepan set over low heat. Beat the softened cream cheese, lemon juice, and lemon zest in a large bowl with an electric mixer set on medium speed until smooth, scraping down sides of bowl occasionally. Add the melted butter and remaining eggs; blend until smooth. Add the powdered sugar; blend until smooth. Stir in the blueberries.

Spread lemon-blueberry mixture over prepared crust. Bake for 42–45 minutes (do not overbake; bars should be slightly gooey). Transfer to a wire rack and cool completely. Cut into bars or squares. Cover and store in refrigerator.

MAKES 24 LARGE OR 36 SMALL BARS.

Variation:

FRESH CRANBERRY ORANGE CHESS SQUARES: Prepare as directed above but substitute orange juice for the lemon juice, orange zest for the lemon zest, and fresh or frozen (thawed) cranberries for the blueberries.

LEMON BUTTERMILK BARS

I'm a firm believer in making the most of the summer months. The living, as an old song suggests, should be easy, the food, light. With that said, these treats are indispensable. The buttermilk brightens the lemon for a very citrusy, very summery bar (plain yogurt can be used in place of the buttermilk for equally good results). The only other items needed are a glass of iced tea, a good book, and a few hours of nothing else to do.

- 1 (18.25-ounce) package lemon cake mix
- 4 large eggs
- ¾ cup (1½ sticks) butter, melted, divided
- ¾ cup buttermilk
- ¼ cup fresh lemon juice
- ⅓ cup sugar
- 1 tablespoon grated lemon zest
- 1–2 tablespoons powdered sugar

Preheat oven to 350°F (or 325°F for dark-coated metal pan). Position oven rack in middle of oven. Spray the bottom only of a 13 x 9-inch metal baking pan with nonstick cooking spray (or foil-line pan; see page xxiv).

Reserve 1 cup of the cake mix; set aside. Place the remaining cake mix, 1 of the eggs, and ¼ cup melted butter in a large bowl. Blend for 1–2 minutes with an electric mixer set on low speed until well blended. Press mixture into bottom of prepared pan.

Mix the remaining eggs, buttermilk, lemon juice, remaining melted butter, sugar, and lemon zest in a medium bowl with electric mixer set on low speed until well blended. Add the reserved cake mix, beating for 2 minutes on medium speed until mixture is smooth; pour over prepared crust.

Bake for 35–38 minutes, until just set and light golden on top. Transfer to wire rack and cool completely. Cut into bars and sift with powdered sugar.

MAKES 24 LARGE OR 36 SMALL BARS.

LEMON COOKIE SQUARES

Brew a cup of Earl Grey when it's chilly or pour a glass of iced tea when it's sizzling—either way, these creamy-crunchy lemon cookies will fit the bill.

- 1⅓ cups white chocolate chips
- ½ cup (1 stick) butter
- 2 teaspoons grated lemon zest
- 1⅓ cups coarsely crushed lemon creme sandwich cookies
- 1 cup chopped pecans, preferably skillet toasted and cooled (see page xviii)

Line an 8 x 8 x 2-inch pan with foil (see page xxiv); lightly spray with nonstick cooking spray. Set aside.

Place the white chocolate chips and butter in a medium saucepan set over low heat. Stir until the white chocolate is completely melted.

Remove from heat; stir in the zest, cookies, and pecans, mixing well. Quickly spread mixture into prepared pan.

Refrigerate bars for 3 hours or until firm. Cut into squares. Store in covered containers between layers of wax paper.

MAKES 16 SQUARES.

LEMON CURD SWIRL CHEESECAKE BARS

A swirl of purchased lemon curd makes all the difference in these simple-to-make, elegant bars. Serve them at your next summertime get-together and let the kudos resound.

- 1 (18.25-ounce) package lemon cake mix
- ½ cup (1 stick) butter, melted
- 1 tablespoon grated lemon zest
- 3 large eggs
- 2 (8-ounce) packages cream cheese, softened
- ⅓ cup sugar
- 1 tablespoon fresh lemon juice
- 2 tablespoons all-purpose flour
- 1 (12-ounce) jar lemon curd, room temperature

Preheat oven to 350°F (or 325°F for dark-coated metal pan). Position oven rack in middle of oven. Spray the bottom only of a 13 x 9-inch baking pan with nonstick cooking spray (or foil-line pan; see page xxiv).

Place the cake mix, melted butter, lemon zest, and 1 of the eggs in a large bowl. Blend for 1–2 minutes with an electric mixer set on medium speed until well blended. Press into prepared pan. Bake for 15 minutes. Remove from oven (leave oven on).

While the crust bakes, place the softened cream cheese and sugar in same large bowl (no need to clean). Blend with an electric mixer set on medium speed until light and fluffy. Add the lemon juice and flour; beat until smooth, scraping down sides with rubber spatula. Beat in remaining eggs, one at a time, until blended. Spread cream cheese mixture evenly over crust. Distribute the lemon curd in spoonfuls evenly over the cream cheese layer. Swirl the lemon curd and cream cheese batter with tip of a knife.

Bake bars in middle of oven for 23–26 minutes or until topping is just barely set when the pan is jiggled (do not overbake). Transfer to a wire rack and cool completely. Chill in refrigerator for at least 3 hours or until firm. Cut into bars or squares.

MAKES 24 LARGE OR 36 SMALL BARS.

LEMON LAYERED BARS

Smooth and cool with the flavor of lemon, these layered citrus bars are home-run hot weather fare.

- 12 tablespoons (1½ stick) butter, softened and divided
- 4 (1-ounce) squares white chocolate, divided use

- 1½ tablespoons pasteurized egg product (e.g., Egg Beaters)
- 1 cup quick-cooking oats, uncooked
- 1½ cups sweetened flake coconut
- ½ cup finely chopped almonds
- 1 teaspoon vanilla extract
- 2½ cups powdered sugar, divided use
- 2 teaspoons grated lemon zest
- 2½ tablespoons lemon juice

Lightly spray a 9 x 9 x 2-inch pan with nonstick cooking spray; set aside.

Melt 8 tablespoons (1 stick) of the butter with 2 squares of the white chocolate in a saucepan, stirring until smooth. Remove from heat and stir in the egg product, oats, coconut, almonds, vanilla, and ½ cup of the powdered sugar. With a large square of wax paper, press mixture into prepared pan. Chill for 1 hour.

Blend the remaining powdered sugar with the lemon zest, lemon juice, and 3 tablespoons of the remaining softened butter in a medium bowl, mixing until it has an icing-like consistency. Spread lemon mixture over the oat mixture in the pan. Chill for 30 minutes.

Melt the remaining butter with the remaining white chocolate in a small saucepan. Spread over the top of the bars. Chill for 1 hour to set chocolate. Cut into bars. Store in covered containers between layers of wax paper.

MAKES 16 SQUARES.

LEMON MACAROON BARS

A memorable dessert is something to be proud of, whether hosting a fancy dinner party or just throwing something together for the family some weeknight or weekend.

No matter what the occasion, this is an easy option that will make any home baker beam and blush from all of the kudos.

- 1 (18.25-ounce) package lemon cake mix
- ⅓ cup butter, softened
- 2 large eggs
- 1 (14-ounce) can sweetened condensed milk
- 2 tablespoons lemon juice
- 1 tablespoon grated lemon zest
- 2⅔ cups (7-ounce bag) flaked sweetened coconut, divided

Preheat oven to 350°F (or 325°F for dark-coated metal pan). Position oven rack in middle of oven. Spray the bottom only of a 13 x 9-inch metal baking pan with nonstick cooking spray (or foil-line pan; see page xxiv).

Place the cake mix, softened butter, and 1 of the eggs in a large bowl. Blend for 1–2 minutes with an electric mixer set on low speed until well blended. Press mixture in bottom of prepared pan.

Whisk the condensed milk, remaining egg, lemon juice and lemon zest in a medium bowl until well blended. Stir in 1⅓ cups coconut; spread mixture evenly over base. Sprinkle with remaining coconut; lightly press into condensed milk layer.

Bake for 28–30 minutes or until center is almost set. Center will firm when cool. Transfer to wire rack and cool completely. Cut into bars.

MAKES 24 LARGE OR 36 SMALL BARS.

Variation:

VANILLA MACAROON BARS: Prepare as directed above but use vanilla cake mix in place of lemon cake mix and use 2 teaspoons vanilla extract in place of the lemon juice and lemon zest.

LINZER BARS

This riff on Linzer torte—in cookie bar form—is impressive enough for company.

- 1 (16.5-ounce) roll refrigerated sugar cookie dough
- 1/3 cup finely chopped almonds
- 2 tablespoons all-purpose flour
- 1/4 teaspoon ground cinnamon
- 1/2 cup seedless raspberry jam

Preheat oven to 350°F. Spray an 8-inch-square baking pan with nonstick cooking spray.

Break up the cookie dough into a large bowl. Sprinkle the almonds, flour, and cinnamon over dough. Mix well with fingers until blended.

Reserve 1/2 cup cookie dough mixture. Press remaining mixture onto bottom of prepared baking pan. Spread jam over dough.

Roll out reserved dough on lightly floured surface into 8 x 5-inch rectangle. Cut lengthwise into 10 equal strips. Lay half the strips over jam, about 1 inch apart. Lay remaining strips crosswise over the first strips.

Bake for 25–30 minutes or until top is golden brown. Cool in pan on wire rack for 10 minutes. Serve warm or cool completely. Cut into squares.

MAKES 16 SQUARES.

LIPSMACKER LEMON BARS

Lemon bars are one of my sentimental favorites. Tart lemon curd on a sugar cookie crust? It's hard to beat, especially with a cup of hot tea and a good book close at hand.

- 1 (16.5-ounce) roll refrigerated sugar cookie dough, well chilled
- 4 large eggs, slightly beaten
- 1 1/3 cups sugar
- 1/4 cup all-purpose flour
- 1 teaspoon baking powder
- 3/4 cup lemon juice
- 1/3 cup sifted powdered sugar

Preheat oven to 350°F. Spray a 13 x 9-inch pan with nonstick cooking spray or line with foil. Cut cookie dough into 1/4-inch-thick slices. Arrange slices in bottom of the prepared pan. With floured fingers, press dough evenly to form crust.

Bake for 10–14 minutes or until light golden brown (dough will appear slightly puffed). Remove from oven.

While crust bakes, whisk the eggs, sugar, flour, and baking powder in a large bowl; blend well. Whisk in lemon juice. Pour mixture over warm, partially baked crust.

Return pan to oven and bake for 22–25 minutes or until filling is just set. Remove from oven and cool completely. Cut into bars and remove from pan; sprinkle with powdered sugar.

MAKES 36 BARS.

Baker's Note

If you cannot get enough lemon, drizzle or spread cooled bars with 1 recipe Lemon Icing (see page 368) in place of sifting with powdered sugar.

MAGIC COOKIE BARS

Call them hello dollies, 7-layer bars, or magic cookie bars—an incredible cookie, no matter the name, tastes just as sweet. A bit of crispy from the toasted coconut and pecans, a touch of buttery from the quick crust, and a good dose of gooey from the condensed milk and chocolate chips guarantee that these will magically disappear from the cookie jar.

- 1 (18.25-ounce) package yellow cake mix with pudding in the mix
- ½ cup (1 stick) butter, softened
- 2 cups semisweet chocolate chips
- 1½ cups sweetened flaked coconut
- 1 cup chopped walnuts (or pecans)
- 1 (14-ounce) can sweetened condensed milk

Preheat oven to 350°F (or 325°F for dark-coated metal pan). Position oven rack in middle of oven.

Place the cake mix and softened butter in a large bowl. Blend for 1–2 minutes with an electric mixer set on medium speed until blended and crumbly. Press mixture into a 15 x 10 x 1-inch jelly roll pan. Sprinkle the crust with the chocolate chips, coconut, and nuts. Pour condensed milk evenly over crust and ingredients.

Bake for 25–28 minutes or until lightly browned. Transfer to wire rack. Cool completely. Cut into bars.

MAKES 48 SMALL BARS.

Variations:

BUTTERSCOTCH MAGIC COOKIE BARS:
Prepare as directed above but use butterscotch baking chips in place of the chocolate chips.

DOUBLE CHOCOLATE MAGIC COOKIE BARS:
Prepare as directed above but use chocolate cake mix in place of the yellow cake mix.

VANILLA MAGIC COOKIE BARS:
Prepare as directed above but use vanilla cake mix in place of the yellow cake mix, vanilla baking chips or white chocolate chips in place of the semisweet chocolate chips, and sliced almonds in place of the chopped walnuts or pecans.

MANDARIN ORANGE CHEESECAKE BARS

Mandarin oranges and cheesecake? Oh yes. This is the kind of recipe home bakers dream about: so simple, so beautiful, and so delicious that everyone will want to linger to have a second or third helping. The fresh flavors of this bar make it a great choice for spring and summer get-togethers.

- 1 (18.25-ounce) package yellow cake mix
- 3 large eggs
- ⅓ cup butter, melted
- 2 (8-ounce) packages of cream cheese
- ⅔ cup sour cream
- ⅓ cup orange marmalade
- 1 (11-ounce) can mandarin oranges, drained

Preheat oven to 350°F (or 325°F for dark-coated metal pan). Position oven rack in middle of oven. Spray the bottom only of a 13 x 9-inch metal baking pan with nonstick cooking spray (or foil-line pan; see page xxiv).

Reserve 1 cup of cake mix; set aside. Place the remaining cake mix, 1 of the eggs, and melted butter in a medium bowl. Blend with an electric mixer set on medium speed until all dry ingredients are moistened. Press mixture into prepared pan. Bake for 10 minutes.

Meanwhile, beat the reserved cake mix, remaining eggs, cream cheese, sour cream, and marmalade in a medium bowl with an electric mixer set on medium speed until smooth; fold in mandarin oranges. Spread cream cheese mixture over crust.

Bake for 30–35 minutes or until just barely set. Transfer to wire rack and cool completely. Refrigerate at least for 2 hours before serving. Cut into bars.

MAKES 24 LARGE OR 36 SMALL BARS.

Variation:
GINGER-LIME CHEESECAKE BARS:
Prepare as directed above but add 2 teaspoons ground ginger to the cake mix-egg-butter mixture, use lime juice in place of the marmalade, and eliminate the mandarin oranges.

MANGO CREAM BARS

A spicy gingersnap crust is the perfect foil for the lush, tropical filling in these bars. For an additional tropical twist, consider sprinkling the bars with ½ cup sweetened flake coconut before chilling.

- 1¼ cups gingersnap cookie crumbs
- ¼ cup (½ stick) butter, melted
- ¼ cup fresh lime juice
- 2 teaspoons unflavored gelatin
- 1 (8-ounce) package cream cheese, softened
- ⅔ cup powdered sugar
- 1½ teaspoons grated lime zest
- 1 cup chopped fresh mango (about 1 large mango)

Line an 8 x 8 x 2-inch baking pan with foil (see page xxiv); lightly spray with nonstick cooking spray. Set aside.

Combine the cookie crumbs and melted butter in a medium bowl with a fork or fingers until well blended. Transfer crumb mixture to prepared pan. Press firmly into bottom of pan with a large square of wax paper. Freeze until ready to use.

Pour the lime juice into small saucepan; sprinkle gelatin over. Let stand for 10 minutes. Stir over very low heat just until gelatin dissolves. Set aside.

Blend the cream cheese, powdered sugar, lime zest, and mango in a food processor or blender until smooth. With machine running, add the warm gelatin mixture; blend well. Pour and spread filling evenly over crust. Cover and chill overnight.

Use foil lining to remove uncut bars from pan to cutting board. Cut into bars. Store, loosely covered with foil or plastic wrap, in refrigerator.

MAKES 16 BARS.

MAPLE CRANBERRY CRUNCH BARS

People often ask, "What's your favorite recipe in the book?" The answer to the question is never easy, but for this collection, these simple bars are it. I love the contrast of the maple with the tart cranberries and crunchy pecans. And although the flavors are fitting for cool autumn days and holiday gatherings, you'll find that these gems are popular year-round.

- ▓ ⅓ cup pure maple syrup
- ▓ 2 tablespoons (¼ stick) butter
- ▓ 4 cups miniature marshmallows
- ▓ 1½ teaspoons maple-flavored extract (optional)
- ▓ 6 cups honey and nut flakes and clusters cereal
- ▓ 1 cup dried cranberries
- ▓ 1 cup chopped pecans

Lightly spray a 13 x 9 x 2-inch baking pan with nonstick cooking spray; set aside.

Cook the maple syrup and butter in a large saucepan set over low heat, stirring until butter is melted and mixture is bubbly. Add the marshmallows; stir until marshmallows are melted. Remove from heat and mix in maple extract, cereal, cranberries, and pecans; stir to coat well.

With a large square of wax paper, press firmly into prepared pan. Cool completely. Cut into bars. Store in covered containers between layers of wax paper.

MAKES 24 BARS.

MAPLE CREAM BARS

Fruitcake may be traditional and candies well-loved, but for a truly special holiday treat, whip up a batch of these very maple bars. Look for the maple-flavored extract in the baking aisle where vanilla extract is shelved.

- ▓ 1¼ cups crisp sugar cookie crumbs
- ▓ ¼ cup (½ stick) butter, melted
- ▓ 1 cup chilled heavy whipping cream, divided
- ▓ 2 teaspoons unflavored gelatin
- ▓ ½ cup pure maple syrup
- ▓ 1 (8-ounce) package cream cheese, softened
- ▓ 1½ teaspoons maple-flavored extract

Line an 8 x 8 x 2-inch baking pan with foil (see page xxiv); lightly spray with nonstick cooking spray. Set aside.

Combine the cookie crumbs and melted butter in a medium bowl with a fork or fingers until well blended. Transfer crumb mixture to prepared pan. Press firmly into bottom of pan with a large square of wax paper. Freeze until ready to use.

Place ½ cup of the cream in a small saucepan; sprinkle gelatin over (do not stir). Let stand for 10 minutes to soften. Add the maple syrup to saucepan and turn the heat under saucepan to medium. Whisk and stir until liquid is very hot (but not boiling) and the gelatin is completely dissolved. Remove from heat and cool for 15 minutes.

Beat the maple extract and remaining chilled cream in a medium bowl with electric mixer on high speed until soft peaks form; set aside momentarily.

Beat the cream cheese in a separate medium bowl with electric mixer on medium until light and fluffy. Gradually add gelatin-maple mixture, beating on low speed and occasionally scraping sides of bowl with rubber spatula, until well blended. Fold in whipped cream with a rubber spatula.

Pour and spread filling evenly over prepared crust. Refrigerate for 3 hours or until firm. Use foil lining to remove uncut bars from pan to cutting board. Cut into bars. Store, loosely covered with foil or plastic wrap, in refrigerator.

MAKES 16 BARS.

MAPLE PECAN BARS

Impressive and unexpected, but still easy to prepare, these maple-accented bars can be made at the last minute when necessary.

- 1 (19.5- to 19.8-ounce) package brownie mix
- ½ cup (1 stick) unsalted butter, melted
- 1 (14-ounce) can sweetened condensed milk
- 1 large egg
- 2½ teaspoons maple extract
- 2 cups chopped pecans
- 1¼ cups milk chocolate chips

Preheat oven to 350°F (325°F for dark-coated metal pan). Position a rack in the lower third of the oven. Spray the bottom only of a 13 x 9-inch baking pan with nonstick cooking spray (or foil-line pan; see page xxiv).

Combine the brownie mix and melted butter in a medium mixing bowl with a wooden spoon until just blended and all dry ingredients are moistened. Press mixture into prepared pan. Bake for 15 minutes. Remove from oven (leave oven on).

Meanwhile, whisk together the condensed milk, egg, and maple extract in a medium mixing bowl; stir in pecans. Spoon and spread pecan mixture over hot crust; sprinkle with milk chocolate chips.

Return to oven and bake 20–22 minutes longer, until golden at edges and just set at the center. Transfer to a wire rack and cool completely. Cut into bars.

MAKES 24 LARGE OR 36 SMALL BARS.

MARGARITA BARS

If you're looking for an all-out summertime dazzler, these margarita- inspired bars, with their salty-sweet crust and cool lime and orange filling, will fit the bill.

- 1⅓ cups crushed pretzels
- ¼ cup (½ stick) butter, melted
- 2 tablespoons sugar
- ¼ cup lime juice
- 2 teaspoons unflavored gelatin
- ¼ cup orange juice
- 1½ teaspoons freshly grated lime zest
- 1 (8-ounce) package cream cheese, softened
- ½ cup sour cream
- ¾ cup powdered sugar
- 3 tablespoons tequila

Line an 8 x 8 x 2-inch baking pan with foil (see page xxiv); lightly spray with nonstick cooking spray. Set aside.

Combine the pretzel crumbs, melted butter, and sugar in a medium bowl with a fork or fingers until well blended. Transfer crumb mixture to prepared pan. Press firmly into bottom of pan with a large square of wax paper. Freeze until ready to use.

Place the lime juice in a small saucepan; sprinkle gelatin over (do not stir). Let stand for 10 minutes to soften. Add the orange juice to the saucepan and turn the heat under saucepan to medium. Whisk and stir until juice mixture is very hot (but not boiling) and gelatin is completely dissolved. Remove from heat and set aside momentarily.

Beat the lime zest, cream cheese, sour cream, powdered sugar, and tequila in a large bowl with electric mixer on medium speed until creamy. Gradually add gelatin mixture, beating on low speed and occasionally scraping sides of bowl with rubber spatula, until well blended.

Pour and spread the filling evenly over prepared crust. Refrigerate for 3 hours or until firm. Use foil lining to remove uncut bars from pan to cutting board. Cut into bars. Store, loosely covered with foil or plastic wrap, in refrigerator.

MAKES 16 BARS.

MAUI WOWIE MACADAMIA BARS

This is a beautifully simple yet very delicious cookie with a big "wow" factor. A little bit crunchy, a little bit chewy, the perfect level of sweetness and lots of big tropical flavors make it ideal summer-dessert fare.

- 1/3 cup honey
- 2 tablespoons butter
- 2 teaspoons ground ginger
- 4 cups miniature marshmallows
- 2 teaspoons grated lime zest
- 6 cups honey and nut flakes and clusters cereal
- 1 cup dried tropical fruit bits
- 1 cup chopped, lightly salted roasted macadamia nuts

Lightly spray a 13 x 9 x 2-inch baking pan with nonstick cooking spray; set aside.

Cook the honey and butter in a large saucepan set over low heat. Stir until butter is melted and mixture is bubbly. Add the ginger, marshmallows, and lime zest. Stir until marshmallows are melted and mixture is blended. Remove from heat and mix in cereal, tropical fruit bits, and macadamia nuts; stir to coat well.

With a large square of wax paper, press firmly into prepared pan. Cool completely. Cut into bars. Store in covered containers between layers of wax paper.

MAKES 24 BARS.

MAUI WOWIE MAGIC BARS

For an imaginative cookie, try this aloha-inspired variation on magic cookie bars. They are definitely summer barbecue fare, so invite the guests and fire up the grill.

- 1 (18.25-ounce) package yellow cake mix with pudding in the mix
- 1½ teaspoons ground ginger
- ½ cup (1 stick) butter, softened
- 1 (14-ounce) can sweetened condensed milk
- 1 tablespoon lime juice
- 2 teaspoons grated lime zest
- 1½ cups white chocolate chips
- 1½ cups sweetened flaked coconut
- 1 cup chopped macadamia nuts
- ½ cup pineapple preserves

Preheat oven to 350°F (or 325°F for dark-coated metal pan). Position oven rack in middle of oven.

Place the cake mix, ginger, and softened butter in a large bowl. Blend for 1–2 minutes with an electric mixer set on medium speed, until blended and crumbly. Press mixture into a 15 x 10 x 1-inch jelly roll pan.

Mix the condensed milk with the lime juice and lime zest in a small bowl. Sprinkle the crust with the white chocolate chips, coconut, and macadamia nuts. Pour condensed milk mixture evenly over crust and ingredients.

Bake for 25–28 minutes or until lightly browned. Transfer to wire rack. Heat preserves in a small saucepan set over low heat until melted; drizzle over baked bars. Cool completely. Cut into bars.

MAKES 48 SMALL BARS.

MILK CHOCOLATE CHEESECAKE BARS

Dedicated chocolate fans will delight in this quick, handheld version of chocolate cheesecake.

- 1¼ cups chocolate wafer cookie crumbs
- ¼ cup (½ stick) butter, melted
- ¼ cup milk
- 2 teaspoons unflavored gelatin
- 1 (8-ounce) package cream cheese, softened
- ½ cup unsweetened cocoa powder
- 1 cup sour cream
- ¾ cup powdered sugar
- 1 teaspoon vanilla extract

Line an 8 x 8 x 2-inch baking pan with foil (see page xxiv); lightly spray with nonstick cooking spray. Set aside.

Combine the chocolate cookie crumbs and melted butter in a medium bowl with a fork or fingers until well blended. Transfer crumb mixture to prepared pan. Press firmly into bottom of pan with a large square of wax paper. Freeze until ready to use.

Place the milk in a small saucepan; sprinkle gelatin over (do not stir). Let stand for 10 minutes to soften. Turn the heat under saucepan to medium. Whisk and stir until milk is very hot (but not boiling) and gelatin is completely dissolved. Remove from heat and set aside momentarily.

Beat the cream cheese, sour cream, cocoa powder, powdered sugar, and vanilla in a large bowl with electric mixer on medium speed until creamy. Gradually add gelatin-milk mixture, beating on low speed and occasionally scraping sides of bowl with rubber spatula, until well blended.

Pour and spread cream cheese mixture evenly over prepared crust. Refrigerate for 3 hours or until firm. Use foil lining to remove uncut bars from pan to cutting board. Cut into bars. Store, loosely covered with foil or plastic wrap, in refrigerator.

MAKES 16 BARS.

MILK CHOCOLATE MACAROON BARS

Don't fuss the next time you need to make dessert for a party crowd. Rather, whip up a batch of these jazzed-up, milk chocolate and coconut-adorned bar cookies. With such a fast and versatile recipe, you'll have plenty of time to celebrate yourself.

- 1 (19.5- to 19.8-ounce) package brownie mix
- ½ cup (1 stick) unsalted butter, melted
- 2 cups shredded coconut
- 1 (14-ounce) can sweetened condensed milk
- 1 cup milk chocolate chips
- 1 teaspoon almond extract

Preheat oven to 350°F (325°F for dark-coated metal pan). Position a rack in the lower third of the oven. Spray a 13 x 9-inch baking pan with nonstick cooking spray (or foil-line pan; see page xxiv).

Combine the brownie mix and melted butter in a medium mixing bowl with a wooden spoon until all dry ingredients are moistened (mixture will be stiff). Press into prepared pan.

Bake for 15 minutes. Remove from oven (leave oven on).

While crust bakes, combine the coconut, condensed milk, chocolate chips, and almond extract in a medium mixing bowl; carefully spread over warm brownie base.

Bake for an additional 16–18 minutes or until topping is set and golden brown. Transfer to a wire rack and cool completely. Cut into bars.

MAKES 24 LARGE OR 36 SMALL BARS.

MILK CHOCOLATE ORANGE BARS

The flavors of chocolate and orange are very good together. These bars are very tasty, very rich, and very much worth every bite.

- 3 cups finely crushed chocolate graham cracker crumbs
- 1½ cups miniature marshmallows
- 1 cup chopped almonds
- ⅔ cup firmly packed light brown sugar
- 1 cup canned evaporated milk
- 2 cups milk chocolate chips
- 1 tablespoon grated orange zest
- ½ teaspoon almond extract

Lightly spray a 9 x 9 x 2-inch pan with nonstick cooking spray; set aside.

Combine the chocolate graham cracker crumbs, marshmallows, almonds, and brown sugar in a large bowl.

Combine the evaporated milk and milk chocolate chips in a medium saucepan set over low heat. Stir until chips are melted and mixture is smooth. Mix in orange zest and almond extract. Pour all but ½ cup of the melted chocolate over crumb mixture; toss and stir to coat evenly.

Immediately spread mixture into prepared pan. Press and smooth surface with a square of wax paper. Drizzle reserved chocolate mixture over bars. Refrigerate for 2–3 hours or as long as overnight. Cut into bars. Store in covered containers between layers of wax paper.

MAKES 24 BARS.

MINT-CHIP CHEESECAKE BROWNIE BARS

Tis the season for delectable cookie making with these festive, peppermint-y bar cookies. Feel free to experiment with other extracts such as rum, almond, orange, or maple—just be sure to leave off the peppermint candies if you do.

- 1 (19.5- to 19.8-ounce) package brownie mix
- ½ cup (1 stick) unsalted butter, melted
- 3 large eggs
- 2 (8-ounce) packages cream cheese, softened
- ½ cup sugar

- 1 teaspoon peppermint extract
- 2 cups miniature semisweet chocolate chips, divided
- 2 teaspoons vegetable shortening
- 16 red and white striped round peppermint hard candies, coarsely crushed

Preheat oven to 350°F (325°F for dark-coated metal pan). Position a rack in the lower third of the oven. Spray the bottom only of a 13 x 9-inch baking pan with nonstick cooking spray (or foil-line pan; see page xxiv).

Combine the brownie mix, butter, and 1 egg in a medium mixing bowl with a wooden spoon until just blended and all dry ingredients are moistened. Press mixture into prepared pan. Bake for 18 minutes or until center is partially set (do not overbake). Remove from oven (leave oven on).

While crust bakes, beat cream cheese and sugar in a medium mixing bowl with electric mixer set on high until smooth. Gradually beat in remaining eggs and peppermint extract until smooth. Stir in 1 cup of the miniature chocolate chips. Pour over partially baked crust.

Bake for 20–22 minutes, until just barely set at center (do not overbake). Transfer to a wire rack and cool completely.

Melt remaining chocolate chips with shortening in heavy saucepan, stirring until smooth; drizzle over cooled bars and sprinkle with crushed mint candies. Chill for at least 3 hours in refrigerator. Cut into bars. Store in refrigerator.

MAKES 24 LARGE OR 36 SMALL BARS.

MOCHA GANACHE WALNUT BARS

A layer of crunchy walnuts, a layer of sugar cookie, and a swath of mocha ganache add up to a terrific cookie bar for java junkies.

- 2½ cups very finely chopped walnuts
- 6 tablespoons packed light brown sugar
- 6 tablespoons (¾ stick) butter, melted
- ½ teaspoon ground cinnamon
- 1 (16.5-ounce) roll refrigerated sugar cookie dough
- 1½ cups bittersweet chocolate chips
- ⅓ cup heavy whipping cream
- 1 tablespoon instant espresso powder

Preheat oven to 350°F.

Combine the walnuts, brown sugar, butter, and cinnamon in a medium bowl until blended. Press mixture evenly onto bottom of an ungreased 13 x 9-inch baking pan.

Bake for 9–13 minutes or until edges are golden. Cool for 30 minutes. Cut cookie dough into ¼-inch slices. Arrange slices to cover walnut crust. With floured fingers, press dough evenly atop walnut crust.

Bake for 20–25 minutes or until golden brown. Cool.

Microwave the chocolate chips, whipping cream, and espresso powder in a medium microwavable bowl on high for 1 minute, stirring every 30 seconds until chips are melted and mixture is smooth. Spread chocolate mixture evenly over bars. Refrigerate for 1 hour. Cut into bars. Store in refrigerator.

MAKES 24 BARS.

MOTHER LODE CHOCOLATE TOFFEE CARAMEL BARS

It seems that something chocolate is nearly everyone's favorite dessert. These quick and easy bars, loaded with caramel, toffee, and even more chocolate, qualify as one such something, effortlessly.

- 1 (18.25-ounce) package yellow cake mix
- 1/3 cup vegetable oil
- 2 large eggs
- 1 cup semisweet chocolate chips
- 1 cup white chocolate chips
- 3 (1.4-ounce) chocolate-covered toffee candy bars, coarsely chopped
- 32 caramels, unwrapped
- 1/2 cup (1 stick) butter
- 1 (14-ounce) can sweetened condensed milk

Preheat oven to 350°F (or 325°F for dark-coated metal pan). Position oven rack in middle of oven. Spray the bottom only of a 13 x 9-inch metal baking pan with nonstick cooking spray (or foil-line pan; see page xxiv).

Place the cake mix, oil, and eggs in a large bowl. Blend for 2 minutes with an electric mixer set on medium speed until well blended. Stir in semisweet chocolate chips and white chocolate chips. Press half of mixture into bottom of prepared pan. Stir toffee pieces into remaining half. Bake crust for 10 minutes.

While the crust bakes, place the caramels, butter, and condensed milk in a medium heavy saucepan. Stir over medium-low heat until caramels are melted and mixture is blended and smooth; pour evenly over partially baked crust and sprinkle with the remaining cake mix mixture.

Bake for 25–28 minutes or until the topping is golden and firm to the touch. Transfer to wire rack. Run knife around edges of pan to loosen; cool completely.

MAKES 24 LARGE OR 36 SMALL BARS.

NANAIMO BARS

They may not be well-known in the States (yet!), but Nanaimo bars are Canadian cookie classics. Although they are named after the town of Nanaimo in British Columbia, no one is quite sure why or how or when the recipe originated. What is certain is they are scrumptious bars, suitable for any time of the year and any occasion.

- 1/4 cup sugar
- 5 tablespoons unsweetened cocoa powder
- 1 cup plus 2 tablespoons (2 1/4 sticks) butter, softened, divided
- 1 large egg, beaten
- 1 1/4 cups graham cracker crumbs
- 1/2 cup finely chopped pecans, walnuts, or almonds
- 1 cup sweetened flake coconut
- 2 1/2 tablespoons milk
- 2 tablespoons vanilla instant pudding and pie filling powder (from a 4-serving-size package)
- 2 cups powdered sugar
- 4 (1-ounce) squares semisweet baking chocolate

Lightly spray an 8 x 8 x 2-inch pan with nonstick cooking spray; set aside.

Combine the sugar, cocoa, and ½ cup (1 stick) butter in the top of a double boiler set over simmering water. Stir until melted and blended. Add the beaten egg; stir for 1 minute. Remove from heat. Stir in the graham cracker crumbs, nuts, and coconut. Press firmly into prepared pan with a large square of wax paper. Refrigerate for 1 hour.

Beat the milk, pudding powder, powdered sugar, and ½ cup (1 stick) of the remaining butter in a medium bowl with an electric mixer set on low speed, beating until light and well blended. Spread over chilled base. Refrigerate for 30 minutes.

Melt the chocolate with the remaining 2 tablespoons butter in a small saucepan over low heat. Remove from heat; cool for 5 minutes. Pour and spread over bars. Refrigerate for 30 minutes. Cut into bars. Store in covered container, in the refrigerator, between layers of wax paper.

MAKES 16 BARS.

Variations:

KAHLUA NANAIMO BARS:
Prepare as directed above but substitute 2½ tablespoons Kahlua or other coffee liqueur for the milk.

CHOCOLATE PEPPERMINT NANAIMO BARS:
Prepare as directed above but add 1 teaspoon peppermint extract and 1–2 drops of red food coloring, if desired, to the pudding layer. Sprinkle the third (chocolate) layer with ½ cup coarsely crushed red and white-striped peppermint candies or candy canes.

PISTACHIO NANAIMO BARS:
Prepare as directed above but substitute 2 tablespoons pistachio instant pudding powder for the vanilla powder. Sprinkle the third (chocolate) layer with ½ cup coarsely chopped pistachio nuts.

NEW YORK CHEESECAKE BARS

Forget the springform pan—you can make an incredible, New York-style cheesecake in a plain 13 x 9-inch baking pan. Not only is it a breeze to make, it is much easier to cut and serve to a crowd—or a small army. Because this silky-rich cheesecake is skyscraper-high, one square will go a long way. For a dressed-up dessert, serve the squares plated with a drizzle of chocolate or caramel sauce, fresh fruit, or a quick berry compote. And for an easy flavor variation, vary the cake mix for the crust. Lemon, chocolate, and spice cake are particularly delicious.

- 1 (18.25-ounce) package vanilla cake mix
- ½ cup (1 stick) butter, melted
- 4 large eggs
- 3 (8-ounce) packages cream cheese, softened
- 1¾ cups powdered sugar, divided
- 3 teaspoons vanilla extract, divided
- 1 (16-ounce) container (2 cups) sour cream

Preheat oven to 350°F (or 325°F for dark-coated metal pan). Position oven rack in middle of oven. Spray the bottom only of a 13 x 9-inch metal baking pan with nonstick cooking spray (or foil-line pan; see page xxiv).

Place the cake mix, melted butter, and 1 egg

in a large bowl. Blend for 1–2 minutes with an electric mixer set on low speed until well blended. Press mixture evenly into prepared pan. Bake crust for 15 minutes.

While crust bakes, beat softened cream cheese, 1¼ cups of the powdered sugar, and 2 teaspoons of the vanilla extract with electric mixer set on medium speed until well blended, scraping down bowl several times. Add remaining eggs, one at a time, mixing on low speed after each addition just until blended. Pour over hot crust.

Bake for 23–26 minutes or until center is just barely set when pan is jiggled (do not overbake); remove from oven (leave oven on).

Whisk the sour cream in a large mixing bowl with the remaining ½ cup powdered sugar and 1 teaspoon vanilla extract; spread evenly over bars. Return bars to oven for 5 minutes. Transfer to wire rack and cool completely. Refrigerate at least 4 hours or overnight. Cut into bars.

MAKES 36 MEDIUM BARS OR 48 SMALL SQUARES.

Variation:
FRESH BERRY CHEESECAKE BARS:
Prepare as directed above but eliminate the final sour cream topping steps. Instead, distribute 2 cups fresh raspberries, blackberries, or blueberries over the cheesecake batter before baking. Sprinkle the cooled, chilled bars with powdered sugar.

NEW YORK CHEESECAKE BROWNIE BARS

Take the silken simplicity of New York–style cheesecake, layer it atop a rich, dark chocolate base, and what have you got? An irresistible bar cookie. But not for long—they will disappear fast. These bars are very rich, very high, and very creamy, as New York cheesecake should be. One batch easily makes forty-eight servings when cut small, enough for a good-sized crowd.

- 1 (19.5- to 19.8-ounce) package brownie mix
- ½ cup (1 stick) unsalted butter, melted
- 4 (8-ounce) packages cream cheese, softened
- 1 cup plus 2 tablespoons sugar, divided
- 4 teaspoons vanilla extract, divided
- 4 large eggs
- 1 (16-ounce) container (2 cups) sour cream

Preheat oven to 350°F (325°F for dark-coated metal pan). Position a rack in the lower third of the oven. Spray the bottom only of a 13 x 9-inch baking pan with nonstick cooking spray (or foil-line pan; see page xxiv).

Combine the brownie mix and melted butter in a medium mixing bowl with a wooden spoon until just blended and all dry ingredients are moistened. Press mixture into prepared pan. Bake for 15 minutes. Remove from oven (leave oven on).

While crust bakes, beat cream cheese, 1 cup of the sugar, and 3 teaspoons of the vanilla with an electric mixer set on medium until well blended. Add eggs, one at a time, mixing on low after each addition just until blended. Pour over hot crust.

Bake for 23–26 minutes or until center is just barely set when pan is jiggled (do not overbake); remove from oven (leave oven on).

Whisk the sour cream with the remaining 2 tablespoons sugar and 1 teaspoon vanilla in a medium mixing bowl; spread evenly over bars. Return bars to oven for 5 minutes. Transfer to a wire rack and cool completely. Refrigerate for at least 4 hours or overnight. Cut into bars.

MAKES 36 MEDIUM OR 48 SMALL BARS.

NO-BAKE HELLO DOLLIES

Ideal for backyard barbecues, this no-bake rendition of the favorite multi-layered bar will garner high praise—and requests for the recipe.

- 1 cup (2 sticks) butter, divided use
- 2½ cups finely crushed graham cracker crumbs
- ½ cup plus 2 tablespoons firmly packed light brown sugar, divided use
- ⅓ cup canned evaporated milk
- 2¼ cups miniature marshmallows
- 1 cup butterscotch baking chips
- 1 cup chopped walnuts or pecans, preferably skillet toasted and cooled (see page xviii)
- 1⅓ cups shredded coconut, skillet toasted and cooled (see page xx)
- 1 cup miniature semisweet chocolate chips

Line a 13 x 9 x 2-inch pan with foil (see page xxiv); lightly spray with nonstick cooking spray. Set aside.

Melt ¾ cup of the butter in a large nonstick skillet set over medium-low heat. Mix the graham cracker crumbs and 2 tablespoons brown sugar in a large bowl with the melted butter until blended. Transfer crumb mixture to prepared pan, pressing down and smoothing surface with a square of wax paper. Refrigerate while preparing topping.

Place the remaining brown sugar, evaporated milk, marshmallows, and remaining butter in a large saucepan; cook on medium heat until mixture comes to a boil, stirring constantly. Boil for 5 minutes, stirring constantly. Add butterscotch chips; cook until completely melted, stirring frequently.

Pour and spread mixture over prepared crust to cover evenly. Immediately sprinkle with nuts, coconut, and miniature chocolate chips; press lightly into chocolate layer. Refrigerate until set, for about 3 hours. Cut into bars. Store in covered containers between layers of wax paper.

MAKES 36 BARS.

ONE BOWL TRIPLE-CHOCOLATE CHERRY BARS

Cherry filling makes these bars moist, cake-like, and cherry all over. I personally refer to these as "procrastination bars" because they are the ideal solution for last-minute baking. Just one bowl, five ingredients, and a bit of stirring are all that's needed to get them in the oven. A gilding of chocolate frosting ensures that these will be surefire hits for any and every occasion.

- 1 (19.5- to 19.8-ounce) package brownie mix
- 1 (21-ounce) can cherry pie filling
- 3 tablespoons vegetable oil
- 2 large eggs, lightly beaten
- 1 cup miniature semisweet chocolate chips
- 1 (16-ounce) tub ready-to-spread chocolate frosting, or
- 1 recipe Chocolate Fudge Frosting (see page 362; 13 x 9-inch pan size), optional

Preheat oven to 350°F (325°F for dark-coated metal pan). Position a rack in the lower third of the oven. Spray a 15 x 10-inch jelly roll baking pan with nonstick cooking spray (or foil-line pan; see page xxiv).

Combine the brownie mix, pie filling, oil, eggs, and chocolate chips in a medium mixing bowl with a wooden spoon until just blended and all dry ingredients are moistened. Spread mixture evenly into prepared pan.

Bake for 28–32 minutes or until just set and firm to the touch (do not overbake). Transfer to a wire rack and cool completely.

If desired, prepare Chocolate Fudge Frosting; spread over cooled bars. Cut into bars.

MAKES 24 LARGE OR 36 SMALL BARS.

ORANGE BUTTERCREAM BARS

The mild bitterness of orange zest and a deep chocolate crust temper the sweetness of these easy, creamy bars. You can prepare these sophisticated treats up to a day ahead.

- 2/3 cup plus 1 tablespoon butter, softened, divided use
- 1¼ cups finely crushed chocolate wafer cookies
- 1½ cups powdered sugar
- 1 tablespoon freshly grated orange zest
- 1 tablespoon milk
- 1 teaspoon vanilla extract
- 1 tablespoon unsweetened cocoa

Line an 8 x 8 x 2-inch baking pan with foil (see page xxiv); lightly spray with nonstick cooking spray. Set aside.

Melt 1/3 cup butter in a small saucepan set over low heat. Combine the melted butter and cookie crumbs in a medium bowl until blended. Transfer crumb mixture to prepared pan. Press firmly into bottom of pan with a large square of wax paper. Freeze until ready to use.

Beat the powdered sugar, orange zest, milk, vanilla, and 1/3 cup of the remaining softened butter in a medium bowl with an electric mixer set on medium speed until creamy. Spread filling mixture over prepared crust.

melt the remaining 1 tablespoon butter in a small saucepan set over low heat. Remove from heat and whisk in cocoa powder until smooth. Drizzle over filling. Refrigerate bars until firm, 1–2 hours. Use foil lining to remove uncut bars from pan to cutting board. Cut into bars. Store, loosely covered with plastic wrap, in the refrigerator.

MAKES 16 BARS.

ORANGE DREAMSICLE BARS

Remember those orange and cream popsicles from childhood? Here is the same flavor combination, captured in cookie bar form. It's even better than you remembered.

- 1 (16.5-ounce) roll refrigerated sugar cookie dough
- 2 tablespoons grated orange zest
- 2 (8-ounce) packages cream cheese, softened
- 2/3 cup orange marmalade
- 2 large eggs
- 2 tablespoons butter
- 2 tablespoons milk
- 2 drops liquid orange food color
- 2/3 cup white chocolate chips

Preheat oven to 350°F.

Break up the cookie dough in an ungreased 13 x 9-inch baking pan. Using floured fingers, press cookie dough evenly on bottom of pan. Sprinkle with the orange zest. Press zest into the dough.

Beat the cream cheese and marmalade with an electric mixer on medium-high speed for about 1 minute or until well blended. Beat in the eggs until just blended and mixture is smooth. Spread evenly in crust.

Bake for 30–35 minutes or until crust is golden brown and center is set. Cool for 1 hour.

Microwave the butter, milk, and food color in a small microwavable bowl on high for about 30 seconds or just until boiling. Add the white chocolate and stir until melted and smooth. Spread mixture evenly over bars. Refrigerate for at least 2 hours. Cut into bars.

MAKES 36 COOKIES.

PANFORTE BARS

These bars are based on the Italian fruit-cake known as panforte, a dense cake rich with candied fruit, spices, cocoa, and nuts. The bars make a great ending to a holiday dinner.

- 2 cups finely ground vanilla wafers (about 44 wafers)
- ¾ cup powdered sugar
- 2 tablespoons unsweetened cocoa powder
- 1 teaspoon pumpkin pie spice
- ½ cup (1 stick) butter, melted
- ¼ cup brandy
- 1 cup chopped mixed candied fruit and peels
- ½ cup chopped dried apricots
- ½ cup chopped dates
- Powdered sugar to coat

Line a 9 x 9 x 2-inch square pan with foil (see page xxiv). Lightly coat foil with nonstick cooking spray.

Combine the ground wafers, powdered sugar, cocoa powder, and pumpkin pie spice in a large bowl. Add the melted butter and brandy; stir to combine and coat well. Add the candied fruit, dried apricots, and dates; mix well to combine.

Turn mixture into prepared pan. Using a

square of wax paper or moist fingers, press into prepared pan (mixture will seem slightly wet and sticky; it will set up as it chills). Loosely cover and refrigerate overnight. Liberally dust with powdered sugar to coat. Cut into bars. Store in covered containers between layers of wax paper.

MAKES 24 BARS.

PB AND J BITES

Here's a delectable cookie—based on the tried-and-true peanut butter and jelly sandwich—that will bring you all of the joy and fulfillment you expect from a homemade cookie.

▨ 3 cups miniature marshmallows
▨ ½ cup (1 stick) butter
▨ 1 cup plus 1½ tablespoons creamy or crunchy peanut butter, divided
▨ 4½ cups crisp rice cereal
▨ ⅔ cup strawberry jam, stirred to loosen
▨ ⅔ cup milk chocolate chips
▨ 1 tablespoon vegetable shortening

Line an 11 x 7 x 2-inch pan with foil (see page xxiv). Lightly coat foil with nonstick cooking spray.

Melt the marshmallows, butter, and 1 cup peanut butter in a large saucepan set over low heat, stirring until smooth. Remove from heat and stir in cereal until well coated.

Turn mixture into prepared pan. Using a square of wax paper or moist fingers, press into prepared pan. Immediately spread strawberry jam over warm cookie base. Set aside momentarily.

Melt the chocolate chips, shortening, and remaining peanut butter in a small saucepan set over low heat, stirring until smooth. Spoon and spread mixture gently over jam layer.

Cover bars loosely with plastic wrap and refrigerate for 2 hours or until firm. Cut into small bars. Store in covered containers between layers of wax paper.

MAKES 32 "BITES."

PEANUT BRITTLE BARS (CAKE MIX)

This satisfying, candy-like finale features all the flavors of homemade peanut brittle. With a few simple steps, you'll impress any dessert lover.

▨ 1 (18.25-ounce) package yellow cake mix
▨ 1⅓ cups creamy peanut butter, divided
▨ 1 large egg
▨ ½ cup vegetable oil
▨ 1 (14-ounce) can sweetened condensed milk
▨ 2 teaspoons vanilla extract
▨ 1 (10-ounce) bag toffee baking bits
▨ 2 cups lightly salted roasted peanuts

Preheat oven to 350°F (or 325°F for dark-coated metal pan). Position oven rack in middle of oven. Spray the bottom only of a 13 x 9-inch metal baking pan with nonstick cooking spray (or foil-line pan; see page xxiv).

Combine the cake mix, 1 cup peanut butter, egg, and oil in a large bowl. Blend for 1–2 minutes with an electric mixer set on low speed, until well blended (mixture will be stiff and crumbly). Press two-thirds of mixture into prepared pan. Bake for 10 minutes.

Meanwhile, whisk the condensed milk, remaining peanut butter, and vanilla extract in a medium bowl until smooth. Stir in half of the toffee bits; pour over crust. Sprinkle with peanuts, remaining crumb mixture, and remaining toffee bits.

Bake for 20–25 minutes or until golden brown and topping is firm to the touch.

Transfer to wire rack and cool completely. Cut into bars.

MAKES 24 LARGE OR 36 SMALL BARS.

PEANUT BRITTLE BARS (COOKIE DOUGH)

Peanut brittle lovers, mark your calendars: January 26th is National Peanut Brittle Day. One taste of these bars—bolstered with both toffee bits and butterscotch chips—and you won't be able to stop celebrating.

- 1 (16.5-ounce) roll refrigerated sugar cookie dough, well chilled
- 1½ cups lightly salted, roasted peanuts
- ¾ cup butterscotch chips
- ½ cup toffee baking bits
- 1 cup jarred caramel ice cream topping
- 2 tablespoons all-purpose flour

Preheat oven to 350°F. Spray a 13 x 9-inch baking pan with nonstick cooking spray or line with foil.

Cut cookie dough into ⅛-inch slices. Arrange slices in bottom of the prepared pan. Using floured fingers, press dough evenly in pan to form crust.

Bake for 8–11 minutes or until light golden brown and slightly puffed. Remove pan from oven and sprinkle peanuts, butterscotch chips, and toffee bits over warm base Combine caramel topping and flour. in a small bowl; blend well. Drizzle caramel mixture evenly over peanut layer.

Bake for an additional 15–18 minutes or until topping is set and golden brown. Remove from oven and cool completely. Cut into bars.

MAKES 36 BARS.

Baker's Note

Milk or semisweet chocolate chips may be substituted for the butterscotch chips.

PEANUT BUTTER AND STRAWBERRY JAM BARS

These old-fashioned bar cookies combine the best of peanut butter and strawberry jam in one delicious mouthful—comfort food to the max.

- 1 (16.5-ounce) roll refrigerated sugar cookie dough, well chilled
- 1 (14-ounce) can sweetened condensed milk
- 1 cup creamy-style peanut butter
- 1 teaspoon vanilla extract
- 3 large egg yolks
- ⅔ cup strawberry jam or preserves

Preheat oven to 350°F. Spray a 13 x 9-inch pan with nonstick cooking spray or line with foil.

Cut cookie dough into ¼-inch-thick slices.

Arrange slices in bottom of the prepared pan. With floured fingers, press dough evenly to form crust. Bake for 10–14 minutes or until light golden brown (dough will appear slightly puffed). Remove from oven.

Meanwhile, combine the sweetened condensed milk, peanut butter, vanilla, and egg yolks in a medium bowl; mix until smooth. Spoon and carefully spread milk mixture evenly over crust; dollop with spoonfuls of jam and swirl slightly with the tip of a knife.

Return to oven; bake for an additional 20–25 minutes or until just set. Remove from oven and cool completely. Cut into bars.

MAKES 36 BARS.

PEANUT BUTTER BLONDIES

Can the butterscotch blondie be made better? For peanut butter fiends, the answer is a resounding yes and involves merely stirring some peanut butter into the batter. Delicious!

- 1 (18.25-ounce) package yellow cake mix
- 1/3 cup butter, melted
- 2 large eggs
- 3 teaspoons vanilla extract, divided
- 2/3 cup plus 1 tablespoon creamy peanut butter (not natural style), divided
- 1 cup powdered sugar
- 2–3 tablespoons milk

Preheat oven to 350°F (or 325°F for dark-coated metal pan). Position oven rack in middle of oven. Set aside a 13 x 9-inch baking pan.

Combine the cake mix, melted butter, eggs, and 1 teaspoon vanilla extract in a large bowl with an electric mixer on low speed for 30 seconds. Stop the mixer and scrape down the sides of the bowl. Increase the mixer speed to medium and beat for 1 to 2 minutes more or until batter is smooth and very thick. Stir in 2/3 cup peanut butter with a wooden spoon.

Spoon the dough into the ungreased 13 x 9-inch pan; spread evenly with rubber spatula or fingers (dough will puff and spread as it bakes).

Bake for 22–25 minutes until just set at center (do not overbake). Transfer to a wire rack and cool completely.

Whisk the powdered sugar, remaining vanilla extract, and remaining peanut butter in a small bowl until blended, adding enough milk to make drizzling consistency; drizzle over cooled bars. Cut into bars or squares.

MAKES 24 LARGE OR 36 SMALL BARS.

Variations:

CHOCOLATE-CHIP PEANUT BUTTER BLONDIES: Prepare as directed above but add 1 cup semisweet or milk chocolate chips to the batter along with the peanut butter.

PEANUT BUTTER BLONDIES DELUXE: Prepare as directed above but add 1 cup peanut butter baking chips to the batter along with the peanut butter. After drizzling blondies with icing, sprinkle with 2/3 cup chopped peanuts.

PEANUT BUTTER– CHOCOLATE GOOEY CHESS SQUARES

oly moly. Yes, the combination of chocolate and peanut butter is a match made in heaven, but it has never been quite so good as in these gooey bars. Part cake, part cookie, they are 100 percent scrumptious.

- 1 cup (2 sticks) butter, divided
- 1 (18.25-ounce) package chocolate cake mix
- 4 large eggs
- 1 (8-ounce) package cream cheese, softened
- 1 cup creamy-style peanut butter
- 1 teaspoon vanilla extract
- 1 (16-ounce) box powdered sugar

Preheat oven to 350°F (or 325°F for dark-coated metal pan). Position oven rack in middle of oven. Spray the bottom only of a 13 x 9-inch metal baking pan with nonstick cooking spray (or foil-line pan; see page xxiv).

Melt ½ cup (1 stick) of the butter in a small saucepan set over low heat. Beat the cake mix, melted butter, and 1 egg in a large bowl with an electric mixer set on medium speed until well blended (mixture will come together as a thick dough). Pat the dough evenly into the prepared pan. Set aside momentarily.

Melt the remaining stick of butter in a small saucepan set over low heat. Beat the softened cream cheese and peanut butter in a large bowl with an electric mixer set on medium speed until smooth, scraping down sides of bowl occasionally. Add the melted butter, remaining eggs, and vanilla extract; blend until smooth. Add the powdered sugar; blend until smooth.

Spread peanut butter mixture over prepared crust. Bake for 42–45 minutes (do not overbake; bars should be slightly gooey). Transfer to a wire rack and cool completely. Cut into bars or squares. Cover and store in refrigerator.

MAKES 24 LARGE OR 36 SMALL BARS.

PEANUT BUTTER CUP BARS

ere's a great everyday cookie, loaded with the favorite flavors of chocolate and peanut butter, quick to make, and sturdy enough for weekday lunch bags.

- ¾ cup (1½ sticks) butter, softened
- 2 cups peanut butter, divided use
- 1 teaspoon vanilla extract
- 2 cups powdered sugar, divided use
- 3 cups graham cracker crumbs
- 2 cups miniature semisweet chocolate chips, divided use

Lightly spray a 13 x 9 x 2-inch pan with nonstick cooking spray; set aside.

Beat the butter, 1¼ cups peanut butter, and vanilla in a large bowl with an electric mixer on medium-high speed until well blended and creamy. Turn mixer speed to low; gradually beat in 1 cup of the powdered sugar. Using a wooden spoon, mix in remaining powdered sugar, graham cracker crumbs, and ½ cup of the chocolate chips. Using a large square of wax paper, press the mixture firmly and evenly into prepared pan.

Melt the remaining peanut butter and 1½ cups chocolate chips in a medium saucepan over lowest possible heat, stirring constantly, until smooth. Spread mixture over graham cracker crust in pan. Chill for at least 1 hour or until chocolate is firm. Cut into bars. Store in covered containers between layers of wax paper.

MAKES 24 BIG BARS.

PEANUT BUTTER CUP CARAMEL BARS

Peanut butter, chocolate, caramel, cake, and frosting in one bar cookie? Gooey-licious.

- 1 (18.25-ounce) package yellow or chocolate cake mix
- ½ cup (1 stick) butter, softened
- 2 large eggs
- 20 miniature peanut butter cups, chopped
- 2 tablespoons cornstarch
- 1 (12-ounce) jar caramel ice cream topping
- ¼ cup creamy peanut butter
- 1 cup lightly salted, coarsely chopped peanuts, divided
- 1 recipe Milk Chocolate Frosting (see page 370)

Preheat oven to 350°F (or 325°F for dark-coated metal pan). Position oven rack in middle of oven. Spray the bottom only of a 13 x 9-inch metal baking pan with nonstick cooking spray (or foil-line pan; see page xxiv).

Combine the cake mix, softened butter, and eggs in a large bowl. Blend with an electric mixer for 1–2 minutes on medium speed until all dry ingredients are moistened and mixture is well blended. Stir in the peanut butter cups. Spread mixture evenly into the prepared pan.

Bake for 18–22 minutes or until golden brown. Meanwhile, combine cornstarch, caramel topping, and peanut butter in a medium saucepan over low heat. stirring until smooth. Continue to stir over low heat until mixture begins to bubble.

Remove from heat and stir in ½ cup of the peanuts; spread evenly over warm crust. Bake for 5 minutes longer. Transfer to wire rack and cool completely.

Prepare Milk Chocolate Frosting. Spread bars with frosting and sprinkle with remaining peanuts. Refrigerate for at least an hour before cutting. Cut into bars. Store in the refrigerator.

MAKES 24 LARGE OR 36 SMALL BARS.

PEANUT-BUTTERCREAM CRUNCH BARS

A thick layer of vanilla buttercream gets sandwiched between a crispy peanut butter cookie base and a white chocolate fudge topping in these incredible bars.

- 1 cup sugar
- 1 cup light corn syrup
- 2 cups creamy peanut butter
- 3 cups crisp rice cereal
- 3 cups cornflakes
- 1¼ cups (2½ sticks) butter, divided
- 4 cups sifted powdered sugar
- 2 (4-serving-size) packages instant vanilla pudding mix
- 2–4 tablespoons milk
- 1 (12-ounce) package white chocolate chips (2 cups)

Lightly spray a 15 x 10 x 1-inch jelly roll pan with nonstick cooking spray; set aside.

Heat the sugar and corn syrup in a large saucepan just until mixture boils on the edge of the pan. Cook and stir for 1 minute more; remove from heat. Stir in peanut butter until melted and blended. Stir in rice cereal and cornflakes until coated. With a large square of wax paper, press into bottom of prepared pan; set aside.

In a medium saucepan, melt ¾ cup (1½ sticks) of the butter. Stir in powdered sugar, vanilla pudding mixes, and enough of the milk to make spreading consistency. Spread over cereal layer; set aside.

Heat the white chocolate chips and remaining butter in a small saucepan over low heat, stirring constantly until melted. Spread over pudding layer. Cover and chill in the refrigerator for at least 1 hour or until set. Cut into bars. Store in covered containers between layers of wax paper.

MAKES 64 BARS.

PEANUT BUTTER FUDGE BARS

Just like politics, dessert preferences are local. Maybe you're partial to Georgia peach cobbler. Or perhaps California coconut-lime ice cream or a New England cranberry betty is your style. But one thing's for certain: these over-the-top peanut butter–chocolate fudge bars bridge all boundaries.

- 1 (18.25-ounce) package yellow cake mix
- 1 cup creamy peanut butter
- 2 large eggs
- ½ cup vegetable oil
- 2 cups semisweet chocolate chips
- 1 (14-ounce) can sweetened condensed milk
- 2 tablespoons butter
- 2 teaspoons vanilla extract

Preheat oven to 350°F (or 325°F for dark-coated metal pan). Position oven rack in middle of oven. Spray the bottom only of a 13 x 9-inch metal baking pan with nonstick cooking spray (or foil-line pan; see page xxiv).

Combine the cake mix, peanut butter, eggs, and oil in a large bowl. Blend for 1–2 minutes with an electric mixer set on low speed until well blended. Reserve ½ cups of the mixture. Press remaining mixture into bottom of prepared pan; set pan and reserved mixture aside.

Meanwhile, melt the chocolate chips with the condensed milk and butter in a heavy saucepan set over low heat, stirring until smooth. Remove from heat and stir in the vanilla extract; pour over crust. Sprinkle with remaining crumb mixture.

Bake for 20–25 minutes or until golden brown and topping is firm to the touch. Transfer to wire rack and cool completely. Cut into bars.

MAKES 24 LARGE OR 36 SMALL BARS.

Variations:

DOUBLE PEANUT BUTTER FUDGE BARS: Prepare as directed above but substitute 2 cups peanut butter–flavored baking chips for the chocolate chips.

DOUBLE CHOCOLATE PEANUT BUTTER FUDGE BARS: Prepare as directed above but use a chocolate cake mix instead of yellow cake mix.

PEANUT BUTTERSCOTCH FUDGE BARS

Loaded with a winning combination of butterscotch, peanut butter, and marshmallows, these incredible treats will tempt one and all.

- 3½ tablespoons butter, divided use
- 4 cups miniature marshmallows, divided use
- 1 cup creamy peanut butter, divided use
- 3 cups toasted rice cereal
- ⅔ cup canned evaporated milk
- 1½ cups sugar
- 1 cup butterscotch baking chips
- ¾ cup creamy peanut butter
- 1 teaspoon vanilla extract
- ¼ cup cocktail peanuts, chopped

Lightly spray a 13 x 9 x 2-inch baking pan with nonstick cooking spray; set aside.

In a medium saucepan set over low heat melt 1½ tablespoons of the butter. Add 2 cups marshmallows and ¼ cup peanut butter and stir until melted and smooth. Remove from heat. Add cereal and stir until blended. With a large square of wax paper, press mixture into bottom of prepared pan.

Combine the evaporated milk, sugar, and remaining butter in a medium saucepan. Bring to a boil over medium heat, stirring constantly. Continue to boil, stirring constantly, for 4–5 minutes. Remove from heat.

Add the remaining 2 cups marshmallows, butterscotch chips, vanilla, and remaining peanut butter to the hot milk mixture; stir vigorously for 1 minute or until marshmallows and chips are completely melted. Pour and spread mixture over prepared crust. Sprinkle with peanuts. Refrigerate for 1 hour to set. Cut into bars. Store in covered containers between layers of wax paper.

MAKES 36 BARS.

PEANUT-BUTTERSCOTCH FUDGE-FILLED BARS

Ultra-rich with chocolate, butterscotch, and a double dose of peanut butter, these are bars everyone will give in to, kids to grown-ups. If it's more peanut buttery-ness you're after, substitute peanut butter baking chips for the butterscotch chips. Or if it's more chocolate you crave, use semisweet or milk chocolate chips.

- 1 (19.5- to 19.8 ounce) package brownie mix
- 1¾ cups peanut butter, divided
- ½ cup (1 stick) unsalted butter, melted, plus
- 2 tablespoons (¼ stick) butter (not melted)
- 2 large eggs
- 1 (14-ounce) can sweetened condensed milk
- 1½ cups butterscotch baking chips
- 2 teaspoons vanilla extract

Preheat oven to 350°F (325°F for dark-coated metal pan). Position a rack in the lower third of the oven. Spray the bottom only of a 13 x 9-inch baking pan with nonstick cooking spray (or foil-line pan; see page xxiv).

Combine the brownie mix, 1 cup peanut butter, ½ cup melted butter, and eggs in a large mixing bowl with electric mixer set on medium until blended and thick. Reserve 1½ cups for topping; press remaining batter into bottom of prepared pan.

In a medium saucepan set over low heat combine the sweetened condensed milk, remaining ¾ cup peanut butter, remaining 2 tablespoons butter, and 1 cup butterscotch chips, stirring until melted and smooth, 3–4 minutes. Remove from heat and stir in vanilla. Pour and spread mixture over prepared crust. Crumble reserved crumb mixture over the top; sprinkle with remaining ½ cup butterscotch chips.

Bake for 25–30 minutes or until topping is firm to the touch. Transfer to a wire rack and cool completely. Cut into bars. Store loosely covered at room temperature.

MAKES 24 LARGE OR 36 SMALL BARS.

PECAN PIE BARS (CAKE MIX)

These decadent dessert bars are dedicated to all my fellow cookie aficionados who cannot resist the pecan pie bars in the coffeehouse pastry case. Great with a cup of coffee at any time of the year, they can also replace traditional pecan pie when you need to serve a crowd.

- 1 (18.25-ounce) package yellow cake mix
- ⅓ cup butter, softened
- 4 large eggs
- ½ cup firmly packed dark brown sugar
- 1½ cups dark corn syrup
- 1½ teaspoons vanilla extract
- 1¼ cups chopped pecans, divided

Preheat oven to 350°F (or 325°F for dark-coated metal pan). Position oven rack in middle of oven. Spray the bottom only of a 13 x 9-inch metal baking pan with nonstick cooking spray (or foil-line pan; see page xxiv).

Set aside ⅔ cup of the dry cake mix. Combine remaining cake mix, softened butter, and 1 of the eggs in a large bowl with an electric mixer set on medium speed until blended and crumbly. Press mixture in bottom of prepared pan. Bake for 15 minutes.

Meanwhile, mix reserved ⅔ cup cake mix, brown sugar, corn syrup, vanilla extract, and remaining eggs in large bowl with electric mixer set on low speed for 1 minute.

Increase speed to medium; blend for 1 minute. Stir in ¾ cup chopped pecans. Pour mixture over hot crust; sprinkle with remaining pecans.

Bake for an additional 30–35 minutes or until filling is set. Transfer to wire rack and cool completely. Cut into bars.

MAKES 24 LARGE OR 36 SMALL BARS.

Variation:

CHOCOLATE-CHIP PECAN PIE BARS:
Prepare as directed above but use chocolate cake mix and add 1 cup miniature semisweet chocolate chips to the filling.

PECAN PIE BARS (COOKIE DOUGH)

Everything you love about pecan pie—perhaps the most famous of all the decadent Southern desserts—is captured in these foolproof bar cookies. Cut them small to serve as bite-sized delights, or cut into big squares to serve "pie style" with vanilla ice cream or whipped cream.

- 1 (16.5-ounce) roll refrigerated sugar cookie dough, well chilled
- 4 large eggs
- 1 cup packed brown sugar
- 1 cup dark corn syrup
- ½ stick (¼ cup) butter, melted
- 1 teaspoon vanilla extract
- 2 cups chopped pecans

Preheat oven to 350°F. Spray a 13 x 9-inch pan with nonstick cooking spray or line with foil.

Cut cookie dough into ¼-inch-thick slices. Arrange slices in bottom of the prepared pan. With floured fingers, press dough evenly to form crust.

Bake for 10–13 minutes or until dough is golden brown (dough will appear slightly puffed). Remove from oven.

Whisk the eggs, brown sugar, corn syrup, melted butter, and vanilla in a medium bowl until blended; stir in pecans. Pour pecan mixture over warm, partially baked crust and spread evenly.

Bake for 25–30 minutes or until filling is just set. Cool completely in pan and cut into bars.

MAKES 36 BARS.

Baker's Note

Chocolate lover? Substitute chocolate-chip cookie dough for the sugar cookie dough in this recipe. Proceed as directed.

PEPPERMINT CHOCOLATE GANACHE BARS

These dark chocolate bars have just the right amount of peppermint freshness. To crush the candy canes or peppermint candies, place the candies in a heavy, resealable plastic bag. Place the bag on a firm, flat surface and use a rolling pin or mallet to crush the candies into pieces.

- 2½ cups finely crushed chocolate wafer or chocolate graham cracker crumbs
- ½ cup (1 stick) butter, melted
- 3 tablespoons sugar
- 1 cup semisweet chocolate chips
- ⅔ cup heavy whipping cream
- 1 cup powdered sugar
- 2 (8-ounce) packages cream cheese, softened
- 1½ teaspoons peppermint extract
- 1 cup frozen non-dairy whipped topping, thawed
- ⅔ cup coarsely crushed peppermint candy canes or red hard peppermint candies

Line a 13 x 9 x 2-inch baking pan with foil (see page xxiv); lightly spray with nonstick cooking spray. Set aside.

Combine the cookie crumbs, melted butter, and sugar in a medium bowl with a fork or fingers until well blended. Transfer crumb mixture to prepared pan. Press firmly into bottom of pan with a large square of wax paper. Freeze until ready to use.

Melt the chocolate chips and whipping cream in a medium saucepan over low heat, stirring occasionally, until smooth. Pour chocolate mixture over crust. Place in freezer for at least 10 minutes while preparing the filling.

Combine the powdered sugar, cream cheese, and peppermint extract in a large bowl. Beat with electric mixer set at low speed, scraping bowl often, until smooth and creamy, for 2–3 minutes. Gently stir in whipped topping. Spread evenly over chocolate ganache layer. Sprinkle with crushed candy, if desired. Cover; freeze 4 hours or overnight. Use foil lining to remove uncut bars from pan to cutting board. Cut into bars. Store, loosely covered with foil or plastic wrap, in refrigerator.

MAKES 36 BARS.

PEPPERMINT WHITE CHOCOLATE CHEESECAKE BARS

The weather outside may be frightful, but your kitchen will be delightful if you bake up these cool mint-y bars come holiday-time. To crush the candies, place in a heavy-duty zippered plastic bag and bang with a rolling pin or can (it doubles as holiday stress relief).

- 1 (18.25-ounce) package vanilla cake mix
- ½ cup (1 stick) butter, melted
- 3 large eggs
- 3 (8-ounce) packages cream cheese, softened
- ⅔ cup sugar
- 1¼ teaspoons peppermint extract
- 2 cups white chocolate chips
- 2 teaspoons vegetable shortening
- 1 cup coarsely crushed red and white striped peppermint candies or candy canes

Preheat oven to 350°F (or 325°F for dark-coated metal pan). Position oven rack in middle of oven. Spray the bottom only of a 13 x 9-inch metal baking pan with nonstick cooking spray (or foil-line pan; see page xxiv).

Place the cake mix, melted butter, and 1 of the eggs in a large bowl. Blend for 1–2 minutes with an electric mixer set on low speed until well blended. Press mixture evenly into prepared pan. Bake crust for 15 minutes.

While crust bakes, beat the softened cream cheese and sugar in a large mixing bowl with electric mixer set on high speed until smooth. Gradually beat in remaining eggs, one at a time, and peppermint extract, until smooth. Stir in 1 cup of the white chocolate chips. Pour over partially baked crust.

Bake for 23–36 minutes, until just barely set at center (do not overbake). Transfer to a wire rack and cool completely.

In heavy saucepan melt remaining white chocolate chips with shortening until smooth; drizzle over cooled bars. Immediately sprinkle with crushed peppermint candies. Chill for at least 3 hours in refrigerator. Cut into bars. Store in refrigerator.

MAKES 24 LARGE OR 36 SMALL BARS.

PERSIAN PISTACHIO BARS

The bright green interiors of the chopped pistachios makes these cookies as striking as they are delicious.

- 1 (16.5-ounce) roll refrigerated sugar cookie dough
- ½ cup honey
- 2 tablespoons all-purpose flour
- ¾ teaspoon ground cardamom
- 1 cup shelled roasted, salted pistachios, coarsely chopped

Preheat oven to 350°F. Spray an 8-inch-square pan with nonstick cooking spray.

Break up ¾ of the cookie dough into prepared pan. With floured fingers, press dough evenly in bottom of pan to form crust.

Bake for 12–17 minutes or until light golden brown.

Meanwhile, mix the honey, flour, and cardamom in small bowl until blended. Mix remaining ¼ of dough and the pistachios in another small bowl,.

Drizzle honey mixture evenly over partially baked crust. Crumble pistachio dough evenly over honey.

Bake for 23–27 minutes longer or until top is golden brown and firm to the touch and caramel is bubbly. Cool completely. Cut into bars.

MAKES 16 BARS.

PINEAPPLE GOOEY CHESS SQUARES

These sunny, golden bars are chock-full of fruits and flavor: zesty lime, chunks of moist, naturally sweet Hawaiian pineapple, and peppery ginger—all baked to perfection in a rich, buttery batter.

- 1 cup (2 sticks) butter, divided
- 1 (18.25-ounce) package yellow cake mix
- 4 large eggs
- 1 (8-ounce) package cream cheese, softened
- 1 (20-ounce) can of crushed pineapple, well drained
- 2 tablespoons fresh lime juice
- 1 teaspoon grated lime zest
- 1 (16-ounce) box powdered sugar
- 1½ teaspoons ground ginger

Preheat oven to 350°F (or 325°F for dark-coated metal pan). Position oven rack in middle of oven. Spray the bottom only of a 13 x 9-inch metal baking pan with nonstick cooking spray (or foil-line pan; see page xxiv).

Melt ½ cup (1 stick) of the butter in a small saucepan set over low heat. Beat the cake mix, melted butter, and 1 egg in a large bowl with an electric mixer set on medium speed until well blended (mixture will come together as a thick dough). Pat the dough evenly into the prepared pan. Set aside momentarily.

Melt the remaining stick of butter in a small saucepan set over low heat. Beat the cream cheese, pineapple, lime juice, and lime zest in a large bowl with an electric mixer set on medium speed until well blended, scraping down sides of bowl occasionally. Add the melted butter and remaining eggs; blend until smooth. Add the powdered sugar and ginger; blend until smooth.

Spread pineapple mixture over prepared crust. Bake for 42–45 minutes (do not overbake; bars should be slightly gooey). Transfer to a wire rack and cool completely. Cut into bars or squares. Cover and store in refrigerator.

MAKES 24 LARGE OR 36 SMALL BARS.

PINEAPPLE MACADAMIA BARS

Whip up a batch of these bars for a mouth-watering tropical escape.

- 7⅓ cups sweetened puffed wheat cereal
- 1 cup roasted, coarsely chopped, salted macadamia nuts
- 1 cup coarsely chopped dried pineapple
- 1 (14-ounce) package caramels
- 2 tablespoons fresh lime juice
- 2 teaspoons grated lime zest
- 1 teaspoon ground ginger

Lightly spray a 13 x 9 x 2-inch baking pan with nonstick cooking spray; set aside.

Mix the cereal, macadamia nuts, and pineapple in a large bowl.

Microwave caramels and lime juice in medium microwavable bowl on high for 2 minutes or until caramels are melted, stirring every minute; stir in lime zest and ground ginger. Immediately pour over cereal mixture; mix lightly until well coated.

With a large square of wax paper, press into the prepared pan. Refrigerate until firm. Cut into bars. Store in covered containers between layers of wax paper.

MAKES 24 BIG BARS.

PINEAPPLE-ORANGE SNACK BARS

Look for dried pineapple slices in the bulk foods section at the grocery store or check out the section of the store where raisins are shelved. In the latter section, the dried pineapple is more likely to be found pre-chopped.

- 2 tablespoons (¼ stick) butter
- ¼ cup sugar
- ¼ cup honey
- 2½ teaspoons grated orange zest
- 1½ cups honey nut cornflakes cereal
- 1 cup chopped dried pineapple (about 4 ounces)
- ½ cup sliced almonds

Lightly spray an 8 x 8 x 2-inch square baking pan with nonstick cooking spray; set aside.

Combine the butter, sugar, and honey in a medium saucepan. Bring to a boil over medium heat, stirring constantly. Reduce heat and simmer for 3 minutes, stirring constantly.

Remove from heat. Carefully stir in orange zest. Add the cereal, pineapple, and almonds to syrup mixture, mixing until thoroughly coated.

With a large square of wax paper, press into prepared pan. Let stand until firm. Cut into bars. Store in covered containers between layers of wax paper.

MAKES 12 BARS.

PINEAPPLE-WHITE CHOCOLATE ALOHA BARS

The dark chocolate brownie base of these island-inspired bars takes beautifully to the contrasting flavors of white chocolate and pineapple in the filling. I highly recommend them for summertime picnics and barbecues.

- 1 (19.5- to 19.8-ounce) package brownie mix
- 2½ teaspoons ground ginger
- 1⅔ cups quick-cooking oats
- 1 cup sweetened shredded coconut
- 1 cup (2 sticks) unsalted butter, melted
- 1 (16-ounce) can crushed pineapple, well drained
- ⅔ cup pineapple preserves
- 2 tablespoons lime juice
- 1 cup white chocolate chips

Preheat oven to 350°F (325°F for dark-coated metal pan). Position a rack in the lower third of the oven. Spray a 13 x 9-inch baking pan with nonstick cooking spray (or foil-line pan; see page xxiv).

Combine the brownie mix, ginger, oats, coconut, and melted butter in a large mixing bowl with a wooden spoon until just blended and all dry ingredients are moistened. Press half of mixture evenly into prepared pan.

Combine the drained pineapple, preserves, and lime juice in a medium mixing bowl. Spoon mixture over prepared crust. Sprinkle reserved topping and white chocolate chips evenly over filling; press down gently.

Bake for 30–34 minutes or until topping is firm. Transfer to a wire rack and cool completely. Cut into bars.

MAKES 24 LARGE OR 36 SMALL BARS.

PINK LEMONADE SQUARES

A smooth texture and tart lemon flavor make these bars a great follow-up to a spicy meal, whether Indian curry or Texas BBQ.

- 1¼ cups crisp sugar cookie crumbs
- ¼ cup (½ stick) butter, melted
- 1 (8-ounce) package cream cheese, softened
- 1 cup jarred marshmallow creme
- 2 tablespoons fresh lemon juice
- 2 teaspoons grated lemon zest
- 1–2 drops red food coloring

Line an 8 x 8 x 2-inch baking pan with foil (see page xxiv); lightly spray with nonstick cooking spray. Set aside.

Combine the cookie crumbs and melted butter in a medium bowl with a fork or fingers until well blended. Transfer crumb mixture to prepared pan. Press firmly into bottom of pan with a large square of wax paper. Freeze until ready to use.

Beat the cream cheese, marshmallow creme, lemon juice, lemon zest, and enough red food coloring to tint mixture pale pink in a medium bowl with electric mixer set on medium until light and fluffy. Spread evenly over crust.

Refrigerate for at least 4 hours until firm. Use foil lining to remove uncut bars from pan to cutting board. Cut into squares. Store, loosely covered with foil or plastic wrap, in refrigerator.

MAKES 16 SQUARES.

PREMIER CRANBERRY CREAM CHEESE BARS

Dazzle those dear to you during the winter holidays, or year-round, with these easy-to-make, beautiful-to-behold bars.

- 1 (18.25-ounce) package spice cake mix
- 1 cup (2 sticks) butter, melted
- 2¼ cups quick-cooking oats
- 1 cup white chocolate chips
- 1 (8-ounce) package cream cheese, softened
- 1 (14-ounce) can sweetened condensed milk
- ¼ cup fresh lemon juice
- 1 teaspoon vanilla extract
- 2 tablespoons cornstarch
- 1 (16-ounce) can whole cranberry sauce

Preheat oven to 350°F (or 325°F for dark-coated metal pan). Position oven rack in middle of oven. Spray the bottom only of a 13 x 9-inch metal baking pan with nonstick cooking spray (or foil-line pan; see page xxiv).

Place the cake mix and melted butter in a large bowl. Blend for 1–2 minutes with an electric mixer set on low speed until well blended. Stir in the oats with a wooden spoon. Press half of mixture evenly into prepared pan. Add the white chocolate chips to remaining oat mixture; set aside.

Beat the softened cream cheese, condensed milk, lemon juice, and vanilla extract in a large mixing bowl with electric mixer set on medium speed until smooth. Spoon and spread cream cheese mixture over prepared crust.

Stir together the cornstarch and cranberry sauce in a small bowl until well blended; spoon over cream cheese mixture. Top with reserved crumb mixture and press down gently.

Bake for 35–38 minutes or until topping is set and firm to the touch. Transfer to wire rack and cool completely.

MAKES 24 LARGE OR 36 SMALL BARS.

PRETTY-IN-PINK STRAWBERRY STREUSEL BARS

Anyone who has had a chocolate-dipped strawberry knows how well this combination of flavors works. The strawberry jam gets used twice here: first to flavor and turn the creamy filling pink, then again dolloped on top before adding the second layer of chocolate streusel. This recipe also works very well with apricot or seedless raspberry preserves.

- 1 (19.5- to 19.8-ounce) package brownie mix

- 2¼ cups quick-cooking oats
- 1 cup (2 sticks) unsalted butter, melted
- 2 (8-ounce) packages cream cheese, softened
- 1¼ cups strawberry jam, divided
- 2 large eggs

Preheat oven to 350°F (325°F for dark-coated metal pan). Position a rack in the lower third of the oven. Spray the bottom only of a 13 x 9-inch baking pan with nonstick cooking spray (or foil-line pan; see page xxiv).

Combine the brownie mix, oats, and melted butter in a large mixing bowl with a wooden spoon until just blended and all dry ingredients are moistened. Press half of mixture evenly into prepared pan.

Beat the cream cheese and ½ cup jam in a medium mixing bowl with electric mixer set on medium until smooth. Beat in eggs until just blended; spread over base layer. Dollop remaining jam, in teaspoons, on top of the filling. Sprinkle with remaining crumb mixture; press gently into filling.

Bake for 32–34 minutes or until topping is firm and center is just set. Transfer to a wire rack and cool completely. Refrigerate for at least 2 hours before serving. Cut into bars.

MAKES 24 LARGE OR 36 SMALL BARS.

PUMPKIN BARS

One taste of these creamy no-bake pumpkin bars may just convince you to start a delicious new holiday dessert tradition.

- 1¼ cups gingersnap cookie crumbs
- ¼ cup (½ stick) butter, melted
- ⅓ cup milk
- 2 teaspoons unflavored gelatin
- ½ cup firmly packed light brown sugar
- 1 cup canned solid pack pumpkin
- 1 (8-ounce) package cream cheese, softened
- 2 teaspoons pumpkin pie spice blend
- 1 teaspoon vanilla extract

Line an 8 x 8 x 2-inch baking pan with foil (see page xxiv); lightly spray with nonstick cooking spray. Set aside.

Combine the cookie crumbs and melted butter in a medium bowl with a fork or fingers until well blended. Transfer crumb mixture to prepared pan. Press firmly into bottom of pan with a large square of wax paper. Freeze until ready to use.

Place the milk in a small saucepan; sprinkle gelatin over (do not stir). Let stand for 10 minutes to soften. Add the brown sugar to saucepan and turn the heat under saucepan to medium. Whisk and stir until liquid is very hot (but not boiling) and both the gelatin and brown sugar are completely dissolved. Remove from heat and cool for 15 minutes.

Beat the pumpkin, cream cheese, pumpkin pie spice, and vanilla in a large bowl with electric mixer on medium speed until creamy. Gradually add cooled gelatin mixture, beating on low speed and occasionally scraping sides of bowl with rubber spatula, until well blended.

Pour and spread cheese mixture evenly over prepared crust. Refrigerate for 3 hours or until firm. Use foil lining to remove uncut bars from pan to cutting board. Cut into bars. Store, loosely covered with foil or plastic wrap, in refrigerator.

MAKES 16 BARS.

PUMPKIN GOOEY CHESS SQUARES

Bye-bye, pumpkin pie—that's what you'll likely croon once you try these out-of-this-world chess squares. Be sure to use pure pumpkin in the filling, not pumpkin pie mix. Both come in a can, but the latter is pre-spiced and presweetened, which will lead to an overly sweet bar with the wrong consistency.

- 1 cup (2 sticks) butter, divided
- 1 (18.25-ounce) package spice or yellow cake mix
- 4 large eggs
- 1 (8-ounce) package cream cheese, softened
- 1 (15-ounce) can pumpkin purée
- 2 teaspoons vanilla extract
- 1 (16-ounce) box powdered sugar
- 2 teaspoons pumpkin pie spice (or ground cinnamon)

Preheat oven to 350°F (or 325°F for dark-coated metal pan). Position oven rack in middle of oven. Spray the bottom only of a 13 x 9-inch metal baking pan with nonstick cooking spray (or foil-line pan; see page xxiv).

Melt ½ cup (1 stick) of the butter in a small saucepan set over low heat. Beat the cake mix, melted butter, and 1 egg in a large bowl with an electric mixer set on medium speed until well blended (mixture will come together as a thick dough). Pat the dough evenly into the prepared pan. Set aside momentarily.

Melt the remaining butter in a small saucepan set over low heat. Beat the softened cream cheese and pumpkin purée in a large bowl with an electric mixer set on medium speed until smooth, scraping down sides of bowl occasionally. Add the melted butter, remaining eggs and vanilla extract; blend until smooth. Add the powdered sugar and pumpkin pie spice; blend until smooth.

Spread the pumpkin mixture over prepared crust. Bake for 42–45 minutes (do not overbake; bars should be slightly gooey). Transfer to a wire rack and cool completely. Cut into bars or squares. Cover and store in refrigerator.

MAKES 24 LARGE OR 36 SMALL BARS.

PUMPKIN PIE BARS (CAKE MIX)

This extra-easy take on everybody's Thanksgiving favorite brings easy entertaining up to date.

- 1 (18.25-ounce) package yellow cake mix
- ¼ cup vegetable oil
- 4 large eggs
- ½ cup chopped pecans
- 1 (14-ounce) can sweetened condensed milk
- 1 (16-ounce) can pumpkin purée
- 2 teaspoons vanilla extract
- 1½ teaspoons pumpkin pie spice

Preheat oven to 350°F (or 325°F for dark-coated metal pan). Position oven rack in middle of oven. Spray a 13 x 9-inch metal baking pan with nonstick cooking spray (or foil-line pan; see page xxiv).

Reserve for ½ cup cake mix. Place remaining cake mix, oil, and 1 of the eggs in a large bowl. Blend for 1–2 minutes with an electric mixer set on low speed until well blended and crumbly; stir in the pecans. Press mixture into bottom of prepared pan.

Place the condensed milk, pumpkin, vanilla extract, pumpkin pie spice, remaining eggs, and ½ cup reserved cake mix in the same large bowl (no need to clean). Blend for 1–2 minutes with an electric mixer set on medium speed until well blended. Pour over crust.

Bake for 40–45 minutes or until filling is just set. Transfer to a wire rack and cool completely. Cut into bars.

MAKES 24 LARGE OR 36 SMALL BARS.

PUMPKIN PIE BARS (COOKIE DOUGH)

My brother is something of a dessert purist, especially around the holidays. So when it comes to pumpkin pie, he eschews any "unnecessary" additions, such as cranberries, nuts, or chocolate. He applauds this handheld version of his favorite toothsome treat, in part because of its "pure" pumpkin pie flavor, but also because it is literally easier than pie to prepare. If you don't have pumpkin pie spice blend, substitute 1¾ teaspoons ground cinnamon, ½ teaspoon ground ginger, and ¼ teaspoon ground cloves.

- 1 (16.5-ounce) roll refrigerated sugar cookie dough, well chilled
- 2 large eggs
- 1 (15-ounce) can pure pumpkin
- 1 (5-ounce) can (⅔ cup) evaporated milk
- ½ cup packed brown sugar
- 2½ teaspoons pumpkin pie spice

Preheat oven to 350°F. Spray a 13 x 9-inch pan with nonstick cooking spray or line with foil.

Cut cookie dough into ¼-inch-thick slices. Arrange slices in bottom of the prepared pan. With floured fingers, press dough evenly to form crust.

Bake for 10–13 minutes or until dough is golden brown (dough will appear slightly puffed). Remove from oven.

Mix the eggs, pumpkin, evaporated milk, brown sugar, and pumpkin pie spice in a medium bowl with wire whisk until smooth. Pour mixture over the partially baked crust.

Bake for 33–37 minutes or until just set. Cool in pan on wire rack. Cut into squares. Store in the refrigerator. Serve room temperature or chilled.

MAKES 24 BIG SQUARES.

Baker's Note

For a chocolate treat, substitute chocolate-chip cookie dough for sugar cookie dough. Prepare as above except sprinkle pumpkin layer with ½ cup miniature semisweet chocolate chips just before baking.

PUMPKIN SWIRL CHEESECAKE BARS

Looking for a tempting alternative to traditional Thanksgiving pumpkin pie? It's right here. The chocolate brownie base is a fine foil for the creamy layer of pumpkin-swirled cheesecake. If you want a formal presentation, cut them into large squares and serve, plated, with whipped cream; if informal is more your style, cut them into small squares to serve as part of a casual dessert buffet.

- 1 (19.5- to 19.8-ounce) package brownie mix
- ½ cup (1 stick) unsalted butter, melted
- 2 teaspoons pumpkin pie spice, divided
- 4 large eggs
- ½ cup canned pumpkin purée
- 1½ tablespoons all-purpose flour
- 3 (8-ounce) packages cream cheese, softened
- ¾ cup sugar
- 2 teaspoons vanilla extract

Preheat oven to 350°F (325°F for dark-coated metal pan). Position a rack in the lower third of the oven. Spray the bottom only of a 13 x 9-inch baking pan with nonstick cooking spray (or foil-line pan; see page xxiv).

Combine brownie mix, melted butter, 1 teaspoon of the pumpkin pie spice, and 1 egg in a medium mixing bowl until just blended and all dry ingredients are moistened. Press into bottom of prepared pan. Bake for 18 minutes. Remove from oven (leave oven on).

Meanwhile, mix the pumpkin purée, flour, and remaining 1 teaspoon pumpkin pie spice in a medium mixing bowl; set aside.

Beat cream cheese in a large mixing bowl with electric mixer set on high until smooth. Add the sugar, beating until blended. Beat in vanilla and remaining eggs, one at a time, until just blended. Stir ½ cup of the cream cheese mixture into the pumpkin mixture. Pour remaining cream cheese mixture over prepared crust, spreading evenly to cover. Distribute large spoonfuls of the pumpkin batter randomly over cream cheese layer. Carefully swirl the batters with the tip of a knife.

Bake for 25–30 minutes or until just barely set at the center. Transfer to a wire rack and cool completely. Chill for 2 hours or overnight in refrigerator; cut into bars. Store covered in refrigerator.

MAKES 24 LARGE OR 36 SMALL BARS.

RASPBERRY AND WHITE CHOCOLATE CHEESECAKE CHUBBIES

My first encounter with raspberry-white chocolate cheesecake was at a bakery located in close proximity to my summer office job. These extravagant bars capture the same exquisite union of flavors in one great big chubby bar.

- 1 (8-ounce) package cream cheese, softened
- ¼ cup sugar
- 1 large egg
- 1 teaspoon vanilla extract
- 1½ cups white chocolate chips, divided
- 1 (16.5-ounce) roll refrigerated sugar cookie dough
- ⅓ cup seedless raspberry jam or preserves
- 1 tablespoon vegetable shortening

Preheat oven to 350°F. Spray an 8-inch pan with nonstick cooking spray or line with foil.

Combine cream cheese, sugar, egg, and vanilla in a medium bowl; beat with electric beaters on high, stopping to scrape down the sides of the bowl with a rubber spatula once or twice, until smooth. Stir in 1 cup white chocolate chips; set aside.

Cut the cookie dough in half. With floured fingers, press half of the dough in bottom of prepared pan. Spread the cream cheese mixture over dough; dollop with teaspoons of jam. Crumble and sprinkle remaining half of cookie dough over cream cheese mixture (need not completely cover cream cheese and jam layer).

Bake for 32–36 minutes or until golden brown and firm to the touch; cool completely. Combine remaining white chocolate chips and shortening in small saucepan over low heat. Stir until melted and smooth. Drizzle over bars. Cut into bars. Serve room temperature or chilled. Store in refrigerator.

MAKES 16 BARS.

RASPBERRY LEMON SQUARES

Raspberries, with their ruby color and lush flavor, have so much going for them that they taste great in pies, in cake, and certainly in these lemon-laced summertime bar cookies.

- 2 cups fresh raspberries, divided use
- 1¼ cups crisp sugar or macaroon cookie crumbs
- ¼ cup (½ stick) butter, melted
- 1 (8-ounce) package cream cheese, softened
- 1 cup jarred marshmallow creme
- 1½ tablespoons fresh lemon juice
- 2 teaspoons grated lemon zest

Line a 9 x 9 x 2-inch baking pan with foil (see page xxiv); lightly spray with nonstick cooking spray. Set aside.

Remove 16 of the raspberries for garnish; place in refrigerator until ready to use.

Combine the cookie crumbs and melted butter in a medium bowl with a fork or fingers until well blended. Transfer crumb mixture to prepared pan. Press firmly into bottom of pan with a large square of wax paper. Freeze until ready to use.

Beat the cream cheese, marshmallow creme, lemon juice, and lemon zest in a medium bowl with electric mixer set on medium until light and fluffy. Gently fold in remaining raspberries; spread evenly over crust. Poke reserved 16 raspberries atop filling in 4 x 4 rows.

Refrigerate for at least 4 hours or until firm. Use foil lining to remove uncut bars from pan to cutting board. Cut into squares with a raspberry centered in each square. Store, loosely covered with foil or plastic wrap, in refrigerator.

MAKES 16 SQUARES.

RASPBERRY LINZER BARS

Reminiscent of the classic Austrian torte of the same name, these bars are elegant enough to serve as a finale to a first-rate supper.

- ¾ cup (1½ sticks) butter, softened
- 1¼ cups almond butter
- 1 teaspoon almond extract
- 2 cups powdered sugar, divided use
- 3 cups graham cracker crumbs
- ⅔ cup seedless raspberry preserves, stirred to loosen
- 1 cup white chocolate chips
- 2 teaspoons vegetable shortening

Lightly spray a 9 x 9 x 2-inch pan with nonstick cooking spray; set aside.

Beat the butter, almond butter, and almond extract in a large bowl with an electric mixer set on medium-high speed until well blended and creamy. Turn mixer speed to low; gradually beat in 1 cup of the powdered sugar. Using a wooden spoon, mix in the graham cracker crumbs and remaining powdered sugar. Reserve 1 cup of the mixture. Using a large square of wax paper, press the remaining mixture firmly and evenly into prepared pan. Spread bars with raspberry jam. Sprinkle with reserved crumb mixture, using fingertips to gently press into jam layer.

Melt the white chocolate chips and shortening in a small saucepan over the lowest possible heat, stirring constantly, until smooth. Drizzle mixture over bars. Chill for at least 1 hour or until chocolate is firm; cut into bars. Store in covered containers between layers of wax paper.

MAKES 24 SMALL BARS.

Variation:

SACHER TORTE BARS: Prepare as directed above but use chocolate graham crackers in place of regular graham crackers, apricot jam or preserves in place of the raspberry preserves, and semisweet chocolate chips in place of the white chocolate chips.

RASPBERRY SWIRL SOUR CREAM BARS

Spring is a season of celebrations. Start the party planning with these quick-to-prepare, but oh-so-impressive bars, perfect for receptions, showers, and graduation parties. Other jams and preserves can be substituted for the raspberry preserves. Consider apricot preserves, orange marmalade, or lemon curd.

- 1 (18.25-ounce) package vanilla cake mix
- ½ cup sour cream
- ⅓ cup butter, melted
- 1 teaspoon vanilla extract
- 2 large eggs
- 1 (12-ounce) jar seedless raspberry preserves, stirred to loosen

Preheat oven to 350°F for metal or glass pan. Position oven rack in middle of oven. Spray the bottom only of a 13 x 9-inch pan with nonstick cooking spray (or foil-line pan; see page xxiv).

Place the cake mix, sour cream, melted butter, vanilla extract, and eggs in a large bowl. Blend for 2 minutes with an electric mixer set on medium speed until well blended. Reserve 1 cup of batter. Spread remaining batter into prepared pan. Distribute raspberry preserves evenly over batter. Drop remaining cake batter by tablespoonfuls over preserves. Swirl batter and jam with tip of knife.

Bake for 23–26 minutes or until toothpick inserted near center comes out clean. Transfer to wire rack and cool completely.

MAKES 36 LARGE OR 48 SMALL BARS.

RASPBERRY TEATIME TRIANGLES

Turn a cup of Earl Grey into a tea party with these elegant raspberry treats. The secret to their success? A crackly brown-sugar layer combined with not-too-sweet raspberry preserves and a scattering of chopped walnuts.

- 1 (16.5-ounce) roll refrigerated sugar cookie dough, room temperature
- 3 tablespoons all-purpose flour
- ¼ teaspoon salt
- ¼ teaspoon baking soda
- 2 large eggs
- ½ cup firmly packed brown sugar
- 1 teaspoon vanilla extract
- ½ cup seedless raspberry preserves
- 1 cup chopped walnuts (or pecans)
- ¼ cup sifted powdered sugar (optional)

Preheat oven to 350°F. Spray a 9-inch square baking pan with nonstick cooking spray or line with foil.

Crumble cookie dough into the prepared pan; press to form one even layer. Bake for 12–15 minutes or until deep golden (dough will appear puffed). Cool completely on wire rack.

Whisk together the flour, salt, and baking soda in a small bowl. Set aside. Beat together the eggs, brown sugar, and vanilla with whisk in a separate bowl until blended. Gradually whisk in the flour mixture just until blended.

Spoon and spread jam evenly over cooled crust. Pour filling on top, then sprinkle evenly with nuts.

Bake for 22–25 minutes, until center is completely set and top is golden. Cool in pan on wire rack. Cut into squares, then halve each square diagonally. Sprinkle with powdered sugar, if desired.

MAKES 32 TRIANGLES.

ROCKY ROAD BARS

A lumpy-bumpy cookie made of marshmallow, chocolate, and nuts? Who wouldn't want to take a stroll down rocky road?

- 1 (18.25-ounce) package chocolate or devil's food cake mix
- ½ cup (1 stick) butter, melted
- ¼ cup water
- 2 large eggs
- 3 cups miniature marshmallows
- 1 cup roasted peanuts (or cashews)
- 1 cup semisweet or milk chocolate chips

Preheat oven to 350°F (or 325°F for dark-coated metal pan). Position oven rack in middle of oven. Spray the bottom only of a 13 x 9-inch metal baking pan with nonstick cooking spray (or foil-line pan; see page xxiv).

Combine cake mix along with the melted butter, water, and eggs in a large bowl with an electric mixer set on medium speed for 1–2 minutes, until well blended and all dry ingredients are moistened. Spread mixture evenly in prepared pan.

Bake for 25 minutes. Remove from oven and sprinkle with marshmallows, nuts, and chocolate chips. Bake 5–8 minutes longer or until marshmallows are puffed and golden. Transfer to wire rack and cool completely. Cut into bars.

MAKES 24 LARGE OR 36 SMALL BARS.

ROSEMARY-WALNUT SHORTBREAD SQUARES

Begin brewing the Earl Grey and Darjeeling—this is one sophisticated tea-time nibble. Be sure to use white cake mix here—it has less fat than other cake mixes, producing just the right consistency.

- 1 (18.25-ounce) package white cake mix
- ½ cup (1 stick) butter, softened
- 1 (3-ounce) package cream cheese, softened
- 1 tablespoon fresh chopped rosemary or 1½ teaspoons dried, crumbled rosemary
- 1 large egg white, room temperature
- 1 teaspoon vanilla extract
- 2 tablespoons powdered sugar
- 1 cup finely chopped walnuts

Preheat oven to 350°F. Position oven rack in middle of oven. Set aside an ungreased 15 x 10 x 1-inch jelly roll pan.

Place the cake mix, butter, cream cheese, and rosemary in a large bowl. Blend for 1–2 minutes with electric mixer set on low speed until a crumbly dough forms. Gather dough together and press into jelly roll pan.

Clean the beaters on the electric mixer Beat the egg white with vanilla and powdered sugar in small bowl with electric mixer set on high speed until stiff peaks form.

Spread dough with egg white mixture; sprinkle with walnuts. Bake for 15–18 minutes until golden brown and firm to the touch. Cool completely before cutting into squares.

MAKES 48 COOKIES.

Variations:

ORANGE-ALMOND SHORTBREAD:
Prepare as directed above but substitute 1 tablespoon grated orange zest for the rosemary, ½ teaspoon almond extract for the vanilla extract, and 1 cup finely chopped almonds for the walnuts.

BROWN SUGAR–PECAN SHORTBREAD:
Prepare as directed above but eliminate the rosemary, ¼ cup firmly packed dark brown sugar to the cake mix dough, and substitute 1 cup finely chopped pecans for the walnuts.

RUM RAISIN BARS

This is definitely an adult cookie. Perfumed with nutmeg and orange zest, they are excellent additions to holiday cookie plates.

- 2 tablespoons butter
- 3 cups miniature marshmallows
- 2 teaspoons grated orange zest
- 2 teaspoons rum-flavored extract
- ¼ teaspoon ground nutmeg
- 1 cup finely crushed crisp sugar cookies
- ¾ cup golden raisins
- ½ cup chopped walnuts, skillet toasted and cooled (see page xviii)

Lightly spray an 8 x 8 x 2-inch pan with nonstick cooking spray; set aside.

Melt the butter in a large saucepan set over low heat. Add the marshmallows, stirring constantly, until marshmallows are melted. Remove from heat; stir in the orange zest, rum extract, and nutmeg.

Stir in the cookie crumbs, raisins, and walnuts; mix until well blended. Transfer mixture to prepared pan, pressing down and smoothing surface with a square of wax paper. Refrigerate for at least 1 hour. Cut into small bars. Store in covered containers between layers of wax paper.

MAKES 16 BARS.

SALTY-SWEET CHEWY POPCORN BARS

Whether for snack time, potluck gatherings, or late-night movie-watching, these salty-sweet, caramel popcorn cookies are popular.

- 8 cups popped popcorn
- 2 cups honey graham cereal
- 1 cup candy-coated chocolate pieces (e.g., M&Ms)
- 1 cup salted pretzel sticks, broken in half
- ½ cup (1 stick) butter
- 1 cup firmly packed brown sugar
- ½ cup light corn syrup
- 2 tablespoons all-purpose flour

Lightly spray a 13 x 9 x 2-inch baking pan with nonstick cooking spray; set aside.

Combine the popcorn, cereal, candy, and pretzels in a very large bowl; set aside.

Melt the butter in a medium saucepan set over medium heat. Stir in all remaining ingredients. Continue cooking, stirring occasionally, until mixture comes to a full boil. Boil for 1 minute without stirring.

Pour caramel mixture over popcorn mixture; toss with wooden spoon to coat well. With a large square of wax paper, press firmly into prepared pan. Cool completely. Cut into bars. Store in covered containers between layers of wax paper.

MAKES 24 BIG BARS.

SALTY-SWEET PEANUT CHEWY BARS

These easy and very delicious bars bear a strong resemblance to one of my favorite candy bars: PayDay. Have fun playing around with the cake and chip flavors. Consider chocolate cake mix and chocolate chips or caramel cake mix (harder to find, but worth the hunt) combined with butterscotch or white chocolate chips.

- 1 (18.25-ounce) package yellow cake mix
- 10 tablespoons butter, softened, divided
- 1 large egg
- 3 cups miniature marshmallows
- ⅔ cup light corn syrup
- 1 (10-ounce) package peanut butter chips
- 2 teaspoons vanilla extract
- 2 cups crisp rice cereal
- 2 cups salted, roasted peanuts

Preheat oven to 350°F (or 325°F for dark-coated metal pan). Position oven rack in middle of oven. Spray the bottom only of a 13 x 9-inch metal baking pan with nonstick cooking spray (or foil-line pan; see page xxiv).

Place the cake mix, 6 tablespoons softened

butter, and egg in a large bowl. Blend for 1–2 minutes with an electric mixer set on medium speed until blended and crumbly. Press mixture evenly into prepared pan.

Bake for 12–15 minutes or until golden brown. Remove from oven and sprinkle with marshmallows. Return to oven and bake 1–2 minutes longer, until marshmallows begin to puff. Remove from oven and transfer to cooling rack. Cool.

Meanwhile, combine the remaining butter, corn syrup, and peanut butter chips in a heavy saucepan set over medium heat; stir until melted and smooth. Stir in vanilla extract, cereal, and peanuts. Evenly spread mixture over marshmallows; refrigerate at least 1 hour. Cut into bars.

MAKES 24 LARGE OR 36 SMALL BARS.

SCOTCHIE-TOFFEE TREATS

When you're ready to make some treats for a Fourth of July gathering or for winter holiday giving, turn to this page—you won't want to go through any of the holidays without them.

- 3 tablespoons butter
- 1 (10-ounce) package regular marshmallows or miniature marshmallows
- 3 tablespoons dry butterscotch instant pudding and pie mix
- 6 cups crisp rice cereal
- 4 milk chocolate–covered English toffee candy bars, chopped

Lightly spray a 13 x 9 x 2-inch baking pan with nonstick cooking spray; set aside.

Melt the butter in a large saucepan set over low heat. Add the marshmallows and butterscotch pudding mix; stir with a wooden spoon until completely melted. Remove from heat. Add the cereal and toffee candy bars, stirring until all of the cereal is well coated.

Using a large square of wax paper, press mixture evenly into prepared pan. Cool completely. Cut into 2-inch squares. Store in covered containers between layers of wax paper.

MAKES 24 SQUARES.

SEVEN-LAYER MAGIC COOKIE BARS

Something magic happens every time these are served: they disappear in the blink of an eye.

- 1 (16.5-ounce) roll refrigerated chocolate chip cookie dough
- ½ cup graham cracker crumbs
- 1 cup butterscotch chips
- 1 cup semisweet chocolate chips
- 1½ cups sweetened flake coconut
- ½ cup chopped pecans or walnuts
- 1 (14-ounce) can sweetened condensed milk

Preheat oven to 350°F. Line a 13 x 9-inch baking pan with heavy-duty foil, extending foil over sides of pan. Spray bottom and sides of foil with nonstick cooking spray.

Break up the cookie dough in prepared pan. With floured fingers, press dough evenly in bottom of pan to form crust.

Sprinkle graham cracker crumbs evenly over crust. Top evenly with butterscotch chips, chocolate chips, coconut and nuts. Drizzle sweetened condensed milk over top.

Bake for 32–38 minutes or until edges are golden brown (center will not be set). Cool completely on cooling rack. Use foil to lift bars from pan. Cut into bars.

MAKES 36 COOKIES.

SOUR CREAM CRANBERRY BARS

These stellar bars are a delicious contrast of flavors and textures, from the chocolate streusel top and bottom to the slightly tart middle layer, smooth with sour cream and loaded with dried cranberries.

- 1 (19.5- to 19.8-ounce) package brownie mix
- 2¼ cups quick-cooking oats
- 1 cup (2 sticks) unsalted butter, melted
- 1¼ cups sour cream
- ⅓ cup sugar
- 2½ tablespoons all-purpose flour
- 1 tablespoon grated lemon zest
- 1 teaspoon vanilla extract
- 1 large egg
- 2 cups dried cranberries

Preheat oven to 350°F (325°F for dark-coated metal pan). Position a rack in the lower third of the oven. Spray the bottom only of a 13 x 9-inch baking pan with nonstick cooking spray (or foil-line pan; see page xxiv).

Combine the brownie mix, oats, and melted butter in a large mixing bowl with a wooden spoon until just blended and all dry ingredients are moistened. Press half of the mixture evenly into prepared pan.

Whisk the sour cream, sugar, flour, lemon zest, vanilla, and egg in a separate medium mixing bowl until smooth; stir in the cranberries and spread over base layer. Sprinkle with remaining crumb mixture; press gently into filling.

Bake for 30–34 minutes or until topping is firm. Transfer to a wire rack and cool completely. Cut into bars.

MAKES 24 LARGE OR 36 SMALL BARS.

SOUR CREAM LEMON BARS

Light and refreshing, these tangy citrus bars are a great finale for a warm weather supper.

- 2 cups crushed creme-filled lemon sandwich cookies (about 24 cookies)
- ⅓ cup butter, melted
- 2 teaspoons unflavored gelatin
- ½ cup fresh lemon juice, divided use
- 1 (3-ounce) package cream cheese, softened
- 1⅓ cups sour cream
- 1½ teaspoons freshly grated lemon zest
- 1 cup powdered sugar

Line an 8 x 8 x 2-inch baking pan with foil (see page xxiv); lightly spray with nonstick cooking spray. Set aside.

Combine the cookie crumbs and melted butter in a medium bowl with a fork or fingers until well blended. Transfer crumb mixture to prepared pan. Press firmly into bottom of pan with a large square of wax paper. Freeze until ready to use.

Place ¼ cup of the lemon juice in a small saucepan; sprinkle gelatin over (do not stir). Let stand for 5 minutes to soften. Add the remaining ¼ cup lemon juice to saucepan and turn heat to medium. Whisk until hot but not boiling and gelatin is completely dissolved. Let cool for 15 minutes.

Beat the cream cheese, sour cream, lemon zest, and powdered sugar in a large bowl with electric mixer on medium speed until creamy. Gradually add lemon mixture, beating until well blended. Pour and spread evenly over prepared crust. Refrigerate for 3 hours or until firm.

Use foil lining to remove uncut bars from pan to cutting board. Cut into bars.

Store, loosely covered with foil or plastic wrap, in refrigerator.

MAKES 16 BARS.

SPICED AND ICED PUMPKIN SNACK BARS

Mayonnaise is the secret ingredient in these tender, moist pumpkin bars. Be sure to use real mayonnaise (mostly eggs and oil) as opposed to salad dressing for optimal results.

- 1 (18.25-ounce) package spice cake mix
- 1 (15-ounce) can pumpkin purée
- 1 cup mayonnaise
- 3 large eggs
- 1½ teaspoons ground cinnamon, divided
- 1 cup dried cranberries (or raisins), optional

- ½ cup (1 stick) butter, softened
- 3½ cups powdered sugar
- 2 tablespoons milk
- 1 teaspoon vanilla extract

Preheat oven to 350°F (or 325°F for dark-coated metal pan). Position oven rack in middle of oven. Spray the bottom only of a 15 x 10 x 1-inch jelly roll pan with nonstick cooking spray (or foil-line pan; see page xxiv).

Place the cake mix, pumpkin, mayonnaise, eggs, and 1 teaspoon cinnamon in a large bowl. Blend for 2 minutes with an electric mixer set on medium speed until smooth. If desired, stir in dried cranberries. Pour and spread batter into prepared pan.

Bake for 18–20 minutes or until toothpick inserted in center comes out clean. Transfer to wire rack and cool completely.

Beat the softened butter, powdered sugar, milk, vanilla extract, and remaining ½ teaspoon cinnamon in a medium bowl with electric mixer set on low speed for 2 minutes. Beat on high speed until light and fluffy. Spread over cooled bars. Cut into bars. Store leftover bars in refrigerator.

MAKES 36 LARGE OR 48 SMALL BARS.

SPICED APPLE BUTTER BARS WITH APPLE BUTTER-CREAM CHEESE FROSTING

After-school snacks have never been better than with this home-style bar. The Apple Butter-Cream Cheese Frosting adds a luxurious smoothness to these moist bars, which happen to keep extremely well.

- 1 (18.25-ounce) package spice cake mix
- 1 large egg
- ¼ cup vegetable oil
- 1 cup apple butter, divided
- 1 cup chopped walnuts
- 1 (8-ounce) package cream cheese, softened
- ¼ teaspoon ground cinnamon
- 3½ cups powdered sugar

Preheat oven to 350°F (or 325°F for dark-coated metal pan). Position oven rack in middle of oven. Spray the bottom only of a 13 x 9-inch metal baking pan with nonstick cooking spray (or foil-line pan; see page xxiv).

Place the cake mix, egg, oil, and ½ cup of the apple butter in a large bowl. Blend for 1–2 minutes with an electric mixer set on low speed until well blended. Spread evenly into the prepared pan. Sprinkle with walnuts.

Bake for 30–35 minutes until lightly browned and firm to the touch. Transfer to wire rack and cool completely.

Beat softened cream cheese, remaining apple butter, and cinnamon in a medium bowl with mixer set on medium speed. Beat in powdered sugar until frosting is fluffy. Spread frosting over cooled bars. Cut into bars.

MAKES 24 LARGE OR 36 SMALL BARS.

SPICY CHOCOLATE AZTEC BARS

Kicked up with cayenne, coffee, cinnamon, and orange zest, these very rich, dark chocolate bars have gone south of the border.

- 1 (18.25-ounce) package devil's food cake mix
- ½ cup (1 stick) butter, melted
- 2 teaspoons grated orange peel
- ¾ teaspoon ground cinnamon
- 1 cup chopped nuts (almonds, pecans, or walnuts)
- 1½ cups semisweet chocolate chips
- 1 (14-ounce) can sweetened condensed milk
- 1 tablespoon instant espresso (or coffee powder)
- ⅛ teaspoon cayenne pepper

Preheat oven to 350°F (or 325°F for dark-coated metal pan). Position oven rack in middle of oven. Spray a 13 x 9-inch metal baking pan with nonstick cooking spray (or foil-line pan; see page xxiv).

Place the cake mix, melted butter, orange peel, cinnamon, and nuts in a large bowl. Blend for 1–2 minutes with an electric mixer set on low speed until well blended and crumbly. Press mixture into bottom of prepared pan. Bake for 15 minutes.

While crust bakes, melt the chocolate chips with the condensed milk in a medium saucepan set over low heat, stirring until smooth. Remove from heat and stir in espresso powder and cayenne until blended. Pour chocolate mixture over partially baked layer.

Bake for an additional 20–22 minutes until just set. Transfer to a wire rack and cool completely. Cut into bars.

MAKES 24 LARGE OR 36 SMALL BARS.

SWEDISH ALMOND BARS

Fragrant, exotic cardamom lends these easy bars Scandinavian flair.

- 1 (16.5-ounce) roll refrigerated sugar cookie dough
- 1 large egg white
- 2 teaspoons water
- 1 teaspoon almond extract
- ¼ cup sugar
- ½ teaspoon ground cardamom
- 1 cup sliced almonds

Preheat oven to 350°F. Spray a 13 x 9-inch pan with nonstick cooking spray.

Break up the cookie dough into prepared pan. With floured fingers, press dough evenly in bottom of pan to form crust.

Whisk the egg white, water, and almond extract in a small bowl with a fork until frothy. Brush over dough. Mix the sugar and cardamom in a small cup. Sprinkle the sugar mixture and almonds even-ly over dough. Gently press almond into dough.

Bake for 18–23 minutes or until edges are light golden brown. Cool completely on wire rack.

MAKES 30 BARS.

TART CHERRY CARAMEL BARS

The tart dried cherries in these bars are the perfect counterpoint to the velvety caramel and crunchy almonds.

- 1½ sleeves (approximately 57 crackers) coarsely broken saltine crackers
- 2 cups white chocolate chips
- 1 cup miniature marshmallows
- ¾ cup tart dried cherries or dried cranberries
- 1 cup chopped roasted, lightly salted almonds, divided
- ½ cup (1 stick) butter
- 1 (14-ounce) package caramels (about 50), unwrapped
- ¾ teaspoon almond extract

Lightly spray a 13 x 9 x 2-inch pan with nonstick cooking spray; set aside.

Mix the crushed crackers, white chocolate chips, marshmallows, cherries, and half of the chopped almonds in large bowl; set aside.

Place the butter and caramels in small saucepan. Stir over low heat until caramels are completely melted and mixture is well blended, stirring frequently. Stir in almond extract. Pour over cracker mixture; toss to coat well.

Working quickly, press the mixture into the prepared pan, pressing down with a square of wax paper; sprinkle with reserved chopped almonds. Refrigerate for 30 minutes or until completely cooled. Cut into bars. Store in cov-ered containers between layers of wax paper.

MAKES 24 BIG BARS.

TENNESSEE JAM CAKE STREUSEL BARS

Tennessee Jam Cake is a classic Southern dessert made with layers of spice cake, blackberry jam (sometimes stirred into the batter, sometimes spread between the layers of cake) and finished with penuche (caramel fudge) frosting. Heaven. Here the same flavor is captured in an impressive, but still easy, streusel bar.

- 1 (18.25-ounce) package spice cake mix
- 1 cup (2 sticks) butter, melted
- 1 teaspoon pumpkin pie spice (or ground cinnamon)
- 2 cups quick-cooking oats
- 1 (12-ounce) jar blackberry jam or preserves
- 1 cup butterscotch baking chips
- ½ cup chopped pecans (or walnuts)

Preheat oven to 350°F (or 325°F for dark-coated metal pan). Position oven rack in middle of oven. Spray the bottom only of a 13 x 9-inch metal baking pan with nonstick cooking spray (or foil-line pan; see page xxiv).

Place the cake mix, melted butter, and pumpkin pie spice in a large bowl. Blend with an electric mixer set on medium speed for 1–2 minutes, until smooth. Mix in the oats with a wooden spoon until combined. Press half of the mixture evenly into prepared pan.

Spoon and spread blackberry jam over prepared crust. Add butterscotch chips and nuts to remaining crumb mixture; sprinkle over bars and press down gently.

Bake for 30–34 minutes or until topping is set and firm to the touch. Transfer to wire rack and cool completely. Cut into bars.

MAKES 24 LARGE OR 36 SMALL BARS.

TIRAMISU BARS

Tiramisu was a nineties hit, seemingly appearing on most every dessert menu around. But while the fad has faded, the popularity of the ambrosial Italian concoction of cream and cake has not. Here it finds new life as inspiration for an easily assembled bar cookie. Buon appetito!

- 2 teaspoons vanilla extract, divided
- 1 tablespoon instant espresso (or coffee powder)
- 1 (18.25-ounce) package white cake mix, divided
- ¼ cup (½ stick) butter, melted
- 4 large eggs
- 1½ cups chocolate-covered toffee baking bits, divided
- 2 cups ricotta cheese
- 1 (14-ounce) can sweetened condensed milk
- 2 ½ tablespoons dark rum

Preheat oven to 350°F (or 325°F for dark-coated metal pan). Position oven rack in middle of oven. Spray the bottom only of a 13 x 9-inch metal baking pan with nonstick cooking spray (or foil-line pan; see page xxiv).

Mix the espresso powder with 1 teaspoon vanilla extract in a large mixing bowl until dissolved. Measure out ½ cup of the cake mix; set aside. Add the remaining cake mix, melted butter, 1 egg, and ½ cup toffee bits into bowl with espresso mixture. Blend with electric mixer set on low speed for 2 minutes; scrape down bowl. Beat 30 seconds longer. Press mixture into prepared pan. Set aside momentarily.

Using the same large bowl, blend the ricotta cheese and condensed milk with electric mixer set on low speed for 1 minute. Add reserved cake mix, remaining 1 teaspoon vanilla extract, remaining eggs, and rum and blend with electric mixer set on medium speed for 1 minute, until well blended. Pour and spread evenly over prepared crust. Sprinkle evenly with remaining 1 cup toffee bits.

Bake for 48–52 minutes or until center is just barely set when pan is jiggled (do not overbake). Transfer to wire rack and cool completely. Refrigerate for at least 4 hours or overnight. Cut into bars.

MAKES 36 MEDIUM BARS OR
48 SMALL SQUARES.

TOASTED ALMOND-APRICOT TRUFFLE BARS

Almonds add crunch, while apricots give these very rich cookies some chewiness. You can vary the bars in any number of ways. For example, vary the type of dried fruit, use lemon or lime zest in place of orange, mix in spices, or change out the type of chocolate chips.

- 1 cup (2 sticks) butter, divided
- 2½ cups finely crushed crisp shortbread or sugar cookie crumbs
- 1 cup sugar
- 1 (5-ounce) can evaporated milk (about ⅔ cup)
- 1 (10-ounce) package miniature marshmallows
- 2 cups white chocolate chips
- ¾ teaspoon almond extract
- 2 teaspoons grated orange zest
- 1 cup chopped dried apricots

- ½ cup sliced almonds, skillet toasted (see page xviii)

Foil-line a 13 x 9 x 2-inch baking pan (see page xxiv); set aside.

Melt ¾ cup (1½ sticks) of the butter in a small saucepan. Mix the melted butter and shortbread cookie crumbs in a medium bowl. With a large square of wax paper, press mixture into bottom of prepared pan. Chill while preparing topping.

Place the sugar, evaporated milk, marshmallows, and remaining butter in a large saucepan. Stir over medium heat until mixture comes to boil, stirring constantly. Boil for 5 minutes, stirring constantly. Remove from heat and add the white chocolate chips, almond extract, and orange zest, stirring until chips are completely melted.

Pour the chocolate mixture over the crust, spreading evenly to cover. Sprinkle with the apricots and almonds; press lightly into white chocolate layer. Refrigerate for 2 hours or until firm. Cut into bars. Store in covered containers between layers of wax paper.

MAKES 36 BARS.

TOASTED ALMOND BUTTERMILK BARS

The toasted almonds are a delicious, crunchy counterpoint to the creamy buttermilk custard in these home-style bars.

- 1 (18.25-ounce) package vanilla cake mix
- ½ cup (1 stick) butter, softened
- 1 (3-ounce) package cream cheese, softened

- 2 cups packed light brown sugar
- 1½ cups buttermilk (not nonfat)
- 4 large eggs
- ½ cup (1 stick) butter, melted
- ⅓ cup all-purpose flour
- 2 teaspoons vanilla extract
- 2 cups sliced almonds
- 2–3 tablespoons powdered sugar

Preheat oven to 350°F. Position oven rack in middle of oven. Set aside an ungreased 15 x 10 x 1-inch jelly roll pan.

Place the cake mix, softened butter, and cream cheese in a large bowl. Blend for 2 minutes with an electric mixer set on low speed until blended and a crumbly dough forms. Gather dough together and press into jelly roll pan. Bake crust for 10 minutes.

Meanwhile, place the brown sugar, buttermilk, eggs, ½ cup melted butter, flour, and vanilla extract in a large bowl and mix with an electric mixer set on low speed until well blended. Stir in almonds. Pour mixture over partially baked crust.

Bake for 25–28 minutes or until golden brown and firm to the touch. Transfer to wire rack and cool completely before cutting into squares. Sprinkle cooled squares with powered sugar.

MAKES 48 BARS.

TOASTED COCONUT CHEESECAKE BARS

Oh, to be basking on a Bahamas beach enjoying the island breezes and tropical treats. Consider these bars your passport.

- 1 (19.5- to 19.8-ounce) package brownie mix

- ½ cup (1 stick) unsalted butter, melted
- 5 large eggs
- 1 (7-ounce) package shredded coconut (about 2⅔ cups), divided
- 2 (8-ounce) packages cream cheese, softened
- ⅓ cup sugar
- ¾ cup canned sweetened cream of coconut
- 2 tablespoons dark rum or 2 teaspoons rum extract

Preheat oven to 350°F (325°F for dark-coated metal pan). Position a rack in the lower third of the oven. Spray the bottom only of a 13 x 9-inch baking pan with nonstick cooking spray (or foil-line pan; see page xxiv).

Combine the brownie mix, melted butter, 2 of the eggs, and ⅔ cup coconut in a medium mixing bowl with a wooden spoon until just blended and all dry ingredients are moistened. Press mixture into prepared pan. Bake for 15 minutes. Remove from oven (leave oven on).

Meanwhile, beat the cream cheese, sugar, cream of coconut, and rum in a medium mixing bowl with an electric mixer set on medium until well blended. Beat in remaining eggs, one at a time, until just blended. Pour the cream cheese mixture over partially baked crust. Sprinkle with remaining coconut; gently press coconut into cheesecake batter.

Bake for an additional 15 minutes. Loosely cover pan with foil (to prevent coconut from over-browning) and bake for 10–12 minutes longer, until just barely set when pan is jiggled. Transfer to a wire rack and cool completely. Refrigerate for at least 3 hours or up to overnight before serving. Cut into bars.

MAKES 24 LARGE OR 36 SMALL BARS.

TOASTED COCONUT FUDGE BARS

These chocolate confections rest on the cusp of cookie and candy. They have a deep chocolate, truffle-like flavor accented by the slightly nutty flavor of toasted coconut. If you have the time and inclination, you can skillet-toast the walnuts, too, to deepen their flavor.

- 1 cup (2 sticks) butter, divided
- 2½ cups finely crushed graham cracker crumbs
- 1 cup sugar
- 1 (5-ounce) can evaporated milk (about ⅔ cup)
- 1 (10-ounce) package miniature marshmallows
- 2 cups semisweet chocolate chips
- 1 cup chopped walnuts
- 1 cup shredded coconut, skillet toasted (see page xx)

Foil-line a 13 x 9 x 2-inch baking pan (see page xxiv); set aside.

In a small saucepan melt ¾ cup (1½ sticks) of the butter. mix the melted butter and graham cracker crumbs in a medium bowl until blended. With a large square of wax paper, press into bottom of prepared pan. Chill while preparing topping.

Place the sugar, evaporated milk, marshmallows, and remaining butter in a large saucepan. Stir over medium heat until mixture comes to boil, stirring constantly. Boil for 5 minutes, stirring constantly. Remove from heat and add the chocolate chips, stirring until chips are completely melted.

Pour the chocolate mixture over the crust, spreading evenly to cover. Sprinkle with the walnuts and coconut; press lightly into chocolate layer. Refrigerate for 2 hours or until firm. Cut into bars. Store in covered containers between layers of wax paper.

MAKES 36 BARS.

TOFFEE CHEESECAKE BARS

Chopped English toffee candy bars and brown sugar create a new and enticing twist on cheesecake. Don't expect leftovers!

- 1¼ cups crisp sugar cookie crumbs
- ¼ cup (½ stick) butter, melted
- ½ cup milk
- 2 teaspoons unflavored gelatin
- ½ cup packed dark brown sugar
- 1 (8-ounce) package cream cheese, softened
- 1 cup sour cream
- 1 teaspoon vanilla extract
- 4 chocolate-covered English toffee bars, chopped

Line an 8 x 8 x 2-inch baking pan with foil (see page xxiv); lightly spray with nonstick cooking spray. Set aside.

Combine the sugar cookie crumbs and melted butter in a medium bowl with a fork or fingers until well blended. Transfer crumb mixture to prepared pan. Press firmly into bottom of pan with a large square of wax paper. Freeze until ready to use.

Place the milk in a small saucepan; sprinkle gelatin over (do not stir). Let stand for 10 minutes to soften. Add the brown sugar to the saucepan. Turn the heat under saucepan to medium. Whisk until milk is very hot (but not boiling) and gelatin is completely dissolved. Remove from heat and set aside momentarily.

Beat the cream cheese, sour cream, and vanilla in a large bowl with electric mixer on medium speed until creamy. Gradually add gelatin-milk mixture, beating on low speed and occasionally scraping sides of bowl with rubber spatula, until well blended. Stir in all but about 2 tablespoons of the toffee bars to the cheesecake mixture.

Pour and spread cream cheese mixture evenly over prepared crust; sprinkle remaining toffee over bars. Refrigerate for 3 hours or until firm. Use foil lining to remove uncut bars from pan to cutting board. Cut into bars. Store, loosely covered with foil or plastic wrap, in refrigerator.

MAKES 16 BARS.

TOFFEE CREAM CHEESE STREUSEL BARS

I do not trust myself alone with these bars. Loaded with brown sugar, cream cheese, and toffee, they are everything a favorite bar cookie should be: simple to make and splendid to eat.

- 1 (18.25-ounce) package yellow cake mix
- ¼ cup packed dark brown sugar
- 1 cup (2 sticks) butter, melted
- 2¼ cups quick-cooking oats
- 2 (8-ounce) packages cream cheese, softened

- ½ cup packed light brown sugar
- 1½ teaspoons vanilla extract
- 2 large eggs
- 1 cup toffee baking bits, divided

Preheat oven to 350°F (or 325°F for dark-coated metal pan). Position oven rack in middle of oven. Spray the bottom only of a 13 x 9-inch metal baking pan with nonstick cooking spray (or foil-line pan; see page xxiv).

Place the cake mix, ¼ cup dark brown sugar, and melted butter in a large bowl. Blend for 1–2 minutes with an electric mixer set on medium speed until smooth. Stir in oats. Press half of mixture evenly into prepared pan.

Beat the softened cream cheese and ½ cup light brown sugar with in a large mixing bowl electric mixer set on high speed until smooth. Add the vanilla extract and eggs, one at a time; beat until just blended. Stir in ½ cup toffee bits. Spoon and spread cream cheese mixture over base layer. Add remaining toffee bits to remaining crumb mixture; sprinkle over cream cheese layer and press down gently.

Bake for 30–34 minutes or until topping is golden and firm to the touch. Transfer to wire rack and cool completely.

MAKES 24 LARGE OR 36 SMALL BARS.

TOFFEE CREAM CHOCOLATE-CHIP BARS

I love the addition of toffee to these over-the-top chocolate chip cheesecake bars. Feel free to vary the type of chocolate chips: white, milk, and bittersweet are equally irresistible.

- 1 (16.5-ounce) roll refrigerated chocolate chip cookie dough
- 1¼ cups toffee baking bits, divided use
- 1 (8-ounce) package cream cheese, softened
- ⅓ cup packed dark brown sugar
- 1 large egg
- 1 teaspoon vanilla extract
- ½ cup miniature semisweet chocolate chips

Preheat oven to 350°F.

Cut cookie dough into ½-inch slices. Arrange slices to cover bottom of ungreased 13 x 9-inch pan. With floured fingers, press dough evenly in bottom of pan to form crust. Sprinkle with ¾ cup of the toffee bits.

Bake for 16–18 minutes or until golden brown.

Meanwhile, beat the cream cheese, brown sugar, egg, and vanilla in a medium bowl with electric mixer on medium speed until smooth.

Using a spatula, gently press edges of partially baked crust down to make surface flat. Spoon and spread cream cheese mixture over crust. Sprinkle with chocolate chips and remaining toffee bits.

Bake 20–25 minutes longer or until edges are deep golden brown and center is set. Cool for 10 minutes on wire rack. Run knife around sides of pan to loosen bars. Cool completely. Store in refrigerator.

MAKES 36 BARS.

TOFFEE SQUARES

When it comes to sweets, my biggest weakness is brown sugar. Hence, toffee bars are definitely favorites on my treat list. This no-bake version comes from the combination of several recipes and lots of trial and error. I think they are as tasty as the ones that take twice as long—or longer—to prepare.

- 1 cup all-purpose flour
- ½ teaspoon baking powder
- ½ teaspoon salt
- 2 cups bran flakes cereal
- ¾ cup plus 2 tablespoons milk, divided use
- 1 cup firmly packed dark brown sugar
- 10 tablespoons (1¼ sticks) butter, softened, divided
- 2 large eggs
- 1½ teaspoons vanilla extract, divided
- 2 cups sifted powdered sugar

Lightly spray an 8 x 8 x 2-inch microwave-safe baking pan with nonstick cooking spray; set aside.

Mix the flour, baking powder, and salt in a medium bowl until blended. Set aside.

Combine the cereal and ¾ cup milk in a small mixing bowl. Let stand for 2–3 minutes or until cereal is softened.

Beat the brown sugar and 8 tablespoons (1 stick) butter in medium mixing bowl with an electric mixer set on medium-high speed until light and fluffy. Add the eggs and 1 teaspoon vanilla. Beat well. Stir in the cereal mixture. Add the flour mixture, stirring until well blended.

Spread the batter evenly in the prepared pan. Microwave on high about for 10 minutes or until wooden pick inserted near center comes out clean. Rotate every 3 minutes. Remove from microwave. Cool completely.

Combine the powdered sugar, remaining butter, remaining milk, and remaining ½ teaspoon vanilla in a small bowl with an electric mixer set on low speed until smooth. Spread frosting evenly over cooled bars. Cut into bars.

Store in covered containers between layers of wax paper.

MAKES 16 BARS.

TRI-LEVEL CARAMEL BARS

These showstopper bars will dazzle your friends. They'll be even more amazed that no baking is required to turn out these triple-decker treats.

- 1 cup (2 sticks) butter, divided
- 4 cups powdered sugar
- 1½ cups graham cracker crumbs
- 1½ cups peanut butter
- 1½ cups coarsely chopped roasted cashews or peanuts, divided use
- 1 (14-ounce) package caramels (about 50 pieces), unwrapped
- ¼ cup milk
- 1⅓ cups milk or semisweet chocolate chips

Lightly spray a 13 x 9 x 2-inch pan with nonstick cooking spray; set aside.

Melt ¾ cup (1½ sticks) butter in a small saucepan. Mix the melted butter, powdered sugar, graham cracker crumbs, peanut butter, and 1 cup of the chopped nuts in a large bowl. Transfer mixture to prepared pan, pressing down and smoothing surface with a square of wax paper. Refrigerate while preparing topping.

Melt the caramels and milk in a large saucepan set over low heat, stirring frequently until mixture is melted and smooth. Pour over crust.

Melt chocolate with remaining butter in large saucepan on low heat, stirring frequently until melted and smooth. Spread over caramel layer.

Immediately sprinkle with remaining nuts. Refrigerate for at least 1 hour. Cut into bars. Store in covered containers between layers of wax paper.

MAKES 36 SMALL BARS.

TRI-LEVEL MOCHA CHEESECAKE BARS

As luscious proof that decadent desserts can be quick and easy too, these delectable espresso-spiked chocolate treats come together in no time. A chocolate lover's delight, they will satisfy even the most intense chocolate cravings.

- 1 (18.25-ounce) package chocolate cake mix
- ½ cup (1 stick) butter, melted
- 3 large eggs
- 1 tablespoon instant espresso or coffee powder
- 3 teaspoons vanilla extract, divided
- 2 (8-ounce) packages cream cheese, softened
- ¾ cup powdered sugar, divided
- 1 (16-ounce) container (2 cups) sour cream

Preheat oven to 350°F (or 325°F for dark-coated metal pan). Position oven rack in middle of oven. Spray the bottom only of a 13 x 9-inch metal baking pan with nonstick cooking spray (or foil-line pan; see page xxiv).

In a large bowl place the cake mix, butter, and 1 of the eggs. Blend for 1–2 minutes with an electric mixer set on low speed until well blended. Press mixture into prepared pan. Bake for 10 minutes. Remove from oven (leave oven on).

While crust bakes, dissolve espresso powder in 2 teaspoons of the vanilla extract in a medium bowl. Add the softened cream cheese and ½ cup of the powdered sugar to the same bowl and blend with electric mixer set on medium speed until well blended and smooth. Add remaining eggs, one at a time, mixing on low speed after each addition just until blended. Pour over hot crust.

Bake for 22–25 minutes or until center is just barely set when pan is jiggled (do not overbake); remove from oven (leave oven on).

Whisk the sour cream with the remaining powdered sugar and 1 teaspoon vanilla extract in a large mixing bowl; spread evenly over bars. Return bars to oven for 5 minutes. Transfer to wire rack and cool completely. Refrigerate for at least 4 hours or overnight. Cut into bars.

MAKES 36 MEDIUM BARS OR
48 SMALL SQUARES.

TRI-LEVEL PEANUT BUTTER MARSHMALLOW CRISPY BARS

Layers of chocolate, marshmallows, peanut butter chips, and crisp rice cereal? Sounds like kid stuff, but think again. The reality is a chewy-gooey, candy bar–like confection that everyone, of every age, will love.

- 1 (19.5- to 19.8-ounce) package brownie mix
- 10 tablespoons (1¼ sticks) unsalted butter, softened, divided
- 2 large egg yolks
- 3 cups miniature marshmallows
- Topping:
- ⅔ cup light corn syrup
- 1 (10-ounce) package peanut butter chips
- 2 teaspoons vanilla extract
- 2 cups crisp rice cereal
- 2 cups lightly salted peanuts

Preheat oven to 350°F (325°F for dark-coated metal pan). Position a rack in the lower third of the oven. Spray the bottom only of a 13 x 9-inch baking pan with nonstick cooking spray (or foil-line pan; see page xxiv).

Combine the brownie mix, 6 tablespoons softened butter, and egg yolks in a large mixing bowl with an electric mixer set on low until mixture is combined and crumbly. Press mixture firmly into the bottom of the prepared pan.

Bake for 18 minutes or until set at edges. Remove crust from oven (leave oven on). Immediately sprinkle with marshmallows. Return to oven; bake for an additional 3–5 minutes or until marshmallows just begin to puff. Transfer to a wire rack and cool while preparing topping.

Combine the corn syrup, remaining butter, and peanut butter chips in a large saucepan. Stir constantly over low heat until the chips are melted and smooth. Remove from heat; stir in vanilla, cereal, and peanuts. Immediately spoon warm topping over marshmallows; spread to cover. Place pan of bars in refrigerator for 1 hour or until firm. Cut into bars or squares.

MAKES 36 MEDIUM BARS OR
48 SMALL SQUARES.

TRIPLE-CHOCOLATE GOOEY CHESS SQUARES

A chocolate lover's dream come true, these decadent chess squares are memorable after one bite. Their deep, rich flavor stems from chocolate times three: chocolate cake mix, cocoa powder in the filling, and miniature chocolate chips throughout.

- 1 cup (2 sticks) butter, divided
- 1 (18.25-ounce) package chocolate cake mix
- 3 large eggs
- 1 (8-ounce) package cream cheese, softened
- 5 tablespoons unsweetened cocoa powder
- 2 teaspoons vanilla extract
- 1 (16-ounce) box powdered sugar
- ¾ cup miniature semisweet chocolate chips

Preheat oven to 350°F (or 325°F for dark-coated metal pan). Position oven rack in middle of oven. Spray the bottom only of a 13 x 9-inch metal baking pan with nonstick cooking spray (or foil-line pan; see page xxiv).

Melt ½ cup (1 stick) of the butter in a small saucepan set over low heat. Beat the cake mix, melted butter, and 1 egg in a large bowl with an electric mixer set on medium speed until well blended. Pat the dough evenly into the prepared pan. Set aside momentarily.

Melt the remaining stick of butter in a small saucepan set over low heat. Beat the softened cream cheese, cocoa powder, and vanilla extract in a large bowl with an electric mixer set on medium speed until smooth, scraping down sides of bowl occasionally. Add the melted butter and remaining eggs; blend until smooth. Add the powdered sugar; blend until smooth. Stir in chocolate chips.

Spread the cream cheese mixture over prepared crust. Bake for 42–45 minutes (do not overbake; bars should be slightly gooey). Transfer to a wire rack and cool completely. Cut into bars or squares. Cover and store in refrigerator.

MAKES 24 LARGE OR 36 SMALL BARS.

TRIPLE CHOCOLATE PUDDING BARS

Elevate your sense of well-being and euphoria with these voluptuous chocolate bars.

- 5 tablespoons butter, divided
- 1 ¼ cups chocolate wafer cookie crumbs
- 4½ tablespoons cornstarch
- ⅔ cup sugar
- ⅓ cup unsweetened cocoa powder
- 2 cups half and half
- ⅔ cup semisweet chocolate chips

Line an 8 x 8 x 2-inch baking pan with foil (see page xxiv); lightly spray with nonstick cooking spray. Set aside.

Melt 4 tablespoons (½ stick) of the butter in a large nonstick skillet set over medium-high heat. combine the cookie crumbs and melted butter in a medium bowl with a fork or fingers until well blended.

Transfer crumb mixture to prepared pan. Press firmly into bottom of pan with a large square of wax paper. Freeze until ready to use.

Combine the cornstarch, sugar, and cocoa powder in a medium saucepan. Whisk in 1 cup of the half and half until smooth and blended; whisk in remaining half and half. Stir over medium high heat until mixture is thick and bubbly. Remove pan from heat; whisk in chocolate chips and remaining butter until chips are melted and mixture is smooth. Let cool for 20 minutes.

Pour mixture over prepared crust, smoothing top with a rubber spatula. Place a piece of plastic wrap directly on filling. Refrigerate for 4–6 hours or until firm. Cut into bars. Use foil lining to remove uncut bars from pan to cutting board. Store, loosely covered with foil or plastic wrap, in refrigerator.

MAKES 16 BARS.

TRIPLE-DECKER CHOCOLATE-CHIP PEANUT BUTTER BARS

Some occasions call for restraint, others for indulgence. Be sure to serve these bars on the latter type of occasion. Everyone knows how good chocolate and peanut butter are in combination, but this layered bar elevates the duo to new hedonistic heights.

- 1¼ cups sifted powdered sugar
- 1¼ cups creamy peanut butter
- 1½ teaspoons vanilla extract
- 1 (16.5-ounce) roll refrigerated chocolate-chip cookie dough, well chilled

Preheat oven to 350°F. Spray an 8-inch pan with nonstick cooking spray or line with foil.

Combine the powdered sugar, peanut butter, and vanilla in a medium bowl; mix well with a wooden spoon (mixture will be stiff).

Cut cookie dough in half. With floured fingers, press half of dough in bottom of the prepared pan. Press peanut butter mixture evenly over dough. Crumble remaining half of cookie dough evenly over peanut butter mixture.

Bake for 27–30 minutes or until golden brown and firm to the touch. Remove from oven and cool completely. Cut into bars.

MAKES 16 BIG BARS.

TURTLE CHEESECAKE BARS

Here pecans, caramel, and chocolate transform a simple cheesecake bar into an extraordinary treat.

- 2½ cups chocolate wafer cookie crumbs
- 3 tablespoons sugar
- ½ cup (1 stick) butter, melted
- ½ cup chopped pecans
- 2 (8-ounce) packages cream cheese, softened
- 1½ cups cold milk
- ¼ cup firmly packed dark brown sugar
- 1 (4-serving-size) package instant butterscotch pudding and pie filling mix
- ⅔ cup caramel ice cream topping
- 1 cup pecan halves

Line a 13 x 9 x 2-inch baking pan with foil (see page xxiv); lightly spray with nonstick cooking spray. Set aside.

Combine the cookie crumbs, sugar, melted butter, and pecans in a medium bowl with a fork or fingers until well blended. Transfer crumb mixture to prepared pan. Press firmly into bottom of pan with a large square of wax paper. Freeze until ready to use.

Beat the cream cheese in a large bowl with an electric mixer set on medium-high speed until light and fluffy. Gradually beat in the milk until smooth and well blended. Add the brown sugar and pudding mix; beat at low speed for 2 minutes. Pour and evenly spread mixture over crust in pan.

Drizzle with caramel topping; swirl into filling with tip of knife. Arrange pecan halves over top of cheesecake. Refrigerate for at least 3 hours or until firm.

Use foil lining to remove uncut bars from pan to cutting board. Cut into bars. Store, loosely covered with foil or plastic wrap, in refrigerator.

MAKES 36 BARS.

ULTIMATE FRESH RASPBERRY CHEESECAKE BARS

I cannot say enough good things about these brownie bars. One bite and you'll agree that they live up to their "ultimate" name. As indicated in the recipe, frozen unsweetened raspberries (individually frozen in bags, not in sweetened syrup) may be substituted for fresh if you're making these when berries are out of season. It is essential, however, that the frozen raspberries are not thawed or the brownie base will become goopy (from extra liquid seeping into the batter) and the topping will not set properly.

- 1 (19.5- to 19.8-ounce) package brownie mix
- ½ cup (1 stick) unsalted butter, melted
- 4 large eggs
- 2 (8-ounce) packages cream cheese, softened
- ⅓ cup sugar
- 1 teaspoon vanilla extract
- 2 tablespoons all-purpose flour
- 2 cups (1 pint) fresh raspberries or frozen (not thawed) unsweetened raspberries
- 1–2 tablespoons powdered sugar (optional)

Preheat oven to 350°F (325°F for dark-coated metal pan). Position a rack in the lower third of the oven. Spray the bottom only of a 13 x 9-inch baking pan with nonstick cooking spray (or foil-line pan; see page xxiv).

Combine the brownie mix, melted butter, and 2 of the eggs in a medium mixing bowl with a wooden spoon until just blended and all dry ingredients are moistened. Spread batter into prepared pan. Bake for 18 minutes. Remove from oven (leave oven on).

While the brownie base bakes, beat the cream cheese and sugar in a medium mixing bowl with an electric mixer set on medium until light and fluffy. Add the remaining eggs, vanilla, and flour and beat until smooth, scraping down sides with rubber spatula.

Spread the cream cheese mixture evenly over batter. Distribute the raspberries evenly over the cream cheese layer.

Bake bars on a middle oven rack for 22–25 minutes, or until topping is just barely set when the pan is jiggled (do not overbake). Transfer to a wire rack and cool completely. Chill in refrigerator at least 3 hours or until firm. Cut into bars or squares and sprinkle with powdered sugar, if desired.

MAKES 24 LARGE OR 36 SMALL BARS.

VERY APRICOT CHOCOLATE STREUSEL BARS

These delicious bars would be right at home in the pastry case of your favorite coffeehouse (for about $2.50 per square). Yet despite having the look and taste of a pedigreed bar cookie, these apricot-filled chocolate bars are deceptively easy to make, proving that elegant does not have to equal time-consuming.

■ 1 (19.5- to 19.8-ounce) package brownie mix
■ 2¼ cups quick-cooking oats
■ 2½ teaspoons ground ginger
■ 1 cup (2 sticks) unsalted butter, melted
■ 2 cups chopped dried apricots
■ 1 (12-ounce) jar apricot preserves
■ 1 tablespoon grated lemon peel

Preheat oven to 350°F (325°F for dark-coated metal pan). Position a rack in the lower third of the oven. Spray the bottom only of a 13 x 9-inch baking pan with nonstick cooking spray (or foil-line pan; see page xxiv).

Combine the brownie mix, oats, ginger, and melted butter in a large mixing bowl with a wooden spoon until just blended and all dry ingredients are moistened. Press half of mixture evenly into prepared pan.

Stir together the chopped dried apricots, apricot preserves, and lemon peel in a medium mixing bowl. Spoon and spread apricot mixture over prepared crust. Top with reserved crumb mixture and press down gently.

Bake for 30–34 minutes or until topping is set and firm to the touch. Transfer to wire rack and cool completely.

MAKES 24 LARGE OR 36 SMALL BARS.

VIENNESE ALMOND TEACAKES

The Berkeley coffeehouse where I worked for many years served a moist, dense almond cake that I have been unable to forget. This very easy version comes very close to replicating the original. An added bonus is that they keep and travel extremely well. The almond filling (not to be confused with almond paste or marzipan) can be found in the baking section of most supermarkets alongside the fruit pie fillings.

■ 1 (18.25-ounce) package yellow cake mix
■ 1 (12.5-ounce) can almond filling
■ ⅓ cup butter, melted
■ 2 large eggs
■ ⅓ cup powdered sugar

Preheat oven to 350°F (or 325°F for dark-coated metal pan). Position oven rack in middle of oven. Spray the bottom only of a 13 x 9-inch metal baking pan with nonstick cooking spray (or foil-line pan; see page xxiv).

Combine half of the cake mix, the almond filling, melted butter, and eggs with in a large bowl an electric mixer set on medium-high speed for 1–2 minutes, until well blended and smooth. Stir in remaining cake mix with a wooden spoon until all dry ingredients are moistened and well blended (mixture will be thick). Press dough into prepared pan.

Bake for 22–25 minutes or until just set at edges. Transfer to wire rack and cool completely. Cut into bars. Sift with powdered sugar.

MAKES 24 LARGE OR 36 SMALL BARS.

> ### Variation:
> **CHOCOLATE CHOCOLATE-CHIP ALMOND TEACAKES:** Prepare as directed above but substitute chocolate cake mix for yellow cake mix and add 1 cup miniature semisweet chocolate chips to the batter.

WAIKIKI WHITE CHOCOLATE PINEAPPLE BARS

Pineapple boosts the flavor of these island-inspired bars. Just be sure to drain the pineapple thoroughly, and pat it dry to keep the crust crisp.

- 1 (16.5-ounce) roll refrigerated sugar cookie dough, well chilled
- 1 (20-ounce) can crushed pineapple, drained and patted dry between paper towels
- 1 cup white chocolate chips
- 1⅓ cups shredded coconut
- 1 cup coarsely chopped macadamia nuts (or blanched almonds)

- 1 (14-ounce) can sweetened condensed milk

Preheat oven to 350°F. Spray a 13 x 9-inch pan with nonstick cooking spray or line with foil.

Cut cookie dough into ¼-inch slices. Arrange slices in bottom of prepared baking pan. With floured fingers, press dough evenly in pan to form crust.

Sprinkle the pineapple, white chocolate chips, coconut, and nuts evenly over prepared dough. Drizzle with sweetened condensed milk.

Bake for 24–27 minutes or until edges are bubbly and center is just lightly browned. Remove from oven and immediately run a narrow metal spatula or table knife around edges of pan to loosen. Cool completely in pan on a wire rack; cut into bars.

MAKES 36 BARS.

WALNUT FUDGE BARS

Having simple luxuries on hand for hungry friends and loved ones who just happen to pop in is a saving grace during the holidays or any time of year. Here is a homey but luxurious treat worth offering any time.

- 1 (19.5- to 19.8-ounce) package brownie mix
- ½ cup (1 stick) unsalted butter, melted
- ¼ cup water
- 2 large eggs
- 2 cups quick-cooking oats
- 2 cups chopped walnuts
- 2 cups semisweet chocolate chips
- 1 (14-ounce) can sweetened condensed milk

Preheat oven to 350°F (325°F for dark-coated metal pan). Position a rack in the lower third of the oven. Spray the bottom only of a 13 x 9-inch baking pan with nonstick cooking spray (or foil-line pan; see page xxiv).

Combine brownie mix, melted butter, water, and eggs in a large mixing bowl with a wooden spoon until just blended and all dry ingredients are moistened; mix in oats and walnuts.

Melt the chocolate chips with the condensed milk in a medium saucepan set over low heat, stirring until smooth.

Spread half of brownie batter in the prepared pan. Spread melted chocolate mixture over batter. Drop remaining brownie mixture by spoonfuls over chocolate layer (brownie mixture will not completely cover chocolate layer).

Bake for 29–33 minutes or until brownie topping feels dry and edges begin to pull away from sides of pan. Transfer to wire rack and cool completely. Refrigerate for at least 2 hours. Cut into bars.

MAKES 24 LARGE OR 36 SMALL BARS.

- 2½ tablespoons lime juice
- 2 teaspoons grated lime zest
- 2 cups white chocolate chips

Preheat oven to 350°F. Spray a 13 x 9-inch pan with nonstick cooking spray or line with foil.

Cut cookie dough into ¼-inch-thick slices. Arrange slices in bottom of the prepared pan. With floured fingers, press dough evenly to form crust.

Bake for 10–14 minutes or until light golden brown (dough will appear slightly puffed).

Sprinkle coconut and almonds over partially baked crust. Combine condensed milk, lime juice, and lime zest in a small bowl. Drizzle mixture over coconut and almonds.

Bake for 21–24 minutes or until edges are golden brown and top is lightly browned. Remove from oven and immediately sprinkle with white chocolate chips. Cool completely. Cut into bars.

MAKES 36 BARS.

WHITE CHOCOLATE AND LIME-LAYERED BARS

These luscious layered bars carry a double dose of lime. For a heavenly summer dessert, cut the bars into larger squares or diamonds and serve with berries and a cloud of whipped cream.1 (16.5-ounce) roll refrigerated sugar cookie dough, well chilled

- 1½ cups unsweetened shredded coconut
- 1 cup sliced almonds
- 1 (14-ounce) can sweetened condensed milk

WHITE CHOCOLATE BERRY BARS

Trust me—it's never a mistake to serve a white chocolate-raspberry confection for dessert.

- 2 cups crushed creme-filled vanilla sandwich cookies (about 24 cookies)
- ⅓ cup butter, melted
- ½ cup heavy whipping cream
- 2 teaspoons unflavored gelatin
- 1 cup white chocolate chips
- 1 cup sour cream
- 1 cup fresh blueberries, raspberries, or blackberries

Line an 8 x 8 x 2-inch pan with foil (see page xxiv). Lightly coat foil with nonstick cooking spray.

Combine the cookie crumbs and melted butter in a medium bowl with a fork or fingers until well blended. Transfer crumb mixture to prepared pan. Press firmly into bottom of pan with a large square of wax paper. Freeze until ready to use.

Place the cream in a small saucepan. Sprinkle gelatin over cream (do not stir). Let stand for 5 minutes to soften. Stir over low heat for 4–6 minutes until cream is hot (but not boiling) and gelatin is dissolved. Remove from heat and add white chocolate chips; stir until melted and smooth. Set aside and let cool for 20–25 minutes until room temperature.

Whisk the sour cream and white chocolate mixture in a medium bowl until smooth. Pour and spread mixture evenly over chilled crust. Sprinkle berries over surface of bars and gently press into filling. Refrigerate for at least 3 hours until firm.

Use foil lining to remove uncut bars from pan to cutting board. Cut into bars. Store, loosely covered with foil or plastic wrap, in refrigerator.

MAKES 16 BARS.

WHITE CHOCOLATE BROWN SUGAR MERINGUE BARS

These elegant bars have a touch of drama. It's dark chocolate versus white chocolate, dense chewy brownie against light, airy meringue. The contrasts add up to a lot of excitement.

- 1 (19.5- to 19.8-ounce) package brownie mix
- ½ cup (1 stick) unsalted butter, melted
- 1 large egg
- 1 (12-ounce) package white chocolate chips
- 4 large egg whites
- 1 cup packed dark brown sugar
- 1 cup slivered almonds

Preheat oven to 375°F (350°F for dark-coated metal pan). Position a rack in the lower third of the oven. Spray the bottom only of a 13 x 9-inch baking pan with nonstick cooking spray (or foil-line pan; see page xxiv).

Combine the brownie mix, melted butter, and egg in a medium mixing bowl with a wooden spoon until just blended and all dry ingredients are moistened. Press mixture into prepared pan.

Bake for about 12 minutes, until partially set at center. Remove pan from oven (leave oven on). Sprinkle with the white chocolate chips. Transfer to wire rack while preparing meringue.

Beat the egg whites in a medium mixing bowl with an electric mixer set on high until frothy. Gradually add the brown sugar; beat until stiff peaks form. Carefully spread meringue over chips and nuts. Sprinkle with almonds.

Bake for an additional 13–15 minutes or until meringue is golden brown. Transfer to a wire rack and cool completely. Cut into bars.

MAKES 24 LARGE OR 36 SMALL BARS.

WHITE CHOCOLATE FUDGE FANTASY BARS

A thick layer of white chocolate fudge nestled between two more layers of chocolate brownie cookie make these quick-to-assemble bars a chocoholic's dream come true. The flavor of the fudge can be tailored to suit your tastes. Consider using maple, rum, brandy, mint, or orange extract in place of the vanilla. Alternatively, milk or semisweet chocolate chips may be substituted for the white chocolate chips. And if you really want to change things up, try butterscotch, peanut butter or cinnamon chips in place of the white chocolate chips.

- 1 (19.5- to 21.5-ounce) package brownie mix
- 1/3 cup vegetable oil
- 1 large egg
- 1 cup chopped pecans or walnuts
- 2 cups white chocolate chips
- 1 (14-ounce) can sweetened condensed milk
- 2 teaspoons vanilla extract

Preheat oven to 350°F (325°F for dark-coated metal pan). Position a rack in the lower third of the oven. Spray the bottom only of a 13 x 9-inch baking pan with nonstick cooking spray (or foil-line pan; see page xxiv).

Combine the brownie mix, oil, and egg in a large mixing bowl with an electric mixer set on medium until blended. Stir in the nuts. Set aside 1½ cups of the crumb mixture. Firmly press remaining crumb mixture into bottom of prepared pan.

Melt the chips with condensed milk in a small saucepan set over low heat, stirring until smooth. Remove from heat and stir in the vanilla. Pour and spread evenly over prepared crust. Sprinkle reserved crumb mixture evenly over top.

Bake for 25–30 minutes or until topping is set and firm to the touch. Transfer to wire rack and cool completely. Cut into bars. Store loosely covered at room temperature.

MAKES 24 LARGE OR 36 SMALL BARS.

WHITE CHRISTMAS CRANBERRY MALLOW BARS

As much as I love it, white chocolate isn't "true" chocolate. Rather, it is a combination of sugar, cocoa butter, and milk solids. Regardless, it is delicious, especially in these pretty, holiday cookies flecked with orange zest and cranberries.

- 2 cups white chocolate chips
- 2 tablespoons vegetable shortening
- 1 cup miniature marshmallows
- ½ cup coarsely chopped honey-roasted almonds
- 1 cup chopped dried cranberries
- 2 teaspoons grated orange zest
- 2 cups crisp rice cereal

Lightly spray an 8 x 8 x 2-inch square baking pan with nonstick cooking spray; set aside.

Melt the white chocolate chips and shortening in a medium saucepan set over low heat, stirring constantly until smooth. Remove from heat. Stir in the marshmallows, almonds, cranberries, orange zest, and cereal, mixing until well coated.

Spread mixture evenly into prepared pan. Refrigerate for about 1 hour until set. Cut into bars. Store in covered containers between layers of wax paper.

MAKES 24 SMALL BARS.

BROWNIES

ALMOND FUDGE BROWNIES

If you can't resist the urge to overindulge, serve the brownies warm with premium ice cream, whipped cream, more almonds, and a cherry.

- 1 (19.5- to 19.8-ounce) package brownie mix
- ½ cup vegetable oil
- ¼ cup water
- 2 large eggs
- 2 cups semisweet chocolate chips
- 1 (14-ounce) can sweetened condensed milk
- 1 teaspoon almond extract
- 1½ cups sliced almonds, toasted

Preheat oven to 350°F (325°F for dark-coated metal pan). Position a rack in the lower third of the oven. Spray the bottom only of a 13 x 9-inch baking pan with nonstick cooking spray (or foil-line pan; see page xxiv).

Combine the brownie mix, oil, water, and eggs in a medium mixing bowl with a wooden spoon until just blended and all dry ingredients are moistened. Spread batter into prepared pan.

Bake for 28–30 minutes or until toothpick inserted 2 inches from side of pan comes out clean or almost clean (do not overbake). Transfer to a wire rack and cool.

Meanwhile, melt chips with condensed milk in heavy saucepan set over low heat, stirring constantly. Remove from heat; stir in almond extract. Spread evenly over brownies. Sprinkle with toasted almonds; press down firmly. Chill for 3 hours or until firm. Cut into squares. Store in the refrigerator.

MAKES 24 LARGE OR 36 SMALL BROWNIES.

ALMOND JOYFUL COCONUT BROWNIES

Inspired by a favorite candy bar of similar name, these moist, almond-, coconut-, and milk chocolate–packed brownies are more confection than brownie. To enhance the almond flavor, lightly toast the almonds before sprinkling onto the brownies.

- 1 (19.5- to 19.8-ounce) package brownie mix
- ½ cup vegetable oil
- ¼ cup water
- 2 large eggs
- 1 teaspoon almond extract
- 2 cups sweetened shredded coconut, divided
- 1½ cups milk chocolate chips
- ½ cup sliced almonds, preferably lightly toasted

Preheat oven to 350°F (325°F for dark-coated metal pan). Position a rack in the lower third of the oven. Spray the bottom only of a 13 x 9-inch baking pan with nonstick cooking spray (or foil-line pan; see page xxiv).

Combine the brownie mix, oil, water, eggs, and almond extract in a medium mixing bowl with a wooden spoon until just blended and all dry ingredients are moistened; stir in 1 cup coconut. Spread batter into prepared pan.

Bake for 28–30 minutes or until toothpick inserted 2 inches from side of pan comes out clean or almost clean (do not overbake). Remove from oven and immediately sprinkle with chocolate chips. Return to oven for 1 minute to soften chips; spread the melted chips evenly over brownies with the back of a metal spoon.

Transfer to a wire rack and sprinkle with almonds and remaining coconut. Gently press into melted chocolate. Cool completely. Refrigerate for 1 hour to set the chocolate. Cut into squares.

MAKES 24 LARGE OR 36 SMALL BROWNIES.

ALMOND TOFFEE-TOPPED BROWNIES

If you like brown sugar (and would anyone who doesn't please step forward?), these are your brownies. With tempting toffee and crunchy bits of brown-sugary almonds, each square tastes like an English toffee chocolate bar transformed into a brownie.

- 1 (19.5- to 19.8-ounce) package brownie mix
- ½ cup vegetable oil
- ¼ cup water
- 2 large eggs
- 1 cup English toffee baking bits
- ⅓ cup unsalted butter
- ½ cup packed dark brown sugar
- 1 tablespoon all-purpose flour
- 2 tablespoons milk
- 1 cup sliced almonds

Preheat oven to 350°F (325°F for dark-coated metal pan). Position a rack in the lower third of the oven. Spray the bottom only of a 13 x 9-inch baking pan with nonstick cooking spray (or foil-line pan; see page xxiv).

Combine the brownie mix, oil, water, and eggs in a medium mixing bowl with a wooden spoon until just blended and all dry ingredients are moistened; stir in toffee bits. Spread batter into prepared pan.

Bake for 28–30 minutes or until toothpick inserted 2 inches from side of pan comes out clean or almost clean (do not overbake).

While brownies bake, combine the butter, brown sugar, flour, milk, and almonds in a medium saucepan. Cook and stir over medium heat until sugar is dissolved, about 4–5 minutes.

Remove brownies from oven and turn oven to broiler setting; position oven rack 4–6 inches from the heat. Pour almond topping over brownies, spreading evenly. Broil 1–2½ minutes, until bubbly and light golden. Transfer to wire rack and cool completely. Cut into squares.

MAKES 24 LARGE OR 36 SMALL BROWNIES.

AMARETTO CAFÉ CREAM BROWNIES

Here the archetypal brownie is taken to new coffeehouse-inspired heights with the enhancement of almonds, coffee, and cream.

- 1 (19.5- to 19.8-ounce) package brownie mix
- ½ cup (1 stick) unsalted butter, softened
- ⅓ cup milk
- 2 large eggs
- 12 ounces (1½ (8-ounce) packages) cream cheese, softened
- 1 (7-ounce) jar marshmallow creme
- 1½ tablespoons instant espresso or coffee powder
- 1 teaspoon almond extract
- 1 cup chopped walnuts

Preheat oven to 350°F (325°F for dark-coated metal pan). Position a rack in the lower third of the oven. Spray the bottom only of a 13 x 9-inch baking pan with nonstick cooking spray (or foil-line pan; see page xxiv).

Combine the brownie mix and softened butter in a large mixing bowl with an electric mixer set on low for 1 minute or until crumbly. Reserve 1 cup of the mixture in a small mixing bowl for topping. Add the milk and eggs to remaining brownie mixture; mix with a wooden spoon until smooth. Spread batter evenly into prepared pan.

Beat cream cheese, marshmallow creme, espresso powder, and almond extract in a medium mixing bowl with electric mixer set on medium until smooth. Spread evenly over brownie mixture. Add walnuts to reserved 1 cup brownie mixture; mix well. Sprinkle evenly over cream cheese mixture.

Bake for 28–30 minutes or until toothpick inserted 2 inches from side of pan comes out clean or almost clean (do not overbake). Transfer to a wire rack and cool completely. Cut into squares. Store in refrigerator.

MAKES 24 LARGE OR 36 SMALL BROWNIES.

APRICOT MACAROON BROWNIES

Te quiero. Je t'aime. S'ayapo. There are many ways to say "I love you," but a batch of these toasty coconut and apricot brownies will do it in any language. They come together in a flash, allowing plenty of time to sit back and savor.

- 1 (19.5- to 19.8-ounce) package brownie mix
- ½ cup vegetable oil
- ¼ cup water
- 2 large eggs
- ⅔ cup apricot preserves
- ⅓ cup butter
- 1 (10-ounce) package marshmallows
- 1 (7-ounce) package shredded coconut, toasted

Preheat oven to 350°F (325°F for dark-coated metal pan). Position a rack in the lower third of the oven. Spray the bottom only of a 13 x 9-inch baking pan with nonstick cooking spray (or foil-line pan; see page xxiv).

Combine the brownie mix, oil, water, and eggs in a medium mixing bowl with a wooden spoon until just blended and all dry ingredients are moistened. Spread batter into prepared pan.

Bake for 28–30 minutes or until toothpick inserted 2 inches from side of pan comes out clean or almost clean (do not overbake). Transfer to a wire rack and cool completely. Spread evenly with apricot preserves.

Meanwhile, melt butter in a large saucepan set over low heat. Add marshmallows; cook until marshmallows are completely melted and mixture is well blended, stirring frequently. Remove from heat; stir in toasted coconut. Spread evenly over apricot layer using back of large spoon or spatula. Cool completely. Cut into squares.

MAKES 24 LARGE OR 36 SMALL BARS.

BEST "BOOSTED" BROWNIES

What's the secret to this incredibly delicious, intensely chocolate batch of brownies? Butter in place of oil for added flavor and richness, buttermilk in place of water for an extra tender-chewy crumb, and a splash of vanilla and a dash of espresso powder, both of which deepen the dark chocolate flavor. And, of course, more chocolate, in the form of bittersweet chocolate chunks.

- 1 tablespoon instant espresso or coffee powder
- 2 teaspoons vanilla extract
- 1 (19.5- to 19.8-ounce) package brownie mix
- ½ cup (1 stick) unsalted butter, melted
- ¼ cup buttermilk
- 2 large eggs
- 4 (1-ounce) squares bittersweet chocolate, coarsely chopped into chunks

Preheat oven to 350°F (325°F for dark-coated metal pan). Position a rack in the lower third of the oven. Spray the bottom only of an 8-inch-square baking pan with nonstick cooking spray (or foil-line pan; see page xxiv).

Combine espresso powder and vanilla in a small cup until dissolved.

Combine the brownie mix, melted butter, buttermilk, eggs, and vanilla-espresso mixture in a medium mixing bowl with a wooden spoon until just blended and all dry ingredients are moistened. Stir in the chopped chocolate. Spread batter into prepared pan.

Bake for 40–44 minutes or until toothpick inserted 2 inches from side of pan comes out clean or almost clean (do not overbake). Transfer to a wire rack and cool completely. Cut into squares.

MAKES 9 LARGE OR 16 SMALL BROWNIES.

BIG-BATCH BROWNIES

Brownies are a perennial hit for great big gatherings. This doubled recipe lets you satisfy the whole gang while keeping your kitchen time minimal. To gild the lily in a matter of minutes, smooth a layer of prepared chocolate frosting over the cooled brownies, or take a few minutes more to prepare and spread with any of the frostings or glazes listed in the chapter "Icings, Frostings, Fillings, and Extras." You can also incorporate any one, or several, of the stir-in options suggested for Classic Brownies (see page 328) but increase the total amount of your ingredient(s) choice to 2 cups (e.g., 2 cups chocolate chips or 1 cup dried cranberries plus 1 cup chopped pecans).

- 2 (19.5- to 19.8-ounce) packages brownie mix
- 4 large eggs
- ½ cup water or buttermilk
- 1 cup vegetable oil or 2 sticks (1 cup) unsalted butter, melted

Preheat oven to 350°F. Position a rack in the lower third of the oven. Foil-line a 15 x 10 x 1-inch pan (see page xxiv), letting the foil overlap just two of the pan's sides.

Combine the brownie mixes, eggs, water and oil in a large mixing bowl with a wooden spoon until well blended. Spread batter into prepared pan.

Bake for 50–55 minutes or until toothpick inserted 2 inches from side of pan comes out clean or almost clean (do not overbake). Transfer to a wire rack and cool completely.

When cool, slide a knife between the pan and the brownies on the unlined sides. Lift the ends of the foil liner and transfer to a cutting board. Cut brownies into squares.

MAKES 36 LARGE OR 48 SMALL BROWNIES.

BLACK AND TAN LAYERED BROWNIES

Old-fashioned brownies get a new treatment with a middle layer of butterscotch and a generous spread of cocoa icing as the crowning touch. For "Black and White" brownies, substitute white chocolate chips for the butterscotch chips.

- 1 (19.5- to 19.8-ounce) package brownie mix
- ½ cup vegetable oil
- ¼ cup water
- 2 large eggs
- 1 cup chopped pecans, divided
- 1 cup semisweet chocolate chips
- 2 cups butterscotch chips, divided
- 2 cups sifted powdered sugar
- ¼ cup unsweetened cocoa powder
- 3 tablespoons hot water
- ¼ cup (½ stick) unsalted butter, melted
- 1 teaspoon vanilla extract

Preheat oven to 350°F (325°F for dark-coated metal pan). Position a rack in the lower third of the oven. Spray the bottom only of a 13 x 9-inch baking pan with nonstick cooking spray (or foil-line pan; see page xxiv).

Combine the brownie mix, oil, water, and eggs in a medium mixing bowl with a wooden spoon until just blended and all dry ingredients are moistened; stir in ½ cup of the chopped

pecans, all of the chocolate chips, and ½ cup of the butterscotch chips. Spread batter into prepared pan.

Bake for 28–30 minutes or until toothpick inserted 2 inches from side of pan comes out clean or almost clean (do not overbake). Remove from oven and immediately sprinkle with remaining butterscotch chips. Return to oven for 1 minute to soften chips; spread the melted chips evenly over brownies with the back of a spoon. Transfer to a wire rack and cool completely.

Whisk the powdered sugar, cocoa powder, hot water, melted butter, and vanilla in a small mixing bowl until smooth (mixture will be thin).

Carefully spoon over butterscotch layer, spreading to cover; sprinkle with remaining pecans. Cool completely to set the glaze. Cut into squares.

MAKES 24 LARGE OR 36 SMALL BROWNIES.

BLACK FOREST BROWNIES

I cannot speak for everyone, but by the time Valentine's Day rolls around, I'm either stumped for ideas or strapped for time. Enter in these Black Forest Brownies, an easy yet extravagant treat that solves any such Valentine's crises. They look gorgeous (and very festive with the contrasts of dark brownie, snowy whipped cream, and bright red cherries) and they taste spectacular. You're sure to earn kudos and win hearts.

- 1 (19.5- to 19.8-ounce) package brownie mix
- ½ cup vegetable oil

- ¼ cup water
- 2 large eggs
- 1 (21-ounce) can cherry pie filling
- 1 (2-cup) recipe for Sweetened Whipped Cream (see page 375)
- 2 (1-ounce) semisweet chocolate baking bars, grated with vegetable peeler

Preheat oven to 350°F (325°F for dark-coated metal pan). Position a rack in the lower third of the oven. Spray the bottom only of an 8-inch-square baking pan with nonstick cooking spray (or foil-line pan; see page xxiv).

Combine the brownie mix, oil, water, and eggs in a medium mixing bowl with a wooden spoon until just blended and all dry ingredients are moistened. Spread batter into prepared pan.

Bake for 40–44 minutes or until toothpick inserted 2 inches from side of pan comes out clean or almost clean (do not overbake). Transfer to a wire rack and cool. Cut into squares. Top each brownie (warm or completely cooled) with pie filling, Sweetened Whipped Cream, and grated chocolate.

MAKES 9 SERVINGS.

BRANDY-LACED "FRUITCAKE" BROWNIES

You have to try these brownies to believe how yummy they are. If you love fruitcake, this may supplant your favorite recipe, and if you're not a fan, you will become a fast convert with one or two bites of these rich, delicious holiday treats, which boast four kinds of dried fruit (no glacé cherries!), toasted walnuts, and a generous pour of brandy.

- 1 (19.5- to 19.8-ounce) package brownie mix
- ½ cup (1 stick) unsalted butter, melted
- ¼ cup brandy or dark rum
- 3 large eggs
- ⅓ cup chopped walnuts, preferably lightly toasted
- ⅓ cup chopped dried apricots
- ⅓ cup chopped dried figs
- ⅓ cup chopped pitted dates
- ⅓ cup dried tart cherries or cranberries
- 1 recipe Cream Cheese Frosting (see page 366)

Preheat oven to 350°F (325°F for dark-coated metal pan). Position a rack in the lower third of the oven. Spray the bottom only of a 13 x 9-inch baking pan with nonstick cooking spray (or foil-line pan; see page xxiv).

Combine the brownie mix, melted butter, brandy, and eggs in a medium mixing bowl with a wooden spoon until just blended and all dry ingredients are moistened. Stir in the walnuts and dried fruits. Spread batter into prepared pan.

Bake for 28–30 minutes or until toothpick inserted 2 inches from side of pan comes out clean or almost clean (do not overbake). Transfer to a wire rack and cool completely.

Prepare Cream Cheese Frosting. Spread frosting over cooled brownies. Cut into squares. Store in refrigerator.

MAKES 24 LARGE OR 36 SMALL BROWNIES.

BROWNED BUTTER CASHEW BROWNIES

Punctuated with velvety bits of roasted cashews and finished with a sleek spread of browned-butter frosting, this is a winning new twist on classic brownies. Prepare for this page to become dog-eared and batter-splattered from repeated use.

- 1 (19.5- to 19.8-ounce) package brownie mix
- ½ cup (1 stick) unsalted butter, melted
- ¼ cup water
- 2 large eggs
- 2 cups coarsely chopped roasted, lightly salted cashews, divided
- 1 recipe Browned Butter Icing (see page 360)

Preheat oven to 350°F (325°F for dark-coated metal pan). Position a rack in the lower third of the oven. Spray the bottom only of an 8-inch-square baking pan with nonstick cooking spray (or foil-line pan; see page xxiv).

Combine the brownie mix, melted butter, water, and eggs in a medium mixing bowl with a wooden spoon until just blended and all dry ingredients are moistened; stir in 1 cup chopped cashews. Spread batter into prepared pan.

Bake for 40–44 minutes or until toothpick inserted 2 inches from side of pan comes out clean or almost clean (do not overbake). Transfer to a wire rack and cool completely.

Prepare Browned Butter Icing. Spread over cooled brownies; sprinkle with remaining cashews. Cut into squares.

MAKES 9 LARGE OR 16 SMALL BROWNIES.

CAPPUCCINO BROWNIES

Think of the layers of a perfect cappuccino and you will understand the construction of these brownies: an espresso/brownie base, a layer of cinnamon-flecked creaminess, and a smooth chocolate finish. Coffee lovers will be transported.

- 1 tablespoon instant espresso or coffee powder
- ¼ cup water
- 1 (19.5- to 19.8-ounce) package brownie mix
- ½ cup vegetable oil
- 2 large eggs
- Topping:
- 1 (8-ounce) package cream cheese, softened
- ¾ cup sifted powdered sugar
- 1 teaspoon vanilla extract
- ½ teaspoon cinnamon
- 1 recipe Shiny Chocolate Glaze (See page 374; prepare full recipe)

Preheat oven to 350°F (325°F for dark-coated metal pan). Position a rack in the lower third of the oven. Spray an 8-inch-square baking pan with nonstick cooking spray (or foil-line pan; see page xxiv).

Dissolve the espresso powder in the water in a medium mixing bowl. Add the brownie mix, oil, and eggs and mix with a wooden spoon until just blended and all dry ingredients are moistened. Spread batter into prepared pan.

Bake for 40–44 minutes or until toothpick inserted 2 inches from side of pan comes out clean or almost clean (do not overbake). Transfer to a wire rack and cool completely.

Beat cream cheese in a medium mixing bowl the with an electric mixer until light and fluffy. Add the powdered sugar, vanilla, and cinnamon; beat until well blended and smooth. Spread mixture evenly over brownie layer. Chill brownies for 1 hour in the refrigerator.

Prepare Shiny Chocolate Glaze. Spread glaze carefully over frosting. Chill brownies, covered, until cold, for at least 3 hours. Cut into squares. Store in refrigerator.

MAKES 9 LARGE OR 16 SMALL BROWNIES.

CARAMEL-BUTTERSCOTCH-LOADED BROWNIES

Wow! If you're a butterscotch and caramel lover (as I am), you'll move these brownies to the top of your must-make-immediately list.

- 1 (19.5- to 19.8-ounce) package brownie mix
- ½ cup vegetable oil
- ¼ cup water
- 2 large eggs
- 2 cups butterscotch-flavored baking chips, divided
- 24 caramels, unwrapped
- 2 tablespoons milk

Preheat oven to 350°F (325°F for dark-coated metal pan). Position a rack in the lower third of the oven. Spray the bottom only of a 13 x 9-inch baking pan with nonstick cooking spray (or foil-line pan; see page xxiv).

Combine the brownie mix, oil, water, and eggs in a medium mixing bowl with a wooden spoon until just blended and all dry ingredients are moistened. Stir in 1 cup butterscotch chips. Spread batter into prepared pan.

Bake for 28–30 minutes or until toothpick inserted 2 inches from side of pan comes out clean or almost clean (do not overbake). Remove from oven and immediately sprinkle with remaining butterscotch chips. Return to oven for 1 minute to soften chips. Transfer to a wire rack and cool (do not spread melted chips).

Combine caramels and milk in a medium saucepan set over low heat, stirring until melted and smooth; drizzle over brownies. Transfer to a wire rack and cool completely. Cut into squares.

MAKES 24 LARGE OR 36 SMALL BROWNIES.

CARAMELICIOUS TURTLE BROWNIES

Because I am crazy for caramel, this recipe is my brownie nirvana. Decked out with gooey caramel, chocolate chips, and pecans, it's hard to find something better—I can't!

- 1 (19.5- to 19.8-ounce) package brownie mix
- ½ cup vegetable oil
- ¼ cup water
- 2 large eggs
- 1½ cups semisweet or milk chocolate chips, divided
- 1 cup coarsely chopped pecans
- 16 caramels, unwrapped
- 1½ tablespoons milk

Preheat oven to 350°F (325°F for dark-coated metal pan). Position a rack in the lower third of the oven. Spray the bottom only of an 8-inch-square baking pan with nonstick cooking spray (or foil-line pan; see page xxiv).

Combine the brownie mix, oil, water, and eggs in a medium mixing bowl with a wooden spoon until just blended and all dry ingredients are moistened; stir in ¾ cup of the chocolate chips. Spread batter into prepared pan.

Bake for 40–44 minutes or until toothpick inserted 2 inches from side of pan comes out clean or almost clean (do not overbake). During the last 10 minutes of baking, sprinkle the top with the pecans (so that they will toast). Remove from oven and immediately sprinkle with remaining chocolate chips. Transfer to a wire rack.

Melt the caramels with the milk in a medium saucepan set over low heat, until smooth. Drizzle caramel over brownies and cool completely. Cut into squares.

MAKES 9 LARGE OR 16 SMALL BROWNIES.

CHOCOLATE CARAMEL BROWNIES

A voluptuous combination of caramel and chocolate comprise these mouthwatering brownies. Share them—it's certain they will create countless new friendships and fond memories.

- 1 (18.25-ounce) package chocolate fudge cake mix
- 1 cup chopped pecans (or walnuts)
- 1 cup canned evaporated milk, divided
- ½ cup (1 stick) butter, melted
- 35 caramels, unwrapped
- 2 cups semisweet chocolate chips

Preheat oven to 350°F (or 325°F for dark-coated metal pan). Position oven rack in middle of oven. Spray the bottom only of a 13 x 9-inch metal baking pan with nonstick cooking spray (or foil-line pan; see page xxiv).

Place half the cake mix along with the nuts, ⅔ cup evaporated milk, and melted butter in a large bowl. Blend with electric mixer on medium speed for 1–2 minutes, until all dry ingredients are moistened and well blended (batter will be thick). Spread half of the batter into prepared pan. Bake for 10 minutes.

Meanwhile heat caramels and remaining evaporated milk in small saucepan over low heat, stirring constantly, until caramels are melted. Sprinkle chocolate chips over partially baked brownie; drizzle with caramel mixture. Drop remaining batter by heaping spoonfuls over caramel mixture.

Bake for 24–27 minutes or until center is set and firm to the touch. Transfer to wire rack and cool completely. Cut into bars.

MAKES 24 LARGE OR 36 SMALL BARS.

Variations:

SNICKERY-GOOD BROWNIES: Prepare as directed above but eliminate the caramel filling (the 35 caramels and the remaining ⅓ cup evaporated milk) and chocolate chips. Instead, sprinkle the partially baked crust with 6 coarsely chopped caramel nougat chocolate bars (e.g., Snickers); drop remaining batter by heaping spoonfuls over chocolate bars. Continue baking as directed above.

PEANUT-BUTTERSCOTCH LAYERED BROWNIES: Prepare as directed above but eliminate the caramel filling (the 35 caramels and the remaining ⅓ cup evaporated milk) and chocolate chips.

Instead, melt 1⅓ cups butterscotch baking chips with ½ cup creamy peanut butter in a saucepan set over low heat. Spoon and spread mixture over the partially baked crust; drop remaining batter by heaping spoonfuls over butterscotch layer. Continue baking as directed above.

CHOCOLATE-CHIP COOKIE BULL'S-EYE BROWNIES

If you're one of those home cooks who is always looking for the "next new thing," place your bookmark here. What's more, these brownies are simple to make since the chocolate-chip "bull's-eyes" are made with refrigerated cookie dough. Whether for a picnic, pitch-in, or your own enjoyment, these chocolate-chip-cookie-bolstered brownies are both excitingly modern and reassuringly conventional.

- 1 (19.5- to 19.8-ounce) package brownie mix
- ½ cup vegetable oil
- ¼ cup water
- 3 large eggs
- 1 cup semisweet chocolate chips
- 1 (16.5-ounce) package refrigerated chocolate-chip cookie dough
- 28 chocolate "kiss" or white chocolate striped "hugs" candies, unwrapped

Preheat oven to 350°F (325°F for dark-coated metal pan). Position a rack in the lower third of the oven. Spray the bottom only of a 13 x 9-inch baking pan with nonstick cooking spray (or foil-line pan; see page xxiv).

Combine the brownie mix, oil, water, and eggs in a medium mixing bowl with a wooden spoon until just blended and all dry ingredients are moistened; stir in chocolate chips. Spread batter into prepared pan.

Cut cookie dough in half, then in half again (for 4 equal pieces). Cut each quarter of dough into 7 pieces. Roll each piece into a ball, then flatten slightly. Evenly space pieces atop brownie layer in rows (4 across, 7 down).

Bake for 28–30 minutes or until just set. Remove from oven and immediately press a chocolate kiss into each cookie mound. Transfer to a wire rack and cool completely. Cut into squares with one "bull's-eye" in the center of each brownie.

MAKES 28 LARGE BROWNIES.

CHOCOLATE-CHIP COOKIE DOUGH BROWNIES

These cookie dough–filled brownies effortlessly pass the "devour in the middle of the night" test. Be careful not to overbake—the cookie dough should maintain a slight ooey-gooey quality when the brownies are done.

- 1 (19.5-ounce) package brownie mix
- 2 large eggs
- ¼ cup water
- ½ cup vegetable oil
- 1 (16.5-ounce) roll refrigerated chocolate-chip cookie dough, well chilled

■ 1 recipe Dark Chocolate Frosting, see page 367, optional

Preheat oven to 350°F. Spray a 13 x 9-inch pan with nonstick cooking spray or line with foil.

Combine brownie mix, eggs, water, and oil in a medium mixing bowl with a wooden spoon until well blended. Spread batter into the prepared pan.

Break up the cookie dough into walnut-size pieces; drop evenly onto brownie batter, pressing down lightly.

Bake for 37–40 minutes or until a toothpick inserted 2 inches from side of pan comes out almost clean. Cool completely. If desired, spread with Dark Chocolate Frosting.

MAKES 48 BROWNIES.

CHOCOLATE-COVERED CHERRY BROWNIES

These brownies remind me of a hard-to-find candy bar from my childhood known as a "mountain bar." It came in several flavors but my favorite was the cherry version, which had a crispy chocolate exterior and a cherry and almond-flavored cream filling. But as good as these candy-shop-inspired brownies are, I guarantee they're even better warm, topped with vanilla ice cream.

■ 2 (6-ounce) jars maraschino cherries without stems, drained, liquid reserved
■ 1 (19.5- to 19.8-ounce) package brownie mix
■ 10 tablespoons (1¼ sticks) unsalted butter, melted, divided

■ 2 large eggs
■ ½ teaspoon almond extract
■ 1½ cups semisweet chocolate chips
■ 1½ cups sifted powdered sugar

Preheat oven to 350°F (325°F for dark-coated metal pan). Position a rack in the lower third of the oven. Spray the bottom only of a 13 x 9-inch baking pan with nonstick cooking spray (or foil-line pan; see page xxiv).

Coarsely chop maraschino cherries; set aside.

Combine the brownie mix, 8 tablespoons (1 stick) butter, ¼ cup reserved cherry liquid, eggs, and almond extract in a medium mixing bowl with a wooden spoon until just blended and all dry ingredients are moistened; stir in cherries and chocolate chips. Spread batter into prepared pan.

Bake for 28–30 minutes or until toothpick inserted 2 inches from side of pan comes out clean or almost clean (do not overbake). Transfer to a wire rack and cool completely.

Combine powdered sugar, remaining melted butter and 2 teaspoons reserved cherry liquid in small mixing bowl; stir. Add enough additional reserved cherry liquid, if needed, to make glazing consistency. Spread over brownies. Cut into squares.

MAKES 24 LARGE OR 36 SMALL BROWNIES.

CHOCOLATE CREAM CHEESE CHOCOLATE-CHIP BROWNIES

Old-fashioned brownies get a triple dose of chocolate in this very easy but very delicious recipe. In case you have any doubts, these are a huge hit with kids.

- 1 (19.5- to 19.8-ounce) package brownie mix
- ½ cup vegetable oil
- ¼ cup water
- 2 large eggs
- 1½ cups miniature semisweet chocolate chips, divided
- 1 recipe Chocolate Cream Cheese Frosting (see page 361)

Preheat oven to 350°F (325°F for dark-coated metal pan). Position a rack in the lower third of the oven. Spray the bottom only of an 8-inch-square baking pan with nonstick cooking spray (or foil-line pan; see page xxiv).

Combine the brownie mix, oil, water, and eggs in a medium mixing bowl with a wooden spoon until just blended and all dry ingredients are moistened; stir in 1 cup of the miniature chocolate chips. Spread batter into prepared pan.

Bake for 40–44 minutes or until toothpick inserted 2 inches from side of pan comes out clean or almost clean (do not overbake). Transfer to a wire rack and cool completely.

Prepare the chocolate cream cheese frosting. Frost brownies with frosting and sprinkle with remaining chocolate chips. Cut into squares. Store in refrigerator.

MAKES 9 LARGE OR 16 SMALL BROWNIES.

CHOCOLATE-GLAZED MINT-FROSTED BROWNIES

Much to my joy, my mother made a version of these layered brownies every Christmas of my childhood. Using brownie mix streamlines her recipe for these festive cookies that are lovely for the winter holidays but also welcome year-round.

- 1 (19.5- to 19.8-ounce) package brownie mix
- ½ cup vegetable oil
- ¼ cup water
- 2 large eggs
- ½ teaspoon peppermint extract
- 1 cup semisweet chocolate chips
- 1 recipe Mint Frosting (see page 374)
- 1 recipe Shiny Chocolate Glaze (see page 374)

Preheat oven to 350°F (325°F for dark-coated metal pan). Position a rack in the lower third of the oven. Spray the bottom only of a 13 x 9-inch baking pan with nonstick cooking spray (or foil-line pan; see page xxiv).

Combine the brownie mix, oil, water, eggs, and peppermint extract in a medium mixing bowl with a wooden spoon until just blended and all dry ingredients are moistened. Stir in the chocolate chips. Spread batter into prepared pan.

Bake 28–30 minutes or until toothpick inserted 2 inches from side of pan comes out clean or almost clean (do not overbake). Transfer to a wire rack and cool completely.

Prepare Mint Frosting. Spread frosting over cooled brownies.

Prepare Shiny Chocolate Glaze; drizzle over frosting. Refrigerate for 1 hour to set the glaze. Cut into squares. Store in refrigerator.

MAKES 24 LARGE OR 36 SMALL BROWNIES.

CLASSIC BROWNIES

Few eating pleasures are greater than biting into a warm, chewy, chocolate brownie. There may be many brownie recipes around, but this classic version is a winner, on its own or doctored with any number of stir-ins. You can also up the flavor ante by making them with buttermilk and melted butter in place of water and vegetable oil. To create your own original brownie, consider stirring in one or two of the stir-in options listed here or adding a special frosting or glaze from the "Icings, Frostings, Fillings, and Extras" chapter.

- 1 (19.5- to 19.8-ounce) package brownie mix
- ½ cup vegetable oil or 1 stick (½ cup) unsalted butter, melted
- ¼ cup water or buttermilk
- 2 large eggs
- 1–2 stir-ins, optional
- Any of the frostings or glazes listed in the Icings, Frostings, Fillings, and Extras chapter, optional

Preheat oven to 350°F (325°F for dark-coated metal pan). Position a rack in the lower third of the oven. Spray the bottom only of an 8-inch-square baking pan with nonstick cooking spray (or foil-line pan; see page xxiv).

Combine the brownie mix, oil (or butter), water (or buttermilk), and eggs in a medium mixing bowl with a wooden spoon until just blended and all dry ingredients are moistened. Spread batter into prepared pan.

Bake for 40–44 minutes or until toothpick inserted 2 inches from side of pan comes out clean or almost clean (do not overbake). Transfer to a wire rack and cool completely. Cut into squares.

Stir-Ins:

Stir in 1 cup of any one of the following options into prepared brownie batter and bake as directed. If adding two stir-ins (e.g., chocolate chips and nuts), decrease the quantity to ½ cup for each stir-in.

BAKING CHIPS AND BITS: Chocolate chips (e.g., semisweet, milk, or white chocolate chips) or other baking chips (e.g., butterscotch, peanut butter, or cinnamon baking chips or English toffee baking bits).

NUTS: Chopped nuts (e.g., pecans, walnuts, almonds, hazelnuts, roasted peanuts, roasted cashews, lightly salted mixed nuts, roasted Brazil nuts, macadamia nuts, or pistachios).

FRUIT AND COCONUT: Coconut or dried fruit (e.g., shredded coconut (sweetened or unsweetened), cranberries, raisins (regular or golden), currants, dried cherries, dried cranberries, chopped dried apricots, dried tropical fruit bits, or chopped banana chips).

MAKES 9 LARGE OR 16 SMALL BROWNIES.

Variation:
CAKE-STYLE BROWNIES: Increase number of eggs to three. Prepare, bake, cool, and cut as directed above.

Baker's Note

9-inch square pan: Prepare as directed above but bake for 38–42 minutes.
13 x 9-inch pan: Prepare as directed above but bake for 28–30 minutes.
9-inch springform pan: Prepare as directed above but bake for 38–42 minutes.

COOKIES 'N' CREAM BROWNIES

This is one of my favorite brownies, at once familiar and newfangled. And if I don't make a batch of them at least once a month, one of my colleagues won't speak to me.

- 1 (19.5- to 19.8-ounce) package brownie mix
- ½ cup vegetable oil
- ¼ cup water
- 2 large eggs
- 3 cups coarsely crushed creme-filled chocolate sandwich cookies, divided
- 1 recipe Cream Cheese Frosting (see page 366)

Preheat oven to 350°F (325°F for dark-coated metal pan). Position a rack in the lower third of the oven. Spray the bottom only of a 13 x 9-inch baking pan with nonstick cooking spray (or foil-line pan; see page xxiv).

Combine the brownie mix, oil, water, and eggs in a medium mixing bowl with a wooden spoon until just blended and all dry ingredients are moistened; stir in 1½ cups cookie crumbs. Spread batter into prepared pan.

Bake for 28–30 minutes or until toothpick inserted 2 inches from side of pan comes out clean or almost clean (do not overbake). Transfer to a wire rack and cool completely.

Prepare Cream Cheese Frosting. Spread brownies with frosting and sprinkle with remaining cookie crumbs. Cut into squares. Store in refrigerator.

MAKES 24 LARGE OR 36 SMALL BROWNIES.

CRAGGY-TOPPED TOFFEE FUDGE BROWNIES

Anything goes with these over-the-(craggy) top brownies. You can, with terrific success, use any variety of chips (e.g., white chocolate, milk chocolate, cinnamon, butterscotch) in place of the semisweet chocolate chips and change out the almonds for your favorite nut—you'll still get a craggy-topped brownie!

- 1 (19.5- to 19.8-ounce) package brownie mix
- ½ cup vegetable oil
- ¼ cup water
- 2 large eggs
- 2 cups semisweet chocolate chips, divided
- 2 cups coarsely chopped almonds
- 4 (1.4-ounce) milk chocolate–covered toffee candy bars, very coarsely chopped

Preheat oven to 350°F (325°F for dark-coated metal pan). Position a rack in the lower third of the oven. Spray the bottom only of a 13 x 9-inch baking pan with nonstick cooking spray (or foil-line pan; see page xxiv).

Combine the brownie mix, oil, water, and eggs in a medium mixing bowl with a wooden spoon until just blended and all dry ingredients are moistened; stir in 1 cup chocolate chips. Spread batter into prepared pan; evenly sprinkle with the almonds.

Bake for 28–30 minutes or until toothpick inserted 2 inches from side of pan comes out clean or almost clean (do not overbake).

Transfer to a wire rack and immediately sprinkle with remaining chocolate chips and chopped candy bars while brownies are still hot. Cover with a cookie sheet for 5 minutes. Remove cookie sheet and cool completely. Refrigerate for 1 hour to set the chocolate. Cut into squares.

MAKES 24 LARGE OR 36 SMALL BROWNIES.

CRANBERRY BROWNIES WITH CRANBERRY GANACHE TOPPING

Cloaked with a layer of chocolate-cranberry ganache, these moist, cranberry-packed brownies are a harmonious marriage of sweet and tart flavors. Although I wouldn't pass on the ganache layer myself, I will readily admit that these are every bit as good without it.

- 1 (19.5- to 19.8-ounce) package brownie mix
- ½ cup vegetable oil
- ¼ cup freshly squeezed orange juice
- 2 teaspoons grated orange zest
- 2 large eggs
- 1¼ cups dried cranberries
- 1 cup semisweet chocolate chips
- ¼ cup heavy whipping cream
- ¼ cup canned jelly cranberry sauce

Preheat oven to 350°F (325°F for dark-coated metal pan). Position a rack in the lower third of the oven. Spray the bottom only of an 8-inch-square baking pan with nonstick cooking spray (or foil-line pan; see page xxiv).

Combine the brownie mix, oil, orange juice, orange zest, and eggs in a medium mixing bowl with a wooden spoon until just blended and all dry ingredients are moistened; stir in the cranberries. Spread batter into prepared pan.

Bake for 40–44 minutes or until toothpick inserted 2 inches from side of pan comes out clean or almost clean (do not overbake). Transfer to a wire rack and cool completely.

In a medium saucepan melt the chocolate chips, heavy cream, and cranberry sauce over low heat, stirring until melted and smooth. Remove from heat and let cool for 5 minutes. Spread over cooled brownies. Let stand in refrigerator for 1 hour to set chocolate. Cut into squares.

MAKES 9 LARGE OR 16 SMALL BROWNIES.

CREAM CHEESE SWIRLED BROWNIES

Take note: the aroma of these luscious brownies baking will quickly lure family and friends to the kitchen. The marbled effect looks elaborate but is in fact simple to accomplish with a few swirls of a kitchen knife. Don't worry about making perfect swirls—"mistakes" look every bit as beautiful. Warm cocoa is the beverage of choice here.

- 1 (19.5- to 19.8-ounce) package brownie mix
- ½ cup vegetable oil
- ¼ cup water
- 3 large eggs
- 1 (8-ounce) package cream cheese, softened
- 3 tablespoons sugar

■ 2 teaspoons all-purpose flour
■ 1 teaspoon vanilla extract

Preheat oven to 350°F (325°F for dark-coated metal pan). Position a rack in the lower third of the oven. Spray the bottom only of a 13 x 9-inch baking pan with nonstick cooking spray (or foil-line pan; see page xxiv).

Combine the brownie mix, oil, water, and 2 eggs in a medium mixing bowl with a wooden spoon until just blended and all dry ingredients are moistened. Spread all but about ½ cup of the batter into prepared pan.

Beat the cream cheese in a medium mixing bowl with an electric mixer set on medium until smooth. Beat in the sugar, flour, vanilla, and remaining egg until well blended and smooth.

Spoon the cream cheese mixture over brownie batter in pan; dollop remaining brownie batter over the spoonfuls of cream cheese batter. Swirl the batters with the tip of a knife to create a marbled design.

Bake for 28–30 minutes or until toothpick inserted in brownie 2 inches from side of pan comes out clean or almost clean (do not overbake). Transfer to a wire rack and cool completely. Cut into squares. Store in refrigerator.

MAKES 24 LARGE OR 36 SMALL BROWNIES.

DAD'S DOUBLE PEANUT BUTTER FROSTED BROWNIES

Oh, that peanut butter/chocolate combination—who can resist? Not me, and certainly not my peanut-butter-loving dad.

To push the envelope, consider sprinkling the frosted brownies with some coarsely chopped peanut butter cups.

■ 1 (19.5- to 19.8-ounce) package brownie mix
■ ½ cup vegetable oil
■ ¼ cup water
■ 4 large eggs
■ ⅓ cup packed brown sugar
■ ⅓ cup creamy peanut butter
■ 1 recipe Peanut Butter Frosting (see page 374)

Preheat oven to 350°F (325°F for dark-coated metal pan). Position a rack in the lower third of the oven. Spray the bottom only of a 13 x 9-inch baking pan with nonstick cooking spray (or foil-line pan; see page xxiv).

Combine the brownie mix, oil, water, and 3 of the eggs in a medium mixing bowl with a wooden spoon until just blended and all dry ingredients are moistened. Spread batter into prepared pan.

Mix brown sugar, peanut butter, and remaining egg in a small mixing bowl until blended. Drop by tablespoonfuls onto batter. Cut through batter several times with the tip of a knife to create a marble effect.

Bake for 32–35 minutes or until toothpick inserted 2 inches from side of pan comes out clean or almost clean (do not overbake). Transfer to a wire rack and cool completely.

Prepare Peanut Butter Frosting. Spread frosting over cooled brownies. Cut into squares.

MAKES 24 LARGE OR 36 SMALL BROWNIES.

DARK CHOCOLATE GINGERBREAD BROWNIES

over warm brownies; cool completely. Cut into squares.

MAKES 9 LARGE OR 16 SMALL BROWNIES.

Rich with redolent spices, these brownies are a perfect autumn day detour or departure from the daily grind.

- 1 (19.5- to 19.8-ounce) package brownie mix
- 2 teaspoons ground ginger
- ¾ teaspoon ground cinnamon
- ½ teaspoon ground nutmeg
- ¼ teaspoon ground cloves
- ½ cup (1 stick) unsalted butter, melted
- ¼ cup dark molasses
- 3 large eggs
- 2 teaspoons vanilla extract
- 4 (1-ounce) squares bittersweet chocolate, coarsely chopped
- 1 recipe Vanilla-Butter Glaze (see page 376)

Preheat oven to 350°F (325°F for dark-coated metal pan). Position a rack in the lower third of the oven. Spray the bottom only of an 8-inch-square baking pan with nonstick cooking spray (or foil-line pan; see page xxiv).

Toss brownie mix with the ginger, cinnamon, nutmeg, and cloves in a medium mixing bowl. Add the butter, molasses, eggs, and vanilla and mix with a wooden spoon until just blended and all dry ingredients are moistened; stir in chopped chocolate. Spread batter into prepared pan.

Bake for 40–44 minutes or until toothpick inserted 2 inches from side of pan comes out clean or almost clean (do not overbake). Transfer to a wire rack.

Prepare Vanilla-Butter Glaze. Spread glaze

DOUBLE CHOCOLATE BROWNIES

Who knew that five ingredients and five minutes of prep time could lead to such chocolate pleasure? Be sure to add another 15 seconds to pour a glass of cold milk. Superb plain, they can be gussied up in numerous ways, as the variations below indicate.

- 1 (18.25-ounce) package chocolate cake mix
- ⅓ cup butter, melted
- 2 large eggs
- 2 teaspoons vanilla extract
- 1 cup semisweet chocolate chips

Preheat oven to 350°F (or 325°F for dark-coated metal pan). Position oven rack in middle of oven. Spray the bottom only of a 13 x 9-inch metal baking pan with nonstick cooking spray (or foil-line pan; see page xxiv).

Combine half of the cake mix along with the butter, eggs, and vanilla extract in a large bowl with an electric mixer set on medium-high speed for 1–2 minutes, until well blended and smooth. Stir in remaining cake mix and chocolate chips with a wooden spoon until all dry ingredients are moistened and well blended (mixture will be thick). Press dough into prepared pan.

Bake for 22–25 minutes or until just set at edges. Transfer to wire rack and cool completely. Cut into bars.

MAKES 24 LARGE OR 36 SMALL BARS.

Variations:

ESPRESSO GANACHE BROWNIES:

Prepare as directed above but eliminate semisweet chocolate chips and add 1 tablespoon instant espresso or coffee powder to batter. After baking, spread completely cooled brownies with Chocolate Ganache (see page 362).

WALNUT FUDGE BROWNIES: Prepare as directed above but eliminate semisweet chocolate chips and add 1 cup chopped walnuts to batter. After baking, spread completely cooled brownies with Chocolate Fudge Frosting (see page 362).

WHITE CHOCOLATE CANDY CANE

BROWNIES: Prepare as directed above but eliminate semisweet chocolate chips. Transfer baked brownies to wire rack and immediately sprinkle with 2 cups white chocolate chips; let stand 5 minutes until softened but not melted. Using a table knife, spread the white chocolate evenly over brownies; immediately sprinkle with 2/3 cup crushed peppermint candy canes or striped peppermint candies.

EASY MISSISSIPPI MUD BROWNIES

Some families believe that blood is thicker than water; others believe chocolate is, and that their shared bond is an intrinsic love of the dark, delicious stuff. This recipe is just the thing for strengthening such familial bonds. Positively sumptuous, these brownies are also a breeze to put together, making them great for last-minute chocolate cravings.

- 1 (19.5- to 19.8-ounce) package brownie mix
- ½ cup vegetable oil
- ¼ cup water
- 2 large eggs
- 1 (7-ounce) jar marshmallow creme
- 1¼ cups ready-to-spread milk chocolate frosting

Preheat oven to 350°F (325°F for dark-coated metal pan). Position a rack in the lower third of the oven. Spray the bottom only of a 13 x 9-inch baking pan with nonstick cooking spray (or foil-line pan; see page xxiv).

Combine the brownie mix, oil, water, and eggs in a medium mixing bowl with a wooden spoon until just blended and all dry ingredients are moistened. Spread batter into prepared pan.

Bake for 28–30 minutes or until toothpick inserted 2 inches from side of pan comes out clean or almost clean (do not overbake). Transfer to a wire rack. Dollop marshmallow creme evenly over hot brownies; gently spread with knife.

Place frosting in small saucepan set over low heat; heat until melted, about 2 minutes, stirring until smooth. Pour frosting over marshmallow creme. Swirl with knife to marbleize. Cool completely. Cut into squares.

MAKES 24 LARGE OR 36 SMALL BROWNIES.

FUDGE-FROSTED WALNUT BROWNIES

Just about every coffeehouse has a version of these classic brownies. Elegant in their simplicity of flavors, they are dressy enough to close out a posh supper party or give as a special gift. To intensify the flavor of the walnuts, lightly toast and cool them before adding to the brownie batter—it's well worth the extra step.

- 1 (19.5- to 19.8-ounce) package brownie mix
- ½ cup (1 stick) unsalted butter, melted
- ¼ cup buttermilk
- 2 large eggs
- 1 teaspoon vanilla extract
- ¼ teaspoon almond extract
- 1 cup coarsely chopped walnuts, preferably lightly toasted
- 1 recipe Chocolate Fudge Frosting (see page 362)

Preheat oven to 350°F (325°F for dark-coated metal pan). Position a rack in the lower third of the oven. Spray the bottom only of an 8-inch-square baking pan with nonstick cooking spray (or foil-line pan; see page xxiv).

Combine the brownie mix, butter, buttermilk, eggs, vanilla extract, and almond extract in a medium mixing bowl with a wooden spoon until just blended and all dry ingredients are moistened; stir in the walnuts. Spread batter into prepared pan.

Bake for 40–44 minutes or until toothpick inserted 2 inches from side of pan comes out clean or almost clean (do not overbake). Transfer to a wire rack and cool completely.

Prepare Chocolate Fudge Frosting. Spread frosting over cooled brownies. Cut into squares.

MAKES 9 LARGE OR 16 SMALL BROWNIES.

GIANDUIA BROWNIES (ITALIAN CHOCOLATE HAZELNUT BROWNIES)

The Italian combination of chocolate and hazelnuts, called gianduia, is used here to create a dense, sumptuous brownie. You can typically find chocolate hazelnut spread (Nutella is the most common brand) in one of two places in the supermarket: in the peanut butter section or in the international foods section.

- 1 (19.5- to 19.8-ounce) package brownie mix
- ½ cup (1 stick) unsalted butter, melted
- ¼ cup water
- 2 large eggs
- 1 (13-ounce) jar chocolate-hazelnut spread (e.g., Nutella), divided
- 2 tablespoons all-purpose flour
- 1 large egg yolk
- 1 cup coarsely chopped, lightly toasted hazelnuts, optional

Preheat oven to 350°F (325°F for dark-coated metal pan). Position a rack in the lower third of the oven. Spray the bottom only of an 8-inch-square baking pan with nonstick cooking spray (or foil-line pan; see page xxiv).

Combine the brownie mix, melted butter, water, and eggs in a medium mixing bowl with a wooden spoon until just blended and all dry ingredients are moistened. Spread batter into prepared pan.

Mix 1/3 cup chocolate-hazelnut spread, flour, and the egg yolk in a small mixing bowl until blended. Drop by spoonfuls onto batter. Cut through batter several times with tip of a knife for a marbled effect.

Bake for 40–44 minutes or until toothpick inserted 2 inches from side of pan comes out clean or almost clean (do not overbake). Transfer to a wire rack and cool completely.

Spread cooled brownies with remaining hazelnut spread and, if desired, sprinkle with chopped hazelnuts. Cut into squares.

MAKES 9 LARGE OR 16 SMALL BROWNIES.

Baker's Note

To skin hazelnuts, boil 3 cups of water; add 1/4 cup baking soda and then the hazelnuts. Boil for 3 minutes; drain and rinse. Under running water pinch off the hazelnut skins. Dry completely. Toast at 350°F for 10–15 minutes.

GOOEY BABY RUTHY BROWNIES

Few sentences are more welcoming when crossing the threshold of home than "there's a batch of brownies just out of the oven." Why not intensify the pleasure and excitement by adding " ...and they're loaded with chunks of gooey Baby Ruthy bars!"

- 1 (19.5- to 19.8-ounce) package brownie mix
- ½ cup vegetable oil
- ¼ cup water
- 3 large eggs
- 3 (2.1-ounce) chocolate covered peanut-nougat candy bars (e.g., Baby Ruth or Snickers), coarsely chopped
- 1 (8-ounce) package cream cheese, softened
- 3 tablespoons packed brown sugar
- 2 teaspoons milk

Preheat oven to 350°F (325°F for dark-coated metal pan). Position a rack in the lower third of the oven. Spray the bottom only of a 13 x 9-inch baking pan with nonstick cooking spray (or foil-line pan; see page xxiv).

In a medium mixing bowl mix the brownie mix, oil, water, and 2 of the eggs with a wooden spoon until just blended and all dry ingredients are moistened. Stir in chopped candy bars. Reserve 1 cup of the batter. Spread remaining batter into prepared pan.

Beat the cream cheese and brown sugar in a medium mixing bowl with an electric mixer set on medium until smooth. Beat in milk and remaining egg. Spoon and spread over brownie batter in pan (need not cover completely). Dollop reserved brownie batter over cream cheese layer. Use the tip of a knife to swirl the batters for a marbled effect.

Bake for 30–35 minutes or until toothpick inserted 2 inches from side of pan comes out clean or almost clean (do not overbake). Transfer to a wire rack and cool completely. Cut into squares. Store in refrigerator.

MAKES 24 LARGE OR 36 SMALL BROWNIES.

JIM AND ANNA'S DARK RUM BROWNIES

My friends Jim and Anna Lynch are two of the most generous people I have ever known. Lucky for me, they are always happy to be thanked with chocolate. They both came close to swooning when they tasted these brownies which, fittingly, are extremely generous in both chocolate and rum.

- 1 (19.5- to 19.8-ounce) package brownie mix
- ½ cup (1 stick) unsalted butter, melted
- ¼ cup dark rum
- 2 large eggs
- ¼ teaspoon ground nutmeg
- 4 (1-ounce) squares bittersweet chocolate, coarsely chopped
- 1 recipe Chocolate Rum Glaze (see page 363)

Preheat oven to 350°F (325°F for dark-coated metal pan). Position a rack in the lower third of the oven. Spray the bottom only of an 8-inch-square baking pan with nonstick cooking spray (or foil-line pan; see page xxiv).

Combine the brownie mix, butter, dark rum, eggs, and nutmeg in a medium mixing bowl with a wooden spoon until just blended and all dry ingredients are moistened; stir in chopped chocolate. Spread batter into prepared pan.

Bake for 40–44 minutes or until toothpick inserted 2 inches from side of pan comes out clean or almost clean (do not overbake). Transfer to a wire rack and cool for 15 minutes.

Prepare Chocolate Rum Glaze. Spread glaze over warm brownies; cool completely. Cut into squares.

MAKES 9 LARGE OR 16 SMALL BROWNIES.

JULIE'S CINNAMON BUTTERMILK BROWNIES

I had my friend Julie Artis—a terrific cook, great scholar, and die-hard cinnamon lover—in mind when I developed these cinnamon-scented treats. The cinnamon chips are an easy way to intensify the cinnamon flavor—look for them in the baking aisle alongside chocolate chips. If you cannot find them, leave them out or substitute semisweet chocolate chips in their place for double the chocolate goodness. And if you don't have buttermilk, plain yogurt may be substituted. Be sure to serve these brownies alongside your favorite hot drink for the epitome of cozy.

- 1 (19.5- to 19.8-ounce) package brownie mix
- ½ cup (1 stick) unsalted butter, melted
- ¼ cup buttermilk
- 2 large eggs
- 1 teaspoon ground cinnamon
- 1 cup cinnamon baking chips

Preheat oven to 350°F (325°F for dark-coated metal pan). Position a rack in the lower third of the oven. Spray the bottom only of an 8-inch-square baking pan with nonstick cooking spray (or foil-line pan; see page xxiv).

Combine the brownie mix, melted butter, buttermilk, eggs, and cinnamon in a medium mixing bowl with a wooden spoon until just blended and all dry ingredients are moistened; stir in cinnamon chips. Spread batter into prepared pan.

Bake for 40–44 minutes or until toothpick inserted 2 inches from side of pan comes out clean or almost clean (do not overbake). Transfer to a wire rack and cool completely. Cut into squares.

MAKES 9 LARGE OR 16 SMALL BROWNIES.

MACADAMIA AND WHITE CHOCOLATE CHUNK BROWNIES

Few can resist these brownies, not that anyone I know has ever tried. Studded with chunks of white chocolate and macadamia nuts, they were inspired by a nearly identical brownie at one of my favorite local coffeehouses.

- 1 (19.5- to 19.8-ounce) package brownie mix
- ½ cup vegetable oil
- ¼ cup water
- 2 large eggs
- 1 cup coarsely chopped macadamia nuts
- 1 (6-ounce) white chocolate baking bar, coarsely chopped into chunks, divided
- 2 teaspoons vegetable shortening

Preheat oven to 350°F (325°F for dark-coated metal pan). Position a rack in the lower third of the oven. Spray the bottom only of an 8-inch-square baking pan with nonstick cooking spray (or foil-line pan; see page xxiv).

Combine the brownie mix, oil, water, and eggs in a medium mixing bowl with a wooden spoon until just blended and all dry ingredients are moistened; stir in the macadamia nuts and two-thirds of the white chocolate chunks. Spread batter into prepared pan.

Bake for 40–44 minutes or until toothpick inserted 2 inches from side of pan comes out clean or almost clean (do not overbake). Transfer to a wire rack and cool completely.

Place remaining white chocolate and shortening in small saucepan set over low heat; stir until melted and smooth. Drizzle melted chocolate over brownies. Refrigerate for at least 1 hour until chocolate is set. Cut into squares.

MAKES 9 LARGE OR 16 SMALL BROWNIES.

MAPLE-FROSTED BROWNIES

You may not have known before now that chocolate and maple make a perfect match. These brownies are indisputable proof. Look for maple flavoring where vanilla extract is sold in the baking section of your supermarket.

- 1 (19.5- to 19.8-ounce) package brownie mix
- ½ cup vegetable oil
- ¼ cup water
- 2 large eggs
- 2 teaspoons maple-flavored extract
- 1 cup coarsely chopped walnuts, preferably lightly toasted
- 1 recipe Maple Frosting (see page 369)

Preheat oven to 350°F (325°F for dark-coated metal pan). Position a rack in the lower third of the oven. Spray the bottom only of an 8-inch-square baking pan with nonstick cooking spray (or foil-line pan; see page xxiv).

Combine the brownie mix, oil, water, eggs, and maple extract in a medium mixing bowl with a wooden spoon until just blended and all dry ingredients are moistened; stir in chopped walnuts. Spread batter into prepared pan.

Bake for 40–44 minutes or until toothpick inserted 2 inches from side of pan comes out clean or almost clean (do not overbake). Transfer to a wire rack and cool completely.

Prepare Maple Frosting. Spread over cooled brownies. Cut into squares. Store in refrigerator.

MAKES 9 LARGE OR 16 SMALL BROWNIES.

MILK CHOCOLATE BUTTERMILK BROWNIES

Rich, moist, and sweet with chocolate, these buttermilk-enhanced, milk-chocolate-frosted brownies are a quick and easy path to chocolate heaven.

- 1 (19.5- to 19.8-ounce) package brownie mix
- ½ cup (1 stick) unsalted butter, melted
- ¼ cup buttermilk
- 3 large eggs
- 1½ teaspoons vanilla extract
- 1½ cups milk chocolate chips, divided
- 2 teaspoons vegetable shortening

Preheat oven to 350°F (325°F for dark-coated metal pan). Position a rack in the lower third of the oven. Spray the bottom only of an 8-inch-

square baking pan with nonstick cooking spray (or foil-line pan; see page xxiv).

Combine the brownie mix, melted butter, buttermilk, eggs, and vanilla in a medium mixing bowl with a wooden spoon until just blended and all dry ingredients are moistened; stir in 1 cup of the chocolate chips. Spread batter into prepared pan.

Bake for 40–44 minutes or until toothpick inserted 2 inches from side of pan comes out clean or almost clean (do not overbake). Transfer to a wire rack and cool completely.

Melt the remaining ½ cup chocolate chips with the shortening until smooth in a small saucepan set over low heat; drizzle over brownies. Refrigerate for 1 hour to set the chocolate. Cut into squares.

MAKES 9 LARGE OR 16 SMALL BROWNIES.

MILK CHOCOLATE MALT BROWNIES

If any brownie can make you feel like a kid again, this is it. It's bound to become a favorite. When baked in the brownies, the malt balls add both old-fashioned flavor and richness.

- 1 (19.5- to 19.8-ounce) package brownie mix
- ½ cup vegetable oil
- ¼ cup water
- 3 large eggs
- 2 cups malted milk balls, coarsely chopped
- 1 cup milk chocolate chips
- 1 tablespoon vegetable shortening

Preheat oven to 350°F (325°F for dark-coated metal pan). Position a rack in the lower third of the oven. Spray the bottom only of a 13 x 9-inch baking pan with nonstick cooking spray (or foil-line pan; see page xxiv).

Combine the brownie mix, oil, water, and eggs in a medium mixing bowl with a wooden spoon until just blended and all dry ingredients are moistened. Spread batter into prepared pan; sprinkle with malted milk balls.

Bake for 28–30 minutes or until toothpick inserted 2 inches from side of pan comes out clean or almost clean (do not overbake). Transfer to a wire rack.

Melt chocolate chips and shortening in a small saucepan set over low heat, until smooth, stirring. Drizzle over topping; cool completely. Refrigerate for about 10 minutes or until chocolate is firm. Cut into squares.

MAKES 24 LARGE OR 36 SMALL BROWNIES.

MINT JULEP GANACHE BROWNIES

Some people (like me) want too much of a good thing. This recipe suits such types by combining just enough of several extremely good things to produce an elegant but still easy-to-assemble brownie inspired by the Kentucky Derby drink of choice. You can use this recipe as a template for other liqueur ganache brownies: simply leave out the peppermint extract and substitute the liqueur or spirit of your choice in place of the bourbon.

■ 1 (19.5- to 19.8-ounce) package brownie mix

■ 2 large eggs
■ 5 tablespoons bourbon or whiskey, divided
■ ½ cup (1 stick) unsalted butter, melted
■ 1 teaspoon peppermint extract
■ Topping:
■ 1 cup semisweet chocolate chips
■ ¼ cup heavy cream

Preheat oven to 350°F (325°F for dark-coated metal pan). Position a rack in the lower third of the oven. Spray the bottom only of an 8-inch-square baking pan with nonstick cooking spray (or foil-line pan; see page xxiv).

Combine the brownie mix, eggs, 4 table-spoons bourbon, melted butter, and peppermint extract in a medium mixing bowl with a wooden spoon until well blended. Spread batter into prepared pan.

Bake for 40–44 minutes or until toothpick inserted 2 inches from side of pan comes out clean or almost clean (do not overbake). Transfer to a wire rack and cool completely. Using a toothpick, poke holes all over the top of the brownies.

To make ganache topping, whisk the chocolate chips and heavy cream in a small saucepan set over medium-low heat until melted and smooth. Remove from heat and whisk in remaining bourbon.

Pour and spread evenly over brownies in pan. Refrigerate brownies until topping is set, about 2 hours (or as long as overnight). Cut brownies into squares. Store in refrigerator.

MAKES 9 LARGE OR 16 SMALL BROWNIES.

MOCHA BUTTERCREAM BROWNIES

Making brownies for a coffee-loving friend? Give them the special treatment by adding embellishments that show you care, namely a swath of smooth Mocha Buttercream. A few extra ingredients from the pantry and several strokes of the spoon are all it takes.

- 1 (19.5- to 19.8-ounce) package brownie mix
- ½ cup vegetable oil
- ¼ cup water
- 2 large eggs
- 1 tablespoon instant espresso or coffee powder
- ½ teaspoon ground cinnamon
- ¼ teaspoon ground cardamom (optional)
- 1 recipe Mocha Buttercream Frosting (see page 370)

Preheat oven to 350°F (325°F for dark-coated metal pan). Position a rack in the lower third of the oven. Spray the bottom only of an 8-inch-square baking pan with nonstick cooking spray (or foil-line pan; see page xxiv).

Combine the brownie mix, oil, water, eggs, espresso powder, cinnamon, and cardamom in a medium mixing bowl with a wooden spoon until just blended and all dry ingredients are moistened. Spread batter into prepared pan.

Bake for 40–44 minutes or until toothpick inserted 2 inches from side of pan comes out clean or almost clean (do not overbake). Transfer to a wire rack and cool completely.

Prepare Mocha Buttercream Frosting. Spread frosting over cooled brownies. Refrig-

erate for at least 1 hour or until frosting is set. Cut into squares. Store in refrigerator.

MAKES 9 LARGE OR 16 SMALL BROWNIES.

MONKEY BUSINESS BANANA BROWNIES

These easy, banana-enhanced brownies are just right for a week's worth of lunch bag goodies or after-school snacks. For a delicious dress-up, consider frosting these with either the Caramel or Milk Chocolate Frosting in the "Icings, Frostings, Fillings, and Extras" chapter, then sprinkle with chopped banana chips.

- 1 (19.5- to 19.8-ounce) package brownie mix
- ¾ cup mashed very ripe bananas (about 2 medium)
- 3 tablespoons vegetable oil
- 2 large eggs
- 1 cup milk chocolate chips
- 1 cup chopped walnuts or pecans

Preheat oven to 350°F (325°F for dark-coated metal pan). Position a rack in the lower third of the oven. Spray the bottom only of a 13 x 9-inch baking pan with nonstick cooking spray (or foil-line pan; see page xxiv).

Combine the brownie mix, mashed bananas, oil, and eggs in a medium mixing bowl with a wooden spoon until just blended and all dry ingredients are moistened. Spread batter into prepared pan; sprinkle with chocolate chips and nuts.

Bake for 28–30 minutes or until toothpick inserted 2 inches from side of pan comes out clean or almost clean (do not overbake). Transfer to a wire rack and cool completely. Cut into squares.

MAKES 24 LARGE OR 36 SMALL BROWNIES.

NO-BAKE BROWNIES

The simplicity of chocolate brownies is one of life's greatest (eating) pleasures. Here the well-loved confection takes shape in a quick and easy no-bake bar. You can doctor this brownie recipe to suit your taste in the same way you would regular brownies. For example, replace the vanilla with a different extract (e.g., peppermint, brandy, rum, orange, maple), use any nut of your choice, spice it up with cinnamon or a dash of red pepper, or a add a favorite purchased or homemade frosting.

- 2½ cups finely crushed chocolate graham cracker crumbs
- 2 cups miniature marshmallows
- 1 cup chopped walnuts or pecans, preferably skillet toasted and cooled (see page xviii)
- 1 cup semisweet chocolate chips
- 1 cup canned evaporated milk
- ½ cup light corn syrup
- ¼ teaspoon salt
- 1 tablespoon butter
- 1 tablespoon vanilla extract

Lightly spray a 9 x 9 x 2-inch baking pan with nonstick cooking spray; set aside.

Mix the crumbs, marshmallows, and nuts in a large bowl; set aside.

Combine the chocolate chips, evaporated milk, corn syrup, and salt in a medium saucepan.

Stir over low heat until chocolate is melted. Increase heat to medium; bring to a full boil. Boil for 10 minutes, stirring constantly. Remove from heat and stir in butter and vanilla until blended.

Immediately stir chocolate mixture into the crumb mixture, mixing until well blended. Spread evenly in prepared pan, pressing down and smoothing surface with a square of wax paper. Refrigerate until set, about 3 hours. Cut into 24 bars. Store in covered containers between layers of wax paper.

MAKES 24 BARS.

OATMEAL COOKIE-BOTTOMED BROWNIES

If there is a way to build on the brownie's old-fashioned, homey goodness, it's by fortifying its foundation with a brown sugar oatmeal base. Pour a glass of cold milk to complement the renovation.

- 2½ cups quick-cooking or old-fashioned oats
- ¾ cup all-purpose flour
- ¾ cup packed dark brown sugar
- ½ teaspoon baking soda
- ¾ cup (1½ sticks) butter, softened
- 1 (19.5- to 19.8-ounce) package brownie mix
- ½ cup vegetable oil
- ¼ cup water
- 2 large eggs
- 1 cup semisweet chocolate chips

Preheat oven to 350°F (325°F for dark-coated metal pan). Position a rack in the lower third of the oven. Spray the bottom only of a 13 x 9-inch baking pan with nonstick cooking spray (or foil-line pan; see page xxiv).

Combine oats, flour, brown sugar, and baking soda; mix in softened butter in a large mixing bowl with wooden spoon or electric mixer set on low until well blended. Reserve 1 cup of the oat mixture; press remaining oat mixture into prepared pan. Bake for 10 minutes; transfer to wire rack and cool for 5 minutes (leave oven on).

Combine the brownie mix, oil, water and eggs in a medium mixing bowl with a wooden spoon until just blended and all dry ingredients are moistened; stir in chocolate chips. Spread batter over partially baked crust; sprinkle with reserved oat mixture.

Bake for 30–35 minutes or until toothpick inserted 2 inches from side of pan comes out clean or almost clean (do not overbake). Transfer brownies to a wire rack and cool completely. Cut into squares.

MAKES 24 LARGE OR 36 SMALL BROWNIES.

OH-SO-ORANGE BROWNIES

A refreshing change of pace from traditional brownies, this recipe features the full flavor of orange throughout. Make sure to choose a relatively thin-skinned navel orange for best flavor.

- 1 large navel orange
- 1 (19.5- to 19.8-ounce) package brownie mix
- ½ cup oil
- 2 large eggs

Preheat oven to 350°F (325°F for dark-coated metal pan). Position a rack in the lower third of the oven. Spray the bottom only of an 8-inch-square baking pan with nonstick cooking spray (or foil-line pan; see page xxiv).

Scrub the orange gently under warm water with a vegetable brush; pat dry. Cut the orange into quarters, trimming off ends (do not remove peel); remove any stray seeds. Place quarters into blender or food processor; purée until smooth.

Combine orange purée, brownie mix, oil, and eggs in a medium mixing bowl with a wooden spoon until just blended. Spread batter into prepared pan.

Bake for 40–44 minutes or until toothpick inserted 2 inches from side of pan comes out clean or almost clean (do not overbake). Transfer to a wire rack and cool completely. Cut into squares.

MAKES 9 LARGE OR 16 SMALL BROWNIES.

ORANGE CREAM-FROSTED BROWNIES

Accented with a creamy orange frosting, these brownies are a heavenly marriage of flavors. One (6-ounce) container of frozen orange juice concentrate is enough to make both the brownies and the frosting.

- 1 (19.5- to 19.8-ounce) package brownie mix
- ½ cup vegetable oil
- ¼ cup frozen (thawed) orange juice concentrate
- 2 large eggs
- 1 recipe Orange Cream Cheese Frosting (see page 372)

- ½ cup semisweet chocolate chips
- 1 tablespoon shortening

Preheat oven to 350°F (325°F for dark-coated metal pan). Position a rack in the lower third of the oven. Spray the bottom only of a 13 x 9-inch baking pan with nonstick cooking spray (or foil-line pan; see page xxiv).

Combine the brownie mix, oil, orange juice concentrate, and eggs in a medium mixing bowl with a wooden spoon until just blended and all dry ingredients are moistened. Spread batter into prepared pan.

Bake for 28–30 minutes or until toothpick inserted 2 inches from side of pan comes out clean or almost clean (do not overbake). Transfer to a wire rack and cool completely.

Prepare Orange Cream Cheese Frosting; spread over cooled brownies.

Place chocolate chips and shortening in small saucepan set over low heat; stir until melted and smooth. Drizzle over brownies. Refrigerate for at least 1 hour, until chocolate is set. Cut into squares. Store in refrigerator.

MAKES 24 LARGE OR 36 SMALL BROWNIES.

PEANUT BUTTER CHEESECAKE SWIRL BROWNIES

These thick, chewy brownies are loaded. With a chocolaty base, a rich swirl of peanut butter-infused cheesecake batter, and a handful of peanut butter baking chips, they're decadence to the max.

- 1 (19.5- to 19.8-ounce) package brownie mix
- ½ cup vegetable oil
- ¼ cup water
- 3 large eggs
- 1 cup peanut butter baking chips
- 1 (8-ounce) package cream cheese, softened
- ¼ cup creamy peanut butter
- 3 tablespoons packed brown sugar
- 1½ tablespoons all-purpose flour

Preheat oven to 350°F (325°F for dark-coated metal pan). Position a rack in the lower third of the oven. Spray the bottom only of a 13 x 9-inch baking pan with nonstick cooking spray (or foil-line pan; see page xxiv).

Combine the brownie mix, oil, water, and 2 eggs in a medium mixing bowl with a wooden spoon until just blended and all dry ingredients are moistened; stir in peanut butter chips. Spread two-thirds of the batter in prepared pan.

Beat the cream cheese, peanut butter, brown sugar, flour, and remaining egg in a medium mixing bowl with an electric mixer set on medium until smooth.

Spoon and spread peanut butter mixture over batter in pan. Drop remaining brownie batter by spoonfuls onto peanut butter mixture; swirl with tip of knife for marbled effect.

Bake for 28–30 minutes or until toothpick inserted 2 inches from side of pan comes out clean or almost clean (do not overbake). Transfer to a wire rack and cool completely. Cut into squares. Store in refrigerator.

MAKES 24 LARGE OR 36 SMALL BROWNIES.

PEANUT BUTTER CUP BROWNIES

If chocolate–peanut butter cravings are part of your genetic blueprint, you'll want to whip up these easy-to-assemble brownies ASAP.

- 1 (19.5- to 19.8-ounce) package brownie mix
- ½ cup vegetable oil
- ¼ cup water
- 2 large eggs
- 28 1-inch chocolate-covered peanut butter cup candies, unwrapped

Preheat oven to 350°F (325°F for dark-coated metal pan). Position a rack in the lower third of the oven. Spray the bottom only of a 13 x 9-inch baking pan with nonstick cooking spray (or foil-line pan; see page xxiv).

Combine the brownie mix, oil, water, and eggs in a medium mixing bowl with a wooden spoon until just blended and all dry ingredients are moistened. Spread batter into prepared pan. Arrange candies in rows (7 across, 4 down) on batter. Press candies into batter slightly.

Bake for 28–30 minutes or until toothpick inserted 2 inches from side of pan comes out clean or almost clean (do not overbake). Transfer to a wire rack and cool completely.

Cut into squares (with peanut butter cup at center of each brownie).

MAKES 28 LARGE BROWNIES.

PECAN PIE BROWNIES

My love of pecan pie was the inspiration for this new-fashioned brownie. The combination of chewy chocolate brownie and familiar brown sugar pecan goodness is out of this world. I prefer a cakey brownie to contrast with the pecan filling (hence the three eggs in the brownie batter) but you can certainly reduce the number of eggs in the brownie batter to two for a fudgy effect. I am confident these will become a fast favorite for you, too.

- ¼ cup (½ stick) unsalted butter
- 2 tablespoons all-purpose flour
- ¼ cup packed brown sugar
- ¼ cup corn syrup
- 5 large eggs
- 1 teaspoon vanilla extract
- 1½ cups very coarsely chopped pecans
- 1 (19.5- to 19.8-ounce) package brownie mix
- ½ cup vegetable oil
- ¼ cup water

Preheat oven to 350°F (325°F for dark-coated metal pan). Position a rack in the lower third of the oven. Spray the bottom only of a 13 x 9-inch baking pan with nonstick cooking spray (or foil-line pan; see page xxiv).

Melt the butter in a medium saucepan set over medium heat; stir in flour until blended. Stir in the brown sugar, corn syrup, and 2 of the eggs until well blended. Cook over medium heat for about 4–5 minutes, stirring constantly, until bubbly. Remove from heat. Stir in vanilla and pecans. Set aside.

Combine the brownie mix, oil, water, and remaining eggs in a medium mixing bowl with a wooden spoon until just blended and all dry ingredients are moistened. Spread batter into prepared pan; spoon pecan mixture evenly over top.

Bake for 32–35 minutes or until toothpick inserted 2 inches from side of pan comes out clean or almost clean (do not overbake). Transfer to a wire rack and cool completely. Cut into squares.

MAKES 24 LARGE OR 36 SMALL BROWNIES.

PEPPERMINT PATTY-FROSTED BROWNIES

The impressive mint and dark-chocolate swirled frosting on these brownies is almost embarrassingly easy to make. The marbled result looks professional and the taste is fantastic. Good luck making them last!

- 1 (19.5- to 19.8-ounce) package brownie mix
- ½ cup vegetable oil
- ¼ cup water
- 2 large eggs
- 28 chocolate-covered miniature peppermint patties, unwrapped

Preheat oven to 350°F (325°F for dark-coated metal pan). Position a rack in the lower third of the oven. Spray the bottom only of a 13 x 9-inch baking pan with nonstick cooking spray (or foil-line pan; see page xxiv).

Combine the brownie mix, oil, water, and eggs in a medium mixing bowl with a wooden spoon until just blended and all dry ingredients are moistened. Spread batter into prepared pan.

Bake for 28–30 minutes or until toothpick inserted 2 inches from side of pan comes out clean or almost clean (do not overbake).

Remove pan from oven and immediately place peppermint patties to cover top of brownies. Return to oven for 3–4 minutes or until patties are softened.

Remove from oven and immediately spread the patties evenly with a small offset metal spatula or butter knife, swirling the melted chocolate and mint of the candies for a marbled design. Transfer to a wire rack and cool completely. Cut into squares.

MAKES 24 LARGE OR 36 SMALL BROWNIES.

RASPBERRY BROWNIES

The combination of raspberry and chocolate has timeless appeal. No one will guess that these beautiful, scrumptious brownies are so easy to prepare.

- 1 (19.5- to 19.8-ounce) package brownie mix
- ½ cup vegetable oil
- ¼ cup water
- 2 large eggs
- ½ cup seedless raspberry jam
- 1 cup white chocolate chips
- 2 teaspoons vegetable shortening

Preheat oven to 350°F (325°F for dark-coated metal pan). Position a rack in the lower third of the oven. Spray the bottom only of an 8-inch-square baking pan with nonstick cooking spray (or foil-line pan; see page xxiv).

Combine the brownie mix, oil, water, and eggs in a medium mixing bowl with a wooden spoon until just blended and all dry ingredients are moistened. Spread batter into prepared pan.

Bake for 40–44 minutes or until toothpick inserted 2 inches from side of pan comes out clean or almost clean (do not overbake). Immediately spread jam over brownies. Transfer to a wire rack and cool completely.

Melt the white chocolate with the shortening in a small saucepan set over low heat until smooth; drizzle over brownies. Refrigerate for 1 hour to set chocolate. Cut into squares.

MAKES 9 LARGE OR 16 SMALL BROWNIES.

RASPBERRY CREAM CHEESE BROWNIES

With a swath of pretty-in-pink frosting and dark chocolate drizzle, small squares of these brownies are perfect for bridal and baby showers or as part of a spring luncheon dessert buffet. The creamy berry frosting is a great foil to the dark chocolate drizzle.

- 1 (19.5- to 19.8-ounce) package brownie mix
- ½ cup vegetable oil
- ¼ cup water
- 2 large eggs
- 1 (8-ounce) package cream cheese, softened
- ½ cup sifted powdered sugar
- ½ cup seedless raspberry preserves
- 1 (1-ounce) square unsweetened baking chocolate, chopped
- 1 tablespoon unsalted butter

Preheat oven to 350°F (325°F for dark-coated metal pan). Position a rack in the lower third of the oven. Spray the bottom only of a 13 x 9-inch baking pan with nonstick cooking spray (or foil-line pan; see page xxiv).

Combine the brownie mix, oil, water, and eggs in a medium mixing bowl with a wooden spoon until just blended and all dry ingredients are moistened. Spread batter into prepared pan.

Bake for 28–30 minutes or until toothpick inserted 2 inches from side of pan comes out clean or almost clean (do not overbake). Transfer to a wire rack and cool completely.

Beat the cream cheese, powdered sugar, and preserves in a small mixing bowl with an electric mixer set on medium until smooth; spread over cooled brownies.

Place chopped chocolate and butter in a small saucepan set over low heat; stir until melted and smooth. Drizzle from the edge of a spoon in decorative swirls or lines over brownies. Refrigerate for at least 1 hour or until chocolate is firm. Cut into squares. Store in refrigerator.

MAKES 24 LARGE OR 36 SMALL BROWNIES.

ROCKY ROAD BROWNIES

Make this marshmallow, chocolate chip, and nut-topped rendering of the all-American brownie on a Saturday afternoon when everyone seems too busy to slow down and enjoy the day. The wafting smells of baking chocolate will silently summon everyone around the kitchen table in no time for some good old-fashioned conversation and commensality.

- 1 (19.5- to 19.8-ounce) package brownie mix
- ½ cup vegetable oil
- ¼ cup water

- 3 large eggs
- 2 cups semisweet chocolate chips, divided
- 2 cups miniature marshmallows
- 1 cup coarsely chopped roasted, lightly salted peanuts

Preheat oven to 350°F (325°F for dark-coated metal pan). Position a rack in the lower third of the oven. Spray the bottom only of a 13 x 9-inch baking pan with nonstick cooking spray (or foil-line pan; see page xxiv).

Combine the brownie mix, oil, water, and eggs in a medium mixing bowl with a wooden spoon until just blended and all dry ingredients are moistened; stir in 1 cup of the chocolate chips. Spread batter into prepared pan.

Bake for 28–30 minutes or until toothpick inserted 2 inches from side of pan comes out clean or almost clean (do not overbake).

Remove pan from oven and immediately sprinkle with the marshmallows, remaining chocolate chips, and peanuts. Cover pan with cookie sheet for about 5 minutes to soften (slightly) the chocolate chips and marshmallows. Remove cookie sheet. Transfer to a wire rack and cool completely.

MAKES 24 LARGE OR 36 SMALL BROWNIES.

RUM RAISIN BROWNIES

Here you have brownies with a grown-up taste and the sophisticated balance of sweetness and rum. Try them warm with vanilla ice cream or, if you can find it, rum raisin ice cream.

- 1 cup raisins, packed
- ½ cup dark rum

- 1 (19.5- to 19.8-ounce) package brownie mix
- ½ cup (1 stick) butter, melted
- 2 large eggs
- 1 cup semisweet chocolate chips

Combine the raisins and rum in a small mixing bowl; soak until raisins are plump, about 30 minutes (do not drain).

Preheat oven to 350°F (325°F for dark-coated metal pan). Position a rack in the lower third of the oven. Spray the bottom only of an 8-inch-square baking pan with nonstick cooking spray (or foil-line pan; see page xxiv).

Combine the brownie mix, melted butter, eggs, and raisins and their liquid in a medium mixing bowl with a wooden spoon until just blended and all dry ingredients are moistened; stir in chocolate chips. Spread batter into prepared pan.

Bake for 40–44 minutes or until toothpick inserted 2 inches from side of pan comes out clean or almost clean (do not overbake). Transfer to a wire rack and cool completely. Cut into squares.

MAKES 9 LARGE OR 16 SMALL BROWNIES.

S'MORES BROWNIES (BROWNIE MIX)

No tents or sleeping bags are required for this brownie rendition of a classic campfire treat. Gooey marshmallows and melted chocolate chips piled atop a graham cracker and brownie base? It doesn't get much better than this.

- 10 whole graham crackers, broken crosswise in half (20 squares), divided

- 1 (19.5- to 19.8-ounce) package brownie mix
- ½ cup vegetable oil
- ¼ cup water
- 2 large eggs
- 2 cups semisweet chocolate chips, divided
- 2½ cups miniature marshmallows

Preheat oven to 350°F (325°F for dark-coated metal pan). Position a rack in the lower third of the oven. Line a 13 x 9-inch baking pan with foil, with ends of foil extending beyond sides of pan; spray bottom of foil-lined pan with nonstick cooking spray.

Place 15 of the graham squares in bottom of pan, overlapping slightly. Break remaining 5 graham squares into large pieces; set aside.

Combine the brownie mix, oil, water, and eggs in a medium mixing bowl with a wooden spoon until just blended and all dry ingredients are moistened; stir in 1 cup of the chocolate chips. Carefully spread batter into graham cracker–lined pan.

Bake for 28–30 minutes or until toothpick inserted 2 inches from side of pan comes out clean or almost clean (do not overbake). Sprinkle evenly with the marshmallows and remaining chocolate chips. Bake for an additional 3–5 minutes or until marshmallows begin to puff. Poke reserved graham pieces gently through marshmallows into the brownie (let them stick out).

Transfer to a wire rack and cool completely. Lift brownies out of pan onto cutting board using foil handles. Cut into bars.

MAKES 24 LARGE OR 36 SMALL BROWNIES.

S'MORES BROWNIES (CAKE MIX)

Here is a delicious brownie-based interpretation of the classic campfire classic.

- 1¾ cups graham cracker crumbs
- 2 tablespoons sugar
- 1 cup (2 sticks) butter, melted, divided
- 1 (18.25-ounce) package chocolate fudge cake mix
- ⅔ cup (1 (5-ounce) can) evaporated milk
- 1 cup miniature semisweet chocolate chips
- 3½ cups miniature marshmallows

Preheat oven to 350°F (or 325°F for dark-coated metal pan). Position oven rack in middle of oven. Foil-line a 13 x 9-inch baking pan (see page xxiv).

Combine the graham cracker crumbs, sugar, and half (1 stick) of the melted butter in a medium bowl until well blended. Press crumb mixture evenly into bottom of foil-lined pan. Bake for 5 minutes.

Meanwhile, combine the cake mix, remaining melted butter, evaporated milk, and miniature chocolate chips in a large bowl with an electric mixer set on medium speed for 1–2 minutes, until all dry ingredients are moistened and well blended (batter will be thick). Carefully spread batter over graham cracker crust.

Bake for 22–25 minutes or until just set at edges. Remove from oven and turn oven to broil setting. Position the oven rack 8–10 inches from heat source. Sprinkle brownies evenly with marshmallows. Broil 1–3 minutes, until marshmallows are puffed and browned (watch carefully to avoid scorching; marshmallows should still hold their shape).

Transfer to wire rack and cool completely. Cut into bars with knife sprayed with nonstick cooking spray.

MAKES 24 LARGE OR 36 SMALL BARS.

SNICKERY SUPREME BROWNIES

Supreme indeed! Take these to any gathering and I guarantee you will come home with an empty plate. Best of all, they are a snap to make.

- 1 (19.5- to 19.8-ounce) package brownie mix
- ½ cup vegetable oil
- ¼ cup water
- 2 large eggs
- 1 cup semisweet chocolate chips
- ¼ cup (½ stick) unsalted butter
- 3 (2.1-ounce) chocolate-covered peanut-caramel nougat candy bars (e.g., Snickers), coarsely chopped

Preheat oven to 350°F (325°F for dark-coated metal pan). Position a rack in the lower third of the oven. Spray the bottom only of an 8-inch-square baking pan with nonstick cooking spray (or foil-line pan; see page xxiv).

Combine the brownie mix, oil, water, and eggs in a medium mixing bowl with a wooden spoon until just blended and all dry ingredients are moistened. Spread batter into the prepared pan.

Bake for 40–44 minutes or until toothpick inserted 2 inches from side of pan comes out

clean or almost clean (do not overbake). Transfer to a wire rack to cool.

Combine chocolate chips and butter in a medium saucepan; stir over low heat until chocolate is melted and mixture is smooth. Pour and spread over brownies and immediately sprinkle with chopped candy bars. Gently press chopped candy into chocolate layer. Cool. Cut into squares.

MAKES 9 LARGE OR 16 SMALL BROWNIES.

SOUR CREAM BROWNIES WITH BROILED BROWN SUGAR TOPPING

These irresistible brownies are the stuff from which the concept "comfort food" is derived. Frankly, I could eat the topping on its own straight from a spoon (it's a brown sugar thing), but it is truly delectable atop the sour cream brownie base.

- 1 (19.5- to 19.8-ounce) package brownie mix
- 3 large eggs
- 1 cup sour cream, divided
- ½ cup (1 stick) unsalted butter, melted, divided
- 1½ cups sweetened shredded coconut
- ½ cup chopped pecans
- 1 cup packed brown sugar

Preheat oven to 350°F (325°F for dark-coated metal pan). Position a rack in the lower third of the oven. Spray the bottom only of an 8-inch-square baking pan with nonstick cooking spray (or foil-line pan; see page xxiv).

Combine the brownie mix, eggs, ¾ cup of the sour cream, and ¼ cup melted butter in a medium mixing bowl with a wooden spoon until just blended and all dry ingredients are moistened. Spread batter into prepared pan.

Bake for 40–44 minutes or until toothpick inserted 2 inches from side of pan comes out clean or almost clean (do not overbake).

While brownies bake, combine the coconut, chopped pecans, brown sugar, remaining sour cream and remaining melted butter in a medium mixing bowl and blend with a wooden spoon.

Remove brownies from oven and turn oven to broiler setting. Spread brownies evenly with the prepared topping. Broil 4 inches from heat for 2–3 minutes or until golden brown (watch carefully to avoid burning). Transfer to a wire rack and cool completely. Cut into squares.

MAKES 9 LARGE OR 16 SMALL BROWNIES.

SOUR CREAM BROWNIES WITH CHOCOLATE VELVET FROSTING

I tested and retested this recipe until I came up with this moist, incredibly flavorful rendition. The velvety sour cream frosting pushes them over the top. One (8-ounce) container of sour cream provides enough to make both the brownies and the Chocolate Velvet Frosting.

- 1 (19.5- to 19.8-ounce) package brownie mix
- ⅓ cup butter, melted

- ½ cup sour cream (not reduced fat)
- 2 large eggs
- 1 recipe Chocolate Velvet Frosting (see page 364)

Preheat oven to 350°F (325°F for dark-coated metal pan). Position a rack in the lower third of the oven. Spray the bottom only of an 8-inch-square baking pan with nonstick cooking spray (or foil-line pan; see page xxiv).

In a medium mixing bowl mix the brownie mix, melted butter, sour cream, and eggs with a wooden spoon until just blended and all dry ingredients are moistened. Spread batter into prepared pan.

Bake for 40–44 minutes or until toothpick inserted 2 inches from side of pan comes out clean or almost clean (do not overbake). Transfer to a wire rack and cool completely.

Prepare Chocolate Velvet Frosting. Spread over cooled brownies. Cut into squares. Store in refrigerator.

MAKES 9 LARGE OR 16 SMALL BROWNIES.

SPICY AZTEC BROWNIES

Melted butter, a handful of dark chocolate, a kick of cayenne, and a sheen of cinnamon glaze makes for one intensely delicious Aztec-inspired brownie.

- 1½ tablespoons instant espresso or coffee powder
- 1 tablespoon vanilla extract
- 1 (19.5- to 19.8-ounce) package brownie mix
- ½ cup (1 stick) unsalted butter, melted

- ¼ cup water
- 2 large eggs
- ¼ teaspoon cayenne pepper
- 3 (1-ounce) squares bittersweet chocolate, finely chopped
- 1 recipe Cinnamon Glaze (see page 365)

Preheat oven to 350°F (325°F for dark-coated metal pan). Position a rack in the lower third of the oven. Spray the bottom only of an 8-inch-square baking pan with nonstick cooking spray (or foil-line pan; see page xxiv).

Dissolve the espresso powder in the vanilla in a small cup. Combine the brownie mix, melted butter, water, vanilla-espresso mixture, eggs, and cayenne pepper in a medium mixing bowl with a wooden spoon until just blended and all dry ingredients are moistened; stir in chopped chocolate. Spread batter into prepared pan.

Bake for 40–44 minutes or until toothpick inserted 2 inches from side of pan comes out clean or almost clean (do not overbake). Transfer to a wire rack.

Prepare Cinnamon Glaze; spread over warm brownies. Cool completely. Cut into squares.

MAKES 9 LARGE OR 16 SMALL BROWNIES.

STRAWBERRIES AND CREAM BROWNIES

Everyone loves traditions because they are familiar and comforting, especially when it comes to food. But to keep things exciting, sometimes you need to inject an element of surprise in even your most steadfast of rituals. Case in point these brownies, which transform the perennial favorite of strawberries and cream into a berry-layered, buttercream-rich chocolate treat.

- 1 (19.5- to 19.8-ounce) package brownie mix
- ½ cup vegetable oil
- ¼ cup water
- 2 large eggs
- ¾ cup strawberry jam, stirred to loosen
- 1 cup white chocolate chips
- ¾ cup (1½ sticks) butter, softened
- ¼ cup sifted powdered sugar

Preheat oven to 350°F for metal or glass pan (325°F for dark-coated metal pan). Position a rack in the lower third of the oven. Spray the bottom only of a 13 x 9-inch baking pan with nonstick cooking spray (or foil-line pan; see page xxiv).

Combine the brownie mix, oil, water, and eggs in a medium mixing bowl with a wooden spoon until just blended and all dry ingredients are moistened. Spread batter into prepared pan.

Bake for 28–30 minutes or until toothpick inserted 2 inches from side of pan comes out clean or almost clean (do not overbake). Transfer to wire rack and cool 10 minutes; spread with jam. Cool completely.

Melt the white chocolate chips according to package directions; cool for 30 minutes.

Beat the butter and powdered sugar in a medium bowl with electric mixer set on medium-high until light and fluffy. Gradually beat in cooled white chocolate until smooth, light, and fluffy. Carefully spread mixture over preserves. Store in refrigerator. Cut into squares. Let stand at room temperature for 5–10 minutes before serving.

MAKES 24 LARGE OR 36 SMALL BROWNIES.

SWIRLED TUXEDO-TOP BROWNIES

The beautifully marbleized pattern on these brownies is surprisingly simple to do, but the result is stunning. Consider making them in a 9-inch round cake pan (reducing the baking time to 38–42 minutes), then cut into wedges and serve with raspberry sauce for an elegant plated dessert.

- 1 (19.5- to 19.8-ounce) package brownie mix
- ½ cup vegetable oil
- ¼ cup water
- 2 large eggs
- 1 cup chopped walnuts, lightly toasted
- 1¼ cups semisweet chocolate chips, divided
- 1¼ cups white chocolate chips, divided

Preheat oven to 350°F (325°F for dark-coated metal pan). Position a rack in the lower third of the oven. Spray the bottom only of an 8-inch-square baking pan with nonstick cooking spray (or foil-line pan; see page xxiv).

Combine the brownie mix, oil, water, and eggs in a medium mixing bowl with a wooden spoon until just blended and all dry ingredients are moistened; stir in the toasted walnuts, ½ cup of the semisweet chocolate chips, and ½ cup of the white chocolate chips. Spread batter into prepared pan.

Bake for 40–44 minutes or until toothpick inserted 2 inches from side of pan comes out clean or almost clean (do not overbake).

Remove pan from oven and immediately sprinkle with remaining semisweet and white chocolate chips; cover with a cookie sheet. Let stand for 5 minutes or until chocolates are melted. Remove sheet and swirl with the tip of a knife for a marbled effect. Transfer pan to a wire rack and cool completely. Refrigerate for 1 hour to set the chocolate. Cut into squares.

MAKES 9 LARGE OR 16 SMALL BROWNIES.

TENNESSEE JAM CAKE BROWNIES

This recipe takes its inspiration from traditional Tennessee jam cake, a rich spice cake made with blackberry jam and a brown sugar "penuche" frosting. The chocolate rendition here is wonderful.

- 1 (19.5- to 19.8-ounce) package brownie mix
- ½ cup vegetable oil
- ¼ cup buttermilk or water
- 2 large eggs
- ½ teaspoon ground cinnamon
- ¼ teaspoon ground cloves
- 1 cup chopped pecans or walnuts
- ¾ cup blackberry jam, stirred to loosen
- 1 recipe Caramel Penuche Frosting (see page 374)

Preheat oven to 350°F (325°F for dark-coated metal pan). Position a rack in the lower third of the oven. Spray the bottom only of a 13 x 9-inch baking pan with nonstick cooking spray (or foil-line pan; see page xxiv).

Combine the brownie mix, oil, buttermilk, eggs, cinnamon, and cloves in a medium mixing bowl with a wooden spoon until just blended and all dry ingredients are moistened; stir in nuts. Spread batter into prepared pan. Dollop jam randomly over top of batter; swirl into batter with the tip of a knife.

Bake for 28–30 minutes or until toothpick inserted 2 inches from side of pan comes out clean or almost clean (do not overbake). Transfer to a wire rack and cool completely.

Prepare Caramel Penuche Frosting. Spread frosting evenly over cooled brownies. Cut into squares.

MAKES 24 LARGE OR 36 SMALL BROWNIES.

TOASTED COCONUT WHITE CHOCOLATE FUDGE BROWNIES

Tropical coconut, white chocolate, and rum flavoring pump up the volume of these part-brownie, part-fudge treats. Semisweet chocolate may be substituted for the white chocolate, if desired.

- 1 (19.5- to 19.8-ounce) package brownie mix
- ½ cup oil
- ¼ cup water
- 2 large eggs
- 3 teaspoons rum extract, divided
- 1 (5-ounce) can evaporated milk
- 3 cups miniature marshmallows
- 1½ cups white chocolate chips
- 2 cups sweetened shredded coconut, toasted

Preheat oven to 350°F (325°F for dark-coated metal pan). Position a rack in the lower third of the oven. Spray the bottom only of a 13 x 9-inch baking pan with nonstick cooking spray (or foil-line pan; see page xxiv).

Combine the brownie mix, oil, water, eggs, and 1½ teaspoons of the rum extract in a medium mixing bowl with a wooden spoon until just blended and all dry ingredients are moistened. Spread batter into prepared pan.

Bake for 28–30 minutes or until toothpick inserted 2 inches from side of pan comes out clean or almost clean (do not overbake). Transfer to a wire rack to cool.

Meanwhile, place evaporated milk and marshmallows in a large saucepan; cook on medium-low heat until mixture is melted and smooth, stirring constantly (to avoid scorching). Remove pan from heat and add white chocolate; stir until completely melted. Stir in remaining rum extract. Immediately pour over brownies, spreading to cover evenly.

Immediately sprinkle with toasted coconut; press lightly into white chocolate fudge layer. Cool completely. Refrigerate for 2 hours or until firm. Cut into bars. Store in airtight container in refrigerator.

MAKES 24 LARGE OR 36 SMALL BARS.

TRIPLE-SHOT ESPRESSO LAYERED BROWNIES

The bold flavor of espresso is a perfect partner to the chocolate in these sophisticated, triple-layered (brownie-brown sugar espresso-chocolate glaze) brownies.

- 1 (19.5- to 19.8-ounce) package brownie mix
- ½ cup vegetable oil
- ¼ cup water
- 3 large eggs

- 2 tablespoons plus 1 teaspoon instant espresso or coffee powder, divided
- 2 teaspoons vanilla extract, divided
- 6 tablespoons unsalted butter, softened, divided
- ½ cup firmly packed brown sugar
- 1 cup coarsely chopped walnuts
- 3 cups semisweet chocolate chips
- 1–2 teaspoons milk

Preheat oven to 350°F (325°F for dark-coated metal pan). Position a rack in the lower third of the oven. Spray the bottom only of a 13 x 9-inch baking pan with nonstick cooking spray (or foil-line pan; see page xxiv).

Combine the brownie mix, oil, water, 2 of the eggs, 1 tablespoon espresso powder, and 1 teaspoon vanilla in a medium mixing bowl with a wooden spoon until just blended and all dry ingredients are moistened. Spread batter into prepared pan.

Bake for 26–28 minutes or until just barely set at center (do not overbake). Transfer to a wire rack momentarily (leave oven on).

Meanwhile, beat 4 tablespoons (½ stick) butter and brown sugar in a medium mixing bowl with an electric mixer set on medium until light and fluffy. Add egg, 1 tablespoon espresso powder, and remaining vanilla; beat with electric mixer set on low until just blended. Mix in walnuts and 2 cups of the chocolate chips.

Spoon and carefully spread brown sugar filling over baked brownies. Return to oven; bake for 17–20 minutes or until light brown. Transfer to a wire rack and cool.

Melt remaining 1 cup chocolate chips and remaining butter in small saucepan over low heat, stirring constantly until smooth. Remove from heat. Whisk in remaining espresso powder and enough milk for desired drizzling consistency. Spread or drizzle over warm brownies. Cool completely. Cut into squares.

MAKES 24 LARGE OR 36 SMALL BROWNIES.

TRUFFLE-TOPPED BROWNIES

Chocolate euphoria? It's right here. These deep chocolate brownies are super rich—a small square goes a long way. Sifting the squares with unsweetened cocoa powder adds to the truffle resemblance.

- 1 (19.5- to 19.8-ounce) package brownie mix
- ½ cup (1 stick) unsalted butter, melted
- ¼ cup water
- 2 large eggs
- 2 cups semisweet chocolate chips
- 1 (14-ounce) can sweetened condensed milk
- 2 teaspoons vanilla extract
- 1–2 tablespoons unsweetened cocoa powder, optional

Preheat oven to 350°F (325° for dark-coated metal pan). Position a rack in the lower third of the oven. Spray the bottom only of a 13 x 9-inch baking pan with nonstick cooking spray (or foil-line pan; see page xxiv).

Combine the brownie mix, melted butter, water, and eggs in a medium mixing bowl with a wooden spoon until just blended and all dry ingredients are moistened. Spread batter into prepared pan.

Bake for 28–30 minutes or until toothpick inserted 2 inches from side of pan comes out clean or almost clean (do not overbake).

During last 10 minutes of brownies baking, prepare topping. Melt chocolate chips with condensed milk in a heavy saucepan set over low heat, stirring until smooth. Remove from heat and stir in vanilla.

Remove brownies from oven and immediately spread with chocolate mixture. Transfer to a wire rack and cool completely. Chill for 1 hour in refrigerator to set topping. Cut into bars. If desired, sift cocoa powder over squares. Store in refrigerator.

MAKES 24 LARGE OR 36 SMALL BROWNIES.

TURKISH COFFEE BROWNIE BARS

Coffee two ways—both instant espresso and coffee liqueur—and a bit of cardamom give these bars their exotic flavor.

- 1 (16.5-ounce) roll refrigerated sugar cookie dough
- 1 (19.5- to 19.8-ounce) package brownie mix
- 2 large eggs
- ½ cup vegetable oil
- ⅓ cup coffee liqueur
- 1 tablespoon instant espresso or instant coffee powder
- ¾ teaspoon ground cardamom
- 1 cup bittersweet chocolate chips (e.g., Ghiradelli brand)

Preheat oven to 350°F. Spray a 13 x 9 x 2-inch baking pan with nonstick cooking spray.

Break up the cookie dough into prepared pan. Press dough on bottom of pan.

Mix the brownie mix, eggs, oil, liqueur, espresso powder, and cardamom in a large bowl until just combined. Spread batter over sugar cookie dough. Sprinkle with chocolate chips.

Bake for 38–40 minutes or until edges are set. Cool in pan on a wire rack. To serve, cut into bars.

MAKES 24 BROWNIES.

TURTLE CHEESECAKE BROWNIES

A rich brownie base, a silken layer of cheesecake, crunchy pecans, and buttery caramel? I call it perfection. These outstanding brownies make a delicious present for a very lucky friend.

- 1 (19.5- to 19.8-ounce) package brownie mix
- ½ cup vegetable oil
- ¼ cup water
- 3 large eggs
- 1 (8-ounce) package cream cheese, softened
- ½ teaspoon vanilla extract
- ⅔ cup caramel ice cream topping
- 1 cup chopped pecans

Preheat oven to 350°F (325°F for dark-coated metal pan). Position a rack in the lower third of the oven. Spray the bottom only of a 13 x 9-inch baking pan with nonstick cooking spray (or foil-line pan; see page xxiv).

Combine the brownie mix, oil, water, and 2 eggs in a medium mixing bowl with a wooden spoon until just blended and all dry ingredients are moistened. Spread batter into prepared pan.

Beat the cream cheese in a medium mixing bowl with an electric mixer set on medium until smooth. Beat in vanilla and remaining egg until thoroughly blended.

Spoon cream cheese mixture over brownie batter in pan (need not cover completely); dollop with spoonfuls of caramel topping. Cut through mixture with knife several times for marbled design. Sprinkle with pecans.

Bake for 32–35 minutes or until toothpick inserted 2 inches from side of pan comes out clean or almost clean (do not overbake). Transfer to a wire rack and cool completely. Cut into squares. Store in refrigerator.

MAKES 24 LARGE OR 36 SMALL BROWNIES.

Bake for 40–44 minutes or until toothpick inserted 2 inches from side of pan comes out clean or almost clean (do not overbake). Transfer to a wire rack. Prepare Vanilla-Butter Glaze; spread over warm brownies and cool completely. Cut into squares.

MAKES 9 LARGE OR 16 SMALL BROWNIES.

VANILLA AND BUTTER-RICH GLAZED BUTTERMILK BROWNIES

Vanilla and chocolate are the yin and yang of the dessert world. Here I match vanilla with butter in the batter and glaze, which brings out the best in the chocolate and leads to a newfangled brownie few can turn down. The glaze seeps into the top half of the brownie, adding to the fudgy-ness of every bite.

- 1 (19.5- to 19.8-ounce) package brownie mix
- ½ cup (1 stick) unsalted butter, melted
- ¼ cup buttermilk
- 1 tablespoon vanilla extract
- 2 large eggs
- 1 recipe Vanilla-Butter Glaze (see page 376)

Preheat oven to 350°F (325°F for dark-coated metal pan). Position a rack in the lower third of the oven. Spray the bottom only of an 8-inch-square baking pan with nonstick cooking spray (or foil-line pan; see page xxiv).

Combine the brownie mix, melted butter, buttermilk, vanilla, and eggs in a medium mixing bowl with a wooden spoon until just blended and all dry ingredients are moistened. Spread batter into prepared pan.

WHISKEY-GLAZED DOUBLE CHOCOLATE BROWNIES

This variation on traditional brownies features a generous dose of whiskey. Not for the faint of heart, they are simple yet wickedly rich. You can use this recipe as a template—substitute the liqueur or spirit of your choice in place of the whiskey.

- 1 (19.5- to 19.8-ounce) package brownie mix
- ½ cup (1 stick) unsalted butter, melted
- ¼ cup whiskey
- 2 large eggs
- 1 cup semisweet chocolate chunks or chips
- 1 recipe Whiskey Glaze (see page 377)

Preheat oven to 350°F (325°F for dark-coated metal pan). Position a rack in the lower third of the oven. Spray the bottom only of an 8-inch-square baking pan with nonstick cooking spray (or foil-line pan; see page xxiv).

Combine the brownie mix, melted butter, whiskey, and eggs in a medium mixing bowl with a wooden spoon until well blended; stir in chocolate chunks or chips. Spread batter into the prepared pan.

Bake for 40–44 minutes or until toothpick inserted 2 inches from side of pan comes out clean or almost clean (do not overbake). Transfer to a wire rack.

Prepare Whiskey Glaze. Spread glaze evenly over warm brownies. Cool completely. Cut into squares.

MAKES 9 LARGE OR 16 SMALL BROWNIES.

FRESH NEW IDEAS

Color—vibrant oranges, scarlet cranberries, fresh green mint. Texture—crunchy nuts, silken frostings, gooey chocolate. Spices—sweet cinnamon, exotic cardamom, fiery chili peppers. An abundance of tastes and flavors awaits your experimentation.

Apple-Cranberry Harvest Cookies
TIME-SAVING SHORTCUT: Cake Mix

Chocolate-Chip Cream Cheese Softies

TIME-SAVING SHORTCUT: Cookie Dough

PAGE 19

Toffee Apple Cookies

TIME-SAVING SHORTCUT: Cookie Dough

PAGE 72

Coconut Macaroonies

TIME-SAVING SHORTCUT:
Cookie Dough

PAGE 25

Cinnamon-Orange Chocolate Chippers

TIME-SAVING SHORTCUT:
Cookie Dough

COOKIE BARS

*Y*et another way to enjoy cookies, these bars range from gooey treats to energy-packed essentials.

Carrot Cake Bars
PAGE 196

TIME-SAVING SHORTCUT: Cake Mix

PAGE 232

Double Berry Streusel Bars

TIME-SAVING SHORTCUT:
Cake Mix

PAGE 243

High-Energy Dried Fruit Bars

TIME-SAVING SHORTCUT:
No-Bake

PAGE 251

Lemon-Blueberry Gooey Chess Squares

TIME-SAVING SHORTCUT:
Cake Mix

PAGE 277

Pecan Pie Bars

TIME-SAVING SHORTCUT:
Cake Mix

Toasted Almond Buttermilk Bars

PAGE 299

TIME-SAVING SHORTCUT:
Cake Mix

PAGE 230, 285

Deep Dark Chocolate Truffle Bars and Pumpkin Gooey Chess Squares

TIME-SAVING SHORTCUT:
Cookie Dough (*Deep Dark Chocolate Truffle Bars*),
Cake Mix (*Pumpkin Gooey Chess Squares*)

INTERNATIONAL DELIGHTS

The names might be hard to pronounce, but baking these cookies is anything but difficult!

PAGE 122 | *Ginger Lime Biscotti*
TIME-SAVING SHORTCUT: Cookie Dough

Classic Madeleines
PAGE 105

TIME-SAVING SHORTCUT: Cake Mix

Mexican Wedding Cakes
PAGE 135

TIME-SAVING SHORTCUT: Cookie Dough

ENJOY!

Visit www.camillacooks.com for more tips, fun, and delicious recipes.

PAGE 149 *Pistachio-Lemon Biscotti*
TIME-SAVING SHORTCUT: Cake Mix

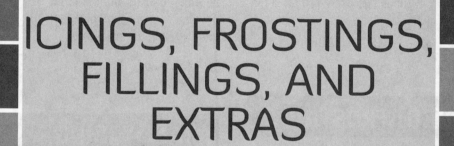

ICINGS, FROSTINGS,
FILLINGS, AND
EXTRAS

ALMOND ICING

- 3 tablespoons hot water
- 1½ teaspoons almond extract
- 1 pinch of salt
- 2¾ cups powdered sugar

Mix water, almond extract, and salt in a small bowl. Whisk in enough powdered sugar to form frosting thick enough to pipe or spread.

MAKES ABOUT 1 CUP.

APRICOT FROSTING

Use this recipe as a template for other fruit frostings, substituting an equal amount of cherry, strawberry, peach, seedless raspberry, or pineapple preserves, for example, in place of the apricot preserves.

- 3 cups sifted powdered sugar
- 3 tablespoons butter, softened
- ⅔ cup apricot preserves

Beat the powdered sugar, butter, and apricot preserves in a medium mixing bowl with an electric mixer on medium until smooth.

MAKES ABOUT 1½ CUPS FROSTING, ENOUGH TO FROST A 13 X 9-INCH PAN OF BROWNIES OR 48–60 COOKIES.

Baker's Note

For an 8-inch-square pan of brownies, halve the ingredients listed above and proceed as directed.

BOURBON FROSTING

- 3 tablespoons butter, softened
- 1½ cups sifted powdered sugar
- 1 tablespoon bourbon
- 1 tablespoon milk

Beat the butter in a medium mixing bowl with an electric mixer until creamy. Gradually add powdered sugar, bourbon, and milk, beating until spreading consistency.

MAKES ABOUT 1 CUP.

BRANDY ICING

- 2 cups sifted powdered sugar
- ¼ cup (½ stick) butter, melted
- 2½ teaspoons brandy-flavored extract, divided
- 2–3 tablespoons milk

In a small bowl combine the powdered sugar, butter, and brandy flavoring. Add just enough milk to make icing of spreading consistency.

MAKES ABOUT ¾ CUP.

BROWNED BUTTER ICING

Be sure to use real butter, not margarine, for this recipe. Margarine will not brown and get the nutty flavor that butter will.

- 6 tablespoons (¾ stick) butter (do not use margarine)

- 3 cups powdered sugar, sifted
- 1½ teaspoons vanilla extract
- 1–2 tablespoons milk

Melt the butter in a medium saucepan set over medium heat until light brown in color (watch butter carefully—it can burn quickly). Remove from heat. Stir the powdered sugar, vanilla extract, and 1 tablespoon milk into browned butter. Stir in just enough more milk to make frosting smooth and spreadable. Stir in more milk if mixture is too thick or more powdered sugar if mixture is too thin.

MAKES ABOUT 1½ CUPS.

Variations:

RUM VARIATION: Substitute rum-flavored extract for vanilla extract.

MAPLE VARIATION: Substitute maple-flavored extract for vanilla extract.

COFFEE VARIATION: Prepare as above adding 2 teaspoons instant coffee powder or espresso powder along with powdered sugar.

CHOCOLATE CREAM CHEESE FROSTING

Here's a dependable recipe I know I can turn to again and again to gussy up just about anything and everything sweet. Always divine on brownies, this tangy chocolate frosting is also delectable on brownie cookies and cupcakes.

- 6 (1-ounce) squares semisweet, milk, or white chocolate, chopped
- ¼ cup heavy whipping cream
- 1 (8-ounce) package cream cheese, softened
- 2 cups powdered sugar, sifted

Melt the chopped chocolate with the heavy cream in a double boiler, mixing until melted and smooth. Remove from heat.

Beat the cream cheese and powdered sugar in a medium mixing bowl with electric mixer set on medium until smooth. Slowly add the chocolate mixture, beating until incorporated and smooth. Cover and refrigerate for at least 30 minutes (frosting will thicken up as the chocolate cools).

MAKES ABOUT 2 CUPS.

CHOCOLATE DRIZZLE OR DIP

Adding vegetable shortening to the chocolate chips makes the melted chocolate smooth, spreadable, and easy to work with. Be sure to keep the pan on very low heat and stir frequently to avoid scorching the chocolate.

- 1 cup semisweet, milk, or white chocolate, or cinnamon baking chips
- 1 tablespoon vegetable shortening

Melt chips and shortening in a small heavy saucepan over low heat, stirring often to avoid scorching.

TO USE AS A CHOCOLATE DIP: Dip a cookie or biscotto into the melted chocolate. Remove the excess chocolate by pulling the cookie across the edge of the pan.

TO USE AS A CHOCOLATE DRIZZLE: Place cookies on a wire rack over wax paper. Dip a fork or knife into melted chocolate and let the first clumpy drip land back in the pan. Then drizzle the chocolate over the edge of the pan onto the cookies.

Let the cookies stand until the chocolate is set or refrigerate until chocolate is set.

MAKES ABOUT 1 CUP MELTED CHOCOLATE, ENOUGH TO DRIZZLE OVER ONE 13 X 9-INCH PAN OF BROWNIES OR 48–60 COOKIES, OR SPREAD ONTO ONE BATCH OF BISCOTTI.

CHOCOLATE FUDGE FROSTING

Anyone who tastes this rich, buttery, and very fudgy frosting will feel very lucky. It's a classic for spreading on plain or fancy brownies, just like what you would find on a premium coffeehouse brownie.

- 4 (1-ounce) squares unsweetened chocolate, coarsely chopped
- 6 tablespoons (¾ stick) butter, cut into pieces
- 3 cups powdered sugar, sifted, divided
- 2–3 tablespoons milk
- 1 teaspoon vanilla extract
- 1 pinch of salt

Melt the chopped chocolate with the butter in a medium double boiler; cook and stir until melted and smooth. Remove from heat and cool for 10 minutes.

Mix the melted chocolate, ½ cup powdered sugar, 1 tablespoon milk, vanilla extract, and pinch of salt in a medium bowl with an electric mixer set on medium until blended. Add the remaining powdered sugar, ½ cup at a time, beating on medium speed until smooth. Add a few more drops milk, if necessary, to make the frosting spreading consistency.

MAKES ABOUT 2 CUPS.

CHOCOLATE GANACHE, AKA CHOCOLATE GANACHE FROSTING

- ¾ cup heavy whipping cream
- 8 ounces semisweet baking chocolate, chopped

Heat the cream in a medium, heavy-bottomed saucepan set over low heat until cream is hot but not boiling; remove from heat.

Place chopped chocolate in a medium bowl; pour the hot cream over chocolate. Whisk mixture until the chocolate is melted and mixture is glossy and smooth. Cool completely (several hours) before using as a frosting.

MAKES ABOUT 2 CUPS.

CHOCOLATE MARSHMALLOW FROSTING

- 2¼ cups powdered sugar, sifted
- ⅔ cup unsweetened cocoa powder
- 6 large marshmallows

- ¼ cup (½ stick) butter, cut into small pieces
- 5–6 tablespoons milk
- 1 teaspoon vanilla extract

Combine the powdered sugar and cocoa powder in a large bowl. Set aside momentarily.

Combine the marshmallows, butter, and milk in a medium saucepan set over low heat, stirring constantly until melted and smooth, 3–4 minutes. Remove the pan from the heat. Pour the marshmallow mixture over the sugar-cocoa mixture. Add the vanilla and stir until the frosting is smooth and satiny. Let stand for 15–20 minutes to cool and thicken.

MAKES ABOUT 1½ CUPS, ENOUGH TO FROST A 13 X 9-INCH PAN OF BROWNIES OR 48–60 COOKIES.

Baker's Note

For an 8-inch-square pan of brownies, halve the ingredients listed above and proceed as directed.

CHOCOLATE-RASPBERRY FROSTING

Silky chocolate-raspberry frosting? It's even better than you can imagine.

- 1 cup semisweet chocolate chips
- 2/3 cup sour cream
- ¼ cup seedless raspberry preserves, whisked to loosen
- 2 tablespoons light corn syrup
- 1 teaspoon vanilla extract
- 1½ tablespoons butter, softened

Stir chocolate in top of double boiler over simmering water until melted and smooth. Pour chocolate into large bowl. Cool to room temperature. Beat in the sour cream, preserves, corn syrup, and vanilla with an electric mixer set on medium, beating until mixture is fluffy, smooth and light in color, about 3 minutes. Beat in the butter.

MAKES ABOUT 2 CUPS, ENOUGH TO GENEROUSLY FROST A 13 X 9-INCH PAN OF BROWNIES OR 48–60 COOKIES.

Baker's Note

For an 8-inch-square pan of brownies, halve the ingredients listed above and proceed as directed.

CHOCOLATE RUM GLAZE

The crowning touch for Jim and Anna's Dark Rum Brownies (see page 336), this spiked glaze is also excellent drizzled over cookies. The glaze may look thin while it is still warm, but it thickens as it cools.

- ½ cup packed light brown sugar
- 3 tablespoons butter (not unsalted)
- 2 tablespoons dark rum
- 1 tablespoon milk
- ½ cup semisweet chocolate chips

Combine the brown sugar, butter, rum and milk in a small saucepan set over medium-low Heat. Stir constantly until the mixture comes to a boil. Boil, stirring constantly, 1 minute longer. Remove the pan from the heat and stir in the chocolate chips. Stir the mixture until the chips are completely melted and the mixture is smooth. Cool for 5 minutes. Pour the glaze over warm or cooled brownies.

MAKES ABOUT ¾ CUP GLAZE, ENOUGH TO GLAZE AN 8-INCH-SQUARE PAN OF BROWNIES.

Baker's Note

For a 13 x 9-inch pan of brownies or 48–60 cookies, double the ingredients listed above and proceed as directed.

CHOCOLATE SOUR CREAM FROSTING, AKA CHOCOLATE VELVET FROSTING

This frosting is everything that its name implies: rich, smooth, luxurious, and, of course, very chocolate.

- 2 tablespoons butter
- ½ cup semisweet chocolate chips
- ¼ cup sour cream
- 1¼ cups sifted powdered sugar

Combine the butter and chocolate chips in a medium saucepan set over low heat; cook and stir until melted and smooth. Remove from heat and cool for 5 minutes; whisk in sour cream. Gradually add the powdered sugar, whisking until blended, shiny, and smooth.

MAKES ABOUT 1 CUP FROSTING, ENOUGH TO FROST AN 8-INCH-SQUARE PAN OF BROWNIES.

Baker's Note

For a 13 x 9-inch pan of brownies or 48–60 cookies, double the ingredients listed above and proceed as directed.

CHOCOLATE WHISKEY FROSTING

Your guess is correct: This frosting is sublime. Southern Comfort and framboise (raspberry liqueur) are equally exquisite substitutions for the whiskey.

- 6 tablespoons (¾ stick) unsalted butter
- ¼ cup whiskey or bourbon
- ¼ cup light corn syrup
- 4 (1-ounce) squares unsweetened baking chocolate, coarsely chopped
- 2 teaspoons vanilla extract
- 2 cups powdered sugar, sifted

Combine the butter, whiskey, and corn syrup in a medium saucepan set over medium-high heat; bring to a boil. Remove from heat. Stir in the chocolate, whisking until melted. With wire whisk beat in vanilla and gradually add the powdered sugar until frosting is of spreading consistency. Cool. Refrigerate for at least 30 minutes before using.

MAKES ABOUT 1½ CUPS, ENOUGH TO FROST A 13 X 9-INCH PAN OF BROWNIES OR 48–60 COOKIES.

Baker's Note

For an 8-inch-square pan of brownies, halve the ingredients listed above and proceed as directed.

CINNAMON GLAZE

Depending on the degree to which you like cinnamon, you can increase or decrease the amount of cinnamon here. Alternatively, use the recipe as a template for other spicy glazes, substituting the ground spice of your choice, or a combination, for the ground cinnamon.

- 1½ cups powdered sugar, sifted
- ¾ teaspoon ground cinnamon
- 1½ tablespoons unsalted butter, melted
- 2–3 teaspoons milk

Whisk the powdered sugar, cinnamon, and melted butter in a small bowl until smooth. Add just enough milk, a teaspoon at a time, to make glaze a thin spreading consistency, whisking until smooth.

MAKES ABOUT ½ CUP GLAZE, ENOUGH TO GLAZE AN 8-INCH-SQUARE PAN OF BROWNIES.

Baker's Note

For a 13 x 9-inch pan of brownies or 48–60 cookies, double the ingredients listed above and proceed as directed.

COCONUT PECAN FROSTING

- ½ (5-ounce) can evaporated milk
- ¼ cup (½ stick) unsalted butter, softened
- ¼ cup sugar
- 1 large egg yolk, beaten to blend
- 1½ teaspoons all-purpose flour
- ½ teaspoon vanilla extract
- ¾ cup chopped pecans
- ¾ cup flaked sweetened coconut

Combine the evaporated milk, butter, sugar, egg yolk, flour, and vanilla in a heavy large saucepan. Whisk constantly over medium-low heat until butter melts and mixture thickens (do not boil), about 10 minutes. Stir in pecans and coconut. Cool until frosting is thick enough to spread but is still warm, about 40 minutes. Generously spread warm frosting onto cookies.

MAKES ABOUT 1 1/3 CUPS.

COOKIE DECORATING ICING

Use this simple icing on the Brownie Cut-outs for a pretty white contrast against the dark chocolate dough or tint with food coloring paste for a rainbow of icing colors. The egg whites act as a stabilizer in this icing, allowing it to harden for decorating the cookies. Because the whites are not cooked, I prefer to use powdered egg whites (e.g., Just Whites). They are available in the baking section of most supermarkets.

- 1 (16-ounce) box powdered sugar
- 4 teaspoons powdered egg whites (not reconstituted)
- 1/3 cup water
- 1 tablespoon fresh lemon juice
- 1 teaspoon vanilla extract
- Food coloring paste, optional

Beat together all ingredients except food coloring in a large bowl with an electric mixer set on medium speed until just blended, about 1 minute. Increase speed to high and continue to beat, scraping down side of bowl occasionally, until it holds stiff peaks, about 3 minutes in a stand mixer or 4–5 minutes with a handheld mixer. Beat in food coloring (if added color is desired).

If you plan to spread (rather than pipe) icing on cookies, stir in more water, a few drops at a time, to thin to desired consistency.

MAKES ABOUT 3 CUPS.

Baker's Note

For a two-color icing variation, spread one color of icing evenly over a baked sliced cookie or cookie cutout. While the first color is still wet, apply dots or lines of a second color of icing. Use a toothpick to pull through the dots or lines, making a design or giving a marbled look.

CREAM CHEESE FROSTING

This very versatile frosting is classic on carrot cake, but I think you will soon agree that it is unbeatable on brownies.

- 6 ounces cream cheese, softened
- ¼ cup (½ stick) butter, softened
- 1 teaspoon vanilla extract
- 2¼ cups powdered sugar, sifted

Beat the cream cheese, softened butter, and vanilla extract in a medium bowl with an electric mixer set on medium speed until smooth. Gradually add the powdered sugar, beating until incorporated and smooth.

MAKES ABOUT 1¾ CUPS.

CREAMY CHOCOLATE COOKIE FROSTING

- 2 cups sifted powdered sugar
- ¼ cup (½ stick) butter, softened
- 1¼ teaspoons vanilla extract
- 2 (1-ounce) squares unsweetened baking chocolate, melted and cooled
- 2–3 tablespoons milk

Mix the powdered sugar and butter in a medium bowl with a wooden spoon or an electric mixer on low speed. Stir in the vanilla and chocolate. Gradually beat in just enough milk to make frosting smooth and spreadable. Add more milk as necessary to make spreadable, or more powdered sugar if mixture becomes too thin.

MAKES ABOUT 1½ CUPS.

Variations:

MOCHA VARIATION: Add 2½ teaspoons instant espresso or coffee powder along with powdered sugar.

WHITE CHOCOLATE VARIATION: Substitute 2 ounces chopped white chocolate baking bar, melted and cooled, for the semisweet chocolate.

THE ULTIMATE SHORTCUT COOKIE BOOK

DARK CHOCOLATE FROSTING

- 3 tablespoons butter (or margarine)
- 2 tablespoons corn syrup
- 2 tablespoons water
- 2 ounces unsweetened baking chocolate, chopped
- 2 teaspoons vanilla
- 1 cup sifted powdered sugar

Combine the butter, corn syrup, and water in a medium saucepan set over medium-high heat; bring to a boil. Remove from heat. Stir in the chocolate, whisking until melted. With wire whisk beat in vanilla and enough powdered sugar until frosting is of spreading consistency.

MAKES ABOUT ¾ CUP.

EASY COCOA ICING

- 5 tablespoons unsalted butter, softened
- 2 cups sifted powdered sugar, divided
- 2–4 tablespoons milk
- ¾ teaspoon vanilla extract
- ½ cup unsweetened cocoa powder

Beat the butter in a large bowl until fluffy. Gradually beat in 1 cup powered sugar. Beat in 1 tablespoon milk and vanilla. Add the cocoa and remaining sugar; beat until blended, thinning with more milk if necessary.

MAKES ABOUT 1⅓ CUPS.

FLUFFIEST CHOCOLATE BUTTERCREAM

Curiously enough, this very fluffy, very buttery, very easy, and very delicious light chocolate frosting comes courtesy of a good friend who is a very avid exerciser and health food junkie and is also a dedicated chocolate aficionado. It is also heavenly on angel food cake.

- 2 (1-ounce) squares bittersweet or semisweet chocolate, coarsely chopped
- ½ (7-ounce) jar marshmallow creme
- ¾ cup (1½ sticks) butter, softened and cut into chunks

Melt the chocolate in a medium double boiler set over simmering water, stirring until melted and smooth. Remove from heat and let cool for 15–20 minutes.

Beat the marshmallow creme in a medium bowl with an electric mixer on high until smooth. Gradually add the chunks of butter, mixing until incorporated, smooth and fluffy. Scrape bowl well and add the melted, cooled chocolate. Mix on high speed until incorporated and smooth. Use immediately.

MAKES ABOUT 2 CUPS, ENOUGH TO GENEROUSLY FROST A 13 X 9-INCH PAN OF BROWNIES OR 48–60 COOKIES.

FRESH CITRUS (LEMON, LIME, OR ORANGE) ICING

- 3 cups sifted powdered sugar
- 2 teaspoons grated lemon, orange, or lime zest
- 5–6 tablespoons fresh lemon, orange, or lime juice

Place powdered sugar in medium bowl. Mix in zest and enough juice as needed to make icing just thin enough to drip off fork.

MAKES ABOUT 1 1/3 CUPS.

FRUITY FROSTING

- 3 cups sifted powdered sugar
- 3 tablespoons butter, softened
- 2/3 cup preserves or jam, any variety

Beat the powdered sugar, softened butter, and preserves in a medium mixing bowl at medium speed with electric mixer until smooth.

MAKES ABOUT 1 1/2 CUPS.

IRISH CREAM FROSTING

- 1/2 cup (1 stick) unsalted butter, softened
- 1 1/2 cups powdered sugar, sifted

- 1 pinch of salt
- 3 1/2 tablespoons Irish cream liqueur

Cream the butter in a medium bowl with an electric mixer until it is smooth. Beat in the powdered sugar, gradually; beat in the salt and the Irish cream. Beat the frosting until it is light and fluffy.

MAKES ABOUT 1 1/4 CUPS.

IRISH CREAM FROSTING (CREAM CHEESE)

This frosting is so good, it's very difficult to keep from eating it straight off the spoon. Once you try it on brownies or chocolate cookies, though, you'll find it's worth the initial restraint.

- 1/4 cup (1/2 stick) unsalted butter, softened
- 1 (3-ounce) package cream cheese, softened
- 2 tablespoons Irish cream liqueur
- 2 cups powdered sugar, sifted

Beat the butter, cream cheese, and liqueur in a medium mixing bowl on medium speed until blended, smooth, and fluffy. Gradually add the powdered sugar, beating on medium until light and creamy. Add a little more powdered sugar if necessary to stiffen frosting.

MAKES ABOUT 1 1/2 CUPS FROSTING, ENOUGH TO FROST A 13 X 9-INCH PAN OF BROWNIES OR 48–60 COOKIES.

KAHLUA COFFEE ICING

This doubly coffee icing can also be used with great success on the brownie biscotti in the "Formed, Filled, and Fancy Cookies" chapter. Simply spread over one side of the biscotto with a butter knife or small offset spatula, then set on wire rack to harden.

- 3½ tablespoons Kahlua or other coffee liqueur
- 2 teaspoons instant espresso or coffee powder
- 1 teaspoon vanilla extract
- 1 pinch salt
- 3 cups powdered sugar, sifted

Combine the liqueur, espresso powder, vanilla, and pinch of salt in a medium bowl until dissolved. Whisk in powdered sugar until smooth.

MAKES ABOUT 1⅓ CUPS ICING, ENOUGH TO ICE A 13 X 9-INCH PAN OF BROWNIES OR 48–60 COOKIES.

LADY BALTIMORE FROSTING

- ½ cup golden raisins, chopped
- ½ cup chopped dried figs (about 8 whole, stems removed)
- 1 tablespoon brandy (or bourbon)
- 3 tablespoons chopped red or green candied cherries
- 1 cup canned creamy white cake frosting

Place chopped raisins and figs in a small bowl. Stir in brandy; let stand for 30 minutes (do not drain). Stir together the brandy-fruit mixture, candied cherries, and white frosting.

MAKES ABOUT 1½ CUPS.

MAPLE FROSTING

Maple and chocolate may sound like an unusual combination, but the proof is in the tasting here. You will wonder why you haven't matched the two before now!

- 3 cups powdered sugar, sifted
- 2 (3-ounce) packages cream cheese, softened
- 2 tablespoons butter, softened
- 1 tablespoon maple-flavored extract

Beat the powdered sugar, softened cream cheese, butter, and maple flavoring in a medium bowl until smooth.

MAKES ABOUT 1¾ CUPS.

MAPLE ICING

- ¼ cup (½ stick) butter, softened
- 2¼ cups sifted powdered sugar
- 1 teaspoon maple-flavored extract
- 3–4 teaspoons milk

Cream butter in a medium bowl with an electric mixer or a wooden spoon; gradually add powdered sugar. Stir in maple extract and enough milk to make frosting of spreading consistency.

MAKES ABOUT ¾ CUP.

Baker's Note

For an 8-inch-square pan of brownies, halve the ingredients listed above and proceed as directed.

MILK CHOCOLATE FROSTING

This is my very favorite chocolate frosting. It's light and buttery with a smooth milk chocolate finish that makes a superb crowning touch to a host of dark chocolate brownie, cupcake, and cookie options.

- 2 (2-ounce) squares unsweetened baking chocolate, coarsely chopped
- ½ cup (1 stick) butter, softened
- ¾ cup powdered sugar, sifted
- ½ cup heavy whipping cream

Put 1 inch of water in a large skillet. Bring to a low simmer over medium-low heat.

Place the chopped chocolate in large metal bowl; place the metal bowl in the skillet of water; stir chocolate until melted and smooth. Remove bowl from heat and cool for 15 minutes. Add the butter to the bowl of melted chocolate. Beat with electric mixer set on medium until blended. Add the powdered sugar alternately with the cream, beating on medium until light and creamy. Add more sugar if too soft and more cream if too thick. Refrigerate for 15 minutes.

MAKES ABOUT 1⅔ CUPS, ENOUGH TO FROST A 13 X 9-INCH PAN OF BROWNIES, 12 CUPCAKES, OR 48–60 COOKIES.

MILK CHOCOLATE SOUR CREAM FROSTING

- 1 cup milk chocolate chips
- ⅓ cup sour cream
- 1 teaspoon vanilla extract

Melt chocolate in a double boiler or a large metal bowl over a saucepan of simmering water, stirring occasionally. Remove bowl from heat, then whisk in sour cream and vanilla. Cool to room temperature, stirring occasionally (frosting will become thick enough to spread). Use immediately to frost cookies.

MAKES ABOUT 1¼ CUPS.

MOCHA BUTTERCREAM FROSTING

Butter plus cocoa plus espresso equals one of the very best frostings for gilding a pan of homemade brownies. It's easy to prepare, too.

- 1 tablespoon coffee powder or instant espresso
- 4 teaspoons hot water

- 2 cups powdered sugar
- 2 tablespoons unsweetened cocoa
- ½ cup (1 stick) butter, softened

Dissolve coffee powder in the hot water in a large bowl. Add the powdered sugar, cocoa, and softened butter; beat with electric mixer on medium until smooth.

MAKES ABOUT 1 CUP FROSTING, ENOUGH TO FROST AN 8-INCH-SQUARE PAN OF BROWNIES.

NO-PREP FROSTINGS FOR BROWNIES AND BROWNIE COOKIES OR SANDWICH COOKIE FILLINGS

A plain batch of brownies can be dressed up quickly and deliciously with any one of these no-prep frosting options. Use approximately ¾ cup to 1 cup for an 8-inch-square batch of brownies, and approximately 1½ to 2 cups to frost a 13 x 9-inch batch of brownies or 48–60 cookies. You can add some final flourishes, too, by sprinkling on shredded coconut, chopped nuts, chocolate chips, toffee bits, or candy nonpareils from the baking aisle in the supermarket. Sometimes the best "recipes" require no work at all. This short list of no-prep frostings can change your chocolate-chip or sugar cookies into masterpieces in minutes. Sandwich chocolate-chip cookies around a thin or thick dollop of peanut butter or chocolate-hazelnut spread; squeeze squiggles, dots, and doodles with tubes of decorating icing; or spread sugar cookies with strawberry-flavored cream cheese for instant cheesecake cookies.

- Peanut butter
- Peanut butter and jelly
- Soft-spread sweetened cream cheese
- Chocolate hazelnut spread (e.g., Nutella)
- Jam, preserves, or marmalade
- Jarred lemon curd
- Ready-to-spread canned cake frosting
- Marshmallow creme/fluff

ONE-STEP CHOCOLATE-CHIP/ BAKING CHIP "FROSTING"

This is one of my favorite ways to dress up a plain pan of brownies. For an even fancier finish, first do this one-step frosting, then do a contrasting chocolate drizzle (for example, white chocolate drizzle over semisweet chocolate chip frosting) in the recipe that follows; drizzle over melted chip frosting in a decorative design. Gorgeous!

1 cup chocolate chips (e.g., semisweet, milk, or white) or baking chips (e.g., butterscotch, peanut butter, cinnamon)

Prepare and bake 8-inch-square pan Classic Brownies (see page 328).

Remove from oven and sprinkle evenly with 1 cup chocolate chips (e.g., semisweet, milk, or white) or baking chips (e.g., butterscotch, peanut butter, cinnamon). Cover baking pan with cookie sheet for 3 minutes. Remove pan and spread melted chips with knife or small offset spatula to cover the brownies.

For thicker frosting on 8 x 8-inch batch: Increase chips to 1½ cups.

For 13 x 9-inch batch of brownies: Increase chips to 2 cups.

ORANGE CREAM CHEESE FROSTING

I developed this recipe for my friend Elizabeth, who is of the mindset that all brownies should be frosted. She has a particular penchant for the combination of orange and chocolate, so this doubly orange frosting makes her very happy, especially when it is smoothed over a batch of Orange Cream-Frosted Brownies (see page 342).

- 1 (8-ounce) package cream cheese, softened
- 3 cups powdered sugar
- 2 tablespoons frozen orange juice concentrate, thawed
- 1 teaspoon grated orange zest
- 1–2 drops yellow food coloring
- 1–2 drops red food coloring

Mix the cream cheese, powdered sugar, orange juice concentrate, orange zest, yellow food coloring, and red food coloring in a small bowl until smooth and spreadable.

MAKES ABOUT 1⅔ CUPS, ENOUGH TO FROST A 13 x 9-INCH PAN OF BROWNIES OR 48–60 COOKIES.

PEANUT BUTTER AND HONEY FROSTING

- ¼ cup creamy-style peanut butter
- 2 tablespoons honey
- 2 tablespoons hot water
- 1½ cups sifted powdered sugar

Combine the peanut butter, honey, and hot water in a medium bowl with a wooden spoon until smooth. Stir in powdered sugar, adding a few more drops of hot water if needed to make icing spreading consistency.

MAKES ABOUT ¾ CUP.

PEANUT BUTTER FROSTING

Peanut butter and brownies are made for each other, and this quick-to-make frosting makes it easy to foster the relationship. And it's very likely you have all of the ingredients on hand.

- 6 tablespoons creamy style peanut butter (not natural or old-fashioned style)
- ¼ cup (½ stick) unsalted butter, softened

- 2 cups powdered sugar, sifted
- 3–4 tablespoons milk

Beat the peanut butter and butter in a medium mixing bowl with an electric mixer set on medium until blended. Gradually add the powdered sugar alternately with the milk, beating on low until smooth. Increase speed to medium and beat 1 minute longer until light and creamy.

MAKES ABOUT 1¾ CUPS, ENOUGH TO GENEROUSLY FROST A 13 X 9-INCH PAN OF BROWNIES OR 48–60 COOKIES.

Baker's Note

For an 8-inch-square pan of brownies, halve the ingredients listed above and proceed as directed.

PEANUT BUTTER ICING

- 6 tablespoons creamy-style peanut butter
- 1½ cups sifted powdered sugar
- 1½ tablespoons milk

Combine the peanut butter, powdered sugar, and milk in a medium mixing bowl. Beat with electric mixer on medium-high speed until combined and smooth. Add more milk, by the teaspoon, if needed to make icing drizzling consistency.

MAKES ABOUT ¾ CUP.

PEPPERMINT FROSTING

This is a classic recipe for holiday brownies and cookies.

- 3 cups powdered sugar, sifted
- ⅓ cup butter, softened
- ¾ teaspoon peppermint extract
- 2–4 tablespoons milk
- 2 drops green food coloring, optional

Beat the powdered sugar, softened butter, and peppermint extract in a medium bowl with an electric mixer set on low speed until smooth. Beat in milk, 1 tablespoon at a time, until smooth and spreadable for frosting. For icing, add more milk until mixture is of drizzling consistency. Beat in green food coloring, if desired.

MAKES ABOUT 1½ CUPS FROSTING, ENOUGH TO FROST A 13 X 9-INCH PAN OF BROWNIES OR 48 COOKIES.

Baker's Note

For an 8-inch-square pan of brownies, halve the ingredients listed above and proceed as directed.

PEPPERMINT ICING

- 1¾ cups sifted powdered sugar
- 2 tablespoons butter, softened
- ¼ teaspoon peppermint extract
- 3–4 teaspoons milk (or cream)

Stir together, in a small bowl, the powdered sugar, softened butter, peppermint extract, and enough of the milk or cream to make icing that is easy to drizzle.

MAKES ABOUT ¾ CUP.

QUICK CARAMEL FROSTING, AKA CARAMEL PENUCHE FROSTING

This delicious frosting is incredible on brownies, cookies, and just about everything else. Be sure to spread while it's still warm. If left to cool completely, it sets up to a fudge consistency which, while still scrumptious, makes it almost impossible to spread.

- ½ cup (1 stick) butter
- 1 cup packed dark brown sugar
- ¼ cup milk
- 2 cups powdered sugar, sifted
- 1 teaspoon vanilla extract

Melt the butter with the brown sugar in a medium saucepan set over medium heat. Stir until the mixture comes to a boil. Add the milk; bring the mixture back to a boil. Remove the pan from the heat and stir in the powdered sugar and vanilla extract. Best if used right away, while still warm.

MAKES ABOUT 2 1/3 CUPS.

RUM ICING, AKA BUTTER-RUM ICING

- 2 cups sifted powdered sugar
- ¼ cup (½ stick) butter, melted
- 2½ teaspoons rum-flavored extract, divided
- 2–3 tablespoons milk

Combine the powdered sugar, butter, and rum flavoring in a small bowl. Add just enough milk to make icing of spreading consistency.

MAKES ABOUT ¾ CUP.

SHINY CHOCOLATE GLAZE

Adding a bit of shimmery glamour to a basic batch of brownies is as easy as making and spreading this glaze.

- 1 cup semisweet chocolate chips
- 2 tablespoons unsalted butter
- 2 tablespoons corn syrup
- 1–3 teaspoons hot water

Melt the chocolate chips, butter, and corn syrup in a small saucepan set over low heat, stirring occasionally, until melted and smooth.

Stir in hot water, a few drops at a time, until mixture is thin enough to drizzle.

MAKES ABOUT 1¼ CUPS, ENOUGH TO GLAZE A 13 X 9-INCH PAN OF BROWNIES.

Baker's Note

For an 8-inch-square pan of brownies, halve the ingredients listed above and proceed as directed.

SOUR CREAM FROSTING

If you like flavor contrasts, you will adore this tangy, creamy frosting lavished over a pan of dark chocolate brownies or a batch of chocolate cookies. Be sure to store the frosted brownies or cookies in the refrigerator.

- ¾ cup powdered sugar
- 1 (8-ounce) package cream cheese, room temperature
- ½ cup sour cream
- 1 teaspoon fresh lemon juice

Beat the powdered sugar, cream cheese, sour cream, and lemon juice in a medium bowl with an electric mixer on high until well blended and smooth.

MAKES ABOUT 1¾ CUPS FROSTING, ENOUGH TO FROST A 13 X 9-INCH PAN OF BROWNIES OR 48–60 COOKIES.

Baker's Note

For an 8-inch-square pan of brownies, halve the ingredients listed above and proceed as directed.

SUGAR COOKIE PAINT

Cookie paint is essentially a colored egg wash. Paint it onto slices of refrigerated sugar cookie dough before baking to produce shiny cookies with brilliant colors and a glossy sheen. This is a wonderful rainy-day activity for children as well as a fun party break for adults. Use small artist brushes—made with natural bristles—to apply the paint and let your inner artist break free!

- 1 large egg yolk
- ⅛ teaspoon water
- Liquid, paste, or powder food coloring of choice

Combine the egg yolk and water in a small bowl. Add a dab or two of coloring if using paste, a pinch if using powder; mix well. Use an artist's brush to apply the paint to the cookies before baking.

MAKES ENOUGH FOR ONE BATCH OF COOKIES.

SWEETENED WHIPPED CREAM

Frozen whipped topping may be fine in a pinch, but the real thing—sweetened whipped cream—is worth the splurge.

FOR 1 CUP:

- ½ cup heavy whipping cream
- 1 tablespoon granulated sugar
- ½ teaspoon vanilla extract

FOR 1½ CUPS:

- ¾ cup heavy whipping cream
- 2 tablespoons granulated sugar
- 1 teaspoon vanilla extract

FOR 2 CUPS:

- 1 cup heavy whipping cream
- 3 tablespoons granulated sugar
- 1½ teaspoons vanilla extract

FOR 3 CUPS:

- 1½ cups heavy whipping cream
- ¼ cup granulated sugar
- 2 teaspoons vanilla extract

Beat the whipping cream, sugar, and vanilla extract in a chilled mixing bowl with electric mixer on high until soft peaks form. Use immediately.

VANILLA BUTTER FROSTING

- ¼ cup (½ stick) butter, softened
- 2 cups sifted powdered sugar
- 1 teaspoon vanilla extract
- 1½ tablespoons milk

Cream the butter in a large bowl with an electric mixer or a wooden spoon; gradually add powdered sugar. Stir in vanilla extract and enough milk to make icing of spreading consistency.

MAKES ABOUT ¾ CUP.

VANILLA BUTTER GLAZE

Vanilla and butter have a transformative effect on chocolate. In particular, this quickly assembled glaze makes already good brownies extraordinarily moist, irresistible masterpieces. For an even richer butter flavor, consider browning the melted butter (see page 361) before whipping up the glaze.

- 1½ cups powdered sugar, sifted
- 1½ tablespoons unsalted butter, melted
- 1 teaspoon vanilla extract
- 1–2 teaspoons milk

Whisk the powdered sugar, melted butter, and vanilla in a small bowl until smooth. Add just enough milk, a teaspoon at a time, to make glaze a thin spreading consistency, whisking until smooth.

MAKES ABOUT ½ CUP GLAZE, ENOUGH TO GLAZE AN 8-INCH-SQUARE PAN OF BROWNIES.

Baker's Note

For a 13 x 9-inch pan of brownies or 48–60 cookies, double the ingredients listed above and proceed as directed.

VANILLA ICING

- 4 cups powdered sugar, sifted
- 2–3 tablespoons whole milk
- ½ teaspoon vanilla extract

Combine the powdered sugar, 2 tablespoons milk, and vanilla extract in a medium bowl. Stir until icing is well blended, smooth, and spreadable, adding more milk by teaspoonfuls if consistency is too thick.

MAKES ABOUT 1½ CUPS.

WHISKEY GLAZE

Three ingredients equals simple perfection here.

- 1¼ cups powdered sugar, sifted
- 1 tablespoon unsalted butter, melted
- 1 tablespoon whiskey or bourbon

In a small bowl combine the powdered sugar, melted butter, and whiskey. Whisk until smooth.

MAKES ABOUT ½ CUP OF GLAZE, ENOUGH TO GLAZE AN 8-INCH-SQUARE PAN OF BROWNIES.

WHITE CHOCOLATE CREAM CHEESE FROSTING

- 1 cup white chocolate chips
- 6 ounces cream cheese, room temperature
- 2 tablespoons unsalted butter, room temperature
- 1 tablespoon fresh lemon juice

Stir white chocolate in top of double boiler over barely simmering water until almost melted. Remove from over water and stir until smooth. Cool to lukewarm. Beat the cream cheese and butter in a large bowl until blended. Beat in lemon juice, then cooled white chocolate.

MAKES ABOUT 1¼ CUPS.

GLOSSARY OF BASIC COOKING AND BAKING TERMS

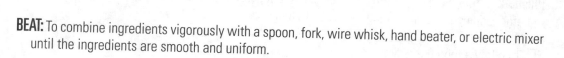

BEAT: To combine ingredients vigorously with a spoon, fork, wire whisk, hand beater, or electric mixer until the ingredients are smooth and uniform.

BLEND: To combine ingredients with a spoon, wire whisk, or rubber scraper until very smooth and uniform. A blender or food processor may also be used, depending on the job.

BOIL: To heat a liquid until bubbles rise continuously and break on the surface and steam is given off. For a rolling boil, the bubbles form rapidly and will not stop forming even when the liquid is stirred.

CHOP: To cut food into small pieces using a chef's knife, food processor, or blender.

DRAIN: To pour off extra liquid from a food, often with the use of a colander or strainer over the sink. To reserve the drained liquid, place a bowl under the colander.

DRIZZLE: To slowly pour a liquid, such as melted butter, melted chocolate, or glaze, in a very thin stream over a food.

FOLD: To combine ingredients lightly while preventing loss of air by using two motions: Using a rubber spatula, first cut down vertically through the mixture. Next, slide the spatula across the bottom of the bowl and up the side, turning the mixture over. Repeat these motions after rotating the bowl one-fourth turn with each series of strokes.

GARNISH: An edible decoration added to food.

GREASE: To rub the inside surface of a pan with solid shortening, using a pastry brush, wax paper, or paper towels to prevent food from sticking during baking. Nonstick cooking spray may also be used. Do not use butter or margarine (especially in a baked recipe); either may burn and/or sticking may occur.

GREASE AND FLOUR: To rub the inside surface of a pan with solid shortening before dusting it with flour in order to prevent food from sticking during baking. After flouring the pan, turn it upside down and tap the bottom to remove excess flour.

MIX: To combine ingredients in any way that distributes them evenly, integrating the ingredients. This can be accomplished using a hand utensil or an electric mixer.

PIPE: A decorating technique that involves forcing frosting, icing, or chocolate from a pastry bag or parchment cone to form specific designs on a cookie.

PREHEAT: To turn the oven controls to the desired temperature, allowing the oven to heat thoroughly before adding food. Preheating takes 10–15 minutes.

SET: To allow a food to become firm.

SOFTEN: To allow cold food, such as butter, margarine, or cream cheese, to stand at room temperature until no longer hard. Generally this will take 30–60 minutes.

STIR: To combine ingredients with a circular or "figure 8" motion until they are of a uniform consistency.

WHIP: To beat ingredients with a wire whisk, hand rotary beater, or electric mixer to add air and increase volume until ingredients are light and fluffy, such as with whipping cream or egg whites.

ZEST: The perfume-y outermost layer of citrus fruit that contains the fruit's essential oils. Zest can be removed with a zester, a small handheld tool that separates the zest from the bitter white pith underneath, or with a grater, vegetable peeler, or sharp knife.

EQUIPMENT AND INGREDIENT SOURCES

BED BATH & BEYOND

(800) 462-3966

www.bedbathandbeyond.com

You might not know it from their name, but Bed, Bath, and Beyond has an extensive cooking and baking department, complete with appliances (e.g., food processors, toaster/convection ovens, and pizzelle irons), general baking equipment (e.g., pans, measuring cups and spoons, bowls, cookie sheets, cooling racks, and silicone mats), and specific cookie tools (e.g., cutters, stamps, madeleine pans, and decorating kits).

BERYL'S CAKE DECORATING EQUIPMENT

P.O. Box 1584

North Springfield, VA 22151

(703) 256-6951

(800) 488-2749

www.beryls.com

Beryl's Cake Decorating Equipment is a particularly good source for original cookie cutters and sets.

BRIDGE KITCHENWARE

49 Eagle Rock Avenue
East Hanover, NJ 07936
(973) 240-7364
www.bridgekitchenware.com

In addition to its wide variety of general cookie-baking equipment and tools, Bridge Kitchenware also offers an extensive selection of cookie sheets and imported European cooking and baking supplies.

CHEF'S CATALOG

3215 Commercial Avenue
Northbrook, IL 60062-1900
(800) 967-2433
www.chefscatalog.com

Cookie sheets, cookie stamps, cookie cutters, multi-decker cooling racks, and just about every other piece of cooking equipment you can imagine is available from Chef's Catalog.

COOKING.COM

4086 Del Rey Avenue
Marina Del Rey, CA 90292
(800) 663-8810
www.cooking.com
Cooking.com is one of my favorite sources for a complete range of cooking and baking tools and small kitchen appliances.

DEAN AND DELUCA

560 Broadway
New York, NY 10012
(212) 431-1691
(800) 221-7714
www.deandeluca.com

Dean and DeLuca carries an upscale assortment of baking tools from spice mills to timers to all manner of goods specific to cookie preparation. They also have cookie ingredient provisions such as imported chocolate, cocoa powder, extracts, and spices.

J.B. PRINCE COMPANY

36 East 31st Street
New York, NY 10016
(212) 683-3553

(800) 473-0577
www.jbprince.com

J.B. Prince Company sells professional-quality baking equipment, mostly imported from Europe.

KING ARTHUR FLOUR BAKER'S CATALOG

P.O. Box 876
Norwich, VT 05055
(800) 827-6836
www.kingarthurflour.com

King Arthur Flour Baker's Catalog offers home bakers a wide range of cookie equipment as well as specialty flours, specialty sugars, and specialty extracts.

KITCHEN COLLECTABLES, INC.

(888) 593-2436
www.kitchencollectables.com

No matter what cookie cutter you are looking for, Kitchen Collectables, Inc. is likely to have it. In addition to more than 2,000 copper cookie cutters, they also stock a wide variety of basic and hard-to-find cookie tools and accessories.

KITCHEN KRAFTS

P.O. Box 442-ORD
Waukon, Iowa 52172-0442
(563) 535-8000
(800) 776-0575
www.kitchenkrafts.com

Kitchen Krafts is a good one-stop supplier for both basic and fancy cookie and other baking supplies. Especially for novice bakers who need to stock up on basic tools, Kitchen Krafts offers competitive prices on all of their equipment.

LA CUISINE

323 Cameron Street
Alexandria, VA 22314
(703) 836-4435
(800) 521-1176
www.lacuisineus.com

In addition to all of the basic cookie baking equipment you may need, La Cuisine also carries cookie decorations, including specialty decorating sugars.

LAMALLE KITCHENWARE

36 West 25th Street
New York, NY 10010
(212) 242-0750
www.foodnet.com/epr/sections/writers/trends/lamall.html

Lamalle's is the source for unique cutters and other specialty cookie tools.

PARRISH'S CAKE DECORATING SUPPLIES, INC.

225 West 16th Street
Gardena, CA 90248-¬1803
(310) 324-2253
(800) 736-8443
www.parrishsmagicline.com/systmpl/door

Parrish's is "cookie baking central," offering a wide variety of cookie equipment, including cutters, presses, molds, and other cookie tools.

PENZEY'S SPICES

P.O. Box 993
W129362 Apollo Drive
Muskego, WI 53150
(800) 741-7787
www.penzeys.com

Look to Penzey's for some of the best and freshest spices at good prices. They also carry assorted extracts and are an especially good source for hard-to-find spices and flavorings.

SUR LA TABLE

1765 Sixth Avenue South
Seattle, WA 93134-1608
(800) 243-0852
www.surlatable.com

Sur La Table has a wide selection of baking equipment and appliances in general and cookie baking and decorating supplies in particular. They also carry a wide variety of fine baking ingredients, including imported chocolates and pure chocolate and vanilla extracts.

SUGARCRAFT

3665 Dixie Hwy.
Hamilton, Ohio 45015
(513) 896-7089
www.sugarcraft.com

Sugarcraft easily lives up to its slogan, "a baker's paradise." They carry a wide array of just about everything you need for baking and decorating.

SWEET CELEBRATIONS

P.O. Box 39426
Edina, MN 55439-0426
(612) 943-0426
(800) 328-6722
www.maidofscandinavia.com

Sweet Celebrations carries a wide range of cake decorating supplies, baking equipment, and imported chocolate for baking.

WILLIAMS-SONOMA

P.O. Box 7456
San Francisco, CA 94120-7456
(415) 421-4242
(800) 541-2233
www.williams-sonoma.com

Williams-Sonoma offers a wide range of baking equipment, including, but not limited to, appliances (mixers, food processors, and combined toaster-convection ovens), cookie accessories (cutters, presses, sheets, silicone liners, cake and cookie decorating tips), and ingredients (decorating sugar and imported chocolate, cocoa, and vanilla).

WILTON ENTERPRISES, INC.

240 West 75th Street
Woodridge, IL 60517
(630) 963-7100
(800) 794-5866
www.wilton.com

In addition to being a leading cake decoration supplier, Wilton Enterprises also carries an extensive selection of cookie cutters and most every other type of cookie baking accessory, from presses to molds to stamps. They also stock a wide variety of decorating accessories, including pastry bags and tips.

METRIC MEASURE CONVERSIONS

Note: The exact equivalents in the following lists have been rounded for convenience.

Liquid and Dry Measures

U.S.	METRIC
¼ teaspoon	1.25 milliliters
½ teaspoon	2.5 milliliters
1 teaspoon	5 milliliters
1 tablespoon	15 milliliters
1 fluid ounce	30 milliliters
¼ cup (4 tbsp)	60 milliliters
⅓ cup	80 milliliters
1 cup (16 tbsp)	240 milliliters
1 pint (2 cups)	480 milliliters
1 quart (4 cups)	960 milliliters
1 gallon (4 qts)	3.84 liters

INDEX

CAKE MIX RECIPES

Cake Mix Drop Cookies

Cake Mix Formed, Filled, and Fancy Cookies

Cake Mix Bar Cookies

Cake Mix Brownies

COOKIE DOUGH RECIPES

Cookie Dough Drop Cookies

Cookie Dough Formed, Filled, and Fancy Cookies

No-Bake Bar Cookies

No-Bake Brownies

ICINGS, FROSTINGS, FILLINGS, AND EXTRAS

ALL RECIPES